CHILD LABOR
AND
HUMAN RIGHTS

CHILD LABOR
AND
HUMAN RIGHTS

MAKING CHILDREN MATTER

edited by
Burns H. Weston

LYNNE
RIENNER
PUBLISHERS

BOULDER
LONDON

Published in the United States of America in 2005 by
Lynne Rienner Publishers, Inc.
1800 30th Street, Boulder, Colorado 80301
www.rienner.com

and in the United Kingdom by
Lynne Rienner Publishers, Inc.
3 Henrietta Street, Covent Garden, London WC2E 8LU

Library of Congress Cataloging-in-Publication Data
Child labor and human rights : making children matter / edited by Burns H. Weston.
    p. cm.
    Includes bibliographical references and index.
    ISBN 1-58826-324-X (hardcover : alk. paper) — ISBN 1-58826-349-5 (pbk. : alk. paper)
    1. Child labor.   2. Human rights.   I. Weston, Burns H., 1933–   II. Title.
HD6231.C454 2005
331.3'1—dc22

                                        2005011011

British Cataloguing in Publication Data
A Cataloguing in Publication record for this book
is available from the British Library.

Printed and bound in the United States of America

The paper used in this publication meets the requirements
of the American National Standard for Permanence of
Paper for Printed Library Materials Z39.48-1992.

5 4 3 2 1

*To the little Cambodian girl in the red dress
scavenging barefoot atop the Stung Meanchey garbage
dump on the outskirts of Phnom Penh, November 2002*

Contents

Part 3   Case Studies

Part 4   Toward Progressive Change

Part 5   Conclusion: Contributors' Consensus

Preface

The genesis of this book lies in a thought-provoking lecture on child labor and human rights by US senator Tom Harkin of Iowa on the occasion of The University of Iowa's commemoration of the fiftieth anniversary of the 1948 Universal Declaration of Human Rights—on the eve, not coincidentally, of the adoption of the 1999 ILO Convention (No. 182) Concerning the Prohibition and Immediate Action for the Elimination of the Worst Forms of Child Labor (see appendix), now ratified by more than 155 countries. It lies also in Senator Harkin's subsequent gracious help, despite some disagreement between us regarding the suitability of children in the workplace, in securing generous congressional funding to make possible this and related research on child labor* under my stewardship at The University of Iowa Center for Human Rights (UICHR) (see http://www.uichr.org), which I then directed. What greater proof of commitment and decency in the cause of human rights does one need? I thank Senator Harkin for his stimulating words and unqualified support. The result is a work, intended for teacher, student, government official, international civil servant, nongovernmental activist, and concerned citizen alike, conceived and executed in an intellectually free, multidisciplinary, and robustly open-ended way.

In late 2001, a visionary group of distinguished faculty and staff from many disciplines at The University of Iowa (Jonathan Carlson, Kenneth Cmiel, Gregory Hamot, Gina McGee, Josephine Gittler, Rex Honey, Daniel Holub,

---

* Throughout this volume, except as otherwise indicated, "child labor" is defined to mean work done by children that is harmful to them because it is abusive, exploitive, hazardous, or otherwise contrary to their best interests—a subset of a larger class of children's work, some of which may be compatible with children's best interests (variously expressed as "beneficial," "benign," or "harmless" children's work).

Maureen McCue, Lon Moeller, Chivy Sok, Shelton Stromquist, Roberta Till-Retz, and Lea Vandervelde) came several times and variously together at the UICHR's invitation to conceptualize and hammer out a working outline for this book and to recommend contributors who could bring intellectual and experiential excitement to it. With help from others, they succeeded admirably. One year later, almost all of the invited contributors were on board and most of the chapters had been drafted and circulated, well in time for a July 2003 colloquium ("Using the Human Rights Framework to Combat Abusive Child Labor") hosted by the UICHR in part to critique and refine the work accomplished to that point. Joining the UI group (now including UICHR fellows Susan Koch, Karen Kubby, and John McLure—and even, for a brief while, students from Shimek Elementary School in Iowa City) were most of the contributors to this volume plus four highly qualified human rights experts (Cynthia Price Cohen, James Gross, Roger Normand, and James Silk) specially invited to challenge and provoke. And so they did, immeasurably helping the book to become richer in substance and more nuanced in detail than otherwise it might have been.

But no less noteworthy, perhaps even more so, is the fact that virtually everyone present and participating in the July colloquium was of different training, experience, expertise, and even persuasion relative to the problem of child labor and what to do about it. Illustrating the diversity were the disciplines represented: anthropology, business management and organization, economics, education, ethics, geography, history, journalism, labor, law, medicine, philosophy, psychology, political science, public health, and sociology.

Many of these disciplines and consequent worldviews are represented in the contributions to this volume. And by conscious design. Because child labor is a quintessentially transdisciplinary problem, any solution to it requires transdisciplinary analysis. Remarkably, as evidenced by the final chapter of the book, a "Contributors' Consensus" proved nonetheless possible—largely if not entirely, I think, because of a strong shared commitment to human rights and, in particular, the human rights of children, even when the particulars about human rights were disputed among us.

But I have a confession to make. Try as I have as editor of this volume to maintain a transdisciplinary outlook throughout, I *am* an international lawyer and thus inevitably influenced by the cognitive perspectives and traditions of the legal profession. I am not, on the other hand, the stereotypic lawyer, given to rule-oriented thinking divorced from context, and this book reflects that fact (particularly in Chapters 1 and 10, which I helped to write). I conceive of law and legal process in far more dynamic terms than do most nonlawyers and even many lawyers when they conjure the term "law." As I have written elsewhere, "law is legitimized politics—a Hydra-headed process of social decision, involving persons at all levels and from all walks of public and private life who, with authority derived both explicitly and implicitly from community consensus or expectation, and supported by formal and informal sanction, effect those codes or standards of everyday conduct by which we plan and go about our lives."[1] The phenomenon we call social etiquette, for example, may readily be viewed as a form of legal process. So, too, can church life, the classroom, the playing field, or, indeed, the workplace be viewed as micro legal systems. Even family life. "Law does not live by executives and legislators and judges alone. It lives also beyond the formal corridors of power among individual human beings such as ourselves, pushing and pulling through reciprocal claim and mutual tolerance in our daily competition for power, wealth, respect, and other cherished values."[2] It is from this perspective that I have helped with this book.

Even so, I am a lawyer, and thus given to seeing the world around me in strong even if liberal jurisprudential terms, a fact that surely has shaped at least some of the organization and content of this work. An anthropologist, economist, political scientist, or sociologist doubtless would have compiled a different text and argued for bringing human rights to child labor in a different way than I do. But not even the anthropologist, economist, political scientist, or sociologist can escape the law entirely. The language of "standards" and "rights" is, after all, legal language, even though not legal language only. Its interpretation and application, as well as its invention or prescription, must therefore be understood, in major part, in juridically analytical and operational terms.

In any event, such are the historical origins and intellectual roots of this unique collection. And for its strengths (I alone am responsible for its weaknesses), I am indebted to many, beginning with every person mentioned above. To all of them I extend my deep, respectful thanks.

Most of all among these persons, however, I thank my co-contributors. Without them and their extraordinary hard work and generosity of time and spirit, manifestly this book would never have been realized. That they would give so generously of their vast knowledge and experience is humbling beyond what words can express. But there is more: they taught me abundantly, they taught me with grace, I learned from them much, and many I now call friend. No finer reward is there; no words of appreciation suffice.

I am grateful, as well, for my Iowa law students of the past three years who joined me and my indefatigably dedicated former UICHR deputy director, Chivy Sok, in an advanced research seminar we called "International Human Rights and Child Labor." I am absolutely convinced that I learned more from them and Chivy Sok than any of them learned from me. Certainly their intellectual contributions figured prominently in the evolution of this work. Certainly, therefore, they too merit my unbounded thanks.

I offer additional thanks to David Parker for allowing us to use his photograph on the cover of the paperback edition of this book.

On final analysis, however, it is those selfless hands behind the scenes that make it possible for the play to go on. To my research assistants and associates of the past three years—Jonathan Amarilio, Gavin Boyles, Anne Burmeister, Maureen De Armond, Megan Dempsey, Jessica Downs, Mary Galligan, Kara Hartzler, Tissetso Russell, and Casie Shorey—I owe very special thanks. Maureen De Armond and Jessica Downs are particularly to be recognized for their diligence, creativity, and generosity. I thank also Dean Emeritus N. William Hines of The University of Iowa College of Law and Vice Dean Bruce Duthu of the Vermont Law School for making it financially possible for one or more of these wonderfully acute and sensitive researchers to come to my daily rescue.

In the same spirit, I thank Brian Harvey, Gina McGee, and Grainne Martin of The University of Iowa Division of Sponsored Programs and, as well, the staff of the university's International Programs, in which the UICHR is administratively housed. Their support and trust were ever noticed, never misprized. I am especially grateful to Gina McGee for her unfailing optimism in times of stress, always helping me to believe that everything will be okay in the end, and that if it's not okay it's not the end. Never to be forgotten either is the steady help I received from my UICHR staff and my exceptional law school secretary, Grace Tully, who in the closing stages helped me to process the final manuscript from afar, as always with a grace for which she is so aptly named.

Last but not least, I want to thank my wife, Marta Cullberg Weston. In Chapters 1 and 10, I have acknowledged her for her acute critiques. Here I thank her for her extraordinarily patient acceptance of this major intervention upon our lives. Never have I taken this for granted, never has it gone unappreciated. On the other hand, I do confess appreciation of late for comforting, distracting Google—not the search engine on which we have all come to rely (though that, too), but our new cat who gets into everything (ergo Google) and thus became Marta's steady, purring friend and companion while I obsessed over deadlines.

Two concluding thoughts. First, you will notice that many of the writings quoted in the ensuing pages are sexist (including official documents) in that they refer often only to men or boys as actors in society, nationally and internationally. This is the inevitable result of the long exclusion of women from public life and even private decisionmaking of consequence, tangible evidence of the patriarchies that dominate much of human life worldwide. I do not value such marginalization and therefore do not welcome "man-made" language; but neither do I believe it easy to remove or revise without distracting demurrers or other graceless interventions. I therefore request you, the reader, to construe the masculine gender used in these passages in the generic sense, always to include women and girls as well as men and boys when syntactically appropriate.

Finally, I write these words only a short while after the catastrophic Indian Ocean tsunamis of December 26, 2004. Immediately after and ever since, one learns of newly parentless children being abducted into forced labor, trafficked into the sex trade, and otherwise exploited and abused. The need to abolish child labor has never been greater, our task never more daunting. Sisyphus comes to mind. But struggle onward we must, again and again. This book, I hope, will help to clarify the way.

—*Burns H. Weston*

■ Notes

1. Weston, "The Role of Law in Promoting Peace and Violence . . . ," p. 117.
2. Ibid.

Introduction

Burns H. Weston

This book is dedicated to the abolition of child labor and advocates its extinction via the language and law of human rights.[1] By "child labor" I mean work done by children that is harmful to them because it is abusive, exploitive, hazardous, or otherwise contrary to their best interests—a subset of a larger class of children's work, some of which may be compatible with children's best interests (variously expressed as "beneficial," "benign," or "harmless" children's work).[2] By "abolition" I mean the eradication of child labor, especially its "worst forms," as completely as human imagination will allow, and with a commitment that recalls the successful (nonviolent) abolitionist movements of the eighteenth and nineteenth centuries that sought the end of slavery—an evil with which, alas, child labor evinces uncomfortable affinity in many respects. And by "human rights" I mean individual and group values or capabilities that are deemed inalienable for being central to human existence, that express both the "is" and the "ought" in human affairs, and that, though seldom absolute, are "quintessentially general or universal in character, in some sense equally possessed by all human beings everywhere."[3]

Before the 1989 United Nations Convention on the Rights of the Child (CRC),[4] however, the problem of child labor, even in its worst forms, was seldom addressed as a human rights problem.[5] The practice of the International Labour Organization (ILO) over the years, though long attentive to the needs and wants of immediate importance to most people, is illustrative. Reflecting the ILO's traditional labor market perspective, no ILO convention addressing issues of child labor prior to the 1989 CRC couched its provisions in the language of rights, let alone mentioned "human rights," to define its mission or achieve its goals—not even ILO Convention (No. 29) Concerning Forced or Compulsory Labour (ILO C29), nor ILO Convention (No. 105) Concerning the Abolition of Forced Labour (ILO C105), nor ILO Convention (No. 138) Concerning Minimum Age for Admission to Employment (ILO C138).[6] The first of these important lawmaking initiatives, concluded in 1930, may perhaps be excused for having been adopted before human rights law began to be taken seriously in world affairs, beginning with the 1945 Charter of the United Nations[7] and the 1948 Universal Declaration of Human Rights.[8] But not so the latter two treaties, concluded in 1957 and 1973, respectively, and joining a long list of ILO conventions that address all sorts of worker issues without engaging human rights discourse.[9] The reason seems clear. Although its roots can be traced to antiquity, the idea of human rights is relatively new on the world stage;[10] and as everyone knows, social change—especially progressive social change—ordinarily takes place slowly, the more so in a context where, both nationally and internationally, command and enforcement mechanisms familiar to mature legal systems are relatively lacking. Yet there are prices—often steep prices—to be paid for such human rights quiescence. As James Gross has observed regarding worker rights specifically: "This lack of [human rights] attention has contributed to workers being seen as expendable in worldwide economic development and their needs and concerns not being represented at conferences on the world economy dominated by bankers, finance ministers, and multinational corporations."[11]

It is important to acknowledge, however, that, since the adoption of the 1989 CRC and particularly the 1999 ILO Convention (No. 182) Concerning the Prohibition and Immediate Elimination of the Worst Forms of Child Labour (ILO C182),[12] a commitment to the abolition of child labor as a human rights imperative has taken hold and begun to spread. Key intergovernmental organizations (IGOs) working in the field now actively affirm the link between child labor and human rights—most prominently, even if sometimes equivocally, the ILO[13] and the United Nations Children's Fund (UNICEF).[14] Also committed to a rights-based approach to child labor is the World Health Organization (WHO), whose Department of Child and Adolescent Health and Development (CAH) recognizes that the basic health needs of children and adolescents are fundamental human rights dependent for their protection and fulfillment on the realization of other rights such as "freedom from all forms of exploitation."[15]

Human rights orientations to child labor are now found also, even more conspicuously, among nongovernmental organizations (NGOs) working in this field—for example, Anti-Slavery International (formerly the Anti-Slavery Society) in respect of an estimated 8 million children suffering in slavery and slavelike circumstances worldwide;[16] the London-based International Save the Children Alliance, established in 1919 but principally focused on child labor in the last decade;[17] and Global March Against Child Labour, begun in 1998 and now headquartered in New Delhi.[18] Also noteworthy: Amnesty International, relative to child soldiering;[19] the Children's Rights Division of Human Rights Watch, largely focused on forced and bonded child labor;[20] and Defence for Children International.[21] Certain regional and local NGOs, too, have become well-known for combating child labor from a rights-based per-spective—Child Workers in Asia, for just one example[22]—and the same is true of some national governments as well.[23]

In sum, both alone and in increasing combination, variously specialized IGOs and NGOs, increasingly in collaboration with national governments, have in recent years placed child labor, especially its worst forms, high among their concerns and, in the process, confirmed its human rights standing. Per-haps not coincidentally, they also have begun to achieve some discernible progress.

But not nearly enough. According to the ILO's newest—though imper-fect—2000 global estimate, approximately 246 million children between the ages of five and seventeen (usefully compared to a current US population of 290 million) are engaged in "child labour."[24] Large though uncertain numbers toil in appalling conditions, are ruthlessly exploited to perform dangerous jobs with little or no pay, and thus are made often to suffer severe physical and emo-tional abuse.[25] They can be found in brick factories, carpet-weaving centers, fishing platforms, leather-tanning shops, mines, and other hazardous places, often as cogs in the global economy. They can be found—most abundantly—in domestic service, vulnerable to sexual and other indignities that escape pub-lic accountability. They can be found on the streets as prostitutes, forced to serve clients against their will. They can be found as soldiers in life-threaten-ing conflict situations. Working long hours under exploitive conditions, often beaten or otherwise abused, and commonly trafficked from one country to an-other, they are unable to obtain the education that can liberate and improve their lives; their health is severely threatened from years of exposure to haz-ardous material; many, if they survive, are deformed and disabled before they can mature physically, mentally, or emotionally.

A primary explanation for this grotesquery is to be found, of course, in the array of economic and political forces worldwide, mostly though not exclu-sively nationally or locally based, whose various interests are served not by the elimination or reduction of child labor but by its perpetuation and proliferation. But let us be very clear: child labor exists also because, except for a valiant few, the world's governing elites have yet to discover not just the political will that is needed to surmount the problem but, as well, the comprehensive under-standing of it upon which solutions adequate to its abolition depend—a critical deficit because such understanding is essential for the vision that is needed to energize the grand political will that so far is lacking.

This book is intended to help offset this deficit and, to this end, is premised on the following five interrelated propositions: first, that child labor—work done by children that is harmful to them for being abusive, exploitive, haz-ardous, or otherwise contrary to their best interests—constitutes a major blight on human civility and welfare worldwide; second, that it therefore begs to be abolished by all who profess ethical-moral conscience and/or pragmatic self-interest in the well-being of present and future generations; third, that it manifests itself in complex and diverse ways and thus requires both coextensive (multidisciplinary, multifaceted, and multisectoral) and singly focused approaches and techniques to achieve its eradication in whole or in part; fourth, that these approaches and techniques must be informed by frank recognition that no form or level of social organization can claim "business as usual"—that is, exemption from meaningful, even fundamental change—if the goal of abolition is genuinely to succeed in situations large or small over time; and fifth, that such change and the benefits to human dignity that can flow from it are not likely to be achieved except episodically without a dedicated and ongoing commitment to the contextual application of human rights law and policy, including the right of children to have a say about their own lives. The time is long overdue, from the most local to the most global circumstance, for the rights of working children—not just their needs—to be taken seriously into account in the making and shaping of agendas pertinent to their lives, and especially, of course, when such agendas affect them directly.

Each of the chapters in this book, though as diverse in substance and style as the identities and experiences of their authors, reflects a common appreciation of these five propositions, more or less. Of course, none of the contributors herein, this writer included, presumes to believe that in this collective enterprise we have devised the definitive solution to the child labor problem. Nor do we naively believe that the publication and dissemination of it will suffice to cause child labor's eradication. We do hope, however, that the many and varied recommendations contained in our chapters will win the responsible attention and sustained action of national governments, intergovernmental agencies, nongovernmental organizations, academic and research institutions, and others who seek to end the workplace abuse and exploitation of children, our future's treasure. For in the end, the task of abolishing child labor belongs to them—and by delegation of responsibility, to you, the reader: teacher, student, governmental official, international civil servant, nongovernmental activist, concerned citizen.

In the remainder of this volume, adhering to the definition of "child labor" set forth in the first paragraph of this introduction except as otherwise indicated,[26] we seek to explain why, how, and subject to what conditions a human rights approach to abolishing child labor can and should be pursued. We do so in four parts.

In Part 1, "Clarifying the Problem," Mark Teerink and I open by confirming that the problem of child labor is indisputably a human rights problem—multidimensional in character—and explaining why a human rights approach to its rollback is pragmatically desirable and theoretically defensible. Our purpose is to set the normative and operational stage for all that follows, demonstrating how human rights discourse and strategy can have substantial beneficial utility when addressing social ills such as child labor and deconstructing the barriers that often are mounted to resist the social justice agendas that such discourse and strategy commonly inspire.

Next, in Chapter 2, Judith Ennew, William Myers, and Dominique Plateau identify the nature and scope of child labor as a social construct that, from the standpoint of children's best interests, is most beneficially defined by reference to human rights doctrines, principles, and rules. The application of a definitional orientation that puts the human rights of children front and center, they contend, requires a balanced consideration of children's work in its various aspects and contexts and, thus, careful and objective study of children's work that empirically reveals precisely how it affects them and their rights.

Finally in Part 1, Hugh Cunningham and Shelton Stromquist trace the evolution of children's work from the early nineteenth century to the present. The lessons from history, they conclude, are that there is nothing inevitable in the elimination or even the decline of child labor, but that success might be achieved when human rights, including social and economic rights, have real purchase in national and international society.

In Part 2, "The Standards-Based Response of the World Community," Holly Cullen opens with a chapter that considers the evolution of international legal standards on child labor, covering both legal (or formal) and extralegal (or informal) standards. Not until the 1989 CRC, she observes, did international standards relative to child labor begin to shift from a labor regulation to a human rights orientation. Even then, she notes, the focus of international standards has remained fixed on the type of employment that children may take up and at what age, not on their rightful entitlements. Like other contributors to this volume, she calls for greater attention to regulation of the conditions of working children, with human rights as guideposts.

Next, in Chapters 5 and 6, respectively, Sarah Bachman and Michael Bourdillon examine how international standards on children's work in general, and child labor in particular, have been translated into practice. Bachman considers the transnational barriers involved (institutional, political, and conceptual) and concludes that the international community has remarkably little direct say in how or whether international labor standards become reality. She thus urges strengthened roles for the two principal IGOs in this field, the International Labour Organization and the World Trade Organization (WTO). At the same time, arguing that no international institution is likely to succeed without the active participation of national governments, she also concludes that it is on individual states that the primary burden must fall, thereby inviting Bourdillon's assessment of local resistance to the elimination of children's work, child labor included. Such resistance, he writes, borrowing from his personal experience in Zimbabwe, comes from at least three categories of people: those who gain from the exploitation of children; those who see the advantage of economic activity by children to the children and their families;

and children themselves, not least because children who engage even in harmful work do so because commonly it is the best option available to them. To break down these barriers to change, Bourdillon concludes, it is necessary that we focus on the needs of children and their families who supply the labor; on why each resists demands for change; on the exact harm we wish to eliminate from children's lives; and therefore, accepting the potential of human rights discourse and strategy, on the exact rights of children we want to ensure.

Bourdillon's concluding chapter in Part 2 links logically to the three case studies that compose Part 3, each of them derived from the Global South, where child labor is most prevalent. Reflecting a continuum of country struggle against child labor from, arguably, the least to the most accomplished to date, they also reflect—not coincidentally—that poverty and underdevelopment have much to do not only with the existence of child labor but, as well, with the ability to battle successfully against it. Thus does each author urge a holistic rights-based approach to child labor, one that values equally and interdependently the civil, political, economic, and social rights of children at the least. Donald Mmari, from the vantage point of one of the poorest economies in the world—Tanzania—calls for poverty reduction accompanied by humane policies in education, health, and other social infrastructures. Victoria Rialp, from the perspective of an economy now striving for "newly industrialized" status—the Philippines—reports and endorses increased participation on the part of Filipino children and youth in the struggle against child labor and a consequent mainstreaming of children's rights in national and local development planning. And Benedito Rodrigues dos Santos, in the context of a national economy that outweighs all other South American economies and competes increasingly successfully in world markets—Brazil—recounts approvingly innovative rights-based strategies invented and promoted by social movements and civil society organizations dedicated to the overall welfare of working children: media mobilization, children's participation, product labeling, school grants, and most recently, the programming and funding of child labor eradication campaigns.

Each of the case studies in Part 3 anticipates and to some extent invades the space reserved for Part 4, "Toward Progressive Change," in which the principal elements of a human rights approach to the abolition of child labor are explored. At the outset in Chapter 10, Mark Teerink and I reunite to propose what we believe a *comprehensive* human rights strategy worthy of abolishing child labor should comprise. To this end, we emphasize first the centrality of a self-conscious commitment to an ethos of empathy and respect that invites a shift away from the statist, elitist, patriarchal, and paternalistic logics that obstruct the genuine promotion and safeguarding of children's best interests as matters of right rather than mere charity. Mindful of the skeptics, however, we leave it to David Post in Chapter 11 to challenge our human rights advocacy by asking whether the conceiving of child labor in human rights terms actually can mobilize progressive change. Relying upon several incidents of progressive change in national experience, Post reviews four perspectives on how social progress may be generated through a rights-based approach and responds affirmatively by citing improved protection and advocacy for children as the result. Additionally, he offers his views about the progressive change potential of state-directed solutions to child labor in contrast to "bottom-up" efforts to promote children's rights through social mobilization by nonstate actors in civil society.

Thereafter, in Part 4's remaining five chapters, especially important "bottom-up" and also "top-down" dimensions of a human rights approach to child labor are scrutinized. In Chapter 12, Victor Karunan argues that mainstream approaches to child labor have proven inadequate to "correct" or even address it for being based on Western conceptions of childhood and child development. He therefore advocates a rights-based approach that puts children at the center of a discourse that presupposes both a "new sociology of childhood"—interdisciplinary, cross-cultural, and humanistically sensitive to the life situations of working children—and a focus on the structural, macroeconomic factors that influence and shape the global economy and trade relations between countries.

In Chapter 13, Ben White assesses the practice of intergovernmental organizations in the anti–child labor struggle (principally the ILO, UNICEF, and the World Bank, with some consideration also of the United Nations Educational, Scientific, and Cultural Organization [UNESCO]) and confirms that the IGOs have so far made little headway in this regard. Rights-based arguments and strategies, he writes, have been, until recently, largely absent in international standard-setting, policy, and practice on child work, and he attributes this fact in no small measure to confusions that have arisen from multiple and contradictory uses of the term "child labor," uses that reinforce counterproductive and largely unnecessary polarizations between "abolitionist" and "protectionist" approaches to children's work. Observing that the principal international commitments on child rights, child labor, and education since the 1980s, though not perfect, provide a workable basis for reorienting child labor policy and practice in ways that can be attuned to the interests, needs, and rights of children, he therefore concludes that the task now is to get the relevant IGOs, as well as national and local governments, political elites, and the general public, to take them seriously and to act on them, in the language of ILO C182, as a "matter of urgency."

For purposes of comparison, White considers briefly the work of some of the transnational NGOs working in the child labor/child rights field. It is for Laurie Wiseberg in Chapter 14, however, to treat this subject at length. Beginning with an overview of the energetic role played by NGOs in the protection and promotion of human rights generally, she considers the universe of NGOs active in the area of children's work specifically, noting that, at all levels—

global, regional, national, and local—the worst forms of child labor have attracted, not surprisingly, the highest degree of NGO attention, while the largest group of child laborers—those who work under parental control—have received the least attention. Wiseberg explores how NGOs get child labor put on the agendas of the likes of the ILO, UNICEF, and the UN Commission for Human Rights, and assesses their work in standard-setting, fact-finding and monitoring, and witnessing and advocacy. Most if not all of these efforts, Wiseberg observes, have been pursued, especially since the late 1980s, with the human rights of children in mind, and on the whole, she concludes, they have been remarkably successful in mobilizing shame, as evidenced by transnational campaigns such as the Global March Against Child Labour and increasing numbers of cutting-edge international conferences. But whether all this NGO activity has altered the situation of working children for the better, she argues, is not clear. Problems about how to evaluate impact, the absence of precise definitions, the noncomparability of data—these and other factors make such an assessment difficult. In any event, she observes, success or failure in combating child labor may be linked more to the general conditions of poverty and inadequate or nonexistent education than to the work of NGOs specifically focused on child labor. And if that be the case and if the impact of globalization remains a widening gap between rich and poor, she concludes, child labor is unlikely to disappear until this trend is reversed, no matter how hard NGOs struggle in this regard.

Chapter 15, by Susan Bissell, follows pertinently on the heels of Wiseberg's observations. Confronting the contemporary debate between those who favor education as a strategy for child labor elimination and those who argue for a more laissez-faire approach, she explores some of the traditional literature and discusses the issue of poverty and some of the economic issues relative to children working. Of particular interest is a brief consideration of the notion of social capital, after which Bissell examines aspects of education quality that actually make children available for work. Finally, relying on her abundant experience with child labor in South Asia, she argues that the complexity of the issue in a human rights context lies not in the incompatibility of earning and learning but in case and situation specificity. At the same time, she posits that if education quality is addressed effectively, then the numbers of abjectly poor—and therefore typically working—children for whom education is immediately unaffordable can be small enough for communities at all levels to accommodate sensitively their best interests. The chapter concludes with a description of a human rights approach to child labor elimination that is championed by a growing number of stakeholders and that is shaping a new child labor discourse.

Chapter 16, by Frank Garcia and Soohyun Jun, closes Part 4 by exploring how international trade law and sanctions, a logical avenue for confronting child labor, could serve as a viable strategy for progressive change.

Acknowledging that domestic child labor sanctions might not survive legal challenge under WTO law as currently interpreted, Garcia and Jun nonetheless demonstrate how a child labor sanction, provided it is "nondiscriminatory," could be held consistent with the exceptions in Article XX of the General Agreement on Tariffs and Trade (GATT) for measures protecting public morals and measures protecting human life and health.[27] By offering a strategy for guiding domestic trade sanctions through a WTO challenge, they explain how the full power of international trade could be deployed in service to the human rights of vulnerable children, enabling WTO members to act affirmatively—and potentially powerfully—against child labor practices.

Finally, by way of formal conclusion, a "Contributor's Consensus," implicit in the foregoing summary, is offered. Initially—and graciously—drafted by Victor Karunan and William Myers at my request, and thereafter agreed to by each contributor to this volume, it sets forth guiding principles and a call to action that take the human rights of working children seriously. In so doing, drawing upon the rich inquiries and recommendations found in each of the chapters that precede it, it delineates clearly what we contributors to this text collectively believe is needed to be thought and done to win the struggle against child labor. It is hoped that in this consensus statement and in all the pages upon which it is predicated, you, the reader, will find insights and strategies worthy of your responsible attention and inspiration worthy of your progressive action.

True, real social change, as previously noted, typically takes place slowly. Not even the scourge of slavery, though outlawed, has been fully eradicated from the face of the earth. But even if we cannot eliminate the problem of child labor overnight, the possibility that we can define it correctly and identify its solutions adequately may do some good. If so, we then dare to believe that our collaborative effort will prove to have been worthwhile.

■ Notes

1. For the origins and perspectives that led to the creation of this volume, see the preface.

2. This definition of "child labor" is consistent with Chapter 2 in this volume and is in keeping with the other chapters that follow, each of which, except for Chapters 3 and 6, likewise accept the definition set forth in Chapter 2.

3. Weston, "Human Rights," p. 5.

4. United Nations, *Convention on the Rights of the Child* (1989). See also United Nations, *Optional Protocol to the Convention on the Rights of the Child on the Involvement of Children in Armed Conflict* (2000); and United Nations, *Optional Protocol to the Convention on the Rights of the Child on the Sale of Children, Child Prostitution and Child Pornography* (2000).

5. An early exception is the 1924 Declaration of Geneva on the Rights of the Child. Paragraph IV of the declaration, reflecting a former concerned era, provides:

"The child must be put in a position to earn a livelihood and must be protected against every form of exploitation."

6. See the bibliography for the official citations to each of these conventions.

7. *Charter of the United Nations* (1945).

8. United Nations, *Universal Declaration of Human Rights* (1948).

9. Accord, Gross, "A Long Overdue Beginning . . . ," p. 3: "Until recently, the international human rights movement and organizations, human rights scholars, and even labor organizations and advocates have given little attention to worker rights as human rights." See also Leary, "The Paradox of Workers' Rights as Human Rights"; Grimsrud, "Too Much Work at Too Early an Age," p. 9. For further discussion of the historical disconnect between, specifically, child labor and human rights, see Chapter 10 in this volume, pp. 236–238.

10. On the history as well as the meaning and scope of human rights, see Weston, "Human Rights."

11. Gross, "A Long Overdue Beginning . . . ," p. 3.

12. See the appendix for Article 3 of ILO C182, which defines "the worst forms of child labour."

13. Demonstrating the ILO's growing commitment is, for example, the 1998 ILO Declaration on Fundamental Principles and Rights at Work, Paragraph 2 of which expressly enjoins ILO members "to promote and to realize . . . the effective abolition of child labour" and to do so in accordance with the constitution of the International Labour Organization—and therefore also the 1944 Declaration of Philadelphia Concerning the Aims and Purposes of the International Labour Organization, which is annexed to, and forms an integral part of, the ILO constitution. In addition to reaffirming worker rights specifically, the declaration commits the ILO and its membership to all manner of human rights generally. Further, the preamble to 1999 ILO C182 expressly recalls, inter alia, the 1989 CRC, the 1998 ILO Declaration, and the 1956 United Nations Supplementary Convention on the Abolition of Slavery, the Slave Trade, and Institutions and Practices Similar to Slavery. See the appendix. Finally, in a 2002 report on child trafficking, the ILO, via its International Programme on the Elimination of Child Labour (IPEC), indicated a pronounced shift to human rights discourse and strategy in at least one major respect. As ILO/IPEC's director put it in his foreword to the report: "The trafficking of human beings is unacceptable under any circumstances, but the trafficking of vulnerable children and young people is a violation of their rights to protection from exploitation, to play, to an education, and to health, and to family life." Röselaers, foreword to IPEC, *Unbearable to the Human Heart* . . . , p. v.

14. UNICEF has worked closely with the ILO in this realm and now is increasingly known for putting rights at the center of its child labor advocacy and fieldwork. See, for example, UNICEF, *Beyond Child Labour* . . . ; and UNICEF, *Human Rights for Children and Women* . . . . See also Beigbeder, *New Challenges for UNICEF* . . . , pp. 163–172.

15. For elaboration, see the WHO website, at http://www.who.int/child-adolescent-health/right.htm, wherein the CAH identifies the following spectrum of child and adolescent rights, essentially within the framework of the 1989 CRC: nondiscrimination; education and access to appropriate information; privacy and confidentiality; protection from all forms of violence; rest, leisure, and play; an adequate standard of living; freedom from all forms of exploitation; and participation, including the right to be heard.

16. See Anti-Slavery International's website, at http://www.antislavery.org.

17. See the alliance's website, at http://www.savethechildren.net/homepage. The alliance describes itself as "the world's leading independent children's rights organization."

18. See the Global March website, at http://globalmarch.org/index.php. See also the website for the International Center on Child Labor and Education, based in Washington, DC, which is the North American secretariat for Global March, at http://www.iccle.org.

19. See Amnesty International's website, at http://web.amnesty.org/web/content.nsf/pages/gbroptionalprotocol.

20. See Human Rights Watch's website, at http://www.hrw.org/children/labor.htm.

21. See the Defence for Children International website, at http://www.defence-for-children.org.

22. See the Child Workers in Asia website, at http://www.cwa.tnet.co.hth/whatiscwa/whatiscwa.htm.

23. See, for example, the country studies in Part 3 of this volume.

24. ILO, *Every Child Counts* . . . , pp. 6, 20. In this report, the ILO defines "child labor" to mean all "economically active children" except "children 12 years and older who are working only a few hours each week in permitted light work" and "[children] 15 years and above whose work is not classified as 'hazardous.'" The ILO's estimate of 246 million children engaged in child labor, however, cannot be called exact. Indeed, because so much child labor takes place in the informal sector, such a verdict probably is impossible. At the same time, as a general proposition, the reported overall dimension of the problem and its regional distribution cannot be summarily dismissed. Of the 352 million children between five and fourteen years of age whom the ILO estimates to be engaged in "economic activity" worldwide (a broader concept than "child labor"), the Asian Pacific region is said to have the largest number (127 million), sub-Saharan Africa the second largest concentration (48 million), and Latin America and the Caribbean the third largest (17 million), followed by the Middle East and North Africa (approximately 13 million). The remaining 5 million "economically active" children are reported to be found in both developed and transitional economies. It is not unreasonable to extrapolate "child labor" proportions and distributions of rough equivalence.

25. It is essential to bear in mind that, just as no one has yet credibly measured precisely all the children engaged in child labor worldwide, neither has anyone yet credibly measured precisely all the children engaged in each category or form of child labor. For example, while estimating the number of children working in industries considered hazardous, the ILO appears not to have determined the number of children working in nonhazardous jobs in such industries.

26. See, for example, Chapters 3 and 6 in this volume.

27. See *General Agreement on Tariffs and Trade* (1947).

Part 1

Clarifying the Problem

1

Rethinking Child Labor: A Multidimensional Human Rights Problem

Burns H. Weston and Mark B. Teerink

It is indisputable. Child labor is a human rights problem,[1] and increasingly recognized as such the world over. Consider, for starters, the 1966 International Covenant on Economic, Social, and Cultural Rights (ICESCR),[2] Article 10(3) of which provides, in part, as follows: "Children and young persons should be protected from economic and social exploitation. Their employment in work harmful to their morals or health or dangerous to life or likely to hamper their normal development should be punishable by law. States should also set age limits below which the paid employment of child labour should be prohibited and punishable by law." Consider also the 1989 United Nations Convention on the Rights of the Child (CRC),[3] so widely adopted (more so than any other human rights compact in history) that it may be said to have entered into customary international law.[4] Article 32(1) of the convention is explicit: "States Parties recognize the right of the child to be protected from economic exploitation and from performing any work that is likely to be hazardous or to interfere with the child's education, or to be harmful to the child's health or physical, mental, spiritual, moral or social development." Article 32(2), requiring the states parties to take "legislative, administrative, social and educational measures" in respect of the foregoing, gives formal muscle to this human rights injunction.

Also explicit, though less directly, is the 1999 International Labour Organization Convention (No. 182) Concerning the Prohibition and Immediate Elimination of the Worst Forms of Child Labour (ILO C182).[5] In its preamble, ILO C182 recalls, inter alia, the 1989 CRC, the 1998 ILO Declaration on Fundamental Principles and Rights at Work,[6] and the 1956 United Nations Supplementary Convention on the Abolition of Slavery, the Slave Trade, and Institutions and Practices Similar to Slavery.[7] Thus it predicates its prohibitions of child labor's "worst forms" on a human rights framework, at least in part.

3

But particularly instructive, especially when accounting for the most egregious forms of child labor, are multiple additional provisions of the 1989 CRC, among them:[8] Article 3, requiring the states parties, "in all actions concerning children," to ensure "the best interests of the child," including "such protection and care as is necessary for his or her well-being"; Article 6, requiring the states parties to ensure "to the maximum extent possible the survival and development of the child"; Article 8, requiring the states parties to respect "the right of the child to preserve his or her identity, including . . . name and family relations"; Article 9, requiring the states parties to ensure that, unless otherwise provided by law, "a child shall not be separated from his or her parents against their will"; Article 11, requiring the states parties "to combat the illicit transfer and non-return of children abroad"; Article 12, requiring the states parties to assure "the child who is capable of forming his or her own views the right to express those views freely in all matters affecting the child," including "in any judicial and administrative proceedings affecting the child"; Article 13, safeguarding the right of children to "freedom of expression," including "freedom to seek, receive, and impart information and ideas of all kinds"; Article 15, recognizing the right of children to "freedom of association" and "peaceful assembly"; Article 16, protecting children against "arbitrary or unlawful interference with his or her privacy, family, home or correspondence"; Article 18, requiring parents to assume "common" and "primary" responsibility for "the upbringing and development of the child," guided by "the best interests of the child"; Article 19, requiring the states parties "to protect the child from all forms of physical or mental violence, injury or abuse, neglect or negligent treatment, maltreatment or exploitation, including sexual abuse"; Article 24, recognizing "the right of the child to the enjoyment of the highest attainable standard of health"; Article 26, recognizing "for every child the right to benefit from social security"; Article 27, recognizing "the right of every child to a standard of living adequate for the child's physical, mental, spiritual, moral and social development"; Article 28, recognizing "the right of the child to education"; Article 31, recognizing "the right of the child to rest and leisure"; Article 34, requiring the states parties "to protect the child from all forms of sexual exploitation and sexual abuse"; Article 35, requiring the states parties "to prevent the abduction of, the sale of or traffic in children for any purpose or in any form"; Article 36, requiring the states parties to protect the child "against all other forms of exploitation prejudicial to any aspect of the child's welfare"; Article 37, protecting children against "cruel, inhuman or degrading treatment"; and Article 38, requiring states parties "to ensure that persons who have not attained the age of fifteen years do not take direct part in hostilities" and to "refrain from recruiting any person who has not attained the age of fifteen years into their armed forces."

In other words, the problem of child labor is and must be recognized as a human rights problem not in a narrow monolithic sense, but as one that is multidisciplinary, multifaceted, and multisectoral—in a word, multidimensional—and involving practices that violate children's human rights both directly (e.g., slavery) and—more commonly—indirectly (e.g., compulsory labor that results in denial of the right to education). It embraces not only "the rights of the child" per se, but as well the broad panoply of entitlements across the whole spectrum of rights with which, at least in theory, *all* members of the human family are endowed—that is, the three "generations" of rights that have evolved since at least the English Bill of Rights of 1689 to the present day: (1) civil and political rights; (2) economic, social, and cultural rights; and most recently (3) community (or "solidarity") group rights.[9] Each has its own historical roots that track the evolution of modern industrial society, including the development of a labor class.[10] Each is thus linked to the problem of child labor in one or more of its manifestations, including such third generation rights as the right to peace,[11] the right to development,[12] and the right to a clean and healthy environment.[13] The exploitive employment of trafficked children for commercial sexual acts, for example, flouts the right to the security of one's person, ergo first generation civil and political rights.[14] The exposure of working children to toxic and otherwise hazardous substances infringes directly upon the human right to health, ergo second generation economic, social, and cultural rights.[15] Child soldiering subverts not only the first generation right to security of one's person but, likewise, the group right to peace, ergo third generation community (or solidarity) rights.[16]

Indeed, few provisions of the three historic instruments that constitute the "International Bill of Human Rights"—the 1948 Universal Declaration of Human Rights (UDHR), the 1966 ICESCR, and the 1966 International Covenant on Civil and Political Rights (ICCPR)—are unaffected by the problem of child labor.[17] This is particularly apparent when one conceives of human rights in terms of "human capabilities" in the manner of Martha Nussbaum and Amartya Sen; that is, by reference less to abstract wants (policy objectives) than to concrete and measurable needs (life functions)[18]—for example, life itself; bodily health and bodily integrity; senses, imagination, and thought; emotions; conscience; affiliation qua friendship and respect; and political and material control over one's environment.[19] It is impossible to disassociate the problem of child labor, especially its worst forms, from any one of these most central of human capabilities and therefore, as well, from any of their human rights correlatives. A mere glance at the 1948 UDHR proves the comparative point.[20]

But it is not only the multidimensionality of the child labor problem that reveals its human rights linkages. Also highly relevant is its interrelatedness with the human rights of the parents or guardians of working children,[21] a point well understood by, for example, the United Nations Children's Fund (UNICEF), which works to advance the rights of children and of women—qua mothers—in tandem.[22] As evidenced elsewhere in this volume, the safeguarding of children's rights depends not merely on the promotion and protection of their rights, but on the promotion and protection of the fundamental human rights of their parents or guardians as well,[23] and "without distinction of any kind, such as race, colour, sex, language, religion, political or other opinion, national or social origin, property, birth or other status."[24] Denying parents or guardians their human rights contributes to the propagation or perpetuation of child labor and thereby to denials of the rights of children.

In sum, the nexus between child labor and human rights is both broad and deep. That a number of states, intergovernmental institutions, and nongovernmental organizations (NGOs) engaged in the struggle against child labor have adopted or begun to adopt rights-based policies to prosecute its abolition is thus not surprising.

Still, as noted in the introduction to this volume[25] and in Chapter 10 as well,[26] a commitment to a rights-based approach to child labor is not yet common in official policy or practice. Skeptics assert that rights-based approaches to social ills such as child labor lack pragmatism because, it is said, they focus on unrealistic, aspirational norms that have little or no connection to the "real world." Indeed, some suggest that, in respect of child labor at least, human rights approaches tend to be counterproductive[27] and, more generally, that the international human rights movement is part of the problem, not the solution.[28]

We demur and contest these claims below. While the skeptics certainly have some valid points (the human rights movement is, after all, a human—ergo imperfect—project), there is no denying that a rights-based approach to child labor, especially when conceived and executed from a multidimensional, holistic perspective, has strong pragmatic underpinnings and thus can have substantial beneficial results.[29] One can point to numerous instances in which human rights discourse and strategy have had real impact,[30] including in the area of child labor.[31] Given the continued skepticism, however, it behooves us to explain why, and to explain also why the skeptics are mistaken.

◼ The Utility of a Human Rights Approach to Child Labor

Why is it important to think and act upon the problem of child labor as a human rights problem? What purposes are served by such an approach?

Human Rights as "Trumps"

In his germinal book *Taking Rights Seriously,* legal philosopher Ronald Dworkin asserts unequivocally—and correctly—that when a claimed value or good is categorized as a "right," it trumps most if not all other claimed values or goods.[32] Rights discourse confers a special status of importance on claimed entitlements, juridically more elevated than commonplace standards or laws, which in contrast to human rights are subject to everyday revision and reci-

sion for lack of such ordination. A proximate analogy is the distinction between a contractual or statutory claim and a constitutional one.

Thus, when child labor is designated as a condition from which children
have a *right* to be free and not merely an option for which regulating (but
comparatively easily revocable) *standards* must be devised, there results an
opportunity for empowerment and mobilization that otherwise is lacking. A
rights-based approach to child labor elevates the needs and interests of children in this context to societal needs and interests—societal goods—with associated claims of legal and political legitimacy. As UNICEF's 1997 *State of
the World's Children* report characterized the organization's strategic decision
to use rights to reduce child labor: "The idea that children have special needs
has given way to the conviction that children have rights, the same full spectrum of rights as adults: civil and political, social, cultural and economic."[33]
Or as UNICEF put it two years later in its 1999 *State of the World's Children*
report: "What were once seen as the needs of children have been elevated to
something far harder to ignore: their rights."[34]

In other words, rights are not matters of charity, a question of favor or
kindness, to be bestowed or taken away at will.[35] They are high-level public
order values or goods that carry with them a sense of entitlement on the part
of the rights-holder and obligatory implementation on the part of the rights-
protector—intergovernmental institutions, the state, society, the family. They
are values or goods deemed fundamental and universal; and while not absolute, they are nonetheless judged superior to other claimed values or goods.
To assert a *right* of a child to be free from abusive, exploitive, and hazardous
work is thus to strengthen a child's possibility for a life of dignity and well-
being. It bespeaks duty, not optional—often capricious—benevolence.

Human Rights as Interdependent
Agents of Human Dignity

Central to the concept of human rights is the notion of a "public order of
human dignity," a public order *(ordre publique)* "in which values are shaped
and shared more by persuasion than by coercion, and which seeks to promote
the greatest production and widest possible sharing, without discriminations irrelevant of merit, of all values among all human beings."[36] This notion of public order is embedded in the preamble of the 1948 UDHR, which proclaims the
concept of human rights to grow out of "recognition of the inherent dignity
. . . of all members of the human family" as "the foundation of freedom, justice and peace in the world."

Thus, in the struggle against child labor, a rights-based approach signals
more than the alleviation of child abuse and exploitation per se. It signals also
that notions of nondiscrimination and justice and dignity must be central in all
aspects of a working child's life, including provision for her or his education,
health, and spiritual, moral, or social development—precisely as the 1989

CRC envisions. A rights-based approach to the child labor problem is part of a complex web of interdependent rights that extends protection beyond one domain to many others in a child's life. Most if not all human rights (e.g., the right to be free from inhumane labor practices) depend on the satisfaction of other human rights (e.g., the right to education) for their fulfillment. Treating freedom from abusive, exploitive, and hazardous child work as a human right thus raises the stakes against those who would put children in harm's way. It transforms the struggle *against* child labor into a struggle *for* human dignity and thus better captures responsible attention and heightened pressure in the search for enduring solutions.

Human Rights as a Mobilizing Challenge to Statist and Elitist Agendas

Because they trump lesser societal values or goods and because they are agents of human dignity, human rights challenge and make demands upon state sovereignty. Scores of human rights conventions entered into force since World War II require states actually to cede bits of sovereignty in the name of human rights. Legal obligations of great solemnity, the 1989 CRC and 1999 ILO C182 are among them.

Proof is found, too, in the many occasions in which states, international governmental institutions, NGOs, transnational professional associations, corporations, trade unions, churches, and others have relied successfully on this "*corpus juris* of social justice"[37] to measure and curb state behavior. The legitimacy of political regimes—hence their capacity to govern noncoercively or at all—is today judged by criteria informed and refined by human rights.

All of this is well-known. Keenly aware of their interdependencies, most states, however much they may resist human rights pressures from within and without,[38] are mindful that their national interests and desired self-image depend on their willingness to play by the rules and especially those rules that weigh heavily on the scales of social and political morality. Even the most powerful states are thus vulnerable to what has come to be called "the mobilization of shame" in defense of human rights.[39] The case of apartheid South Africa is perhaps the best known in this regard. There is no reason why states that encourage or tolerate abusive, exploitive, and hazardous child work cannot or should not be similarly targeted and shamed.

But not just states. For the same reasons that human rights challenge and make demands upon state sovereignty, so also do they challenge and make demands upon the particularist agendas of private elites.[40] Why? Because human rights have as their core value the value of respect, by definition possessed equally by all human beings everywhere.[41] They insist upon equality of treatment across the board. Writes Virginia Leary, "[e]quality or non-discrimination . . . is a leitmotif running through all of international human rights law."[42] True, no observant person would dispute the widespread disregard of these principles. Still, there is no denying the potential power of human rights discourse and strategy to stand up, dare, and defy the special economic and political interests, private as well as public, that, usually for selfish reasons, dismiss the equal treatment of all human beings and thus contribute to social ills such as child labor.

In sum, ordinary norms, institutions, and procedures are not defined, typically, by the language of human rights and therefore do not have the same gravitas as their human rights counterparts. They therefore do not carry with them the same moral authority upon which, in democratic societies at least, governing elites depend to exercise and retain legitimacy and power. The potential for human rights discourse and strategy to dislodge or seriously burden those private exclusive interests that help to perpetuate child labor is likewise manifest.

Human Rights as Empowerment for Children
As noted, human rights carry with them a sense of entitlement on the part of the rights-holder. Indeed, human rights law embraces not only this sense of entitlement, but also "the right of the individual to know and act upon his rights,"[43] hence a sense of duty and redress on the part of the state and other actors. The essence of rights discourse (or human rights law) is that, in Michael Freeman's pointed alert, "if you have a right to x, and you do not get x, this is not only a wrong, but it is a wrong against *you*."[44] This extends inexorably to children as rights-holders. CRC Article 12 expressly requires that states parties "assure to the child . . . the right to express [her or his] views freely in all matters affecting the child" and that "the views of the child [be] given due weight."[45]

At least four specific ways have been identified by which human rights accomplish this empowerment.[46] Each bears obvious relevance to children and others who seek the abolition of child labor. First, human rights provide a level of accountability that transcends that of other legal obligations. Like those obligations, human rights provide victims of rights violations with the authority to hold violators accountable, even to the point of criminal liability. However, because human rights entail fundamental values of "superior" moral order, their violation correspondingly entails greater moral condemnation than other wrongs. This is what distinguishes "rights" from "benefits" or from being the beneficiary of another's obligation,[47] and thus what makes possible, for example, "the mobilization of shame" and the condemnation of the international community, commonly without even having to go to formal court. The "truth and reconciliation" processes of Argentina, Chile, El Salvador, Ghana, Guatemala, Haiti, Malawi, Nepal, Nigeria, the Philippines, Serbia and Montenegro, South Africa, South Korea, and elsewhere are proof enough.[48] On occasion, they can be more effective than their more formal legal counterparts in overcoming impunity.[49]

Second, human rights provide access to international institutions dedicated specifically to their promotion and vindication, including the human rights mechanisms of the United Nations[50] and the regional human rights regimes of Europe, the Americas, and Africa.[51] The effectiveness of these institutions as enforcement mechanisms is not consistent and often cumbersome and time-consuming, particularly at the global level. Nevertheless, they confirm that human suffering is and can be taken seriously, providing formal legal tools to remedy or otherwise mitigate abuses and thereby help to prevent future abuse. Like less formal techniques (e.g., a civil society mobilization of shame), their use can result in both specific and general deterrence, potentially ensuring individual and group rights.[52]

Third, human rights generate legal grounds for political activity and expression because, as already noted, they entail greater moral force than ordinary legal obligations. This is abundantly seen in the many global and regional conferences and other gatherings commonly called under the auspices of the United Nations (including the UN's Commission on Human Rights) and such regional organizations as the Council of Europe, the Organization of American States, and the African Union, each providing a forum in which the voices of human rights victims and advocates can be heard. The history of the antiapartheid movement is replete with examples. Also illustrative are the annual conferences of the ILO and the high-level meetings of UNICEF and other intergovernmental organizations. All contribute to political empowerment, from the adoption of new resolutions and treaties to the recommendation of new norms and mechanisms to the reinterpretation of existing international and domestic rules and procedures—according to which, in Mary Robinson's pithy characterization of the 1989 CRC, "[t]he more fortunate are called upon to assist the less fortunate as an internationally recognized responsibility."[53] In turn, the resulting rights vocabulary and action plans help to refine the theoretical and operational foundations for human rights projects of all sorts, reinforced by the authority with which the sponsoring organizations and attending participants are regarded.

Finally, human rights discourse and strategy, which exist to promote and protect human capabilities of all sorts, encourage the creation of initiatives both within and beyond civil society that are designed to facilitate the meeting of basic needs. Excepting the 1975 Helsinki Accords,[54] such initiatives were not easy to find before the fall of the Berlin Wall in 1989, when tensions sacrificed these concerns on the altar of Cold War rivalries. But since then they have proliferated, especially in the human rights advocacy and scholarly communities.[55] All of which is of profound importance because the provision of basic needs provides the material basis for people to act on their rights— the very definition of empowerment.

Despite the relevance of these (and possibly other) forms of empowerment to children and others who seek child labor's abolition, however, some scholars question whether they can in fact extend to children. Onora O'Neill, for one, is skeptical, because "[y]ounger children are completely and unavoidably dependent on those [adults] who have power over their lives."[56] Beyond perhaps the first six to eight years of childhood, we respectfully disagree, as would also most modern anthropologists, historians, and sociologists of childhood. While usually dependent on adults when very young, children are no longer "completely and unavoidably" dependent on them as they mature in age and experience. In fact, children may exhibit considerable independence and self-initiative well before adolescence. Their growing independence may be collective as well as individual. As Michael Freeman has argued, "there are prototypes or at least germs of children's movements already in existence."[57] Indeed, children's movements have long been noted among working children. In early-twentieth-century US cities, for example, the self-organization of child newspaper vendors to defend what they saw as their interests and rights attracted much public attention, and in some places was even supported by far-sighted and creative city officials who linked it to public child protection mechanisms.[58]

Present-day working children's organizations and movements in Africa, Asia, and Latin America have been amply noted and discussed in recent literature,[59] among them organizations linked in an international children's movement (the World Movement of Working Children and Adolescents) that maintains contact between countries and has had two international "summit" conferences, the first in 1996, the most recent in Berlin in April–May 2004, organized with adult assistance. The final declaration from the latter summit, in which the assembled working children reaffirmed their commitment to "practice protagonism" and fight for "recognition as social actors so that our voices be heard in the whole world," is noteworthy: "We value our work and view it as an important human right for our personal development. We oppose every kind of exploitation and reject everything that hurts our moral and physical integrity. . . . [W]e reaffirm our will to continue constructing a world movement that not only fights for, defends and promotes the rights of working children, but of children in general."[60]

In addition, nonworking children also have organized specifically to combat child labor. A prominent example is the Free the Children network, founded by Canadian youth Craig Kielberger, the work and motto of which ("Often assumed to be the leaders of tomorrow, our generation must be the leaders of today") also challenge skepticism of the sort expressed by O'Neill.[61] Further, the Global March Against Child Labour, while an adult-led initiative to mobilize international opinion against child labor, includes ample opportunity for the participation of both working and nonworking children to make their views known. At the Children's World Congress on Child Labor, organized by Global March in Florence in mid-May 2004, some 200 young persons from age ten to seventeen shared their opinions and perspectives and supported the creation of a "network for worldwide, youth-driven action to press international and national efforts towards integrating world resources and responses on poverty, child labour, and education, [including] the development of strategies to enhance national support for implementation of ILO conventions 138 and 182, as well as the 2015 commitment for education for all children."[62]

To be sure, there is room for debate over the extent to which children can or should be self-empowered, as evidenced by the manner in which the above-noted Berlin and Florence events were organized and conducted—the first primarily by working children, the latter primarily by adults. The fact remains, however, that children—including working children—are today demonstrating increasing resolve to assert their own interests and to do so as a self-conscious expression of their universal civil and political rights to access and participate in the decisionmaking and policy-implementing processes that affect their lives. Indeed, direct involvement by children in the defense and promotion of their interests and rights often is key to the validity and vitality of their claims. They are themselves often the best witnesses to the harm that results from violations of their rights and thus are uniquely well positioned to provide the most compelling evidence of the need for redress. Which is why, of course, the 1989 CRC and human rights values generally mandate the right of children to express their views freely and where it counts. Empowerment of children is not only a result of a rights-based approach to child labor; it is, subject to their evolving capacities, virtually a requirement of it.

■ Contesting Resistance to Human Rights Strategy

However manifest the premise and virtues of a human rights approach to the problem of child labor, our advocacy of it would be incomplete were we not to confront the conceptual, psychosocial barriers that all too commonly are mounted to resist human rights agendas and thwart their potential often from the start (testimony, of course, to the potential of human rights law and policy in the first place). Below, therefore, we respond to these conceptual barriers and to the vested interests that cluster behind them. Also, believing that there is nothing as practical as a good theory except the debunking of bad theory, we urge that human rights vis-à-vis child labor be taken seriously and actualized in everyday planning and programming. This may seem an obvious or even redundant thing to say, but it is important to appreciate completely the artfulness of one's detractors in order to weigh in confidently with a human rights orientation to child labor and thereby reap fully its benefits in the making of daily decision and policy. Much hangs in the balance.

Contesting the Claimed Immutability of State Sovereignty

There is no disputing that the state has diminished in relative influence in the past half century. Nevertheless, the classical international law doctrine of territorial sovereignty and its corollary of nonintervention remain the central props of our inherited state-centric system of world order. The values associated with these doctrines, however—a legal license to "do your own thing" and an injunction to "mind your own business"—resist the values associated with human rights, which tell us that "you are your brothers' and sisters' keeper" and therefore invite international scrutiny and outside interference in what otherwise would be internal matters.[63]

In other words, "human rights qualify state sovereignty and power,"[64] and as a consequence governments are naturally resistant to embracing the language of human rights, let alone rights-based agendas. Even governments that have voluntarily consented to human rights treaties, such as the 1989 CRC and 1999 ILO C182, are inclined to demur when it comes to implementation. However, it is disingenuous of them to tarry when they have committed officially to these legal promises. More important, after more than a half century of mounting international rejection of the claim that "the king can do no wrong," it is no longer tenable for them to do so—least of all when, as in the case of the CRC and ILO C182, the treaty obligations involved command the support of the vast majority of the world's states.[65]

In short, a sovereignty defense against human rights violations, particularly of the worst sort, is now, at least theoretically, a thing of the past. To be sure, the radical foundation upon which the scaffolding of contemporary international human rights law and policy has been erected is yet new and fragile. But as evidenced on at least the formal agendas of most international institutions and foreign offices, to say nothing of the agendas of global civil society, the world no longer deems impunity from human rights wrongs acceptable.

Contesting the Claimed Sanctity of Corporate Sovereignty

Also explaining resistance to a rights-based approach to child labor is what may be called "corporate sovereignty."[66] Just as states seek to control the territory and populations of their claimed jurisdictions, so business enterprises, in pursuit of market shares and profits, seek sovereignty over the means of production that principally define their more or less private jurisdictions (including of course their labor forces). Human rights agendas, however, tend to be costly and otherwise inconvenient to this fundamental objective and thus often are downplayed or ignored.[67] Not infrequently, business enterprises actively resist human rights agendas—as when, for example, to curry favor with host governments, they break sanctions against repressive regimes, cooperate with such regimes economically, or lend them internal political support of some kind.[68]

In these circumstances especially, human rights discourse itself is avoided lest it encourage outside scrutiny, possibly intervention. True, many—perhaps most—business enterprises strive to be "good corporate citizens" and thus to accept if not actually promote human rights agendas when called upon to do so.[69] True also, corrupt governmental practices often force business enterprises to comply with discriminatory and otherwise repressive legislation. Still, the impulse of corporate sovereignty remains a powerful deterrent to a rights-based strategy opposed to abusive, exploitive, and hazardous child work, especially when large-scale enterprises with great influence are involved.[70]

Corporate sovereignty, however, is an impulse to which public policy need not and should not defer. Throughout the world, governments adopt and enforce laws to limit factory emissions, regulate product content, set minimum wages, establish occupational safety standards, and the like. Indeed, labor conditions may be the most heavily regulated of business matters. Business enterprises should not therefore expect that a problem such as child labor should be subject to any less scrutiny and control. Nor should they, in their own self-interest, want such an outcome. Most business enterprises care more about stable production and marketing climates than they do about ideology, and the surest way to guarantee that such climates prevail is to safeguard the fundamental rights of the populations on which they depend for economic reward.[71]

Contesting the Claimed Irrelevance of Public International Law to Private Actors

Closely related to notions of state and corporate sovereignty as explanations for resistance to a rights-based approach to child labor—indeed supportive of them—is the orthodox theory that, by definition, public international law applies only to public—not private—actors.[72] Given that the vast majority of the world's working children labor on behalf of private—not public—actors, this theory is of no small consequence to the present discussion. Public international law (which includes international human rights law) simply does not apply, so the argument goes, to private business associations, including ones that employ children.

Of course, theories are but intellectual paradigms, prototypes of thought that define not only what we look at but also how we go about looking at what we look at. They do not necessarily mirror reality. So when the facts of life no longer fit the theory, it is time, as Copernicus taught us, to change the theory. In recent years, feminist scholars have urged this kind of rethinking, successfully, relative to the theoretical structure of international law, particularly in relation to the status of women internationally.[73] There is no reason why the same cannot be done relative to the status of working children in private business enterprises, making such enterprises directly accountable to international human rights norms relevant to them.

In any event, there is UDHR Article 30: "Nothing in this Declaration may be interpreted as implying for any State, *group or person* any right to engage in any activity or to perform any act aimed at the destruction of any of the rights and freedoms set forth herein."[74] Additionally, reflecting an emerging consensus that the large economic and political power of at least multinational corporations must be subjected to heightened international accountability, the UN Global Compact launched by Secretary-General Kofi Annan in 1999, the UN Commission on Human Rights, the UN High Commissioner for Human Rights, and growing numbers of legal scholars now categorically endorse theories of international transparency and responsibility that rewrite the relationship between international law and the private sector, including in relation to human rights.[75] As key beneficiaries of the new economic world order created by international law (e.g., the World Trade Organization [WTO], the North American Free Trade Agreement [NAFTA], etc.), private business enterprises have no standing, it is appropriately argued, to claim immunity from the corresponding obligations established by international law; and trends in actual decision, both national and international, suggest that human rights responsibilities on the part of private persons are being increasingly recognized and enforced.[76]

Expressly or by implication, many of the most fundamental human rights instruments recognize human rights obligations on the part of private actors per se,[77] while others and cognate treaties require states parties to ensure and enforce the rights enumerated against violations by private perpetrators.[78] States often adopt laws giving domestic effect to human rights norms and standing to seek redress for their violation by private actors.[79] And with increasing frequency, corporations commit themselves at least morally to human rights obligations via voluntary "codes of conduct"[80] while consumers and other members of civil society invoke nonjuridical mechanisms to hold private actors accountable by voting with their pocketbooks and otherwise mobilizing shame against private human rights violators.[81]

True, legal scholars differ over the extent to which developments such as these confer "international legal personality" upon corporations and other nonstate actors. Moreover, old canons die hard. But resistance to a rights-based approach to child labor can no longer be justified on the basis of orthodox theory about the "subjects" and "objects" of international law. The world is now far too interpenetrating a place for that.

Contesting the Claimed Indeterminacy of Human Rights

Some scholars criticize the language of human rights as lacking conceptual clarity, noting that there are conflicting schools of thought as to what constitutes a right and how to define human rights.[82] For this reason, they claim the concept to be "indeterminate"[83] and therefore distrust its capacity to address pragmatic, "real world" social ills effectively or at all.[84] They observe that there are many unresolved theoretical questions about rights: "whether the individual is the only bearer of rights" (in contradistinction to such entities as families, groups of common ethnicity, religion, or language, communities, and nations); "whether rights are to be regarded as . . . constraints on goal-seeking action or as parts of a goal that is to be promoted"; "whether rights—thought of as justified entitlements—are correlated with duties"; and not least, "what rights are understood to be rights to" a certain level of well-being, a certain access to certain resources in one's life pursuit, and a certain quality of opportunity in that pursuit.[85] The recent debate over "Asian values" and its underlying tension between cultural relativist and universalist approaches to human rights make clear that all this questioning is no idle intellectual chatter.[86] It is very much present in the political arena as well and thus serves as another possible explanation for resistance to a rights-based approach to child labor.

The claimed indeterminacy of human rights, however, is less problematic than perceived. The core of the human rights concept is as well defined and clearly articulated as any social or legal norm,[87] a fact proven by the numerous widely accepted—and increasingly enforced—human rights norms already noted. Moreover, even conceding that unresolved theoretical issues relating to human rights remain, this fact should not be allowed to distract from the broadest and most effective actualization of the fundamental principles and values on which there is virtually universal agreement—for example, the right of children to be free from abusive, exploitive, and hazardous labor.

Thus, while the concept or language of rights, like most legal language, sometimes suffers ambiguity, it is not to be discarded in the anti–child labor struggle (or any other) simply for this reason. Rather, as with any human— that is, incomplete and imperfect—system, one must make use of those elements that are established and effective while working to finalize and perfect those that remain still vague or incomplete, just as we do all other legal norms as a matter of course all the time.

Contesting the Claimed Absence of Human Rights Theory

Perhaps the most confounding of the alleged unresolved theoretical issues about human rights is the claimed absence of a theory to justify human rights.[88] In the presence of ongoing philosophical and political controversy about the existence, nature, and application of human rights in a multicultured world, a world in which Christian natural law justifications for human rights are now widely deemed obsolete, one must exercise caution when adopting a human rights approach to social policy lest one be accused of cultural imperialism. It is not enough to say, argues Michael Freeman, that human beings possess human rights simply for being human, as does, for example, the 1993 Vienna Declaration and Programme of Action, which proclaims that "[h]uman rights and fundamental freedoms are the birthright of all human beings."[89] Writes Freeman: "It is not clear why one has *any* rights simply because one is a human being."[90]

We do not disagree. But neither do we accept that there exists no theory to justify human rights in our secular times, ergo no theory to justify a human rights approach to child labor. The concept of human rights is or can be firmly established on sound theoretical ground.

First, there is the proposition, formally proclaimed in both the 1948 UDHR and the yet more widely adopted and revalidating 1993 Vienna Declaration, that human rights derive from "the inherent dignity . . . of all members of the human family"[91] or, alternatively, from "the dignity and worth inherent in the human person."[92] While this proposition informs us little more than the assertion that human rights extend to human beings simply for being human, it does point the way. Unless one subscribes to nihilism, it is the human being's inherent dignity and worth that justify human rights. Of course, the obvious question remains: How does one determine the human being's inherent dignity and worth?

Noteworthy in this regard is the previously noted work of Nussbaum and Sen on "capabilities and human functioning." In their search for a theory that answers at least some of the questions raised by rights talk, they have pioneered the language of "human capabilities" as a way to speak about, and act upon, what fundamentally is required to be human—that is, life; bodily health; bodily integrity; senses, imagination, and thought; emotions; affiliation (friendship and respect); other species; play; and control over one's environment (political and material).[93] While Nussbaum and Sen do not reject the concept of human rights as such[94]—indeed, they see it working hand in hand with their concept of capabilities, jointly signaling the central goals of public policy[95]—they propose emphasis on human capabilities as the theoretical means by which to restore "the obligation of result"[96] and thereby move the discussion from the abstract to the concrete without having to rely on controversial transempirical metaphysics to cut across human differences.[97] There remains, however, the question of how to distinguish those capabilities that are central to human existence—hence worthy of the title "human rights"—and those that are not.[98] Control over one's political and/or material environment, for example, can lead to some very nasty results.[99]

Thus we dig deeper and find the work of the late John Rawls compelling.[100] Rawls proposed a thought experiment, akin to Kant's "categorical imperative," in which a group of thinking men and women of diverse characteristics (race, class, creed, etc.) come together in their private capacity (i.e., not as state representatives) in some "original position" to construct a just society with their personal self-interests in mind, but without knowing their own position in it (economic, social, racial, etc.). Behind this "veil of ignorance," these "original position" decisionmakers, rationally contemplating their own self-interest, freely choose a society that is fair to all, one in which benefits (rights) and burdens (duties) are distributed equally and in which a core of fundamental liberties (freedom of conscience, speech, movement, religion, etc.) and equality of opportunity are protected. This social constructionism, however, need not be restricted to Rawls's historically Western core values favoring individual civil and political rights. Accounting for *all* the voices assembled, the "original position" decisionmakers, transcending personal self-interest even while accounting for it, could equally well choose a set of basic but diverse values (rights and/or capabilities) that would win the general assent of human beings *everywhere*—a set of universal basic values of human dignity that, grounded in principles of reciprocal tolerance and mutual forbearance, define the human rights society. It is such a society that can most guarantee the fairest distribution of basic wants (rights) and needs (capabilities) among all human beings and thereby ensure that all will benefit as much as possible and, by the same token, suffer the least possible disadvantage.

And therein lies, we believe, the theoretical justification for human rights in our secular age: a kind of share-and-share-alike Golden Rule that, in an "original position" behind a "veil of ignorance" and as rational human beings contemplating our own self-interest, we would choose for ordering a society in which all of us would want to live. However interpreted and applied in real world conflict and contestation, they are theoretically justified because they satisfy the fundamental requirements of socioeconomic and political justice. In the words of UN High Commissioner for Human Rights Louise Arbour before a working group on economic, social, and cultural rights of the Commission on Human Rights in January 2005, "[h]uman rights are not a utopian ideal. They embody an international consensus on the minimum conditions for a life of dignity."[101] When joined to the struggle against abusive, exploitive, and hazardous child work, they can be a uniquely powerful tool.

Conclusion

In the preceding pages, we have challenged a palpable if diminishing reluctance to use human rights to combat child labor. We have done so, first, by calling attention to the multidimensional human rights nature of the problem; next, by detailing the virtues of human rights discourse and strategy to combat the problem; and finally, by contesting claims that would prevent or curtail resort to such rights talk and maneuver. These latter claims, we submit, are as unconvincing as the virtues of human rights law and policy are convincing. And thus we are driven to conclude that the core questions demanding responsible attention are not why or whether to bring human rights to the prosecution of child labor, but how and how quickly.

These core questions, we hasten to add, demand urgent as well as responsible attention. Economic globalization, which can be no more arrested than the transition from agrarian to industrial society,[102] is proceeding apace, and while it has its bright sides, it has also its dark sides, negative aspects that threaten human rights generally and the rights of working children in particular. A human rights approach to child labor, we believe, one that foresees a true culture of respect for children's rights, can help to offset these darker forces if urgently as well as responsibly embraced and pursued.

In Chapter 10, therefore, we resume this discussion by proposing a comprehensive, multifaceted solution to child labor's abolition. Once the human rights of working children are recognized and their legal content understood, their provisions, both national and international, must be translated into effective policies, programs, and projects—measures that foresee, it bears repeating, a true culture of respect for children's rights. Both before and after we engage this discussion, however, experts from a wide variety of disciplines and professional experience lend their insights to a deeper understanding of child labor as a human rights problem, to the complexities that accompany it, and to some of the solutions they see as critical for it. Our purpose is to draw upon the extensive knowledge and experience of our co-contributors and, through them, bring human rights to child labor in a way that no longer can be denied. A hugely multidimensional human rights problem, child labor begs for a coextensively multifaceted human rights solution that, in whole or in part, can contribute to child labor's abolition.

■ Notes

We are grateful to Gavin Boyles, Susan Bissell, Kenneth Cmiel, Dorian Gossy, Teresa May Teerink, Willam Myers, Marta Santos-Pais, Chivy Sok, and Marta Cullberg Weston for gracious, insightful counsel.

1. In this chapter, we adopt the definition of "child labor" set forth in the introduction to this volume, in turn derived from Chapter 2, that is, "work done by children that is harmful to them because it is abusive, exploitive, hazardous, or otherwise contrary to their best interests—a subset of a larger class of children's work, some of which may be compatible with children's best interests (variously expressed as 'beneficial,' 'benign,' or 'harmless' children's work)."

2. United Nations, *International Covenant on Economic, Social, and Cultural Rights* (1966).

3. United Nations, *Convention on the Rights of the Child* (1989). See also United Nations, *Optional Protocol to the Convention on the Rights of the Child on the Involvement of Children in Armed Conflict* (2000); and United Nations, *Optional Protocol to the Convention on the Rights of the Child on the Sale of Children, Child Prostitution, and Child Pornography* (2000).

4. As of July 1, 2005, 191 states plus Niue (a self-governing island in free association with New Zealand) were party to the CRC, a process of ratification and accession that took just a little over seven years, with Ghana being the first to ratify, on February 5, 1990, and Switzerland the most recent, on February 24, 1997. Only Somalia and the United States among the signatories to the CRC have yet to ratify it.

5. ILO C182. See the appendix for Article 3 of ILO C182, which defines "the worst forms of child labour."

6. ILO, *Declaration on Fundamental Principles and Rights at Work* (1998). See also endnote 13 in the introduction to this volume.

7. United Nations, *Supplementary Convention on the Abolition of Slavery . . .* (1956).

8. For the full text of each of the provisions hereinafter quoted as well as other relevant provisions, see the appendix.

9. The notion of three "generations" of human rights is the brainchild of French jurist and former UNESCO legal adviser Karel Vasak, inspired by the three themes of the French Revolution, *liberté* (civil and political rights), *égalité* (economic, social, and cultural rights), and *fraternité* (community or "solidarity" rights). See Vasak, "Pour Une Troisième Génération des Droits de l'Homme." For extensive explication, see Marks, "Emerging Human Rights . . . ." See also Weston, "Human Rights," p. 5: "Vasak's model is, of course, a simplified expression of an extremely complex historical record, and it is not intended to suggest a linear process in which each generation gives birth to the next and then dies away. Nor is it to imply that one generation is more important than another. The three generations are understood to be cumulative, overlapping, and, it is important to note, interdependent and interpenetrating."

10. This history is summarized in Weston, "Human Rights," pp. 5–7.

11. On the right to peace, see, for example, Alston, "Peace as a Human Right." See also United Nations, *General Assembly Declaration on the Preparation of Societies for Life in Peace* (1978); and United Nations, *General Assembly Declaration on the Right of Peoples to Peace* (1984).

12. On the right to development, see, for example, Alston, "The Right to Development . . ."; Marks, "The Human Right to Development . . ."; Sengupta, "On the Theory and Practice of the Right to Development"; and Udombana, "The Third World and the Right to Development . . . ." See also United Nations, *General Assembly Declaration on the Right to Development* (1986).

13. On the right to a clean and healthy environment, see, for example, Boyle and Anderson, *Human Rights Approaches to Environmental Protection;* and Weiss, *In Fairness to Future Generations . . . .*

14. See, for example, United Nations, *Universal Declaration of Human Rights* (1948) [hereinafter "UDHR"], art. 1; and United Nations, *International Covenant on Civil and Political Rights* (1966) [hereinafter "ICCPR"], arts. 7–10.

15. See, for example, UDHR, art. 25. See also United Nations, *International Covenant on Economic, Social, and Cultural Rights* (1966) [hereinafter "ICESCR"], art. 12.

16. See, for example, United Nations, *General Assembly Declaration on the Preparation of Societies for Life in Peace* (1978); United Nations, *General Assembly Declaration on the Right of Peoples to Peace* (1984); and United Nations, *Security Council Resolution 1325* (2000).

17. Among the UDHR's rights provisions, see, for example, arts. 1, 3–9, 11–15, 22, 25.

18. See, for example, Sen, *Commodities and Capabilities;* Nussbaum, "Capabilities and Human Rights"; and Sen, "Capability and Well-Being." But see especially Nussbaum, "Capabilities, Human Rights, and the Universal Declaration." In the policy-oriented jurisprudence of Myres S. McDougal and Harold D. Lasswell, the distinction would be between "goal values" (rights/wants) and "base values" (needs/capabilities). See, for example, McDougal, Lasswell, and Chen, *Human Rights and World Public Order . . . .* See also note 97 and accompanying text.

19. See Nussbaum, "Capabilities, Human Rights, and the Universal Declaration," pp. 44–46.

20. Thus: *life* (UDHR art. 3 on the right to life, liberty, and security of the person); *bodily health* (UDHR arts. 12 and 25 on the right to privacy, family, and home and on the right to the highest attainable physical and mental health); *bodily integrity* (UDHR arts. 3–5 and 13 on the right to security of the person, to freedom from slavery or servitude, to freedom from cruel, inhuman, or degrading treatment, and to free-

dom of movement and residence); *senses, imagination, and thought* (UDHR art. 26 on the right to education and associated arts. 18, 19, and 27 on the right to thought, conscience, religion, opinion, and expression and to participate, enjoy, and share in cultural life); *emotions* (UDHR art. 12 on the right to privacy); *conscience* (UDHR arts. 18 and 19 on the right to thought, conscience, religion, opinion, and expression); *affiliation qua friendship and respect* (UDHR arts. 1, 20, and 29 on the right to peaceful assembly and association and to community duties for the free and full development of personality, all in a "spirit of brotherhood"); *play* (UDHR art. 24 on the right to rest and leisure); *political and material control over one's environment* (UDHR arts. 12, 17, 19–21, and 23 on the right to privacy, property, speech, association, political participation, and to work and free choice of employment).

21. See, for example, Article 2 of the CRC, safeguarding children "against all forms of discrimination on the basis of the . . . activities . . . of the child's parents."

22. See, for example, UNICEF, *Human Rights for Children and Women* . . . .

23. See, for example, UDHR, arts. 3, 6, 7, 13, 17, 23, 25, and 26.

24. Ibid., art. 2.

25. See pp. xv–xvi.

26. See pp. 236–238.

27. See, for example, O'Neill, "Children's Rights . . . ," p. 37.

28. See, for example, Kennedy, "The International Human Rights Movement . . . ," pp. 102–104. For convincing rebuttal, see Charlesworth, "Author! Author! . . ." But see also Kennedy, *The Dark Sides of Virtue* . . . .

29. See, for example, Charlesworth, "Author! Author! . . . ," p. 130.

30. See, for example, Cassel, "International Human Rights in Practice . . ."; and Slye, "International Human Rights Law in Practice . . . ." See also infra "Contesting the Claimed Irrelevance of Public International Law to Private Actors" in this chapter.

31. See, for example, the country studies in Part 3 of this volume.

32. Dworkin, *Taking Rights Seriously,* pp. 91–93, 189–191, 269.

33. UNICEF, *The State of the World's Children 1997,* p. 9.

34. UNICEF, *The State of the World's Children 1999,* p. 8.

35. Accord, Santos Pais, *A Human Rights Conceptual Framework for UNICEF,* p. 5.

36. McDougal, "Perspectives for an International Law of Human Dignity," p. 987.

37. Van Boven, "Survey of the Positive Law of Human Rights," p. 88.

38. See infra "Contesting the Claimed Immutability of State Sovereignty" in this chapter.

39. See, for example, Drinan, *The Mobilization of Shame.*

40. See, for example, the statement of common understanding developed at the UN interagency workshop on a human rights–based approach in the context of UN reform, May 3–5, 2003: "In a human rights–based approach, human rights determine the relationship between individuals and groups with valid claims (rights-holders) and State *and non-state actors* with correlative obligations (duty-bearers). It identifies rights-holders (and their entitlements) and corresponding duty-bearers (and their obligations) and works towards strengthening the capacities of rights-holders to make their claims, and of duty-bearers to meet their obligations." UNICEF, *The State of the World's Children 2004,* Annex B, p. 92 (emphasis added).

41. "[I]f a right is determined to be a human right, it is understood to be quintessentially general or universal in character, in some sense equally possessed by all human beings everywhere." Weston, "Human Rights," p. 5. The universality of human

rights has been much debated in recent years. For pertinent discussion, see Weston, "The Universality of Human Rights in a Multicultured World . . . ."

42. Leary, "The Right to Health . . . ," p. 37.

43. *Final Act of the Conference on Security and Co-operation in Europe . . . ,* para. 7.

44. Freeman, *Human Rights . . . ,* p. 61 (emphasis in original).

45. See CRC, art. 12(1) (emphasis added), quoted in the appendix to this volume.

46. For much of what follows, we are indebted to Slye, "International Human Rights Law in Practice . . . ," pp. 73–76.

47. Donnelly, *The Concept of Human Rights,* pp. 1–13; Donnelly, *Universal Human Rights in Theory and Practice,* pp. 9–12.

48. See, for example, the website of the United States Institute of Peace, at http://www.usip.org/library/truth.html.

49. See Rotberg and Thompson, *Truth v. Justice . . . .* See also Minow, *Between Vengeance and Forgiveness . . . ,* chap. 4; and Dugard, "Reconciliation and Justice. . . ."

50. See Marks, "The United Nations and Human Rights . . . ."

51. Stated in chronological order. See, generally, Shelton, "The Promise of Regional Human Rights Systems."

52. For pertinent discussion, see Chapter 10 in this volume.

53. Robinson, foreword to Marta Santos Pais, *A Human Rights Conceptual Framework for UNICEF,* p. v.

54. See *Final Act of the Conference on Security and Co-operation in Europe . . . .*

55. See, for example, Chapter 14 in this volume.

56. O'Neill, "Children's Rights and Children's Lives," p. 38. O'Neill asserts skepticism also because, she writes, "the ranks of childhood are continuously depleted by entry into adult life" (p. 39). Surely, however, this second argument is neutralized by the truism, curiously disregarded by O'Neill, that children, absent catastrophes such as AIDS and genocidal conflicts, continuously maintain the ranks of childhood by entering into life itself, replacing their seniors who mature into adulthood.

57. Freeman, "Taking Children's Rights More Seriously," p. 57.

58. See Nasaw, *Children of the City . . . ,* pp. 62–87.

59. See, for example, Black, *Opening Minds . . . ;* Miljeteig, *Creating Partnerships . . . ;* Swift, *Working Children Get Organised . . . ;* and Tolfree, *Old Enough to Work . . . .*

60. See *Final Declaration of the Second Meeting of the World Movement of Working Children and Adolescents.*

61. See the Free the Children website, at http://www.freethechildren.org. See also Kielburger, *Free the Children . . . .*

62. Quoted from the website of the Children's World Congress on Child Labour, at http://www.globalmarch.org/worldcongress/why_new.php3. A resulting children's declaration ("We Are the Present, Our Voice Is the Future") bears witness to these youth-defined intents. See http://globalmarch.org/worldcongress/dec.php3.

63. Claude and Weston, *Human Rights in the World Community . . . ,* p. 3.

64. Weston, "Human Rights," p. 4.

65. The CRC registered 192 parties as of February 1, 2005, one more than were party to the UN Charter (i.e., members of the United Nations) at the same time. As of February 1, 2005, 142 states were party to 1999 ILO C182.

66. We coin the term "corporate sovereignty" to cover a multitude of private business formations, not to single out corporations per se.

67. See, for example, Jennings and Entine, "Business with a Soul . . . ," p. 72. See also, generally, Mock, "Human Rights, Corporate Responsibility, and Economic Sanctions . . . ."

68. See, for example, ibid. See also Lippman, "Multinational Corporations and Human Rights," pp. 256–259; Monshipouri, Welch, and Kennedy, "Multinational Corporations . . . ."

69. See, for example, Jennings and Entine, "Business with a Soul . . . ," pp. 10–17.

70. As Richard Barnet and Ronald Müller pointed out in their germinal exposé of the power of multinational corporations three decades ago, "[a] global corporation is able to pay an annual retainer to a Wall Street law firm to represent its worldwide interests, which is perhaps five times the entire budget of the government agencies in poor countries that are supposed to regulate it." Barnet and Müller, *Global Reach . . .* , p. 138. See also Zia-Zarifi, "Suing Multinational Corporations . . . ," p. 84, n. 6 and documents cited therein.

71. See Jennings and Entine, "Business with a Soul . . . ," pp. 35–36, 41–46, 60–61.

72. According to this theory in its purest form, reflecting the dominance of the state as the primary organizational unit of human communities on the world stage since at least the Peace of Westphalia of 1648, states are the sole "subjects" of international law, the only actors with "standing" in the international legal order, the only beings competent to create and be bound by international legal obligations. See, for example, Shaw, *International Law,* p. 126; and Janis, *An Introduction to International Law,* p. 238.

73. See, for example, Charlesworth and Chinkin, *The Boundaries of International Law . . . .* See also Charlesworth, Chinkin, and Wright, "Feminist Approaches to International Law"; Orford, "Contesting Globalization . . ."; and Shelton, "Protecting Human Rights . . . ."

74. Emphasis added.

75. Regarding the Global Compact, see Global Compact, *The Nine Principles.* Regarding the United Nations Commission on Human Rights, see United Nations Sub-Commission on the Protection and Promotion of Human Rights, *Norms on the Responsibilities of Transnational Corporations.* Regarding the UN High Commissioner of Human Rights, see the OHCHR website, at http://www.ohchr.org/english/issues/globalization/business/index.htm ("Business and Human Rights"). And for scholarly commentary, see, for example, Monshipouri, Welch, and Kennedy, "Multinational Corporations . . ."; Paust, "Human Rights Responsibilities of Private Corporations"; Ratner, "Corporations and Human Rights . . ."; and Zia-Zarifi, "Suing Multinational Corporations . . . ."

76. Ibid.; Shelton, "Protecting Human Rights . . . "; Office of the UN High Commissioner for Human Rights, *Business and Human Rights . . . .* See also the following pertinent websites: Business for Social Responsibility, at http://www.bsr.org; Business and Human Rights Resource Centre, at http://www.business-humanrights.org/home; and Amnesty International, at http://web.amnesty.org/web/web.nsf/pages/ec_home.

77. See, for example, ICCPR, arts. 8 (slavery, servitude, forced or compulsory labor) and 17 (privacy, family, home, or correspondence); ICESCR, arts. 7 (just and favorable conditions of work) and 8 (trade unions); and *American Convention on Human Rights,* arts. 6 (slavery and involuntary servitude) and 11 (privacy).

78. Labor treaties that have emerged from the ILO, for example, have long required governments to enact domestic legislation affecting private businesses.

79. Examples include *US Alien Tort Claims Act,* 28 USC sec. 1350; also the German federal system's concept of *Völkerrechtfreundlichkeit,* or "friendliness" to human rights, whereby treaties are adopted by federal statute and treated as federal law. See Oeter, "International Human Rights Law . . . ."

80. See, for example, Schrage, *Promoting International Worker Rights . . . .* See also Chapters 4 and 5 in this volume.

81. See, for example, Jennings and Entine, "Business with a Soul . . . ," pp. 10–16. See also Gonzales, "Latin Sweatshops Pressed by U.S. Campus Power" (discussing the impact of US student actions on sweatshops); Kelly, "For Some, an Uncomfortable Fit" (discussing antisweatshop actions against various footwear companies); and Mannion, "Lobby Groups Open Ethical Attacks" (discussing lobby groups' efforts to persuade pension funds to pull investments from companies accused of not being socially responsible).

82. For an insightful account, with discussion of other views, see Gewirth, *The Community of Rights.*

83. The concept of indeterminacy has been much discussed in several modern approaches to language and literature, contending that the meaning of a text never can be fully determined because its author's original intention is subject to the unfixed nature of the author's makeup and experience, because it is the consequence of the particular cultural and social background of the reader, and because language itself generates its own meaning over time. This contention, Michael Freeman points out, is prominent particularly when it comes to concepts such as "human rights"—abstract, oftentimes ambiguous, and therefore "a challenge" to the philosophical discipline of conceptual analysis, which "can seem remote from the experiences of human beings." Freeman, *Human Rights . . . ,* p. 2.

84. For a seemingly nihilistic critique and a convincing rebuttal to it, see references in supra endnote 28.

85. Nussbaum, "Capabilities, Human Rights, and the Universal Declaration," pp. 26–27.

86. On cultural relativism versus universalism in human rights law and policy, see Weston, "The Universality of Human Rights in a Multicultured World . . . ."

87. See, for example, Weston, "Human Rights," pp. 4–9, especially pp. 4–5.

88. Richard Rorty, for one, contends that there is no theoretical basis for human rights on the grounds that there is no theoretical basis for any belief. See Rorty, "Human Rights . . . ," pp. 116, 126.

89. *Vienna Declaration and Programme of Action . . .* [hereinafter "Vienna Declaration"].

90. Freeman, *Human Rights . . . ,* pp. 60–61 (emphasis in original).

91. UDHR, Preamble, para. 1.

92. Vienna Declaration, Preamble, para 2. The declaration was adopted by acclamation by 171 states. "Because the [Declaration] was agreed to by virtually every nation on earth," opines Robert Drinan, "the document constitutes customary international law." Drinan, *The Mobilization of Shame . . . ,* p. x.

93. See Nussbaum, "Capabilities and Human Rights" and other references cited in supra endnote 18. See also Sen, *Equality of What?* For an early advocacy of a capabilities approach to human rights, see Williams, "The Standard of Living . . . ," p. 100.

94. In her essay linking the capabilities approach with the UDHR, Nussbaum acknowledges that the language of rights retains an important place in public discourse, providing a normative basis for discussion, emphasizing the important and basic role of the entitlements in question and people's choice and autonomy, and establishing the

parameters of basic agreement. See Nussbaum, "Capabilities, Human Rights, and the Universal Declaration," p. 59.

95. Regarding this symbiosis between capabilities and rights, see supra endnote 18 and accompanying text.

96. Nussbaum, "Capabilities, Human Rights, and the Universal Declaration," p. 56.

97. Similar efforts, distinguishing between "goal values" (rights) and "base values" (capabilities), have been articulated in the policy-oriented jurisprudence of the so-called New Haven School. See McDougal, Lasswell, and Chen, *Human Rights and World Public Order* . . . . Likewise for research on the intersection of human rights and basic needs. See, for example, Galtung, *Human Rights in Another Key;* and Galtung and Wirak, *Human Needs, Human Rights, and the Theories of Development* . . . . See also Claude and Weston, *Human Rights in the World Community* . . . , chap. 3. But see Donnelly, *The Concept of Human Rights,* pp. 28–31. Donnelly rejects the claim that human rights are justified by human needs because there is not, he argues, any scientific way to determine a universally agreed-upon set of needs.

98. Nussbaum and Sen go to considerable lengths to substantiate their choice of human capabilities on the basis of historical evidence, but history does not of itself answer this differential question.

99. Accord, Freeman, *Human Rights* . . . , p. 67.

100. See Rawls, *A Theory of Justice,* secs. 1–4, 9, 11–17, 20–30, 33–35, 39–40.

101. *Statement by Ms. Louise Arbour* . . . .

102. See Sen, *Development and Freedom,* p. 240: "The one solution [to the problems caused by globalization] that is not available is that of stopping globalization of trade and economics." See also Howard-Hassmann, "The Second Great Transformation . . . ," p. 1.

2

Defining Child Labor as if Human Rights Really Matter

Judith Ennew, William E. Myers, and Dominique Pierre Plateau

There is no one universally accepted way to define "child labor." Concepts and definitions are so many, so varied, and frequently so vague that the term has now been devalued beyond technical usefulness. This can be seen in the following list of some of the ways it commonly is used in the literature:

All work of any kind performed by children.
Economic participation by children.
Full-time work performed by children.
Work that is harmful to children.
Work that interferes with schooling.
All paid work.
Waged employment.
Work that exploits children.
Work that violates national child labor laws.
Work that violates international standards.[1]

Different usages describe very different observable facts, and people campaigning to "eliminate child labor" are not all talking about the same thing. That matters greatly in practice, because different definitions lead to different policies.

We argue in this chapter that there is no single, correct definition of child labor because it is a social construct, not a natural phenomenon, and social constructs are cultural ideas that differ between actors, histories, contexts, and purposes. This implies that, to understand child labor, one first must explore the ways it is constructed as a problem by various actors and in different situations. In our discussion, we use as a framework several distinct discourses (sets of closely interlinked ideas about childhood and work) representing the most common ways child labor is currently constructed, each of which results in different policies and practices. We raise the question of how such constructs relate to human rights, especially the main international human rights conventions as they apply to children. Particular attention is devoted to the most recent international convention on child labor and the issue of defining the so-called worst forms of child labor. The practical significance of different ideas about the meaning of child labor is then illustrated by a case study of the Lower Mekong subregion of Southeast Asia, one of the few regions about which there is sufficient information to make such a comparison. Finally, we turn to the question of what construction of child labor might best serve human rights values and objectives.

■ "Child Labor" Is a Social Construction

Although children can be seen working all over the world, their activities are perceived in a wide variety of ways, resulting in multiple, competing definitions of child labor. This means that, however it is used, the term is not an objective, technical description of a single, observable set of human relations, but rather a rhetorical label that blends description with negative value judgments. Identifying a situation as child labor involves mixing observations about what children do with ideas about the nature and value of their activities. The process of identifying child labor is an exercise as much cultural and political as scientific. This means that, as with all social constructs, it is difficult to provide a factual justification for any definition of child labor or to prove that one definition is better than any other.

Four distinct constructs of child labor are particularly common and influential today. They are the products of specific discourses, or sets of ideas with their own internal logic, which we have labeled "labor market," "human capital," "social responsibility," and "children-centered" according to the central ideas about childhood and work used in each one.[2] These are all produced and reproduced through organizations and agents that give them expression in the world of practice. Each is something of a world unto itself, defining and acting upon a particular view of reality, which seems obvious to insiders but is not necessarily shared by everyone.

The "labor market" discourse is the oldest, the most widely known, and currently dominant. It is the basis of 1973 International Labour Organization Convention (No. 138) Concerning Minimum Age for Admission to Employment (ILO C138) as well as most national laws affecting working children, and has been the main source for child labor intervention for over a century and a half. A legacy of nineteenth- and early-twentieth-century European and North American industrialization, it conceives of child labor (without using the term) primarily as the participation of children in what "should be" exclusively adult labor markets, and seeks "the abolition of child labor" through the exclusion or removal of children from those labor markets. The main means of doing this is the exercise of state power in the form of legislation such as minimum age laws, workplace inspection by government agents, prosecution of law violations, and provision of compulsory public education. This is a legalistic approach that tends to explain child labor through the theory that the weak are exploited by the strong, who must be controlled through legislation and its enforcement. This discourse also regards work and education as incompatible and insists that children should not be allowed to work until they have finished their basic education (one latent purpose of compulsory education being to keep children out of the labor market). In this discourse, children are regarded as unaware of their own best interests, highly vulnerable to workplace exploitation, and completely dependent on adults for protection, especially through the actions of the state. Because the labor market discourse demands that children under the legal minimum age not be economically active at all, it refuses such children both the right to work and the right to join or form trade unions. This perspective is typically predominant in the ILO, national ministries of labor, trade unions, and the legal profession.

A second common social construction of child labor is the product of "human capital" discourse, which is a relatively recent phenomenon much influenced by the language that economists use to discuss economic development, for example, "poverty alleviation," "the productivity of labor," and "developing human resources with marketable skills." It is a discourse particularly at home in the World Bank and regional and national development banks, in the United Nations Development Programme (UNDP), in national economic development agencies, and in education systems. From this perspective, child labor is seen as the result of underdevelopment and defined as work and/or working conditions that undermine development of the health status, knowledge, and skills that children will require to contribute in adult life to both national economic development and their own prosperity. In this discourse, there is no fundamental objection to children being economically active, as long as their "human capital" is not threatened and is properly nurtured (through apprenticeships, for example). Thus, children are viewed as human potential that must be prepared for productive adulthood, and childhood as a period of economic investment that produces future returns through taxes paid, increased productivity, and an expanded economy. The human capital discourse places great importance on education, at least insofar as this is focused on schooling and skills training, and supports programs that ensure access by all children, including working children.

The third discourse, on "social responsibility," looks at children in the context of social (or human) rather than economic development, and is concerned with the separation of children from mechanisms of social protection, participation, and opportunity. It conceptualizes child labor as a problem of social exclusion leading to work that exploits, alienates, and oppresses children, often because they are socially excluded in the first place. The problem of child labor is explained as the result of social breakdown of family, community, or nation so that support does not reach marginalized groups of children. The remedy, according to this discourse, is to mobilize society to reach and include those who are excluded. Not surprisingly, this construction of child labor has generated innovations in reaching and assisting working children, including "street education" and the participation of children themselves in devising solutions to their problems. This discourse is primarily the product of civil society, often nongovernmental organizations (NGOs) in developing countries, many of which have a religious orientation or a democratic ideology that stresses human rights. In Latin America, for example, it is associated with the Christian labor movement and liberation theology. In some industrialized countries and development agencies, this construction has been also associated with the idea of "social capital," which emphasizes the importance, for political and economic development, of civil society structure, informal networks, and relationships built on trust. In this discourse, children are regarded as both a social product and a social project, with the well-being of children ultimately resting on the care and moral values of their society.

The fourth and most recent social construction of child labor is the product of "children-centered" discourse. At the international level, it is represented by the child rights approaches of organizations such as the United Nations Children's Fund (UNICEF) and the International Save the Children Alliance, and at national levels by an increasing number of local organizations promoting children's rights and welfare. Similarly, 1999 ILO Convention (No. 182) Concerning the Prohibition and Immediate Elimination of the Worst Forms of Child Labour (ILO C182), although linked with ILO C138 (1973) via its preamble and the 1998 ILO Declaration on Fundamental Principles and Rights at Work, is consistent with the children-centered discourse; its preamble explicitly recalls the 1989 United Nations Convention on the Rights of the Child (CRC) as well as other historic human rights treaties. Organizations with this perspective assess children's work according to the effect it has on children, so that child labor is defined as work that is harmful to them. Interventions are intended to guarantee children's well-being as well as to safeguard their rights. This point of view is directly linked to human rights discourses through the CRC and commentaries on its provisions, particularly those using the language of "entitlements" and "duty-bearers." Occasionally drawing on recent sociological and philosophical work on childhood, the children-centered discourse proposes that children are resilient, capable, and knowledgeable in some ways while vulnerable and dependent in others. Children are conceptualized as active participants in their own defense when given the chance. Children-centered programs tend to value practical knowledge about children and their lives, to focus on children's rights and best interests according to the CRC, and to encourage children's own initiatives and their participation in planning and conducting activities on their own behalf.

■ Childhood and Work

Each social construction of child labor makes use of two other well-recognized social constructs much studied by historians and social scientists: "child" (and childhood) and "labor" (and work). Both need to be examined because of the clues they provide to different definitions and understandings of child labor.

The Social Construction of Childhood

Although "childhood" is socially constructed in different ways, all are based on the same observable, physical fact: children are biologically immature human beings who, initially, are highly dependent on others for survival yet gradually develop capacities that decrease dependency. It is universally true also that biological survival and development are closely tied to the social arrangements through which children are nurtured from infancy to adulthood, arrangements that vary according to culture, climate, historical period, status, and so forth. These social arrangements are complex systems of rules and expectations about who children are, what their role is, and what childhood is or ought to be. Such cultural ideas are often related to religion or other beliefs, family status, personal experience, tradition, and other community factors. Any society's perspective on, and management of, child work is highly dependent on the way it constructs childhood, as we illustrate later in our case study of four countries in the Lower Mekong subregion.

Current scientific evidence suggests that no one construct of childhood or child-raising merits adoption as a universal model. Yet a Northern cultural construction of childhood and child-rearing, which is now globally dominant, is incorrectly assumed to represent a scientific understanding of children valid everywhere and is the driving force behind many universalized social policies, including those governing child work; and this is so even in developing societies where often these policies do not fit. Constructive "Southern" or "non-Western" ideas of childhood and child-rearing tend to be ignored or treated as inferior. Some social scientists studying childhood point out that, even though contributions from wealthy countries—such as improvements in child health care—clearly benefit children, the "globalization of childhood" through the extension and imposition of the Global North model unfairly disadvantages and stigmatizes children in Southern countries who are being raised according to different but equally rational views of children and childhood.

Human Rights and Childhood

Children's access to the protection of human rights depends on how people and organizations defining those rights conceive of children and childhood. A central issue is whether children are defined to be part of humanity as a whole, sharing fully and equally in any fundamental rights claimed for all human beings, or whether they are categorized as a separate group having more, fewer, or different rights than people who are older. The 1948 Universal Declaration of Human Rights (UDHR) emphasizes universality, stating that "everyone is entitled to all the rights and freedoms set forth in this Declaration, without distinction of any kind, such as race, colour, sex, language, religion, political or other opinion, national or social origin, property, birth, or other status." Empowering children as bearers of equal human rights—for example, political rights (Article 21)—is such a radical departure from law and custom almost everywhere that many assume the declaration was never intended to apply to children. Others insist that it means what it says and is inclusive of everyone, which would have important practical implications for considering child labor. Some working children and child rights advocates claim a universal right to work if they wish to do so, as well as the right to form and join trade unions, both of which are clearly guaranteed by Article 23 of the UDHR, without age qualification. However, in 1966 the International Covenant on Economic, Social, and Cultural Rights (ICESCR) and the International Covenant on Civil and Political Rights (ICCPR) took significant preliminary steps toward modifying human rights according to age, by defining childhood as a state requiring special protection, with rights distinct from those of adults.[3] It can be (and is) debated whether children gained or lost with this shift, the answer depending on the construct of childhood being used.

In 1989 the CRC attempted to unite the empowerment and protection visions in a single instrument. While it was drafted specifically to spell out the rights of children by defining them as a special class apart from adults, at the same time it reinforced the idea of children as citizens who should enjoy rights of expression and action. These two concepts of childhood are intertwined throughout the CRC, not always in harmony. This raises the question of whether separate rights are equivalent to lesser rights. Does defining children as a distinct, less competent, and more dependent class, to be protected separately from adults and often in preference to them, ultimately extend their rights or isolate them from the full force of rights originally guaranteed to everyone under the UDHR, ICESCR, and ICCPR?

Some critics of the CRC claim that the international legal construction of children as world citizens with rights of action gave way, between 1948 and 1966, to a construction of them as passive and vulnerable victims completely dependent on adults. They argue that defining children as a special category trivializes their rights, reducing what should be rights of empowerment to mere entitlements to government protection and services, thereby suggesting that this leaves children *more* vulnerable because it reinforces the idea that they are wholly dependent on adults and reduces their capacity for autonomy.

Indeed, we have personally observed that working children sometimes report that putting too much emphasis on the identity of young workers as children exposes them to arbitrary treatment, abuse, and exploitation by the authorities and other adults. Many say that they would prefer to be regarded simply as workers and be accorded the same rights extended to adult workers, which they find to be more protective in practice than are special rights intended to protect only children. They and their adult advocates also point out that "protective" laws prohibiting children from voluntary work are actually used to forbid them to form or join trade unions for their own protection, which is a clear violation of the UDHR, ICESCR, and ICCPR.[4]

Defenders of the CRC reject the charge that it weakens basic human rights, arguing that children gain more rights, or at least more observance of their rights, by being defined as a special group, with legally recognized interests that are specific to their stage in the life cycle. They emphasize that the provisions of the CRC are simply the rights and principles of the UDHR, ICESCR, and ICCPR, adapted to meet the particular status of children. For example, CRC Article 32, which addresses children's economic exploitation, is clearly derived from ICESCR Article 10(3). Therefore, to promote compliance with the CRC is to promote wider observance of the full range of human rights as they apply to children.

It is beyond the scope of this chapter to detail the complex arguments of this debate, but it serves to demonstrate that the way childhood is defined and constructed socially has enormous impact on the kinds and extent of rights available to children in practice. It could be argued that the controversies surrounding conflicting ideas of rights come more to the fore with respect to child work and working children than in any other sphere of childhood. These controversies challenge the much repeated cliché that all human rights (or child rights) are indivisible, in harmony, and mutually reinforcing. Experience teaches that even the most basic rights are not compatible in every situation and cannot be always simultaneously maximized. When working children insist that it is more advantageous for them to be defined as workers with full worker rights than as children with child rights, they raise a basic question that goes beyond the relatively narrow field of child labor and deserves further thorough and sophisticated consideration.

Child Labor and the Social Construction of Work

The many everyday meanings of "work" complicate its use as a universally understood technical term. It can mean anything from household chores, to formal sector employment, to any kind of purposeful activity—and of course children do all of these. In a summary of results from a study of children's views, the International Save the Children Alliance states that "we recognize that there are often no shared beliefs about what work is. For girls and boys work means many things. For some, unpaid activities are not considered work, for others it is important to include these activities to ensure that the housework of girls is recognized. Some working children argue that work is something that is 'dignified' and contributes to their own or their family's survival. Others see work as harmful or exploitive."[5]

The extensive literature on work presents its various forms as ranging from the cruel to the sublime. Work is widely understood across cultures not only as a way of making a living, but also as a vehicle of socialization, independence, and self-realization. However, the dominant official construction of work within Northern discourses on child labor tends to be particularly narrow and bleak in its view of work. By reducing work to "employment," this definition, in economic terms, shrinks work to a "disutility" (a pain or cost) that must be endured to gain an income with which workers can acquire "utilities" (goods and services that they wish to consume), with the result that a key objective of labor law is to reduce the disutility of work to workers. In this context, work is not credited with qualities that would make it desirable in its own right—although, even in advanced industrial societies, much work is popularly considered to render personal and social rewards well beyond its economic benefits.

Although many children regard their work as an unpleasant burden, many others defend it as intrinsically rewarding and claim a right to engage in it if they wish. However, the currently dominant international discourse on children's work virtually ignores both children's views about and research results on the benefits of work, focusing instead almost exclusively on the dangers and costs. Both are real and important, and both need to be taken into account when properly analyzing the effects of different kinds of work on children. It is unwise to ignore the fact that many working children insist that they enjoy their work, learn a lot from it, develop self-confidence, and find it a valuable source of pride and self-esteem, in addition to gaining much needed income and a sense of satisfaction by helping to support themselves and their families. In many cases, children's testimony of this kind is dismissed as a sure sign that they are misled and unable to recognize their own exploitation. It is as though working children have to suffer to have their opinions taken seriously. What this negative view disregards is the evident fact that work can provide pleasure, a sense of community, self-esteem, and training, as well as mental and physical health and other benefits; it can be, returning to the language of economists, a *producer utility.* Most of the extensive research that has been carried out on the psychological and sociological impact of working (and not working) has been conducted with adults, but the findings closely parallel what working children often say about their own experiences. Generally, this research indicates that work is among the most powerful sources of self-esteem, human capital development, intellectual enhancement, and even of overall happiness and contentment. Factory and other organized work has been shown in some developing countries to be the most effective modernizing influence for individuals, to an even greater extent than education. Some longitudinal research suggests that one of the best predictors of adult success, happiness, and good mental health is having worked as an adolescent.[6] We are not suggesting that work always does children more good than harm. In fact, there is evidence from the ILO that more kinds of child work may harbor more dangers than is commonly realized.[7] But there is also at least equally strong evidence that work in some circumstances can benefit children.[8] The failure to consider thoroughly what children gain as well as lose through their work results in a distorted construct of work as primarily threatening to children and their welfare, even though work by children has also been, throughout history, an important vehicle of their socialization and development.

Further complications arise when official definitions narrowly equate work with "economic participation," a term associated with the economic accounting of gross domestic product (GDP), in which the contributions of women, children, and illegal workers, and of workers engaged in domestic work, unpaid agricultural production, and informal-sector activities, are ignored or undervalued. Child labor is understood in this perspective as economic participation by underage workers, "underage" being defined by the ILO as younger than the minimum age norms for employment established in various ILO conventions, including ILO C138. These have long been the international standards by which national ministries of labor are expected to set national child labor laws and regulations even though they exclude many common activities that children and most others would reasonably consider as work.

A further practical difficulty is that other international languages, to say nothing of local languages, do not make the subtle English distinction between "labor" and "work," which results in confusion when campaigns condemning child *labor* are translated from English and appear to be seeking the elimination of all child *work*. Not surprisingly this can lead to local vested interests claiming that prohibition of child labor is an imposition of Northern values and contrary to local custom. Partly to avoid such confusion and partly because the old dichotomy of child labor versus child work is increasingly regarded as too crude for considering the advantages and disadvantages of working, it is now suggested in some circles to avoid using the word "labor" altogether and to refer instead to different kinds and qualities of children's "work." This approach may be the most precise alternative available, but it is not always useful because the term "child labor" is now so widely used in whatever sense that it is difficult to avoid. It is perhaps most practical to promote consensus around its meaning as work incompatible with the best interests of the child.

Constructing the "Worst Forms of Child Labor"

Since the early 1990s, the search has been on for a functional concept of child labor that can be widely agreed upon. A general consensus has gradually emerged that some kinds and conditions of child work are so detrimental or demeaning that international agencies, governments, and nongovernmental organizations can agree they are unacceptable and take priority action against them. ILO C182, adopted in 1999 to codify this common purpose, introduced the phrase "worst forms of child labor" to denote such unacceptable work. This phrase is worth considering in some detail because it is increasingly linked to rights discourses and because it represents an attempt to solve the seemingly endless debates about defining "child work" and "child labor."

When one begins to examine the ways the four discourses work themselves out in global, regional, and national practices, areas of overlap stand out. The same reference points, data, and legal instruments, such as the CRC and ILO C182, are used in all four, but to support different points of view that match varied constructions of "child," "work," "rights," and "human being." This is inevitable. Facts do not lie around the world waiting to be picked up and recognized as "the truth." They are constructed and conceptualized in discourses so that they provide appearances of reality. The labor market discourse is currently dominant, which means that it influences other major discourses, particularly through its latest category, the worst forms of child labor.

As in the case of the CRC, the drafting process for ILO C182 resulted in deliberately vague wording to bring about universal ratification. The CRC does not define "child labor"—indeed, it does not use this term. ILO C182, on the other hand, attempts to define the worst forms of child labor in Article 3, making an effective distinction between two types, which we distinguish as "unconditional" and "unresolved." Unconditional worst forms are defined by their violation of already existing human rights standards, while unresolved worst forms can be defined only through the application of theories of child development, which, as already pointed out, tend to be based on imposed Northern models.

Two Kinds of Worst Forms: Unconditional and Unresolved

The distinction between unconditional and unresolved worst forms of child labor is implicit in Article 3 of ILO C182. The first three subparagraphs of this article are devoted to the unconditional forms that are already prohibited by numerous instruments of international law. ILO C182 thus effectively equates some labor standards with some human rights applicable to children and adults alike. The key to these worst forms is "unfreedom," a core human rights theme. In subparagraphs (a), (b), and (c) of Article 3, ILO C182 acknowledges that the way work is organized may be as hazardous to children as the kind of work they perform. While a denial of freedom violates the human rights of children just as it may violate the human rights of all human beings of any age, children are particularly vulnerable to slavery and slavery-like practices because of their lack of strength, power, and understanding. Forced labor, bonded labor, and trafficking, which are absolutely forbidden relative to all workers under international law, are ways of organizing the labor force and labor process that bring about the worst forms of child labor. Sexual exploitation is also a violation of the provisions of existing human rights instruments. Other unconditional worst forms are connected to illegal activities.

Subparagraph (d) of ILO C182 Article 3 loosely defines what we call the "unresolved" worst forms of child labor, that is, "work which, by its nature or the circumstances in which it is carried out, is likely to harm the health, safety or morals of children." ILO Recommendation No. 190 (1999) provides broad criteria for identifying these worst forms: work that exposes children to physical, psychological, or sexual abuse; that takes place in dangerous and unhealthy environments; or that includes long hours of work by day or night. We suggest, however, that it may be more productive to focus on the effects on a child rather than list different kinds of work. Even "light work" can be dangerous for children who are exhausted. The length of the working day (or night) may be a hazard for children and young people in itself. Tasks that are light for robust, well-nourished children may be hazardous for others who are stunted or malnourished. Work that is not dangerous for adults can be unsafe for children either because it, or the environment in which it takes place, has specific effects on developing bodies or because the tools and equipment involved are the wrong size or type for a child or adolescent to use. In addition, the unresolved worst forms may not only be harmful in themselves; they also can do lasting social harm, because the workers tend to be some of the most socially excluded children.

"Worst Forms" in Other Discourses

As far as many actors in developing countries are concerned, "worst forms" language just adds to an already confusing list of imposed terminology. For example, within the human capital discourse, which focuses on childhood as preparation for productive adult contributions to national economic development, the idea of worst forms has not taken root because the reasons for concern are not the same. Child labor is described by the World Bank as a "serious threat to the future of humanity";[9] but this is largely because of the harm done to long-term national investment rather than to children themselves. Quantification of the global health impact of child labor shows that the occupational injury and mortality rates of children exceed those of adults. While claiming that its figures are underestimates of a "hidden epidemic," a 1998 World Bank study reported 6 million work-related child injuries a year, resulting in around 2.5 million disabilities and 32,000 deaths, referring to "the economic implications of these health impacts on growth and development [and] the cost . . . in terms of the statistical value of lives lost and in health costs."[10] In this perspective, child labor reduces the cost effectiveness of investments in education and child health. Thus there are both powerful economic arguments and urgent welfare reasons for taking action to reduce, and eventually abolish, child labor. Yet the link with human rights is very tenuous.

Unresolved worst forms are increasingly becoming the focus of debates within two other remaining discourses. The social exclusion aspect of the social responsibility discourse is probably most comprehensively expressed in the largely bureaucratic construction of a mixed bag of vulnerable children first described by UNICEF in the mid-1980s as "children in especially difficult circumstances" (CEDC). When first formulated, the CEDC concept included working and street children, unaccompanied children in disasters and conflicts, refugee children, children affected by war, and children with disabilities. Over the years, other groups were informally included, sometimes an expression of regional concerns (as with "the girl child"), at other times locally defined categories that may be as specific as, for example, the *talibe* of Senegal.[11] In 1996 the notion of CEDC was revised in a UNICEF policy review to take into account the concept of "special protection measures" formulated by the Committee on the Rights of the Child,[12] yet the category persists within the terminology of some UNICEF field offices, local NGOs, and some governments. People facing practical challenges on the ground appear to find "children in especially difficult circumstances" easier to conceptualize than "worst forms."

One of the reasons for these bureaucratic constructions is the historical association between "children in especially difficult circumstances" and "street children." Throughout the 1980s and well into the 1990s, this group of children seemed often to stand for the entire range of children in difficult circumstances. Even though the numbers of street children are far smaller than those of other groups of working children, information about them and studies of their lives often dominated (and in some places still dominate) the field of child labor at local levels, especially through the interest of civil society. Yet "street child" is neither a worst form of child labor nor a worst form of organization of child labor. At best it might be described as one of the worst forms of environment for children, whether working or not, with health impacts that often have little to do with the working activities of children on the street.

The children-centered discourse constructs "children" as subjects of rights, and "work" as purposeful human effort, be it in the formal workplace, the informal sector, or the household. Moreover, children are not reduced to objects of charity and concern, as is so often the case with the social responsibility discourse. Nevertheless, in practice, the chief international players in the child welfare field still strive to define the ideas of both rights-based programming and children's participation. With respect to child labor, considerable discussion, internationally and particularly in Latin America, is based in misunderstandings of what is described as the claim by certain organizations of working children to a "right to work." In our experience, the most common position is best summed up as "We don't prefer to work, but we have to be-cause of the economic situation of our parents, so at least let us work in dig-nity." Some children do demand the right to work as a matter of learning or self-realization, but seldom without the qualification that they wish to be treated with dignity and the same respect given to other workers.

From Counting to Measurement

The quantification of both unconditional and unresolved worst forms is not particularly difficult. Nevertheless, the literature within all discourses tends to report that child labor (or whatever "form" is under discussion) is "unmea-surable" while quoting with absolute certainty figures based on estimates and/or poor data and stating that it is difficult to draw the line between labor and work. As with most social data about children, the child labor field is dominated by two contrasting tendencies, both of which can lead to incorrect conclusions and inappropriate policies. The first might be called an obsession with numbers. The second is the tendency of available information to refer-ence the same limited set of poorly researched or anecdotal data.

Legal definitions need to be translated into concrete scientific definitions if they are to be useful in counting and measuring the nature and incidence of a phenomenon. It is not possible to count accurately unless there is an exact op-erational definition of what is being counted, which may not be a universal def-inition for all time but rather an agreed definition by scientific researchers for use in gathering information for specific purposes. To write "the ILO says that there are 250 million child laborers" can be misleading unless it is clear (a) what definition of "child labor" was used for measuring; (b) when (what year) the measurement was made; (c) where measurements were made; (d) what age groups were included as "child laborers"; and (e) what measurement methods were used. In this case, the 250 million figure was based on estimates from ILO child labor surveys carried out by or with the support of the ILO Sta-tistical Information and Monitoring Programme on Child Labour (SIMPOC), using various methods, assumptions, and sources. The reference year was 1995. The main limitations were that the data sets used were incomplete; the populations under fifteen (or in some cases ten) years of age were not covered by many responding countries; and the instruments used by national statistics offices underestimated children's economic activity.[13]

Thus, rather than being a measure of child labor as it might be reasonably defined, the 250 million estimate referred to "economically active" children aged five to eleven in the developing world based on a definition of "eco-nomic activity" used by the United Nations system of national accounts. This includes "all production and processing of primary goods whether for the market or barter or for own consumption, the production of all other goods and services for the market and, in the case of the households which produce such goods and services for the market, the corresponding production for own consumption."[14] In brief, this includes a considerable amount of purposeful human activity. Then as now, to be counted as economically active in a SIMPOC survey, a person must have worked for pay, profit, family gain, or personal consumption for at least one hour on any day during the preceding seven days (one week); or the individual must have such work from which he/she was absent during this reference period. Some argue that this is too short a period, and many national labor force (and child labor) surveys use a longer period (ranging from seven to twenty-four hours), including some countries currently working with SIMPOC. Accordingly, there still is no agreement on a precise operational definition to be used in measurement exercises, and obviously this must be taken into account when assessing the usefulness of global figures based on different data sets.

An alternative method is to use children's own criteria for establishing worst forms and hazards. A simple but telling example is research carried out by children in India giving practical reasons for the work they "can and cannot do" at various ages.[15] In 2001, showing their agreement with this approach, children in India provided qualitative evidence to ILO staff, reporting days that began in the hours of darkness in which they experienced many hazards.[16] Yet even statistical accounts can be sensitive to these factors. A 1999 survey conducted by Statistics South Africa, in cooperation with SIMPOC, found that the most common economic activities of children were fetching water and wood. Although children did not fail to attend school because of this work, they reported more illness, injuries, tiredness, and environmental discomfort (too hot/cold) than did children working in formal and informal activities in urban areas or children working on commercial farms.[17] However, because the collection of water and wood is commonly regarded as necessary family chores in traditional rural settings, some countries may not include these activities in labor force surveys, or may include them only if they are carried out by men, with the result that the collection of wood and water for family use is often not included or categorized as child labor. Nevertheless, these tasks are considered "economic activity" by SIMPOC because the UN system of national accounts considers them productive activities. At the same time, as the above examples demonstrate, one way of addressing the difficulty of defining child labor and worst forms is to ask children, although this must be done systematically and using scientific techniques of data collection and analysis rather than by collecting isolated testimony and anecdotes.

Data on Unconditional Worst Forms

To move from the somewhat crude counting currently taking place both nationally and internationally and to establish secure grounds for identifying both child labor and worst forms, it is necessary to move from counting children to measurement of hazard and harm. Only thus can worst forms be determined. However elegantly drafted, legal instruments require interpretation for effective implementation, the more so if they are drafted with the intention of being inclusive of different cultural meanings. Even unconditional worst forms require further definition before the provisions of ILO C182 can be implemented. Child prostitution and child domestic work, which tend to be high on current agendas for abolition, illustrate that more (and better) information may be necessary to establish grounds and means for program intervention.

On first impression, child commercial sex work should need no further clarification because the definitions already exist in human rights law. Nevertheless, program activities arise out of different discourses. In addition, there are two common and contradictory assumptions about the commercial sexual exploitation of children: that there is a strong economic base for quantifying it; and that, at the same time, the problem itself is unmeasurable but undoubtedly very large indeed.

In contrast to the certainty that child commercial sexual exploitation is a worst form, the case of child domestic servants is an anomaly. Like child prostitution, this informal sector work is a hidden form of child economic exploitation, but it is seldom the subject of national legislation, even for adults, and efforts to have it defined in international law as a worst form have not been successful. Child domestic work often includes violations of other child rights, such as the rights to education and to protection from physical, sexual, and verbal abuse. Child domestic servants appear to suffer from many psychosocial hazards, not least of which are alienation and loss of self-esteem.[18] Although this is difficult to research, the numbers involved are thought to be very large and there appear to be clear links with trafficking and bonded labor. It is worth noting that the 2001 ILO report on forced labor specifically mentions child domestic work, which effectively identifies it as an unconditional worst form.[19] Child domestic work could be described as "unconditional" when it is associated with trafficking and bonded and other forced forms as well as with sexual exploitation, but "unresolved" if children are able to go to school and are not abused (unless psychosocial evidence can be used to establish the harm that is believed to result).

Identifying Unresolved Worst Forms

To define "unresolved" worst forms requires accurate occupational health information and workplace inspection (or surveillance) focusing on child labor, both of which are almost entirely lacking, especially in the Global South. Theoretical discussion of discourses provides few clues about the effects of work on children's bodies and minds and despite the fact that a considerable literature on child development—and a vast array of tools for measuring it—were worked out during the twentieth century. While it is true that the majority were made for use with children in the Global North, the mechanisms for adapting them for other social groups are well established within the human sciences. What appears to be lacking is the will to support the work of scientists in establishing the proofs for identifying particular work, conditions of work, and labor processes as "harmful" to children's development. Yet if this were done, it would render "labor" versus "work" debates redundant.

Definitions of worst forms, whether unconditional or unresolved, tend to rely on case study evidence, which focuses on the more obviously harmful types of work. There is sparse information about the effects of particular working environments, repetitive or heavy tasks, using tools intended for adults, or contact with pollutants and toxic substances. In a review of the literature of the 1980s, Elihu Richter and Janice Jacobs stated that "the subject of crippling injuries in working children and their risks and prevention is an epidemiologic wasteland,"[20] a situation that has changed little in well over a decade. Most of the literature on child occupational health consists of isolated studies, although it is thought that children are uniquely susceptible to work hazards.[21] Beginning work in childhood also means a longer exposure to cumulative hazards. For example, a child working in an auto repair shop at age six will have ten additional years to develop lung disease from asbestos in brake lining compared with someone who starts work at age sixteen.[22] An ILO Task Force on Harmful Forms of Child Labour that met in Geneva in October 2002 showed how occupational health for children is conceptualized within the labor market discourse. Focusing on work deemed unacceptable for fifteen- to seventeen-year-olds, with all work under age fifteen ruled out as "zero tolerance" through the minimum age perspective of ILO C138, discussion concentrated on physical rather than psychosocial hazards and consisted of attempting universal lists of unacceptable work based largely on adult ranges of tolerance. It eschewed trying to establish processes by which children-centered national lists might be developed, which arguably would have been more in the spirit of ILO C182 and its associated Recommendation 190.

One problem in establishing the extent of worst forms according to occupational health criteria is that labor inspectors are usually insufficiently orientated to the developmental needs of children or the relevant rights issues. As with the assumption that child work within the family is a harmless part of socialization, so many forms of work require more detailed proof that an identifiable hazard is involved. Field-level instruments designed for use by labor inspectors show a practical way forward. In the Philippines, for example, a "hazardous rating matrix" demonstrates that, among other working activities previously regarded as benign, vegetable farming in a family undertaking is hazardous.[23] The matrix assesses level of safety of working conditions and intensity of work. A similar diagnostic tool developed in Cambodia distinguishes among "child chores," "child work" (or "light work"), "semi-hazardous child labor," "hazardous child labor," and "worst forms of child labor." The indicators for assessment are the views of children themselves (why they work, their relationship to coworkers, migration status, education status, and income); working conditions (hours, days, breaks); tasks performed; appropriateness of work for age; and frequency of injury.[24] Using such tools, it could well turn out that there are many more worst forms than originally were envisaged, indicating that defining both "child labor" and "unresolved worst forms" probably should be undertaken in local contexts rather than through theoretical debates at the international level.

■ Local Constructions of Child Labor: Case Study of the Lower Mekong Subregion

In this section, we illustrate the problematic effect of confusing discourses through ideas about human rights, childhood, and child labor in the four countries of the Lower Mekong subregion of Southeast Asia (Cambodia, Lao PDR, Thailand, Vietnam). We focus on this region because it offers opportunities for reviewing both unconditional and unresolved worst forms in a variety of different economic and cultural contexts, including considerable ethnic and religious diversity. Study of texts from the subregion also shows how the values of international human rights are viewed and interpreted in local cultures. Focus on international standards set for child labor can illustrate that debates about the apparent contradictions between Asian values and "Western" human rights are far from settled. Some claim that not to work in childhood is contrary to tradition and culture, and that Western definitions of unacceptable child work/labor are interpreted as cultural imperialism, even if work is as obviously harmful as prostitution.

Nevertheless, it is difficult to construct a unitary childhood for the subregion. In many rural areas, children are valued for their current and future contribution to the support of their elders, to whom obedience is a lifelong duty.[25] Yet there are also examples of dependent, costly children in the wealthy, urban middle classes of Thailand, similar to the "little emperors" who are the result of China's one-child family policy. The limited literature on children in all four countries concentrates almost exclusively on socially excluded groups, but with confusing perspectives. Depending on the agency involved, one discourse or another dominates information, analysis, and planning and evaluation on child labor issues.

Constructions of child labor in the Lower Mekong subregion parallel discussions about Asian values and human rights. For example, government spokespeople may argue that child work is an unfortunate but necessary activity in the pursuit of a competitive economic position in the global economy. Others may claim that the understanding of labor and work has to be different in the subregion because its history of development and its cultural understandings differ from those of the "West." However, it is difficult to support either line of reasoning in the absence of a sustained literature on the meaning and value of "work," which in subsistence agriculture cannot be contrasted directly with urban work values, as if both worlds were discrete.

Global values penetrate, with varying meanings, into even remote villages, bringing ideas about employment, profit, and trading as well as opportunities to benefit from working in all economic sectors (including illegal activities), from skills acquisition, and from becoming part of cash-dominated consumer society.

Discourses on Child Labor in the Lower Mekong Subregion

Texts of national and international agencies in the subregion, including governmental and intergovernmental publications, show a variety of conflicting constructions of child labor and worst forms, in which even UN agencies do not appear to apply definitions consistently. Broadly speaking, each country reveals the domination of a particular discourse. In Cambodia, the picture of children's economic activities concentrates on specific urban forms within a social responsibility discourse. In Lao PDR, there is no labor market discourse at all, but some interest in the social responsibility discourse. Vietnam wavers between discourses, but finds a fit between the construction of CEDC and the ideological construction of "social evil." Thailand (and international agencies in the region) officially champions the children-centered discourse, but focuses on two particular worst forms: trafficking and sexual exploitation.

Labor market discourse. In all four countries, official texts take into account the minimum age aspect of the labor market perspective, but with different emphases according to the realities of national labor markets. UNICEF's 2003 *Atlas for the East Asia and Pacific Sixth Ministerial Consultation* claims that the overall characteristic of child labor in Cambodia is that "[c]hildren start working too young," even though Cambodian minimum age is sixteen years, except for hazardous occupations, which are defined by ministerial decrees. The claim that many very young children are working is said to be based on a 2001 survey conducted by the ILO and the International Programme on the Elimination of Child Labour (IPEC), according to which 26 percent of five- to nine-year-olds and 67 percent of ten- to fourteen-year-olds were working.[26] Yet the contradictions between this and other surveys of working children in Cambodia illustrate the effects of different constructions and definitions. It is a feature of child labor figures in most countries that such discrepancies are seldom noted or discussed. Reports using secondary data tend to seize the figures from the most recent survey and seldom try either to explain inconsistencies or to analyze trends.

Trade union sources in Cambodia, working to a large extent within the labor market discourse, make no claims about the socializing benefits of a rural tradition of child labor in the family: "Families engaged in such work are usually poor, lack decent health care, and lack decent education."[27] The one benefit referred to is that child labor is one way of ensuring survival through subsistence agriculture, with the danger that economic development, in association with the globalization of labor markets and the search for cheap labor, will "commodify" child labor. Thus it is suggested that, although economic development in the long term should eliminate child labor, in the short term it will exacerbate it.

A labor market discourse, on either adults or children, is barely evident in Lao PDR, largely because there is effectively no labor market. Economically active people are mostly self-employed in subsistence farming. There are no reliable figures for unemployment and underemployment, although in 2000 the ILO projected 178,000 economically active children aged ten to fourteen years (a quarter of this age group), mostly in family enterprises, but particularly mentioning shop work, which is allowed by law.[28] The main labor market for Lao children and adults is in Thailand.

The explanations in all discourses for the almost universal association between child sexual exploitation and Thailand tend to be based on cultural constructions of childhood, family, and Buddhism. Yet this contrasts with the fact that the globalized "Western" image of childhood is now the model used in national policymaking, and thus also for the construction of official statistics on the labor market model, which assumes child dependency. The virtual abolition of child labor in Thailand is both a product and a construction of this globalized perspective within official discourse, and even beyond the labor market construction. These discursive practices indicate that child commercial sex work is dissociated in many ways from child labor, and constructed as a very different type of problem.

Combining the minimum age qualifications (at age fifteen) of ILO C138 and the definition of "child" as a person under eighteen years of age in both the CRC and ILO C182, official discourse in Thailand is explicit that, although there is a child work force, this involves children only in the fifteen- to eighteen-year-old age group and that thus there is no child labor. A rapid reduction in participation even within this age group is ascribed to technological developments in production, which have reduced the demand for a submissive, cheap labor force, together with increasing enrollment in secondary schools. Yet this ignores the demand for cheap labor, for example in construction, which is met by adults and children from migratory groups, some from impoverished regions of Thailand, but also largely illegal work forces from Lao PDR, Cambodia, and Myanmar. This labor force perspective prioritizes work conceptualized as legal employment in the labor market perspective, and workers of Thai nationality as the bearers of rights. Thus the false conclusion is that the participation of a child labor force is low because there is no market demand for it. A closer look at the literature reveals anomalies, however, in which certain factors seem to be invisible—constructed out of the picture. For example, the national sport of Thai boxing includes protagonists under the age of ten, yet the idea that this might be included as "child labor" was treated as a joke by one policymaker in discussions about worst forms. In addition, the minimum school-leaving age is twelve years, but the minimum age for employment is fourteen years, and not all children enroll in secondary school, leaving a potential child labor force that does not appear in the statistical records.

Human capital discourse. In contrast to the dominance of the labor market discourse, the idea of human capital is not particularly evident in the Lower Mekong subregion. The Asian Development Bank, which might be expected to adopt this perspective, has recently revised its social protection policy in line with ILO/World Bank ideas on poverty alleviation but also incorporating principles of the CRC and ILO C182 respecting children.[29] Thus the main regional bank approach could be characterized as human capital discourse with a human face. Although the labor market discourse is not very evident in Vietnam, many programs of governmental and intergovernmental organizations target poverty reduction, in keeping with the human capital discourse. In contrast, the Lao PDR government spokesperson, at an international meeting, explicitly denied the human capital argument about poverty relative to unconditional worst forms:

> In general poverty and economic disparity seem to be the push factors for child labor, which may lead to the worst forms of child labor and trafficking of children and women. However, it is also true that by eradicating poverty, child labor or the problem of children and women will not disappear. Poverty alleviation may lessen the problem but will not solve the problem. Additional concerns are the role of the recruitment agents and the separation between trafficking as stipulated by the ILO and illegal migration for the pursuit of economic interest.[30]

Social responsibility discourse. All agencies in the region show evidence of social responsibility discourse, particularly—though not limited to—the nongovernmental sector and UNICEF. There are wide wealth disparities between and within countries, which fosters analyses based on ideas of social exclusion, particularly where female children of ethnic minorities in remote rural areas are concerned, but with program focus on CEDC.

This can be contradictory. According to most surveys, the greatest proportion of Cambodian working children, especially among younger age groups, is to be found in rural areas; but both research and program provision tend to focus on the 9.4 percent of children working in urban areas, in street trades, or as ragpickers.[31] IPEC projects on hazardous labor in Cambodia focus on brick, rubber, and salt manufacture; fishing; and sexual exploitation and trafficking. There is an equally contradictory element in one of the emphases on urban employment. Rural work in the family is not regarded as problematic, yet ragpicking, which is a family enterprise in Cambodia as elsewhere, is regarded as hazardous. Our point is not to deny the hazards of rag-picking, but to question the idea that there are no hazards in subsistence agri-culture. Only tools such as a hazardous rating matrix might prove this. The as-sumption that rural agricultural families are able to protect their children from hazards, whereas urban family-based labor is devoid of protection, cannot be supported by global evidence that agricultural child labor produces the great-est proportion of child deaths and injuries.

The social responsibility discourse in Lao PDR is demonstrated by the es-tablishment of a CEDC program in 1997. UNICEF's 2003 *Atlas* characterizes Lao child labor as taking place far from home through internal migration and having long working hours in agricultural work and begging, basing this on regional and national UNICEF surveys using different definitions.[32] A joint report of UNICEF and the Lao government on street begging and street chil-dren uses the terminology of both "children in especially difficult circum-stances" and "children in need of special protection" (CNSP) (the former most frequently). There appears to be very little consideration of the unresolved worst forms, the distinction between labor and work being made in conven-tional fashion, using similar phrases to those in regional UNICEF publica-tions—for example: "During training for youth researchers it was emphasized that not all child work is harmful. Child labor is any work that endangers the life, health, well being and development of a child whereas child work is con-structive and beneficial to both them and their families."[33]

In Vietnamese official constructions, child labor threatens the moral fab-ric of society and becomes defined as a "social evil," the particularly bad man-ifestations of which are street children and child commercial sex workers, both of which breach public order. The construction of social evils indicates the relative dominance in the region of the social responsibility discourse, which places considerable emphasis on CEDC, especially in governmental texts in which, often, it is synonymous with "street children." The Vietnamese national discourse on social evils, on the other hand, merges with regional in-tergovernmental concerns about sexual exploitation and trafficking, according to which at least 3,000 girls from South Vietnam have been trafficked to Cam-bodia for prostitution, en route often to Thailand or Taiwan, more than 15 per-cent of them younger than fifteen.

Children-centered discourse. Where it exists at all in the Lower Mekong subregion, children-centered discourse is found usually in the texts of inter-national NGOs, which focus on developing rights-based programming on a variety of issues, such as corporal punishment and juvenile justice. Child labor is becoming a decreasing focus of these organizations (even at local lev-els) despite the presence of regional NGOs such as Child Workers in Asia and the Regional Working Group on Child Labour. While the region is notable for the degree of theorization it produces on child rights programming, this tends to focus on organizational and institutional issues, or on children's participation rather than on child labor, despite the production of interesting children-centered research on child labor. Also noteworthy is that the organizations of child workers in the Southeast Asian region as a whole are few and relatively scattered, not being integrated into the child-organized international movement of child workers to the extent found in Africa, Latin America, and South Asia.

Worst forms of child labor. All four countries in the Lower Mekong subregion are working with IPEC on the definition of "worst forms of child labor" to differing degrees, so it is interesting to see how national discourses frame the debates as well as to find out if the provisions of ILO C182 provide a framework for solving child labor/child work debates on the ground. Vietnamese texts sometimes put a particular twist on the "bad child labor" and "good child work" distinction. The benefits to children of work within the family are said to be part of socialization as well as enabling in terms of growth and development: Work "develops the personality," "building confidence and self-esteem." Labor, on the other hand, has "negative effects" by impeding child development.[34]

Worst forms are less discussed in the Vietnamese literature on child labor than hazards, for which there are two constructions. In the first, a legal framework is quite rapidly being established, on the model of ILO C182 and Recommendation 190, including a detailed list of hazardous working conditions in which the employment of minors is prohibited. This is associated with an impressive production of child labor statistics influenced by labor market discourse and focusing largely on work defined as "employment" or "economic activity," which uses various statistical means to show impressive decreases of child labor, even though there seems to be an increase in family-based and informal-sector work performed by children. The second construction of "hazard" is interesting because it reflects traditional attitudes and values. Whereas ILO C182 Article 3(d) refers to harm to the "health, safety, or morals" of children, Vietnamese official reports sometimes reverse this order, referring first to hazards that "affect badly a [child's] personality" and then to hazards that "harm their physical and intellectual development."

Regional literature and programming as a whole have been dominated for over two decades by two child labor concerns, now defined as worst forms: commercial sexual exploitation and trafficking. In contrast to the low-profile of child labor as a whole in the subregion, research, funding for, and programming on these two issues seem to be growing unstoppably.

Sexual exploitation is neither dealt with under the heading "child labor" nor referred to in the context of ILO C182, but may take up twice as much space in a text. Typical statements in regional publications are: "UNICEF believes one million children . . . enter the multibillion dollar commercial sex trade in Asia every year"; "[i]n East Asia, the sex industry is such a huge money spinner that the . . . ILO estimates it to be worth between 14% and 16% of Thailand's gross domestic product"; and "[h]igh on the hillsides of Thailand's famous Golden Triangle lies the epicenter of a modern day slave trade." Other publications repeat the same themes: "extensive networks" are "rampant," with children "moved like chattel" in "this iniquitous slave trade," although "[t]he extent of commercial sexual exploitation of children [in the region] is largely unknown due to its clandestine nature." In these (sometimes contradictory) tendencies, UNICEF publications simply reflect the emphases present to greater or lesser extent among all agencies working for children in the region.

These four country studies show the extent to which discussion of worst forms in the region has been overlaid with a construction of "sexual exploitation and trafficking," which refers to ILO C182 but which, concentrating on two unconditional worst forms, relegates unresolved worst forms to a minor interest, especially if not connected to existing concern for CEDC. In any event, the construction certainly does not allow much space for defining unresolved worst forms via definitions of "hazard" that are based on scientific principles from child development theory, or for establishing institutionalized bases for labor inspection that are based on a body of knowledge about child occupational health. Arguably this gap is a function of the labor market discourse. This follows from a regional concern about migration, which in turn seems inevitable within a labor market perspective given the dominant economic position of Thailand, by far the richest country in this group. The gloss from trafficking to sexual exploitation appears to be a feature of all four child labor discourses.

Whatever the case, in the Lower Mekong subregion the emphasis among international organizations is on trafficking and the commercial sexual exploitation of children. Within countries, the effects of this emphasis are muted by local contexts, although the labor market discourse is particularly evident in the way the concept of child labor is constructed nationally. Yet we must repeat that the construction of work is not universally connected to the idea of "job" or "employment," except perhaps among urban elites, especially in Thailand. The human capital discourse is unevenly represented in the literature, although necessarily linked to governmental considerations, especially in Cambodia, Lao PDR, and Vietnam in their negotiations with the World Bank, the Asian Development Bank, and bilateral donor governments. The social responsibility discourse is evident with respect to the literature on CEDC and street children but takes varied forms—a social evil in Vietnam, street begging in Lao PDR, and ragpicking in Cambodia. Very little attention is paid to identifying the unresolved worst forms, and almost no attention is paid to children working in agriculture, even though these are the children who are probably the most likely to migrate or be trafficked. Despite the development of a diagnostic tool for unresolved worst forms in Cambodia and the attempts of the Vietnamese government to establish a list of hazardous occupations, almost no attention is paid to developing an information base for the occupational health of children.

■ Reflections and Conclusions

The Mekong Delta case suggests the cost of leaving "child labor" so undefined that it can be manipulated to mean whatever a government, multilateral organization, or other group finds politically, ideologically, or otherwise convenient. Lack of disciplined definition leads to lack of accountability. By simply juggling constructs instead of focusing directly on the rights and well-being of children, governments have concentrated their activities in a few high-visibility situations while ignoring large numbers of children in equally worrisome conditions. If we are to use the term "child labor" seriously, it is essential to invest it with agreed meaning that will discipline the discussion.

One way to achieve that is through consensus. Global consensus produced the idea of worst forms of child labor, which could be helpful and which, in principle, is consistent with human rights concepts. But in implementation the emphasis has so far been primarily on subjective constructions of the unconditional worst forms, and the relationship of those constructions to real children is highly problematic. At the same time, children in the unresolved worst forms, in situations perhaps no less dire, are ignored even though diagnostic techniques exist to establish levels of harm and thus to identify them. Governments lack either the knowledge or the political will to use these tools, and as a consequence bureaucratized constructions of child labor trump attention to children's reality and compromise their human rights. Without grounding in solid empirical information about actual working children and their situation, disagreement over exactly what the much-called-for "abolition of child labor" should eliminate continues unabated.

We have attempted to suggest through our deconstruction of the most common discourses on child labor that it would be more useful to speak of "children's work," and then to seek objective measures of harm (or benefit) to development resulting from such work, remaining conscious of the different constructions of "work" and "child" involved. But the world will follow custom and continue using the term "child labor." Thus the twin issues at the definitional center of the problem commonly called "child labor" become unavoidable: how to conceptualize the work of children and how to identify the work they do that is socially unacceptable—the essential first step to assuring working children their human rights.

At present, it is true, the link between child labor and human rights is not one that is widely perceived or understood, despite the "hijacking" of ILO C182 into discussions that refer to "human rights." To a large extent this is due to the conceptual or definitional muddle surrounding "child labor" that has been at the heart of our critique in this chapter. But as we have noted, key human rights instruments—the 1948 UDHR, the two 1966 covenants, the 1989 CRC, and the like—have played an important role in shaping as well as reflecting ideas about children and work and thus social constructions of "child" and "work." The challenge is how best to define the rights of children in relation to work in ways that will both protect and empower them, that will make, in the language of CRC Article 3, "the best interests of the child" a matter of "primary consideration." And this, of course, signals a human rights approach to the problem of child labor and its definition. Taken together and broadly interpreted, basic human rights instruments suggest that socially unacceptable child work (sometimes referred to as "worst forms") should be defined as work that harms children by hindering their holistic development.

The UDHR articulates the empowering right of every human being to work, to receive fair and equal recompense, and to form and join trade unions. The 1966 covenants introduce the notion of a right of special protection for children, indicating that the key concern is exploitive work that is harmful to children. The CRC picks up and expands upon this, particularly by extending the period of "childhood," but also by constructing children as a separate group that, some might argue, is not included in the full range of rights in the UDHR.

A concept of child labor merely as work below a legally designated minimum age does not find support in these human rights instruments, especially if it limits the human right of children to work without proof that this limitation is necessary for their protection. That necessity must be demonstrated by proper research meeting professionally accepted social science standards. The three instruments that compose the "International Bill of Human Rights," together with elaborations and interpretations of the CRC, do not justify agebased modification of rights to work, to fair and equal wages, and to membership in workers' organizations for purposes other than the protection of children. The scientifically doubtful argument that children should be excluded from economic participation in order to protect adult wages and labor markets may or may not have separate merit, but it certainly does not have a solid basis in fundamental human rights instruments. The concept of child labor behind ILO C138, together with most national legislation based upon it, is therefore suspect from a human rights point of view. The question is the relative weight of human rights instruments compared with the labor standards of the ILO. Our answer is that common sense and normal legal procedure suggest that rights defined in fundamental human rights documents should not be undermined by the provisions of instruments that apply only to a specific sector and are meant to be regarded as supplements to universal rights documents.

On the other hand, ILO C182, on the worst forms, is based on the idea that child labor is work damaging to children, a definition that is fully consistent with the basic instruments guiding children's rights. The practical implication is that when the ILO defines international standards and when ILO member states bring their national laws into line with those standards, the children-centered concept and definitions of ILO C182 should be privileged over the older labor market approach of ILO C138. The time has come to make a decisive move from a child labor concept originally intended at least in part to protect adult labor markets to one that directly responds to the rights and well-being of children.

A human rights approach to child labor should pay attention to the empowering aspects of basic human rights instruments, including the rights of children to express themselves and take action on their own behalf. This entails viewing children as capable *as well as* vulnerable, and of work as fulfilling and developmental *as well as* harmful and exploitive. The requirement is to be rigorously empirical and use scientific data to establish hazards and harm, and at the same time be sensitive to the influence of dominant social constructions. This would ensure a focus on real problems rather than on the misguided constructions of popular rhetoric. A human rights–based approach to child labor should also be inclusive of children, establishing institutional space for them to participate in defining and addressing work-related problems that merit concern and intervention. A trend toward defining child labor as work that is seriously harmful to children is already observable in international discussion. What is needed now is to consolidate that definition in action through establishing children-centered information about child occupational health.

Finally we ask how well such a definition of children's work fits into practical national and international efforts to implement human rights. Accumulated international experience in defining and addressing child labor strongly suggests that it is beneficial and empowering for children if rights principles are defined flexibly, to defend and promote their evolving capacities. On the other hand, using rights texts rigidly to force children to fit into inappropriate universal models is likely to injure them and, ironically, to violate their rights. Children's best interests depend on their diversity being treated with as much respect as their universality. Defining child labor as work prejudicial to them is the best definition for accommodating both approaches. Respect and dignity are the basic criteria of human rights, which means that the rights and well-being of children depend above all on profound respect both for who they may become and for who they are right now.

▨ Notes

We wish to acknowledge the generous assistance of David Parker in providing additional information for this chapter, as well as comments on earlier drafts from Harriot Beazley, Sharon Bessell, Rachel Bray, Antonella Invernizzi, Victor Karunan, Brian Milne, Heather Montgomery, and Virginia Morrow.

1. This list comes from Myers, "Valuing Diverse Approaches to Child Labour."
2. Ibid.
3. ICESCR, art. 10; ICCPR, art. 25(2). Note that Paragraph 3 of the former provides that "States should also set age limits below which paid employment of child labour should be prohibited and punishable by law." This denies certain children, many of whom may wish to be employed, access to the 1948 UDHR Article 23 provision that "[e]veryone has the right to work, to free choice of employment." Therefore, under the 1966 ICESCR, it can be argued, the right to work no longer applies to "everyone" as set out in the UDHR.
4. In common with many others, we have at various times presented the idea of letting child workers form or affiliate with trade unions to officers or staff of trade unions and federations (including the ICFTU, the largest international federation of trade unions), to trade union representatives inside the ILO, and to personnel of the US Department of Labor. From these quarters we have met only implacable opposition to the notion that children under the legal minimum age of employment should be allowed to form or join unions. The usual argument is that if they are not legal workers, they cannot be members of organizations dedicated to protecting worker rights.
5. Save the Children–UK, *Save the Children's Position on Children and Work* (summarizing views of children from consultations and other sources).
6. See, for example, the argument developed in Lane, *The Market Experience,* pp. 246–259.
7. ILO, *A Future Without Child Labour,* p. 12.
8. For examples, see Boyden, Ling, and Myers, *What Works for Working Children,* pp. 27–110.
9. Fallon and Tzannatos, *Child Labour . . . ,* p. 5.
10. Graitcer and Lerer, *Child Labor and Health,* p. 1. In other surveys, conducted by the ILO, it has been calculated that as many as one child in five working in hazardous occupations suffers illness and injury. Ashagrie, *Statistics on Working Children in Brief,* p. 11.
11. *Talibe,* from the Wolof for "discipline," originally referred to pupils in quranic schools, who traditionally begged for alms on Fridays. Use of the term widened to apply to all child beggars, and finally to all street children.
12. United Nations Economic and Social Council, *Review of UNICEF Policies . . . .*
13. ILO, *Current International Recommendations on Labour Statistics; ILO, Report IV;* Ashagrie, *Methodological Child Labour Surveys and Statistics;* Ashagrie, *Economically Active Children in 1995/6 . . . .*
14. Ashagrie, *Economically Active Children in 1995/6 . . . .*
15. See Bhima Sangha, *Work We Can and Cannot Do.*
16. Geetha, representing working children from Udupi district, Kundapur Taluk, and Uppunda Panchayath, in an unpublished study presented to a meeting between Bhima Sangha and ILO officials from Geneva and India, May 2001, Bangalore. Translation by Kavita Ratna.
17. Statistics South Africa, *Child Labour in South Africa . . . .*
18. Blagbrough and Glynn, "Child Domestic Workers . . . ," pp. 52–54.
19. ILO, *Stopping Forced Labour,* pp. 30–31.
20. Richter and Jacobs, "Work Injuries and Exposures . . . ," p. 750.
21. Berger, Belsey, and Shah, "Medical Aspects of Child Labor in Developing Countries," p. 698.
22. Ibid.
23. See Subida, *Defining Hazardous Undertakings for Young Workers . . . ,* p. 24.

24. Gourlay, LICADHO, and RCG Labour Inspectorate Staff, *Child Labour Matrix.*

25. This conceptualization is a feature of both patrilineal society in Vietnam and matrilineal structures in Thailand. See Socialist Republic of Vietnam, *National Report* . . . ; and UNICEF, *Children and Their Families* . . . .

26. UNICEF, *Towards a Region Fit for Children* . . . , p. 21.

27. Asian American Free Labor Institute, *Child Labor in Cambodia,* p. 2.

28. ILO, *Economically Active Population 1950–2010,* p. 1.

29. ADB, *Social Protection Strategy;* ADB, *Working with Street Children* . . . .

30. Vongsavath, "Lao People's Democratic Republic Country Paper," p. 2. Vongsavath was at the time deputy director of the Labor Protection Division and deputy chief of the Child Labor Office, Ministry of Labor and Social Welfare.

31. Asian American Free Labor Institute, *Child Labor in Cambodia,* p. 2.

32. UNICEF, *Towards a Region Fit for Children* . . . .

33. Lao PDR Ministry of Labour and Social Welfare, Department of Social Welfare, *Street Children and Child Beggars* . . . , p. 22.

34. Socialist Republic of Vietnam., "Interministerial Circular 09/TT-LB . . ."; UNICEF, *Children and Women* . . . , p. 120.

Child Labor and the Rights of Children: Historical Patterns of Decline and Persistence

Hugh Cunningham and Shelton Stromquist

A link between rights and the work of children was first forged in the 1830s in the industrial revolution in Britain. This chapter traces the emergence and articulation, on a global scale, of rights-based arguments and assesses the weight given to them compared with other arguments against child labor.[1] It examines factors that have caused child labor and that may explain the fluctuations of its extent in the world's North. It then examines the process by which, from the late nineteenth century, debates on child labor and attempts to control it became global in scope, providing a background to the explosion of concern about child labor in the late twentieth century. The chapter concludes with reflections on the enduring links between poverty and child labor within a capitalist world order, and on the significance of the assertion of rights as a counterbalance to market and other forces. What has become particularly clear in more recent debates surrounding child labor in the developing world is that the rights of child workers are inseparable from the rights of all workers to adequate protections, to a living wage, and to dignity and respect. Our starting point is a review and critique of currently dominant ways of understanding the history of child labor.

▪ Understanding the History of Child Labor

The conventional understanding of the history of child labor is informed, explicitly or implicitly, by a modernization model of development based on the experience of societies in the world's North. Such models have a long history in Western social science. They became especially popular and widespread in their application to development policies in the 1950s, however, and they continue to influence the way many Western policymakers perceive postcolonial "nation building" to the present day. Modernization theory posits a preindustrial world in which "child labor," with its negative connotations, did not exist. Children worked, but their work was their education, useful to their families, and an excellent training for the adult world. The work was gendered—boys tending to be out in the fields, scaring the birds off crops or looking after farm animals; girls helping their mothers nearer the home, sometimes engaged in domestic industry, normally textiles. No one could imagine a world in which children did not work; their work seemed "natural," in accordance with the sometimes harsh dictates of nature.

The history of child labor, in this view, starts with the industrial revolution in Britain. In the late eighteenth century and lasting through the mid–nineteenth century, employers recruited children to work in the industrializing economies of northern Europe and the eastern United States. Two key industries, textiles and coal mining, employed large numbers of children; and the conditions in which children worked provoked outrage: "child labor" was born. By the mid–nineteenth century, however, child labor was in retreat, though by no means eliminated. The causes of the retreat continue to be debated, but the fact of it is undisputed. Much attention is thereafter devoted to explaining how childhood was reformulated as a period of schooling rather than work, and how this model of childhood became global in scope.

The long contribution on child labor in the 1930 *Encyclopaedia of the Social Sciences* exemplifies this way of thinking. Each country in turn, it was assumed, would go through the same process as did Britain. Most of the space was given to histories of child labor and attempts to control it in Britain and the United States. In these countries the exploitation of young children in industry was now over. Less advanced countries were at an earlier developmental stage, undergoing child labor abuses similar to those "in the darkest period of England's industrial history."[2] Persia and Algeria might in due course experience the spread of child labor, as had China and Japan, but with the help of the International Labour Organization (ILO), "[m]ore backward countries" might take initiatives to raise their standards, as some had already done.[3] This modernization framework is evident also in more recent writing. Carolyn Tuttle linked her sophisticated analysis of child labor in the British industrial revolution to observations that "[t]he ILO is aware that history is repeating itself in many developing countries today," an analysis she herself endorses.[4] And Hugh Hindman overtly looks for lessons from history in his study of child labor in the United States. All industrialized countries, he claims, have gone through a "'dirty' phase of development,"[5] using child labor; but since they have come through it, their example makes it "now possible to embrace and express an optimism that is grounded in historical fact."[6]

Modernization theory, or its bastardization, had an enormous impact on social science in the United States, particularly in the post–World War II era. As development of the "third world" became a preoccupation of Western social science in the 1950s, policymakers took comfort in what they believed was the inevitable, organic development of societies toward something approximating those of Western Europe and the United States. Critics of modernization theory have suggested that such a trajectory is by no means inevitable. Perhaps the most influential antimodernization theorist of the developing world has been Andre Gunder Frank, who suggested that the "development" promoted by Western, anticommunist powers after World War II was really a scheme for perpetuating dependency and underdevelopment. Far from disappearing, critics of modernization theory argue, such systems of labor exploitation represented by child labor took on a life of their own, perpetuated by the logic of neoliberal markets and financial dependency in less developed countries.[7]

In at least three respects, the modernization model does not seem adequately to capture the direction of historical change relative to child labor. First, child labor in Europe was neither so transitory nor so necessary and benign a stage in industrial evolution as the model implies. Second, in mature industrial or postindustrial societies of the West, child labor has persisted in ways the model did not predict. Periodic infusions of immigrants, often occupying a netherworld of illegal status, have populated low-wage, highly competitive niches in developed economies, making it necessary for unskilled immigrant families to generate additional income for survival.[8] To the extent that social safety nets proved inadequate for such immigrant populations, most notably in the United States, child labor appeared repeatedly as a family income-maintenance strategy, despite compulsory school attendance and state child labor laws. The US case illustrates both the failure of child labor reformers to attack root causes—general impoverishment—and the problems of regulation in a "weak state" environment.[9] Third, in large portions of the developing world—the former colonies of metropolitan industrial powers—child labor has become widespread and its eradication extremely problematic. Far from progressing up some smooth path of modernization, these former colonies continue to function in economically dependent ways within a highly stratified global economy. As fertile fields for Western capital investment, burdened with chronically debt-ridden, politically unstable states, these societies and their citizens resort to child labor to stabilize family income on a long-term basis with little prospect of seeing the fruits of rising income and productivity.[10] Under the weight of international debt and the structural adjustment requirements of international financial institutions, these societies cut public spending for education and social services. Even if they possess laws that formally prohibit child labor or require school attendance, they lack the capacity to enforce such regulations. The low wages paid to adult workers in the "formal" sectors of their economies make necessary and inevitable the widespread employment of children in "informal" sectors.[11] (These trends are discussed in some detail for India below and for Tanzania in Chapter 7.)

Can we imagine a history of child labor that escapes the thrall of the modernization model? It is easiest, perhaps, to say what a new model will avoid. There will be no assumption that child labor may end, or that the occurrence of child labor in one economy at a particular point in time will bear a resemblance to its occurrence elsewhere at a different time. On the positive side, the aim perhaps should be, given the weight of the existing model, deliberately to see if there are differences in child labor in different places and different times.

It is useful, then, to consider some discrete historical cases and what they can tell us about the circumstances that give rise to child labor and its decline or persistence. Though other cases might work equally well, we have chosen to focus on: (1) child labor during the industrial revolution in Europe, with a particular emphasis on Britain; (2) child labor in the industrial economies of the Western world in the late nineteenth and twentieth centuries, particularly in Britain and the United States; and (3) child labor in the context of the globalization of capital and technology in the colonial and postcolonial developing world, particularly in India. Together, the case studies suggest that no single model can explain the character and durability of child labor across time and societies and that the modernization model has serious flaws.

The Industrial Revolution in Europe

On the eve of the industrial revolution, it was almost axiomatic among opinion-leaders and policymakers in Europe that work should be the lot of children of poor families, and that it should begin at an early age. John Locke wanted them to begin at age three, the Committee on the Relief and Settlement of the Poor in England at four.[12] Only very rarely do we find any criticism of this early work; it was taken for granted that such work in industry would be advantageous to the child, to the child's family if he or she had one, and to the local and national economy. It had the sanction of religion and morality. As J. F. Feddersen wrote in his *Life of Jesus for Children* (1787): "It is God's will that people avoid all idleness and should work from their earliest years."[13] With such a climate of opinion, it is not surprising that manufacturers met with encouragement rather than resistance when they sought to employ children in the increasingly mechanized textile industries. As Austrian empress Maria Theresa put it, the children of the poor "should grow accustomed to hard work. . . . Our manufacturers are in great need of spinners, and they would gladly employ children for this purpose."[14]

Why did manufacturers want to employ children? Partly because they were cheap; but also because the work to be done seemed naturally to be children's work—or put another way, that it did not seem to be work that adults, especially adult men, should or could easily be asked to do. The advantages that children possessed as workers were manifold.[15] First, they were small of stature. The early machines, made of wood, had to be built small and close to the floor to avoid excessive vibrations. They were designed for children to use.[16] Second, though recent work has concluded that the "nimble fingers" argument is and was bogus, contemporaries believed in its truth—to such an extent that they saw no point in putting it to the test.[17] Third, much of the work, especially that of the piecers, was ancillary to that of adult workers, and for that reason particularly suited to children. Fourth, children were much more likely than adults to be amenable to the work discipline that attendance on machinery required; to adults, accustomed to working at their own pace, the work seemed akin to slavery. The demand for children as workers was therefore strong. Manufacturers did not see how they could carry on their businesses without it.

If manufacturers wanted children for their work forces, was it inevitable that parents would supply them? Manufacturers initially looked to institutional sources of supply such as workhouses or orphanages, rather than working-class families; but by the early nineteenth century in Britain, employers turned to what they called "free labor," children who were not bound to the work by parishes or other institutions, but sent by their parents. The pressures on parents were considerable, the overriding one being poverty. Employers sometimes held out the bribe of employment for the adults in the family if they could be guaranteed the children. There is now substantial evidence, after decades of bitter debate, that levels of poverty remained high through the first half of the nineteenth century. Figures for real wages support this conclusion, as does evidence on height and diet: the British became smaller because their diets were deteriorating. The pressures of unfilled stomachs could erase any doubts about the desirability of sending young children to work for long hours.[18]

Britain served as the cradle of the industrial revolution, and it is therefore not surprising that controversies surrounding the impact of industrialization on the lives of workers and their children have been centered there. While in one sense the issue of child labor cannot be separated from broader controversies about the industrial revolution and its impact on standards of living, recent controversies about child labor have revolved around a few specific questions.[19] Were children in large numbers recruited into industrial employment? Did the conditions of their employment produce harmful effects on their health and well-being? Who was responsible for the fact that large numbers of children went to work for wages (employers, parents, children themselves)? And over what period of time and by what means did child labor decline?

The most recent and vigorous intervention in this debate has come from so-called neoclassical economic historians, especially Clark Nardinelli.[20] Nardinelli has challenged the pessimists in their answers on each of these questions. English historian Edward P. Thompson voiced the moral outrage of the pessimists when he asserted "that the exploitation of little children, on this scale and with this intensity, was one of the most shameful events in our history."[21] Nardinelli, reflecting the optimists' views, argued that the extent of child labor has been exaggerated. But in his view, to the extent that children did work, they contributed directly to improvements to the standard of living of themselves and their families. Nardinelli sees child labor as a rational choice by parents given the supply and demand constraints with which they were faced. The needs of employers for factory labor and the needs of families to increase their incomes and improve the prospects for their children intersected. Finally, Nardinelli sees a rapid decline in child employment as technology improved in ways that favored the use of adult workers and as families enjoyed rising incomes and the choices that permitted them to improve the "quality of their children" through education. The "rising opportunity cost" of children's labor was thus the "most important long-term change in the economic role of children."[22] In other words, the return on investment in human capital within the family (i.e., schooling) increased to a point where the "reallocation of children's time" from work to school made economic sense. But such a proposition has many hidden assumptions—to wit: (1) that schooling of a type that would generate perceptible economic returns was readily available; (2) that families could forgo the immediate return from children's work in the interest of long-term benefits (How long-term? Ten, twenty, thirty years?); (3) that those benefits would be returned to the birth family; (4) that such calculations yielded uniform results regardless of workers' status or degree of economic insecurity. The precariousness of working-class life—unemployment, injury, death, desertion—does not fall within Nardinelli's field of vision.

Contemporary observers, as we have seen, made a positive assessment of child work in industry in the early modern period before the industrial revolution. What was it, then, that changed to produce, at least in some minds, outrage at the very existence of child labor over the half century from the 1780s to the 1830s? The simple answer is that both the amount of child labor and the exploitation of it increased, although this fact in itself provokes a critique; the simple answer does contain part of the truth, but not all of it. What also changed in this period was the perception of what constituted childhood, and it was this new view of childhood that informed contemporary critiques of child labor. In the 1760s, Jean-Jacques Rousseau argued that children had a right to childhood and a right to enjoy it. This was in marked contrast to accepted advice on child-rearing, which focused either on the production of the good adult or on saving the souls of young children. Initially adopted by better-off parents, Rousseau's ideas were by the 1830s being applied by reformers to all children.

The rights of children that began to be voiced in the early nineteenth century stemmed from ideas of nature cultivated during the Enlightenment. Childhood had been set aside as a time for growth and play. There was an "order of nature" whereby the adults in a family should provide for the fledg-

ling children. That order of nature seemed to be inverted in the cotton factories.[23] The response of those who saw the laboring children was one of
"pity,"[24] which could transmute into anger directed against those thought responsible for the children's condition. It led in Britain to something that was
perhaps unique: a mass movement of protest in opposition to child labor. Consider the meeting held at the Castle Yard in York on April 24, 1832. Many
thousands, "not only men, but factory boys and girls, mothers with infants in
their arms," walked between twenty and fifty miles from the factory districts
to protest, and heard speeches in dire weather conditions for five hours.[25]
Later in the same year, Michael Sadler and Richard Oastler, two leaders of the
agitation, attended a meeting in Manchester, where there were, it was said, "at
least one hundred thousand persons," including "thousands of poor factory
children" with banners, and seventeen bands of music.[26] It was much more
usual, then and subsequently, for opposition to child labor to be voiced in the
respectable press and in representative assemblies, and for the case for action
to be demanded by committees, or for the control of child labor to be dealt
with by civil servants without any attendant publicity.

The sense of pity was also evident in the way contemporaries listened to
what children had to say. The British parliamentary papers are forbidding-
looking documents, stretching yard after yard across archival shelves. Yet
within them are to be heard children recounting to investigators the conditions
of their work, and telling them what they felt about it. It is perhaps a fair measurement of how alert adults in different contexts are to the rights of children
to ask how far they listen to children. Many writers, echoing Elizabeth Barrett Browning's famous poem, were to claim to give voice to "the cry of the
children,"[27] but few actually listened to and recorded what children said. In
the 1830s and 1840s, by contrast, children had their say, and were heard, to an
extent that, as later essays in this collection indicate, has not been repeated
until very recently.[28]

Some people in the early and middle nineteenth century imagined a brave
new world where children never worked. Much more common were efforts to
eliminate the worst forms of child labor, without pretending that it was either
possible or desirable to eliminate the work of children altogether. But for both
groups there was a sense, often explicit, that children possessed fundamental
human rights. T. B. Macaulay gave expression to it, as something new, in his
comparison of England in 1685 and in his own day, 1848:

> [T]he practice of setting children prematurely to work, a practice which the
> state, the legitimate protector of those who cannot protect themselves, has, in
> our time, wisely and humanely interdicted, prevailed in the seventeenth cen-
> tury to an extent which, when compared to the extent of the manufacturing
> system, seems almost incredible. At Norwich, the chief seat of the clothing
> trade, a little creature of six years old was thought fit for labor. Several writ-
> ers of the time, and among them some who were considered eminently benev-

olent, mention, with exultation, the fact that in that single city boys and girls of very tender age created wealth exceeding what was necessary for their own subsistence by twelve thousand pounds a year. The more carefully we examine the history of the past, the more reason shall we find to dissent from those who imagine that our age has been fruitful of new social evils. The truth is that the evils are, with scarcely an exception, old. That which is new is the intelligence which discerns and the humanity which remedies them.[29]

If we are looking for the beginnings of a view that children have special rights in the labor market, Macaulay's robust statement can stand as a foundation text. A wise and humane state now protects children, "those who cannot protect themselves," in Macaulay's words. There is outrage that profit, £12,000 a year, should be made from their labor, and conviction that intelligence and humanity unite to remedy an old social evil. Children, it is being asserted, now have a right not to work. Since they are defined as unable to protect themselves, they have an additional right to rely on the protection offered by a paternalist state. And like other critics, Macaulay believed the evil that had been remedied was an old one, fully evident in the seventeenth century.

Child Labor in the Industrial
Economies of the Western World
In the dominant modernization model considered above, the story of child labor in Europe after the middle of the nineteenth century is one of decline. The much-debated causes of the decline include a contemporary belief in the importance of the passage of labor laws, embodying a sense of the rights of the child, and a more recent view emphasizing market factors that are presumed to have influenced the behavior of both entrepreneurs and working-class families. The statistics and other evidence tend to cover all forms of work by children, but we may draw conclusions that have relevance for the worst forms of child labor.

Confining the analysis initially to England and Wales, we do see a general pattern of decline in the proportion of children counted as employed (see Table 3.1). Reliance on these figures needs to be accompanied by multiple cautions. For example, we should not assume that girls worked less frequently or less hard than boys; rather, the work that they did, often in the home, was less likely than that of boys to be counted as employment by the census enumerators. By the same token, there is very likely to be undercounting of part-time and casual work for both sexes.

Despite their inadequacies, however, a conclusion can be drawn from the figures: the decline trend was inconsistent and at times agonizingly slow. Looking at those aged ten to fourteen, the highest incidence of employment was not in 1851, but in 1861 for boys, and 1871 for girls. As Geoffrey Best put it, "[o]ne cannot too much emphasise that the fifties and sixties were not in general decades of liberation for working children."[30] The sharpest decennial

Table 3.1 **Percentage of Children Recorded as Working, England and Wales, 1851–1911**

	1851	1861	1871	1881	1891	1901	1911
Boys 5–9	2.0	2.0	0.8				
Girls 5–9	1.4	1.1	0.7				
Boys 10–14	36.6	36.9	32.1	22.9	26.0	21.9	18.3
Girls 10–14	19.9	20.2	20.5	15.1	16.3	12.0	10.4

Source: Censuses of England and Wales.

Note: In 1881 and subsequently, it was assumed that there were no working children under the age of 10.

decline was between 1871, when the state moved rapidly toward compulsory schooling, and 1881. Surprisingly, the figures for 1891 are higher than those for 1881. As a result, a boy aged ten to fourteen in 1891 was very nearly as likely to be at work as one of the same age in 1871. We could take back the beginnings of concern about child labor in Britain at least to the early 1830s, and, in its origins, to the late eighteenth century. Only in 1931 do figures for child employment disappear from the census—and there was something like a determination to show in the interwar period that children's labor was a thing of the past despite evidence to the contrary.[31] On the most optimistic interpretation, it took a century to get rid of child labor, and it was done by slowly raising the age of entry to certain key childhood occupations. The contrast with the 1973 ILO Convention (No. 138) Concerning Minimum Age for Admission to Employment (ILO C138)[32] is marked. The ILO laid down ages below which child work should be categorically illegal. Its deliberations took little account of how long it had taken to reduce child labor in the industrialized world or the actual child labor conditions that had appeared in many less developed countries around the world.

More detailed examination of the census returns and other data reinforce and elucidate this basic fact, that the decline of child labor in Britain and the West extended over a long time period. The decline was intimately linked with the geography of child employment; the chances of being employed as a child and the age at which you started work depended very much on where you lived. Thus in the 1851 census there was a range for girls aged ten to fourteen from 50.6 percent employed in Bedfordshire to only 7.6 percent employed in Durham. For boys the range was not so great but still substantial, from 51.6 percent employed in West Riding of Yorkshire to 18 percent employed in Middlesex.[33] Even within counties the differences could be considerable. Thus in the high-employment county of Lancashire in 1911, over 80 percent of fourteen-year-old girls were employed in many textile towns, but only 20 percent in the glass-making town of St. Helens.[34]

There was consistency over time in areas of high and low child employment. Of twenty-one counties in the bottom half of the 1851 county figures for employment of boys aged ten to fourteen, fifteen recur in 1921. While some counties moved up or down the table, the consistency of position is the dominating feature. Further illustration of this fundamental point is to be found by examining figures for child employment by industrial area. As late as 1921, about 15 percent of twelve- and thirteen-year-olds were employed in the textile areas of Lancashire and Yorkshire, traditionally areas of high child employment, compared with 1.5 percent in the northeast and 0.2 percent in Greater London, equally traditionally areas of low employment.[35] Once child labor has become established in a particular geographical area, it is peculiarly difficult to dislodge it. As Margaret McMillan put it, "[i]n certain districts where child-labor is a tradition and custom, the very idea of associating it with inhumanity does not occur to the people."[36]

The census figures, up until 1911, were drawn up on the assumption that each child could be allocated to one of the categories in the census: from 1881 onward children were either in employment or at school. There were at least two ways in which this was misleading. First, employment might be part-time or intermittent. Second, being at school did not preclude also being employed part-time. We can get a more accurate picture of the child employment market as a whole from some figures calculated by Frederic Keeling in 1912: nearly half a million children under fourteen worked, 41 percent of them full-time, 8 percent part-time in factories and other employment; the majority of them, over 50 percent, both attended school and worked.[37] If we translate this into a typical career for a child growing up, a period of school combined with employment becomes the norm. Nonetheless, as late as 1911 a significant number of children under fourteen left school early to work full-time.

The finding that most children at some point combined school with work has obvious bearing on twenty-first-century debate. It is easy to imagine that compulsory schooling laws, particularly when effectively implemented, could or should bring an end to child work, but the British experience shows that child employment before and after school was normal, particularly as the school leaving age neared. Nor was the British experience in any way unusual; there is good evidence also of the part-time work of schoolchildren in Austria, Prussia, and Norway, where, in contrast to Britain in the early twentieth century, its effects were thought to be beneficial.[38]

What prompted children who were by compulsion attending school full-time also to work? Boredom at school, peer group pressure, the custom of the region, the wish to be more adult, and other motives—all doubtless played their part. But the overriding reason was the need to contribute wages to the family economy. It often is claimed that in the second half of the nineteenth and first half of the twentieth centuries an adult male breadwinner economy came close to reality. Such a claim focuses on the low level of employment of married women as if they alone might be supplementary wage earners. But in fact, adult male wages were rarely sufficient for most working-class families with children, and it was the children who were under pressure to enter the labor market to make ends meet. Across Europe and North America the evidence is consistent: children were the key supplementary wage earners, their percentage of total family income rising as the adult male got older and their own earning potential increased. By the time an adult male was in his fifties, children's contributions to family income were typically between one-third and nearly one-half. Children knew, from the moment they started working, that their earnings were for the family. Thus, in early-twentieth-century Scotland, "[i]t was taken for granted that earnings [of schoolchildren] would be handed over 'to the house.'"[39] For households without a male head, children's earnings were even more critical. Until the pressure to contribute to the family eased, probably in the middle decades of the twentieth century, it was highly unlikely that schoolchildren would not also be working. When that pressure did ease, and schoolchildren could be permitted to keep all or most of their earnings, entrepreneurs appreciated the potential of the "teenage consumer," and children faced a different kind of pressure to work: to pay for their own consumption needs.[40]

The conclusion that most contemporary commentators drew from figures of the kind we have been examining was a positive one. Child labor was in decline. The most abusive forms of it had been dealt with in laws specially targeted at particular industries: climbing boys cleaning the chimneys, children working underground in mines, gang employment of children in agriculture, and the labor of children in brickworks. The Factory and Workshops Act of 1878, wrote T. H. S. Escott,[41] represented the point at which legislation had reached, after three-quarters of a century, "a culminating point of efficiency and comprehensiveness, beyond which, in the present century, it is not likely to advance." The laws had "certainly cured all the evils existing in the first half of the century" and they had been "the foundation of the Factory Acts of all other countries." True, there were "abuses" that still needed to be dealt with, but the processes to deal with them were in place. Moreover, the assertion that children had rights had become a commonplace.[42]

A century and more on, we may be more cautious. We may be struck by the length of time it took to achieve success, by the persistence of child labor in particular industries and areas, and by the frequently false hopes that a problem had been dealt with only for it to emerge again years later—the story of the climbing boys is replete with such happenings. If we broaden the analysis beyond Britain, it becomes more rather than less difficult to be confident of the decline and eventual disappearance of child labor. Even in the textile industries, where child labor was most often used and where the technology became relatively standardized, the proportion of children in the work force across or within national boundaries showed no dominant trend. In Ghent,

Belgium, for example, the firm of Voortmans was well-known for its employment of children, employing more than rival manufacturers, with the proportion rising sharply in the 1840s and 1850s. And yet the 10 percent of the work force who were under fifteen in 1859 looks distinctly modest compared with the figures for Britain or France. Similarly in northern Massachusetts and New Hampshire, where young women rather than children were the preferred factory labor force, child employment levels were low.[43] French figures comparing the early 1840s and early 1860s suggest that women were replacing children in industrial employment, a trend for which there is little evidence elsewhere.[44] If we can conclude anything from this, it is that there was nothing in any way inevitable about high levels of child employment at a particular stage of economic development or its decline, and that analysis (yet to be carried out) must compare not only countries, but also regions and firms.

Looking ahead from the time Escott wrote in the early 1880s, we know that the early twentieth century was to see renewed concern about exploitive child labor in forms not easily dealt with by legislation—the part-time work of schoolchildren and the work of children in the home-based sweatshop industries. What had been acceptable and praiseworthy for Escott—for example, the part-time system in the textile areas, where, he believed, "the wits of children working half-time are sharpened"[45]—had become widely condemned as abusive and exploitive twenty years later. Early-twentieth-century commentators were horrified also by the stultifying effects on older children of attending machinery. It was, said one commentator, "a more insidious form of cruelty" than that prevalent in the factories and mines of the early nineteenth century.[46] Abusive and exploitive child labor had a tendency to rear its head in new and unexpected forms.

Child labor in the United States, while exemplifying many of the same patterns as in Western Europe, departs notably from them. First, with the exception of the southern textile industry, which in some ways replicated the problem of first generation industrialization in the United States and Britain, the US "child labor problem" shifted substantially in the late nineteenth century to become a problem associated with the employment of growing numbers of "new immigrant" children. Children were employed as auxiliary wage earners within low-wage households, either in mainline industrial jobs (coal mining, glass making, canning, etc.) or as "informal sector" workers ("newsies," errand boys, ragpickers) outside basic industry. The 1900 census reported a sobering increase of 1 million in the number of child laborers between the ages of ten and fifteen over the previous thirty years; the 1,750,178 reported child laborers included none under age ten because their labor was not enumerated.[47] The advent of "mature industrialization" showed little diminution in the demand for child labor or in the willingness of hard-pressed new immigrant families to supply that demand.[48] Second, regulating child labor in the United States was encumbered by two problems. In the first place, unlike Britain and much of Western Europe, the United States continued to be characterized by a peculiarly weak central state.[49] The inability to achieve and maintain effective federal regulatory control over child labor was chronic until the passage of the Fair Labor Standards Act (FLSA) in 1938,[50] and even then agricultural and informal sector employment lay beyond federal regulatory control. State-level regulation was uneven and inconsistent, as was the enforcement of mandatory school attendance. Large segments of the child labor market lay beyond effective regulatory control.[51]

The second problem associated with the regulation of child labor in the United States had to do with the ideology of child labor reformers. The progressive reform community that organized to combat child labor did so primarily through "protective legislation" as it applied to the conditions under which women and children worked.[52] That movement specifically eschewed addressing the conditions faced by male workers in low-wage employment, where dangerous conditions and long hours were also characteristic. The reformers believed, as have child labor reformers generally, that the problem of child labor could be addressed in isolation from the general impoverishment of laboring families. Minimum wage or shorter hours regulation for all workers in private industry might have addressed the central causes of family poverty and child labor, but reformers failed to support these demands.[53] Economist and future US senator Paul Douglas of Illinois was unrepresentative of reformers in his claim that

> the most effective way in which society protects children is in providing their parents with sufficient income so that they can be brought up properly. It is foolish to expect the wage earner with unduly low income to feed, cloth [*sic*] and rear their children in adequate fashion. Give a family of average intelligence sufficient money and it will be able to take care of its children. The most pressing obligation is for the industry to put its system of wage payment on an adequate basis and until this is done, social reform will swing against the child.[54]

The regulatory movement in the United States was further handicapped by a labor movement, dominated in the early twentieth century by the American Federation of Labor (AFL), wary of state meddling in labor relations. While the AFL officially opposed child labor, it failed to provide the kind of political muscle that might have led to a more concerted and successful national campaign to abolish it.[55]

The limits of child labor reform in the United States in the face of the expanding employment of children are revealed in the history of the National Child Labor Committee (NCLC), the leading advocacy organization on behalf of child workers after 1904. No crusade tapped the moral outrage of the reform community more deeply than the campaign to abolish child labor. While child labor reformers mobilized a constituency that crossed class lines and embraced some forward-looking businessmen, other corporate leaders associated with the National Civic Federation believed that sensational literature on child labor was purveyed by "socialistic writers" and that it had done "a great injustice to many fair-minded and humane employers in the South."[56]

The national campaign against child labor developed along parallel but distinct paths in the southern and northern United States. The Knights of Labor had succeeded in pressuring some states in the 1880s to pass laws setting age limits and restricting hours of work for children in factories. Lacking enforcement mechanisms, such laws had become by the 1890s dead letters or had been repealed. A new effort in Alabama, spearheaded initially by AFL organizers and then taken over by an Episcopalian minister, Edgar Gardner Murphy, built a new, more formidable campaign. New legislation, passed in 1903, banned children under twelve from working in factories and prescribed a maximum sixty-six-hour workweek for children under sixteen, the most advanced child labor standard in any southern state.[57] Parallel efforts in New York pushed through amendments to existing state laws in 1903 that required documentation of age for child workers, increased the number of days of compulsory school attendance, reduced hours to nine, and extended application of the law to the "street trades."[58]

Nationalizing the child labor movement followed quickly on the heels of the successes in Alabama and New York. A provisional national committee organized a founding convention in New York on April 15, 1904. Reformer Felix Adler focused the attention of delegates squarely on what he termed "a holocaust of the children—a condition which is intolerable."[59] In so doing, he prescribed strict limits to the concerns that would guide the new NCLC:

> That for which the Committee stands should be the absolute minimum which the enlightened public sentiment of the community demands. It should be plainly said that whatever happens in the sacrifice of adult workers, the public conscience inexorably demands that the children under twelve years of age shall not be touched; that childhood shall be sacred; that industrialism and commercialism shall not be allowed beyond this point to degrade humanity.[60]

Child labor reformers thus framed their arguments in moral terms, but they did so pragmatically, in ways that rationalized the existing economic order. Leading reformer and settlement house activist Jane Addams argued that the work of children "robs the assets of the community . . . it uses up those resources which should have kept industry going on for many years."[61] Samuel McCune Lindsay described his fellow child labor reformers as "meliorists" occupying a middle ground in the reform movement:

> With the muckraker and the socialist who gloats over the indecencies revealed by child labor as evidences of the unalterable rottenness of our in-

dustrial society, and with the mere sentimentalist who sees none of the practical difficulties or underlying causes of the Child Labor problem, North or South, the National Child Labor Committee has no sympathy . . . I think I may safely say that the National Committee are meliorists, one and all, that is, persons who have a sincere faith in the power of a united effort to ameliorate the conditions brought about by any industrial development or situation, however bad, through the better guidance and application of laws of natural and economic evolution.[62]

But even understood as a discrete social problem, child labor had spread—not receded—with the maturation of the industrial order. The use of child laborers in southern textile mills had grown in the 1890s to a staggering 30 percent of the work force by the turn of the century. They constituted, in Edwin Markham's powerful phrases, "a gaunt goblin army" of cheap laborers, "a pygmy people sucked in from the hills."[63] The textile industry of New England and the piedmont South were inextricably interconnected by ownership and investment. These connections fed a sense of common cause among the reformers witnessing the spreading plague of child labor.

The NCLC expanded from a modest organization of 50 members in 1904 to a membership of more than 6,400 and a budget of $60,000 in 1912. Marshaled in the child labor phalanx were state and national organizations, unions, and a broad cross section of the reform community. In 1912 these reform interests pushed US president Theodore Roosevelt's Progressive Party to adopt a platform that included at its heart a call for federal prohibition of child labor.[64] Federal legislation—the Keating-Owen Act—signed into law by President Woodrow Wilson in September 1916,[65] provided the most tangible achievement the movement could claim to that point. But the law tested the limits of US legal regulatory culture and was declared an unconstitutional expansion of federal authority over interstate commerce in 1918.[66] A subsequent law, passed in 1919, attempted to abolish child labor through taxation but was also declared unconstitutional.[67] A combination of employer, rural, and conservative antistatist interests continued to thwart effective federal regulation. With each defeat, the number of child laborers surged. And with the Great Depression deepening and adult employment falling to new lows, the numbers of child laborers had risen again to over a million in 1932. The same pattern followed the 1935 Supreme Court decision declaring the National Industrial Recovery Act (NIRA) and its codes of fair practice (including bans on child labor) unconstitutional.[68] Finally, in 1938, the Franklin Roosevelt administration succeeded in getting Congress to pass a new measure—the FLSA—that promised for the first time truly effective elimination of child labor.[69] Two features of this effort are particularly noteworthy. First, it occurred in a new legal environment, since a Roosevelt-appointed Court had declared the Wagner Act and other key pieces of New Deal regulatory legislation constitutional. Second, President Roosevelt insisted that a child labor ban be part of a legislative package that set minimum wage and maximum hours for adult workers. In so doing, he departed from the child labor reform orthodoxy that consistently sought to single children out as a special protected category of workers. In the context of the depression, a revived labor movement, reflecting the organizing surge among mass production workers, had dropped the AFL's long-standing opposition to such federal government regulation of the terms of employment.[70]

The slow and interrupted decline of child labor in Europe and its persistent reappearance in the United States, with each phase of economic transformation and each major influx of cheap immigrant labor, suggest that no simple causal connection links industrial modernization and the elimination of the scourge of child labor. And this "lesson" has some relevance to contemporary campaigns to combat child labor in the global economy of the twenty-first century.

Capitalism, Globalization, and Child Labor in the Developing World

Since the problem of child labor first came to public attention in the 1830s, its implications have, in two respects, been global in scope. First, children's most notorious work lay in export industries. Half of the cotton goods manufactured with the aid of young children in Britain were exported and 70 percent of all Britain's exports were textiles, in all of which child labor was prominent. These exports had effects that stretched beyond the beneficial one of supplying people across the world with cheap textiles; they also disrupted industry in the importing countries. It may have been an exaggeration for critics to claim that the plains of Bengal were white with the bones of Indian weavers starved to death by the competition from child-run machinery in Europe, but the image conveyed an element of truth.

Second, any attempt to control child labor had to be considered from an international as well as national perspective. Reformers often had a global perspective. From Massachusetts in 1840, Horace Mann wrote to an English counterpart, hoping that factory and other reforms "may lead to human amelioration all over the globe."[71] From a different perspective, employers demanded a level playing field, across international boundaries as well as within national ones. In 1840 the leading British factory inspector, Leonard Horner, pressing for further legislation, published a short book whose chief purpose was

> to show, and especially to our manufacturers, that it is not now in this country alone that the employment of children in factories is restricted by law. The inhumanity, injustice, and impolicy of extorting labor from children unsuitable to their age and strength—of subjecting them, in truth, to the hardships of slavery (for they are not free agents)—have been condemned by the public voice in other countries; and their governments have either already applied, or are now engaged in preparing, a remedy for this vice of modern times.[72]

This, Horner hoped, "may reconcile our manufacturers to the interference to which they are subjected, when they see that the example of England has been followed by other nations."[73] The "other countries" whose proceedings he outlined were Austria, France, Prussia, Russia, Switzerland—and Massachusetts.[74]

From the outset, then, there was an awareness both of the global implications of the use of children as workers and of the desirability of common action across national boundaries to deal with it. It took another half century, however, before there was anything approaching concerted international action. "Progress" in restricting, let alone eliminating, child labor came slowly and unevenly. In 1890, the Kaiser convened a meeting in Berlin where delegates from twelve European countries met to discuss an agenda focused around Sunday work and the work of children, young persons, and women in mines and factories. Despite "good-humored scepticism" about the likely outcome, agreements did emerge, though without legal sanction to enforce them. It is possible to trace a more or less direct line from this moment through to the foundation, following World War I, of the ILO with its commission to secure "the abolition of child labor."[75] The initiative came from trade unions during World War I. The French Confédération Générale du Travail prepared a document to "fix 14 years as the age of the admission of children to industrial, commercial and agricultural work."[76] The Leeds Conference of Allied Trade Unions in June 1916 adopted this standard, and allied governments, aware of the strength of labor, and anxious to reduce the appeal of socialism after the 1917 Bolshevik Revolution, gave it their backing.[77]

Until 1918, international discussions on child labor were confined largely to Europe and areas of white settlement outside it. The series of conventions concluded by the ILO in the interwar period gave nearly worldwide scope to the issue, but two key countries stood outside the ILO: the United States and the Soviet Union. The ILO perforce was restricted to confronting child labor in only a portion of the capitalist world. We know next to nothing about the extent of, and attitudes toward, child labor outside the capitalist world. The Soviet Union made two legislative attempts to control child labor, in 1918 and 1922, and in the 1920s these laws, together with unemployment, discouraged the employment of the young. But the Soviet Union was faced with the problem of millions of homeless children living in the streets, and in the 1930s it showed willingness to send them to work in the countryside or to engage them in "socially useful work." The rhetoric asserted that children should be at school; how much it matched reality remains uncertain.[78] US absence from the ILO conventions on child labor may have been compensated in part by a vigorous domestic debate in the interwar period that led eventually to more effective state regulation.

The typical thinking in the period between the foundation of the ILO and the mid-1970s was that the experience of the European countries over almost a century had shown the necessity of legislative interference to protect working children and, where necessary, to prevent them from working. Reformers convinced themselves that there could be a progressive realization of the ideal that child labor could be abolished. This was itself closely linked to a belief in children's rights, and specifically to the right of a child not to be subjected to exploitation in any kind of productive relationship. Both the global ambition to abolish child labor, and the limitations in the achievement of it, are evident in the attempts in the first half of the twentieth century to export labor legislation to the colonies of the European empires.

The ILO set the pace here, but accepted that some gradualism was necessary, especially in the face of opposition from colonial administration. Thus the 1919 ILO convention banning the employment of children under fourteen in industrial employment[79] was to be applied in colonies "except where owing to the local conditions its provisions are inapplicable" or "subject to such modifications as may be necessary to adapt its provisions to local conditions."[80] Even so, colonial administrations and Western capital operating in the colonies often protested the inappropriateness of what was being proposed, and dragged their feet. In Gold Coast (now Ghana), although there was some concern in the early twentieth century about "immature children" acting as headloaders in cocoa, the response to ILO conventions in the 1920s was that "steps will be taken . . . as local conditions may decide."[81] Such labor legislation as was passed remained a dead letter, and in 1956, the year before independence, it was thought that "[t]he time is not yet ripe for progressive legislation to rationalize conditions of service on cocoa farms."[82] In 1937, Malcolm MacDonald, the British secretary of state for the colonies, asked colonial governments to consider the application of ILO conventions: "all necessary steps," he wrote, "should be taken to induce legislation to give effect to the conventions in question."[83] The Nyasaland government dutifully responded with a "Women, Children, and Young Persons" bill that set sixteen as the working age, though by the time the bill became law in 1939 the age of sixteen had been reduced to twelve, the obligation to control night work had been circumvented by defining night as the period from sunset to sunrise (a solution also adopted by the Dutch in Indonesia), and tea and tobacco had been excluded from the definition of "industrial undertaking" despite the fact that it was in the sheds where tea and tobacco were sorted that there was extensive employment of young workers and most cause for concern over conditions.[84] As the director of medical services put it in 1941, after examining the tobacco sheds, he was "quite satisfied that in England work of this nature would be very strongly controlled."[85] MacDonald had in fact objected to the exclusion, and insisted that the law be changed, but no sooner was this done than the law was suspended for the duration of the war. In any event, difficulties continued after the war. Employers claimed that without child workers they could not compete, and officialdom, under pressure to do something, prevaricated: "As regards the employment of children," wrote the chief secretary in 1948, "it is a matter of very considerable difficulty, and one which will have to be very carefully examined," an admission that employers were mounting pressure to be allowed to continue employing children.[86]

The ILO approach to the child labor issue reached its apogee in 1973 with the adoption of the Minimum Age Convention.[87] The overall aim was to set a standard with global reach and to rely on individual countries to implement it. The minimum age for employment was set at fifteen or the age at which compulsory schooling ended, whichever was higher; and while developing countries were allowed to reduce this to fourteen, the recommendation that accompanied the convention suggested a minimum target age of sixteen. The mood was upbeat: the convention and recommendation, it was reported, "represent a new effort by the ILO to eliminate child labor, a problem which has always been one of its main concerns and one that it has tackled with appreciable success in the past, but whose solution remains a matter of urgency in many parts of the world."[88]

Over a quarter of a century later, the optimism underlying the decisions of 1973 looks at best naive. There had of course been much in the international economy between 1918 and 1973 to suggest that it was unrealistic to place reliance on a "modernization" model that presumed, as a consequence of steadily advancing capitalist development, that legislative advance to control child labor could take place. But it was only after the oil crisis of 1973 that the inherent instability of the capitalist world forced itself on world consciousness. That instability had its roots not only in the ability of some nations to ration the supply of oil, but also in the removal of controls on capitalism that allowed it to exploit to the full new technologies and the speed of global communications. Some economies blossomed in this new environment, others suffered. The gap between rich and poor widened.

It is difficult to assess the effects of all this on child labor. But the problem is perhaps best examined in a specific context, that of India, which, in the eyes of many, represents the most serious, intractable case and the one that is best documented. Indeed, child labor in India has generated an enormous literature.[89] A further reason for selecting India is that it is the subject of a particularly provocative study that has been widely influential, namely Myron Weiner's *The Child and the State in India and Pakistan*.[90] By focusing largely on state failure to provide basic education and enforce compulsory education laws, Weiner discounts what he calls "society-centered explanations" and in so doing contributes to a narrowing of focus that misses the critical structural and economic causes.

First, it is important to establish the dimensions of the problem. While estimates of the extent of child labor in India and the less developed world vary enormously, we can speak of ranges. The estimates of child workers worldwide, but predominantly in developing countries, reach as high as 250 million, with perhaps 120 million children between ages five and fourteen working full-time. For India, the conservative estimate is about 11.3 million (according to the 1991 census) and the higher estimate is 23.2 million (according to the ILO in 1996). Both estimates include full-time and "marginal" child workers. Mishra estimates that in 1991, 5.2 percent of children five to fourteen years old were child workers, down from 7.6 percent in 1981, and that as a percentage of all workers, children in India constituted 5.2 percent, significantly lower than some developing countries (Turkey 27.3 percent, Thailand 20.7 percent, Indonesia 12.4 percent, Egypt 8.2 percent).[91] We might note, for the sake of comparison, that almost all of these percentages of working children fall below levels for England and Wales during the period 1851–1911, reported earlier in this chapter. The presence of large numbers of what one commentator called "nowhere children"—that is, children who are neither in school nor officially working—suggests that actual magnitudes of "working" children may be significantly higher. Finally, in India, as in much of the developing world, the vast majority of child workers are in rural areas, though not exclusively in agricultural cultivation activities. Roughly 90 percent of India's child workers dwell in rural areas; of the 10 percent in urban areas, nearly 9 percent work in manufacturing or related activities but under 1 percent in "factories."[92]

Of course, the circumstances under which the children work vary enormously; but we can define, for the purposes of analysis, three broad sectors: agriculture (both export-oriented and subsistence), formal sector, and informal sector. While the formal sector is often defined as those employments that are covered by the Factories Act of 1948 and include electrified places of employment with ten or more workers or nonelectrified units with twenty or more workers, in fact many "formal" sector workers labor under "informal" conditions (casual, temporary, or contract) without protection of the labor laws.[93] This blurring of the lines between formal and informal sectors is a crucial feature of child labor in India. Children work in both sectors and participate in family economies that straddle the two worlds. A significant share of Indian agricultural production is for export and involves the work of children; in manufacturing, the data on children working in the export-oriented carpet manufacturing, diamond cutting and polishing, glassware, and footwear industries suggest as many as 1 million children in these four industries alone.[94] G. K. Lieten sees the growth of "segmented labor markets" as a critical development in the economies of less developed countries. He notes studies of the match industry in India, where "working families often combined factory work with work in the home and/or service in other business sectors."[95] Segmented labor markets mean that "the most vulnerable and marginalized families" must "fend for survival at the lower end of the income scale," often below the level of family reproduction.[96]

Many analysts acknowledge the fundamental fact of family poverty and family strategies for economic survival as primary determinants of children working for income. As Lakshmidhar Mishra notes of the parents of children working in Bidi establishments, "[l]andless with virtually no source of subsistence, they feel they have no alternative other than to pledge the services of their children to survive."[97] Virtually every study of child labor in India argues that the central cause lies in the economic insecurity of families. As Shakuntala Gupta and Sangeeta Nagaich assert, "inadequate, irregular or no family income" is the cause of child labor.[98] And Mishra observes that the research supports the primary finding that children work to "augment household income" and to "safeguard against the uncertainties of income" that result from job loss, natural calamities, or sickness of parents in poor families that are often in debt and have no savings.[99] The contributions of children to family income are not incidental. One study estimates that 23 percent of family income for India as a whole is contributed by children; another study that surveyed working children found that 40 percent worked because adult wage earners in the family were unemployed and one-third because of cuts in adult wages.[100] The acute needs of migrating families make utilization of child labor almost a necessity. Legal requirements for minimum wages and for residential accommodation of recruited migrants and their families routinely go unenforced, leading frequently to abominable, temporary housing. Under these circumstances children are deployed as household servants or in the informal economy to supplement low wages.[101]

The growth of the "informal economy," as it has come to be understood, represents a significant departure from the standard pattern of Western economic modernization envisioned for the developing world by a previous generation of social theorists. The persistence of immigrant children in the "street trades" during the Progressive era in the United States and to a lesser degree in Britain suggests a parallel informal sector in the West as well. Considerable evidence, most notably from India, shows that informal sector growth, at the expense of formal sector production and employment, is widespread. Such employment is characterized by a "casualization" of employment relations, small units of production, extensive subcontracting, the absence of regulation, high turnover, and low wages. The informal sector is not strictly an urban phenomenon but describes a large sphere of employment in rural industry and in agriculture as well. Anthropologist Jan Breman has argued that "informalization" has increased by leaps and bounds over the past few decades to the point where as few as 10 to 15 percent of industrial workers inhabit the formal sector. "Flexibilisation" has led to a contraction in formal sector work and expansion of the informal sector.[102] Arvind Das has shown that growth in formal sector employment has lagged significantly behind growth in gross domestic product (GDP).[103] But such conditions have fit very nicely the prescribed path of liberalization imposed through programs of structural adjustment by the World Bank and the International Monetary Fund (IMF). Breman summarizes the current condition: "[M]ore production and higher productivity but all that without labor legislation and with the abolition of whatever government machinery had been set up for that purpose in the past; no minimum wages and protected employment; no regulation of work conditions and hardly any trade unions daring to mobilize and unite the fragmented workforce."[104] The new informal terrain that child labor inhabits globally makes even more imperative the rethinking of international regulatory policies and situating the rights of children within a human rights framework that upholds the rights of all workers, as is argued in Chapter 17.

In contrast to these analyses, political scientist Myron Weiner has put forward a case that the child labor problem (in India and South Asia) stems primarily from state failure to provide adequate education facilities and the failure of states to enforce compulsory school attendance. Drawing on an implicit free market model, Weiner argues that policies, like compulsory education, will "deny parents the income of their children" with salutary results. "Children cease to be regarded as economic assets and there is less incentive for increasing their number. In time, a social transformation takes place, with financial resources within the family flowing not from the very young to their parents, but rather downward from parents to children."[105] However, to imply that solving the education problem in the absence of a solution to the problem of poverty and economic dependency will eliminate the child labor problem is both myopic and ludicrous. Lieten has criticized the cultural myopia and ethnocentrism of Weiner's analysis and his failure (with others) to give sufficient attention to the demand side of the child labor equation by privileging supply side analysis. In particular, he disputes the notion that poor people maintain high fertility in order to enhance family income. Quoting demographer Tim Dyson, he suggests that "children work because people have children, rather than people have children because children work."[106]

The focus on literacy as the single key to solving the problem of child labor misses the point. Do children work because they are illiterate? Hardly. They work because of family poverty. Literacy is offered as a panacea that presumably creates the appetite for individual self-improvement (a very Western, modernizing notion), but in the absence of secure, remunerative adult employment and the accompanying reduction in poverty, literacy alone cannot do the trick. A possible alternative view (not one that Weiner shares) is that literacy might contribute to the politicization of peasants and the poor in ways that can foster the kinds of mass movements that could organize politically to challenge the existing economic structure. But that would require a particular kind of literacy campaign, such as that pioneered by Paulo Freire in Brazil or carried out in revolutionary Cuba.[107]

While Weiner finds the simple failure of the Indian state to impose compulsory education and invest in the literacy of its population as the sole cause of the high rates of child labor, others see a more complicated equation, exacerbated by global economic conditions. As Parveen Nangia observes, "[t]he poor economic conditions make conflicting demands upon the children between work participation and schooling. Thus, even the easy accessibility to schools does not increase the enrollment of children if their economic status does not permit it."[108] Survey data suggest both children and parents report that in the vast majority of cases low parental earnings are the cause of children working. "When parents were asked if they would like their children to work in case their own earnings go up . . . , 72.4% of the respondents were of the view that they would withdraw their children from the labor force if their own earnings increased."[109]

■ Capitalism, Child Labor, and Human Rights

Historically, the causes of child labor have been fundamentally economic, rooted in a capitalist marketplace that perpetually transforms work and puts downward pressure on wages. In Britain (and Western Europe), strong traditions of state regulation (mercantilist to laborist), strong labor movements, and social democratic or labor activism have to some extent deterred the reinvention of child labor. In the United States, weak state regulation and a relatively weak labor movement combined with the periodic reintroduction of economically vulnerable immigrant workers have led to the episodic return of low-wage regimes in which child labor flourishes, albeit in new forms. In the developing world, dependent postcolonial economies have been in a weak position to eliminate child labor, which flourishes especially in the informal sectors spawned by dependent, low-wage industrialization. Postcolonial regimes have shown little interest in or capacity to regulate child labor through the enforcement of existing legislation; postcolonial dependency and divergent "economic development" have meant that debtor nations have had to welcome foreign investment under conditions that perpetuate low-wage dependency and widespread use of child labor. Persistent poverty has meant that families—often dislocated from the countryside—continue to rely on family economic strategies that require the use of children's labor. Efforts to institute universal education as a deterrent to child labor have been hobbled by market pressures within the global economy and pressures from international financial policies to curtail social spending and infrastructure investment. Under such conditions, we have no reason to expect that child labor will soon diminish or that states in the developing world will show any capacity to regulate it.

The implications of this analysis are that child labor will only recede from the developing world and not be reinvented in Western regimes, especially those with weak state regulation, if states strengthen their capacity to negotiate a greater degree of economic independence from global capitalist firms and Western-dominated financial institutions. Breaking the cycle of dependency is critical. Of some assistance in that process will be the development of effective labor movements and state structures staffed by nationals committed to enhancing the social level of their populations and limiting the dictation of transnational corporations and international financial institutions (World Bank and IMF). Indeed, one might argue that the most consistent and politically effective opponents of child labor have been labor movements that battle against child labor to protect the interests of their members as well as fundamental human and worker rights. Trade unions initiated the movement for the abolition of child labor enshrined in the ILO.[110] International agencies and nongovernmental organizations (NGOs) can also be of some assistance in this process, though the resistance of global, cartelized capital and its state allies (preeminently the United States) will likely continue to be massive and will distort the efforts of those NGOs that operate under the influence of global capital.[111]

In the face of these conditions, what is the role of human rights in the efforts to combat child labor? Campaigners against child labor have always used arguments based on rights. Until recently, however, the rights they have argued for have not been, *tout court,* human rights, but rather rights specific to children. The reaction against child labor, first voiced in the industrial revolution in the United Kingdom, has itself contributed to a new view of childhood as properly dependent, protected, and happy. Adults, by contrast, particularly if they are fully functioning adults, have no rights to these things. For children at work, the downside to this protectiveness was that they lacked access to the bargaining rights that adults might succeed in winning. Whether in the 1830s or in the 1990s, pictures of children at work are designed to provoke pity for the child as a child rather than outrage at the exploitation of labor.

A language of rights has been integral to all attempts to control child labor, but it has not been, on its own, instrumental in achieving that control. Alongside it, and often more influential, has been a language of utilitarianism. Here the argument is that child labor has harmful effects both on individual children and on society as a whole. Individual children suffer in their health, and they learn skills that serve them in childhood but for which there is no useful outlet in adult life. Society as a whole needs adults able to work in a wide variety of roles, both domestic and in the labor market, and child labor hindered the development of such adults. Children therefore have a right, from which society benefits, to be trained in skills that will provide them with an adult livelihood. The utilitarian argument is in many ways an appeal to fear: if child labor is allowed to continue, the successful reproduction of society is threatened. Women, too, have been at times the subject of such protectionist policies. Since human rights advocacy on its own is unlikely to achieve success, an appeal to utilitarian arguments has been able to widen the constituency of those campaigning for some control of child labor.

It would be naive to suppose that the strongest combination of human rights and utilitarian arguments will necessarily achieve success. In addition, economic actors need to feel that control of child labor is in their interests.

Child workers themselves are among those economic actors and face the problem that the approach to child labor that has the most sanction from history allows them no place in the labor force. It is true that the 1989 UN Convention on the Rights of the Child and subsequent thinking acknowledge children as social actors, but there still remains a large residue from the romantic conception of childhood as economically useless. Part of its appeal was that it was simple to understand and led to clear policies. The attempts to modify it by allowing children access to some adult human rights while insisting also on a degree of protectiveness not accorded to adults leaves gray areas where policymakers can flounder. And it has little purchase on the imagination of a world that likes its child laborers to be pitiable.

One challenge for the twenty-first century is to imagine a childhood as free as possible of the romantic conception. This will mean a childhood that does not place a taboo on productive activity, but at the same time ensures that the child worker is not exploited. Human rights, to which a child is entitled, like the rights workers generally deserve, must include the right to a living wage, the right to organize collectively, and the right to the provision of social benefits from states that claim the prerogative to regulate corporate behavior. Unless those rights are guaranteed to all, we can foresee no end to exploitive child labor.

Notes

1. In this historical chapter, the term "child labor" is used in the ways it was used by people in the nineteenth and twentieth centuries, and as it has been used by historians who have discussed the issues involved during those times. The term as we use it describes the work that children did and, in some instances, embodies a criticism of it. Current usage, as explained in Chapter 2 of this volume, typically defines "child labor" to mean, as stated in the introduction to this volume, "work done by children [generally youth under age 15 or 18 depending on the nature of their work] that is harmful to them because it is abusive, exploitive, hazardous, or otherwise contrary to their best interests—a subset of a larger class of children's work, some of which may be compatible with children's best interests (variously expressed as 'beneficial,' 'benign,' or 'harmless' children's work)." We prefer here to conform to the usage of historically contemporary actors and of historians rather than to impose a distinction rooted in our own judgment about what was or should have been deemed harmful to children's best interests.

2. Fuller, "Child Labor," p. 416.

3. Ibid.

4. Tuttle, *Hard at Work in Factories and Mines . . .* , pp. 5, 244, 254–255.

5. Hindman, *Child Labor . . .* , p. 5.

6. Ibid., p. 7.

7. Within a vast literature, see Gilman, *Mandarins of the Future . . .* , pp. 1–27, 241–277, on the origins of modernization theory. See Frank, *Capitalism and Underdevelopment in Latin America . . .* , and Frank, *The Underdevelopment of Development.* See also Ghosh, *Dependency Theory Revisited,* on dependency theory; and Scott, *Gender and Development,* for a critique of both.

8. Foner, *From Ellis Island To JFK* . . . , pp. 89–107; Sassen, *Globalization and Its Discontents,* pp. 63–105.

9. For data on increasing rates of child labor in the United States and United Kingdom, see Mishra, "Multi-Dimensional Approach to Child Labour in India," p. 31. See also Hobbs, McKechnie, and Lavalette, *Child Labor* . . . , pp. 236–240.

10. For a discussion of the role of transnational corporations in the perpetuation of child labor, see Sawyer, *Children Enslaved,* pp. 151–152.

11. Nangia, *Child Labor* . . . . See also Breman, *Footloose Labor* . . . .

12. Cunningham, *The Children of the Poor* . . . , pp. 22–32.

13. Quoted in Cunningham, *Children and Childhood* . . . , pp. 130–131.

14. Ibid., p. 130.

15. Tuttle, *Hard at Work in Factories and Mines* . . . , pp. 80–81; Kirby, *Child Labour in Britain* . . . , p. 72.

16. Berg and Hudson, "Rehabilitating the Industrial Revolution," p. 36.

17. See, for example, McMillan, "Child Labor," p. 93.

18. For a summary of the debate, see Mokyr, *The British Industrial Revolution* . . . , pp. 115–120.

19. Ibid.

20. See Nardinelli, *Child Labor and the Industrial Revolution.*

21. Thompson, *The Making of the English Working Class,* p. 349.

22. Nardinelli, *Child Labor and the Industrial Revolution,* p. 63.

23. Cunningham, *The Children of the Poor* . . . , pp. 83–84.

24. Horner, *On the Employment of Children in Factories,* p. 41.

25. Alfred, *The History of the Factory Movement,* vol. 1, pp. 235–252.

26. Ibid., pp. 254–256.

27. Forster, *Selected Poems* . . . , p. 179. For evidence of its impact, see Smith, *The Cry of the Children* . . . , esp. p. 6.

28. Karunan, Chapter 12 in this volume. See also Chapter 8 in this volume.

29. Macaulay, *The History of England* . . . , p. 323.

30. Best, *Mid-Victorian Britain* . . . , p. 111.

31. Cunningham, "The Problem That Doesn't Exist? . . . ," pp. 139–172.

32. 1015 UNTS 297, reprinted in Weston and Carlson, *International Law and World Order,* vol. 3, III.O.5.

33. Cunningham, "The Employment and Unemployment of Children . . . ," pp. 144–145.

34. Winstanley, *Working Children* . . . , p. 16.

35. Cunningham, "The Employment and Unemployment of Children . . . ," pp. 144–145.

36. McMillan, "Child Labor," p. 94.

37. Keeling, *Child Labour in the United Kingdom,* p. xxviii.

38. Weiner, *The Child and the State in India* . . . , pp. 128–129, 134–135; Schrumpf, "From Full-Time to Part-Time . . . ," pp. 47–78.

39. Quoted in Cunningham, "The Decline of Child Labor . . . ," p. 422–423.

40. Ibid., pp. 422–425.

41. Escott, *England* . . . , pp. 138–149.

42. Cunningham, "The Rights of the Child . . . ," pp. 7–8, 11–12.

43. Cunningham, "The Decline of Child Labor . . . ," pp. 411–412.

44. Heywood, "The Market for Child Labor . . . ," p. 37.

45. Escott, *England* . . . , p. 144.

46. Quoted in Cunningham, *The Children of the Poor* . . . , p. 186.

47. Trattner, *Crusade for the Children* . . . , p. 41.

48. Keil and Usui, "The Family Wage System . . ."; and Robinson, "Economic Necessity and the Life Cycle . . . ."

49. See Skocpol, *Protecting Soldiers and Mothers* . . . , also for a discussion of the limits imposed on central state capacity in the United States. See, additionally, Skowronek, *Building the New American State* . . . ; and Keller, *Affairs of State* . . . .

50. Fraser, *Labor Will Rule* . . . , pp. 161, 240. See also Kennedy, *Freedom from Fear* . . . , p. 28, n. 28.

51. On the limited opportunities for education as an alternative available to would-be child laborers in the United States, see Walters and James, "Schooling for Some. . ."; and Horan and Hargis, "Children's Work and Schooling . . . ."

52. Kessler-Harris, *Out to Work* . . . , pp. 184–198. See also Stromquist, *Reinventing "The People."*

53. On the limits of progressive reformers' support for state regulation, see Stromquist, *Reinventing "The People."*

54. Quoted in Patel and Talati, "Child Labor in India . . . ," p. 67.

55. For a recent discussion of the limits of AFL's politics and its antistatism, see Greene, *Pure and Simple Politics* . . . . By comparison, Nardinelli notes the key role played by the labor movement in child labor campaigns in Western Europe. See Nardinelli, *Child Labor and the Industrial Revolution,* pp. 138, 151.

56. Ralph Easley to Nelson Aldrich (July 20, 1906), quoted in Weinstein, *The Corporate Ideal* . . . , p. 28.

57. Trattner, *Crusade for the Children* . . . , pp. 51, 55; Bremner, *From the Depths* . . . , pp. 217–218.

58. Felt, *Hostages of Fortune* . . . , pp. 42–47; Yellowitz, *Labor and the Progressive Movement* . . . , pp. 89–93; Trattner, *Crusade for the Children* . . . , pp. 56–57.

59. Minutes, First General Meeting of the National Child Labor Committee (1904), quoted in Trattner, *Crusade for the Children* . . . , p. 58.

60. Ibid., pp. 58–59.

61. Quoted in Bremner, *From the Depths* . . . , p. 216 (from Addams, *Child Labor and Pauperism*).

62. Quoted in Trattner, *Crusade for the Children* . . . , pp. 66–67 (from Lindsay, *The Work, Policy, and Plans of the National Child Labor Committee*).

63. Quoted in Bremner, *From the Depths* . . . , p. 217 (from Markham, "The Hoe-Man in the Making").

64. See Trattner, *Crusade for the Children* . . . , pp. 95–131; Bremner, *From the Depths* . . . , pp. 220–229; and Muncy, *Creating a Female Dominion of Reform* . . . , pp. 38–60.

65. For a detailed discussion of the legislative history of the Keating-Owens Act, see Wood, *Constitutional Politics in the Progressive Era* . . . , pp. 47–80. See also Hindman, *Child Labor* . . . , pp. 65–70; and Abbott, *The Child and the State,* pp. 483–486.

66. *Hammer v. Dagenhart,* 247 US 251 (1918), discussed in Wood, *Constitutional Politics* . . . , pp. 81–110, esp. pp. 105–110.

67. The Child Labor Tax Act, an amendment to the Revenue Act of 1919, was declared unconstitutional in *Bailey v. Drexel Furniture,* 259 US 20 (1922). See Hindman, *Child Labor* . . . , pp. 70–74; Wood, *Constitutional Politics* . . . , pp. 193–219, 254–299, esp. pp. 277–288; and Abbott, *The Child and the State,* pp. 517–525.

68. *Schechter Poultry Corporation v. United States,* 295 US 495 (1935), declared the NIRA (and its child labor prohibition) unconstitutional. See discussion in Kennedy,

Freedom from Fear . . . , pp. 325–329. See also Hindman, *Child Labor* . . . , pp. 81–84; Fraser, *Labor Will Rule* . . . , pp. 319–326; and Trattner, *Crusade for the Children* . . . , pp. 159–160, 185, 195, 200.

69. For a discussion of the 1938 Fair Labor Standards Act, see Forsythe, "Legislative History of the Fair Labor Standards Act," pp. 464–490. See also Kessler-Harris, *In Pursuit of Equity* . . . , pp. 101–117, esp. pp. 104–105.

70. Trattner, *Crusade for the Children* . . . , p. 203; Fraser, *Labor Will Rule* . . . , pp. 329–330, 392–395; Dubofsky, *The State and Labor in Modern America,* pp. 165–166; Kennedy, *Freedom from Fear* . . . , pp. 344–345, 371.

71. Horner, *On the Employment of Children in Factories,* p. 113.

72. Ibid., p. v.

73. Ibid., p. vi.

74. Ibid., pp. v, vii.

75. Shotwell, *The Origins of the International Labor Organization,* vol. 1, p. 449.

76. Ibid., vol. 2, p. 15.

77. Cunningham, "The Rights of the Child and the Wrongs of Child Labour . . . ," pp. 18–19; Shotwell, *The Origins of the International Labor Organization,* vol. 2, pp. 15, 25, 95, 113, 186, 214, 217.

78. Hobbs, McKechnie, and Lavalette, *Child Labor* . . . , p. 269; Schwarz, *Labor in the Soviet Union,* pp. 76–78; Goldman, *Women, the State, and Revolution* . . . , pp. 59–100; Stolee, "Homeless Children . . . ," pp. 64–83. Also, private email from Catriona Kelly to Hugh Cunningham, Aug. 14, 2003 (on file with the author).

79. ILO, *Convention* (No. 5) *Fixing the Minimum Age for Admission of Children to Industrial Employment* (1919).

80. Ibid., art. 8(1)(a)–(b).

81. Van Hear, "Child Labor and the Development of Capitalist Agriculture in Ghana," pp. 500–501.

82. Ibid., p. 504.

83. Chirwa, "Child and Youth Labour . . . ," p. 676.

84. Ibid., pp. 676–678.

85. Ibid., p. 676.

86. Chirwa, "Child and Youth Labor . . . ," pp. 662–680; for the Dutch in Indonesia, see White, "Children, Work, and 'Child Labor.' . . ."

87. ILO, *Convention* (No. 138) *Concerning Minimum Age for Admission to Employment* (1973).

88. ILO, *International Labor Review* (1972), 106:296–298; (1973), 108:264–266.

89. For an overview of the child labor literature in India, see Jain, *Child Labor in India* . . . . See also extensive bibliographies in numerous recent works—for example, Mishra, *Child Labor in India.*

90. Weiner published a later version of this 1991 book that focused on both India and Pakistan. See Weiner and Noman, *The Child and the State in India and Pakistan* . . . .

91. For various statistical estimates, see National Resource Centre on Child Labor, *Child Labor in India* . . . , pp. 16–18, 21; Rehman, Rehman, and Begum, *Child Labor and Child Rights,* pp. 21–22; and Mishra, "Multi-Dimensional Approach . . . ," pp. 23–26.

92. National Resource Centre on Child Labor, *Child Labor in India* . . . , pp. 18, 22; Mishra, "Multi-Dimensional Approach . . . ," pp. 24–25.

93. See very helpful discussion of these issues in Hensman, *The Impact of Globalisation* . . . , pp. 6–7.

94. FOIL, *Those That Be in Bondage* . . . .

95. Lieten, "Child Labor and Poverty . . . ," p. 463.

96. Ibid., p. 16.

97. Mishra, *Child Labor in India,* pp. 3–4.

98. Gupta and Nagaich, "Child Labor in India . . . ," p. 78.

99. Mishra, *Child Labor in India,* p. 28.

100. The studies cited are discussed in Gupta and Nagaich, *Child Labor in India* . . . , p. 78; Mishra, *Child Labor in India,* p. 28; and Singh, *Child Labor in India* . . . , p. 14.

101. Mishra, *Child Labor in India,* pp. 30–32; Nangia, *Child Labor* . . . , pp. 39–40.

102. Breman, "The Study of Industrial Labor in Post-Colonial India: The Informal Sector . . . ," p. 427; Breman, "The Study of Industrial Labor in Post-Colonial India: The Formal Sector . . . ," pp. 35–36. For a particularly insightful treatment of the phenomenon of work in the informal sector—not limited to children—see Breman, *Footloose Labor* . . . ; also, most recently, Breman, *The Laboring Poor in India* . . . .

103. Das, epilogue to Breman and Das, *Down and Out* . . . , p. 155; and Breman, "The Study of Industrial Labor in Post-Colonial India: The Informal Sector . . . ," pp. 428–429.

104. Breman, prologue to Breman and Das, *Down and Out* . . . , p. 10.

105. Weiner, *The Child and the State in India and Pakistan* . . . , p. 186.

106. Lieten, "Child Labor and Poverty . . . ," p. 460.

107. On Paulo Freire's popular education ideas, see Taylor, *The Texts of Paulo Freire;* and Street, *Literacy in Theory and Practice.* On the Cuban literacy campaign, see Keeble, *In the Spirit of Wandering Teachers* . . . .

108. Nangia, *Child Labor* . . . , p. 43.

109. Ibid., pp. 184–185; see also pp. 174, 176.

110. See text accompanying supra endnotes 68–77.

111. See Hobbs, McKechnie, and Lavalette, *Child Labor* . . . , pp. 177–178; Stiles, "Grassroots Empowerment . . . ," pp. 39, 42; Hulme and Edwards, "NGOs, States, and Donors . . . ," pp. 9–11; and Smillie, *The Alms Bazaar* . . . , pp. 167–169. See also Smillie, "Changing Partners . . . ," pp. 13–43. One particularly prominent and controversial example has been the effort of the Fair Labor Association (FLA), the White House Apparel Industry Partnership, and the Collegiate Licensing Company to push through anemic codes of fair employment. See Howard, "Partners in Sweat." See also Benjamin, "A Critique of the Fair Labor Association."

Part 2

The Standards-Based Response of the World Community

4

Child Labor Standards: From Treaties to Labels

Holly Cullen

This chapter examines international legal and quasi-legal standards on child labor.[1] My focus is on evaluating how and how much this standard-setting on child labor has moved toward a human rights approach.

Early international legal efforts to address child labor tended to be abolitionist in tone, and treated it as just another aspect of the labor market to be regulated. It was the approach of the International Labour Organization (ILO) over several decades and reached its ultimate refinement in 1973 ILO Convention (No. 138) Concerning Minimum Age for Admission to Employment (ILO C138).[2] This convention attracted very little support from states initially, however, and the issue of child labor was lost for a time.

Recent efforts in child labor standard-setting have seen the ILO take on broad developments in human rights, particularly children's rights. As a result of the 1989 United Nations Convention on the Rights of the Child (CRC)[3] and other international developments such as the United Nations World Summit on Social Development,[4] child labor began to be considered as more a human rights than a labor regulation issue. This had consequences for how international standards have been drafted in recent years. First, not all child labor was seen to be violative of human rights, so international standards began to focus on those aspects of child work that are truly abusive or exploitive, as now expressed in 1999 ILO Convention (No. 182) Concerning the Prohibition and Immediate Elimination of the Worst Forms of Child Labour (ILO C182).[5] Second, in respect of child work deemed morally acceptable, there later developed, albeit only very recently, a concern for labor rights issues that impinge on the well-being of working children. Third, the child labor agenda became part of the wider children's rights agenda so as to include issues of child soldiering and the commercial sexual exploitation of children, both of which have been the subject of recent optional protocols to the CRC.[6]

Several international actors have influenced this merger of child labor and human rights. Some exert influence from within the international system, such as the ILO's International Programme on the Elimination of Child Labour (IPEC) and the special rapporteurs and representatives on children's rights issues. Some exert influence from outside the system, such as nongovernmental organizations (NGOs) and NGO networks. It also has been recognized that children themselves should be participants in the processes that determine and implement their rights.[7]

Paralleling these essentially legal standard-setting approaches to child labor has been, in recent years, an expansion of quasi-legal standard-setting, involving the development of theoretically nonbinding initiatives—for example, corporate codes of conduct and product labels. Often these initiatives derive much of their content from the relevant binding treaties—that is, ILO C138, the CRC, and ILO C182. Also, they perform different functions. The 1998 ILO Declaration of Fundamental Principles and Rights at Work, for example, serves as an informal monitoring tool for states that balk at binding legal rules. Or like memoranda of understanding signed with IPEC,[8] they may be country- or situation-specific guidelines on how to address particular kinds of child labor problems.

In this chapter, I review the history of legal and quasi-legal standard-setting relative to child labor, taking into account the policy approaches to child labor that have shaped these initiatives. Several different approaches can be identified. Two of these, labor regulation and human rights, relate to the substantive content of standards, while two others, prioritization and consensus, relate to the political processes leading to the adoption of those standards.

A *labor regulation approach* to child labor refers to the approach taken by ILO conventions on the subject up to and including ILO C138, treating child labor as an issue to be resolved via the setting of agreed legal rules concerning minimum ages for employment, similar to the regulation of such other aspects of the employment relationship as the health and safety of workers. A *prioritization approach* refers to the development of legal rules that, rather than attempting to abolish all forms of child employment below a given age, focus on those forms that cause children the greatest harm, ILO C182 being a prime example. Closely related is a *consensus approach,* which refers to the articulation of child labor rules in a way that attracts the greatest support, particularly in the international legal community of states. Finally, a *human rights approach* refers to the development of legal and quasi-legal rules that are premised on the human rights of children, particularly as set forth in the CRC. Such rules focus not only on the avoidance of harm to children but, as well, on the regulation of the employment relationship in which working children find themselves and, beyond that, on the right of children to education and to participate in decisions that affect their lives, including those relating to their employment. This holistic view of child labor as only part of a child's life is principally what sets the human rights approach apart from the labor regulation approach.

▨ Legal Approaches to Child Labor

ILO Standards up to ILO C138 (1973)

From the early days of the ILO until the adoption of the CRC in 1989, ILO standard-setting on child labor was informed not by notions of children's rights as a matter of legal entitlement, but rather by notions of child welfare as a matter of labor regulation.[9] In keeping with the ILO's 1944 Declaration of Philadelphia, which proclaimed the "provision for child welfare" to be one of the ILO's priority aims,[10] all but a few ILO conventions and recommendations that implicated working children before 1989 were conceived from this regulatory perspective. These instruments, therefore, do not distinguish between harmful and benign child work, but aim to abolish all child labor.

The vast majority of these regulatory initiatives, it is important to note, were dedicated to the proposition that children below a certain age, although varying over time and depending upon circumstance, should be kept out of the work force altogether and their employment below such age therefore prohibited altogether.[11] The first ILO convention to address the issue—1919 ILO Convention (No. 5) Fixing the Minimum Age for Admission of Children to Industrial Employment (ILO C5)—set the age for admission into employment at fourteen. While this general standard later rose to age fifteen as the average age for leaving full-time education climbed higher, and while it was based primarily, if not exclusively, on the experience of the wealthiest countries, it nonetheless reflected the public outcry against the employment of children in construction, factory, mining, transport, and similar work in the nineteenth century. Ratifying states had only one basic obligation: to ensure that "[c]hildren under the age of fourteen shall not be employed in any public or private industrial undertaking."[12] Only technical schools and, more significantly, the family enterprise (defined as "an undertaking in which only members of the same family are employed") were exempted,[13] an exception that does not appear in some of the later ILO conventions, notably ILO C138.

Reflecting an agricultural tradition of children combining work and education, Article 1 of 1921 ILO Convention (No. 10) Concerning the Age for Admission of Children to Employment in Agriculture (ILO C10) provides that "[c]hildren under the age of fourteen years may not be employed or work in any public or private agricultural undertaking, or any branch thereof, save outside the hours fixed for school attendance [in which case] the employment shall not be such as to prejudice their attendance at school"[14]—a provision sufficiently flexible to make express exceptions for family enterprises unnecessary. In addition, Article 2 of the convention allows ratifying states to arrange the periods and hours of school attendance to permit the employment of children in light agricultural work (first appearance of the "light work" concept) provided the total annual period of school attendance is at least eight months.

Similarly, 1932 ILO Convention (No. 33) Concerning the Age for Admission of Children to Non-Industrial Employment (ILO C33),[15] defining non-industrial employment to mean any employment not covered by any previous convention on minimum age,[16] set a minimum age of fourteen years and exempted technical schools and family enterprises from it.[17] To this fact must be added several innovative qualifications, however. Employment by technical schools and family enterprises was not to be "harmful"—a rare example of harm used as a factor in early ILO instruments.[18] The minimum age of fourteen for employment was to be set higher if it was within school attendance age.[19] A lower minimum age, twelve, was set for light work outside of school hours.[20] And in this last connection, the convention developed the category of permissible light work by setting several conditions designed to protect the children engaged in it.[21] Additionally, introducing yet a third category of minimum age, ILO C33 required the specification of a higher minimum age where the work is dangerous to a child's life, health, or morals;[22] likewise for employment in itinerant occupations such as outdoor trading.[23] Also, because of the complexity of the standards, ILO C33 imposed obligations of adequate supervision and enforcement. For the first time in respect of the employment of children, a convention was supplemented by a recommendation to provide guidance on the types of work that fall within the light work and dangerous work categories.[24]

Thus, as of the adoption of ILO C33 in 1932, ILO standards on child labor were more or less established, and they remained substantially unchanged until ILO C182 in 1999. The textual inflexibility of the minimum age conventions appears to be, in fact, a principal reason why, even after being ratified, they have been marked by a large number of compliance problems.[25] In his 1966 survey of the first thirty years of ILO supervision, A. E. Landy noted that countries often did not avail themselves of specific flexibility clauses in the ILO conventions.[26]

Raising the basic minimum age from fourteen to fifteen is part of the problem. The most frequently cited school-leaving age is fourteen, and twelve and thirteen are not uncommon.[27] Thus, even where the law on school-leaving age or minimum age for employment has been changed, the enforcement of the stipulated age has often been lax, as found, according to Lammy Betten, by the ILO Committee of Experts.[28]

Unrealistic rules on minimum age can have the effect of driving child work underground, where employers conceal the use of the underaged and the conditions under which they work.[29] Moreover, precisely because minimum age conventions focus on preventing the employment of underage workers, they naturally do not encourage states to adopt protective legislation (minimum wage, health, and safety) on behalf of such workers, as adopting protective rules for working children acknowledges their existence.

ILO C138

ILO C138, adopted in 1973, is the ultimate refinement of the labor regulation approach. Revising the earlier conventions on minimum age in particular sectors, it is a general convention that brought together in one place the rules from the previous sector-specific treaties and applies to all types of work. It has been argued, however, that the convention was poorly drafted, failing to take into account the actual practice of child employment in developed and developing countries,[30] which perhaps explains a very low number of ratifications until after the initiation of the ILO's 1998 Declaration on Fundamental Principles and Rights at Work[31] and accompanying ratification campaign.

Many of the problems with ILO C138 were simply carried over from the earlier minimum age conventions. The scope of the light work exception was drawn from ILO C33, adopted in 1932, and its successors, and as a consequence ILO C138 is based on a near-absolute prohibition on the employment of school-age children. Article 1 requires the states parties to make "the abolition of child labour" a national policy, with the general minimum age for employment to be not less than the school-leaving age but at least fifteen (fourteen in developing countries).[32] The minimum age for light work that is not likely to be harmful to a child's health or education is thirteen (twelve in developing countries).[33] And the minimum age for hazardous work is eighteen (sixteen if adequate protective measures have been guaranteed).[34]

These absolute rules are moderated somewhat by Articles 4 and 5 of the convention. Article 4 allows some sectors to be excluded; requires employer and worker organizations to be consulted; and makes no exception for any work that might be hazardous to the health, safety, or morals of children. Article 5 allows developing countries to restrict the convention's application to a small number of industries (mostly those where physical hazards to children are present) and likewise requires employer and worker organizations to be consulted. The ILO has argued that it is lack of awareness of the potential of Articles 4 and 5 that is partly to blame for deterred ratifications.[35] This is to be questioned, however, at least insofar as Article 5 is concerned. Article 5 lists commercial agriculture as one of the sectors to which ILO C138 must apply, yet commercial agriculture is the industry in which most children work and the one most frequently exempted from national minimum age legislation.[36]

There are two major problems for monitoring compliance with ILO C138. One is the tendency of states parties to disregard their obligation to notify the ILO of their use of exemptions (which must be set out in national law) under Articles 4, 5, and 8 (artistic performances).[37] Without this notification, the task of the ILO in monitoring compliance is made more difficult. The second problem is one of monitoring and enforcement within states, which means that failures to observe the law never come to light.[38] Labor inspection is often inadequate and underresourced, leading to impunity for the employers of child workers. Enforcement mechanisms may be complex and time-consuming, thus deterring families and children's advocates from using them.

In brief, the blanket approach of ILO C138 is not in keeping with the approach taken by states in their domestic laws, where a minimum age for employment may apply only to the industrial sector or may vary according to occupation.[39] It also falls short of the realities of children at work. Its inflexibility fails to distinguish between exploitive and nonexploitive work, such as genuine apprenticeships. The ILO Committee of Experts rejected as incompatible with ILO C138 the legality of apprenticeships for children under fourteen in Brazil and Singapore.[40] Similarly, Italy's laws allowing children to combine school and agricultural work were considered contrary to ILO C138.[41]

The Human Rights Shift

From the standpoint of international law at least, the issue of child labor went silent between ILO C138 of 1973 and the early 1990s. This is demonstrated by the low level of ratifications of ILO C138. Arguably, by this stage, a labor regulation approach to child labor issues had run its course in the sense that existing standards fully reflected that approach. Nonetheless, the ILO and some NGOs continue to advocate the labor regulation approach of seeking to abolish all child labor.

The first signal came with the adoption of the 1989 CRC. In a major shift regarding children's rights, it separates children's rights from the family. Earlier human rights provisions, such as Article 24 of the 1966 International Covenant on Civil and Political Rights (ICCPR), either contextualized the child within the family or provided for rights of families only, such as in Article 8 of the European Convention on Human Rights.

The idea of children themselves having rights was, for some, controversial. Some commentators continue to argue that the status of children is not the same as for adults and that talking about the human rights of children is therefore erroneous, even dangerous for children.[42] However, the idea of children's rights, particularly the right of children to choose or to participate in choices made on their behalf, is consistent with recent research demonstrating the diversity of children's lives, especially as revealed in the inapplicability of Northern ideas of childhood dependency to the lives of many working children in the Global South.[43]

Children's rights may be understood to rest on two protective principles that often are in tension with one another: the *child welfare principle,* involving the right of children to the goods or capabilities that are necessary for their well-being; and the *child agency principle,* involving the right of children autonomously to choose their own goods or capabilities. It is the failure of the critics of children's rights to recognize this duality and tension that is partially responsible for the controversy.[44] The 1989 CRC, however, does recognize this duality through the inclusion of both principles in its text. This suggests that the CRC does not recognize a universal solution to the tension between agency and welfare.

Article 3 of the CRC, calling upon states to take the best interests of the child into primary consideration and to "ensure the child such protection and care as is necessary for his or her well-being," expresses the child welfare principle. CRC Article 12, giving children the right to express their views on matters affecting them and, more significantly, obligating states to take those views into account "in accordance with the age and maturity of the child," expresses the child agency principle. The CRC thus embraces a concept of childhood that sees it as a developmental phase during which children are to be protected while simultaneously respecting their developing capabilities.

Especially noteworthy, however, is CRC Article 32. While recommending the first new minimum age provision since 1973 ILO C138 (setting the age for defining a child as "every human being below the age of eighteen"),[45] it indicates the emergence of a new human rights approach to working children in international law. Following Article 10(3) of the 1966 International Covenant on Economic, Social, and Cultural Rights (ICESCR), CRC Article 32(1) also provides that children have the right to be protected from economic exploitation and harmful work. Two important points are to be made here. First, though it draws primarily if not exclusively on the child welfare principle rather than the child agency principle, the CRC uses, for the first time since the ICESCR, the language of rights to define the prohibition on child labor. Second, it implicitly distinguishes between benign (permissible) and harmful (impermissible) child work. This point was made explicit by IPEC a few years later, in distinguishing between "child work" (benign and permissible) and "child labor" (harmful and impermissible). It is this distinction or approach that went on to inform the content of ILO C182.

The CRC has been a source of profound inspiration for many children's rights advocates worldwide and on a number of complex issues, including abusive and exploitive child work. As noted by William Myers, "much of the most effective advocacy for the CRC (1989) is by non-governmental organizations and mobilized civil society."[46] Working children themselves have been mobilized in local and national organizations specific to them,[47] which of course reflects the more active model of childhood that informs the CRC. And this undebatable fact is not changed by the puzzling fact that CRC Article 1 defines childhood to mean all persons under age eighteen, an unusual determination considering that most minimum age provisions have been based on school-leaving ages, not admission-to-adulthood ages, and thus is subject to criticism for being overly bureaucratic and too tied to contemporary Western conceptions of childhood.

The ILO was (and remains) deeply influenced by these changes to the international legal-political environment,[48] arguably best reflected in its establishment of IPEC, a technical assistance program focused on countries with significant child labor problems that is the ILO's principal means of addressing child labor.[49] Begun in 1992, it quickly integrated advocacy of more direct, pragmatic methods of combating child labor into its work by actively campaigning for, along with children's advocates outside the ILO, a new child labor convention to supplement the essentially moribund ILO C138.[50] IPEC accepted that it was impossible, or at least unrealistic, to try to ban all instances of work by children.[51] Instead, it argued for focusing on those types of work that are abusive or harmful. The result: ILO C182 Concerning the Prohibition and Immediate Elimination of the Worst Forms of Child Labour, adopted in 1999, now the most rapidly and widely ratified convention in ILO history. The priorities identified by IPEC from its 1996 report onward formed the basis for identifying the "worst forms" of child labor, now standardized in ILO C182's Article 3: (a) "all forms of slavery or practices similar to slavery, such as the sale and trafficking of children, debt bondage, and serfdom and forced or compulsory labor, including forced or compulsory recruitment of children for use in armed conflict"; (b) "the use, procuring, or offering of a child for prostitution, for the production of pornography or for pornographic performances"; (c) "the use, procuring, or offering of a child for illicit activities, in particular for the production and trafficking of drugs as defined in the relevant international treaties"; and (d) "work which, by its nature or the circumstances in which it is carried out, is likely to harm the health, safety or morals of children." Referencing the CRC in its preamble, ILO C182, it may be argued, causes violations of these prohibitions to be violations of children's rights.

Integrating the Child Labor Agenda and the Child Rights Agenda

The ILO has an equivocal relationship with human rights. Even though it contributes materially to the sessions of human rights monitoring bodies such as the Committee on Economic, Social, and Cultural Rights (which monitors the 1966 ICESCR) and to the Committee on the Rights of the Child (which monitors the 1989 CRC), it does not ordinarily use the language of rights in its conventions. ILO C182, however, might well be described as a human rights treaty masquerading as a labor regulation treaty. Not only does its preamble reference the CRC, but its contents reflect unequivocally important developments in children's rights elsewhere in international law and policy. Below, I examine how in this ambiguous setting the integration of child labor and child rights has taken place and to what extent it has succeeded.

The process. The crucial players in the drafting and adoption of ILO C182 were IPEC, NGOs, certain actors within the United Nations, and several ILO member states. Not surprisingly, therefore, the "worst forms" priorities adopted in ILO C182 reflect their respective though sometimes overlapping agendas. They reflect also, however, an unprecedented engagement with the worldwide human rights movement and particularly that part that focuses on children's rights. Implicitly demonstrating this link is the fact that two of ILO C182's priority areas—the sexual exploitation of children and the use of children in armed conflict—are also the subject of optional protocols to the CRC,[52] each of whose drafting processes were influenced in part by ILO C182[53] and adopted only a year after its adoption. When in 1998 the International Labour Conference began discussing what became ILO C182, Canada and Zimbabwe, responding to questionnaires discussing then-proposed ILO C182, raised the issue of child soldiering,[54] which at the time was the subject of discussions at the UN relative to the CRC's optional protocol on the same subject.[55] The issue was controversial, but it was pursued with sufficient vigor as an example of forced labor (a human rights violation) to be included finally in Article 3(a) of ILO C182. This, however, was the only instance of a major change to the original draft of the convention. In other respects, the ILO was resistant to pressures for substantive amendment.[56]

The role of NGOs in the drafting of international treaties is the subject of much academic interest and, in the case of labor conventions at least, somewhat controversial.[57] Some ILO social partner organizations see NGO involvement as a threat to the ILO's traditional tripartitism in which worker and employer groups are given a privileged role in the implementation of ILO conventions such as ILO C138 and ILO C182 and on matters left open by them. They seem to fear that, if other NGOs are given greater status, they will be downgraded to the status of "ordinary" NGO. This fear, however, overlooks the important role that national and international NGOs have played in IPEC and unnecessarily demeans the important example that the ILO's tripartitism itself serves for the potential of integrating nonstate actors into reformist international legal processes. Article 6 of ILO C182, requiring states, in respect of time-bound programs targeting the worst forms of child labor, to consult workers and employers but only to consider the views of "other concerned groups as appropriate," thus seems unduly restrictive.[58]

In fact, NGOs and NGO coalitions have been much more active in the development of child labor–related standards outside the ILO. Illustrative are the Campaign to End Child Prostitution in Asian Tourism (ECPAT)[59] and the Coalition to Stop the Use of Child Soldiers (CSC),[60] groups that have actively campaigned for strong standards in the CRC's two optional protocols adopted in 2000. Their success specifically in standard-setting has been mixed, however.

The optional protocol on the sale of children, child prostitution, and child pornography arguably adds little to the existing range of standards in the area, although it does flesh out the obligations set out in the CRC. Therefore, ECPAT has concentrated its efforts on monitoring state compliance with the

Stockholm Declaration and Agenda for Action adopted at the First World Congress Against the Commercial Sexual Exploitation of Children in 1996.[61] The idea that the Agenda for Action can give content to CRC Articles 34 and 35 is frequently mentioned, however,[62] and one area of great ECPAT concern has been, consistent with CRC Article 12, the participation of children in decisionmaking in this realm.[63]

The CSC was formed to fulfill a particular, limited standard-setting agenda in the drafting of the CRC optional protocol on the involvement of children in armed conflict—that is, to guarantee a "straight-eighteen" approach to the recruitment of children into armed forces. The rule would require that all forms of recruitment into armed forces and participation in hostilities (including forced and voluntary recruitment, state and nonstate armed forces, and direct or indirect participation) be restricted entirely to those aged eighteen or older. The optional protocol does not take a "straight-eighteen" approach, but it does go quite far in that direction.[64] Although states may prescribe ages sixteen to eighteen for voluntary recruitment, the minimum age for participation in hostilities, forced recruitment by states, and all recruitment by nonstate forces must be at least eighteen.[65] ILO C182 is the first treaty to set age eighteen as a minimum age for recruitment into armed forces, and while this minimum age is only for forced or compulsory recruitment, this initial success was used by the CSC and others as part the campaign to strengthen the optional protocol.

Further demonstrating the integration of the child labor agenda and the child rights agenda has been the important role and impact of the special rapporteurs and representatives of the United Nations Commission on Human Rights relative to child labor issues (along with the Office of the UN High Commissioner for Human Rights and, in the case of child soldiering, the Secretary-General of the United Nations). Both the special rapporteur of the Commission on Human Rights on the Sale of Children, Child Prostitution, and Child Pornography and the special representative of the Secretary-General for Children and Armed Conflict regularly produce annual reports on these subjects and typically with arguments for strong new standards, taking advantage of their privileged access to the working groups of the Commission on Human Rights that draft the standards. Unfortunately, the special rapporteur's report on the sale of children, child prostitution, and child pornography[66] was not successful in persuading states to adopt a broad definition of the sale of children so as to cover all instances of trafficking, whether for the purpose of sexual exploitation or otherwise. The optional protocol ended up prohibiting the sale of children for use in prostitution or pornography only.

The special representative on children in armed conflict, along with the Secretary-General, argued consistently for the "straight-eighteen" position.[67] Probably the special representative's documentation of the harms faced by child soldiers helped to push through the comparatively strong standards that were adopted in the final version of the Optional Protocol to the Convention on the Rights of the Child on the Involvement of Children in Armed Conflict. Although several states, including the United Kingdom and the United States, argued for a lower age basis for the optional protocol, the basic minimum age for recruitment and participation ended up at eighteen years, and when ratifying the optional protocol, states must declare what age they set for voluntary recruitment, the only condition being that it must be higher than fifteen, as required by CRC Article 38.

The integration of the child labor agenda and the child rights agenda is yet further seen, finally, in the growth of groups directly representing and including children—a natural outgrowth of the child agency principle that lies at the heart of the CRC, particularly in Article 12. The Global March Against Child Labour, an initiative involving child workers from throughout the world, was received by the ILO secretary-general and included at the International Labour Conference of 1998.[68] However, Global March was not admitted to speak at the conference deliberations on the draft of ILO C182. The Second World Congress Against Commercial Sexual Exploitation of Children, held in Yokohama in December 2001, did have a strand of child participation, including a final document produced by the child delegates.[69] But by and large, children themselves, particularly working children, have so far had a very minor role in official standard-setting on child labor. While the preamble to ILO C182 references the CRC (and therefore its Article 12), and while its accompanying Recommendation No. 190 requires states to take into consideration the views of "the children directly affected by the worst forms of child labor [and] their families,"[70] ILO C182 itself contains no obligation to listen to children affected by it. Nor is there any mention in either of the optional protocols of an obligation to consult children in implementing the standards they contain.

The result. The result of all these efforts at integrating the child labor agenda with the child rights agenda, successful and less so, is a prioritization approach to child labor, involving the drawing of distinctions among "child work" (generally benign), "child labor" (harmful), and "worst forms of child labor" (abusive, inherently rights violating).[71] Child labor, according to this analysis, includes some element of harm or exploitation that goes beyond mere employment. Insofar as the prioritization approach emphasizes harm as the focus of child labor standards, it is a beneficial move. However, it arguably defines harm too narrowly.

In part this result is a consequence of widespread dissatisfaction with ILO C138, which prevents distinguishing between benign and abusive forms of child labor. Its prohibition is overly broad, covering child labor on the basis of age rather than of harm to children, and thus it became somewhat discredited.[72] For this reason (though also because of the influence of the actors noted in the above subsection, IPEC especially), as well as the gravity of the harms prohibited, ILO C182 takes the prioritization approach to child labor.

The prioritization approach to child labor taken by ILO C182 results from a consensus sought, and to some extent imposed, by the ILO on the priority areas for an absolute prohibition on child labor, with states preferring to adopt the necessary means to eliminate the condemned practices rather than argue over norms that are too inflexible or that do not take account of the differing socioeconomic conditions of states. As a consequence, except for the catch-all clause in Article 3(d), the types of prohibited child labor involve practices that are inherently human rights violations and that, in some cases, would be such even if the victims were adults. On final analysis, in other words, the prioritization approach adopted in ILO C182 is for the most part a human rights approach to child labor in international law. It is not the only conceivable conclusion to be reached, but it is fully consistent with a human rights understanding of the child labor problem.

Not surprisingly, the prioritization approach has its critics, at least some of whom appear skeptical of the shift from a labor regulation approach to a human rights approach to child labor. The types of child labor addressed in ILO C182 are not the product of an analysis of what types of work interfere with a child's development. They were driven, rather, by the gravity of the harms involved and the need for political consensus.[73] This need for political consensus may have the effect of oversimplifying norms, meaning that such norms run the risk of again reflecting only a Western view, ignoring, for example, that some slavery-like practices may be deeply culturally embedded.

It is yet too early to tell whether this pressure for consensus has resulted in anything more than a warm glow of textual achievement. Nevertheless, one may legitimately ask whether consensus is worth the cost. For example, with neither agriculture nor domestic service—two important sectors with substantial child labor—explicitly covered in ILO C182, is it reasonable to conclude that formal legal standards are ignoring the informal sector and agriculture because of family sensitivities, as in early ILO conventions? Are the formal legal standards of ILO C182 ignoring sectors such as domestic service simply because they may be difficult to monitor? Or can it be assumed that catchall Article 3(d) will be interpreted liberally to extend to these realms where the best research tells us that the work that children do commonly harms their "health, safety, or morals"? Only time will tell. However, it does not bode well that, during the drafting of ILO C182, there was little political support within the International Labour Conference for a link between child labor and education[74] even though IPEC had asserted that child labor, in the sense of a violation of human rights, interferes with a child's development.

The debates surrounding the drafting of ILO C182 resembled the debates going on at the same time at the United Nations surrounding the drafting of the two optional protocols to the CRC. Also, they implicated the 1998 Rome

Statute of the International Criminal Tribunal[75] (child soldiering, sexual exploitation of children) and both the 2000 United Nations Protocol to Prevent, Suppress, and Punish Trafficking in Persons, Especially Women and Children[76] and the 2000 United Nations Protocol Against the Smuggling of Migrants by Land, Sea, and Air[77] (forced labor, trafficking for sexual exploitation), each supplementing the 2000 United Nations Convention Against Transnational Organized Crime.[78] In these formal legal ways, through the actions of numerous organizations—governmental, intergovernmental, and nongovernmental—the child labor agenda has been integrated into the children's rights agenda of the past decade. In these formal legal ways, the shift from a labor regulation approach to a human rights approach to child labor may be noted.

Concededly, the shift is relatively particularistic and therefore limited. Concededly, too, the emerging human rights approach, at least as so far manifested in formal legal mechanisms and procedures, risks losing some of the advantages of the labor regulation approach, which, before ILO C138 (1973) at least, was capable of focusing on sectors such as agriculture and domestic service where it is known that harmful child labor occurs in abundance. Still, a human rights approach to child labor, broadly conceived to honor all the rights to which children are entitled under international law, can identify clearly those who need the law's protection, fill in the sectoral gaps between the various formal legal prohibitions so far developed, distinguish between work that is harmful and work that is not, and otherwise enhance the lives of working children everywhere. Along the way, however, it is important to remember that, when approached from a perspective that seeks to integrate child labor standards with the wider child rights agenda established since the 1989 CRC, international child labor standard-setting will necessarily be informed by both child welfare and child agency principles. And as these principles are not infrequently in competition with one another, they will necessarily require a balancing between them. Certainly the child welfare principle predominates in respect of the worst forms of child labor inasmuch as standard-setting choice is taken away from children regardless of age or maturity in this context. Probably this is defensible in most cases. But it must be acknowledged—especially when invoking and applying 1999 ILO C182 Article 3(d)—that the effect of such bans is to reduce child agency and thus to risk damaging capabilities upon which, ultimately, the elimination of child labor depends.

Afterword

The prioritization approach of ILO C182 focuses on some of the harmful forms of child work. Even where child work is not harmful in itself, child workers, like all workers, require regulatory systems to protect them from abuse.

CRC Article 32(2) calls upon states to regulate the hours and conditions of work of young workers. However, this aspect of Article 32 has received comparatively little attention and analysis. ILO C138 attempts to regulate working conditions, but only indirectly through the definition of "light work" and the conditions attached to allowing older children to engage in hazardous work.

An alternative approach is found in the distinction made by IPEC between child work (benign) and child labor (harmful). If we accept this distinction, rather than the approach of setting a blanket minimum age for employment, we are led to protect children in work. If there is scope for permissible child work, then, on at least moral grounds, protection is necessary. As for all workers, the terms and conditions of work for child workers need to be regulated for their benefit. Otherwise, children will be exploited not in terms of the work they do, but in their conditions of work.

European measures are the most detailed in this respect. Community Directive 94/33 on Young Workers,[79] although it draws to some extent on ILO C138, contains provisions on the protection of young workers as well as banning children from harmful work. The European Social Charter of 1961 and the Revised European Social Charter of 1996, adopted by the Council of Europe, contain extensive provisions on the protection of children in work.[80]

It often is argued that the attraction of child workers for employers is that they are easier than adults to abuse. A network of rights within the employment relationship, including for children who are not engaged in child labor in the negative sense, is necessary to protect them from other forms of abuse and exploitation and consequent violation of their human rights. Therefore, regardless of whether one approaches child labor from the standpoint of labor regulation or human rights, neither is complete if it does not address the rights of working children.

▪ Quasi-Legal Approaches to Child Labor

Just as formal legal initiatives have moved increasingly to regulate child labor from a human rights perspective, so also have quasi-legal initiatives (i.e., norms, institutions, and procedures that, while lacking the imprimatur of formal legal process, are nonetheless capable of ordering social behavior, sometimes even more effectively than the formal law itself). And over the past decade they have grown in number and sophistication as well. Some are located in intergovernmental organizations—particularly the ILO—generally in the form of "soft law" (i.e., theoretically nonbinding) standards or as part of technical assistance programs. Others are purely private, resulting largely from NGO pressure on multinational corporations to respect human rights doctrines, principles, and rules.

Among the advantages of these informal, quasi-legal initiatives is that they bring nonstate actors more responsibly into the standard-setting and standard-applying process than do formal measures of national and international law. Additionally, quasi-legal initiatives are able to integrate standard-setting with flexible approaches to implementation.

The foundation of many of these quasi-legal initiatives on child labor is the ILO's 1998 Declaration on Fundamental Principles and Rights at Work.[81] This declaration, though theoretically nonbinding, recasts certain ILO conventions as human rights measures rather than as labor regulation measures. The declaration is itself somewhat ambiguous, using the terms "principles" and "rights" disjunctively. However, the use of "rights" makes explicit what is implicit in the conventions: that the conventions are concerned with human rights. ILO conventions pertinent to child labor are not drafted to invoke the phrase "every child has the right." Not even the CRC does that at every turn. But the substance of their provisions transmits essentially the same human rights messages we find in the CRC. The significance of the declaration lies in its ability to make the child labor–human rights link for ILO member states and to facilitate a common standard of minimum respect for labor-related human rights outside the ILO generally. A somewhat fuller treatment of the declaration, especially as it relates to the work of IPEC, is thus warranted.

The ILO Declaration on Fundamental Principles and Rights at Work

The declaration is a new type of legal instrument within the ILO. Previously the legal standard-setting forms used by the ILO had been conventions (theoretically binding treaties), recommendations (theoretically nonbinding supplementary guides to the conventions), and the ILO constitution itself. Like a recommendation, the 1998 declaration is in theory a nonbinding measure. But it serves a different function. The ILO's intention in adopting the declaration was to empower itself to monitor the compliance of ILO member states with fundamental principles—or "core" labor standards—contained in existing conventions *whether or not ratified by the member states.* And to this end, though conceived as a promotional instrument, the declaration proclaims four principles—freedom of association, freedom from forced labor, nonuse of child labor, and nondiscrimination in employment—derived in part from eight ILO conventions deemed "fundamental,"[82] including 1973 ILO C138 and 1999 ILO C182 (on child labor).[83] It is worth noting that the "child labor" (i.e., harmful child work) principle includes both the elimination of the worst forms of child labor and the broader minimum age approach.[84]

As already noted, the declaration's title indicates that the four core areas of key concern involve not only principles, but also rights. This is the first time that an ILO measure has used the language of rights in the context of child labor per se. While the idea of rights did not filter into ILO C182's body text, both the declaration and the CRC are referenced in ILO C182's preamble. The declaration may be considered evidence of a move toward a human rights approach to child labor, which accepts the idea of child agency as well as child welfare as a foundation.

The four principles that form the basis of the declaration derive not only from ILO conventions but from the 1995 Program of Action of the Copenhagen World Summit on Social Development as well.[85] Child labor was at the time the least widely accepted of the four principles inasmuch as ILO C138 then had the lowest number of ratifications of all the conventions referenced in the declaration and ILO C182 had yet to be concluded. However, its position is now much more secure; like all the "fundamental" ILO conventions, ILO C138 and ILO C182 now boast well over 100 ratifications each.[86]

For the ILO, the main point of the declaration was to encourage greater acceptance of, and compliance with, the rights and principles set out in the "fundamental" conventions. The declaration, therefore, sets out a follow-up program of promoting the rights proclaimed in it rather than enforcing them.[87] The program includes two elements of reporting: an annual follow-up and a global report.

It is not my task to discuss implementation matters in detail in this chapter, as this theme is taken up by others elsewhere in this volume. However, to ensure true understanding of how a quasi-legal standard-setting instrument can have genuine force and effect, the example of the enforcement of the 1998 declaration is instructive. It is important to bear in mind, of course, that it is an instrument of an officially recognized intergovernmental organization, membership in which requires good faith cooperation lest the organization's purposes and the formal legal rules it establishes to achieve them are vitiated.

Annual follow-up reports. In November 1998 the ILO's Governing Body decided that the first requests to states would be sent following the Governing Body meeting in March 1999 with a view to their first annual review taking place at the March 2000 Governing Body meeting.[88] The annual review is a simplified procedure, covering all four rights confirmed in the declaration though requiring each state to report only on ILO conventions it has not ratified. The focus of the reports is on changes in law and practice within the state involved measured against reference data provided in the first reports (states being required to submit information only on changes in subsequent years).

States are required to indicate whether their laws provide for a minimum age for admission to employment, whether they allow for any exemptions, and whether there is a higher minimum age for hazardous work. In addition, they are expected to provide information on indicators or statistics on the factual situation regarding child labor. This is especially important because, in almost all countries, there is some law on child labor, but in many countries, including countries in the Global North (the United Kingdom, for example), there is inadequate enforcement. Finally, states must provide information on measures to eliminate child labor, such as removal and rehabilitation programs and preventative and protective measures. In this regard, states are asked what conditions are necessary to achieve the effective abolition of child labor within their jurisdictions.

The annual follow-up reports are reviewed by the ILO Governing Body after a preliminary review by a group of experts appointed by the ILO.

Global reports. The global reports are the responsibility of the ILO director-general, who must base them on official information, particularly information from the annual reports and reports on ratified fundamental conventions of the member states, or information gathered and assessed in accordance with established procedures (in principle, this does not include information from NGOs). The global report is thus intended to provide an overview of the situation in all ILO member states.

The first global report on child labor, *A Future Without Child Labour* (2002),[89] drew heavily from the ILO's work within IPEC and from ILO's emphasis on the worst forms of child labor as defined by ILO C182. Despite the declaration's focus on improving state compliance with core labor rights to achieve universal or near-universal ratification, the 2002 global report places more emphasis on the social and economic obstacles to the elimination of harmful child employment than it did on legal compliance, referring more to IPEC than to formal processes for monitoring state compliance with ILO conventions. As such, the 2002 global report is proof that the 1998 declaration plays essentially a promotional role within the ILO system and thus does not alter the formal legal obligations of the member states within it. All the same, consistent with ILO intention, increased ratification of the core conventions to which it refers has been one important outcome of its follow-up process. From this perspective, the declaration and its follow-up program may be said to be so far reasonably successful.

IPEC Memoranda of Understanding and Time-Bound Programs

Clearly, the ILO's work on child labor cannot be neatly separated into the drafting of ILO C182 and Recommendation No. 190, the activities associated with the 1998 declaration, and IPEC. Each has informed the others. To some extent, however, IPEC is the principal locus of the ILO's efforts to implement the child labor prohibition that is listed among the core labor standards articulated in the declaration. A proper understanding of IPEC's Memoranda of Understanding (MOUs)—its primary means of implementing its child labor work—is thus in order.

IPEC was the first administration within the ILO to effect a prioritization approach to child labor, moving toward a concentration on the worst forms of child labor such as are proscribed in ILO C182. Early in its work, IPEC rarely referred to what was the main convention on child labor at the time—that is,

ILO C138 (1973)—although this is not surprising given the low level of ratification at that stage. Now, however, IPEC actively links to all the ILO standards relevant to its work.

In its 2002–2003 implementation report,[90] IPEC defines the scope of the child labor problem with reference to both ILO C138 and ILO C182, calling for its elimination as defined by these two conventions. This does not mean, however, the elimination of every form of work by children under eighteen years of age. The ILO's "Decent Work Agenda," with which IPEC coordinates and to which the report refers, alone makes this clear.[91]

IPEC's main regulatory tools are MOUs signed with governments that wish to focus on the child labor problem, although usually a particular aspect of it—perhaps a regulatory area such as labor inspection, perhaps a particular geographic region or industry or both. IPEC describes its country program method of work under these MOUs as a "multisectoral strategy" embracing many elements.[92]

Following the signing of a memorandum of understanding with a government, IPEC support is based on a phased, multisectoral strategy with the following elements:

1. Encourage ILO constituents and other partners to begin dialogue and create alliances.
2. Determine the nature and extent of the child labour problem.
3. Assist in devising national policies to counter it.
4. Set up mechanisms to provide in-country ownership and operation of a national program of action.
5. Create awareness in the community and the workplace.
6. Promote development and application of protective legislation.
7. Support direct action aimed at preventing child labor or withdrawing children from work.
8. Replicate successful projects.
9. Integrate child labor issues systematically into social and economic development policies, programs, and budgets.
10. Undertake comprehensive and integrated projects.

Successful MOUs commonly involve several of these elements simultaneously, including numerous activities to mobilize government and social actors against abusive and exploitive child labor.

Successful MOUs also have resulted in some governments agreeing to "time-bound programs" (TBPs) for the elimination of the worst forms of child labor[93] expressly in compliance with ILO C182.[94] In fact, each of the first three TBPs—in El Salvador, Nepal, and Tanzania—had previously been a party to MOUs with IPEC.[95] By the end of 2003, fourteen countries had negotiated

MOUs with IPEC and secured funding to develop a TBP.[96] TBPs, planned and executed within an MOU framework, are comprehensive and integrated programs covering legal measures and enforcement, the economic environment facing families with working children, education issues, and social policy, including assistance and rehabilitation of children working in the worst forms of child labor.[97] TBPs are intended to involve a wide range of stakeholders, public and private, and to have built-in flexibility.[98] As a result, they have advantages over formal legal initiatives, which tend to lack detail or, where they are detailed, possibly lack flexibility. Also, it is often difficult to ensure accountability of nonstate actors in the formal international law context. TBPs must have monitoring and evaluation built into their program design.[99]

Through its country-specific MOU initiatives and TBPs, IPEC enables a range of actors in the participating country to be mobilized: public authorities, UN specialized agencies, social partner organizations, and international and national NGOs. As a technical assistance program, it can address the causes of child labor. Which is not to say that legal measures are unimportant. Indeed, during 2004–2005, one part of IPEC's support to countries will focus on "formulation, promotion, enforcement, and monitoring of relevant national legal frameworks."[100] In particular, IPEC, as an indicator of progress, has set as a target that at least forty ILO member states "will have drawn on ILO support" to make "significant progress" in applying ILO C138 and ILO C182 "as reflected in the implementation of at least two interventions associated with Time-Bound Programmes."[101] With full ratification of ILO C182 well on its way to being achieved, IPEC will focus on ratification of ILO C138, with a target of getting at least twenty additional member states to ratify it during 2004–2005.[102] It is not clear, however, why such an emphasis is placed on ILO C138, given its flaws.

Like all technical assistance programs, IPEC requires long-term monitoring to determine its true impact. However, there have been limited independent evaluations of its effectiveness, primarily by donor countries,[103] and generally these reviews have been positive, though they have recommended greater emphasis on capacity-building and phasing-out strategies. The ILO itself conducted a major review of IPEC in 1999 and pointed out the need to integrate child labor concerns into mainstream policymaking and implementation to ensure that the changes accomplished by IPEC projects are sustainable over the long term (a potential problem identified in the independent evaluations as well).[104] There are reasons to expect, however, that with local institutions having been established to monitor progress, sustainability will be achieved in at least some participating countries.[105] And on the level of standard-setting, IPEC seems to have contributed to raising the profile of ILO child labor conventions, particularly ILO C182, where the worst forms of child labor are a large part of IPEC's work.

The Cocoa Protocol of September 21, 2001

International conventions (i.e., treaties) are agreements between states (and sometimes between states and international organizations) deemed binding under international law. However, it is often the case that states cannot deliver on the results promised in them without the cooperation of nonstate actors, including business enterprises and worker organizations. In theory, they can regulate activity only within their own borders. Thus, within the existing state system, there is invariably the potential for a regulatory gap such that international standards, including child labor standards, may have little or no impact on the actors for whom they are intended. The so-called Cocoa Protocol of September 21, 2001, between the Chocolate Manufacturers Association and the World Cocoa Foundation relative to the growing and processing of cocoa beans, an industry much infused with child labor, illustrates how that regulatory gap can be effectively closed.[106] Referencing the legal standards of ILO C182, it establishes a quasi-legal regime among relevant actors concerned to eliminate abusive child labor in the cocoa industry.[107]

The agreement was initiated by US senator Tom Harkin (D–Iowa) and member of the US House of Representatives Elliot Engel (D–N.Y.) following a wave of news reports, beginning in late 2000, on the presence of child workers on cocoa farms in West Africa working in slaverylike conditions.[108] The subsequent pressure on the Western chocolate manufacturers who rely on West African cocoa resulted in their willingness to address the issue. The Cocoa Protocol, also known as the Harkin-Engel Protocol, was signed by the Chocolate Manufacturers Association and the World Cocoa Foundation and witnessed by a wide range of interests, including, in addition to Harkin and Engel, the Côte d'Ivoire ambassador to the United States and representatives of the ILO and nongovernmental organizations, among them the International Union of Food, Agricultural, Hotel, Restaurant, Catering, Tobacco, and Allied Workers' Associations; the US-based National Consumers League; the Child Labor Coalition; and Free the Slaves. In addition, eight chief executives of major chocolate brands and cocoa processors expressed their personal support for the protocol, and the International Cocoa Organization and two European trade associations endorsed it.[109]

The protocol, which was followed on November 30, 2001, by a "common statement" of the parties and governmental and nongovernmental representatives creating a "broad consultative group" to work collaboratively with the ILO to implement the protocol,[110] makes compliance with ILO C182 the first of its guiding principles and calls for "(a) a survey of the affected areas; (b) an advisory council to oversee the survey; (c) a consultative group comprising industry, non-governmental organizations, government agencies, and labor groups; (d) a pilot program; (e) a monitoring group; (f) an international foundation; and (g) public certification that cocoa used in chocolate or related products has been grown and processed without forced child labor."[111] The guiding principles acknowledge "the ILO's unique expertise" and accept that the ILO must have an active role in all aspects of addressing the problem of child labor in cocoa plantations. The goal is to develop and implement by July 1, 2005, "credible, mutually-acceptable, voluntary, industry-wide standards of public certification, consistent with (United States) federal law, that cocoa beans and their derivative products have been grown and/or processed without any of the worst forms of child labor."[112]

The international foundation envisioned in the protocol led to the establishment, in July 2002, of a Geneva-based foundation called the International Cocoa Initiative—Working Toward Responsible Labour Standards for Cocoa Growing.[113] The foundation's aims are to provide financial and operational support to field projects, to serve as a clearinghouse for best practices, to conduct a joint research program, and to develop a means of monitoring and public reporting. As of mid-2003,[114] the follow-up to the protocol included pilot programs in cocoa-growing countries, efforts to help cocoa farmers to increase their incomes (and thereby be less dependent on abusive child labor), and moves toward a credible certification program to ensure that cocoa is grown responsibly. This certification will be limited to guaranteeing the nonuse of the worst forms of child labor.

Social Labeling and Corporate Codes of Conduct

Increasingly within the framework of international standards for human rights protection in the employment context—the 1998 ILO Declaration on Fundamental Principles and Rights at Work, for example—social labeling and corporate codes of conduct have grown remarkably and become more and more sophisticated both in their definition of relevant labor standards (including nonuse of the worst forms of child labor) and in their implementation and monitoring methods. I focus here on child labor standard-setting, although some discussion about these schemes in the round is necessary.

The interest in social labeling and codes of conduct that has conspicuously marked international trade in recent years arises from a growing recognition that private business enterprises as well as states can be violators of human rights and that multinational corporations in particular can be very difficult to regulate through formal legal processes in this and other respects. Consumer pressure for "corporate responsibility," including the voluntary adoption of policies attuned to human rights, thus has grown, affecting business concern about public image and reputation. The September 2001 Cocoa Protocol, discussed in the preceding subsection, is illustrative. At the same time, there is ever present a fear that voluntary schemes of claimed social responsibility may be no more than exercises in public relations if monitoring is not intense.[115] Also disconcerting to many is that such initiatives, which tend to target export-oriented industries, may have limited impact on reducing child labor overall,[116] although this is not to say that, within that limited context at least, they cannot have positive impact.[117]

Social labeling is the private voluntary initiative most associated with child labor, due partly to the RUGMARK label for child labor–free hand-knotted carpets.[118] RUGMARK certifies producers and retailers who agree to produce carpets without illegal child labor. The criteria for the label require producers not to employ children under age fourteen, although, in family-run loom businesses, family members may work if they also attend school.[119] RUGMARK therefore appears to rely for its basic standard on minimum age per ILO C138 rather than harm per ILO C182. However, as RUGMARK also supports community-based projects for children, particularly in the area of education, it appears that positive support for the health and education of child workers and former child workers is now as much part of RUGMARK's social labeling as is the guarantee of a child labor–free product.[120] Nonetheless, the focus on removing children even from benign work may be criticized for ignoring child agency.

Some social labels have a closer relationship with the formal international initiatives than others. As already noted, RUGMARK does not refer explicitly to ILO conventions or to the CRC in its criteria. The Abrinq Foundation in Brazil, on the other hand, has worked with IPEC as well as the United Nations Children's Fund (UNICEF) on its Empresa Amiga da Criança label, and consequently takes into account the human rights standards that help to define IPEC and UNICEF in the child labor field.[121] All private voluntary initiatives, however, are dependent on rigorous monitoring for their credibility, and most give details of their monitoring systems on their websites.[122] There are concerns that these initiatives, social labeling in particular, involve the imposition of labor standards and conceptions of childhood conceived in the wealthy countries of the Global North inasmuch as many early social labeling initiatives began in these countries.[123] However, as is evident from the Brazilian social label Empresa Amiga da Criança, some are now based in other parts of the world.

Corporate codes of conduct are motivated by the same goals as social labels: the assurance that goods, usually internationally traded goods, are made in accordance with certain ethical standards. However, they are usually more comprehensive. While labels such as RUGMARK attest specifically to the absence of child labor in the manufacturing process, codes of conduct ordinarily contain standards on a range of labor rights along with other social responsibility standards. At the same time, codes of conduct, unlike social labels, usually are invisible to consumers unless they are well informed about the practices of the company from which they purchase.

Corporate codes of conduct have a history going back about thirty years,[124] and particularly those designed before the 1998 ILO Declaration on

Fundamental Principles and Rights at Work do not always include child labor as an area of concern and, indeed, may not even be based on international legal standards.[125] Codes of conduct adopted in the late 1990s, however, relied on a child labor standard inspired by ILO C138 if any international standard was used at all.[126] The adoption of the 1998 ILO declaration and ILO C182 has brought limited change. More recent codes, increasingly oriented toward the four categories of rights in the 1998 declaration, reflect both ILO C138 and ILO C182—for example, the Base Code of the UK-based Ethical Trading Initiative,[127] and the Netherlands-based Fair Wear Principles and Policies[128]—but some still refer only to ILO C138, for example, the Clean Clothes Campaign[129] and the SA8000 Standard Elements.[130] Very few codes do more than simply ban child labor, either on the basis of a minimum age standard or on the basis of harm or exploitation. A few include standards on working conditions for young workers under eighteen, such as limited hours or standards on apprenticeship.[131] One particularly detailed code—that of Swedish clothing retailer H&M—sets out obligations for the rehabilitation of child workers and recommends provision of child care at facilities with largely female work forces, this recommendation having been designed in part to prevent child labor.[132]

As noted above, one weakness of codes of conduct is that they are largely invisible, serving as a dialogue more between companies and NGOs (who monitor the workplace activities) than between companies and consumers. One way to fuse the advantages of social labels (publicity) and of codes of conduct (wide-ranging ethical standards) is to develop certifications modeled on those initiated by the International Standards Organization (ISO) to authorize labels that manufacturers can attach to their products to communicate a demonstrated commitment to corporate social responsibility.[133] Social Accountability International (SAI) operates an accreditation system for monitoring corporate social responsibility, certifying compliance with a number of labor rights, including child labor, used also by others, that has been described as an "organizational integrity" approach, emphasizing prevention and remedy rather than punishment.[134]

UN Initiatives on Corporate Social Responsibility

A final demonstration of the integration of the child labor agenda and the child rights agenda via quasi-legal initiatives is seen in the adoption by the UN Sub-Commission on the Promotion and Protection of Human Rights on August 13, 2003, of "Norms on the Responsibilities of Transnational Corporations and Other Business Enterprises with Regard to Human Rights."[135] Its sixth paragraph, the commentary which refers to both ILO C138 and ILO C182,[136] stipulates that "[t]ransnational corporations and other business enterprises shall respect the rights of children to be protected from economic exploitation as forbidden by the relevant international instruments and national legislation as well as international human rights and humanitarian law." Based as it is on the first paragraph of CRC Article 32 and ICESCR Article 10(3), its basic standard thus may be said to take the human rights rather than labor regulation approach to child labor and not to seek the banning of all child labor, focusing on exploitation rather than harm. As such, it is an instrument that holds out the potential of replacing the 1998 ILO Declaration on Fundamental Principles and Rights at Work as the basis for future codes of conduct.

It also has been suggested that the United Nations Global Compact might form the basis of corporate social responsibility measures in future.[137] The Global Compact, Principle 5 of which calls for the "effective abolition of child labour," goes beyond labor and human rights issues to include environmental principles. There is a strong argument that an international code of conduct rather than individual ones designed for each company is preferable, as it would constitute a uniform standard that would be less easy for companies to evade or manipulate.[138] However, there is the danger that a uniform code, even one designed by the UN, would be seen as reflecting Northern and Western values only and would exclude companies with limited ability to comply fully in the short to medium term.

■ Conclusion

Recent international law rules on child labor have been inspired by a human rights discourse and action. Their content is significantly different from previous standards, which were overinclusive, taking an abolitionist approach to child labor. This is a development that represents a fundamental change from the labor regulation approach exemplified by ILO C138, and in two important respects. First, it presupposes that for child labor to be a human rights issue there must be some element of harm to, or exploitation of, the child worker. Second, drawing on developments in children's rights, it expects that there will be some element of choice or participation by child workers in their future. To varying degrees the increasingly dominant CRC and its two optional protocols and ILO C182 reflect this human rights approach.

Much the same has happened also with quasi-legal measures bearing upon child labor, particularly in the realm of voluntary initiatives in the private sector. These quasi-legal measures are often based on the formal international law rules, such as the CRC and the ILO conventions, but bring them into a context where they can create obligations for private actors as well as states. While ILO C138 continues to play a role, despite its abolitionist ethos,[139] the prioritization approach epitomized by ILO C182 and rooted in human rights principles appears more and more to be gaining the upper hand.

New child labor initiatives increasingly reflect the language of children's human rights, drawing from the holistic approach of the CRC. There is consensus on the language to be employed, although the level of commitment to the underlying principles may vary between actors. What remains to be asked is how this consensus and the legal and quasi-legal measures that flow from it can be converted to universal or near-universal standards that will better address and find solutions to the situations of abuse and deprivation to which working children throughout the world are all too frequently subjected.

▧ Notes

1. In this chapter, I adopt the definition of "child labor" set forth in the introduction to this volume, in turn derived from Chapter 2, that is, "work done by children that is harmful to them because it is abusive, exploitive, hazardous, or otherwise contrary to their best interests—a subset of a larger class of children's work, some of which may be compatible with children's best interests (variously expressed as 'beneficial,' 'benign,' or 'harmless' children's work)."

2. ILO, *Convention* (No. 138) *Concerning Minimum Age for Admission to Employment* (1973) [hereinafter "ILO C138"].

3. United Nations, *Convention on the Rights of the Child* (1989) [hereinafter "CRC"].

4. United Nations, *Copenhagen Declaration on Social Development and Programme of Action* . . . (1995).

5. ILO, *Convention* (No. 182) *Concerning the Prohibition and Immediate Elimination of the Worst Forms of Child Labour* (1999) [hereinafter "ILO C182"].

6. United Nations, *Optional Protocol to the Convention on the Rights of the Child on the Involvement of Children in Armed Conflict* (2000); United Nations, *Optional Protocol to the Convention on the Rights of the Child on the Sale of Children, Child Prostitution, and Child Pornography* (2000).

7. See Myers, "The Right Rights? . . ." See also Chapters 8 and 12 in this volume.

8. See infra "IPEC Memoranda of Understanding and Time-Bound Programs" in this chapter.

9. Valticos and von Potobsky, *International Labour Law*, p. 216.

10. ILO, *Declaration Concerning the Aims and Purposes* . . . , pt. III(h).

11. See ILO, *Convention* (No. 5) *on Fixing the Minimum Age for Admission of Children to Industrial Employment* (1919) [hereinafter "ILO C5"]; ILO, *Convention* (No. 6) *Concerning Night Work of Young Persons (Industry)* (1919) [hereinafter "ILO C6"]; ILO, *Convention* (No. 7) *Fixing the Minimum Age for Admission of Children to Employment at Sea* (1920); ILO, *Convention* (No. 10) *Concerning the Age for Admission of Children to Employment in Agriculture* (1921) [hereinafter "ILO C10"]; ILO, *Convention* (No. 15) *Fixing the Minimum Age for the Admission of Young Persons to Employment as Trimmers or Stokers* (1921); ILO, *Convention* (No. 16) *Concerning the Compulsory Medical Examination of Children and Young Persons Employed at Sea* (1921) [hereinafter "ILO C16"]; ILO, *Convention* (No. 33) *Concerning the Age for Admission of Children to Non-Industrial Employment* (1932) [hereinafter "ILO C33"]; ILO, *Convention* (No. 58) *Fixing the Minimum Age for the Admission of Children to Employment at Sea (Revised)* (1936); ILO, *Convention* (No. 59) *Fixing the Minimum Age for Admission of Children to Industrial Employment (Revised)* (1937); ILO, *Convention* (No. 60) *Concerning the Age for Admission of Children to Non-Industrial Employment (Revised)* (1937); ILO, *Convention* (No. 77) *Concerning Medical Examination for Fitness for Employment in Industry of Children and Young Persons* (1946) [hereinafter "ILO C77"]; ILO, *Convention* (No. 78) *Concerning Medical Examination of Children and Young Persons for Fitness for Employment in Non-Industrial Occu-*

pations (1946) [hereinafter "ILO C78"]; ILO, *Convention* (No. 79) *Concerning the Restriction of Night Work of Children and Young Persons in Non-Industrial Occupations* (1946) [hereinafter "ILO C79"]; ILO, *Convention* (No. 90) *Concerning the Night Work of Young Persons Employed in Industry (Revised)* (1948) [hereinafter "ILO C90"]; ILO, *Convention* (No. 112) *Concerning the Minimum Age for Admission to Employment as Fishermen* (1959); ILO, *Convention* (No. 123) *Concerning the Minimum Age for Admission to Employment Underground in Mines* (1965); ILO, *Convention* (No. 124) *Concerning Medical Examination of Young Persons for Fitness for Employment Underground in Mines* (1965) [hereinafter "ILO C124"]; ILO, *Convention* (No. 138) *Concerning Minimum Age for Admission to Employment* (1973) [hereinafter "ILO C138"]; ILO, *Recommendation* (No. 41) *Concerning the Age for Admission of Children to Non-Industrial Employment* (1932); ILO, *Recommendation* (No. 52) *Concerning the Minimum Age for Admission of Children to Industrial Employment in Family Undertakings* (1937); ILO, *Recommendation* (No. 96) *Concerning the Minimum Age of Admission to Work Underground in Coal Mines* (1953); ILO, *Recommendation* (No. 124) *Concerning the Minimum Age for Admission to Employment Underground in Mines* (1965); and ILO, *Recommendation* (No. 146) *Concerning Minimum Age for Admission to Employment* (1973). The texts of each of these ILO conventions and recommendations may be found online in the ILO's ILOLEX database of conventions and recommendations, at http://www.ilo.org/ilolex/english.

12. ILO C5, art. 2.
13. Ibid.
14. ILO C10, art. 1.
15. ILO C33.
16. Ibid., art. 1(1).
17. Ibid., art. 1(2)(b), art. 1(3), and art. 2.
18. Ibid., art. 1(2).
19. Ibid., art. 2.
20. Ibid., art. 3(1).
21. Ibid., art. 3.
22. Ibid., art. 4.
23. Ibid., arts. 5 and 6.
24. See ILO Recommendation No. 41 (1932).
25. See Landy, *The Effectiveness of International Supervision . . .* , pp. 68–69.
26. Ibid., p. 124.
27. Valticos and von Potobsky, *International Labour Law,* p. 220.
28. Betten, *International Labour Law . . .* , pp. 302–308.
29. Ibid., pp. 316–317.
30. Meyers, "The Right Rights? . . ."
31. ILO, *Declaration on Fundamental Principles and Rights at Work* (1998).
32. ILO C138, art. 2.
33. Ibid., art. 7.
34. Ibid., art. 3.
35. ILO, "Child Labour . . . ."
36. Creighton, "Combating Child Labour . . . ," p. 376.
37. When a general survey of the application of ILO C138 was undertaken in 1981, no state had given notice of the enactment of any exemption law as required by these articles. Creighton, "Combating Child Labour . . . ," p. 376.
38. ILO, *Background Document Prepared for the Amsterdam Child Labour Conference.*
39. Valticos and von Potobsky, *International Labour Law,* p. 220.

40. Betten, *International Labour Law* . . . , pp. 302–305.

41. Ibid., pp. 306–307.

42. For a review of theoretical debates on children's rights, see Fortin, *Children's Rights* . . . .

43. See research cited by Myers, "The Right Rights? . . . ," pp. 40–43.

44. See Lucy, "Controversy over Children's Rights," pp. 215–216, 238–240.

45. CRC, art. 1.

46. Myers, "The Right Rights? . . . ," p. 50.

47. See Invernezzi and Milne, "Are Children Entitled to Contribute . . . ?" See also Chapters 8 and 12 in this volume.

48. Myers, "The Right Rights? . . . ," pp. 52.

49. See http://www.ilo.org/public/english/standards/ipec/index.htm.

50. See ILO, *Report VI (1)*.

51. Myers, "The Right Rights? . . . ," pp. 52.

52. United Nations, *Optional Protocol to the Convention on the Rights of the Child on the Involvement of Children in Armed Conflict* (2000); United Nations, *Optional Protocol to the Convention on the Rights of the Child on the Sale of Children, Child Prostitution, and Child Pornography* (2000).

53. Sheppard, "Child Soldiers . . . ," p. 48; Becker, "If the US Opposes Child Labor . . . ."

54. ILO, *Report VI (2)*.

55. Sheppard, "Child Soldiers . . . ," pp. 48, 54–60.

56. See, for example, ILO, *Report of the Committee on Child Labour, International Labour Conference* (1998), paras. 148, 155; ILO, *Report of the Committee on Child Labour, International Labour Conference* (1999), para 8.

57. See, for immediate example, Chapter 14 in this volume.

58. Similar language is found in Paragraph 2 of ILO Recommendation No. 190. Consultation of workers and employers, by contrast, is mentioned in several paragraphs: 2, 4, 8, and 16.

59. ECPAT addresses issues of commercial sexual exploitation of children in all its forms and has national ECPAT groups worldwide. See http://www.ecpat.net/eng/ecpat_network/history.asp.

60. See the CSC website, at http://www.child-soldiers.org/cs/childsoldiers.nsf/displaysmessage/about_the_csc?opendocument.

61. *Stockholm Declaration and Agenda for Action* (1996).

62. ECPAT International, *Annual Report 2001–2002*.

63. This is one of ECPAT's project areas and is reflected in its materials. See http://www.ecpat.net/eng/ecpat_inter/projects/youth_participation/youth.asp.

64. Sheppard, "Child Soldiers . . . ," p. 62.

65. United Nations, *Optional Protocol to the Convention on the Rights of the Child on the Involvement of Children in Armed Conflict* (2000), arts. 1–4.

66. United Nations, *Report of the Special Rapporteur (Ms. Ofelia Calcetas-Santos)* (1999).

67. United Nations, *Report of the Special Representative of the Secretary-General (Mr. Olara A. Otunnu)* (1999–2002).

68. See Global March Against Child Labour, "About Us."

69. See *Final Appeal of Children and Young People* (2001).

70. ILO Recommendation No. 190 (1999), para. 2.

71. ILO, *Report VI (1)*.

72. Creighton, "Combating Child Labour . . . ," pp. 378–379; Myers, "The Right Rights? . . . ," pp. 47–48.

73. Smolin, "Strategic Choices . . . ," pp. 975–977.

74. See ILO, *Report of the Committee on Child Labour* . . . (1998); and ILO, *Report of the Committee on Child Labour* . . . (1999).

75. *Rome Statute of the International Criminal Tribunal* (1998).

76. *Protocol to Prevent, Suppress and Punish Trafficking in Persons, Especially Women and Children* . . . (2000).

77. *Protocol Against the Smuggling of Migrants by Land, Sea, and Air* . . . (2000).

78. United Nations, *Convention Against Transnational Organized Crime* (2000).

79. *European Communities: Community Directive 94/33* . . . .

80. See Harris and Darcy, *The European Social Charter,* pp. 113–262 passim.

81. ILO, *Declaration on Fundamental Principles and Rights at Work* (1998).

82. See the ILO website, at http://webfusion.ilo.org/public/db/standards/normes/index.cfm?lang=en.

83. ILO C138; ILO C182.

84. See ILO, *Report of the Director-General: A Future Without Child Labour* . . . , paras. 26–27.

85. United Nations, *Copenhagen Declaration on Social Development and Programme of Action* . . . (1995).

86. As of June 13, 2005, ILO C138 had 139 ratifications and ILO C182 had 156 ratifications. See the ILO website, at http://www.ilo.org/ilolex/english/newratframee.htm.

87. ILO, *Declaration on Fundamental Principles and Rights at Work* (1998), Annex.

88. ILO, *Follow-Up Action* . . . .

89. ILO, *Report of the Director-General: A Future Without Child Labour* . . . .

90. See IPEC, *IPEC Action Against Child Labour, 2002–2003* . . . .

91. Ibid., p. 7.

92. See http://www.ilo.org/public/english/standards/ipec/governments/index.htm.

93. Article 7(2) of ILO C182 specifically mentions TBPs as a way to implement the convention.

94. See IPEC, *Eliminating the Worst Forms of Child Labour* . . . , p. 1.

95. See the following IPEC country profiles: http://www.ilo.org/public/english/standards/ipec/timebound/salvador.pdf (El Salvador); http://www.ilo.org/public/english/standards/ipec/timebound/nepal.pdf (Nepal); and http://www.ilo.org/public/english/standards/ipec/timebound/tanzania.pdf (Tanzania).

96. IPEC, *IPEC Action Against Child Labour, 2002–2003* . . . , p. 34.

97. See IPEC, *TBP Map Guide Book II* . . . .

98. Ibid., p. 56.

99. IPEC, *IPEC Action Against Child Labour, 2002–2003* . . . , p. 59.

100. Ibid., p. 75.

101. Ibid., p. 77, Indicator 3.

102. Ibid., p. 76, Indicator 1. See also p. 29 of the report.

103. IPEC, *IPEC Action Against Child Labour, 2002–2003* . . . .

104. Ibid.

105. Ibid. In Tanzania, for example, child labor committees were set up in twenty villages. On child labor in Tanzania, see Chapter 7 in this volume.

106. *Protocol for the Growing and Processing of Cocoa Beans* . . . (2001). See also ILO, "ILO Welcomes New Foundation . . . ."

107. See Schrage, *Promoting International Worker Rights* . . . , pp. 148–150.

108. For example, Blunt, "The Bitter Taste of Slavery."

109. As reported in Schrage, *Promoting International Worker Rights . . . ,*" pp. 149, nn. 92–93.

110. The common statement is available at http://www.iuf.org.uk/cgi-bin/dbman/db.cgi?db=default&uid=default&id=105&view_records=1&en=1.

111. Schrage, *Promoting International Worker Rights . . . ,* p. 149.

112. ILO, "Agreement to End Child Labour on Cocoa Farms."

113. See ILO, "ILO Welcomes New Foundation . . . ."

114. World Cocoa Foundation, *Progress Report.*

115. On the issue of public relations versus public policy, see, generally, Schrage, *Promoting International Worker Rights . . . .*

116. IPEC, *Working Paper 2000 . . . ,* p. 25. See also Chapters 5, 9, and 16 in this volume.

117. See Schrage, *Promoting International Worker Rights . . . ,* pp. 165–180.

118. See the RUGMARK International website, at http://www.rugmark.de/english/index.htm; and the RUGMARK USA website, at http://www.rugmark.org.

119. See RUGMARK International website, at http://www.rugmark.de/english/navi/frnauest.htm.

120. See, for example, IPEC, *Working Paper 2000 . . . ,* p. 21.

121. Ibid., pp. 33–40. See also Chapter 9 in this volume.

122. See, for example, the RUGMARK International website, at http://www.rugmark.de/english/index.htm.

123. IPEC, *Working Paper 2000 . . . ,* p. 2.

124. See Schrage, *Promoting International Worker Rights . . . ,* pp. 2–4; and Monshipouri et al., "Multinational Corporations . . . ," p. 978.

125. Jacobs, "Child Labour," pp. 199–200. This is based on an analysis of fifty codes of conduct.

126. Ibid. See also Cullen, "The Right of Child Workers to Protection . . . ."

127. Ethical Trading Initiative, "The Base Code."

128. Fair Wear Foundation, *The Fair Wear Code of Labour Practices,* chap. 6, para. 3.3.

129. Clean Clothes Campaign, *Code of Labour Practices . . . .*

130. Social Accountability International, *SA8000 Standard Elements.*

131. See Jacobs, "Child Labour," pp. 201–203.

132. Ibid., p. 202.

133. The International Standards Organization, a network of national standards institutes, describes itself as "the world developer of standards," particularly in the area of technical standards. See http://www.iso.ch/iso/en/aboutiso/introduction/index.html.

134. Santoro, "Beyond Codes of Conduct and Monitoring," pp. 413–415.

135. United Nations Sub-Commission on the Promotion and Protection of Human Rights, *Norms on the Responsibilities of Transnational Corporations . . . .*

136. United Nations, *Commentary on the Norms . . . .*

137. United Nations, *Global Compact . . . .* See also Monshipouri et al., "Multinational Corporations . . . ," pp. 980–992.

138. See Monshipouri et al., "Multinational Corporations . . . ," pp. 979–980.

139. See Myers, "The Right Rights? . . . ," p. 47, who notes the continued advocacy of ILO C138 by labor unions.

5

Translating Standards into Practice: Confronting Transnational Barriers

S. L. Bachman

The terms for today's international debate over labor standards and children are set in two labor conventions: 1973 International Labour Organization Convention No. 138, which establishes minimum working ages (ILO C138),[1] and 1999 ILO Convention No. 182, which defines the "worst forms" of child labor and calls for their elimination (ILO C182).[2] These ILO conventions parallel international human rights standards, notably the 1989 United Nations Convention on the Rights of the Child (CRC).[3]

International debate over labor standards gained momentum in the 1990s as trade accelerated. International debate over children's rights, spurred by adoption of the CRC, also picked up momentum in the last decade of the twentieth century. Countless meetings, official discussions, and publications, however, led to curiously little immediate change in the lives of millions of children in the homes, fields, streets, factories, quarries, and other places where they work. International labor standards, along with all human rights conventions, face a paradox: no matter how many governments have ratified international standards, or how heartily the international community declares them to be universal, the international community has minimal direct say in how or whether the standards become reality. That job falls to individual states. As Jeffrey Sachs, a Columbia University economist, has written, the "international order" depends on "international exchange and enforceable international contracts in a global system of nation states, without an overarching politico-legal authority."[4]

International bodies that formulate international standards and define rights have criticized states for failing to live up to labor and human rights standards. And yet, all too often, nations that ignore or neglect international standards face almost no risk of punishment from international agencies. At most, a "scofflaw" state may be publicly embarrassed for falling short. It is as if signs that read "Stop!" have been posted at international crossroads, but no traffic patrol waits nearby to catch those who drive through the intersection without braking.

This chapter does not define or call for a new "overarching politico-legal authority" that might do more to make international labor and other human rights standards a reality for ordinary people. Instead, it looks at international institutions that already exist and asks why their powers or capacities are not exercised more, or more effectively, to persuade nations to adopt and enforce laws, and implement policies and programs consistent with international labor standards.

■ Defining Transnational Barriers

Why are international agencies, and international treaty bodies and trade agreements, not more active promoters and defenders of labor standards? Several obstacles that stand in the way are addressed by other chapters in this volume. This chapter addresses obstacles that involve multilateral organizations, or relationships between the organizations and states, or ideas and ideologies that are persuasive among internationally significant segments of opinion. I call such obstacles "transnational barriers."

Several possible transnational obstacles—greed, corruption, collusion, inefficiency, apathy—are so huge or difficult to quantify that this chapter can only acknowledge their existence. Instead, I focus on obstacles that can be easily identified, quantified, or described. They fall into three categories:

- *Institutional obstacles.* Existing institutions with responsibility for setting standards against child labor, but that have weak or underused enforcement tools. The reasons for this weakness, or underutilization, include institutional internal dynamics, counteracting purposes among institutions, and differing functions and memberships, which cause institutions to favor some policies, programs, and strategies and reject others.
- *Political obstacles.* Friction among governments, organizations, and individual officials that can be traced to power relationships, partisanship, or other differences within national governments.
- *Conceptual obstacles.* Conflicting theories of how change occurs, or should and should not occur. Pertinent theories include the set of ideas surrounding free markets, but also the set of ideas surrounding the utility and purpose of trade unions. Some of these ideas could be termed "ideologies." These theories, sets of ideas, and ideologies are influential not only within institutions but also among interest groups, national leaders, business executives, and other actors on the international stage.

Simply listing items in each category, however, fails to tell the full story as it unfolded in the late twentieth century and early twenty-first century. Transnational obstacles sometimes fit in more than one category, or overlap or reinforce each other.

I therefore focus on the most vigorous debate over labor standards in international affairs—that is, the debate over whether trade and financial institutions should change their rules to punish nations—or companies—that ignore or neglect labor standards. Through the lens of the trade-labor debate, it is possible to see how an international organization might go beyond merely criticizing states and make them pay a price (i.e., lost trade) for their inattention to labor standards.

The debate's two principal interlocutors are the ILO, which establishes international labor standards, and the World Trade Organization (WTO), whose approaches to labor standards and labor rights I contrast below. The differences between the two organizations reflect a debate begun before the 1948 entry into force (provisionally) of the General Agreement on Tariffs and Trade (GATT),[5] the WTO's predecessor, that has continued well after the WTO's 1994 inception.

I then use institutional, political, and conceptual obstacles as a general template to explain roles played by other important multilateral institutions: the Committee on the Rights of the Child, which oversees the CRC, and the International Monetary Fund (IMF) and World Bank, which are the two largest multilateral financial institutions.[6]

I also discuss how the policy climate is evolving, in the light of several turning points in the 1990s trade-labor debate. Finally, I reflect on whether the evolving policy climate will strengthen or diminish any of the institutional, political, or conceptual barriers.

■ Transnational Barriers and the Trade-Labor Debate

At least four types of international actors play important roles in the global trade-labor debate: individual states; multilateral organizations; multinational or transnational business enterprises and business organizations of all sizes; and civil society organizations, from trade unions to think tanks to lobbying groups. The ILO encompasses three: states, business, and trade unions. The WTO has only states as members. Both the ILO and WTO are lobbied and influenced by all four types of international actors.

Institutional Barriers: Operational Constraints and Inhibitions

The ILO, founded in 1919, is a specialized agency of the United Nations. The WTO came into being in 1996, but its predecessor, the General Agreement on

Tariffs and Trade, came into force (provisionally) in 1948 as part of the UN family of institutions and agreements that were designed to stabilize international relations after World War II.[7] Mapping the principal qualities of the ILO and WTO sheds important light on the key institutional, political, and conceptual obstacles to strong transnational enforcement of labor standards.

The International Labour Organization—key points. ILO membership encompassed 178 states as of April 25, 2005. Delegates representing the member states are usually labor ministers (e.g., the secretary of labor in the United States) or hail from labor ministries (e.g., the Department of Labor in the United States). The ILO also has two other categories of members: business and trade unions. Each member state may send to the ILO's parliamentary-diplomatic assembly (the ILO's annual International Labour Conference) two government delegates, one business delegate, and one trade union delegate. Each of the four delegates may cast a single vote. Delegates operate independently, and worker and business delegates may vote against their governments. This so-called tripartite structure is unique among multilateral agencies. No other agency gives official standing to civil society (nongovernmental or private sector organizations).

ILO conventions are adopted by a two-thirds vote of the yearly ILO conference and often are accompanied by "recommendations," which also must be approved by the conference. Each member state is expected to submit new conventions to its appropriate parliamentary body for ratification. The ratified convention then becomes binding on the member state. Recommendations are advisory only and thus, in theory, are not binding. At the same time, member states do not lose their ILO memberships if they fail to ratify all ILO conventions.

Compliance with ILO standards is fundamentally voluntary. The ILO cannot force members to conform to the labor standards established by conventions, or the more detailed instructions in recommendations. The ILO does have four ways of bringing pressure on its government members to live up to the letter of conventions they ratify:[8]

- *Technical assistance.* ILO members that wish to implement the provisions in labor standards may ask for "technical assistance" to help national and local officials, trade unions, and businesses learn about ways to improve their own policies and practices.
- *Regular supervision.* Member states that ignore conventions they have ratified may pay the price of public exposure. The ILO's "regular supervisory system," involving a naming-and-shaming strategy, requires member states to submit reports on conventions they have ratified (as well as any of the eight core conventions[9] that they have not yet ratified). The reports are public, so countries that are not living up to their obligations must admit as much to the world.

- *Special supervision.* The ILO's "special supervisory systems" authorize workers' or employers' organizations and member states (under Articles 24 and 26 of the ILO constitution, respectively) to bring specific allegations of failure to apply a ratified convention. Also, the ILO may adopt, as needed, "ad hoc supervisory mechanisms" (including the appointment of special representatives of the ILO's director-general) to oversee the enforcement of international labor standards in particular circumstances.
- *Direct action.* Under Article 33 of the organization's constitution, the ILO conference, upon the recommendation of the ILO's Governing Body, can take "such action as it may deem wise and expedient to secure compliance" with ratified conventions.

This ILO system of essentially voluntary compliance is strong in theory, but weak in practice. In the form of members' self-reporting and Article 33 actions, it has proved famously weak when put into motion. More often than not, it simply has not been put into motion. The familiar cliché points out that international organizations are as strong as their members want them to be, and in the ILO's case that conventional wisdom holds more than a kernel of truth. The ILO's weakness can be traced both to the structure of the institution and to the motivations of its members.

The ILO's tripartite membership can be a source of strength when conventions are adopted by large majorities of the membership and therefore can claim broad support both among governments and civil society. The tripartite membership can be also a weakness, however, when, as often happens, governments, business, and trade unions clash, resulting in conventions being passed by slim majorities and ratified by few governments. Until the 1999 adoption of ILO C182, no ILO convention had been adopted unanimously. In other words, of the two conventions deemed "fundamental" by the ILO and aimed specifically at child labor, only ILO C182 was universally approved by ILO members and won rapid ratification around the globe. That is why, as I explain later, ILO C182 has become the more influential of the two fundamental child labor conventions.

Another ILO weakness stems from members' traditionally "shallow" commitment to the institution.[10] For instance, many governments fail to submit their self-monitoring reports on time. Sheer volume of paperwork may be part of the problem.[11] Another may be that governments perceive no measurable benefit from self-reporting their failures to live up to labor standards.

Put another way, the ILO's standards would be perhaps more widely applied if the benefits of applying them were more obvious. Judging from the available literature, the benefits of complying with international labor standards are obvious only to one of the ILO's three classes of members: labor unions. ILO labor standards are written primarily from a labor union perspective and for the benefit and welfare of workers. As mentioned above, officials from labor or trade ministries usually head government delegations. By contrast, government and business members typically perceive less immediate benefit from adherence to labor standards. And in an even more telling contrast, states and businesses perceive a direct monetary benefit from joining the WTO and abiding by its rules to reduce trade barriers. Some of the ideas and ideologies behind this perception are explained below.

With this institutional weakness in mind, it becomes easier to explain why, despite the ILO's paper powers to investigate and sanction states that ignore labor standards, Article 33 sanctions were not imposed until 2000.[12] The Article 33 sanctions imposed on Burma allowed ILO members to review their relations with Burma and to decide what they could do to ensure that continued relations did not continue or increase the use of forced labor. The sanctions decision followed a long period of ILO investigation and international condemnation of Burma's labor practices.

This Article 33 action illustrated some of the truth in the conventional wisdom that the ILO is only as strong as its members want it to be. The world's only superpower, the United States, championed the sanctions against one of the world's weakest and poorest nations, Burma. In part, the decision was easy because Burma had made itself a ready target through years of labor and political rights abuses. Also, crucially, US businesses supported the sanctions as an extension of the trade-labor debate. Ambassador Thomas M. T. Niles, president of the U.S. Council for International Business, told his colleagues that applying Article 33 aimed not only at correcting labor abuses in Burma but also at establishing "the idea that the ILO has the preeminent role in dealing with such violations. . . . [The decision to impose sanctions] refutes the view held by some that international institutions in this area are weak, and that we therefore need to mix labor issues into U.S. trade agreements or impose upon American business the primary responsibility for upholding labor standards abroad."[13]

There is one other way in which the ILO is only as strong as its members want it to be. The governments, business, and trade unions represented within the organization usually account for most of the formal sector employers, workers, and regulators. Yet in many countries, the informal sector both is larger than the formal sector in monetary terms and employs more people. More to the point, the vast majority of child labor occurs in the informal economy.[14] Unions typically do not work in the informal sector. In many countries, too, "independent" or "free" trade unions have been founded in opposition to established trade unions, leaving child workers unrepresented among the trade union organizations that occupy seats in the ILO.

In yet another—this time welcomed—instance of members shaping the organization according to their wishes, child labor gained new prominence within the ILO with the 1992 establishment of the International Programme on Elimination of Child Labour (IPEC). The separate office and budget reserved specifically for child labor research and programs came about as a German initiative. The United States became the primary source of IPEC funds during the administration of President Bill Clinton.

Clinton's support for IPEC, which has largely continued under the subsequent administration of George W. Bush, was bolstered by the support of US business. Niles, the US business representative quoted above, said why:[15] Business does not want labor standards to be linked to trade agreements. Business would much prefer that international labor standards be debated, and any enforcement action imposed, by the ILO rather than by the WTO.

The World Trade Organization—key points and history. The ILO's weaknesses have led labor rights supporters for many years to suggest an alternative: restricting exports from countries that failed to live up to ILO labor standards. The theory is this: Many governments collect taxes (customs duties, tariffs, etc.) on exports and imports. Why not also use the bottleneck at the border as a place to identify and stop the export of goods made by workers who cannot organize unions, or who suffer discrimination or who are at risk, harmed, or even enslaved because they are children? The answer to date has been shaped in part by the WTO's institutional structure and in larger part because of the wishes of its members.

The WTO had 148 member countries as of February 16, 2005. Delegates are usually cabinet ministers of commerce or trade or both, or else they are officials in charge of trade negotiations (e.g., the US trade representative, a cabinet-level official directly responsible to the president and Congress). Although business and labor representatives may be part of national delegations, and often are influential, they and other nongovernmental organizations (notably trade unions) have no formal standing in the organization.

WTO agreements are adopted by consensus by the WTO's Ministerial Conference, which meets every two years. Countries may bring disputes to the WTO's Dispute Settlement Body, an officially neutral panel that deliberates in private but issues public rulings and suggested remedies. Parties to a dispute may appeal to the WTO's Appellate Body. Parties that do not agree to abide by decisions of WTO dispute resolution and appeals panels may be subject to retaliatory sanctions imposed by individual members.[16]

Members agree to give other members "most-favored-nation" status, which means that nations cannot discriminate against products imported from other WTO member nations. All trading nations must abide by the WTO rules or they will likely wind up in a dispute with one or more other WTO member nations. However, no disputes between WTO members over labor rights have ever been brought to the dispute resolution and appeals panels. This is not because of a shortage of disagreements among member nations over how labor standards are observed or not observed. It is because WTO members have reached a consensus that labor rights are not "trade-related" and so should not be subject to disputes that the WTO's dispute and appeals panels arbitrate.[17]

Key ideologies and concepts underlie the WTO's consensus about what is and is not "trade-related," and in turn these concepts shape the organization's behavior. Below, I discuss these ideologies and concepts further, but first more about the institutional behavior of the WTO in contrast to the ILO.

How institutional differences shape approaches to labor rights. Institutional differences between the ILO and WTO profoundly shape the institutions' behavior, including their approaches to labor and trade standards and rights. To summarize:

- *Membership.* The ILO has three types of members (states, trade unions, businesses). The WTO has one type of member (states).
- *Adoption of legal instruments.* The ILO adopts conventions by majority vote. The WTO adopts rules by consensus.
- *How and why states become members.* ILO membership is achieved by communicating to the ILO director-general formal acceptance of the obligations of the ILO constitution, including a promise to vote on ILO conventions and resolutions but not necessarily to ratify them. Members benefit modestly in a financial sense if they receive technical assistance. By contrast, WTO membership is achieved by agreeing to follow WTO rules, bringing with it the possibility that a nation and its businesses will increase income, foreign investment, and influence on international trade rules. This possibility is supported by mainstream economic theory.

States are not coerced to join or remain members of the ILO or the WTO; they join and stay in the hope that membership will, on balance, benefit them. If they are willing to withstand international criticism and perhaps retaliatory tariffs or other sanctions, nothing can force them to comply save their own sense of enlightened self-interest. This is the meaning of state sovereignty.

Sovereign states as institutional actors. It is important to underscore the role played by state sovereignty in international institutions.[18] Two reasons stand out, using the WTO as example. One is that any attempt to levy fines or otherwise punish nations for violating or ignoring international standards or rules runs up against the reluctance of most states to give up their freedom of action. Membership in the WTO involves subjecting a nation's trade policies and practices to the WTO's exceptionally strong dispute resolution system. That system—involving legally binding rulings and an appeals process—is widely recognized as effective in bringing about compliance with the WTO's decisions. Most other international law relies more heavily on voluntary compliance for legitimacy and relevance.[19] Why do states accept the diminution of their sovereignty in return for WTO membership? The obvious answer lies in the quantifiable benefits noted above.

Second, sovereignty questions, like beauty, are commonly a matter of perspective. Protectionist interests routinely resent antisovereignty WTO rules that force a nation to open its economy. Traders typically welcome the WTO's rules as a way to get around the protectionists. For example, advocates of WTO rules that punish countries for failing to live up to ILO labor standards believe that a heavy international hand is the only way to win compliance by reluctant, lazy, or corrupt government officials. Also, in countries with inadequate laws against child labor, corrupt and inefficient enforcement of those laws, ineffective or corrupt labor unions, or all of the above, a WTO rule against trading goods made by children may be seen as an opportunity. They might be able to use international pressure to force local change.

On the other hand, advocates of laws that protect local customs, economic patterns, or values may resent the heavy international hand that forces compliance with international trade rules or labor standards. Many developing countries believe a WTO rule banning trade in goods made by children would be counterproductive: in punishing businesses and industries that continue to employ children, it could require children to find new jobs, without providing them with any replacement income or other assistance.

Are labor "standards" labor "rights"? Discussion within the WTO about labor standards has often foundered on the question over whether international labor standards establish universal rights. In the first place, in the absence of explicit language, it is not clear that standards are rights or, in any event, which standards are rights.[20] Furthermore, critics point out that many ILO conventions have failed to pass by large majorities, or to win widespread acceptance and ratification.[21] As already noted, except for ILO C182, on the "worst forms" of child labor, no ILO convention has been adopted by unanimous vote, and several key ILO conventions conspicuously lack ratifications by large countries. ILO C138, establishing minimum working ages, has not been ratified by major countries such as Canada, India, and the United States.

What is more, until 1998 at least, skeptics complained that it was hard to know which conventions were the most important or of the highest priority. Thus, in 1998, the ILO grouped seven "core" conventions into the Declaration on Fundamental Principles and Rights at Work[22] (ILO C182 was added in 1999), calling upon member states to "respect and promote" the principles and rights proclaimed in the four areas covered in the core conventions "even if they have not ratified the Conventions in question."[23] This commitment is supported by a follow-up procedure by which "Member States that have not ratified one or more of the core Conventions are asked each year to report on the status of the relevant rights and principles within their borders, noting impediments to ratification, and areas where assistance may be required."[24]

The declaration is now clear. Skeptics no longer have grounds on which to assert ambiguities about the ILO's core priorities. The eighth core convention, ILO C182, shifts the pace into higher gear by placing higher priority on ending the worst forms of child labor than on ending labor performed by underage children. ILO C182, thus, has an unofficial first-among-equals designation. That has changed the policy climate in a subtle but important way (explained below).

Still, the ILO has little more than naming-and-shaming tools to persuade members who have not ratified one or more conventions to consider ratifying them, translating them into law, and enforcing those laws. This reality, coupled with the fact that a two-thirds majority is required from among the ILO's large and diverse membership to adopt international labor standards, virtually guarantees that their adoption and implementation at the national level will never be uniform around the world.

For instance, federal democracies such as Canada, India, and the United States must translate international standards into national laws, and separately into state and local laws. The process is complex and unpredictable. National governments and state, provincial, or other subnational governments typically have separate legal powers and responsibilities, and typically respond separately and sometimes differently to local political interests and power centers. State, provincial, or other subnational legislative and executive bodies are thus not unlikely to disagree on whether to conform national law policies and practices to standards set internationally.[25] This devolution of powers is potentially a source of opposition to any attempt to use WTO rules to enforce labor standards.

Institutional weaknesses. A final institutional obstacle relates to the question of how to investigate allegations that child labor has been used in workplaces making goods for export. One refrain of the opposition to WTO enforcement of ILO labor standards is that the WTO simply does not have the expertise, or the personnel, to perform the due diligence that would be required to enforce a rule outlawing trade in goods made by children (or adults whose working conditions fell short of the other core standards). The WTO prides itself on maintaining a relatively small staff.[26] By contrast, the ILO's secretariat (i.e., the International Labour Office) is a large bureaucracy with satellite offices in member countries and more than eighty years of experience investigating and reporting on labor issues. While the ILO does not have a system for comprehensively monitoring the presence of child labor in the export (or domestic) sectors of national economies, it does have, through its International Programme on the Elimination of Child Labour, several programs to improve statistics and data collection about child labor and to offer technical assistance to ILO members.

In short, the ILO simply has a larger institutional capacity to investigate child labor allegations,[27] and this poses a paradox for the organization. If the

ILO allows the WTO to investigate alleged uses of child labor in exports, thus handing off the responsibility to another agency, the ILO might diminish its own international role and importance.[28] Yet if the WTO does not have an institutional stake in investigating child labor allegations, will the WTO take the issue seriously? This paradox might be resolved if WTO dispute resolution panels agreed to consider ILO investigations as evidence in trade disputes— if, that is, as a first step, WTO members would agree to interpret its rules or write a new rule disallowing trade in goods made with child labor.[29]

Political Barriers: People, Ideas, and Political Power
The political strengths and weaknesses of the people and political interest groups involved in the ILO and WTO differ in three important ways:

- *As a general rule, the national ambassadors to the ILO and the WTO come from different ministries.* Often, therefore, they differ profoundly in their own roles in national politics, economics, and society, in their beliefs about society, and in the nature of economic and social change.
- *As a general rule, the ambassadors to the ILO and WTO, and the natural political constituencies of each organization, do not wield the same amount of power in their home governments.* Ministries or departments of labor may be dominated by, or politically beholden to, organized labor. Ministries or departments of commerce may be politically dominated by, or beholden to, the management of major industry.
- *As a general rule, the natural political constituencies of the ILO and WTO do not see eye-to-eye on social philosophy, economics, or the importance of generating economic growth compared to the importance of redistributing wealth or power.* Despite the ILO's tripartite membership, its political constituency and ideological leanings traditionally have hewed toward trade unions. In the WTO, business interests typically hold sway. Relations between labor and management in many, if not most, societies have been polarized for more than 100 years. It is no surprise, then, to find discussions in the ILO about enforcing labor rights favored by trade unions raising hackles among management-oriented negotiators at the WTO. Nor is it a surprise when observers say that, despite the cooperative rhetoric in the Singapore Ministerial Declaration, cooperation between the two international agencies is weak at best.[30]

Conceptual Barriers: How Ideas Shape Behavior
Some of the ideological differences between the ILO and WTO already have come into view. Do ILO conventions establish universal labor rights even though most conventions are not adopted by unanimous vote and are not ratified by all ILO members? Is failure to adhere to labor rights "non-trade-related"

or does it unfairly lower production costs? Are sovereign states solely responsible for adhering to international labor rights and, if they fail, should they be subject to sanctions applied by an international agency?

Economic growth before rights? Or rights realization before trade? Between the labor-oriented ILO and the business-oriented WTO lies a deep gulf of disagreement about how best to bring about economic growth and improve social welfare. To important questions, the two groups offer different answers. For instance, ILO members (especially labor unions) might argue that blocking trade in goods made by exploited workers will give nations a financial incentive to crack down on worker exploitation. WTO members might argue that allowing trade in goods made by exploited workers nevertheless would spur economic growth—and, in the process, expand the probability that workers will have both jobs and the wherewithal to fight for their own rights.

Historical roots of institutional disagreement. Labor rights questions have come up in international trade discussions for at least forty years, since the GATT started operations in 1948. The same questions have been asked repeatedly: Should international trade rules disallow trade in goods made by workers, including children, laboring in substandard conditions? Should GATT or WTO member countries be allowed to ban imports of goods made by those workers, on the grounds that nations that turn a blind eye to such practices are allowing companies or industries to sell goods with low prices achieved through labor exploitation? At a minimum, because the relationship between labor and trade is obvious and compelling to some WTO members but not to others, should the WTO take an initial step by simply studying possible trade-labor links? On at least three occasions, during eight multilateral negotiations (known as "rounds") on GATT rules, from 1948 to 1994, the GATT considered limiting trade to nations that adhered to ILO labor standards.[31] Each time, the trade body's answer was no.

By the time of the Uruguay Round (1986–1995), an era of burgeoning trade, the GATT's provisional status had become a liability. Negotiators decided to establish a more formal organization and, in 1995, the WTO came into being, establishing a set of rules that would govern how trade disputes would be managed and opening the door to new discussion of the controversial trade-labor questions that had been left unresolved for four decades. The GATT's rules already allowed companies to block imports of goods made by prisoners. Why not allow countries to block imports of goods made by child laborers?[32]

Faced with the familiar trade-labor questions, the WTO's members again, overwhelmingly, uttered a familiar answer: no. The WTO governing body explained why in the meeting's final document, the Singapore Ministerial Declaration:

> We renew our commitment to the observance of internationally recognized core labor standards. The International Labour Organization (ILO) is the competent body to set and deal with these standards, and we affirm our support for its work in promoting them. We believe that economic growth and development fostered by increased trade and further trade liberalization contribute to the promotion of these standards. We reject the use of labor standards for protectionist purposes, and agree that the comparative advantage of countries, particularly low-wage developing countries, must in no way be put into question. In this regard, we note that the WTO and ILO Secretariats will continue their existing collaboration.[33]

Many WTO members believed then, and continue to believe today, that the Singapore Ministerial Declaration had put to rest the persistent trade-labor questions.[34] The trade-labor debate nevertheless arose again when the Doha Round, the current round of trade talks, began in 2001. The round's discussion agenda cut off debate, however, by declaring that labor standards are non-trade-related.[35]

Labor standards supporters have not given up. The reasons why lie in the differences between the underlying philosophies and beliefs not only of the WTO and ILO members but also of a large supporting cast of people, businesses, nongovernmental organizations, and other groups whose philosophies, and interests, are at stake.

The WTO, economists, and labor rights opponents—history and attitudes intertwined. By declaring labor issues non-trade-related, WTO members signaled that their views are in line with mainstream economic thought about the relationship between labor conditions and trade. Mainstream economists dismiss the notion that there is a meaningful relationship between the conditions under which products are made and the economic benefits of trade. As one leading text on international economics puts it: "It can seem hard-hearted to try to justify the terrifyingly low wages paid to many of the world's workers. If one is asking about the desirability of free trade, however, the point is not to ask whether low-wage workers deserve to be paid more but to ask whether they and their country are worse off exporting goods based on low wages than they would be if they refused to enter into such demeaning trade. And in asking this question, one must also ask, what is the alternative?"[36]

The non-trade-related judgment also carries historical baggage. One of the GATT's founding goals was to reduce barriers to trade. The GATT's founders followed the Ricardian theory of "comparative advantage," which holds that an economic surplus will be created that can be put to productive use if countries trade what they make most efficiently. The GATT's founders also were chasing big political game: they hoped that by reducing disputes over trade and thereby stabilizing international relations, they could head off a third world war.

The WTO has maintained the reduction of trade barriers as a central raison d'être, and consequently many WTO members are reluctant to tinker with the old formula. Enforcing labor standards by blocking trade in goods made by children or other exploited workers would invite protectionism, impose new costs, and in turn, reduce economic growth.

The free trade goal remains, moreover, far away. More than four decades of trade negotiations have managed to dismantle most tariffs, but nontariff barriers to trade continue to exist, and new ones are still being created. For instance, countries that wish to protect their markets from imported goods often reject imports because of the way a product was manufactured. In the eyes of many WTO members, allowing countries to reject imports on the grounds that they have been manufactured by exploited workers would give protectionists another excuse to exclude imports for essentially protectionist reasons. The WTO's sister agencies, from the United Nations Children's Fund (UNICEF) to the World Bank and the IMF, are responsible for some piece of the economic development puzzle, and the WTO, it is argued, should remain specialized to opening markets.

Many skeptics of linking labor and trade rights through WTO rules believe that discussing labor rights in relation to trade, or even researching the links in detail, would take time and energy away from the bigger task of reducing trade barriers. As one trade analyst has put it, the politics involved in such a discussion would be "poisonous."[37]

Furthermore, since fewer than 5 percent of child laborers make products for export, even trade analysts who acknowledge that some children, the most vulnerable workers, are harmed in the production of exports doubt that protecting those children is worth the trouble. Many also argue that trade policy is not an effective way to make social policy, because blocking trade does not get at the root of the child labor problem.[38]

Finally, skepticism within the WTO about the ILO's labor standards was compounded during most of the 1990s by disagreement about ILO C138. Objections to this minimum age convention ranged from the cultural to the practical. Cultural arguments included the observation that some countries allow children younger than the official working ages to assume adult roles. Other poor countries, for instance in South Asia, do not have thorough records of children's births and therefore would not be able to determine accurately whether children were of legal working age. Those arguments have not gone away, but they have been trumped by ILO C182's call for eliminating the worst forms of child labor first. The way ILO C182 has changed the policy climate is further discussed below.

Labor rights advocates—history and attitudes intertwined. Trade critics have not given up on the idea of conditioning trade on respect for labor rights, and their stubbornness reflects their own history and beliefs.[39] Labor unions support the notion that ILO conventions establish universal worker rights, and increasingly international union leaders are couching their arguments in the language of universal human rights.

Thus the International Confederation of Free Trade Unions (ICFTU) is conducting an international campaign against child labor, which dovetails with the confederation's campaign to persuade the WTO to adopt rules requiring members to respect fundamental "worker rights."[40] The International Garment, Textile, and Leather Workers Federation (IGTLWF) lists "linking trade and worker rights" as one of its top priorities and calls for "workers rights clauses in the agreements and procedures of the World Trade Organization, [including] freedom of association and protection for the right to organize, [prohibition of] forced labor and child labor, and [the outlawing of] discrimination."[41] Barbara Shailor, director of the International Affairs Department of the American Federation of Labor–Congress of Industrial Organizations (AFL-CIO), the largest US trade union federation,[42] has said, "the intellectual debate has been won and, in the near future, the notion of tying respect for basic labor rights to trade agreements, and ensuring their enforcement, will be generally accepted."[43]

History is key. Labor unions have been struggling for more than a century to establish labor rights, at high cost. Blood has been shed—and lives lost—in the process. The campaign for labor rights is an unabashedly moral struggle.

Labor union arguments reflect also an economic ideology. For many years, unions and other labor rights supporters have condemned "social dumping" and the "race to the bottom."[44] Social dumping refers to the practice of entering a market with low-priced imported products manufactured in countries where low wages and labor abuses are tolerated in order to depress labor prices and, subsequently, prices paid by end-users. The race to the bottom is a theory that capital moves to wherever prices are cheapest, such as countries where poor labor practices keep prices low, thereby encouraging countries to maintain low labor standards and discouraging adherence to labor standards. Companies that engaged in social dumping and the race to the bottom, and then traded their goods on the international market, the critics said, were engaging in unfair trade. And countries that went along, by blocking workers from realizing their rights, were also engaging in unfair trade. The best remedy for these problems, the critics argued, would be for all trading nations to agree that the goods they traded would be produced under conditions that conformed to international trade standards.

Children, the social critics pointed out, were among the most vulnerable of workers. Growing numbers of journalists and academic and civil society researchers have been reporting on children in developing nations who made products such as shoes, hand-loomed rugs, and soccer balls for export to industrialized countries where laws banned children from making such goods. By employing children, the critics argued, manufacturers in developing countries were keeping labor costs unfairly low. Such employers could easily mistreat their typically poverty-stricken, docile, malleable child workers in other ways as well.[45]

To remedy this situation, labor rights supporters have called upon the WTO to adopt a "social clause" among its rules for international trade. The proposed clause would require that countries trading by WTO rules respect basic ILO labor standards (rights) or be subject to a variety of disciplinary measures.[46] But most mainstream economists argue that empirical evidence of the race to the bottom is too slim, by their measurements, to justify transnational enforcement of such rights.[47] Some argue, too, that few social policies have been successfully imposed from outside national boundaries.[48]

■ Children's Rights and International Affairs: An Uneasy Fit

The disagreement about the role of labor standards in economic development, as outlined in the trade-labor debate described above, mirrors deep disagreements about the role of children's rights in global affairs. Evidence can be found in observing how key institutions in the international order address, or fail to address, labor issues.

Committee on the Rights of the Child— Key Aspects and History

The UN Committee on the Rights of the Child, the body authorized by the CRC to monitor how well states meet their CRC obligations,[49] is the only body that the world community has designated to be specifically responsible for overseeing state adherence to children's rights. The committee's work, however, is poorly integrated into international trade-labor debates over how or whether to improve adherence to international labor standards.

States parties to the CRC, which has been ratified by all the world's nations except for Somalia and the United States, are obligated by it to submit reports to the committee on "the measures they have adopted" to give effect to the rights recognized in the CRC.[50] In turn the committee, made up of eighteen "experts," reviews these reports, requests further information as needed, invites expert advice to enhance a reporting state's implementation of the CRC, makes suggestions and general recommendations based on information received from a wide variety of sources, and submits every two years to the UN General Assembly, through the Economic and Social Council, reports on its activities. The committee also holds annual one-day discussions, called "Days of General Discussion," on designated topics. Thirteen have been conducted since 1992, one addressed to the economic exploitation of children.[51] However, the committee does not perform its own investigations or studies. Also, unlike other treaty bodies, it has no authority to adjudicate complaints of human rights abuse under the CRC. Essentially, it is a naming-and-shaming oversight body whose limited powers appear to have prevented it from producing reports that could be viewed widely as informative and, when derogatory, as profoundly embarrassing.

In any event, though the committee has been working steadily for over ten years, one is hard-pressed to find evidence that it has influenced the trade-labor debate. For example, though the UN's landmark child rights convention was already ten years old when ILO C182, on the worst forms of child labor, was adopted, ILO C182, except for passing recognition in its preamble, makes no mention of or even tangential reference to any of the children's rights spelled out in the CRC, not even the right of children "to express [their] views freely in all matters affecting [their lives]."[52] On occasion, children have been allowed to address the ILO secretary-general—for instance, when Global March children addressed him in 1998. But generally speaking, children's input has not been routinely welcomed by the ILO. Trade unions, in particular, tend to be uncomfortable with, if not downright hostile to, the notion that working children might wish to do some work or even form their own unions.[53]

Notably, the nation with the greatest potential to make children's rights and the work of the committee a force to be reckoned with in the trade-labor debate is the United States. But it takes no crystal ball to see that the United States will not promote the CRC until the White House succeeds at prodding the US Senate to give its "advice and consent" to ratification of the treaty. Until that time, the WTO is unlikely to discontinue its pattern of avoiding discussion of labor rights, much less children's rights.

International Financial Institutions and Trade Agreements

Child labor has come under increasing discussion in the major financial institutions as controversy has erupted over global financial transactions and international monetary turmoil.[54] If the International Monetary Fund and the World Bank argued in favor of local enforcement of labor standards, they could play a major role in increasing state adherence to standards. The IMF remains uninterested in changing its policies or procedures, but the Bank has taken several steps forward.

The International Monetary Fund. The IMF's founding purposes are to promote international monetary cooperation and exchange stability; to be a lender of last resort; to minimize international financial disruptions; and "[t]o facilitate the expansion and balanced growth of international trade, and to contribute thereby to the promotion and maintenance of high levels of employment and real income and to the development of the productive resources of all members as primary objectives of economic policy."[55] The IMF has come under considerable criticism, however, for the alleged rigidity of the conditions it imposes on countries that accept its lender-of-last-resort loans. The criticism rose to a crescendo in the wake of the 1997 Asian currency crisis, when many critics complained that the IMF's policies slowed the economic recoveries of South Korea and Indonesia.[56] Yet significantly, there is no explicit mention in the IMF's founding documents that the Fund's role is any way related to economic or other human rights. Also noteworthy is the IMF's viewpoint that its basic prescriptions for countries trying to recover from currency shocks are sound, and that much of the blame for inept policies and consequent damage to a country's poor belongs with the national governments that adopt politically expedient but economically inefficient policies.[57]

The World Bank. The World Bank lends money to low- and middle-income developing nations for the purposes of economic development. Conditions that the Bank places on its loans, like the conditions on IMF loans, have led to considerable controversy.[58]

The Bank responded in 1998 by creating a special program to study and formulate policies to address child labor: the Global Child Labour Program (GCLP) in the Human Development Network's Social Protection unit. It claims that the GCLP has made significant contributions toward identifying the Bank's "comparative advantage" in addressing child labor, in "proactively address[ing] the issue of child labor in its lending and non-lending operations," and in facilitating more cooperation among multilateral agencies.[59] In fact, the GCLP has produced new child-oriented research in cooperation with the ILO and UNICEF.[60] Also, in 2004, the World Bank held a dialogue with the ILO and other partners (e.g., the US Department of Labor) to encourage investment.[61] Without a comprehensive, outside review of the effectiveness of the World Bank's programs since 1998, however, it is hard to say how the Bank's official concern about child labor has, or has not, translated into better programs in the villages, towns, cities, and rural areas of the developing world.

Two hopeful observations can be made: the Bank has supported several important research papers relating to child labor; and the Bank's large and growing education lending makes it the world's largest external education lender.[62] Still, with regard to labor standards and trade, as is made clear in the document the Bank published that introduced the reasoning behind the new GCLP, the Bank considers its role to be primarily problem analysis, policy formulation, and program funding aimed at building human resources.[63] The document observes that in 1996, the WTO rejected the idea that child labor and trade are related. The Bank document then says that "[r]equiring its member countries as a general proposition to enforce certain labor law standards regardless of their relevance to Bank operations would raise broader issues with respect to the Bank's mandate and cannot be limited only to the subject of child labor. Therefore, the Bank can only impose conditionalities in this area to the extent that an absence of consistency with child labor standards un-

dermines the execution or the developmental objective of its specific programs and projects."[64] In other words, the Bank considers the human resources aspects of child labor important to its activities, but analyzing and
promoting rights are functions outside the institution's core mission.

■ Other International Actors and the Changing Policy Climate

Many of the institutional, political, and conceptual barriers to progress toward
the elimination of child labor outlined above will never go away. Nevertheless, since the end of the Cold War in 1989 and continuing through a series of
key turning points during the 1990s, the policy climate changed in important
ways.

1989–2004: Growing Understanding of Child Labor and Its Remedies

In the early 1990s, as international discussion about the long-neglected issue
of child labor gained momentum, some governments denied that child labor
existed within their borders. The naysayers backed down in the face of a bliz-
zard of journalism, advocacy reports, and academic scholarship. Since then,
evidence of child laborers working around the world has mushroomed.

As of 1992, IPEC became an international center for research on child
labor. The US Department of Labor, IPEC's major source of funds as previously noted, also produces its own series of studies about child labor.[65] Even
if this level of funding does not continue, the increased scholarship on child
labor already has played a positive role. In addition, IPEC, other agencies
such as UNICEF and the World Bank, international NGOs such as Oxfam and
Radda Barnen, and academic and many other social actors have produced significant research.

Along with the increased scholarship, IPEC and bilateral assistance have
paid for many new on-the-ground programs to address child labor. IPEC
began some new cooperative actions—memoranda of understanding (MOUs)
and "time-bound programs"—that require countries to set deadlines for completing steps to focus attention and action on child labor at several levels of
government, society, and economy. IPEC's early reports on results from the
MOUs and time-bound programs claim that the new programs have been successful, but a few more years will have to pass before any truly reliable assessment of their lasting impact (or lack thereof) can be made.[66]

In addition, several countries—although far from enough—have started
programs to remove children from individual industries or to improve education and educational opportunities.[67] The United States has included in bi- and
trilateral trade treaties increasingly specific carrot-and-stick policies to encourage adherence to international labor policies. Private companies, including

companies that denied employing children, have either adopted new codes of conduct or joined programs to eliminate child labor from their workplaces and industries.[68]

Whether all this new activity has reduced child labor appreciably or will lead to its effective elimination is not clear. Skeptics of specific approaches, programs, and policies have lobbed stinging criticisms at the new scholarship, programs, and strategies.[69] Clearly, there is ample room for improvement.

Evolving Theories About Labor, Trade, and Economic Growth

The flowering of child labor scholarship mentioned above has featured a particular increase in scholarship on the economics of child labor, trade, and economic growth.[70] This is significant because so much of international development policy, specifically trade policy, is formulated according to the theories, assumptions, and observations of mainstream economics. At the end of the twentieth century, several ideas that gained currency in mainstream economics were directly relevant to studies of child labor.

The new economics scholarship calls into question some of the arguments against the transnational enforcement of labor standards. Just a decade ago, labor economists were among the only mainstream economists who believed that investing in labor would produce positive economic returns. Now, "human capital investment" has become a popular buzzword and theory, and is close to being conventional wisdom.[71] One recent, important IPEC contribution to this line of thinking is a study showing that increased spending on education would cost nations more money in the short run but would have high economic returns in the long term.[72] The new interest in investing in human capital is reflected in the World Bank's increased education lending.

Mainstream economic philosophy about labor and trade, however, remains unchanged. The best way to achieve social change, mainstream economists insist, is through economic growth, and the best way to boost economic growth is by expanding trade. A few economists, such as Joseph Stiglitz and William Easterly, who have worked in the multilateral financial institutions, have attracted international attention with their critiques of the conventional economic wisdom.[73] In a nutshell, they say that the economic policies pursued by the international financial institutions in the 1980s and 1990s have not produced as much growth as hoped, and what growth they have produced has not led to as great an increase in human welfare as was hoped.

1999: ILO C182, on the Worst Forms of Child Labor

Perhaps the single most important change in the policy climate surrounding labor standards has been the International Labour Organization's 1999 adoption of ILO C182 defining (and calling for immediate efforts to eradicate) the "worst forms" of child labor. The ILO did not abandon an age-based definition of the appropriate working age, but it did put first priority on addressing four categories of children's work: slavery, sex work, forced work (including children for use in armed conflict), and work that is harmful, hazardous, or morally objectionable.

Countries around the world have been ratifying the convention at a rapid pace.[74] If eventually the convention is universally ratified, or nearly so, it could become the first ILO convention, as even the most caustic of labor standards skeptics would have to admit, to establish a universal child labor standard. That, in turn, could stimulate a rethinking of existing WTO rules. In Chapter 16 of this volume, Frank Garcia and Soohyun Jun argue that the WTO's existing Article XX could be interpreted to allow countries to block imports of products made by the most abused or exploited children. Universal or near-universal ratification of the convention would significantly bolster their argument.

An even more significant development, however, is a growing consensus among economists of all stripes that the new, popular definition of the "worst forms" of child labor has put unexpected pressure on the WTO. Economists from both liberal and conservative camps agree that the convention's popularity has eaten away the WTO's reasons to resist adopting a rule to block trade in goods made (or services provided) by children or other ways to incorporate measures against the forced labor and other worst forms into trade law. If the rest of the world agrees that the worst forms should be eliminated immediately, how, in good conscience, can the WTO allow trade in goods or services made or provided by children working in the worst forms? The WTO will have to respond willingly to the worst cases of child labor—or else public pressure will force it to act.[75]

■ Conclusion: Stalemate . . . and Slow Movement Forward

For now, the stalemate over WTO enforcement of worker rights seems set in concrete. The wisdom of imposing social change from outside, using WTO rules—and by extension, any other multilateral agency's rules or conditions—as an enforcement tool, continues to be vigorously debated. There is at present no clear consensus in sight.

And yet the 1990s saw an explosion of scholarship on, and programs to reduce, child labor. In addition, the unanimous adoption in 1999 of ILO C182, on the worst forms of child labor, together with its rapid rate of ratification since then, is undermining critics' arguments that no ILO conventions comprise truly universally accepted labor rights. Because the convention is still relatively new, the way it has changed the policy environment did not make much of an impression in 2001 when WTO members set the agenda for the Doha Round. Both liberal and conservative economists have warned, however, that the WTO is on notice: if the WTO refuses to limit trade in goods made by workers in the universally recognized worst forms of child labor, the organization will be seriously out of step, and pressure for the WTO to act will build.

The global economy has been orchestrated, to date, without regard to children's human rights. Children's human rights as recognized by the international community have not been incorporated into international financial practices, specifically international trade law. The political will has been lacking to consider children's human rights as central to international economic organization. If ILO C182 becomes the first universally ratified ILO convention, there is reason to hope that it will strengthen efforts to organize international financial and trade rules and practices as if children's rights really matter.

▆ Notes

1. ILO, *Convention* (No. 138) *Concerning Minimum Age for Admission to Employment* (1973) [hereinafter "ILO C138"].

2. ILO, *Convention* (No. 182) *Concerning the Prohibition and Immediate Elimination of the Worst Forms of Child Labour* (1999) [hereinafter "ILO C182"]. In this chapter, I adopt the definition of "child labor" set forth in the introduction to this volume, in turn derived from Chapter 2, that is, "work done by children that is harmful to them because it is abusive, exploitive, hazardous, or otherwise contrary to their best interests—a subset of a larger class of children's work, some of which may be compatible with children's best interests (variously expressed as 'beneficial,' 'benign,' or 'harmless' children's work)."

3. United Nations, *Convention on the Rights of the Child* (1989) [hereinafter "CRC"].

4. For this quote, and a longer explanation of Sachs's theory about the weakness of the rule of law in a globalized economy, see Sachs, "Globalization and the Rule of Law."

5. *General Agreement on Tariffs and Trade* (1947) [hereinafter "GATT"].

6. This chapter's focus is limited to efforts that would be effective worldwide. Considerable scope exists—and progress has been made—toward using regional institutions to promote labor standards in conjunction with children's rights. For instance, each non-WTO trade agreement, from the North American Free Trade Agreement (NAFTA) to bilateral trade agreements, offers an opportunity to improve adherence to international labor standards in a variety of ways. Also, among the regional banks, the Asian Development Bank is notable for emphasis on promoting ILO labor standards. Its website (http://www.adb.org) contains statements unusual, for a bank, in endorsing the goals of the CRC and in linking observance of labor rights to economic development: "A failure to respect labor standards carries specific and measurable costs to national economies, harms economic development, and violates the rights of working people throughout the region. Failure to respect laws is also a grave governance issue. Enforcing labor into the ADB's policies and practices these ideas have penetrated is unclear." See ADB, "Child Protection," and ADB, "Labor Standards . . . ."

7. GATT.

8. See ILO, *International Labour Standards . . . .*

9. The ILO has designated as "fundamental conventions" two conventions on forced labor, the 1930 Convention (No. 29) Concerning Forced or Compulsory Labour

(ILO C29) and the 1957 Convention (No. 105) Concerning the Abolition of Forced Labour (ILO C105); two conventions on freedom of association, the 1948 Convention (No. 87) Concerning Freedom of Association and Protection of the Right to Organize (ILO C87) and the 1948 Convention (No. 98) Concerning the Application of the Principles of the Right to Organize and to Bargain Collectively (ILO C98); two conventions on discrimination, the 1951 Convention (No. 100) Concerning Equal Remuneration for Men and Women Workers for Work of Equal Value (ILO C100) and the 1958 Convention (No. 111) Concerning Discrimination in Respect of Employment and Occupation (ILO C111); and two conventions specifically on child labor, 1973 ILO C138 and 1999 ILO C182.

10. Elliott, "Getting Beyond No . . . ," p. 190.

11. Ibid., p. 192.

12. In 1998 the ILO reported on forced labor in Burma (Myanmar), and in 2000, for the first time in the ILO's eighty-one-year history, ILO members voted unanimously to invoke Article 33 of the ILO constitution to impose "sanctions" on Burma. The Burmese government subsequently promised to work with the ILO to correct the abuses. Burmese authorities, however, are prosecuting nine individuals for alleged treason, citing those individuals for having contacted the ILO. See Jay, "ILO Resolution on Burma . . ."; and ICFTU, "WTO Ignoring Workers' Rights . . . ."

13. US Council for International Business, "Business Representative . . . ."

14. For pertinent discussion, see Bachman, "New Economics of Child Labor . . . ," pp. 545–575.

15. See US Council for International Business, "Business Representative . . . ."

16. On WTO dispute settlement procedures, see the WTO's website, at http://www.wto.org/english/tratop_e/dispu_e/dispu_e.htm#dsb.

17. For pertinent discussion, see Chapter 16 in this volume.

18. For related discussion, see Chapter 1 in this volume.

19. Hudec, "The Role of the GATT Secretariat . . . ," p. 101.

20. For pertinent discussion, see Chapters 1 and 4 in this volume.

21. A detailed discussion of the differences between concepts of human rights held by trade experts and human rights advocates can be found in Howse and Matua, "Protecting Human Rights in a Global Economy . . . ."

22. ILO, *Declaration on Fundamental Principles and Rights at Work* (1998). The declaration covers four areas: freedom of association and the right to collective bargaining; the elimination of forced and compulsory labor; the abolition of child labor; and the elimination of discrimination in the workplace.

23. Ibid.

24. ILO, "About the Declaration."

25. Franck, "Are Human Rights Universal?" pp. 191–193.

26. Hudec, "The Role of the GATT Secretariat . . . ," p. 115.

27. For full information about the ILO's Geneva headquarters and country offices, see the ILO's website, at http://www.ilo.org.

28. Elliott, "Getting Beyond No . . . ," p. 203.

29. On how this might be done, see Chapter 16 in this volume.

30. Elliott, "Getting Beyond No . . . ," p. 203.

31. See, for example, Charnovitz, "The Influence of International Labor Standards . . . ."

32. See Chapter 16 in this volume, in which Frank Garcia and Soohyun Jun contend that WTO Article XX may be so interpreted and applied.

33. WTO, *Singapore Ministerial Declaration* (1996), sec. 4.

34. "Labor Summary."

35. WTO, "Joint Communiqué," para. 17.

36. For the full argument, see Krugman and Obstfeld, *International Economics* . . . , p. 26.

37. Elliott, "Getting Beyond No . . . ," p. 188.

38. Anderson, "Environmental and Labor Standards . . . ," p. 244.

39. See, for example, Chapter 16 in this volume.

40. ICFTU, "WTO Ignoring Workers' Rights . . . ."

41. IGTLWF, "Linking Trade and Workers Rights . . . ."

42. The AFL-CIO is a voluntary federation of sixty-four national and international labor unions whose member unions represent 13 million workers. AFL-CIO, "This Is the AFL-CIO."

43. Statement of Barbara Shailor, director, International Affairs Department, AFL-CIO, in Ulewicz, *Monitoring International Labor Standards* . . . , p. 20.

44. See, for example, Lim, "The Social Clause . . . ," secs. 1.0–1.3.

45. Ibid., sec. 1.1 ("Liberalization of International Trade and Capital Flows").

46. The social clause, from the worker's (or advocate's) position, is comprehensively explained in Lim, "The Social Clause. . . ."

47. Ibid., p. 248.

48. Ibid.

49. CRC (1989), art. 43.

50. Ibid.

51. Topics with an obvious or potential link to child labor have included the rights of indigenous children (2003); the private sector as a service provider (2002); violence against children within the family and in school (2001); state violence against children (2000); HIV/AIDS (1998); children with disabilities (1997); the girl child (1995); economic exploitation (1993); and children in armed conflict (1992).

52. ILO C182, art. 12.

53. See Henn, "Child Labor Unions" (quoting Neil Kearney).

54. For additional discussion of this and related points, see Chapter 13 in this volume.

55. IMF, *Articles of Agreement,* art. I(ii).

56. For extended discussion, see Stiglitz, *Globalization and Its Discontents.*

57. See Rogoff, "The IMF Strikes Back."

58. Trenchant publications of criticism have appeared for more than a decade. Among the best are Caufield, *Masters of Illusion* . . . ; Hancock, *Lords of Poverty* . . . ; and Stiglitz, *Globalization and Its Discontents.*

59. World Bank, "The Global Child Labour Program . . . ."

60. The World Bank, the ILO, and UNICEF jointly support a website called "Understanding Children's Work Project," at http://www.ucw-project.org.

61. World Bank, "World Bank Forum on Child Labor . . . ."

62. Education lending increased from $1.488 billion in fiscal year 1999 to $2.349 billion in fiscal 2003, according to World Bank, "Education Lending."

63. See Fallon and Tzannatos, *Child Labor* . . . .

64. Ibid., p. 18.

65. Most of the studies have been posted online at http://www.dol.gov/ilab/media/reports/iclp/main.htm.

66. UNICEF and the ILO jointly prepared an assessment of the effectiveness of the 1995 UNICEF/ILO/Bangladesh Garment Manufacturers' Association memorandum of understanding that removed children from garment factories. The assessment, which lists several lessons learned by the ILO and UNICEF from the experience of the MOU, was made public in 2004. It is available at http://www.ilo.org/public/english/

standards/ipec/index.htm. For an overall assessment, see IPEC, *IPEC Action Against Child Labour* . . . .

67. Among the many reviews of new anti–child labor programs, see US Department of Labor, *By the Sweat and Toil of Children.*

68. For a solid review of scholarship on economics and child labor, see US Department of Labor, *By the Sweat and Toil of Children.*

69. See Boyden, Ling, and Myers, *What Works for Working Children,* pp. 284–345; and Schrage, *Promoting International Worker Rights* . . . , pp. 180–265.

70. For a solid review of scholarship on economics and child labor, see the series of studies of the US Department of Labor, *By the Sweat and Toil of Children.*

71. Ulewicz, *Monitoring International Labor Standards* . . . , contains a helpful summary of arguments in favor of investing in human capital.

72. See IPEC, *Investing in Every Child* . . . .

73. See Stiglitz, *Globalization and Its Discontents;* and Easterly, *The Elusive Quest* . . . .

74. As of May 6, 2005, 153 countries, 86 percent of the ILO's members (177), had ratified ILO C182.

75. See Anderson, "Environmental and Labor Standards . . . ," pp. 245–246; and Elliott, "Getting Beyond No . . . ," p. 201.

6

Translating Standards into Practice: Confronting Local Barriers

Michael F. C. Bourdillon

We are concerned to understand why, at the local level, communities so often resist pressure to adopt international standards and instead continue to tolerate working children in their midst. We are concerned to know the answer to this question particularly in relation to work that is in any way harmful or potentially harmful to children.

Discourse on children's rights has been developed largely in Europe and North America, regions of relative affluence. In Chapter 1 of this volume, Burns Weston and Mark Teerink show how abusive and exploitive child labor[1] impinges on a variety of children's human rights.[2] These rights are interrelated, and few, if any, are independent of the rest. An overriding right in decisions concerning children is that the best interests of the child must be given primary consideration, and for this reason different rights can be in tension and need to be balanced against one another. Poverty complicates this balance. The rights of children to education and leisure must be balanced against their right to material livelihood. Their rights to guidance and protection must be balanced against their right to have a say in decisions that affect their lives. The rights of individual children must be balanced against the rights of the family or community.

An assessment of the best interests of children requires a detailed understanding of the situations in which children live. When interventions on behalf of children's rights meet resistance to change, we must examine both the intervention and the resistance. Broad changes that may seem sensible to outsiders do not always work in the best interests of children when applied to the particular situations in which children must live their lives. If we are to improve the lives of working children, international standards must be adapted to the children, their families, and their communities. Differing values and beliefs about what is best for children constitute a significant obstacle to change.

143

Those who assume they have superior knowledge on how to raise children are unlikely to help children in social and material environments that are very different from their own.

Even where there is widespread consensus about the problem being addressed, as there is about the "worst forms" of child labor, there may be differences relative to what strategies best serve the best interests of children. Poverty and a consequent lack of services for children may make it difficult to remove children from harmful situations with assurance that their plight will not become even worse. Additionally, confusion abounds between paying children for the work they do, on the one hand, and compelling them to work in situations that hinder their health and development, on the other. People resist excluding children from economic activity they do not consider harmful, and people commonly ignore harmful work that is not targeted by international standards as "labor."

At the local level, resistance to the elimination of children's work comes from at least three categories of people. In one category are people who do not wish to lose what they gain from the exploitation of children, whether in financial enterprises or through cheap services. The rights of children need to be asserted and defended against the large number of such employers, who are responsible for the worst abuses of working children. While the motives of such people are clear and need little discussion, it is not always so clear who precisely falls into this category, since their primary motive may be concealed by expressions of concern for the children's needs. Indeed, motives are usually mixed: businesspeople cannot ignore the need for profit even while they may have genuine concern for their child employees.

A second category comprises people who see the advantage of economic activity by children, both to the children and to their families. The range of people in this category is broad, including, among others, families and communities of the children, persons in government and in organizations supporting working children, and indeed some employers. Even when they agree that ideally, children should not work as they do, these people argue that such work is unavoidable when families lack material resources; they see international standards conceived in wealthy countries as impossible to maintain in poorer nations. Such people regard these standards as inappropriate to their cultural values or economic situation, and thus look for ways to circumvent them without incurring a stigma from appearing to support anything that might be called "child labor," which now is widely condemned internationally.

Finally, much resistance comes from children themselves, who either want to work or who do not want their source of livelihood removed or hindered. This phenomenon has not been widely reported in the mainstream press and by organizations advocating the elimination of child labor, and so deserves mention here. The National Movement of Working Children and Adolescents of Peru, for example, produced in 1999 a "Declaration on the

New ILO Convention Concerning Child Labour"[3] in response to the 1999 International Labour Organization Convention (No. 182) Concerning the Prohibition and Immediate Elimination of the Worst Forms of Child Labour (ILO C182).[4] They pointed out that for twenty-five years they had campaigned for the dignity of children working in homes, on the streets, in fields, and in the cities. They campaigned against language that treats work as unacceptable for children and working children as if in need of "rehabilitation." They opposed raising the minimum age of employment and argued that working children are better protected if their work is recognized and legislated for (as adults are protected) than if their work is made illegal and therefore difficult to monitor.

Elsewhere, too, working children have organized themselves to gain recognition as workers. The African Movement of Working Children and Youth[5] asserts a child's right to choose whether or not to work, and decided in 1998 not to participate in the Global March Against Child Labour because its members believed they would be marching against their means of subsistence.[6] A report from Indian working children included complaints about the conditions under which they had to work and the poor pay they received, but the children insisted that they should not be pulled out of work unless better alternatives were available. Children have a right to survive, and if they need to work, government should protect them and see to it that they receive a just wage and humane treatment.[7]

In this chapter, I point to the advantages that children and their adult communities see in economic activity by children, and why they resist efforts to stop children from working. I also note that children are commonly involved in harmful work outside formal employment. I consider these issues with particular reference to my experience and interest in Zimbabwe, and broadly in Africa, where sweatshops for children are rare but where many children are heavily involved in economic activities and other work that interferes with their schooling and social development, and at times harms them physically. I first discuss why relatively wealthy children seek more or less benign forms of employment, raising troubling issues for a broad campaign against child labor. I then discuss the situation of poorer children, whose work is often essential for family livelihood but commonly is harder, longer, and less voluntary. Consideration of the benefits of work will help to answer the key question we are addressing: Why are children still employed in harmful and exploitive forms of labor?

▣ Work and Employment of Children in Relatively Wealthy Contexts

In most cultures, children are expected to work. Children in relatively wealthy families, however, do not need economic activity for their livelihood. For them, paid work is a means of accessing luxury goods and acquiring skills necessary for autonomy. Most unpaid work required of them is intended for their mental development in the context of school. They might be expected to help with household chores as part of their socialization, giving them competence and self-confidence;[8] but time spent on such work is not normally a significant part of their lives, and rarely impinges on schoolwork.

There is a fuzzy line, however, between work in the context of a child's home that is acceptable and work that is harmful and unacceptable. In certain situations, even schoolwork can impinge on the rights of children to social life and recreation and so can be harmful to the health and development of children.[9] Then, schoolwork meets the criterion of "child labor" according to ILO definitions—work that is harmful.

Similarly, and more widely, domestic chores can involve long hours and impinge on schoolwork. This is a particular problem for girls, who often are assigned the bulk of housework not performed by parents. In one fee-paying school catering for middle- and upper-class children in Zimbabwe, teachers investigating problems with children's schoolwork found several cases of parents, away from home, leaving their teenage schoolchildren in charge of shopping, housework, and care of younger siblings. In one case, a girl student was sent to live with and care for a sick relative. Such work interferes with children's development, yet because no formal employment is involved, it is not covered by legislation on the employment of children, and in civil society people associate it rather with cultural responsibilities.[10] Many cultures take for granted that children should contribute to the running of the home. Work in the home is often justified as training the children for future life, and particularly as training girls for their assumed domestic role in marriage.[11]

Employment in light work, though often called "child labor," is commonly more benign. Many children in developed countries obtain employment, frequently against legislation controlling the employment of children. Resistance to legislation outlawing this kind of work comes largely from the children themselves, who wish to work for an income, with the support of their families when they regard the work as benign. Ben White has pointed out that in the Netherlands the majority of children in the fourteen- to sixteen-year-old age range, and many younger children as well, break the laws that are supposed to protect them by working at jobs that are technically prohibited.[12] In Britain, employment for pay appears to be a majority experience by the time children reach age sixteen, and legislation to control such employment is largely ineffective.[13] Several studies of working children in the United States point to the benefits of light employment as a standard feature of adolescent development.[14]

In Virginia Morrow's British study,[15] the paid and unpaid work of children varied from helping in family businesses to informal contract jobs such as baby-sitting. The children gave a variety of reasons for seeking employment, the principal one being that they wanted to earn spending money. Children are under pressure from peers and advertisers to have cash for consumer goods and for leisure activities. Even in the developed world, children's income can relieve pressure on families struggling to maintain lifestyles on stagnant incomes.[16] Kathleen Call argues that both recreation and work can provide relief from stress in the home.[17]

Many children list other benefits from paid employment.[18] It gives them confidence and experience for future work. The work is enjoyable. Children work for the benefit of charities. They acquire a sense of independence and responsibility in their work, a sense that becomes stronger as they grow older.

Light employment does not necessarily interfere with schoolwork. The context and type of work are relevant: while rural children typically spend more hours in employment than do urban children, their schoolwork often suffers less. While studies in Scotland have shown a negative correlation between employment of more than twenty hours of work per week and school performance (due partly to the differing interests of children and their academic inclinations),[19] they also have shown a positive correlation between employment of less than five hours weekly and certain categories of school performance.[20] The work may be beneficial to the children in other ways also. A study of schoolchildren in Lagos, Nigeria, has shown that, while there was a small negative correlation between school performance and economic work, working children were overrepresented in leadership positions in the schools.[21]

Even in relatively wealthy contexts, however, there are problems, both direct and indirect, in employing children under age eighteen. Much work that children do (such as delivering newspapers) is unskilled and poorly paid, allowing employers to avoid expensive adult labor.[22] The employer usually dictates terms and wages. Legal minimum wages are often lower for children than for adults, and are sometimes not defined for children. Although children may initially be happy to take on a little light work, once employed they can be pressured to work longer hours. Furthermore, the work can interfere with schooling indirectly. When children earn increased incomes through their work, they have money to spend on activities such as frequenting nightclubs or consuming recreational drugs that can distract from schooling; employment sometimes correlates with increased alcohol and drug abuse among children.[23] A degree of independence obtained from employment, together with the time and energy it consumes, can lead to tensions and even conflict within families.[24]

We need to balance the harm that can come from employment against the rights of children to the benefits that can come to them and their right to have a say in decisions affecting their lives. Apart from material gains and useful experience that children can acquire from work, employment can be a source of self-esteem and value in the eyes of others.

■ Work and Employment of Children in Poorer Contexts

The issues become more acute when we consider the situation of poorer children, particularly children in less developed countries. On the one hand, their families have greater need of their labor, both for day-to-day living and for any income they can earn. On the other hand, the labor required of and available to children is more demanding and more likely to interfere with education and social activities. For the majority of working children, work is an essential part of life, perceived as conveying important benefits for the children and their families, and sometimes even as being enjoyable.[25] It is from these families, primarily, that resistance to efforts aimed at eliminating children's work arises.

In subsistence economies throughout the ages, children have contributed their labor to the family livelihood insofar as they have been able. Children help with household chores and on the family farm as soon as they are physically and mentally able to do so. Children as young as five years old have been observed herding domestic animals, caring for even younger children, and helping with the cooking. This kind of family work frees older people for productive tasks. Where families have specific skills, such as music or healing or the making of crafts, such children learn the specialized skills and participate in the family enterprise from an early age. These patterns continue in contemporary countries where the bulk of the population remains in agriculture.[26]

Although the roles of children change as they move into a monetary economy and a formal system of schooling, expectations persist that children should contribute to the family's needs. In small family businesses, children are often expected to help. In Zimbabwe, we find children helping their parents in such activities as contract agriculture, vending, and various crafts.[27] In England, we find them helping in a retail store or other family business.[28] The children, like the adults, take for granted that they should be involved in this kind of work.

Among the urban poor, families are obliged to deploy all their members to earn enough for survival. In a study of a Harare suburb, we found young girls helping their mothers run informal vending stalls.[29] In rural areas, we found children spending hours before and after school in family entrepreneurial activities.[30] Such children recognize the importance of their work to their families, while acknowledging that it interferes with their schoolwork. Although these children take on paid employment primarily to help meet basic family needs, some children mention other benefits. Of children involved in stitching footballs in Pakistan, 81 percent said that the reason for this work was to meet basic household needs, 11 percent mentioned skills, and 25 percent mentioned personal spending money.[31]

Apart from generating income, the services of children are required to help with running the household. In poorer households, children have no option but to perform even the tasks they dislike. They collect water and firewood, clean the home and utensils, cook, care for younger children, and work in the fields and with domestic animals. These tasks may take up as much as forty hours weekly. Girls, who shoulder the bulk of the housework tasks that children perform, have less free time than their brothers; many have little free time at all.[32]

One of the strategies of poor households to maintain their livelihood is the fostering of children with relatives or even friends.[33] In such arrangements, children receive shelter and food, usually in exchange for services. Sometimes the reason is insecurity in their parental home, or the movement of one or both parents in search of employment. Teenage children, especially girls, are often fostered out to relatives or friends needing domestic help, in particular to single or elderly relatives. Such coping strategies are important for the families concerned, and may benefit the children by providing a home and adult care when their parents are unable so to provide. Particularly in the context of HIV/AIDS, extended kinship networks become overstretched and children have to accept foster care wherever they can. The line is not always clear, however, between chores that can reasonably be demanded of children and exploitive demands on their labor; as I observe below, the fostering arrangements can result in severe abuse, transforming a child into a virtual domestic slave.[34]

Children often have to take on the roles and responsibilities of adults, particularly in communities affected by HIV/AIDS or war. In some groups, there are not enough productive adults to care for all the children. In Zimbabwe in 1997, around 35,000 households were headed by persons under age twenty and over 3,000 households by persons under fifteen years of age.[35]

Even when they have adult support, children sometimes have heavy responsibilities toward their households. In one case, for instance, a fourteen-year-old girl and her three younger siblings, whose parents had recently died, were taken in by her grandmother. The grandmother had no income and could not grow enough food for the whole family. At age fourteen, the girl entered an "earn-and-learn" school, where she earned money working on a tea plantation and with that money paid for her own schooling. With the rest of her income, she paid for provisions and schooling for her younger brother and sisters.[36]

In such situations, children must work so that their families can live. While work may interfere with schooling and recreation, it brings material benefits to the children and their families, and often other benefits for the children, such as pride in their achievement and a sense of responsibility toward their family. Children in an Indonesian textile factory did not appear to regard their work as a burden; it brought them both wages and friends and they saw no reason why children should not be allowed to work.[37]

The benefits of paid work for wealthier children often apply to poorer children. The experience of earning and handling money can be useful for later life, as is the training in self-reliance. The luxury goods that children can buy from their wages are even more outstanding among poor children. The children who worked long hours on the tea plantations were proud to show off their fine clothes when they visited their families in the surrounding villages, clothes that children without employment could only dream about.

Independence can be important for poor children also. One girl I knew was able to escape family pressure to marry an elderly friend of her father's by going to an earn-and-learn school. Children at such schools spoke appreciatively of not having to answer to others for their performance and choices of activity.

The status that working children acquire from their employment is easily overlooked. Ellen Scrumpf points out that in some cases in Norway, industrial labor brought children from isolation in the fields into protective factory environments, providing them with skills that would benefit them through their life.[38] Fatima Zalami's 1998 study in Morocco pointed to advantages girls gained from working in the clothing industry, such as access to skills, financial independence, and respect within their families—even while many of them worked as a result of discrimination against girls when they were taken out of school to help the family.[39] When employers were pressured into removing children from their work force, many poor families suffered from loss of income, and many girls were devastated at suddenly losing both income and status.

Much of the language against child labor assumes that employers are simply exploiting a cheap and pliable form of labor. While this is frequently the case, some employers take on children in response to requests from the children and their communities. This is illustrated by earn-and-learn schools in southeastern Zimbabwe, which provided an opportunity for education—and superior facilities—to children who could not otherwise afford it. The controlling tea company ran the schools on condition that pupils contracted to work on the estate, and the company gave priority to local children at the request of the local communities. While there was justifiable criticism of these schools on grounds of long hours and certain conditions of work, the surrounding communities appreciated the standard of education they provided. Virtually all the children were there by choice. One of the pupils had previously attended a more relaxed day school, but often missed school at the beginning of term for want of school fees, and he noticed that the estate schools had much better examination results. Despite the heavy workload on the tea estates, he therefore asked his father to allow him to transfer. The company paid the children the same rates for their work as they paid the adults, and subsidized their schools and their meals besides. This was not particularly cheap labor.

Many of the children in these schools found in them their only chance for secondary education. They described how they had dropped out of school for lack of funds until they were accepted into one of the estate schools. The work on the estates undoubtedly interfered with their schoolwork, particularly in the peak tea-picking season when both teachers and pupils complained of the problem of dozing in class. Nevertheless, without these institutions the children would have had no schooling at all, and their right to education must be balanced against the resources available to them.

Employers sometimes express altruistic reasons for employing children, especially when they employ their parents, who want their children to maximize the family income.[40] Some commercial farmers in Zimbabwe responded to requests by children and their families for employment during the school holidays by giving the children tasks for wages. In many cases, where whole families are employed, the wages paid to children are the same, or very little lower, than those paid to adults for the same work.[41] Expressions of altruism cannot be an excuse for employing cheap and pliant labor. In some cases, the reason why families need income from their children is that the wages paid to the adults are insufficient to support a family. The point remains that when children need income, we should not be overeager to condemn those who provide them with a chance to earn it.

Harmful Work

While work can be both necessary and beneficial to children, we need to consider why so many children are engaged in work that is harmful to their development, and in exploitive work that brings them little in the way of benefits. In some cases, the work is clearly harmful, and the issue is one of law enforcement. In many cases, however, it is not so clear when work becomes harmful; benign forms of work can slide into harmful forms of work. We need to understand how this happens.

Profit. One reason why children find themselves in harmful work is that unscrupulous adults exploit them for their own gain and with little consideration of the interests of the children. There are adults who trade in children for virtual slavery in cheap labor or for the sex trade. This may include blatant kidnapping or persuading poor parents to let their children go through false promises about their children's future. Impoverished parents may give up their children to child traffickers who promise a better life for children elsewhere, but once out of their homes, the children find themselves enslaved and abused.[42] As in all criminal activity, the incomes available prompt some people to take part in it and others, including sometimes politicians and those who should be protecting children, to turn a blind eye.

Off the northeast coast of Sumatra, for example, about two and a half miles or more from shore, thousands of children are trapped on small fishing rigs where they work for long hours with poor food and pay, insufficient sleep, and no recreation or education. Sometimes children are lured into this employment without the knowledge of their parents, with promises of good food and high pay from brokers. It is assumed that some of the owners of these rigs have contacts in high places, and the practice continues in spite of various campaigns to bring it to an end.[43]

In Harare in Zimbabwe, street children are heavily involved in sexual activities. With rare exception, girls cannot survive on the streets without the support of men or boys, and this support is given in exchange for sex.[44] Both boys and girls find it hard to reject the comforts of a bath, a good meal, and a bed in exchange for sex with well-off businesspeople. Children find places to sleep by befriending underpaid security guards of various premises; the security guards increase their incomes by offering the sexual services of the children. Certain adults claim to look after a group of children but make their living by selling the sexual services of children in their care.

Children may choose illegal and hazardous occupations for quick and easy incomes. Girls and boys are attracted to prostitution, drug trafficking, or thievery (whether on an individual basis or as members of teams) by high returns in cash and goods. Poor children may undertake such activities in a desperate bid to find sustenance for themselves and their families; others may want luxuries. Scavenging on rubbish heaps is dangerous work for children; they are exposed to a variety of infections, to sharp and dangerous objects that cause festering wounds, to extremes of weather, and to disorders from poisons and from eating leftover foods. Yet six hours working on the rubbish dumps of Manila can earn a child more than an adult earns from ten hours of work in a factory.[45]

More subtle forms of exploitation—domestic work. In developing countries, another reason for resistance to change is that working children are exploited frequently in subtle ways in which the rights and wrongs are not plainly evident. The trafficking of children, for example, may not be blatant and may not be recognized as trafficking by people participating in it. In Zimbabwe, certain people who have connections with the country's poor rural areas negotiate for urban families to obtain child domestic workers from these areas. Through these connections, the rural families believe that their children will be looked after, while the urban families acquire cheap and pliant labor, trustworthy because of the child's total dependence on the employer. Indeed, children from poor families may benefit from having regular meals and opportunities for education in an urban school. Often, however, the brokers play on the common strategy of fostering out children from poor families, entice the children and their families with false promises of high wages, and take no responsibility for the children once they are employed.

The child may be welcomed into a caring family, and children so treated often express gratitude to their employers for improving their lives and resist being sent home. The situation of such a child mingles patronage and employment in a way that cannot always be disentangled. Employers and brokers point to the benefits the children receive, and talk about the child being treated as one of the family.[46] Since they regard the children as part of the family, they fail to notice the children's needs for time off or for recreation and socialization with equals.

Discourse about "becoming family" conceals the right of children having their employment defined in terms of hours and duties.[47] In practice, they are on call from early morning to late at night, and rarely get formal time off. Their living conditions are frequently not the same as those of other family members; they may sleep in the kitchen or a living area so that their hours of sleep are limited to when no other household member wants to use the space. Often, child domestics work in exchange only for food and accommodation; often they may be referred to in derogatory terms and beaten or abused in other ways; frequently girls in particular are sexually abused. Sometimes, indeed, children are imprisoned in their place of work during the day to ensure they do not take things out of the house, or simply run away.[48] Rarely do employers attend to the education of these children.

Employment of this kind is not legally recognized and therefore not formally controlled. It is rare to find a code on the employment of child domestic workers that employers can consult. Even employers who genuinely take responsibility for the welfare of the children they employ receive no guidance regarding the problems children face and the difficulties they may have in airing their problems. Consequently, an institution that is perceived as beneficial to the children, and often is so, becomes easily a source of abuse.

Moreover, this form of labor is commonly hidden. In Zimbabwe, for example, it is illegal to employ children under fifteen years of age, and as a consequence people are not open about employing child domestic workers. The children are addressed with fictive kinship terms, and to the casual visitor may appear to be relatives, perhaps poor relatives informally fostered by richer kin. Children who are afraid of returning to an impoverished home uphold the pretense of kinship and do not speak out against the way they are being treated. In any case, they have no adult support and often no one to speak to in confidence.

Foster parents may exploit children in a similar way. They perceive fostered children as family, simply doing the normal chores of children. In practice, when families find themselves burdened with increasing numbers of children (as often happens in the context of HIV/AIDS), their resources are stretched and the children are then obliged to contribute to family livelihood. The foster parents are reluctant to see their own children deprived in any way, and the foster children frequently receive fewer and cheaper resources than do children born into the family. They are treated as family in that they are not assigned formal hours of work and are never paid for the work they do, but much work may be expected of them nonetheless. In the course of my study of working children in southeastern Zimbabwe, I met one adolescent boy whose kin were openly resentful of having to support him. They demanded that he work long hours, unpaid, on the family fields. When able to do so, he preferred to spend the odd day working on a coffee estate, where at least he would earn something to spend on himself. Another orphaned adolescent was taken in by one of his mother's kindly patrons. Both the adolescent and the patron spoke of him being a member of the family, with full access to the home and its resources. Unlike the other children of the household, however, he worked hard on his patron's lands, and he was constantly running errands for his patron. In town, children are sometimes sent by their stepparents into the streets to earn their keep, and beaten if they do not bring home sufficient income.

Additionally, a change in a patron's household can result in well-intentioned fostering becoming harmful labor. A kindly pastor in a rural community offered to take in three street children from Harare. Initially all went well, and then the pastor died. The surviving family treated the children harshly, demanding much work and giving them little in return, until one of the children managed to get back to Harare to return to the streets and seek help for the others.

Other factors conducive to harmful work by children. There are several specific factors that may lead children into potentially harmful work situations.

Poverty. Children in poor communities must work long hours often because light work will not meet the needs of their families. Where the need is great, children have little choice over the type and manner of their work. Parents who encourage—or force—their children to take up employment at an early age are usually from the poorest strata of society.

Children from families in difficult circumstances often must work within the home whether or not they are formally employed outside the home. Laina is an example from a poor rural household in Zimbabwe. Her mother was in the hospital when we met the girl. Consequently, at age sixteen, Laina had to do all her mother's household chores, amounting to over thirty hours a week, which left her exhausted for her schoolwork and unable to concentrate in class.[49] We have met teenage children spending long hours taking on the tasks of a sick mother. Catherine was eleven when she dropped out of school to run her mother's stall while the mother recuperated from illness and the elder sister completed her secondary schooling.[50]

In Harare, we find increasing numbers of children on the streets as unemployment increases and the economy collapses. Guardians and occasionally parents push children to earn on the streets to supplement household incomes in whatever way they can.

Much of the economic activity of children occurs in the informal economy, which constitutes between one-third and two-thirds of the economies of most developing countries.[51] In the informal sector, people commonly work long hours for small returns; their work is a survival strategy (particularly of the urban poor), often providing goods and services for poor people whose inability to pay limits the margins of profit that can be charged. When people in this sector employ helpers, whether children or adults, the long hours and low wages reflect problems with the economic environment rather than a deliberate exploitation. Regulatory labor laws are seldom observed, and employers often earn little more than their low-paid employees. Since such activities constitute a survival strategy, children can be prevented from taking part only if other sources of survival are made available. For example, if children or their families can be paid for schoolwork, school becomes attractive. When the governor of Brazilia introduced a scheme that paid poor families a minimum wage if none of their children missed school more than twice a month, absenteeism fell from 7 to 0.5 percent, and repetition rates in school dropped by 10 percent.[52]

Lack of alternative forms of income. One reason why poor children are involved in low-paid and exploitive employment is the lack of alternative sources of income, in particular employment under conditions that can be controlled and monitored. For children who need an income, child unemployment rather than child labor is the major problem.[53]

In Chapter 15, Susan Bissell discusses problems of child textile workers in Bangladesh when they were thrown out of work.[54] In Zimbabwe, one of the results of the international campaign against child labor is that exporting tea estates raised the minimum age for entry into their earn-and-learn schools to fifteen. Children who need income to help them get through school must now wait two or three years until they reach the minimum age. While they are thus waiting, some are able to obtain lower wages in small-scale agriculture. One of the recommendations of child domestic workers in Dakar, Senegal, is that employment opportunities be created for them in their home communities so that they are not compelled to leave the protective environment of their homes.[55]

At a workshop in Harare, there were representatives from children working in informal mining for long hours, in dangerous underground conditions, and for low pay.[56] They pointed out that they had to take on this work or starve, and they appealed to be allowed to work in the formal underground mines where pay and safety are much better. Such underground mining has been designated internationally as one of the worst forms of child labor. To the children, however, it appeared very much better than what they had.

Our study of street girls in Harare showed that girls are more restricted than boys in earning money. Boys often derive reasonable incomes from helping to park and guard cars, controlling queues for transport, and mobile vending. These activities are considered unsuitable for girls, whose principal ready source of income is sex.[57] One way of relieving children from having to work in hazardous conditions and for poor pay is to provide work with better pay and less harsh conditions.

Lack of recognition. I have pointed out that, commonly, the employment of child domestic workers is not formally recognized as labor and that this fact leads to significant problems for the children involved. Among these is the fact that such children have no one to whom they can complain about unjust treatment by their employers without risk of losing their jobs. Lack of recognition serves, thus, to impede progressive change.

A contributing factor to this lack of recognition, however ironic, is national legislation that bans the employment of children. In many countries, the illegality of employing children means that their work, domestic and otherwise, is seldom formally acknowledged,[58] and it is because of this disregard that, for example, children in the streets—such as bootblacks and petty vendors—become particularly vulnerable to extortion by the police and other authorities. Indeed, for lack of formal recognition, their work is sometimes denigrated and they are said to be in need of "rehabilitation." The children see as work all activities that support their livelihood and that of their families, whether they be parking or washing cars, scavenging in dustbins, or entreating passersby to give them money. Society, however, labels such activities as parasitic or unproductive and consequently shuns them, commonly to the detriment of those engaged in them. Society denigrates, even criminalizes, the survival strategies of the poor,[59] and in so doing fails to acknowledge them as legitimate and worthy of responsible attention.

Poor access to services. Welfare services needed by children are typically geared for adults only. As a result, abused or exploited children often have no one to call upon for help or relief, and their concerns are left unheard. Progressive change is thus made the more difficult.

The situation of young caregivers is illustrative.[60] In Zimbabwe, for example, older children may be sent to relatives who need care in sickness, an arrangement that, in the absence of adequate welfare services, allows for the care of adults sick with HIV/AIDS. There are other benefits. Children often say positive things about their caring roles. One girl spoke of the privilege of getting to know her grandmother before she died. Such work sometimes offers a different and privileged kind of education.

At the same time, benefits such as these help to disguise the adversities involved. A child may have to drop schooling to care for the sick parent or other relative. Child caregivers also sometimes complain of having little opportunity for recreation and socialization with their peers. Rarely, however, is their plight acknowledged, let alone treated. When child caregivers and other children try to access social services on their own, they usually are met with a brusqueness that is daunting. If they are in some way deviant, like street children, they have little hope of sympathy if and when they approach officials for help. Thus they tend to be marginalized or overlooked. In a country like Zimbabwe, even adults have difficulty in accessing government services, which are typified by much queuing and long processing with little sympathy from officials who are poorly paid and often overworked in very cramped conditions and with insufficient resources at their disposal.

The caring work of children is widespread and often unrecognized. In Britain, about 25 percent of children live in households where at least one member has chronic illness or disability and needs care, and many thousands of children provide substantial care to them within their households. Although unpaid, the work is similar to the paid work of community care assistants.[61] In addition to providing care to the persons in need, these children typically provide domestic work and often care for younger siblings,[62] and this caring role restricts opportunities for social activities and sometimes stigmatizes the children among their peers, especially when they are dealing with mental illness or with a disease like HIV/AIDS. Also, it creates widespread problems for education, with children missing school and being prevented from partaking in further education, thereby limiting their opportunities in later life and, like harmful employment, entrapping them in a cycle of poverty.[63]

Children are pushed into this kind of work, and largely unacknowledged for it, partly because welfare services are under pressure and not geared for access by children, especially underprivileged poor children. While a number of projects designed specifically with child caregivers in mind have improved the situation in Britain, young caregivers still are much less likely to be able to access social services than are adult caregivers.[64] Government welfare is not sufficient to meet the demands placed upon it, there is heavy competition for any welfare that is offered, and where resources are scarce it is politically easier to ignore the children and favor the adults. Thus, with little chance of winning access to welfare on their own, it is easier for children to earn their own livelihood—and usually, as it happens, in the informal sector, where they tend not to be a statistic.[65]

Inadequate and inappropriate education. While governments provide formal education for children, seldom do they adapt it to the needs of working children—such as children in Zimbabwe who must work to raise the funds they need for their formal schooling. The result is a perpetuation of disadvantaged life that changes little if at all over time. Usually mediated by adults in cooperation with parents or other caregivers who arrange for the placement of children in school, formal educational systems are rarely accessible by children who lack support of this kind.

Conditions such as these challenge the 1989 United Nations Convention on the Rights of the Child (CRC),[66] which repeatedly affirms the right to education[67] and states explicitly that children shall be protected from work that is likely to interfere with their education.[68] This right to education is often taken to mean, erroneously, a right to *formal* education, such that work should not interfere with the formal school system. Where there is a clash between education and work, therefore, it is easy to condemn work rather than consider the failure of educational systems to meet the needs of working children. As African working children put it, however: "We should not only go to school, but school should also come to us, in order to learn more."[69]

Positive initiatives do exist. In the state of Karnataka, India, for example, the formal state schools once required children to be present from 9:00 A.M. to 5:00 P.M. These hours did not allow time sufficient for economic activities before or after and therefore were impossible for the many poor children who needed to work to survive. Working children were thus denied access to knowledge and skills that might enable them to escape from their situation of poverty and harmful work. In October 2002, however, Karnataka state responded by proposing a system of "flexi schools" intended to meet the temporal needs of working children, including flexible timetables and schedules, and also stipends for children losing earning time. In so doing, it lowered a barrier to progressive change.

In Harare, Zimbabwe, schools in the poor urban areas often operate in shifts, with some children attending in the mornings and others in the afternoons. Children are able to perform their economic activities during the other half of the day. The Zimbabwean education system, however, takes no account of the agricultural seasons when determining the dates of school terms and vacations in the rural areas. Teachers in rural schools often excuse absences when they believe children are being held back by parents for essential work and falsely record them as present in the school register. While this practice demonstrates an appealing empathy on the part of the teachers, such absences are not monitored, such that parents can make, on occasion, excessive demands of their children.

Apart from the timing of formal education, there is the issue of its quality and its relevance to the lives of the poor. In many countries, public education is overcrowded and lacks facilities. Teachers become demoralized having to teach large classes with inadequate books and other resources. Children and parents complain that teachers are lazy or stupid, and that they beat the children too frequently.[70] And children drop out of school due to, among other reasons, bad treatment from teachers and other pupils, inability to cover expenses, even pressure from adults to earn an income.

Another factor is the perception by both children and adults that school education is of no use to them, that it will not win them employment at the end. Accordingly, we find a child working at her mother's vending stall, claiming that, unlike school, this work is teaching her to make an adequate living; or a boy working in his father's sewing business, happy that he is learning a profitable craft, unlike his peers still at school. According to a 1995 report, many mothers in India thought girls should learn something useful by working rather than waste their time going to school.[71] When child workers in

Paraguay were asked what they liked most about their lives, the most popular response was their jobs, well ahead of school.[72] In Lima, Peru, a third of a study sample of working children did not prioritize between work and school: both were considered important, but about half said they would not like to stop working.[73] In a study of working children's perspectives in four countries, 69–79 percent preferred to combine work and school; the remainder in Central America and the Philippines largely preferred school only, but work only in Bangladesh and Ethiopia.[74]

One of the problems with school is the curriculum. Much formal education derives from the European middle class, often ill adapted to the local environment. Consequently, it focuses on obtaining certificates rather than on understanding the world in which children live. When on occasion street children have been offered more practical types of education in which the benefits are clear, they have responded with enthusiasm. Child domestic workers in Senegal were happy to give of their sparse free time to courses that would improve their capability and status in their work.[75]

Some analysts have advocated compulsory education as a way to remove children from hazardous work.[76] Compulsion, however, removes potential options and strategies from poor people. Improving the quality and relevance of education would give the poor people an option worth choosing. An alternative to formal schooling, for example, is training in specific crafts or skills (some children regard their work in this way), which can be of permanent benefit. But when providing for such training, one must take caution; though authorized by law, it sometimes can be used to justify the employment of children and potentially, therefore, their exploitation. In the gemstone industry in India, for example, an apprentice is not paid for the first two years, and in subsequent years receives a fifth to a third of what adults would be paid for the same work.[77]

Cultural values. In the contemporary, globalized world, it is fashionable to consider cultures as equal and not to be criticized except from within. On the other hand, some cultures accept the bonding and slavery of children, allowing minimal if any rights, and thus we criticize. If our criticism is to be effective, however, it must be made with sensitivity to, and understanding of, the local situation, including local values and needs. People are understandably defensive when their culture is criticized. Frequently in Zimbabwe I have heard the complaint that the campaign against child labor is an attempt by the "first world" to impose its values and their conditions on other countries without understanding local cultures and the needs of children and their families. Such a perception avoids scrutinizing cultural practices that may hurt children. So another reason for resistance to change is that people perceive that their cultures are being denigrated; they are being criticized, they believe—sometimes rightly—without valid justification or sensitivity.[78]

One aspect of culture that outsiders are assumed not to understand comprises the strong ties of family and kin. African cultures, it is said, emphasize the group rather than the individual, such that individual interests are subordinated to the interests of the family. The strength of family ties provides security for children within the family, and the value that children place on their work often relates to their commitment to their families and to the value their parents place on the incomes they bring to the family.[79]

On the other hand, children sometimes assume heavy responsibilities under this system, and when family support breaks down children are left vulnerable. In many cultures, children are regarded as belonging to, even the property of, the family, and their interests are subordinated to family interests. They can be bonded to pay family debts or as security for loans. Girls can be made to marry a benefactor to the family. In other words, discourse on the rights of children has not reached many people, or it is dismissed as belonging to foreign cultures.

A 1995 study in India pointed out that parents often believe that children are born to serve and support them, seeing nothing wrong in children not being in school or not being able to play.[80] We find parents in Zimbabwe commenting that children are there to work and relieve adults of their burden. A boy earning income in contract work was also at the beck and call of his father and his father's elder brothers, none of whom had children to call upon; and though he was doing over thirty hours of work per week during the school term, neither the boy nor the adults thought to question the demands made on him.[81] A girl might be assigned to keep house for a kinsperson who has no child to call upon; and parents say that, as a matter of cultural obligation, they cannot refuse a request for such assistance from kin, especially in the case of a sick relative.

Culture also sometimes dictates that certain activities are the domain of children. Many domestic chores are considered the domain of girls, although boys may have to help in the absence of girls. In pastoral societies, herding is the work of boys. When I was living in a rural Shona village over thirty years ago, one man herded his cattle himself while his children went to school, but for this he was rewarded with much laughter from the rest of the community. Now, school might have a higher priority in people's perceptions, but herding cattle is still children's work. In one case, a family earned much of its income from hiring out draught oxen, and leading them was children's work, the two eldest children often having several hours of work with the family's cattle before they went to school.[82] On a visit to a rural school, the teachers alerted me to the fact that attendance was poor that day because children were bringing family animals to visiting veterinary services. A man drinking through the morning at a bar explained without shame that his children were taking his cattle to be treated; this was their task and so they had to miss school that day.[83]

Related to the importance of belonging to a family is a lack of responsibility toward people outside it. When children are abused, outsiders are reluctant to interfere. When we were researching rural child workers, many of the adult community were quick to point out children who were being overworked and exploited.[84] They did not like what was happening to the children, but did nothing about it since they were in no way related to the families concerned and consequently felt that they were unable to intrude on family affairs. In some cases, the children were employees and not members of the family; but they were given fictive kinship names that, in the eyes of their neighbors, put them in the family arena.

There were formal structures that should have provided some protection for the children. Local authorities affirmed their responsibility for children in their domain, especially orphans. In practice, however, their concern for children depended on their relationships with relevant adults, and children of people who had not previously shown adequate deference to the authorities could expect little support. Where mutual cooperation exists between families, it is based on reciprocity between the family heads. Loyalty to the community is not strong; still less is loyalty to the government or the state.

A culture that emphasizes the family to the exclusion of the broader community is likely to emphasize also the authority of the head of the family. This reinforces the authority of adults over children. Those who control household wealth can neglect women and children and drive them into poverty, which in turn drives the children to excessive and sometimes harmful work. We found street girls trading sex whose problems started when their mothers were expelled from their marital homes.[85]

Related to adult control over children is the perception that children are ignorant and unable to make decisions. The incompetence attributed to children—and often accepted by them—is largely determined by cultural expectations and norms, which in turn are influenced by the interests of different groups in society. In industrialized societies with established school systems, children are deemed incapable of serious contributions to society: their role is to learn. In other societies, elders and particularly male elders justify their authority by pointing to their knowledge gained from experience, with the knowledge of schoolchildren dismissed as "book knowledge," not relevant to practical issues. Thus we find the heads of farming households simply telling their children what to do in the fields and the children complaining that they do boring work, that they are taught nothing, and that the knowledge they have gained from school is ignored. The assumed incompetence of schoolchildren sometimes protects them from labor in the competitive world, which may reinforce their incompetence in certain areas. The assumed incompetence of working children may be used to justify very low wages. It also can undermine children's self-esteem and job satisfaction.

Sometimes adults justify making children work, whether in school or any other place, by cultural perceptions of what is good for children, and particularly in relation to their preparation for life as adults. While there is widespread agreement that children need to discipline themselves and to develop skills that will help them later in life, the argument sometimes leads to work that hinders the child's general development, as when excessive pressure is put on children to excel in schoolwork, or to star in some sporting activity—or to take on excessive economic activity. In some societies, such perceptions relate to perceptions of social status. High-status people sometimes regard manual labor as appropriate for children of low status, perhaps because they belong to particular disadvantaged ethnic groups, or because of their descent from slaves or other marginalized persons.[86] In India, for example, such perceptions may result from the caste system; employers of bonded labor, to some extent supported by bureaucrats, believe that the social system depends on low-caste children working rather than going to school.[87] They argue that, if the children of poor families do not work, the social structure will break down. This is no easy barrier for child rights to overcome.

Lack of political will. Occasionally political leaders take a share of profits resulting from the exploitation of children, or are socially associated with the profiteers, and consequently fail to enforce legislation that should protect children. In weak economies and where democratic institutions are fragile, caring for marginalized children is often low among the priorities of those in power. Indeed, officials are often poorly paid and sometimes supplement their salaries by exploiting the people they are supposed to be serving.

There is another dimension to the failure to enforce protective legislation. Throughout the world, political discourse is often concerned more with persuasion than with conveying accurate information. When politicians sign conventions and pass legislation, therefore, we need to be alert to true intentions of the politicians so as to understand better the hurdles that must be surmounted locally to enhance children's human rights in the realm of work.

In fairness, it must also be acknowledged that sometimes the lack of political will works in the interests of children. In developing countries, politicians depend not only on their citizens but, as well, on outsiders for personal support or support for their countries; indeed, their citizens sometimes have little power over them. Such politicians are consequently under pressure to appease the values of these outsiders. In terms of aid, it thus is important to show concern for the welfare of children—for example, through signing and ratifying appropriate conventions and supporting them with policy statements and legislation to match.[88] In less public situations, however, the same politicians may indicate privately that the implementation of such policies must take account of local situations, reflecting their perception that it is not always in the interests of children to prevent them from earning an income.

▪ Conclusion

There remain situations in which children are endangered or seriously hurt by their work. We cannot tolerate such situations. We cannot allow children to choose them. We cannot allow, for example, children to trade their sex in a context of widespread HIV/AIDS.

More frequently, children find themselves involved in work that interferes with their physical, social, and mental development because they find themselves in situations where such work is the best option available to them. But they find themselves required to do excessive work also because of the difficulty of drawing boundaries between beneficial and harmful work. Both children and adults see advantages in economic activity for children, but at what stage does this become exploitive and abusive? People value strong family ties, but at what stage do these detract from the rights of children? Informal fostering can help poor children, but at what stage does this become domestic servitude? Children rightly care for disabled relatives, but how much should they reasonably do? Talk about the elimination of child labor in a manner that focuses on the interests of employers and on discouraging them from employing children does not resolve these questions, and is consequently frequently ignored. If we want to help working children, we need to find better options for them, not take away the ones they have chosen to survive; and if we are to do this effectively, we must take their opinions seriously. If we listen to the children, we focus less on formal employment and more on how children are treated, even within the confines of private homes and families.

In other words, while a reduction of poverty levels will result in fewer children needing to be economically active, the economic circumstances and contributions of children should be acknowledged and respected in the meanwhile. If we wish to break down resistance to change, we need to focus not on work and its payment; we need, rather, to focus on the needs of children and their families who supply the labor, on why each resists demands for change, and from these vantage points, on the exact harm we wish to eliminate from children's lives and therefore the exact rights of children we want to ensure. This is an inquiry that requires us to question assumptions about what to expect from children, both in types of work that children can and cannot reasonably do at different ages and in how much or little time they can reasonably spend on work. The kinds and amount of work children can handle depend on their social environment as much as on their physical age. Their individual needs must be balanced against their service to their communities. It is right to recognize and acknowledge the value of children's work. In the end, it makes for greater transparency and thus helps us to overcome the barriers to change in our struggle to eliminate the harm done to children in so much of their work.

■ Notes

I am grateful to many people for responding to questions and helping with criticisms and ideas, in particular Sarah Bachman, Jo Boyden, Julian Kramer, William Myers, Nandana Reddy, and Ben White.

   1. In the introduction and elsewhere in this volume, notably Chapter 2, the term "child labor" is used to mean "work done by children that is harmful to them because it is abusive, exploitive, hazardous, or otherwise contrary to their best interests—a subset

of a larger class of children's work, some of which may be compatible with children's best interests (variously expressed as 'beneficial,' 'benign,' or 'harmless' children's work)." In this chapter, I depart from this usage because I believe that, no matter how carefully one defines the term, many readers will understand it differently. For this reason, and to avoid denigrating children's work, I avoid the term where possible. When I do use it, I do so in an unrestricted sense, modified by qualifying adjectives as needed.

2. See pp. 3–6.

3. *Declaration by the National Movement* . . . .

4. ILO, *Convention* (No. 182) *Concerning the Prohibition and Immediate Elimination of the Worst Forms of Child Labour* (1999) [hereinafter "ILO C182"].

5. The African Movement of Working Children and Youth (AMWCY) grew from a program for child domestic workers starting in the early 1990s. See Swift, *Working Children Get Organised,* pp. 25–30. It now claims over forty associations in twenty-three countries, and an overall membership of around 20,000 children employed in a wide variety of work. For AMWCY particulars, see http://www.enda.sn/eja/anglais/index.htm.

6. Enda Tiers-Monde, *Working Children of Africa,* p. 85.

7. The Concerned for Working Children, *Working Children's Report: India—1998,* pp. 47, 40.

8. Call, "The Implications of Helpfulness . . . ."

9. See, for example, Field, "The Child as Laborer and Consumer . . ."; and Hie-Joang, "Children in the Examination War in South Korea . . . ."

10. A recent survey on child labor, Government of Zimbabwe, *Zimbabwe 1999* . . . , excluded domestic work in a home in which a parent or grandparent or guardian is present. See also Nilsen, "Negotiating Children's Work . . . ," p. 115.

11. See, for example, Blanchet, *Lost Innocence* . . . , p. 99; O'Connell, *Women and the Family* . . . , p. 14; and Pflug, *An Overview of Child Domestic Workers* . . . , p. 17.

12. White, "Children, Work, and 'Child Labour' . . . ," p. 860.

13. McKechnie and Hobbes, "Child Labour . . . ," pp. 92, 94.

14. Mortimer and Finch, "Work, Family, and Adolescent Development," pp. 16–17.

15. Morrow, "Responsible Children? . . ."

16. Ibid.

17. Call, "Adolescent Work . . . ."

18. Morrow, "Responsible Children? . . ."

19. Steinberg, Fergley, and Dornbusch, "Negative Impact of Part-Time Work . . . ," pp. 175–178; McKechnie, Stack, and Hobbes, "Work by Secondary School Students . . . ," p. 297.

20. McKechnie, Stack, and Hobbes, "Work by Secondary School Students . . . ," p. 297.

21. Oloka, "Children's Work in Urban Nigeria . . . ," p. 21.

22. Lavalette, *Child Employment* . . . , pp. 1–2.

23. Mortimer and Finch, "Work, Family, and Adolescent Development," p. 15.

24. Manning, "Parenting Employed Teenagers," p. 192.

25. Glasinovich, "Trabahar o Estudiar . . . ," p. 82.

26. See, for example, Reynolds, *Dance Civet Cat* . . . , especially pp. 62–67, 87–89; and White, "The Economic Importance . . . ," especially pp. 200–203.

27. Bourdillon, "Children at Work . . . ," p. 156; Chirwa and Bourdillon, "Small-Scale Commercial Farming . . . ," pp. 131–133; Mapedzahama and Bourdillon, "Work-

ing Street Children . . . ," pp. 31–32, 37–38; Mutisi and Bourdillon, "Vendors at a Rural Growth Point," pp. 86–97, 91–92.

28. Morrow, "Responsible Children? . . . ," p. 133.

29. Mapedzahama and Bourdillon, "Working Street Children . . . ," p. 33.

30. Chirwa and Bourdillon, "Small-Scale Commercial Farming . . . ," pp. 131–133; Mangoma and Bourdillon, "The Work of Children . . . ," pp. 18–21.

31. Save the Children–UK, *Stitching Footballs* . . . , p. 23.

32. See, for example, Mangoma and Bourdillon, "The Work of Children . . . ," pp. 19–20, 24–26; Reynolds, *Dance Civet Cat* . . . , pp. 41–92; and UNICEF, *The State of the World's Children 1997*, pp. 44–45.

33. Van der Waal, "Rural Children and Residential Instability . . . ," pp. 43–45.

34. See infra "More Subtle Forms of Exploitation—Domestic Work" in this chapter.

35. See Government of Zimbabwe, *Zimbabwe 1999* . . . , tabs. 2.3a, 5.7.

36. See Bourdillon, "Children at Work . . . ," p. 165.

37. White and Tjandraningsih, *Child Workers in Indonesia*, p. 39.

38. Schrumpf, "Attitudes Towards Child Work in Industry . . . ," p. 220.

39. Zalami, *Forgotten on the Pyjama Trail* . . . , pp. 29–30.

40. Bachman, "A New Economics of Child Labor . . . ," p. 560.

41. White, "The Economic Importance of Children . . . ," pp. 196–197.

42. Illustrated by Josephine Effah's account of child trafficking in Nigeria, in Effah, *Modernised Slavery* . . . .

43. White and Tjandraningsih, *Child Workers in Indonesia*, pp. 52–56.

44. Rurevo and Bourdillon, *Less Visible Street Children*, pp. 55–56.

45. UNICEF, *The State of the World's Children 1997*, pp. 41–43.

46. Thérèse Blanchet points out that employers of child domestic workers in Bangladesh see themselves as saviors of poor children, and that there are parallels between employment and adoption or fostering. Blanchet, *Lost Innocence* . . . , pp. 102–103.

47. The idiom of kinship is sometimes used to justify keeping child domestic employment outside the normal labor legislation, even when most domestic servants were previously unknown to their employers. See White and Tjandraningsih, *Child Workers in Indonesia*, pp. 28–89.

48. Pflug, *An Overview of Child Domestic Workers* . . . , pp. 32–33.

49. Mangoma and Bourdillon, "The Work of Children . . . ," pp. 26–28.

50. Rurevo and Bourdillon, *Less Visible Street Children*, pp. 42–45.

51. Bachman, "A New Economics of Child Labor . . . ," p. 550.

52. Green, "Child Workers . . . ," p. 25. For a general account of using economic incentives to reduce the number of children working, see also Anker and Melkas, *Economic Incentives for Children* . . . , especially pp. 13–34.

53. Andvig, "Child Labour in Sub-Saharan Africa . . . ," p. 327.

54. See p. 381, n. 26.

55. Enda Tiers-Monde, *Les Mbindaam sans Mbindou* . . . , p. 45.

56. By "informal mining" I refer to small-scale and undercapitalized mining, characteristically operated by retrenched mine workers or itinerant entrepreneurs and rarely earning enough to sustain a family adequately. See Save the Children–UK, *Children in the Informal Mining Sector* . . . , p. 1.

57. Rurevo and Bourdillon, *Less Visible Street Children*, p. 55.

58. UNICEF, *The State of the World's Children 1997*, p. 26.

59. See Richter and Swart-Kruger, "Society Makes Survival a Crime."

60. Caregivers are commonly called "carers" in Britain and the Commonwealth.

61. Becker, Dearden, and Aldridge, "Children's Labour of Love . . . ," pp. 75, 71–73.

62. The young caregivers in Britain range from five to eighteen years old, and a quarter of them receive no external support. Dearden and Becker, *Young Carers in the United Kingdom,* p. 8; Dearden and Becker, "The Experiences of Young Carers . . . ," p. 274.

63. One study in Britain suggests that about 70 percent of young caregivers, sometimes suffering health problems of their own and frequently suffering from stress, develop psychological problems as adults. Frank, Tatum, and Tucker, *On Small Shoulders,* p. 15, cited in Dearden and Becker, "The Experiences of Young Carers . . . ," p. 273.

64. Dearden and Becker, *Young Carers in the United Kingdom,* p. 83.

65. In the context of the HIV/AIDS epidemic, which leaves so many children with no adults to care for them, the need to make welfare services accessible to children is therefore particularly important.

66. United Nations, *Convention on the Rights of the Child* (1989).

67. Ibid., arts. 23, 24, 28, 29.

68. Ibid., art. 32.

69. African Movement of Working Children and Youth, *"A World Fit for and by Children"* . . . , p. 8.

70. See, for example, Save the Children–UK, *Big Business, Small Hands* . . . , p. 25 (on Pakistan); and White and Tjandraningsih, *Child Workers in Indonesia,* p. 44.

71. Burra, *Born to Work* . . . , pp. 210–213.

72. Green, "Child Workers . . . ," p. 24.

73. Glasinovich, "Trabahar o Estudiar . . . ," p. 81.

74. Woodhead, "The Value of Work and School . . . ," p. 106.

75. Coulibaly and Faye, *Le Programme AEJT–ENDA–Gouvernement–IPEC/BIT* . . . .

76. See, for example, Weiner, *The Child and the State in India* . . . , pp. 114, 186–187.

77. Korgaokor and Myrstad, "Child Labour in the Diamond and Gemstone Industry . . . ," p. 52.

78. For a nuanced treatment of the interface between cultural relativism and the universality of human rights, see Weston, "The Universality of Human Rights . . . ," esp. pp. 83–98.

79. See Woodhead, "The Value of Work and School . . . ," pp. 109–110.

80. Burra, *Born to Work* . . . , p. 170.

81. Mangoma and Bourdillon, "The Work of Children . . . ," pp. 31, 27.

82. Chirwa and Bourdillon, "Small-Scale Commercial Farming . . . ," pp. 131–133.

83. This incident occurred on a visit to Chituuta School. See Bourdillon, "Children at Work . . . ," pp. 151–153.

84. This was our observation when collecting the material described in Chirwa and Bourdillon, "Small-Scale Commercial Farming . . . ."

85. For example, Rurevo and Bourdillon, *Less Visible Street Children,* pp. 21, 24.

86. UNICEF, *The State of the World's Children 1997,* pp. 30–31.

87. Burra, *Born to Work* . . . , pp. 228–229; Weiner, *The Child and the State in India* . . . , pp. 5–6.

88. Myers, "The Right Rights? . . . ," p. 47. See also Chapter 1 in this volume, among others, especially those in Part 4.

Part 3

Case Studies

7

Combating Child Labor in Tanzania: A Beginning

Donald Mmari

Following its independence in 1961, Tanzania, under the leadership of a one-party government headed by Julius Nyerere, pursued a mixed economy that entailed the coexistence of a private sector and a centrally planned economy. In early 1967 the government issued the Arusha Declaration, a major call for "egalitarianism, socialism, and self-reliance" that involved state domination of economic planning and commercial activity and a resulting creation of cooperative farm villages; the nationalization of banks, factories, and plantations; and major investments in primary schools and health care. This policy choice was regarded by national leaders as critical to achieving the economic and social rights of its people, stressing a more equitable distribution of the country's wealth and resources. The creation of new social institutions and redistribution policies caused Tanzania's performance on key indicators of capability and well-being such as literacy, school enrollment, and child mortality to improve dramatically during the 1970s.

By the mid-1980s, however, it was clear that the economic policies launched with the Arusha Declaration had failed. Cycles of alternating floods and droughts reduced agricultural production and exports and generally the economy deteriorated. Major international donors, including the International Monetary Fund (IMF), the World Bank, and providers of bilateral assistance, began to condition aid on the adoption of programs for economic adjustment, and by the end of the 1980s and early 1990s, political adjustment became an added prerequisite for assistance.[1] The adopted adjustments included economic and social reform programs, including the removal of price controls on factors of production, privatization of public enterprises, liberalization of foreign exchange markets, and generally the creation of an environment conducive to the growth of the private sector. Modest growth resumed.

While significant achievements were made on some economic funda-

169

mentals during the 1990s, poverty levels and external debt continued to be major challenges. Toward the end of the 1990s the government stepped up efforts to reduce the burden of debt by borrowing reduction and repayment of outstanding loans. At the same time, poverty reduction strategies became the government's central preoccupation as it did also for the government's development partners. These efforts led to the birth of a poverty reduction strategy (PRS), a locally developed poverty reduction effort supported by the Bretton Woods institutions and other development partners under the Highly Indebted Poor Countries Initiative (HIPC). By 2003, Tanzania had begun its third year of implementation of the PRS, the principal objectives of which are to ensure broad-based growth and reduction of income and nonincome poverty.

Politically, Tanzania enjoys a fairly stable political atmosphere. In 1992 the constitution was amended to allow opposition parties and in 1995 the country's first multiparty elections were held. Today, Tanzania boasts a multiparty democracy that commands growing respect and legitimacy because of its deference to the National Assembly and the country's other institutions of governance. No conditions currently exist that would suggest other than continued peace and political tranquillity, an essential ingredient for social development and the realization of human rights.[2]

The economic and social transformations since independence have had, and continue to have, an important bearing on realization of children's rights, especially those related to access to education and health. The universal public provision of health and education ensured access to a large number of children, both from poor and nonpoor households. Deteriorating economic conditions and consequent reforms during the mid-1980s and 1990s reversed some of the social gains that resulted from the universal provision, including limited access to education for children from poor households. The ongoing implementation of the PRS is expected to ensure broad-based growth and renewed drive to increase spending on education and health for the poor. In addition, the impact of this transformation on household economic activities and income could have important bearing on the choices children have for their livelihoods, and therefore on child labor.

This chapter provides some indication of the status of social development and human rights perspectives in Tanzania, especially with regard to child labor,[3] and discusses review efforts and constraints toward elimination of child labor in Tanzania.

▓ The Status of Social Development and Human Rights in Tanzania

Unemployment, Poverty, and Human Development

Poverty plays a significant role in propagating child labor in Tanzania and thus provides useful context within which the problem of child labor in the country can be better understood. According to a 2002 report on poverty and human development,[4] levels of poverty in Tanzania are high and show no signs of significant decline, especially in the rural areas where income poverty is high.

Similarly, nonincome poverty[5] levels are high, and for many indicators no signs of decline were observed during the 1990s. For example, infant and under-five mortality, which had declined in earlier decades, leveled off in the mid-1980s and seems to have reversed in the 1990s. The rapid spread of HIV/AIDS is likely to be a major cause of this reversal. Access to reproductive health care (as measured by the proportion of births attended by skilled personnel) showed significant deterioration over the 1990s as well. However, a few indicators of nonincome poverty have responded positively to new policy initiatives. Primary school enrollment rates, for example, have responded quickly to the abolition of the universal primary education fee and to ongoing campaigns to facilitate enrollment of young primary school–aged children. It is worth noting that the levels and manifestations of both income and nonincome poverty vary significantly between urban and rural areas, and among the regions of the country.

In addition, employment has not kept pace with the macroeconomic performance that has been recorded in the past decade. According to a 2001 survey on the labor force,[6] unemployment *increased* from 3.6 percent in 1990–1991 to 5.1 percent in 2000–2001. The absolute number of unemployed persons doubled during the same period. If this trend continues, the chances of children engaging in labor in order to support themselves and others in the household will increase.

The magnitudes, characteristics, and disparities of poverty observed in Tanzania have important implications on the nature and character of child labor in the country just as they do elsewhere. Clearly, close relationships—for example, between income poverty and education—create synergies that perpetuate child labor inasmuch as children from poor households are more likely to attain less education, to drop out of school, and to engage in child labor than those who are more fortunate. Similarly, there is a tendency for children to migrate from marginal geographical areas to economically active areas, where they lose parental and community protection against harmful and exploitive activities. Thus it is clear that the problem of child labor in Tanzania must be considered in a broad socioeconomic context within which, from a human rights perspective of equitable relations, the roles of individuals, households, and communities can be demystified.

Human Rights and Social Provisioning

Before looking to the character of social provisioning in Tanzania, it is imperative that a framework for human rights be conceptualized and put into the context that is applicable or easily understood in Tanzania. Universally agreed human rights, developed in the wake of World War II and the grief of the Holocaust, form the basis upon which the states of the world have agreed to underpin social relations and organizations. A large number of states are now bound by the principles first proclaimed at the global level in the 1948 Universal Declaration of Human Rights (UDHR),[7] built on codes related to slavery, discrimination, labor, women, and children, among others.

Article 22 of the UDHR states that "[e]veryone, as a member of society, has the right to social security and is entitled to realization through national effort and international cooperation and in accordance with the organization and resources of each state, of the economic, social, and cultural rights indispensable for his dignity and the free development of his personality." Embedded in this article is the link between human rights and development, and it is reconfirmed in the 1966 International Covenant on Economic, Social, and Cultural Rights (ICESCR), widely adopted throughout the world.[8]

Evidence from research is leading to a consensus that poverty goes beyond the confines of income, and that it includes deprivation of basic capabilities, freedom, and other fundamental human rights. Human rights, including peace and security and sustainable development, are integral components of poverty eradication, and this is evidenced by the shift toward a rights-based approach to development that is characterized by a mix of equitable and distributive processes, resource allocations, participatory decisionmaking, and effective justice systems. In the absence of quality social institutions, poverty remains the key obstacle to the achievement of fundamental human rights.

As noted above, data from poverty studies in many developing countries indicate clear disparities in access to major social services on various welfare indicators between the rural and urban and between the poorer and richer households. For example, evidence from a 2001 household budget survey[9] indicated that households with heads who had either no education or only primary education constituted 37 percent and 55 percent of the poor, respectively. It further showed that two-thirds of children aged seven to thirteen in households not considered poor were attending school, compared with only half the children in the poorest households. In the health sector, about 200,000 children under five years of age die every year from preventable diseases in combination with malnutrition; a 1996 demographic health survey indicated that diarrhea and respiratory illnesses were common causes of child death,[10] and a 2002 report on poverty and human development revealed that children of the richest quintile are significantly less likely to die in infancy and early childhood as compared with the national average.[11]

These disparities bear significant implications for the duration, multidimensionality, and severity of poverty, which impede the realization of the right to development of the majority of the poor. It is obvious from the disparities between the richer and poorer households and the complexity of their poverty that it is difficult for poor people to emerge out of poverty and that they are therefore likely to remain chronically poor, a situation likely to perpetuate child labor.

Child labor, not child work, viewed without regard to its contributing factors, impedes the realization of children's rights.[12] Potentially, child work can assist the realization of children's rights, but seldom does child labor generate positive effects. According to the Save the Children–UK, "work can have both positive and negative effects on the realization of a range of child rights, and this effect will vary greatly with the type of work and with the maturity, gender, and other status of the child."[13] However, just as child labor, especially in its worst forms as defined in conventions and statutes,[14] merits serious concern, the often hidden consequences of child work on the pretext of socialization and self-development also deserve attention.[15] Most children in rural areas help with household chores, especially on family farms, but the extent of their work is frequently beyond what is necessary and oftentimes impinges on their right to adequate schooling and leisure.

In many respects, child labor impacts on children's right to survival and personal development, both physically and mentally. Physically, child labor exposes children to injuries, diseases, harassment, and unfairly long hours of work. Mentally, children are subjected to psychological effects arising from isolation, abuse, and their poor status in the community. Their rights to personal development are significantly impaired when their education is denied because of their engagement in labor. Children working in certain industries, particularly those defined to include the worst forms of child labor (e.g., mining, commercial sex, commercial agriculture, and certain domestic and other informal sector work), usually are exposed to extreme conditions and denied their rights to protection from abuse, and to health, education, and recreation.

At the same time, while it is an indispensable role of government to ensure that basic social services are sufficiently available to ensure the fundamental rights of every individual, the actual provision of these services occurs through the interplay of various institutions—namely families, communities, markets, and the state. The concept of the rights of individuals and groups is related to values and capabilities. Community values vary over time and in space, and so do the capabilities of institutions of social provisioning. Different institutions consider their human rights roles differently, and so their interpretations of children's rights differ as well.[16]

Families and communities in Tanzania traditionally have considered child work to be a means of socialization. But increasingly the line between child work and child labor in the familial and neighborhood context is becoming blurred, as more children are being engaged in activities that go beyond this social context to contribute to their own or family income, both inside and outside their homes. In poor families, all members are expected to contribute to the survival and well-being of families, often resulting in conflict between children's short- and long-term needs; and in the presence of deteriorating family values and traditional safety nets, the risk of diminishing attention to children's rights has increased. A recent survey on child labor indicates that communities in Tanzania do not perceive domestic work and agricultural work to have harmful effects on children. While this may imply that community awareness of children's rights is low, it is important also to note that judgments about what work is appropriate for children differ with age, type of work, and the socioeconomic profile of different households and communities.

The increasing role of markets as the providers of basic social services in Tanzania also must be factored in, given that market-based pricing typically determines who has access to these services. Education (especially basic education) is considered to be a fundamental human right, but access to private primary education, which is qualitatively superior to its public counterpart, is restricted to those who can afford to pay; because rural areas generally are poor relative to urban areas, the rural areas have less access to quality education. Other market processes, too, must be taken into account. Income generation is especially important; when markets do not function properly, the effects can be distressing. For example, the falling prices of major agricultural products in Tanzania, especially export crops, have impaired the capacity of households to support child education initiatives. At the same time, lower household incomes have compelled children to work to meet shortfalls. While income generally determines the status of school attendance, the question of whether schooling contributes to enhanced earning potential remains a determinant of whether households will invest in schooling or engage their children in labor, and especially so for households in which the opportunity cost of child education is high.

The state's role in the provision of basic services has become increasingly important in the fight against poverty in Tanzania. The poverty reduction strategy adopted in 2000 focuses the government's attention on sectors of agriculture, education, health, HIV/AIDS, rural roads, water, and the judiciary. However, while the PRS addresses many of the challenges currently facing Tanzania, the thrust in the education sector may be considered one of the pivotal strategies to combat child labor.[17]

In the long run, investment in quality education for children probably is the best way to combat child labor and thereby enhance children's rights—better, arguably, than is resort to the enactment of laws against child labor that by themselves would be ineffective.[18] It is key to ensuring that children from poor and vulnerable households are not condemned to cycles of unskilled labor and poverty. Evidence from empirical research has shown that even in the absence of absolute poverty, children may work because economic returns may be greater than the returns that may accrue from low-quality and inaccessible schools. It is important to note, however, that there are types of works that are considered unskilled only because the skills are acquired informally through apprenticeships (e.g., carpentry, mechanics, etc.). But these jobs tend in fact to provide permanent earnings to those engaged in them. Some choices that poor children make about their livelihoods are not necessarily or always irrational.

The Status of Child Labor in Tanzania

Having considered the socioeconomic context within which child labor persists in Tanzania and how human rights are embedded in the phenomenon, I turn now to the magnitude of the child labor problem in the country, beginning with Tanzania's 2001 survey of child labor, implemented as a module of its 2001 survey of the labor force.[19] The child labor survey estimated that there were about 11.9 million children between the ages of five and seventeen in Tanzania, accounting for 36 percent of the national population. The majority, 79 percent, of these children lived in rural areas, and of these children, an estimated 4.7 million were working or engaged in economic activities. This estimate included children reported to be working in the familial and neighborhood context and attending school. However, taking into account a number of factors that distinguish child labor from child work,[20] the survey reported that about 1.2 million children, one in every four, were involved in child labor. The majority of working children were unpaid family nonagricultural workers and those who worked on their own family farms. The sectors with relatively high proportions of paid workers were construction, mining and quarrying, and manufacturing.

Some rapid assessments conducted in 2000 revealed a prevalence of the worst forms of child labor.[21] It was estimated that there were about 11,605 children engaged in the informal sector in the three major cities of Dar es Salaam, Mwanza, and Arusha; about 500 children engaged in commercial sex in Dar es Salaam; and about 150 children working in the three mining sites of Geita, Ngapa, and Chunya. Unfortunately, no comprehensive estimates of the worst forms of child labor have been made for the whole country. However, other recent estimates derived from baseline and attitude surveys carried out by the Tanzania-based nongovernmental organization (NGO) Research on Poverty Alleviation (REPOA)[22] (on behalf of the International Labour Organization [ILO] in eleven districts under the first phase of the ILO's timebound program on the elimination of the worst forms of child labor) determined that, in 2002, there were 97,930 and 57,833 children engaged in child labor and in its worst forms, respectively.

Efforts to Combat Child Labor in Tanzania

During the past two decades, there have been several initiatives at the international, regional, and national levels to mitigate some of the problems faced by working children. Efforts to promote these initiatives have been based on the recognition that children have rights and that these rights and children's development are linked and mutually reinforcing. In Cairo in May 2001, a decade after the adoption of the 1989 United Nations Convention on the Rights of the Child (CRC),[23] the Pan-African Forum for Children agreed on a common position relative to the rights of children and, in so doing, drew upon the 1990 African Charter on the Rights and Welfare of the Child,[24] which reflected the principles and objectives of the CRC. The African Charter was adopted by the member states of the Organization of African Unity (OAU), of which Tanzania was a member. It consists of thirty-one articles addressing children's rights ranging from protection, survival, and recreation to education, freedom of thought, and freedom of expression, all of them together reflecting concern for the critical situation posed for most African children due to unique factors relating to their socioeconomic, cultural, traditional, and developmental circumstances; natural disasters; armed conflicts; and exploitation and hunger resulting from inadequate safeguards, care, and attention to their physical and mental immaturity. Article 15 of the African Charter provides for specific protection of children from all forms of economic exploitation and from performing any work that is likely to be hazardous or to interfere with their physical, mental, spiritual, moral, or social development. It calls upon all member states to take appropriate legislative and administrative measures to ensure its full implementation, inclusive of both the formal and informal sectors of employment and with due regard to the relevant provisions of the ILO instruments relating to children. Later, 1999 ILO Convention (No. 182) Concerning the Prohibition and Immediate Elimination of the Worst Forms of Child Labour (ILO C182), to which Tanzania is a party, is now particularly relevant to the development and protection of children's rights.[25]

Tanzania has begun efforts to combat child labor both at the national and local levels as part of its national commitment to implement the regional and global conventions it has ratified. Many of the rights of children are included in Tanzania's key long-term development goals.[26] Efforts are being carried out in partnership among the government, intergovernmental organizations, and civil society to ensure the realization of those rights. These efforts include the creation of a policy framework, legislation and regulation, and direct intervention.

The Policy Framework

The government of Tanzania has been keen to support the fight against child labor through the establishment of an institutional and policy framework conducive to program implementation. In 1990 it formed a ministry responsible for women's and children's affairs, now transformed into the Ministry of Community Development, Gender, and Children Affairs. Since then, under its auspices, a number of initiatives have been undertaken. Various programs have been developed and are being implemented, drawing from this policy and the nation's long-term development goals.

In recognition of the importance of a comprehensive policy framework on child labor, the government has prepared a child development policy, currently in draft form, the objective of which is to facilitate an environment conducive to the development of children and the realization of their rights consistent with the provisions of the CRC. This policy will provide a national framework to guide the implementation of various programs and activities by various social partners and stakeholders; and in accordance with this policy framework the Ministry of Labour, Youth Development, and Sports is now in the process of drafting a comprehensive strategy for the elimination of child labor, which will identify specific areas of intervention, activities, and key implementing agencies, as well as indicators, targets, and resource requirements, to implement the strategy.

In collaboration with other development partners, the government also is implementing a poverty reduction strategy that aims to contain one of the root causes of child labor: widespread poverty.[27] As an integral part of the PRS, the enhancement of household income-earning opportunities has the potential to reduce the opportunity cost of sending children to school. Recognizing the potential of education to strengthen poverty reduction and consequent human capability, the PRS accords high priority to the education sector, with particular emphasis being given to basic education to ensure that all children of school age are enrolled, as is their fundamental human right. Accordingly, fees for primary schools have been abolished. Additionally, a program known as Complementary Basic Education (COBET) is being put in place to provide basic education opportunities to children who are overage for primary school enrollment.[28] The Primary Education Development Plan (PEDP)[29] and the Education Sector Development Program (ESDP)[30] are also important milestones in education sector development, and substantial gains in enrollment have been realized to date.

In addition to education sector reform, the government is strengthening vocational training. The Vocational Education Training Authority (VETA)[31] is being reformed into a more demand-driven, decentralized institution that relates to both formal and informal sectors and is flexible and responsive to a changing labor market.

The government of Tanzania is also stepping up efforts to contain the spread and minimize the consequences of HIV/AIDS, which has been found to contribute significantly to the rising incidence of child labor in recent years. The Tanzania Aids Commission (TACAIDS)[32] and the National Aids Control Programme (NACP)[33] are important elements of the government's initiatives in this realm.

Finally, civil society organizations such as Save the Children–UK are working with the government in policy development and intervention. In general, Save the Children is engaged in development work that focuses on protecting children from dangerous and exploitive work. Save the Children's priority is to tackle poverty that pushes children into work, through support of good-quality and relevant education, improvement of working conditions when children must work, and consultations with children and communities on how to take children out of dangerous work without lowering their incomes or skills. In Tanzania, specific Save the Children interventions have focused on the advocacy of policies that incorporate the views of children, improve the quality of education, and facilitate the health of households in relation to the livelihood of children.

Legislation and Regulation
The government of Tanzania has shown substantial commitment to fighting abusive and exploitive child labor through legislative and regulatory activities. This includes ratification of conventions related to child labor and the rights of children, and participation in the ILO's International Programme on the Elimination of Child Labour (IPEC).

Tanzania has ratified both ILO C138, which sets the minimum age for non-hazardous work at fourteen, and ILO C182, on the worst forms of child labor, which sets the minimum age for hazardous work at eighteen. Tanzania also has ratified the 1989 CRC. Additionally, supporting the work of IPEC, Tanzania has adopted various laws that have as their objectives the protection of children from exploitive work and recognition of their rights. The national employment policy prohibits the employment of children below the age of fifteen,[34] and a number of laws prohibit the involvement of children in some social and economic activities below a designated age. These include the Age of Majority Ordinance (cap. 413) of 1960, which defines a child as one who has not attained the "age of majority" (i.e., eighteen); the Law of Marriage Act of 1971, which prevents the marriage of children under the age of fifteen; and the Employment Ordinance (cap. 366) of 1957, which defines a child as a person under the age of fifteen and ineligible for employment, gainful or otherwise.[35]

Direct Intervention
Various intergovernmental and nongovernmental actors are engaged in the prevention, withdrawal, and rehabilitation of working children in Tanzania. ILO/IPEC and the United Nations Children's Fund (UNICEF) are among the major international partners collaborating with the government and NGOs.

The major emphasis of the IPEC programs has been on capacity building of the government and other social partners, including employer organizations, trade unions, and NGOs, to design and implement specific actions to protect working children and eliminate abusive and exploitive child labor. Actions have involved identification and analysis of child labor in the context of ILO C138; strategic interventions in protection, prevention, and withdrawal of children from exploitive and hazardous work sites in the context of ILO C182; rehabilitation and provision of alternative life opportunities of withdrawn children; raising public awareness on the nature, negative effects, and possibility of eliminating child labor; and community mobilization and information to promote the understanding of the problem and a sense of ownership of the programs at the community level.

Within this IPEC framework and focus, the Tanzanian government is implementing a time-bound program (TBP) intended to aid in the elimination of the worst forms of child labor. The TBP functions within a broad policy approach that emphasizes the need to increase the supply and demand of education by addressing educational access and quality issues; to reduce the opportunity cost of education to poor households through targeted poverty reduction interventions; to put in place efforts to protect the rights of children by implementing various laws in keeping with ILO C138 and ILO C182; to introduce measures to improve the functioning of labor markets; and to address the sociodemographic and gender dimensions of the child labor problem. The TBP engages the central government, local government, and civil society under the overall guidance of the TBP's National Intersectoral Coordination Committee (NISC),[36] which meets quarterly to strategize, plan, review, and advise on the implementation of the project.[37] District authorities participate actively in the process through the formation of committees on child labor issues and the designation of government officers as district coordinators of child labor elimination programs.

In support of the TBP, the Education Development Center (EDC) is working with the ILO to broaden educational opportunities for working children by developing a delivery system for high-quality basic education accessible to working children.[38] At present, the EDC delivers basic education to child laborers via radio, supported by mentors at community-owned centers in three pilot districts: Iringa, Mufindi, and Simanjiro. The EDC project also complements COBET, which provides education opportunities for out-of-school children who are overage for formal school enrollment. The project focuses on basic education in standard levels one to four (age cohort of eleven to fourteen); those children who become eligible for standard five then join the COBET program.

UNICEF has been working with the government and NGOs in support of children and young people in education, health, and other aspects of their lives. UNICEF's support of children with limited access to basic social services, especially in education, is particularly important in addressing persistent child labor. One of the major programs supported by UNICEF, Child Survival and Protection Development (CSPD), has as its overall objective the creation and maintenance of an environment that places the highest priority on the human rights of children; recognizes and respects their right to a dignified and productive existence; ensures their survival, protection, development, and participation; and improves their prospects for social and economic advancement.[39] To these ends, it emphasizes the following four functions:

mainstreaming the human rights of children in policies and national budgeting processes through advocacy activities based on research and monitoring results; improving community development processes and systems to ensure good governance, enhanced community-based systems for vulnerability analysis, mapping, social security provision (in the context of local government reforms and human rights principles), and running community development activities; enhancing maternal well-being and the best possible start for growth and development for all children in Tanzania through early childhood development activities; and striving (through basic education and life skills for adolescence) for a society in which young people thrive and are respected, recognized, and valued.

Some NGOs, such as the Kiota Women's Health and Development (KIWOHEDE),[40] are actively involved in the withdrawal of children from prostitution and in the promotion of attitude change in this regard through the use of a theater group of withdrawn children using music, drama, and dance to stimulate public awareness. Similarly, the Conservation, Hotels, Domestic, and Allied Workers Union (CHODAWU) has been campaigning against the widespread practice of domestic labor by using drama, posters, demonstrations, and marching.[41]

Another direct intervention initiative is that of KULEANA, an NGO actively advocating for children's rights in Tanzania under the framework of the regional and international conventions on the rights of children.[42] Its efforts focus on promoting awareness and advocacy about child rights, with emphasis on the girl child; facilitating the right of children to voice and self-expression; strengthening programming capacity in children's rights; promoting universal primary education in Tanzania and otherwise improving essential services; and supporting the rights of street children.

Other programs being implemented by NGOs and international agencies indirectly complement efforts to combat child labor. One example is the World Food Programme (WFP).[43] In Tanzania, the WFP focuses on conservation work. Through one of its components on environmental education, however, schools are involved, with the result that its school feeding program helps to generate interest among schoolchildren and keeps them from dropping out. Regrettably, this program is being piloted in only two districts, Morogoro and Ifakara.

■ Constraints on Combating Child Labor in Tanzania

While there have been some achievements in the fight against child labor in Tanzania, a number of constraints remain that prevent substantial or faster realization of children's rights. A key constraint, as we have seen, is widespread poverty. Most surveys and studies carried out in Tanzania have identified poverty as one of the most important factors contributing to the persistence of child labor.[44] Poor children often face a terrible dilemma. If they do not work, they do not eat, sleep, or dress. If they do work, they will be subjected to child prostitution, heavy workloads, abuse, and gross underpayment. Further, they will miss out on the development of important educational and social skills. They thus have to choose the lesser of evils. In the absence of adequate safety nets and social institutions, poor children choose to work to survive. As long as strategies addressing poverty as a root contributing factor are not robust, the fight against child labor will continue to be elusive and challenging. Simply put, as long as children from poor households have no real choice, no law or regulation can stop child labor.

Despite considerable efforts to ensure basic education enrollment, the quality of education and relevance of the skills taught in schools raise questions about the effectiveness of education to eliminate child labor. Increased enrollment without corresponding increases in the number and quality of teachers and facilities tends to increase pressures on teacher workload and quality, resulting in poor knowledge and skills on the part of schoolchildren. Such an environment and outcome can result also in increased dropout rates. Although the government of Tanzania is opening up a whole range of vocational facilities, vocational training hardly seems a feasible option amid widespread poverty, as many of the youth cannot afford these facilities, and even their primary school education has not trained them sufficiently to get them through vocational education. In addition, the COBET program has not been able to cater to the education needs of out-of-school children. The present capacity of COBET is only 600,000 children, while there are about 2 million out-of-school children.

The devastating effects of HIV/AIDS pose significant challenges to the achievement of various development targets. Tanzania's 2002 report on poverty and human development[45] and its poverty assessment reports[46] note that the HIV/AIDS pandemic has resulted in a reduction in economic growth; an enormous social burden imposed by illness, death, and orphanhood; and serious implications for the operation and financing of government services. Out of 2 million people currently estimated to be HIV-infected, more than 700,000 are reported to be suffering from AIDS.[47] Although no reliable data on HIV/AIDS orphans exist, it is estimated that they may number up to 1 million. According to a UNICEF study, the number of children who became orphans in Tanzania in 2000 was estimated to be around 1.2 million, mostly as a result of the HIV/AIDS pandemic. This represented about 9 percent of all children under age fifteen.[48] In addition to biological orphans, it is useful to note, from the human rights perspective, the existence of children who were not living with their parents for other reasons, referred to as "social orphans." Children who were socially orphaned by both parents, according to the UNICEF study, totaled 10.3 percent of all children, and those socially orphaned by single parents totaled

24.2 percent. Unable to obtain support from weakening and overstretched, extended families, and in the absence of strong social institutions and safety nets, orphaned children are unable to keep up with school and thus resort to work as a sole means of survival.

The implementation of policies and regulations against child labor is slow and sometimes ineffective due to lack of adequate funding and low capability on the part of the implementing agencies. The district authorities, which should be key movers in the process, lack resources and capacity to deal with multiple pressing priorities.

The absence of adequate social protection policies that would enable children to enlarge their choices in the short run make the poor children even more vulnerable. Children have a right to survival, a right to protection from harmful work, and a right to education. But while human rights are indivisible, the struggle for the right to survive always prevails for the poor children, who from early childhood are often subject to limited opportunities in education and marginalization by teachers and other pupils, and are vulnerable to disruptions. These conditions create psychological effects that often lead to self-exclusion from schools, physically or mentally.

Community attitudes still pose impediments for efforts to combat child labor. Cultural practices that prevent children from attending school, especially girls, and those that encourage early marriages are still in place; and the majority of the people do not consider domestic and agricultural work to be harmful. Any intervention to withdraw children from harmful activities is considered to be the government's responsibility, making community involvement difficult to mobilize. In addition, some communities continue with practices that perpetuate poverty, including the maintenance of large households and polygamy. The key challenge for the government and its development partners is to help communities understand their role in defining rights, social protection, and appropriate work for children.

■ Conclusion

The problem of child labor is indeed a problem of development in its totality. Poverty reduction efforts, which include policies on education, health, and other social infrastructures, are critical to ensuring that the rights of children are realized through broad-based and equitable social development. Such efforts are key to ensuring effective elimination of abusive and exploitive child labor. A number of efforts are being made to address child labor in Tanzania, jointly by the government, international partners, and civil society. However, the problem of child labor is massive, due mainly to pervasive poverty, insufficient funding, inadequate implementing capacity on the part of the government and civil society, and community attributes and traditions. Major social transformation is required. But without large-scale resource reallocations on a global scale, presently not on the horizon, this is unlikely to happen anytime soon. Only a new way of thinking is likely to bring about the just results that are so desperately needed.

■ Notes

1. Barkan, "Divergence and Convergence . . . ," p. 29.

2. On the meaning, nature, and content of international human rights, see Weston, "Human Rights."

3. In this chapter, I adopt the definition of "child labor" set forth in the introduction to this volume, in turn derived from Chapter 2, that is, "work done by children that is harmful to them because it is abusive, exploitive, hazardous, or otherwise contrary to their best interests—a subset of a larger class of children's work, some of which may be compatible with children's best interests (variously expressed as 'beneficial,' 'benign,' or 'harmless' children's work)."

4. United Republic of Tanzania, *Poverty and Human Development Report.*

5. "Nonincome poverty" refers to deprivation in well-being, measured according to parameters other than income such as an individual's health, nutrition, education, housing, and certain rights in a society such as freedom of speech.

6. United Republic of Tanzania, *Integrated Labour Force Survey.*

7. United Nations, *Universal Declaration of Human Rights* (1948).

8. Ratified by 151 countries as of June 18, 2005.

9. United Republic of Tanzania, *Household Budget Survey.*

10. United Republic of Tanzania, *Demographic Health Survey,* pp. 118–119.

11. United Republic of Tanzania, *Poverty and Human Development Report,* p. 27.

12. See supra endnote 3.

13. Save the Children–UK, *Save the Children's Position on Children and Work,* p. 5.

14. See especially ILO, *Convention* (No. 182) *Concerning the Prohibition and Immediate Elimination of the Worst Forms of Child Labour* (1999) [hereinafter "ILO C182"]. Article 2 of ILO C182 defines "child" to mean any person under age eighteen.

15. See Chapter 2 in this volume for a useful discussion of child labor and the social construction of work.

16. The issue is one of cultural relativism. On cultural relativism versus universalism in human rights law and policy, see Weston, "The Universality of Human Rights . . . ."

17. In his address to the launch of the Time-Bound Program on the Worst Forms of Child Labour in Geneva in June 2002, Tanzania's president described child labor and the denial of children's right to basic education as "cruelty, a negation of our common humanity, an insult to the dignity of the human person, and a veritable waste of human capital." United Republic of Tanzania, *His Excellence Benjamin William Mkapa . . . ,* p. 2.

18. See Chapter 15 in this volume for an insightful discussion of the vital relationship between education and child labor.

19. United Republic of Tanzania, *Integrated Labour Force Survey.*

20. Factors considered to distinguish child labor from child work were: children under age fifteen, schooling status, status in employment, hours of work, type of work (hazardous work and risky occupation), working conditions (pay level, medical attention), and risks and dangers at work.

21. Sectors considered to involve the worst forms of child labor in Tanzania are commercial agriculture, domestic service, mining, and the informal sector generally.

22. REPOA is a Tanzania-based NGO, established in 1994, with the mandate to undertake and facilitate research in the area of poverty and poverty-related issues. See REPOA's website, at http://www.repoa.or.tz.

23. United Nations, *Convention on the Rights of the Child* (1989).

24. *African Charter on the Rights and Welfare of the Child* (1990).

25. See ILO C182.

26. United Republic of Tanzania, *Tanzania Development Vision 2025.*

27. United Republic of Tanzania, *Poverty Reduction Strategy . . . .*

28. United Republic of Tanzania, *Non-Formal Education Strategy.*

29. United Republic of Tanzania, *Primary Education . . . .*

30. United Republic of Tanzania, *The Education Sector . . . .*

31. VETA is a semiautonomous institution under the Ministry of Labour, Youth Development, and Sports.

32. TACAIDS is a semiautonomous body under the Prime Minister's Office, responsible for coordinating the implementation of the National Multisectoral Strategy on HIV/AIDS.

33. The NACP is a program under the Ministry of Health responsible for coordinating and monitoring interventions of the Ministry on HIV/AIDS.

34. United Republic of Tanzania, *The National Employment Policy.*

35. The relevant provisions of these laws are conveniently assembled and accessed in the Child Labor Research Initiative legislative database of The University of Iowa Center for Human Rights, available at http://www.childlaborlaws.org/projects/database/search.shtml.

36. NISC membership includes senior-level representatives from key government institutions, including the Prime Minister's Office, the Ministry of Labour, Youth Development, and Sports, the Vice President's Office, the President's Office–Planning and Privatization, the Ministry of Education and Culture, the Ministry of Community Development Women Affairs and Children, and the President's Office–Regional Administration and Local Government. Also included are the Association of Tanzania Employers, the Trade Union Congress of Tanzania, and assorted NGOs. IPEC, the United Nations, and other global and regional institutions, agencies, and donors participate as observers and advisors.

37. See ILO and United Republic of Tanzania, *Project Document . . . .*

38. For details about the EDC, see http://main.edc.org.

39. UNICEF, *Country Programme 2002–2006.* As stated by UNICEF on its website, "[t]he country programme consists of three sectors: Health Programme; Education Programme; and Water and Sanitation Programme. Each is in turn made up of a number of projects and activities. At every one of these levels, there are objectives whose performance and expenditures can be monitored against relevant indicators." See http://www.unicef.org/saotome/projects.htm.

40. KIWOHEDE is a local NGO that engages in the withdrawal and rehabilitation of children from prostitution. For more information, contact: Secretary-General, P.O. Box 15549, Dar es Salaam, Tanzania.

41. CHODAWU is a trade union that has been active in the campaign against child labor, especially domestic child workers. For more information, contact: Executive Director, P.O. Box 10127, Dar es Salaam, Tanzania.

42. KULEANA is a local NGO that advocates for children's rights, especially in education. For more information, contact the director via email, at admin@kuleanatz.org.

43. The World Food Programme is self-described as "the world's largest humanitarian agency." For details, see http://www.wfp.org.

44. See Chapter 6 in this volume, in which Michael Bourdillon notes that the dominant reason for child labor in developing countries is to help meet basic needs, supporting the view that poverty remains the major root cause of child labor.

45. United Republic of Tanzania, *Poverty and Human Development Report.*

46. Economic and Social Research Foundation, *Summary of the Participatory Poverty Assessment . . . .*

47. United Republic of Tanzania, Prime Minister's Office, *National Multi-Sectoral Strategic Framework . . .* , p. 13.

48. United Nations Children's Fund and Social Welfare Department, *Reaching the Most Vulnerable . . .* , p. 13.

8

Combating Child
Labor in the Philippines:
Listening to Children

Victoria V. Rialp

This chapter presents features of a rights-based approach in the current struggle against child labor in the Philippines.[1] It highlights, in particular, the involvement of Filipino children and youth in raising public awareness about child rights, in understanding the phenomenon of child labor in the country, and in framing more appropriate program responses to it; and as the 1989 United Nations Convention on the Rights of the Child (CRC)[2] and its Article 12[3] have grown in the Filipino public's consciousness, this involvement has helped to produce tangible results. Policy pronouncements and plans of action for children by governmental as well as nongovernmental organizations (NGOs) are now setting Filipino child labor issues more and more in the context of child or children's rights—categorized into survival, development, protection, and participation rights. Also, development programs and projects for children have begun to move away from a needs-based to a more rights-based approach, or moved at least to a point of reconciliation of the two approaches. To date, however, program implementers and involved children agree that, while advocacy programs have raised public awareness of child rights and child labor significantly, the enhanced rhetoric has not translated sufficiently into action that effectively protects child rights, and many are disappointed by the results.

Relying upon the current literature, upon recent program reports and documents pertaining to child rights advocacy, and upon efforts to curb child labor in the Philippines, this chapter attempts to give examples of how programs to combat child labor have drawn from children's perceptions about child rights and about child labor; describe efforts to mainstream child rights into local development planning within the context of the Child-Friendly Movement; relate what children say about their experiences in these efforts to engage them as child rights advocates; review the overall assessment of the efforts; and suggest some implications for reflection.

◼ Drawing from Children's Perceptions

National Surveys

Program initiatives in support of child rights and against child labor in the Philippines, historically adult-led, have increasingly involved children, organized to become their own advocates. The earliest instances of involvement by children who work had them merely responding to survey questions about their work and their working conditions. Later efforts to "listen to the children" asked such questions as: What rights do children have? Which of children's rights are respected? What is unacceptable child work? What are the causes and the solutions that children suggest?

Situation studies on child labor are considered important in "making the invisible visible." Descriptive case studies and anecdotal evidence from a handful of communities known to have working children were available as early as the late 1980s. With the start of the International Labour Organization's International Programme on the Elimination of Child Labour (IPEC) in the Philippines, there was a push for a nationwide sample survey to begin to understand the nature and magnitude of child labor.

Such a survey was conducted by the Philippines' National Statistics Office nationwide in 1995 as a rider to the July labor force survey and was subsequently updated in 2001.[4] The 2001 child survey estimated about 4 million economically active children aged five to seventeen years, or 16.2 percent of the total population of children in this age group, compared with its 1995 estimate of a little more than 3.5 million. About a third of the children surveyed said they were not in school, citing unaffordable costs of schooling or long distances from school. Of those in school, about one-fourth reported that their work contributed to poor school performance, frequent absenteeism, and tardiness. The children surveyed spoke of unsanitary and unsafe surroundings, lack of clean water, and frequent flooding of their work areas. About 60 percent, or 2.4 million, said they were exposed to hazardous working environments, particularly in mining and quarrying, construction, farmwork, and fishing. About 23.4 percent of working children said they suffered from work-related injuries. Still, more than half of the working children said they preferred to continue working, citing improvement in the living conditions of their households as the main reason for working.

Based on the nationwide surveys of the child labor situation in the Philippines, in combination with earlier case studies of child labor and surveys of street children, the Philippine government and some NGOs embarked on what they called a unified plan of action. Funding agencies, such as the International Labour Organization (ILO) and the United Nations Children's Fund (UNICEF) and other international donors, found the studies useful for funding decisions as well as for raising more resources for expanded programming. More important, groups already involved with working children utilized what they considered the now more reliable facts and figures about child labor in their own advocacy and fundraising activities, and in reorienting their program focus as well.

Organizing Children Against
Commercial Sexual Exploitation

Different piecemeal situation studies taken together formed the basis for setting policy and program frameworks and intensifying advocacy efforts. This can be seen in the Philippine National Plan of Action Against Commercial Sexual Exploitation of Children,[5] which relied heavily on the 1999 study *Commercial Sexual Exploitation of Children in the Philippines,* commissioned by the Philippine Department of Social Welfare and Development and UNICEF,[6] plus an earlier study on the psychosocial profile of sexually exploited street children. Personal accounts of children were compiled also to promote children's participation in assessing and redressing their situation.

A 2000 report titled *Proceedings: Changing Our Lives—International Conference on Young People's Participation Against Commercial Sexual Exploitation of Children*[7] includes the report of a youth delegation from the Philippines who saw themselves as a coalition of young people against sexual exploitation of children. They described their participation in a series of local, national, and then international discussions and conferences, exchanging information and insight (among themselves and between themselves and the adult organizers) about the lives of sexually exploited children. During a national conference in October 1999, they drew up their own youth plan of action, adding that "in these consultations, we understood better the issue of commercial sexual exploitation of children (CSEC) and further realized that there is indeed an increasing incidence of child abuse and sexual exploitation in the Philippines. We have appreciated, recognized and reaffirmed how young people's action is crucial in the struggle to end sexual abuse and exploitation of children."[8] They also related their activities as a young people's coalition:

So far, we have done the following:

1. Gathered signatures to ratify the International Labour Organisation Convention No. 182[9]
2. Participated in the anniversary celebration of the Global March Against Child Labour
3. Participated in the International Young People's Film Festival
4. Held forums on CSEC in schools, communities, and parishes
5. Distributed information materials on child rights and CSEC
6. Conducted workshops on various issues affecting children
7. Conducted leadership and skills training
8. Carried out media campaigns
9. Referred victims to child-care centers and institutions
10. Had immersion and outreach programs
11. Organized groups in communities.[10]

Initial Efforts to Organize
Children in Commercial Plantations

Another effort to involve working children was a consultation workshop on child labor in commercial plantations, held in September 2002 in southern Mindanao. The workshop was organized by two of the most active rights-based NGOs working with children: the Kamalayan Development Foundation, and Exodus from Child Labor to Integration, Play, Socialization, and Education (ECLIPSE). Its purpose was to "(a) Provide the working children in various plantations the opportunity to know each other, build a group that unites them for their cause, and increase their awareness with regard to their situation, problems, rights, and responsibilities; (b) Start the nationwide organizing of children in rural commercial plantations and the local organizing of those who have not yet organized themselves for the nationwide and local promotion of their rights and their struggle for a better future; and (c) Come up with a scientific picture of the national situation of the working children in Philippine rural commercial plantations and a plan of action for the promotion and realization of their rights."[11] Participants included fifty-three children working in commercial crop plantations in sixteen provinces, together with parent delegates and representatives from women's associations, people's organizations, and NGOs working with child labor, donor agencies, departments of labor and social development, and local media. A number of adult participants said they expected to learn from the children's views and experiences.

Participants described the work children do in commercial plantations for sugar, rice, tobacco, rubber, onion, corn, durian, tiger grass, asparagus, and pineapple—from plowing to seeding, weeding to spraying chemicals, applying fertilizer to harvesting. They explained that the small pay that children earn in the plantations helps some to continue schooling, or to help their families buy food and other necessities, to save for the future, or just simply to survive. When asked who is served by child labor in the various plantations, their responses included capitalists, landlords, farm owners, buyers, factories, and corporations. They cited damage to their health in terms of physical abuse, malnutrition, wounds and fractures, fatigue, stunted growth, body pains, chemical poisoning, cancer, and tuberculosis. And to eliminate the worst forms of child labor they recommended strongly the following actions:

- Raise the consciousness of the children, parents, and other sectors with regards [to] the children's situation and problems, their rights and responsibilities, and what needs to be done in order to achieve genuine development;
- Conduct training, seminars, symposia, and the like concerning the CRC (1989), ILO C182 (1999), other international standards and also the Philippine national and local laws, policies, and programs related to child labor;
- Organize the working children and unite all the children against the worst forms of child labor;
- Organize the parents and other significant sectors;

- Build the trust and confidence among the members and cooperation among them;
- Study the negative and positive effects of elimination and plan accordingly;
- Establish networks with the government, NGOs, and other interested organizations;
- Persevere in the work of child labor elimination and not lose hope.[12]

When the Family Forces Children to Work

A research project on children's concepts about child abuse found that children consider as potentially abusive those situations in which they are forced to work.[13] Participating in this study were forty-three street children, among whom twenty-five lived on the streets and the rest in a shelter in a poor Manila neighborhood. In focus group discussions, they talked extensively about children who were forced to work because of economic needs. Some said that this could not be considered abuse because the children took the initiative to find work because their parents could not support them. Others said it was abusive because a child should not work at all, but instead play and study. Given a choice, some children said they still wanted to work and help their families. After much debate, the children agreed that the following situations can be considered abusive: "(1) When the child is told to work regularly and it causes him/her hardship and is forced to quit schooling; (2) When a child works like a slave at home while the youngest sibling is not given work to do; (3) A child is not through doing one chore and is already asked to do another."[14] The children also said that being forced into prostitution or into becoming a "runner" for drug dealers was abusive.

They said, too, that abusive situations arise when parents argue and one vents her or his anger on the children; when a parent is a drug user, alcoholic, or gambler; and when children encounter the police. Some added that adults abused the children because adults were stronger or were influenced by a demon.

Similar insights about children who are forced to work in the family setting came from children at a 1997 Bangkok forum on intolerable child work in which children from Asian countries, including the Philippines, participated.[15] As reported in the proceedings: "Family duty was mentioned many times. Housework was described as an 'obligation,' and it was generally accepted that it is a child's duty to help their families—but perhaps only up to a certain limit. One child asked, 'It is children's duty to help parents; but if the work is harmful to them, is it child labour?' Another answered: 'If parents ask, it is not forced. It is a kind of sharing. As long as it is not forced.'"

Unacceptable Child Labor

The language constructed by adults—"most intolerable forms of child labor"—was modified by the eleven children aged thirteen to seventeen who participated at the same 1997 Bangkok children's forum. Aside from differentiating between "child work" and "child labor," the participating children chose the word "unacceptable" over the word "intolerable":

> We, the children of Southeast and Northeast Asia, have come together for two days and we have come up with tĬhe following statements:
>
> Child work is different from child labour.
> Child work does not have negative effects on the children's development because it is either voluntary work, not a profit-oriented activity or jobs within the household.
> Child work also opens opportunities in life and gives children new experiences. On the other hand, child labour is profit-oriented. The child needs to work for the whole day everyday, continuous work and is geared towards produced industries and it is mentally and physically exhausting.[16]

Children said that the most "unacceptable" forms of labor are those that are just "too hard" for them—by nature of the work or the difficult working conditions. The children described situations where work interfered with their health, education, leisure time, and future development as they looked at what they do on a daily basis.

When pointing out the most dangerous things they do, the children said they preferred the word "unacceptable" because it was easier for children to understand than "intolerable." Among the kinds of work they said posed dangers were:

> Herding cattle, you can fall off the horse.
> In farm work, you can injure your leg and arms with sharp tools.
> Factory work gives you a stiff neck, back pain, and hurt fingers.
> Working in a fireworks factory, you can get blown up in an explosion.
> In Mongolia, summer is very hot and winter is freezing. Working outside means being out in extreme weather. You can be abused by strangers.
> Working on the streets, you may become involved in crime even if you are not a criminal.
> You may get hit by a bullet.
> In mines you are in danger of being caved in.
> Prostitutes are beaten by clients and sometimes even get killed.
> In domestic work you are exposed to sexual abuse and no one may ever know. Your situation is hidden from the public.
> When diving, you go deep into the sea without protection.[17]

While the children recommended that governments stop the most unacceptable forms of child work, they also insisted that "the children should be allowed to do light work, voluntary, and community work."[18] They added that children and adults must know, understand, and respect children's rights in the situation of child workers. They emphasized that their countries have laws that protect their rights, but the problems are in implementing and monitoring them, and insisted that violators and abusive employers be punished.

The children also said that children working in unacceptable forms of child work "should be rescued and not be punished [for working], given recovering and healing programs and livelihood programmes, [and] the communities should be prepared to welcome back the rescued working children in their communities."[19] Because a major cause of child labor is poverty, children and their families, they said, should be given livelihood opportunities.

Child Rights and the Child-Friendly Movement

Ten years after the Philippines ratified the CRC in 1990, the policy environment and public awareness on child rights had improved significantly to warrant a program strategy that the government and UNICEF agreed to call the "Child-Friendly Movement." The *Fifth Country Programme for Children: Programme of Cooperation for Child Survival, Protection, Development, and Participation in the Philippines, 1999–2003,* "aimed at promoting and assisting in the implementation of a Child-Friendly Movement to mainstream and operationalize the Convention on the Rights of the Child."[20] The UNICEF-Philippine agreement invoked a programming context of children's rights based on the 1987 Philippine constitution,[21] the Philippine Plan of Action for Children for the Year 2000 and Beyond,[22] and the Philippine Child and Youth Welfare Code.[23] The code defines the rights of children, the rights and liabilities of parents, and the role of institutions—for example, the community, religious institutions, and schools—in promoting the welfare of Filipino children.[24] It also recognizes the special categories of children who need immediate, rehabilitative, and development services, and establishes local coordinating mechanisms such as the Barangay (Village) Councils for the Protection of Children.[25]

The UNICEF-Philippine agreement also cited the Social Reform and Poverty Alleviation Act R.A. No. 8425.[26] The act provides "the adoption of area-based, sectoral and focused interventions to poverty alleviation wherein every poor Filipino family shall be empowered to meet its minimum basic needs of health, food and nutrition, water and environmental sanitation, income security, shelter and decent housing, peace and order, education and functional literacy, participation in governance, and family care and psychosocial integrity."[27]

Mainstreaming Child Rights
in Local Development Planning

In 1991 the Philippine government adopted the Local Government Code and devolved most social services to local government units of cities, municipalities, and provinces. Between 1993 and 1997, commitments to the CRC were received from local governments through, respectively, the League of Cities

(1993), the League of Provinces (1994, 1995), and the League of Municipalities (1997), stating their support of national and local goals for children and the pursuit of child-friendly policies. The current UNICEF-Philippine agreement's objectives to strengthen the capacity of national and local governments to implement the CRC and to contribute to a massive mobilization in support of the Child-Friendly Movement at all administrative levels, local communities, and within the family resulted in a project for mainstreaming child rights in local development planning.[28]

Under this project, a municipal plan for children can be completed through a six-month participatory process. A three-day local planning exercise is preceded by months of preparatory studies during which a core planning committee gathers information on the local child situation and invites key officials and community representatives to participate in the planning process. They gather baseline information through secondary data and direct observations of children using a matrix that incorporates child rights and life cycle stages developed for use in the planning exercise. In the planning exercise, participants and resource persons review and assess the information prepared by the core committee to establish the key contents of the Local Plan for Children by consensus.

The proposed plan is prepared together with an annual investment plan and budget. Formal endorsement and adoption by the local legislature and local chief executive, and budget allocation complete the process. Representatives from the children's sector (e.g., student leaders or presidents of local children's associations), local people's organizations and NGOs, and church and civic organizations join planning participants from the local government agencies.

The discussions on the framework for the Local Plan for Children help participants understand the CRC as the legal framework for promoting the rights of Filipino children and are based on the indicators compiled earlier on the status of children according to the four major categories of children's rights: survival, development, protection, and participation, including the auxiliary rights and the indicators associated with these major categories. Of these, indicators about school participation, incidence of child labor, number of street children, incidence of child abuse, and sexual exploitation of children are among those most directly related to child labor. There are also indicators around the right to information and participation of children.

Discussions follow in reply to the question: "What do you perceive to be the problems or negative conditions confronted by children in your province/city/municipality in the areas of survival, development, protection, and participation?" The facilitator distributes the situation analysis matrix and asks the small groups to discuss (a) the direct causes of the problems identified per major rights category, associated right, or life cycle category of the child; (b) the national and local interventions that support child rights; and (c) the weaknesses of the existing interventions. Box 8.1, constituting the situa-

Box 8.1   Situational Matrix of Children's Rights

1. Right to life
   Prenatal Period
   - Quality of prenatal care
   - Maternal health
   Infancy
   - Neonatal mortality rate
   - Maternal mortality rate
   - Birth weight
   - Infant mortality rate
   - Prevalence of diseases
2. Right to a name, nationality, and identity
   - Number of infants registered at birth
3. Right to health (infancy to adolescence)
   - Child mortality rate
   - Under-five mortality rate
   - Rate of low birth weight
   - Prevalence of severely and moderately underweight preschoolers
   - Nutritional deficiencies
   - Prevalence of diseases
   - Immunization
   - Health morbidity
   - Adolescent sexuality
   - Adolescent-focused health programs
4. Right to be protected from abuse and neglect
   - Incidence of child abuse
   - Number of street children
   - Number of families unable to provide adequate protection to child
   - Protection and rehabilitation of abused children
5. Right of the disabled child to special care
   - Number of children with disability
   - Programs for disabled children
6. Right to social security
   - State provisions in absence of family
7. Right to be protected from commercial and sexual exploitation (early childhood to adolescence)
   - Incidence of child labor
   - Number of children engaged in sexual or commercial exploitation
   - Protection and rehabilitation of exploited children
   - Presence/implementation of adequate laws and programs
8. Right to education
   - Literacy rate
   - Cohort survival rate/dropout rate

continues

Box 8.1   continued

- Achievement rate
- Participation rate: day care, elementary, secondary, tertiary students
- Presence of educational infrastructure
- Educational programs

9. Right to rest and leisure
   - Number of schools with playgrounds
   - Number of municipalities with parks/playgrounds

10. Right to opinion (childhood to adolescence)
    - Provision of venue for children's opinions to be heard and considered in planning

11. Right to freedom of association

12. Right to freedom of expression
    - Membership of children in associations and organizations (throughout the life cycle)

13. Right to enjoy one's culture and religion

14. Right to adequate standard of living
    - Access to potable water
    - Access to sanitary toilets
    - Family members with basic clothing
    - Housing conditions
    - Employment and income

15. Right to parental care and support
    - Early separation from mother
    - Violence in family and/or community

16. Right to information
    - Maternal and family illiteracy

17. Right to privacy

18. Right to be safe in emergency or especially difficult circumstances (e.g., armed conflict, child without family)
    - Incidence of terminated pregnancies
    - Incidence of displacement due to armed conflict, natural disasters, crime
    - Provision of basic services to children in situation of armed conflict
    - Physical and psychological recovery and social reintegration of children in especially difficult circumstances

19. Right to legal assistance and appropriate judicial processes
    - Implementation of laws for child protection

20. Right to freedom of thought, conscience, and religion
    - Family members able to vote in elections

21. Right to freedom of association
    - Family members involved in at least one people's association/organization, community development

tional matrix worksheet distributed, shows in detail the headings and sub-headings of the indicators explored.[29]

When, thereafter, plans of action more specific to child labor are framed, they are guided by the implementation checklist suggested by UNICEF's *Implementation Handbook on the Convention on the Rights of the Child,*[30] as presented in Box 8.2.

Box 8.2   Implementation Checklist: Article 32—Protection from Economic Exploitation

General and specific measures of implementation
   Reminder: The Convention is indivisible and its articles are interdependent. Article 32 should not be considered in isolation. Particular regard should be paid to:
The general principles
   Article 2: all rights to be recognized for each child in jurisdiction without discrimination on any ground
   Article 3(1): the best interests of the child to be a primary consideration in all actions concerning children
   Article 6: right to life and maximum possible survival and development
   Article 12: respect for the child's views in all matters affecting the child; opportunity to be heard in any judicial or administrative proceedings affecting the child
Closely related articles
   Articles whose implementation is related to that of article 32 include:
      Article 15: freedom of association (trade unions)
      Article 27: adequate standard of living
      Article 28: right to education
      Article 31: right to leisure, play, and recreation
      Article 33: illicit production and trafficking in drugs
      Article 34: sexual exploitation
      Article 35: sale, trafficking, and abduction
      Article 36: other forms of harmful exploitation
      Article 39: rehabilitation care for child victims

Project: Expanding Children's Participation in Social Reform

Children's participation in planning exercises such as the Local Plan for Children has accelerated as a result of a specific project started in 1997 for the purpose of organizing children as a distinct sector in the policymaking arena. In 1995, four child-focused NGOs in the Philippines—the Christian Children's Fund, the World Vision Development Foundation, Plan International, and the

Educational Research and Development Assistance Foundation—made the case for children to be represented alongside other sectors in the 1995 national Anti-Poverty Summit. The government had created the National Anti-Poverty Commission to implement its poverty alleviation and social reform agenda, identifying "basic sectors" that were to be officially represented in the commission (e.g., farmers, fisherfolk, women, indigenous peoples, etc.). During the succeeding two years, these four NGOs organized local consultation workshops with children in preparation for the creation of a separate Children's Basic Sector within the National Anti-Poverty Council (NAPC).

In 1997 the four NGOs collectively obtained funding support from the US Agency for International Development (USAID) to start a project called "Expanding Children's Participation in Social Reform," undertaken specifically to "organize the children as a sector and increase their participation in the public policy arena; create and establish national and local coalitions of NGOs and people's organizations to collectively address issues and concerns affecting children; intensify advocacy efforts for and on behalf of the children in the legislative process."[31] They organized children's associations, held children's assemblies, worked with the local Village Councils for the Protection of Children (with children participating), and undertook research and advocacy activities. The children's associations were federated eventually into the National Coalition of Children's Associations in the Philippines. The NGOs that had organized them likewise established themselves as the National Committee on Child and Youth Participation as a support group to the children's coalition. Between the two coalitions of adults and children, they represent the children's sector in the National Anti-Poverty Council. They also draw on their members to sit in local councils for the protection of children and in meetings with local officials, and to mobilize for advocacy activities such as child rights rallies and marches, and Children's Day celebrations.[32]

▨   Perceived Results

Heightened Public Awareness
By 2001, awareness of children's rights among Filipino children themselves was already high. A regional opinion survey among young people aged nine to seventeen years ("Speaking Out!")[33] examined, among other things, the extent to which children know that they have rights and are aware of specific rights. Among those sampled in the survey were 500 Filipino children and youth.

When asked, "Do you think children, like adults, have rights?" 82 percent said yes, compared to the regional average of 62 percent who also said yes. Of the specific child rights of which they were spontaneously aware, the children cited the following: the right to education (42%); the right to express opinions/ideas (19%); the right to play/amusement (14%); the right not to be hurt or mistreated (11%); the right to be loved (9%); the right to health care

(2%); the right to adequate food (1%); the right to a clean environment (5%); and the right to information (1%).[34] When read a list of nine rights and asked how much they knew about these rights, their answers for those rights they knew "a lot" or "something" about were the right to be loved (95%); the right to adequate food (93%); the right to play/amusement (91%); the right to health care (91%); the right to a clean environment (91%); the right to education (88%); the right to express opinions/ideas (84%); the right not to be hurt or mistreated (76%); and the right to information (75%).[35]

Most of the Filipino children and youth also believed that child rights were respected in their country. They indicated that the following rights were "totally" or "quite" respected: the right to be loved (97%); the right to play/amusement (96%); the right to health care (94%); the right to education (93%); the right to adequate food (89%); the right to a clean environment (88%); the right to express ideas/opinions (87%); the right to information (86%); and the right not to be hurt or mistreated (81%).

Strengths and Weaknesses

The generally promising picture described above was counterbalanced by what was said at an assessment workshop in September 2001 by children who were involved in local and national children's associations and by adults who had been representing the children's sector in the National Anti-Poverty Council.[36] The assessment workshop posed the following question: "What were the 'sweet' things that made you happy and the 'sour' things that made you unhappy in the National Anti-Poverty Council–Children's Basic Sector?" They also were asked what they considered the helping and hindering factors in their efforts to influence policies. Children's responses were complemented by adult participants' responses.[37]

Children replied that the opportunities for training, exposure, and travel had helped their personality development and that they were happy about the bonds of friendship that they had established. They gained much satisfaction in providing services to other children. They were happy also to have been involved with various working groups in local and national governments, in formulating organizational guidelines for children's associations organized by the NGOs, and in the signature campaign for the ratification of 1999 ILO Convention (No. 182) Concerning the Prohibition and Immediate Elimination of the Worst Forms of Child Labour (ILO C182).

Adult participants said that the children became more responsible, more confident, more aware, and more vigilant about child rights. They saw children gaining respect in the community as well as internationally, and adults becoming more sensitive to children's issues and concerns. They were happy about strengthened cooperation between the government and the NGO sector.

When it came to the "sour" issues regarding their experience as representatives of the Children's Basic Sector in the NAPC, the children were forthright and critical. Topping the list was "unmet promises, especially of local government support." They were unhappy about political instability and changes in government administration, and about the "lack of enforcement in the grassroots level." They saw divisions among the other basic sectors making up the NAPC and complained about delayed communication from other agencies and groups. They questioned the viability of what came out of the National Anti-Poverty Summit. Interesting, as well, was their dilemma in dividing their time and being torn between two priorities: their studies and their children's sector activities.

The adults in the group agreed with the children that choosing between studies and involvement in the NAPC had troubled many child representatives and their parents, and created tensions with school authorities as well. They shared children's frustrations with the local implementers, particularly when they saw children become victims of political battles in government. They were unhappy with "long meetings without concrete actions taken," with the freezing of already limited funds, and with inconsistent laws and policies. They were unhappy with some adult attitudes and were uncertain about exposing children to the adult world.

These disappointments were described by the children and adults together as they talked of factors that helped or hindered them from attaining their objectives. For instance, in lobbying for a resolution from lawmakers regarding children in war and in implementing instructions from the Philippine Department of Education encouraging children's sector participation in the NAPC, they found strong grassroots support and assurances of support from some high-ranking officials. But in the end, they found, among the agencies that were supposed to implement the new measures, that the "resolutions fell on deaf ears, were disregarded; no action taken on their requests, standstill in government offices."[38]

As to their contribution to the NAPC agenda, the children and adults had submitted the results of their consultative workshops to various local government agencies. They were happy to have aired children's issues and concerns and to assert a clear identity for the Children's Basic Sector. Local councils for the welfare of children incorporated the Children's Basic Sector proposals into the NAPC program plans. However, in most cases, the children saw their program proposals remaining on the level of a "broad agenda" or "modified in favor of the implementers" or implemented too slowly.

Saying that constant follow-up and monitoring were necessary to ensure implementation of plans and proposals, the children also contended that monitoring and evaluation were part of their responsibility. This viewpoint allowed them to communicate with local government authorities directly, to promote the Children's Basic Sector more actively, and to measure results against stated objectives. But they were seriously limited in this work because of the conflicting schedules between school and their NAPC activities, the lack of support from some NGOs, and the absence of practical guidelines they could use for monitoring.

Children saw their role as child rights advocates as most significant. They valued their participation in consultative meetings, in local policy discussions, in national and international activities, in campaigns and grassroots organizing, in forming a pool of child facilitators, and in lobbying in legislative and executive offices. They said that their strengths included the fact that the "children's voice is heard" and that "the idea of children having rights is slowly being accepted." But they also pointed out that "child participation is not yet well developed, that activities are mostly adult-led or driven," and that many times they did not get the adult support they needed. They also faulted the means by which child representatives were selected in local and international activities, saying that at times children were used in politics, and that budgetary support for their activities was always very limited.

Commenting on the commemoration of the tenth anniversary of the CRC with the National Summit on Children, the children were enthusiastic about the national media exposure. "We instantly got the commitment; we had the chance to tell authorities what we want; more children were involved." But then disappointment came as they saw that "adults dominated in number. There was a commitment . . . but there was no action on issues presented."[39]

◼ Overall Assessment of the National Program Against Child Labor

Both the children's satisfaction and their disappointment with the results of efforts to promote child rights in the Philippines in general, and to combat child labor in particular, find resonance in the overall assessment of the so-called National Program Against Child Labor (NPACL).[40] During 2000–2001, the Philippine Department of Labor and Employment, which heads the National Child Labor Committee, convened a series of consultative assessment workshops with the many government agencies and NGOs that were involved in child labor projects, most of which were funded by the ILO and UNICEF. Around this time also, UNICEF undertook a program review of the initiatives it supported to combat child labor in the Philippines, particularly with respect to children involved in trafficking and commercial sexual exploitation.[41]

The assessment report on the NPACL cited as a major accomplishment increased public awareness about child labor (with survey results finding an increase from 57 percent in 1995 to 71 percent in 2000). The NPACL was said to have mobilized broad alliances across sectors and had "improved services; increased research on child labor; built capabilities of partners, children, families and communities; used workplace monitoring and occupational safety and health issues as entry points; highlighted child participation as a strategic practice."[42] It listed the elements of the program that were considered "worth sustaining" by its network of governmental and nongovernmental program implementers:

- Reliable, comprehensive information on child labor
- Broad-based and target-specific advocacy
- Laws on child protection and enforcement
- Issue-based community organizing, participation, and empowerment
- Innovative approaches to surveillance and rescue
- Alternative educational modalities
- Quality capability-building interventions using head, heart, hands strategy
- Efforts to document, monitor, and evaluate programs
- Child participation, organization, and empowerment
- Using occupational safety and health issues in workplace monitoring
- Partnering, inter-agency, multidisciplinary approaches.[43]

It also pointed up program gaps in research, communication, and capacity building; uncoordinated resource allocation and service delivery; and inadequate documentation, monitoring, and evaluation. The assessment also indicated concern about the "inadequate enabling environment" and about the fact that "caring in service delivery was not yet fully recognized as a collective value."[44] Major challenges, which the NPACL continues to face, were said to be those of "influencing family and community values," providing economic opportunities for families of child laborers, and ensuring adequate education for children.[45]

The UNICEF project review (in which I participated) brought out persistent problems and challenges that previous program reviews had enumerated. Program participants and children themselves pointed out the need to reduce more proactively the demand for child labor by targeting the perpetrators even though this concern is couched often in terms of "weak law enforcement" or "influencing family and community values." Project strategies, project activities, and project results tended to be defined much more in terms of what to do with the children and much less in terms of what to do with those who harm and exploit them. Although the circumstances surrounding the trafficking and sexual exploitation of children are increasingly known, even to the extent of pinpointing illegal recruiters, erring employers, and other vested interests that impede child protection, little is usually done about them.[46] The reports and studies raise the important question about what to do with the information on the perpetrators of trafficking and sexual exploitation of children.

The assessments stressed that advocacy messages about child labor in general, and victims of trafficking and sexual exploitation in particular, graphically portray only children and their sorrowful plight. In very few instances are the perpetrators depicted, nor is their criminal behavior even suggested, much less exposed. When bars are raided, for example, it is the girls who are rounded up, photographed, and shamed in newspapers and on television. Little fingerpointing, if any, is directed toward the bar owners or their customers. Similarly, in project communities, there is little analysis done to identify which economic and political interests inside and outside of government are culpable in, or accountable for, perpetrating child labor.

Among the NPACL's objectives is the goal of "appropriate physical and psychosocial services to child labour victims as well as safety nets and employment opportunities to children and their families."[47] Scattered project reports give examples of very limited results in terms of providing recovery and rehabilitation services, educational assistance, training and support for parents, community organizing and advocacy, and training for service providers. The review reported that some recovery and rehabilitation services were provided by the Department of Social Welfare and Development and a few NGOs, but these temporary shelters and their services were far from adequate. It therefore stressed the need to improve the quality of service—more specifically, the quality of caring given to child victims, including health and medical care.

Only a few thousand children were estimated as receiving educational assistance from projects under the NPACL. There were spotty reports about organizing parents and training them for livelihood projects and more effective parenting. There was a wide range of activities involving or affecting different kinds of people, but almost always limited to small numbers of actual beneficiaries. More than the concern about the limited numbers was the concern about the limited knowledge of the effects or outcomes of the interventions. A major conclusion of the project review was that much more needs to be done in terms of providing the basic services (especially health and education) for child laborers and the safety nets and alternative income opportunities for their families.

There were reports of local advocacy activities for local government officials, community leaders, and multisectoral groups including employers and labor groups. "Advocacy" was the most frequent project intervention by both governmental and nongovernmental agencies alike. Although there were reports of positive results, it was not always clear which advocacy activities yielded which results, or whether or not specific advocacy activities were particularly effective in raising public awareness. For raising public awareness about child labor, posting information materials at strategic points, such as the entry and exit points of illegal recruitment activities, was thought effective. Forging memoranda of agreement with port authorities, employers' groups, and other watchdog groups increased the number of vigilance groups. Children's theater was found appealing in terms of raising community consciousness about the risks and dangers that working children face. Some groups reported working with their municipal planning offices and successfully linking advocacy work with local development planning and budgeting.

The review of the overall NPACL and of the specific project on child victims of trafficking and sexual exploitation showed clearly that some headway had been made but also that certain problems and constraints persisted. Inadequate support toward psychosocial recovery and reintegration services for child victims sometimes resulted in children ending up worse off than before they were rescued or "assisted" by well-meaning but not wholly competent or equipped service providers or by those who were not truly caring toward the children in their custody.

During recent economic downturns, increasing economic difficulties for families in the Philippines have pushed more children to work, thus causing them to withdraw from school, with serious implications for a national program that will have to address a problem that is growing rather than abating despite best efforts. Resistance and pressure from power groups and those with vested interests, including parents and children themselves, constitute the most formidable challenge for those in the program, especially when no other options or alternatives to the exploitation of children are discernible to them. In addition, slow and ineffectual adjudication and prosecution processes for child labor cases reflect the power wielded by those who are apt to exploit children in contrast to the powerlessness not only of the children themselves but even of those who work to protect them. Inadequate technical expertise among implementers—especially in legal and policy matters—hampers efforts to enforce existing laws and guidelines and to raise public awareness about these laws and policies.

The review emphasized the need for continuing assessment through children's participation, to find out from children themselves how they perceive and experience the protection and care that the projects and implementers purport to give. Children's perceptions are often different from those of the adult caregivers, and have serious implications for effective care for these children—all the more reason, it must be added, to take Article 12 of the CRC seriously.[48]

▨ Implications

A significant feature in the Philippine experience of combating child labor on the basis of child rights is that of "embedding" child labor issues—hence also children's rights—in the country's wider poverty and social reform agenda. Pursuing this rights-based strategy implies efforts toward more serious and effective involvement of children and youth as the Children's Basic Sector of the National Anti-Poverty Council. It signals also poverty and power structure analyses, especially at the grassroots, community, and local government levels in places where child labor is known to exist. Poverty reduction and social reform measures at the local level can then be more focused on combating the poverty and powerlessness of families and preventing communities from generating child labor. The challenges to child rights advocates are more formidable than ever, as all indicators point to a worsening poverty and income distribution picture. Civil strife and political insecurity continue as local governance deteriorates in many parts of the Philippines.

One positive indication that such a rights-based approach to development programming is taking shape and enjoying some success in the country is the training manual drafted by the United Nations Country Team in the Philippines.[49] The training design aims "to provide U.N. staff with a conceptual and operational understanding of a rights-based approach and its importance to development programming."[50] It further explains:

> A rights-based approach can be traced back to the U.N. Charter and is linked to the Right to Development and the Sustainable Human Development paradigm. It is consistent with the human rights mandate of all U.N. Agencies. A rights-based approach to development views development as the process of realization of fundamental human rights and freedoms. It understands poverty as a question of powerlessness rather than mere lack of commodities and services, and consequently recognizes the need to bring political, economic, social and cultural dimensions into the analysis of poverty. Development programming should adopt a human rights perspective: the approach proposes the use of human rights concepts and standards in the analysis of development problems and in the design of projects and programmes, including mechanisms to assess the impact of these programmes and the process by which they are developed and implemented. In a rights-based approach, the process is as important as the outcome. A rights-based approach puts the poor, marginalized, vulnerable groups at the core of policy and the focus of capacity development strategies. Gender analysis is an intrinsic part of a rights-based approach to development, not an add-on. The four broad benefits of a human rights approach can be described as: (1) holistic and multidimensional analysis of development issues; (2) enhanced accountability; (3) genuine empowerment; and (4) greater normative clarity.[51]

Another interesting development in child rights advocacy is the alliance building promoted by the UNICEF-initiated Child-Friendly Movement. Even while it builds on the country's experience with the "minimum needs approach" to development planning, it introduces a child rights framework for gaining allies with various sectors. Hence there are projects in support of child-friendly municipalities, child-friendly schools, child-friendly churches, and so forth. Instead of assuming an adversarial relationship between those who advocate child rights and those who do not, the strategy seems to be that of "constructive engagement" of the relevant local power structures. It will be interesting and useful over the long term to see how effective this approach turns out to be, especially at the local levels.

Finally, in all the plans and activities undertaken to advocate child rights and to combat and eliminate child labor, the bottom line for children seems to be the need for love and trust between children and adults. Some are sensing already that they are being used and manipulated by the grown-ups or sometimes unwittingly jeopardized by them. Others end up in situations worse off than before adults (even well-meaning ones) came around to help or rescue them. Children cannot help but see all the plans and programs and projects as promises by adults. They are quick to see when adults keep their promises and when they do not.

Notes

1. In this chapter, I adopt the definition of "child labor" set forth in the introduction to this volume, in turn derived from Chapter 2, that is, "work done by children that is harmful to them because it is abusive, exploitive, hazardous, or otherwise contrary to their best interests—a subset of a larger class of children's work, some of which may be compatible with children's best interests (variously expressed as 'beneficial,' 'benign,' or 'harmless' children's work)."

2. United Nations, *Convention on the Rights of the Child* (1989).

3. Article 12 provides: "(1) States Parties shall assure to the child who is capable of forming his or her own views the right to express those views freely in all matters affecting the child, the views of the child being given due weight in accordance with the age and maturity of the child. (2) For this purpose, the child shall in particular be provided the opportunity to be heard in any judicial and administrative proceedings affecting the child, either directly, or through a representative or an appropriate body, in a manner consistent with the procedural rules of national law."

4. Government of the Philippines, *Survey . . . .*

5. Government of the Philippines, *Philippine National Plan of Action . . . .*

6. Government of the Philippines and UNICEF, *Commercial Sexual Exploitation . . . .*

7. *Proceedings: Changing Our Lives . . . .*

8. Ibid., p. 81.

9. ILO, *Convention* (No. 182) *Concerning the Prohibition and Immediate Elimination of the Worst Forms of Child Labour* (1999).

10. *Proceedings: Changing Our Lives . . . ,* p. 84.

11. *Report of National Consultation on Child Labor in Commercial Plantations.*

12. Ibid., p. 19.

13. See de la Cruz, *Trust and Power . . . .*

14. Ibid., p. 81.

15. *Report on Children's Forum and Regional Consultation . . . ,* p. 21.

16. Ibid., p. 11.

17. Ibid., p. 21.

18. Ibid., p. 12.

19. Ibid.

20. Government of the Philippines and UNICEF, *Country Programme of Cooperation for Child Survival . . . ,* p. 1.

21. *Constitution of the Republic of the Philippines* (1987), art. II ("Declaration of Principles and State Policies"), sec. 13; art. XV ("The Family"), sec. 3.

22. Government of the Philippines, *Philippine National Plan of Action for Children . . . .*

23. *Philippine Child and Youth Welfare Code.*

24. Ibid., art. 1 ("Declaration of Policy"); art. 3 ("Rights of the Child").

25. Ibid., chap. 2, sec. A, art. 87.

26. *Philippine Social Reform and Poverty Alleviation Act.*

27. Ibid., sec. 4.

28. Council for the Welfare of Children and UNICEF, *Guidelines Mainstreaming Child Rights . . . ,* p. iv.

29. Ibid., pp. 39–41.

30. UNICEF, *Implementation Handbook* . . . .

31. UNICEF, *National Child and Youth Participation Framework* . . . , p. 16.

32. Ibid., pp. 16–18.

33. UNICEF, *Speaking Out!* . . .

34. Ibid., p. 66.

35. Ibid., p. 67.

36. *Proceedings of National Anti-Poverty Council* . . . .

37. Ibid., p. 9.

38. Ibid., pp. 9–10.

39. Ibid., p. 12.

40. Mante and Mante, *Overall Assessment* . . . , pp. 1–5.

41. UNICEF, *Making a Difference* . . . .

42. Mante and Mante, *Overall Assessment* . . . , p. 2.

43. Ibid., p. 3.

44. Ibid., p. 4.

45. Ibid., p. 5.

46. The perpetrators not only include recruiters and owners of brothels and bars, but also bar and club customers who demand and pay for the services of young "guest relations officers." Parents who accept the offers of recruiters, if they do not offer their children in the first place, are another set of perpetrators, although perhaps much more difficult to blame outright.

47. Government of the Philippines, *Redefining the Strategic Directions and Thrusts* . . . , p. 5.

48. See supra endnote 3.

49. UNDP Philippines, *Training Manual* . . . .

50. Ibid., p. 2.

51. Ibid., p. 23.

9

Combating
Child Labor in Brazil:
Social Movements in Action

Benedito Rodrigues dos Santos

*Around 3.5 million children under the age of 14 work in Brazil. More than
70% of them make around half of the minimum wage. Many of them have
semi-slave work conditions: they work long hours, up to 12 hours a day,
without receiving any money for that work. Many of them cut up to 2 tons
of sugar cane per day or carry heavy orange boxes damaging their health
incurably. Others have their lungs damaged by working in charcoal mines
or by inhaling glue at the shoe factories. These types of work are not isolated cases from the backwards periphery of the productive system. Big
multinational and national corporations such as Mercedes, Volkswagen,
Bombril, GM, Ford, Fiat, Cofap, Cosip, Cultrale, Dharma and Petrobs are
just some of the many companies that benefit from the exploitation of a
workforce of children. These companies are consumers of the raw material
produced by children or goods made from child labor.*
　　　　　　　　—Oliveira et al., "Nossas Crianças . . . ," p. 8

Until the mid-1980s, child labor, though legally prohibited, was fully tolerated
by the government, nonprofit organizations, and grassroots movements in
Brazil.[1] It was the dissemination of the children's rights paradigm, building
upon the principles of human rights, that generated the basis for intolerance
of child labor after that time.

In 1990, an estimated 8 million young people between ages ten and seventeen were working throughout Brazil—a strikingly high number. Brazil has
one of the biggest youth populations in the world. While the 1989 United Nations Convention on the Rights of the Child (CRC) defines a child as a person
under age eighteen,[2] the Brazilian Estatuto da Criança e do Adolescente
(ECA; Statute of the Child and Adolescent)[3] makes a distinction between a
child, who is a person under age twelve, and an adolescent, who is a person

between ages twelve and eighteen. The child and adolescent population constitutes around 40 percent of Brazil's 160 million inhabitants. Distribution among the age brackets indicates that more than 60 percent of young people are between seven and seventeen years old. Around 70 percent of all youths live in urban settings.[4] The country follows a school-age demarcation similar to that in most Western countries: preschool, ages three to six; mandatory school, ages seven to fourteen, with fourteen as the age of apprenticeship, sixteen as the age for optional voting and entering the job market, and eighteen as the age of full citizenship and mandatory voting.

The number of working children in Brazil represents 30 percent of the youth population between ages seven and seventeen, and around 12 percent of the entire economically active population. In 1990, 3.4 million workers, around 40 percent of the total Brazilian work force, were between ten and fourteen years old, an age bracket for which working was legally prohibited (the minimum age to begin working was not raised from fourteen to sixteen until 2001). A little more than half of working children and adolescents were situated in agriculture, picking citrus fruit, tea leaves, tobacco, coffee beans, and vegetables, and cutting sugar cane. While some of them worked on their families' small properties, others worked as paid-by-day workers in agrobusiness, migrating according to the harvest seasons. Normally they worked from sunrise to sunset, making misery wages.

The second largest group of working children is engaged in activities in the informal market of the service and commerce sectors; they form the legions of street vendors, domestic workers, car watchers and washers, paper collectors, junk dealers, and manual laborers performing unskilled jobs. A third group engages in industry as unskilled workers at tile, brick, and shoe factories. Most of them struggle with low wages, long work hours, and unhealthy working conditions.[5]

If we classify the work performed by Brazilian children according to the distinction between "child labor" (unacceptable work that does not contribute to the healthy development of children) and "benign child work" (acceptable to be performed by children), there is no doubt that the vast majority of the occupations, jobs, and tasks performed by children in Brazil fit into the first category. The 2000 Ministry of Labor Act (No. 20) of September 13, 2001, describing the most hazardous forms of work for children in Brazil, lists around ninety jobs, occupations, or tasks children are performing that are arduous and harmful to their full development.

However, the picture of child labor changed significantly during the last decade of the twentieth century, with researchers showing a substantial reduction in child labor rates by the end of the 1990s. According to the 2001 *Pesquisa Nacional de Domicilio* (National Household Research), developed by the Instituto Brasileiro de Geografia e Estatísticas (IBGE; Brazilian Institute of Geography and Statistics), child labor in Brazil has been reduced by 35 percent in the past ten years. Even after accepting that statistics fail to capture hidden child labor, a reduction by 35 percent in the number of working children seems to constitute an indisputable confirmation of the impact of a decade of collective effort to combat child labor.

What were the factors responsible for the changes? Some researchers have attributed the reduction of child labor in Brazil overwhelmingly to programs providing financial support to families of poor and working children such as the Programa Bolsa-Escola (School Grant Program), aimed at keeping children in school and preventing them from performing child labor.[6] The Brazilian office of the International Labour Organization (ILO Brazil) provides a broader explanation, arguing that law enforcement in the formal sector of the economy and income programs associated with schools were responsible for the reduction in child labor rates.[7]

The hypotheses of both the researchers and ILO Brazil's director are plausible explanations for the decrease in child labor. Taken individually, however, they are insufficient. Comparing the number of working children who labor with the number covered by social programs, it becomes clear, as I demonstrate later in this chapter, that the latter account for just one-third of the drop in rates. The reduction in the child labor figures calls for more substantial, deeper analyses. Missing, for example, is the attitude shift that has taken place in the past three decades in the perception of child labor in Brazilian society, with the meaning of child labor having changed radically from one of "virtue" to one of a "rights violation."[8]

From my anthropological and activist perspective and in the context of postdictatorship/redemocratized Brazil, I emphasize the role of social mobilization in bringing about changed attitudes toward child labor among certain key organizations advocating on the behalf of and with children—organizations that have exercised strong influence over the design and implementation of social policies such as the School Grant Program. Further, I contend that this attitudinal shift was part of a worldwide cultural "revolution" regarding the meaning of childhood in postindustrial societies and that, in Brazil, a new political actor—the children's rights movement—was largely responsible for it. That is, a new politics of childhood (involving changes in assumptions, attitudes, laws, policies, strategies, and practices) emerged in Brazil at a particular and significant historical moment when an interpretation of human rights principles mediated by the philosophical tenets of liberation theology became a strategy to confront the dictatorship. I detail the trajectory of this development below.

The unique combination of human rights principles and liberation theology that has shaped my own academic and activist work informs my analysis in this study. In this chapter I analyze the shift made by social movements in their strategies to combat child labor by way of a short chronology of the children's rights movement in Brazil; I review the process by which child labor became part of the agenda of social movements, leading them to new campaigns and intervention strategies; I focus on the lessons learned from child labor eradication campaigns; and I consider the impact of these campaigns on Brazilian social policies through the creation of the Brazilian federal government's Programa de Erradicação do Trabalho Infantil (PETI; National Program for Child Labor Eradication) in 1996. I conclude by noting new challenges and tendencies in programming and funding child labor eradication campaigns.

▓ From Child Labor as Virtue to Child Labor as Social Problem

Until the mid-1980s, Brazilian public and private institutions active in children's and adolescents' work traditionally used two strategies: (a) training poor children for the "survival occupations" most characteristic of the informal market by developing "alternative" income generation programs carried out by nonprofit organizations; and (b) training children from the fourth grade on up and adolescents for jobs in the formal labor market, mainly in private companies through national apprenticeship systems coordinated by the Sistema Nacional de Aprendizagem Industrial (SENAI; National System for Industrial Apprenticeship) and the Sistema Nacional de Aprendizagem Comercial (SENAC; National System for Commercial Apprenticeship). In the early 1990s, however, nongovernmental organizations (NGOs) changed their child labor objectives and strategies significantly, moving to eliminate child labor and safeguard working adolescents rather than prepare them for the labor market. The principal demands of the children's rights movement were for children to stay in school, for families to be supported, and for adolescents to have a right to vocational training.[9]

The following factors combined to produce this change in objectives and strategies: the inhumanity of the military dictatorship of the 1970s; the emergence of a broad-based, prochild social movement; the dissemination of the child rights paradigm and the creation and redesign of new social policies for children; criticisms of the two principal strategies for combating child labor; and finally, technical and financial support from the International Labour Organization through its International Programme on the Elimination of Child Labour (IPEC) and the United Nations Children's Fund (UNICEF), each of which played a fundamental role in establishing new objectives and strategies for the prochild social movements.

A Short Chronology of the Children's Rights Movement in Brazil

Beginning in the 1980s, a broad pro–children's rights movement for and with poor children and adolescents assumed responsibility not only for setting an agenda to eradicate child labor in Brazil in the 1990s but also for generating an environment favorable to implementing that agenda. The seeds were sown during the time of the military dictatorship of the 1970s.

The 1970s: Military dictatorship. The 1970s in Brazil saw a "strange combination of economic advance and democratic reversal."[10] While experiencing the so-called economic miracle with gross domestic product (GDP) growth rates of 12 percent per annum, it also experienced the dismantling by the military regime of social and popular movements, severely repressing the political expression of civil society. By the mid-1970s, the social policies adopted by the military to modernize the country showed signs of fatigue. The development process exacerbated social inequalities, increasing disparities between Brazil's rich and poor and its different regions and bringing with it high infant mortality rates, decreased life expectancy, premature entry into the labor market, school evasion, and an increasing presence of children working and living on the streets.

At the same time, the military increased its interventions in respect of children and adolescents, with two childhoods recognized officially in two systems of social policies aimed at children and adolescents. On the one hand, the education and health ministries elaborated general policies for "children," whose responsibilities were carried over from the former national Departamento da Criança (Children's Department). On the other hand, the welfare ministry elaborated social policies for "minors" (children of the poor under eighteen years of age), to whom was given "social problem" status in the Doctrina de Segurunça National (Doctrine of National Security), the ideological foundation of the military dictatorship.

The 1980s: Creation of the children's rights movement. The situation of the 1970s was reversed in the 1980s as the dictatorship faltered. While economically the 1980s were characterized by disastrous cycles of inflation and recession, legal advances in this period were both positive and significant. Broad-based social movements, including the children's rights movement, reemerged. "The legislature was, at least partly, able to recover its force and some gains were achieved especially in social rights."[11]

To a significant extent these developments arose out of indignation toward the violence against minors and children, an indignation that took the form of a specific social movement in defense of children and adolescents, which in turn became a new political actor in the process of the country's redemocratization. Guided by principles of human rights, liberation theology, and popular education, a few years later this movement would incorporate the children's rights agenda explicitly. It took place in two phases.

1980–1984: Gestation phase—the movement of community alternatives. Between 1980 and 1984, various programs emerged advocating the construction and dissemination of the so-called alternative model for minors, particularly street children. These experiences, structured by a dialogical pedagogy from a community perspective, developed initiatives and services in the areas of health, nutrition, education, work, and leisure that had in common an underlying philosophy that the child should be considered a subject of the pedagogical process, not merely an object in the socializing and policymaking processes.[12] The Projeto Alternativas Comunitárias de Atendimento a Meninos de Rua (Community Alternatives for Care of Street Children Project), developed by UNICEF, the National Foundation for the Welfare of Minors (FUNBEM), and the Secretaria de Assistência Social do Ministério da Previdência e Assistência Social (SAS; Social Action Secretariat of the Ministry of Social Security and Action), took on the job of systematizing and disseminating the pedagogical proposal and methodology for these new social agents. During the 1980s, programs following this model proliferated.

1985–1989: National organizations set up and develop the rights paradigm. In the process of mobilizing these alternative programs, the Movimento Nacional de Meninos e Meninas de Ruas (MNMMR; Brazilian National Movement of Street Boys and Girls) was formed, and after its creation in 1985 other networks of organizations emerged on the national scene. The Frente Nacional dos Direitos da Criança (National Front for the Defense of Children's Rights), made up of progressive municipal administrations, existed briefly in 1985. Then the Pastoral do Menor (Pastoral of Minors) of the Conferência Nacional dos Bispos do Brasil (National Bishops' Conference) set up its own national coordination, using as a model the original Pastoral do Menor established in São Paulo in 1978. From this point on, the movement broadened, intensifying and diversifying its activities with the inclusion of new participants and the creation of coalitions coordinating their efforts.

The Forum Nacional Permanente de Organizações Não-Governamentais de Defesa dos Direitos da Criança e do Adolescente (Forum DCA; Permanent National Forum of Nongovernmental Organizations in Defense of Children's Rights) was created as the main national coalition. It focused on two main agendas: combating violence against children and lobbying Congress to include children's rights in the 1988 Brazilian constitution. The Forum DCA succeeded in its campaign to insert articles protecting children's rights into the constitution, and its struggles against violence were reinforced with legal tools to protect children's rights based on human rights norms and strategies. In 1989, the Forum DCA had another big achievement: the approval of the ECA statute, the national version of the 1989 CRC. The guiding philosophy at this time was "the child as a subject of rights." From then on in Brazil, children legally acquired the "right to have rights."

The 1990s: From the alternative to the alternative—the building of new forms of institutionalism and the redesigning of social policies for children. The 1990s were marked by tension between sustainable economic growth and the consolidation of constitutional gains. Economic adjustment "with a human face" did not occur as promised. Rather, during these years, a stable currency with low inflation was achieved at the expense of social policies.

Nevertheless, new actors from the private sector emerged, including foundations linked to private corporations, and were incorporated into the broad social movement on behalf of children. Their espousal of the children's rights paradigm gave them a different profile from earlier charitable and philanthropic organizations. Despite the adverse circumstances, the broad children's rights social movement continued to focus on implementing the ECA statute. This required the creation of new institutions: the *conselhos dos direitos da criança e do adolescente* (child and adolescent rights councils) and the *conselhos tutelares* (children's guardianship councils), each of which was put in charge of designing and monitoring social policies for children in Brazil. The dissemination and implementation of the ECA statute therefore led to a shift in the movement's focus from the national to the local level (states and municipalities).

By the mid-1990s, as a new millennium neared, there was a tendency increasingly to concentrate efforts at the national level against three specific forms of violations of children's rights: child labor, child prostitution, and the treatment of adolescents in conflict with the law. At the same time "child-protagonism" (children as political actors) also became part of the agenda of the children's rights movement. The social construction of children as political subjects is surely one of the greatest conquests for youth in the last century.

A Critique of Social Programs That Tolerate or Reproduce Child Labor

The social movements provided the country with the main political energy to develop a child labor eradication agenda. However, changes in production methods and in labor relations in both the national and international arenas, together with the implementation of the ECA statute, created new standards that demanded that Brazil's two main approaches to child work and child labor be critiqued and rethought.

During the 1980s, the debate around child labor took place in terms of *educação para o trabalho* (education *for* work) and *educação pelo trabalho* (education *through* work). Programs designated "education for work," aimed at training for the world of work, were criticized as merely molding and adapting children for the labor market without any concern for changing the status quo of children and adolescents in that market. That was the criticism made, for example, of the national apprenticeship systems, SENAI and SENAC. They were criticized also for their selectiveness, since they targeted only children and adolescents from the working-class elite, therefore excluding underclass children.

On the other hand, social programs designated "education through work," run by a more progressive faction of nonprofit organizations, were based on the concept of work as an educative force. Approaching the relationship between capital and labor critically, they tried to train workers to question the prevailing system of production. Activities were based on three basic principles: the participation of the trainee in planning and production decisions; proper scientific and technical know-how about what they were producing, in contrast to the *aprender fazendo* (learning on the job) principles of "education for work"; and participation in defining the destination of jointly produced profits.

The new ECA statute reiterated the constitutional prohibition of working under the age of fourteen (later extended to sixteen): (a) universalized adolescents' rights to professional training and labor safeguards; (b) reconceptualized apprenticeship as technical and professional training to be given following guidelines from current education legislation; (c) reinforced educational work in line with Article 1(2) of 1932 ILO Convention (No. 33) Concerning the Age for Admission of Children to Non-Industrial Employment (ILO C33);[13] (d) prohibited differences of salary for sex, age, color, or civil status (ensuring labor rights that were equivalent to those of adults); and (e) reinforced mechanisms that guaranteed compatibility between school and work. At the same time, work conditions changed; there was a reduction of positions in the job market at the same time that schooling became an increasingly important requirement in the competition for existing positions.

Based on new standards set by the Children's Act and the changes in work conditions, the following critique of "alternative" income generation programs for poor children and adolescents was added to the children's rights discourse: (a) they do not respect the legal norms regarding the age young people may start working and enter the labor market; (b) there was a gap between types of work developed or goods produced and market demands (the selection of what will be produced was often based more on preconceived ideas about what occupations are traditionally allotted to the poor, rather than on market research); (c) the activities selected were mechanical and repetitive tasks and therefore did not constitute real apprenticeships because they did not require methodical teaching; (d) the work was seen as a form of "social control" with a disciplinary role in the socialization of children with rules and timetables for each activity; (e) children and adolescents were trained to be subordinate, not to participate in decisionmaking processes; (f) the programs developed unsystematic and incoherent education on labor rights and citizenship because these rights were not practiced in the workplace nor in the organizations running the programs; (g) the programs had difficulties fitting into municipal public policies because of lack of interest in doing so and even resistance among some of the philanthropic and charity programs that had dominated the assistance to children and adolescents for a long time; and (h) the programs failed to provide adequate youth training for self-employment and setting up of small businesses. The goal of the majority of these programs was to occupy children's time on the theory that idleness leads to delinquency. Under these conditions, children were unlikely to perceive that work might be a tool for personal and social realization and a source of pleasure and human development.[14]

There are no available studies of the impact of these alternative income generation programs. However, an assessment of them based on my own experience indicates little effectiveness in breaking the cycle of poverty. Some of them have played simply a disciplinary role relative to the work force (e.g., shoeshine associations, tour guide associations). Many others have had a contrary effect, proving to be an "incentive" to keep children and adolescents working on the streets and thus vulnerable to the hazards of street life. Their "socializing" benefits are also questionable. The rules and schedules are so informal and improvised that they do not offer preparation for real work relationships.

A positive evaluation of these types of social programs could show that they have contributed to "survival arrangements" that have "saved" some lives from death. In addition, it is possible that they were an expression of solidarity with impoverished children who have been excluded even by government assistance programs, albeit from a philanthropic—not a citizenship—perspective. It also is true that many children and adolescents found support in these social networks for their professional and social mobility, although it seems this was not true for the vast majority of them. Finally, these programs do appear to have worked as social pressure sounding boards for better work conditions for the parents and for a more democratic and comprehensive system of professional qualification.[15]

The criticisms of both perspectives, "education for work" and "education through work," provided the technical and programmatic ammunition to combat child labor. By the beginning of the 1990s, many who were involved in alternative income generation programs for children were convinced by the experience that the logic of the welfare programs should be changed from *ajudar as crianças ajudar os seus pais* (helping children to help their parents) to *ajudar os pais a ajudarem os seus filhos* (helping parents to help their children).

◼ Child Labor Reaches the Agenda as a Campaign Issue

In the 1990s, activities to implement children's rights legislation led various Brazilian NGOs to include the issue of children on their agendas and to create or to specialize institutional space for children's rights advocacy or for providing services to children. Trade unions and members of the business sector joined forces with other organizations specifically dedicated to defending children's rights to find solutions to the problem of child labor. UNICEF and the ILO's IPEC program stimulated this search for solutions by offering technical support and funding social mobilization, government statistical research, academic research and case studies, social mobilization, social policy designing, and service provision.

These initiatives contributed both to the modification of strategies from the 1980s and to the creation of new ones. Modifications in existing strategies included: (a) increasing the number of studies on child labor and changing the focus from exploratory studies to the analysis of interventions considered to have brought about changes in strategic thinking; (b) giving funding priority to education and assistance programs that emphasized citizenship building and vocational training relevant to the job market (including several hundred initiatives and programs carried out by private enterprises and NGOs); and (c) broadening activities for the legal and social defense of children and adolescents (denunciations, legal aid, participation of civil society in monitoring child labor). The last began to attract new participants (trade unions, children's defense centers, and NGOs). Trade unions in particular played a central role in mobilizing working adults and children against child labor.

The new strategies that began to be adopted had a holistic vision of children's needs and rights that implied, further: (d) the development of consciousness-raising campaigns to change cultural perceptions of child labor; (e) the participation of civil society in the process of drawing up legal norms, demanding law enforcement and formulating social policies; (f) the involvement of family and schools to remove children from dangerous, arduous, or inappropriate work environments; (g) the development of economic and socioeducational interventions to keep children in school; (h) the mobilization of children themselves against child labor and the organization of working adolescents; and (i) the mobilization of companies through the inclusion of social clauses in commercial and labor contracts and through labels for companies that neither employ child labor nor exploit adolescent labor and that contribute to professional training for adolescents.

Brazilian organizations in partnership with multilateral organizations undertook scores of mobilization activities and education campaigns on the issue of child labor. One of the National Children's and Adolescent Rights Council's guiding principles—*o lugar da criança é na familia, escola e comunidade* (the place of children is in the family, the school, and the community)—became a theme for many campaigns. For example, the Central Única dos Trabalhadores Brasileiros (CUT/CEAP; National Trade Union) undertook the campaign *Diga Não ao Trabalho Infantil* (Say No to Child Labor) and the CUT/Shoemakers Union of Franca adopted the campaign *Lugar de Criança e na Escola não no Trabalho* (A Child's Place Is in School Not at Work). The CUT also established other initiatives, including a telephone hotline for receiving denunciations of child labor. The Força Sindical (Trade Union Force) issued leaflets on *Crianças e Adolescentes no Trabalho* (Children and Adolescents at Work) plus two others on children's rights for trade unionists, including *Brazil: Vai para a Escola Agora* (Brazil: Go to School Now). The Confederação dos Trabalhadores na Agricultura (CONTAG; Agricultural Workers Confederation) issued two special publications including a children's bulletin (with a printing of 2,000 copies) and produced six radio programs transmitted in most states via more than 160 radio stations sponsored by rural workers' trade unions and federations. A symbolic National Independent Tribunal on Child Labor was held in October 1995 in response to the appeal of the Daca Conference against Child Labor and in preparation for the First International Tribunal, held in Mexico in April 1996.

From 1991 to 1994, union campaigns sought to give visibility to the issue of child labor in general and to place its elimination as well as the protection of working adolescents on the national agenda. The objectives of these campaigns may be classified as follows: (a) denouncing violations of human rights and the impact of arduous and unhealthy work on children; (b) raising awareness of the issue among their own members and the external public with whom they had relations as well; (c) generating methods for eradicating child labor and protecting the work of adolescents by eliminating arduous and dangerous work environments.

By the end of 1995, a coalition was created specifically to combat child labor: the Fórum Nacional de Prevenção e Erradicação do Trabalho Infantil (FNPETI; Brazilian National Forum on the Prevention and Eradication of Child Labor), a coalition of forty governmental and nongovernmental organizations funded and supported by the ILO and UNICEF. With the establishment of the FNPETI, the campaigns from the mid-1990s to the present became more focused and targeted: combating child labor in charcoal camps in Mato Grosso do Sul; in sugar cane cutting in São Paulo, Rio de Janeiro, and Pernambuco; in shoe manufacturing in Franca; and against commercial sexual exploitation of children and adolescents, especially in major cities.

■ Four Brazilian Strategies to Eradicate Child Labor

Of all the Brazilian strategies to eradicate child labor, however, four have presented the most innovative methodologies and engaged the greatest number of organizations in their implementation: media mobilization, children's participation, labeling child labor products, and school grants.

Mobilizing the Media

Child labor has been in the Brazilian media for more than three decades. Some studies report that media coverage began as early as the 1970s, at the beginning of the so-called *menor trabalhador* (working minor) phenomenon. Programs aimed at educating and mobilizing the media for a more children's rights–centered approach toward poor children were being advanced already in the 1980s by some international agencies (e.g., the ILO, the United Nations Educational, Scientific, and Cultural Organization [UNESCO], UNICEF) and some nongovernmental organizations (e.g., the Brazilian National Movement of Street Boys and Girls). However, the creation in 1992 of the Agência de Notícias dos Direitos da Infância (ANDI; News Agency for Children's Rights) was a watershed in media education in Brazil. Specialized in mobilizing the media, this organization, along with other NGOs working to eradicate child labor, was among the principal actors that contributed to increasing the media's coverage of child labor, improving the quality of its child labor articles, and changing its view about child labor from one of "virtue" to one of a "human [children's] rights violation."

In a 1985 article, Lia Fukui analyzed 512 articles published during the 1970s in three São Paulo newspapers (*O Estado de São Paulo, Folha de São Paulo,* and *Notícias Populares*) and found that there was very little coverage of the issue of child labor in the media at that time[16]—and this despite the fact that the 1970s saw a mass entry of ten- to fourteen-year-old children into the labor market even though such labor was prohibited by law. According to Fukui, child labor was "tolerated because it was seen as a means of preventing delinquency."[17] Coverage increased somewhat during the 1980s. Yet further research by Fukui on media articles aimed at different classes in São Paulo, Rio de Janeiro, and Porto Alegre between 1990 and 1992 revealed that there was a great distance between research work on child labor and information in the media that did not present the issue critically. Fukui concluded: "the media, as a sounding board for society, is caught between denunciations arising out of research efforts and the ambiguities of the law; it is unable to problematize the issue of child labor because it is not guided by citizenship actions that affirm children's rights."[18]

Research by ANDI confirms Fukui's thesis but shows a change in media behavior beginning in the mid-1990s. According to *Criança na Mídia 1999* (Children in the Media 1999), while its coverage of the subject has been uneven since 1996, the press has been a great "ally" in all child labor eradication projects. Though in tenth place relative to all child-related media coverage, "material published on the exploitation of child labor has a strong impact and is generally placed on the front page."[19] At the same time that the media began denouncing situations of child labor, it began also to report on the various efforts by government and nongovernmental organizations to find solutions to the problem. "It is not rare to find alongside denunciations (on the same page or in the same report) news of successful experiences in combating the problem."[20] A statistic illustrates this balance: of all reports on child labor in 1999, 31.78 percent were denunciations of the exploitation of child labor and 42.99 percent addressed the search for solutions. In contrast to the situation in the 1970s and 1980s, child labor in the 1990s began to be presented as a social "problem" by the media. A turning point was reached when investigative reporting began to examine the exploitation of child labor at the end of the production chain, focusing on those who benefit from it.

In ten years, ANDI's institutional capacity has grown in size, experience, and influence. Similar agencies have been created in Brazil. By the end of 2003 there were nine new agencies in the country and similar agencies had been formed in eight other Latin American countries as well (Argentina, Bolivia, Colombia, Costa Rica, Guatemala, Nicaragua, Paraguay, and Venezuela). These agencies have created the Brazil ANDI Network (2000) and the Latin America ANDI Network (2003), and ANDI and its affiliated organizations and partners have been doing basic daily work supporting the efforts of journalists and turning the press's attention to issues related to children and adolescents. Since it is not linked to governments, a media outlet, or company, ANDI is able to achieve autonomy and independence in disseminating information.

Mobilizing Children, Adolescents, and Youth Against Child Labor

There is in Brazil a growing movement to mobilize children, adolescents, and youth to defend their own rights and to engage in social solidarity activities. Lately, in areas such as health, communication, social mobilization, and education, youth have participated in actions that reveal their potential for creativity and for contributing to political mobilization. The principal characteristic of these initiatives is that they are developed, coordinated, and implemented by the adolescents themselves, a participatory and decisionmaking process called *protagonismo infanto-juvenil* (youth protagonism). The role of adults is to guide but not to direct them.

According to ANDI, youth protagonism has received only modest attention from the media (only 32.34 percent of the reports in 1999 were on this issue). Nevertheless, creating alternatives to the culturally determined idea of work as a cultural "virtue" is one of the most innovative strategies being developed by and with children and adolescents themselves in Brazilian organizations. There are at least three types of strategies for mobilizing working children in the struggle for child labor eradication: social movement strategies, trade union strategies, and service-provider strategies.

The Brazilian National Movement of Street Boys and Girls, an example of a social movement, seeks to organize youth by age group. The subjects of their political mobilization are poor children and adolescents, primarily street children, regardless of whether they work or not. The movement's focus is on their condition of social exclusion. However, because the organization seeks to approach the child as a full person, child labor, albeit important, is viewed as only one dimension of their lives. The general strategy is to group children and adolescents by type of activity, workplace, or in the case of street children, main locus of survival and struggle. These groups, managed by the boys and girls themselves, debate their social condition and acquire knowledge and awareness about their rights, the public services available, and alternative solutions for their own lives. These groups of street children have two aims: education for citizenship and developing forms of collective solidarity through the exercise of mutual help and solidarity.

The Brazilian trade union movement began to seek the involvement of child and adolescent workers in its own mobilization and organizational activities only in the first half of the 1990s. Beginning at that time, a number of activities were organized to mobilize children, adolescents, and youth themselves, to hear their opinions about work, and to discuss alternatives for the problems they were encountering as well as how they might defend their rights. Prior to that time, from the end of the 1980s to the beginning of the 1990s, trade unions had allied themselves with the broad social movement in defense of children's and adolescents' rights. Stimulated by this social movement, particularly based on the methodology used by the National Movement of Street Children, trade unions developed a specific set of activities with children themselves. An example for that experience was the "Project Guidance on Children Laboring in Industry and Other Sectors: Training Union Leaders and Developing Awareness in Society," developed by the Central Headquarters of Laborers–CUT-Brazil in agreement with the ILO, between 1992 and 1994. The project organized activities with children in the footwear sector in Franca, in sugar cane cutting in Sertãozinho, and in babaçu coconut splitting in Maranhão. The main steps of their methodology were raising awareness among trade union leaders about the consequences of child labor and the need to conceive of children as a part of the solution, mobilization and gathering working children, nomination of a steering committee, and development of follow-up activities.

Many service providers (governmental or nongovernmental organizations) normally run the PETI child labor eradication programs as after-school programs. The array of activities offered to children varies from program to program. The programs necessarily include activities such as homework, art education, and recreational activities.[21] Some of the programs also include political consciousness raising. However, these programs are directed more at service providing than movement building.

In Brazil, in contrast to countries like Peru and India, where some nongovernmental organizations seek to organize children and adolescents as workers, both governmental and nongovernmental organizations seek to eliminate child labor and protect the work of adolescents, and they do so by way of discussions concerning the consequences of child labor and by building alternative solutions to keep children and adolescents in school.

One of the main by-products of the mobilization approach is the very process of mobilizing children and adolescents and encouraging their participation in the process of making decisions about social issues pertinent to their lives. This methodology arose from a concept of childhood and adolescence in which children and adolescents are political subjects that can be included in discussions about policies and strategies for the eradication of child labor. The most successful child labor eradication strategies have been those that regard children and adolescents as part of the solution, among them trade union approaches to the problem. Trade unions sensitized by consciousness-raising activities began to approach child laborers first as children and adolescents and second as workers, a sequential approach that is fundamental to dealing with human beings who are in the process of maturation and development.

The approach involved the creation of a methodology for mobilizing children and adolescents that is different from traditional forms of organization used with adults in popular and trade union movements. With children and adolescents, meeting agendas dedicate more time to playfulness and cultural activities than to more formal and openly political discussions.

Social Labeling and Social Clauses as Strategies for Eliminating Child Labor

The engagement of entrepreneur foundations providing low wages and unskilled jobs, job training programs, and charitable actions for children began in Brazil in the mid-1940s. The mobilization of private enterprise toward the eradication of child labor, however, is a relatively new phenomenon in Brazil that dates only from the early 1990s. The Fundação Abrinq Pelos Direitos da Criança (Abrinq Foundation for Children's Rights) was the pioneer in this field and today is joined by other organizations and foundations such as the Instituto Pro-Criança (Prochild Institute) and the Fundação Ethos (Ethos Foundation), which bring together some 100 companies committed to more socially responsible behaviors.

Two innovative strategies have been used to combat child labor. One is the authorization of labels to companies that do not use child labor and that invest in the implementation of social policies for children and adolescents. The label provides a differential for goods and services in a competitive market.[22] The other is the advocacy of social clauses and codes of conduct in commercial and labor contracts. Through these clauses and codes, companies make the commitment to combat child labor in their particular production chain by not purchasing goods and services from companies that use child labor or exploit adolescent labor[23]—and underpinning them are three innovative and fundamental strategies: (a) rather than view entrepreneurs only as part of the problem, entrepreneurs are seen as part of the solution; (b) actions to eliminate child labor target the full production chain; and (c) enlightened consumers are deemed important to combat violations of human rights effectively.

Social labels. The label of the Abrinq Foundation "is a kind of ISO-900" (or international standardization device) that can be used on the packaging, dissemination, and advertising materials of companies receiving it. Currently there are two types of labels used as a mobilizing strategy among companies seeking to eradicate child labor: one for the company and one for the product. The granting of labels depends on the following requirements: (a) nonemployment of children; (b) a statement that the use of child labor has not been found in the production of goods and services; and (c) the use of part of the product sales for funding social programs that benefit children and adolescents.

Studies indicate that one of the principal results of this strategy is the mobilization of entrepreneurs. Labeling and other campaigns to increase business citizenship have slowly and gradually contributed to increased social action by companies,[24] particularly in relation to promoting and defending children's rights and implementing social policies. However, it still is difficult to obtain information from companies about the scale and relevance of this funding in terms of both its proportion of company spending and its contribution to the solution of priority problems, and it appears not to have had any significant effect on social inequalities.

From the companies' viewpoint, the label adds value though it does not generate increased profits. While they allege to have contributed to social problem solving prior to receiving the labels, companies believe that the labels help to legitimize and give visibility to their products and social programs. Another possible benefit, though unverified and undeclared, is the use of labels to protect business against external pressure from competitive sectors and exporters within a globalized economy.

In any event, it appears that considerably more work on the education of consumers still is necessary. According to specialists, only a minority of consumers recognize the labels.[25] However, another study by Kanitz & Associates and the University of São Paulo indicated that 84 percent of Brazilian consumers would choose a product associated with a good social cause over one that is not. In relation to expensive products, 34 percent would choose products associated with a good social cause. These percentages increase to 65 percent for inexpensive products and 95 percent for very cheap products.[26]

Evaluating child labor labeling is a complex and difficult task, but especially important when it is the sole strategy relied upon to reduce child labor. Indicators point to a reduction in child labor in Brazil as a result of social labeling. However, to understand the causes a number of other variables must be taken into account: economic measures and performance, the implementation of social policies, the profile of child labor in certain production activities not yet measured (e.g., agricultural work), and cultural factors such as an increase in awareness of the negative impacts of child labor.

Developing systems, methodologies, and indicators for monitoring and assessing results could improve evaluations of efficiency and effectiveness of labeling as a social mobilization strategy. A central challenge is how to increase the political impact of the label by expanding the numbers of certified companies while at the same time ensuring the quality of services offered. As the efficacy of a label depends on the *credibility* of those awarding it and the *singularity* of those who receive it, one must face the twin questions: (a) how to maintain quality control for certification in a cost-effective way; and (b) how to reconcile the distinctive nature of the label, which is part of its objective, with a more generalized mass application.

Social clauses and codes to eliminate child labor. The insertion of social clauses in commercial and labor contracts to guarantee benefits for workers and their families has been debated for almost a century.[27] In Brazil, the Abrinq Foundation was a pioneer in proposing the use of social clauses as a strategy for eliminating child labor, and in the years since, social clauses have been used within a movement of voluntary codes of conduct and commitments made among companies, governments, and nongovernmental organizations to reduce and eradicate child labor. Social clauses are inserted in purchasing contracts between companies and their suppliers. Various companies and productive sectors have adopted codes and included social clauses in contracts for a range of motives, but they converge in their objective of reducing and eliminating child labor.

Codes to roll back child labor and achieve other social functions have been adopted in important productive sectors in Brazil. These include the shoe-manufacturing industry in Franca; the citrus-producing sector in São Paulo; the tobacco-producing sector in the states of Paraná, Santa Catarina, and Rio Grande do Sul; and the sugar-alcohol sector in the states of São Paulo, Goiás, Mato Grosso do Sul, Paraná, Pernambuco, and Alagoas. However, it is noteworthy that the main companies in the sugar-alcohol–producing region of the northeast, which continue to have a high incidence of child labor, have not adopted such codes.

The Brazilian government's motives for promoting these codes arise out of its duty to guarantee compliance with norms and laws prohibiting labor of people under sixteen and to ensure that the working conditions of adolescents are not arduous, dangerous, or unhealthy. From an official perspective, this kind of mobilization is important for consolidating the rule of law and the implementation of children's rights as expressed in law. For the workers, it may be seen also as a tool to fight unemployment among parents and a chance to improve the quality of the labor of their children through schooling. Entrepreneurs adopt socially redemptive codes of conduct for the same reasons they choose social labeling. A new conception of their responsibility and role in seeking solutions to problems affecting child laborers and their families merges with the increasing importance of social marketing and a consequent demand for visibility of social actions supported by private initiative. Parts of the business sector see their social engagement as a way of changing the image of the company or productive sector, attending to more demanding consumers and citizens through social responsibility and by following a vision of development with a more "human face" for excluded members of the population.[28]

The use of social clauses and codes of conduct in labor contracts began in 1996. However, there has been as of this writing very little systematic evaluation of their efficiency and efficacy because of difficulties in establishing monitoring and evaluation systems for this purpose. The main reason given for this lack of evaluation is the "pioneering" and "embryonic" nature of these interventions and lack of clarity about how they might work. Some studies are being undertaken, but to date they lack a systematizing methodology.[29] Still, there are self-evident problems for social clauses and codes of conduct with each participant inspecting and controlling its own production chain. Also, there are at least two practical challenges: first, companies must make a simple internal decision to ensure that the social clauses are effectively written into contracts to afford legal authorization for not buying suspect products; second, there is a need to create mechanisms for inspection and control of agreements between companies and their suppliers. On the other hand, those who promote social clauses and codes of conduct emphasize that their principal value is political pressure inasmuch as those who refuse to endorse or adopt them get a bad image among both consumers and producers. The spirit driving businesses to keep to clauses and codes is thus largely connected to fears related to their image rather than to fears of inspection and punishment.

Brazilian authorities have stated that child labor has been reduced in areas where this form of social mobilization has taken hold. In the state of São Paulo, for example, the use of child labor accounted for 25 percent of the labor force employed in sugar production in 1992 but was practically zero by 1999. Since reduction of child labor cannot be explained by a single strategy alone, however, it is necessary to take other factors into account, even if these have not been fully evaluated: (a) economic and technical changes in productive sectors; (b) the possibility that child labor has migrated; and (c) links made between the adoption of a label, the inclusion of social clauses, the adoption of codes, and public policies, which if maintained may be among the most effective strategies for eliminating child labor in Brazil, particularly if these are extended to other productive sectors and chains.

The possibility that child labor is migrating to other productive sectors is real. When analyzing the viability of the social clause/code of conduct strategy as a solution for child labor in Brazil, Oded Grajew (founder of Abrinq Foundation and the Ethos Foundation) has pointed out both its limitations and potential. The strategy is limited by the fact that social clauses and codes apply only to the private sector, leaving informal networks of production outside their scope. The potential of the clause and code is the "multiplier or demonstrative effect" that it may have on other production chains. The efficacy of the strategy depends on its combination with the actions of other forces, especially governmental and civil society policies.

Public Policies for the Eradication of Child Labor

It should not be assumed from the foregoing focus on strategies carried out by nongovernmental organizations in Brazil that the federal government has been absent from social mobilization on the issue of child labor. Some agencies of the federal government have participated in coalitions, such as the National Forum for Child Labor Eradication. Pressured by this social mobilization, other federal agencies have paid attention to some of the children's rights movement's proposals for child labor eradication policies. Consequently, after more than a decade of effort, the state at the federal level and at the state and municipal levels in many instances as well has (a) modified and enhanced its body of laws to provide the juridical infrastructure to combat child labor and protect the work of adolescents; and (b) designed social policies, specialized organs, sections, and departments within institutions responsible for policy implementation and law enforcement focusing on child labor eradication. These initiatives are human rights–based and otherwise completely in accordance with UN norms and international agreements regarding child labor. Despite enormous operational and financial problems, gradually Brazilian institutions have implemented policies that seek the wholesale eradication of child labor.

The Conselho Nacional dos Direitos da Criança e do Adolescente (CONANDA; National Council for Child and Adolescent Rights) is an example of the new institutions created by the Statute of the Child and Adolescent in the spirit of the postdictatorship democracy. It is a public institution by nature and a hybrid institution by composition: half of its members are from the government and the other half are from NGOs and grassroots movements, and it has subsidiary power to formulate and monitor social policies for children and adolescents. In 2003, CONANDA approved the Plano Nacional de Prevenção e Erradicação do Trabalho Infantil (PNETI; National Plan for the Prevention and Eradication of Child Labor), which was based on the National Forum for the Prevention and Eradication of Child Labor's "2000 Guidelines for the Formulation of a National Policy to Combat Child Labor." The guidelines covered six strategic areas: (a) integration and systematization of the data about child labor; (b) analysis of the juridical corpus related to child labor; (c) a four-part interinstitutional coordination of government, worker organizations, employer organizations, and nongovernmental organizations; (d) ensurance of good-quality public schools for all children and adolescents; (e) law reinforcement through inspection; and (f) the improvement of minimum income programs and incentives for integrated and self-sustained local development. Some of the social policies established in the plan had begun to be implemented in 1995, during Fernando Henrique's administration, and were continued throughout his two terms in office.

School grants. In 1996 the Brazilian federal government created PETI, a program for the eradication of child labor that is run by the Ministry of Social Welfare. The key component of PETI is a families grant, a modality of school grant called a *bolsa criança cidadã* (child-citizen grant). Several social programs that have been implemented in Brazil provide financial support to complement the income of poor families. These grants were originally given as a social welfare benefit to ensure the so-called social minimum benefits. After the 1990s, they have been employed to keep children in school and to take children off the streets and out of child labor. Schools became, in this strategy, "key" services provided to children and adolescents. The concept of *bolsa escola* (school grant) started as a pilot project developed by the Government of Brasília in 1995. Originally, it was developed only as a mechanism to correct lack of school attendance, dropping out, repetition, and grade/age disparities but later was also associated with child labor eradication.

Before becoming PETI's key component, the school grant strategy was promoted and disseminated by ILO Brazil and UNICEF Brazil and undertaken by state governments to combat child labor. In association with other strategies (such as local social mobilization, law enforcement, alternative income and employment generation for parents, and job requalification training), the school grants have been lauded as effective measures to combat child labor in the mineral charcoal mines in Mato Grosso do Sul, sugar cane cutting in Pernambuco and São Paulo, and wicker growing in Bahia.[30]

In the beginning of 2001, PETI was expanded to become a joint program with state and municipal governments. The federal government provides the school grants and the state and county fund the extracurricular activities associated with the program. The program now pays R$45 per child per month in urban areas (approximately US$17) and R$25 per child per month in rural areas (approximately US$9). According to federal government data, the number of children and adolescents between ages seven and fourteen who were assisted by PETI increased from 3,710 in 1996 to around 800,000 in 2002. The financial investments made by the federal government increased from US$300,000 to US$100 million by the end of 2000.[31]

The Ministry of Education has also implemented several policies to put and keep all children in school and to improve their performance while in school. Although these programs do not necessarily target working children, they have assisted poor working children. In 2001, President Fernando Henrique Cardoso set ambitious goals for these programs: assistance to 11 million children living in at-risk situations. UNICEF has designated the program a success because it has contributed to families paying more attention to children's performance at school, to reduced absences and dropouts, and to improving families' self-esteem.[32] However, the studies have not demonstrated the program's impact in the reduction of child labor as strongly as they have demonstrated its impact on children's performance at school. Therefore, prognostics or rumors that the child labor eradication program would lead working children to migrate to even worse forms of labor, in Brazil, are still a hypothesis under the scrutiny of scholars and policymakers.

Law enforcement. Two of the state's main labor law enforcement institutions at the federal level have offices specialized to combat child labor. One is the Ministry of Labor. The other is the General Attorney's Office for Labor.

The Ministry of Labor, in addition to its participation in the forums for the prevention and eradication of child labor (in which many Brazilian states have taken leadership roles), has convened the Comissão Nacional de Erradicação do Trabalho Infantil (CONAETI; National Commission for Child Labor Eradication), which works with the Grupos de Combate ao Trabalho Infantil e Proteção ao Trabalho do Adolescente (GECTIPA; Special Group for the Combat of Child Labor and the Protection of the Work of Adolescents) in each of its state's branches. Every year, the state branches of GECTIPA send an operational plan to the national office, which determines the areas for child labor inspections. Through these plans, the Ministry of Labor draws an indicator map of child labor, which serves as the basis for the federal government's policies on child labor. It then acts, first, through what is called *fiscalização repressiva* (repressive inspection), which aims at taking children immediately out of work situations in accordance with Brazil's labor laws. However, according to the ministry's own analysis, there are, despite all efforts, "several situations in which the coercive power of an inspection agent is constrained by the limits of the laws. For example, when a child is working in the informal market or in a family economy regime or in domestic service, among other types of work. In these cases, we seek solutions to take children out of work by setting up partnerships with other governmental institutions and nongovernmental organizations."[33]

The Ministério Público do Trabalho (MPT; Procurator-General for Labor) has also constituted a specialized section for combating child labor. Its contribution has been to propose the legal actions necessary to protect children's rights. Since 1999 the MPT has made child labor eradication its first priority and in 2000 it created a national coordination strategy to combat the exploitative work of children and adolescents. In Paraná, for example, the MPT conducted an unannounced inspection of the Central de Abastecimentos S.A. (CEASA) and found 229 children and adolescents loading and unloading trucks. In Pernambuco, one farm was ordered to pay a R$222 million fine (approximately US$30,000) for employing children in pepper farming.[34]

▨ Conclusion

Of course, the recent drop in the rates of child labor has been good news; but this good news must be qualified by the sobering fact that the number of children and adolescents working in Brazil is still enormous: 5.4 million children. The vast majority are working in rural areas and receiving no pay for their work. Child labor has taken at least 1 million children away from school. Around 1.8 million of them work forty hours per week, equivalent to adult working hours. These numbers indicate that Brazil has a long way to go in eradicating child labor.

Monitoring and evaluation systems for child labor eradication programs are still much needed in Brazil as well as elsewhere. My emphasis on the change of the symbolic meanings of child labor in Brazilian society from one of "virtue" to one of a "rights violation" and the influence that key organizations have exercised over the design and implementation of social policies as key factors to understand the reduction of child labor should not be viewed as disregard of other factors that might have been intervening. A deeper evaluation of the impact of child labor policies and strategies should necessarily correlate the changes in the national and international macroeconomies and the effect of these macroeconomies on the local labor market with social policies and law enforcement, and not least important, with the changes in the perception of child labor, as I hope to have demonstrated in this chapter.

My arguments here are in tune with those of ILO Brazil's director. He has stressed that the changes in statistics on child labor in Brazil are important not because they show a decrease in the absolute numbers, which are still huge, but rather because they indicate a steady rate of reduction.[35] In addition, the ILO in Brazil believes that "the success of this whole process can be attributed, mainly, to the Brazilian people's desire for progressive social change as well as to its creativity when it comes to facing a situation that can no longer be tolerated, such as child labor. Such creativity has been made concrete through the actions carried out by social actors that are vitally committed to the advocacy of rights of children in the country."[36]

In the social movement for the eradication of child labor, there are now three very difficult priorities: domestic work, sex work, and drug dealing. Although the campaigns against domestic work currently target conditions of de facto slavery, their failure so far to distinguish clearly between domestic work and household chores worries many parents. Furthermore, the elimination of children's domestic work will affect the adult domestic work system, which ultimately supports the work of middle- and upper-class people. Changes to this system might generate negative public opinion and restrict public support given thus far to child labor eradication. The controversies around sex and drug dealing are, first, whether they can be considered "work," and second, whether the state should extend the school grant benefit to eliminate them. Additionally, there are questions about whether the small state grant would really encourage children involved in the sex and drug trade to change their survival strategies.

▓ Notes

I wish to thank Anna More for her valuable contributions in editing this work.

1. In this chapter, I adopt the definition of "child labor" set forth in the introduction to this volume, in turn derived from Chapter 2, that is, "work done by children that is harmful to them because it is abusive, exploitative, hazardous, or otherwise contrary to their best interests—a subset of a larger class of children's work, some of which may be compatible with children's best interests (variously expressed as 'beneficial,' 'benign,' or 'harmless' children's work)."

2. United Nations, *Convention on the Rights of the Child* (1989), art. 1.

3. Brasil, Congresso Nacional, *Estatuto dos Direitos da Criança e do Adolescente* (1990), art. 2.

4. Governo Brasileiro, IBGE, *Crianças e Adolescentes,* pp. 1–2.

5. Cervini and Burger, "O Menino Trabalhador . . . ," pp. 23–24.

6. See infra "Four Brazilian Strategies to Eradicate Child Labor" in this chapter.

7. ANDI, *Análise do Clipping No. 471,* p. 1.

8. Dos Santos, "Da 'Virtude' . . . ," pp. 69–102.

9. Dos Santos, *Mobilização Empresarial . . . ,* pp. 15–16.

10. Costa, "O Novo Direito da Criança . . . ," p. 27.

11. Farías, "A Montanha e a Pedra . . . ," p. 198.

12. Some examples of these alternative programs were the Movement for the Republic of Small Street Sellers in Belém Pará (1970); the Salesian Center for Minors CESAM, in Belo Horizonte, Minas Gerais (1978); the Big Meeting Hall, Betim, Minas Gerais; the Boa Nova Educational Pottery Works, Ipameri, Goiás; the Pastoral do Menor in São Paulo; the Movement in Defense of the Minor in São Paulo (1978); and the association of ex-pupils of FUNABEM-ASSEAF.

13. ILO, *Convention* (No. 33) *Concerning the Age for Admission of Children to Non-Industrial Employment* (1932).

14. See dos Santos, "A Regulamentação do Trabalho Educativo."

15. de Oliveira, *O Menino, o Trabalho e a Lei,* p. 6.

16. Fukui, "A Questão do Trabalho Infantil na Grande Imprensa . . . ," p. 28.

17. Fukui, "Por que o Trabalho de Crianças é Tolerado?" p. 34.

18. Ibid., p. 37.

19. ANDI, *Análise do Clipping No. 471,* p. 94. The Child Rights Information Agency annually produces "Children in the Media," a study based on news coverage in forty-eight newspapers and eight magazines.

20. Ibid., p. 95.

21. Governo Brasileiro, Ministério da Previdência e Assistência Social, *Manual Operacional . . . ,* p. 13.

22. On product labeling, see Chapters 4 and 14 in this volume.

23. Dos Santos, *Mobilização Empresarial . . . ,* p. 27. For more extensive consideration of codes of conduct in this volume, see Chapters 4 and 14 in this volume.

24. Revista Claudia, *Responsabilidade Social,* p. 12.

25. Fischer, "Estudo Avalia Selos Socais," p. 12.

26. Revista Claudia, *Responsabilidade Social,* p. 12.

27. Information on the use of social clauses to defend the rights of minority or marginalized groups in Europe and the United States dates from the 1980s.

28. For an extended treatment of these and related issues, see Schrage, *Promoting International Worker Rights . . . .*

29. But see ibid.

30. Raphael, "Eliminando o Trabalho Infantil no Brasil," p. 17; dos Santos et al., *Report: O Trabalho Infantil no Brasil,* p. 4; OIT Brasil, *Boas Práticas . . . ,* p. 2.

31. Governo Brasileiro, Ministério do Trabalho e Emprego, *Trabalho Infantil no Brasil,* pp. 4–5; OIT Brasil, *Boas Práticas . . . ,* p. 47.

32. Raphael, "Eliminando o Trabalho Infantil no Brasil," p. 25.

33. Governo Brasileiro, Ministério do Trabalho e Emprego, *Trabalho Infantil no Brasil,* p. 2.

34. See the Ministério Público do Trabalho website, at http://www.pgt.mpt.gov.br/trab_inf/geral/mpt_agente.html.

35. ANDI, *Análise do Clipping No. 471,* p. 1.

36. Quoted in OIT Brasil, *Boas Práticas . . . .*

Part 4
Toward Progressive Change

10

Abolishing Child Labor: A Multifaceted Human Rights Solution

Burns H. Weston and Mark B. Teerink

As hopefully we made clear in Chapter 1 of this volume,[1] both the premise and virtues of a human rights approach to the multidimensional problem of child labor are manifest.[2] They are also compelling. When taken seriously, they lead to the kind of strategy—purposeful and multifaceted—that can generate the social transformations that are needed to generate a culture of respect for children's rights and thus to eliminate, in whole and in part, the abuse and exploitation of working children in enduring fashion.

In this chapter, we outline such a strategy. Using an established typology of decisionmaking functions, we recommend a series of concrete policies and courses of action that, in various combinations especially, can be effective in combating child labor when done from a human rights perspective. Mindful, however, of the richly developed chapters that precede and follow, we limit much of our "nuts and bolts" discussion to descriptive outline, leaving it to more knowledgeable others to fill in the gaps and flesh out the details. Moreover, such recommendations as we do offer are tendered more in tentative than definitive spirit. Making human rights work for the abolition of child labor must be understood as a continuing process of reflection and debate, open to reappraisal and redirection as time and experience dictate. It is risky to be categorical. At the same time, it is irresponsible to rest content with expressions of theoretical commitment only. Once human rights are recognized and their legal content understood, their formal expressions must be made operational.

Before engaging our "nuts and bolts" discussion, however, we choose to underscore the two central injunctions we made earlier in Chapter 1: first, to accept—self-consciously and proactively—the premise and virtues of human rights law and policy on all topical and tactical fronts; second, to reject—again self-consciously and proactively—the psychosocial (conceptual) barriers that all too commonly are mounted to resist human rights initiatives and thus thwart their potential from the start. We choose to do so in the first instance because we believe that self-conscious and proactive *acceptance* of human rights as child labor's moral and legal reference point can effectively counter practices that contradict children's best interests and, at the same time, promote those practices that facilitate their human dignity, including their rights to a reasonable standard of living, to education, even to the right to work. And we choose to do so in the second instance as well because we believe that self-conscious and proactive *rejection* of the conceptual barriers to human rights thought and action in the child labor context unleashes the contributions that states, intergovernmental organizations, nongovernmental organizations (NGOs), and others can and must make toward the solution of this complex and pervasive problem. These injunctions—to take children's human rights *seriously*—are critical "nuts and bolts" in their own right, necessary first steps in any human rights strategy worthy of child labor's abolition and of the social transformations required to make that happen. As Marta Santos Pais has put it relative to the operationalization of UNICEF's approach to development, "[t]he expression of a solemn commitment to human rights legitimizes our work and constitutes a catalyst for our actions."[3]

▣ Taking Working Children's Human Rights Seriously

Although there exists already an emerging commitment to a rights-based approach to child labor—as in the case of the United Nations Children's Fund (UNICEF), for example—the fact is that it is not common in official policy or practice, especially on the national plane, nor a conspicuous feature even of official rhetoric on the international plane. In contrast to other approaches, it appears to be marginalized or less favored than, for example, the labor market perspective, long "the dominant international paradigm of government child labour intervention"; the human capital perspective, which "views the work of children through the lens of national economic development"; and the social responsibility perspective, which is centrally concerned "with the 'exclusion' of disadvantaged groups from full participation in the protection, benefits and opportunities of society" and which thus proposes "greater social inclusion of those being excluded" by way of remedy.[4]

The International Labour Organization (ILO), for a key example, has been generally marginal in expressly engaging human rights law and policy over the years—except recently in respect of child trafficking[5]—and for this reason, we believe, limited in its ability to ameliorate labor problems of a human rights nature. Virginia Leary, a longtime authority on ILO policy and practice, agrees.[6] Leary, it is important to acknowledge, reached this conclusion in 1992, and not with reference to child labor specifically. Her assessment, therefore, must be weighed against the ILO's current avowed commitment (along with UNICEF and others) to a rights-based approach to child labor. When this is done, however, ILO practice even in relation to child labor appears more to confirm than to invalidate Leary's judgment of more than a decade ago, emphasizing, as the ILO tends to do, negotiable "standards" more than inalienable "rights." The recent—and useful—ILO study titled *Action Against Child Labour*[7] underscores the point dramatically. Responding to no less than "the need for comprehensive and practical information on planning and carrying out action against child labour,"[8] it mentions human rights only in circumstantial passing and thus seems to eschew the very idea of mainstreaming a rights-based approach to child labor. Not even the more recent report of the ILO director-general explicitly following up on the ILO's 1998 Declaration on Fundamental Principles and Rights at Work[9] takes the forthright human rights step.[10] Only the 2002 report of the ILO's International Programme on the Elimination of Child Labour (IPEC) on the more conceptually limited (though huge) problem of child trafficking, it appears, has taken such a self-conscious stand.[11]

Indeed, even activists and scholars sympathetic to a rights-based approach to child labor have eschewed the language of rights when making the very point. "Although its intellectual and organizational influence seems to be growing," William E. Myers has written, "the *'child-centered perspective'* [that is, a rights-based approach to child labor] remains surprisingly marginalised in official national policy and programmes guiding child labour action. . . . One might expect from virtually universal ratification of the [Convention on the Rights of the Child] that *a child-centered view* of child labour would have by now become more present in official child labour policy."[12]

In sum, despite a newfound commitment to combat child labor from a human rights perspective, evident since the adoption of the 1989 Convention on the Rights of the Child (CRC)[13] and especially since the adoption of 1999 ILO Convention (No. 182) Concerning the Prohibition and Immediate Elimination of the Worst Forms of Child Labour (ILO C182),[14] the idea of human rights discourse and strategy as an effective tool in this struggle still meets with palpable hesitancy, even among well-wishers. Doubtless this uncertainty is a function of bureaucratic inertia or even general disinterest at least in part—and surely, as well, of incomplete understanding of the virtues of human rights discourse and strategy in the first place. It probably is a function, too, of strongly held beliefs in the minimum age/labor market approach to children's work represented by 1973 ILO Convention (No. 138) Concerning Minimum Age for Admission to Employment (ILO C138).[15] We believe, however, that it is also—perhaps even primarily—a function of the statist, elitist, patriarchal, and paternalistic logics that shape our worldviews and lives. Through many years of psychosocial acculturation, they have come to define not only what, specifically, we see to be possible but also, more generally, how we go about seeing what is possible.

As long as we continue in this way, however, we never will achieve the social transformations that are needed to abolish the abuse and exploitation of working children, in whole or in part, on an enduring basis. The time is long past when we must unreservedly champion the rights of children not simply as *children's* rights, so labeled at risk of marginalization, but as *human* rights that, at their core, evince concern for the alleviation of *all* human suffering—and therefore also, in Costas Douzinas's evocative phrase, "concern for the unfinished person of the future for whom justice matters."[16] UNICEF's Innocenti Research Center comes close in its call for "a new global ethic for children."[17] But not, we sense, close enough. Needed is a wholesale paradigm shift not only in the way we think about children specifically, but also—guided by an ethos of species identity—in the way we think about social governance generally, and therefore a shift away from the statist, elitist, patriarchal, and paternalistic logics that stand in the way of the genuine alleviation of child and other human suffering. The need is for an internalized worldview or mind-set that, on behalf of working children and in continuously persevering ways, actively embraces the premise and virtues of human rights discourse and strategy,[18] consistently contests the psychosocial (conceptual) barriers that impede their operation,[19] and systematically mainstreams the full human rights agenda (civil, political, economic, social, cultural, and communitarian) in each and every policy that is devised and in each and every measure that is taken—all to ensure that children's best interests are served, not as a matter of charity or privilege that may benefit some but as a matter of right that can benefit all. In short, the need is for a culture of respect for children's human rights.

It is, indeed, this kind of rethinking that appears first to have shaped the Declaration and Programme of Action of the 1993 Vienna World Conference on Human Rights;[20] that later guided United Nations Secretary-General Kofi Annan's 1997 summons to all UN system entities to mainstream human rights into the activities and programs that fell within their mandates (part of his program for United Nations reform); and that, as a result, found expression ultimately in the Statement of Common Understanding of a May 2003 UN interagency workshop outlining a human rights–based approach to the development planning and programming of UN agencies.[21] While intended specifically for United Nations development agencies, this Statement of Common Understanding points the way for all who would seek to abolish child labor by way of human rights discourse and strategy.

First, here citing and quoting from UNICEF's edition,[22] the statement identifies several key "human rights principles" to "guide all programming in all phases of the programming process."[23] Specifically, it articulates and explains the following principles: "universality and inalienability; indivisibility; interdependence and interrelatedness; non-discrimination and equality; participation and inclusion; accountability and the rule of law."[24]

Next, but first cautioning that "the application of good programming practices does not by itself constitute a human rights–based approach,"[25] the statement cites four "required additional elements" deemed by the May 2003 UN interagency workshop to be "necessary, specific, and unique to a human rights–based approach":

a) Assessment and analysis [to] identify the human rights claims of rights-holders and the corresponding human rights obligations of duty-bearers, as well as the immediate, underlying, and structural causes when rights are not realized.
b) Programmes [to] assess the capacity of rights-holders to claim their rights, and of duty-bearers to fulfill their obligations, [and the development of] strategies to build these capacities.
c) Programmes [to] monitor and evaluate both outcomes and processes guided by human rights standards and principles.
d) Programming [that] is informed by the recommendations of international human rights bodies and mechanisms.[26]

Finally, the statement lists thirteen other elements deemed "essential" for a human rights–based approach to development planning and programming. We quote them in full, modestly amended to demonstrate their especial relevance to the struggle against child labor:

1. People *[including all working children]* are recognized as key actors in their own development, rather than passive recipients of commodities and services.
2. Participation is both a means and a goal.
3. Strategies are empowering.
4. Both outcomes and processes are monitored and evaluated.
5. Analysis includes all stakeholders.
6. Programmes focus on marginalized, disadvantaged, and excluded groups *[including working children]*.
7. The development process *[relative to working children]* is locally owned.
8. Programmes aim to reduce disparity *[between working and non-working children and others]*.
9. Both top-down and bottom-up approaches are used in synergy.
10. Situation analysis is used to identify immediate, underlying, and basic causes of development problems *[including the causes of child labor]*.
11. Measurable goals and targets are important in programming.
12. Strategic partnerships are developed and sustained.
13. Programmes support accountability to all stakeholders.[27]

All of the foregoing "required" and "essential" elements of the May 2003 Statement of Common Understanding can and should be understood to be part of the human rights discourse and strategy that can and should be directed against child labor. At a minimum, a human rights approach to the abolition of child labor requires: (1) reliance upon human rights criteria and norms when selecting and establishing anti–child labor program priorities, standards, tactics, and strategies; (2) the identification of child labor claims-holders and whether they have the capacity to articulate and advocate for their rights and participate in the process; (3) the identification of duty-bearers and their capacity to meet their anti–child labor obligations as well as constraints on their ability to perform; and (4) the establishment of mechanisms for monitoring, assessing, and redressing child labor situations, with human rights norms all the while in mind, shaping one's outlook and purpose. Proceeding according to this or like-minded designs, programs and projects directed toward the abolition of child labor, even if not conceived initially in human rights terms, become, ipso facto, human rights programs and projects by virtue of their deliberate conceptual reorientation. To the extent that the strategic design is adhered to, and regardless of the substantive measures implemented, it works naturally to protect, promote, and fulfill children's human rights, including the human rights of working children.

In sum, an ethos of species identity that takes working children's suffering seriously is what is needed if the abolition of child labor is to succeed—a primary even if evolutionary first step in any human rights strategy worthy of child labor's abolition and of the social transformations that it requires. It is children's human *rights* we are defending, not just their human *wants* and *needs*. And we must do so not only in matters of substance but, as well, in matters of procedure—in the invention, design, implementation, monitoring, and evaluation of policies and programs directed against child labor, giving particular consideration to such core human rights values as transparency, accountability, participation, and nondiscrimination.[28] If the abolition of child labor is truly the goal, nothing less will do. Even incremental measures, if they are to succeed enduringly, depend on such human rights outlook and strategy.

■ Invoking and Inventing Legal and "Extralegal" Means and Mechanisms

This chapter and section, to minimize redundancies in this volume, focuses on the promotion and protection of the rights of working children largely on the international plane. It is essential to appreciate, however, that all that has been said up to now and that much of what has yet to be said apply as well to national policy- and decisionmaking. Indeed, the implementation of human rights doctrines, principles, and rules on behalf of working children is, generally speaking, probably most efficiently and effectively achieved at the national or even subnational level via the institutions and procedures that obtain within each country's own legal system—broadly defined to include *both* the formal and informal mechanisms that avail human rights in this setting. The authority of a domestic public order system that provides effective formal and informal "remedies" for violations of international human rights obligations (and their national counterparts) can serve richly the promotion and protection of human rights where there is moral and political will. This is as true for working (and nonworking) children's human rights as it is for any other category of human rights.[29] And the examples abound: in the formulation and execution of national strategies and agendas for the implementation in the 1989 CRC and 1999 ILO C182, in efforts at national and subnational policy and law reform based on these same and cognate human rights instruments, in the development of independent governmental institutions at the national level for promoting and protecting the rights of working (and nonworking) children,[30] and so forth. Further examples are suggested below. Still others are found in the chapters that precede and follow. The majority and probably most effective are "extralegal" in kind and therefore merit the lion's share of responsible attention.

Partly for editorial reasons, however, we here focus first, even primarily overall, on the formal legal mechanisms available at both the global and regional levels for the promotion and protection of human rights (including the human rights of working children). But there is another, more important reason for so doing. Perhaps for lack of sufficient knowledge about them, or because of a preference for consensual diplomacy over adversarial advocacy, or perhaps for both reasons, a comparative few appear to have been pressed into anti–child labor service so far. It seems therefore useful to explicate, however briefly, the explicit human rights enforcement arrangements that, on the international plane and in appropriate instances, can assist in child labor's abolition in fact—and potentially to genuine profit.

Human Rights Action via Formal
Legal Mechanisms and Procedures

While resort to formal legal mechanisms may seem inconsistent with goals of social transformation because they represent established officialdom, they should not be dismissed for this reason. To the contrary, if used wisely and with tolerance for quasi- and nonlegal devices, they have the potential to assist the anti–child labor struggle nobly, both as change agents in their own right and as catalysts for change. Indeed, resorting to them even only occasionally among the many elements that comprise a human rights approach to child labor's abolition can send a much needed signal that the anti–child labor movement means to be taken seriously, sending ripples of persuasion that cut across all levels of resistance in the world system, from the most global to the most local. They deserve, therefore, thoughtful consideration, particularly among persons not trained in the law who tend often to be skeptical (not altogether without justification) about the capacity of legal process to mete out justice and otherwise serve humane values. Some of these formal mechanisms are found at the global level, others at the regional level. In each case, we make specific recommendations that we believe can enhance their ability to help end child labor.

Human rights action within the United Nations system. Within the United Nations, the only forum in which *any* country's human rights violations can be challenged, three arenas available specifically to monitor and enforce human rights present themselves as obviously relevant to the abolition of child labor (apart from UNICEF as the UN's chief systemwide promoter of children's well-being and rights): the Committee on the Rights of the Child; the UN Commission on Human Rights and its Sub-Commission on the Promotion and Protection of Human Rights; and though largely without resort to the language of rights, the ILO relative to the implementation of 1973 ILO C138 and 1999 ILO C182 (as well as other ILO conventions). Also available within the UN system, though presently in a supervisory rather than enforcement mode, is the Committee on Economic, Social, and Cultural Rights, established in 1987 by the Economic and Social Council.

The Committee on the Rights of the Child. The Committee on the Rights of the Child, established under the 1989 CRC to oversee its implementation,[31] has no mandate to receive and consider in quasi-judicial manner "communications" (i.e., complaints, applications, or cases) from individuals or groups of individuals who claim to be victims of violations of the CRC. Instead, the committee recommends that children or their representatives refer to the four UN "treaty bodies" that have such competence to date and that are relevant to the claim or claims involved: the Committee on the Elimination of All Forms of Racial Discrimination; the Human Rights Committee; the Committee Against Torture and Other Cruel, Inhuman, or Degrading Treatment or Punishment; and the Committee on the Elimination of Discrimination Against Women.[32] Also, since 1992, when it adopted an "urgent action procedure" to deal with "serious" CRC violations though in nonaccusatory fashion,[33] the committee has several times responded diligently to urgent children's appeals always on an ad hoc basis and mostly confidentially with a view to sensitizing the states parties to their treaty obligations so as to prevent a further deterioration of the contested situation and thereby safeguard children's rights as much as possible under the circumstances.

Beyond these limited interventions, however, the committee's competence is reportorial and recommendatory only. It receives reports required to be submitted to it by states and other parties to the CRC on measures taken to give effect to the rights set forth in the convention;[34] it may request further information from the parties if it so chooses;[35] and on the basis of these communications, it reports to the UN General Assembly every two years on its activities.[36] Additionally, it is authorized to "invite . . . competent bodies as it may consider appropriate to provide expert advice on the implementation of the Convention [and] United Nations organs to submit reports on the implementation of the Convention."[37] Further, it may recommend that the General Assembly request the Secretary-General to study "specific issues relating to the rights of the child" and may "make suggestions and general recommendations based on the information received," which recommendations are to be transmitted to any party concerned and reported to the General Assembly.[38] A recent example, highly pertinent to the issue of child labor, was the committee's request for an international study on the question of violence against children, honored in February 2003 by the UN Secretary-General's appointment of an "independent expert" (Paulo Sergio Pinheiro) to lead a global study on the subject, ongoing in 2005.[39]

These measures afford the committee, which is at the hub of child labor activities in the UN system, significant opportunity to pressure states that engage in, or fail to take steps to correct, violations of the rights enumerated in the CRC and its two optional protocols on the involvement of children in armed conflict[40] and on the sale of children, child prostitution, and child pornography.[41] This includes, of course, Article 32, which proclaims "the child to be protected from economic exploitation and from performing any work that is likely to be hazardous or to interfere with the child's education, or to be harmful to the child's health or physical, mental, spiritual, moral or social development." To enhance the struggle against child labor, however, we recommend that the committee significantly increase its surveillance and exposé not only of violations of the CRC's child labor–specific Article 32 but, as well, of violations of all those CRC provisions that are implicated by child labor.[42] To the same end, we urge that the committee appoint special rapporteurs and/or working groups to study, report on, and recommend solutions to all forms of abusive and exploitive child work, and not only the most scandalous. Particularly helpful, we believe, would be a focus on child labor at the intersection of international human rights law and economic globalization.

Finally, we recommend—strongly—that the CRC be amended to empower the committee to receive and consider individual and group complaints in quasi-judicial manner and to sanction those countries that are found to be in CRC violation.[43] Without prejudice to the committee's "urgent action procedure" noted above, the precedent of the 1999 Optional Protocol to the 1967 Convention on the Elimination of All Forms of Discrimination Against Women (CEDAW), belatedly extending quasi-judicial authority to receive and act upon complaints to the Committee on the Elimination of Discrimination Against Women, is instructive.[44] This step would measurably enhance the opportunity for children themselves, as well as their representatives, to defend and promote their rights against abusive and exploitive child work. The direct involvement of claims-holders in the defense and promotion of their rights usually is key to the validity and vitality of their claims.[45]

The Commission on Human Rights and its Sub-Commission on the Promotion and Protection of Human Rights. Pursuant to Resolution 1235, adopted by the UN Economic and Social Council (ECOSOC) on June 6, 1967[46]; ECOSOC Resolution 1503, adopted on May 27, 1970[47]; and "special procedures" put in place by resolutions first adopted in 1979 to address "country" situations and "thematic" issues involving specific violations of human rights, the UN Commission on Human Rights and its Sub-Commission on the Promotion and Protection of Human Rights are authorized to perform several different operations on behalf of human rights generally.[48] Ergo they are authorized to act also on behalf of those rights implicated by child labor.

Under ECOSOC Resolution 1235, the commission and its subcommission are empowered "to examine information relevant to gross violations of human rights and fundamental freedoms."[49] Precisely what it means to "examine information" and precisely what constitute "gross violations" are not explicitly clarified by Resolution 1235, but in Paragraph 3 the resolution authorizes the commission "[to] make a thorough study of situations which reveal a consistent pattern of violations of human rights, as exemplified by the policy of *apartheid* . . . and racial discrimination . . . and [to] report, with recommendations thereon, to the Economic and Social Council." The widespread abuse and exploitation of working children would seem to fit this mold. In any event, the operational essence of "the 1235 procedure," as it has come to be called, is a public debate that, though entirely in the hands of UN member states (not private individuals or groups) and thus influenced by political considerations, can lead to the establishment of a mechanism (working group, observer delegation, special rapporteur, special representative, special envoy, or representative of the Secretary-General) for study of a country's human rights situation and to the adoption of a resolution concerning the country situation examined or studied. In addition, the subcommission can debate specific country situations and adopt resolutions expressing concern about them. These resolutions, while not comparable to judicial orders, are not without consequence. They therefore can assist the anti–child labor struggle. "Even a Sub-Commission resolution that does no more than express concern about a particular country's human rights situation," writes Nigel Rodley, "can serve . . . important functions"[50]—especially, he adds, "where the Commission has not yet dealt with it."[51] Rodley continues: "first, it may give political impetus to further action by the Commission; second, even if the Commission is unwilling to act, a Sub-Commission resolution represents the opinion of a formally-constituted UN body of human rights experts (which is not without independent influence); and, third, it may build up an official documentary record by requesting a report from the Secretary-General on the situation."[52]

ECOSOC Resolution 1503, a direct response to the subcommission's reliance upon information derived from nongovernmental organizations under the 1235 procedure, gave the human rights complaint initiative for the first time to individuals and NGOs and initially, in contrast to the 1235 procedure, in strict confidence. Limited to general situations that reveal "a consistent pattern of gross and reliably attested violations of human rights and fundamental freedoms" (a "worst form" of child labor?), it nevertheless was seen by many around the time of its adoption as "an enormously valuable precedent, a breach in the citadel of the mutual protection society, one that could be progressively enlarged."[53] In practice, however, the 1503 procedure, though not without some notable successes, has fallen short of its promise. While it has sometimes facilitated gradually increased pressure on offending governments (often as a precursor to action under ECOSOC Resolution 1235), it is, in the words of Frank Newman and David Weissbrodt as long ago as 1990, "painfully slow, complex, secret, and vulnerable to political influence at many junctures."[54] The utility of the 1503 procedure relative to, say, a "worst form" of child labor is therefore open to serious doubt. Nevertheless, with the subcommission formally authorized to receive and act upon complaints and the commission empowered to make "a thorough study" or to initiate "an investigation by an ad hoc committee" subject to "the express consent of the State concerned,"[55] the 1503 procedure is available to the struggle against child labor at least in principle. If a pattern of human rights abuse in a country remains unresolved in the early stages, it can be brought to the world's attention through the Economic and Social Council, the procedures of which are more or less transparent. At a minimum, therefore, the potential of the 1503 procedure in relation to child labor should be explored. Given the almost unanimous endorsement of the 1989 CRC and the rapidly growing popularity of 1999 ILO C182, it is not beyond credulity to imagine that the struggle against child labor could even result in the 1503 procedure's reform and reinvigoration.[56]

Unlike the public procedures authorized by ECOSOC Resolution 1235 and the confidential procedures authorized by ECOSOC Resolution 1503, each of which deals with general *situations* of human rights violation, the thematic mechanisms (or mandates) developed since 1979 to investigate specific violations of human rights can deal with individual *cases* of human rights violation, both actual and threatened. And for the most part they do so, typically via special rapporteurs and working groups and particularly in countries where the violations are widespread. Generally they operate impartially, such that their annual reports to the commission reveal no bias based on the identity of the country being investigated. They operate also relatively efficiently. In these ways, too, they contrast sharply with the 1235 and 1503 procedures, which, as indicated, often are influenced by political considerations and tend to be cumbersome and slow. They thus are ripe for use in the anti–child labor struggle.

To our best knowledge, however, only one of the above three human rights enforcement techniques of the UN Commission on Human Rights has been pressed into service on behalf of the worldwide struggle against child labor. Several of the thematic mechanisms (mandates that have proliferated markedly in recent years) have dealt with child labor issues or issues related to child labor, for example, the right to education (2002),[57] children and armed conflict (2002),[58] and the sale of children and child prostitution and pornography (2001).[59] Probably the fact that the 1235 and 1503 procedures are cumbersome and slow, and perhaps also that the 1503 procedure is secret, has dissuaded child labor abolitionists from invoking them. Additionally, direct participation in the commission's and subcommission's Geneva-based sessions is expensive. "Engaging rapporteurs or working groups is easier," Rodley writes, "and such an approach is more likely to lead to success in individual cases."[60] Nevertheless, the problem of child labor is of such magnitude as to require, as part of a comprehensive abolitionist strategy, at least consideration of all the enforcement techniques that are provided by the commission and its subcommission, and certainly sensitivity to the fact that there are occasions when child labor issues or issues related to child labor must be addressed vis-à-vis countries that are not party to treaty-based complaint procedures. In any event, there can be no question that at least some of the worst forms of child labor, as defined by 1999 ILO C182, meet the 1235 and 1503 jurisdictional test of "a consistent pattern of gross violations of human rights."[61] At the least, the commission's country and thematic mandates should be given increased and more diverse responsibility for child labor issues—including, in collaboration with the Committee on the Rights of the Child as suggested above,[62] a focus on child labor at the intersection of international human rights law and economic globalization, an intersection in which dwell, we believe, not a few consistent patterns of gross violations of children's rights.

The International Labour Organization.[63] "The procedures developed by the International Labor Organization," writes Lee Swepston, chief of the Equality and Employment Branch and coordinator for human rights questions of the Geneva-based International Labour Office, "form part of what may be the most effective and thorough international mechanism for the protection of human rights"[64]—though almost completely, it must be added, without benefit of rights language per se. The procedures, predicated on the adoption of conventions and declarations enunciating principles and standards pertinent mainly to organized and unorganized labor[65] (including 1973 ILO C138 and 1999 ILO C182), are of two distinct but interdependent types: (1) regular and systematic monitoring by the ILO Committee of Experts on the Application of Conventions and Recommendations and the ILO Conference Committee on the Application of Conventions and Recommendations; and (2) complaint procedures premised on the ILO constitution[66] and ILO basic principles.[67]

The first of these procedures is defined more by advocacy, encouragement, and technical cooperation than by adversarial confrontation. It involves mainly five sequential monitoring operations, the first three at the hands of the ILO Committee of Experts: (1) the examination of governmental reports on ILO convention compliance;[68] (2) essentially quiet diplomacy in the form of "direct requests" where compliance is found wanting; (3) published "observations" where noncompliance is deemed serious or persistent; and in the most severe cases of noncompliance, either (4) mandatory appearance before the ILO Conference Committee (which reflects the ILO's tripartite structure of governmental, workers', and employers' representatives) for a public accounting of the reasons for noncompliance or (5) "direct contacts" between the International Labour Office and the delinquent government to resolve the problem without public criticism.

The second (complaint) procedure entails any one of three essentially adjudicative operations. They include: (1) "representations" to the ILO Governing Body by trade unions or employer organizations (not necessarily associated with the subject of the complaint) as authorized by Article 24 of the ILO constitution whenever a country "has failed to secure in any respect the effective observance within its jurisdiction of any Convention to which it is a party"; (2) "complaints" to the ILO Governing Body (and an assisting ILO Commission of Inquiry usually established by the Governing Body) by governments, International Labour Conference delegates, or the Governing Body itself on its own motion, as authorized by Article 26 of the ILO constitution, alleging that a country is not "securing the effective observance" of a convention it has ratified; and (3) "complaints" directly to the ILO Governing Body's Committee on Freedom of Association (CFA) and indirectly via the CFA to an assisting Fact-Finding and Conciliation Commission on Freedom of Association (FFCC) by governments or by employers' or workers' organizations alleging violations of the ILO's basic principles on freedom of association whether or not the state concerned is a party to any ILO convention on the subject.[69]

The last mechanism mentioned above—the complaint procedure involving the ILO Governing Body's CFA—is reliably reported to be "one of the most widely used international complaint procedures for the protection of human rights,"[70] and "[t]he most widely used ILO petition procedure."[71] This comes as no surprise. The principle of freedom of association, including but not limited to the right to form trade unions and to collective bargaining, is fundamental to the protection of worker rights generally.[72] It also is critical to children who are the victims of abusive and exploitive labor practices. Not only do they or their surrogates need its protection to resist particular abuses, they need its protection also to safeguard the right of children under CRC Article 12 "to express [their] views freely in all matters affecting the child," including "in any judicial and administrative proceedings affecting the child."[73] It is essential to the empowerment of child workers and to their direct involvement in the vindication of their rights. A strategy that seeks the abolition of abusive and exploitive child work on a comprehensive basis must therefore embrace the ILO's CFA procedure to the maximum extent needed.

Much the same may be said of the ILO's "representations" and "complaints" procedures under Articles 24 and 26 of the ILO constitution. It appears, however, that these procedures have not been widely used, although for reasons that have more to do with the ILO's successful monitoring and supervision of its many standard-setting conventions than with any ineffectiveness that might be attributed to these procedures. Writes Swepston:

> If these procedures are used relatively infrequently, it is because they are but one part of a comprehensive and active system of regular supervision. . . . It is . . . rare that governments do not cooperate fully in the ILO's investigations. . . . Even if a government does not implement the ILO's conclusions immediately, in the longer term the government often adopts legislation and practices that closely follow the recommendations made.[74]

When it comes to the implementation of ILO C138 and ILO C182, however, credit must be given particularly to the ILO's International Programme on the Elimination of Child Labour, established in 1992 and, as of 2005, active in sixty countries worldwide. Working toward the elimination of child labor through a phased, multisectoral strategy of technical cooperation that includes a legal unit for monitoring and evaluation, it reinforces the ILO's supervisory system and, along the way, confirms that technical cooperation and normative action can be complementary.[75] In fact, in part because of its monitoring and evaluation procedures, IPEC has hastened ratifications of both 1973 ILO C138 and 1999 ILO C182.[76] True, in the years preceding IPEC, work to eliminate child labor barely existed at the global level even after the entry into force of ILO C138 in 1976, and when it did it was slow and incoherent. Still, it is wise not to leap hastily to the conclusion that the ILO's "representations" and "complaints" procedures need never be pressed into service on behalf of the struggle against child labor. To the contrary, a comprehensive strategy to abolish child labor, by definition multifaceted, requires that they be placed in active reserve. The ILO's supervisory procedures probably would not be nearly as effective as they are without the threat of its adversarial procedures lying in waiting.

Finally, as it is not easy for human rights NGOs to gain access to the ILO's enforcement machinery, cooperation with trade unions is strongly recommended, especially with those that are human rights oriented. At the same time, however, we urge greater ILO leniency toward human rights advocacy groups, preferably as part of an ILO policy shift that, like UNICEF in 1999,[77] would signal a strategic decision to use rights discourse to abolish or at least reduce child labor.

Committee on Economic, Social, and Cultural Rights. Article 10 of the 1966 International Covenant on Economic, Social, and Cultural Rights (ICESCR), which provides for the "widest possible protection and assistance . . . to the family,"[78] decrees, as noted earlier, that "[s]pecial measures of protection and assistance should be taken on behalf of all children and young persons";[79] that "[c]hildren and young persons should be protected from economic and social exploitation";[80] that "[t]heir employment in work harmful to their morals or health or dangerous to life or likely to hamper their normal development should be punishable by law";[81] and that "States should also set age limits below which the paid employment of child labour should be prohibited and punishable by law."[82] Like all the other provisions of the ICESCR that bear upon the problem of child labor,[83] the implementation of this provision is monitored by the Committee on Economic, Social, and Cultural Rights (CESCR).

Established in 1987 by ECOSOC,[84] the CESCR is not, as of mid-2005, empowered to receive and adjudicate complaints of violations of the ICESCR, as is, for example, the Human Rights Committee under the companion International Covenant on Civil and Political Rights (ICCPR). The absence of a direct complaint procedure, the CESCR has noted, "places significant constraints on the ability of the Committee to develop jurisprudence or case-law and, of course, greatly limits the chances of victims of abuses of the ICESCR obtaining international redress."[85] Accordingly, the CESCR has promoted the adoption of an optional individual complaints protocol similar to the one provided for in the first optional protocol to the ICCPR.[86] Thus far unsuccessfully, however, and as a consequence the CESCR has signaled that, "[p]ending the addition of an optional protocol, beneficiaries of the rights contained in the Covenant may still have recourse to the general procedures of the Committee, and may utilize what has been called an 'unofficial petition procedure' based on the modalities of the Committee."[87] Also, the committee has drawn up a "Plan of Action to Strengthen the Implementation of the International Covenant on Economic, Social and Cultural Rights" with emphasis on "substantive, analytical, expert, and general support (a) to facilitate the Committee's work with States parties in relation to the reporting process; (b) for the preparation of various substantive background papers to enable the Committee to contribute effectively to the various activities which it is increasingly being called upon to perform; [and] (c) to enable the Committee to work constructively with States parties and United Nations agencies and others in following up on its recommendations designed to enhance the realization of economic, social and cultural rights."[88]

Meanwhile, the CESCR's legal competence is to oversee the ICESCR's state reporting process.[89] Pursuant to ICESCR Articles 16 and 17, the states parties to the ICESCR are obligated to submit periodic reports to the CESCR on the programs and laws they have adopted and on the progress they have made in protecting the rights pronounced in the ICESCR. With the help of state delegations, specialized UN agencies, and relevant NGOs on behalf of civil society, the CESCR reviews the reports, entertains both written and oral testimony, and then concludes its consideration of a state party's report by issuing "concluding observations," which constitute the CESCR's decision and variously include both positive and negative assessments of a state party's performance together with suggestions and recommendations for improvement. A possible committee conclusion is that a state party has failed to comply with an ICESCR obligation and hence is in violation of the covenant.[90] It is important to note, however, that the CESCR's concluding observations are not technically binding and that, to date, there is no method to enforce them. At the same time, the CESCR has stated that "for States parties to ignore or not act on such views would be to show bad faith in implementing their Covenant-based obligations" and that "in a number of instances, changes in policy, practice and law have been registered at least partly in response to the Committee's concluding observations."[91]

Finally, it is important to note that, at its third session in 1988, in response to an invitation from ECOSOC, the CESCR began to prepare and issue "general comments" on the rights and provisions contained in the ICESCR for the purpose of assisting states parties to fulfill their ICESCR reporting obligations, and also to provide greater interpretative clarity as to the intent, meaning, and content of the covenant. The CESCR views the adoption of such comments as a way to promote the ICESCR's implementation of the covenant. It also sees them as a way to generate a consensual jurisprudence relative to the ICESCR's substantive provisions.

To date, however, the CESCR has issued no general comment on Article 10's proscription of child labor. We urge it to do so as an important and potentially persuasive further element in a comprehensive human rights strategy for child labor's abolition. Additionally, and to the same end, we urge the CESCR to move swiftly in winning acceptance of its proposed individual complaint procedure. Even though many economic, social, and cultural rights are perhaps best secured via group action, individual complaints as victims or representatives of victims of abuse can speak with unmatched moral authority. Meanwhile, we urge the CESCR to fulfill its action plan and use its existing supervisory power over the state party reporting process to heighten its scrutiny of dubious labor practices involving child workers and thereby energize states parties, international organizations, and civil society to work yet harder at Article 10's full realization.

Concluding thoughts on the UN human rights system. While the Committee on the Rights of the Child, the ILO, and UNICEF, along with several rapporteurs and working groups, currently dominate anti–child labor activity within the UN system, there is no apparent reason why responsibility for this issue should not extend to other United Nations mechanisms and procedures where appropriate. For example, it is well-known that children of lower socioeconomic status, especially when from unfavored ethnic or tribal groups, often suffer severe discrimination and other abuse at the hands of unscrupulous parties and that, as a consequence, they commonly end up working on the street and in other abusive contexts rather than going to school. In such a setting, it seems appropriate that the Committee on the Elimination of Racial Discrimination (CERD), established under the 1965 International Convention on the Elimination of All Forms of Racial Discrimination[92] and with authority to adjudicate claims of violation under that convention, could and should have a role to play in the anti–child labor struggle. Equivalent conclusions might be reached about the similarly constituted Committee Against Torture, established under the 1984 Convention Against Torture and Other Cruel, Inhuman, or Degrading Treatment or Punishment.[93] Our point is simple. Given the multidimensionality, interrelatedness, and interdependencies of the worldwide child labor problem, the entire UN human rights system, especially at the committee level, should be brought to bear in the anti–child labor struggle in a comprehensive and coordinated way; and what is more, in a fashion that invites the active participation of interested governments and civil society. It is this kind and degree of reordering and mobilization that is needed to ensure child labor's abolition, perhaps with the help of a working children's ombudsperson in the form, say, of a new UN High Commissioner for Children (analogous to, for example, Norway's cabinet-appointed Ombudsman for Children).[94] The Committee on the Rights of the Child, the ILO, and UNICEF are indispensable actors, without a doubt. But they cannot alone win the day. Needed are a kind and degree of reordering and mobilization within the UN system that can raise the moral and legal stakes dramatically higher on the scales of human aspiration and endeavor.

Human rights action within regional human rights systems. There exist today three regional human rights systems, each with state-to-state and individual complaint procedures for judicial or quasi-judicial redress of human rights violations: in Europe, pursuant to the 1950 European Convention for the Protection of Human Rights and Fundamental Freedoms[95] and the European Social Charter (Revised);[96] in the Americas, pursuant to the 1948 Charter of the Organization of American States (OAS)[97] and the 1969 American Convention on Human Rights;[98] and in Africa, pursuant to the 1981 African Charter on Human and Peoples' Rights[99] and 1990 Charter on the Rights and Welfare of the Child.[100] Space does not allow a detailed analysis of these complaint procedures.[101] A brief summary, however, is helpful, as all are relevant to child labor's abolition.

The European human rights system. Of the three regional human rights systems, the most established is the European. After more than four decades of implementing the European Convention for the Protection of Human Rights and Fundamental Freedoms via both a commission and a court, Protocol 11 to the European Convention[102] established a unified, full-time European Court of Human Rights with jurisdiction extending to both interstate and private petitions alleging convention violations. What matters here, of course, is that this juridical machinery—involving the encouragement of "friendly settlements" and the rendering of final and binding judgments on the merits enforced by the Committee of Ministers to the Council of Europe, even to the point of threat of expulsion from the council—is available for the adjudication of the rights of working children. While the convention focuses primarily on "first generation" civil and political rights, it is nonetheless relevant to the consideration of child labor in that, as we argued in Chapter 1 in this volume, child labor practices impinge potentially on *all* human rights (for example, freedom of speech and expression). Moreover, specific rights enumerated in the convention—for example, the right to life[103] and the prohibition of slavery and forced labor[104]—manifestly are implicated by certain "worst forms" of child labor.

In contrast to the convention and its focus on civil and political rights, the European Social Charter (Revised) specifically covers "second generation" economic, social, and cultural rights, including many that are of particular relevance to working children.[105] Again, therefore, the anti–child labor movement should take notice. Under the charter, the parties commit to the rights set forth in it "by all appropriate means, both national and international in character."[106] Under an additional protocol that provides for a system of collective complaints,[107] nongovernmental organizations of employers, trade unions, and others may file a complaint with a Committee of Independent Experts alleging violations of the charter by a state party[108] (indeed, the first complaint filed in this context alleged violation of the charter's Article 7, prohibiting the employment of children below age fifteen).[109] The committee reviews the complaint, may hold a hearing, and reaches a decision on the merits.[110] The decision is forwarded to the Committee of Ministers of the Council of Europe, which may recommend specific measures to redress any violation.[111]

The inter-American human rights system. The American Convention on Human Rights also addresses primarily civil and political rights, calling only for the "progressive development" of measures by the states parties to achieve the "full realization" of economic and social rights.[112] However, among the civil and political rights enumerated in the convention are the right to life, freedom from slavery, freedom of association, and measures of protection specifically for children.[113] Moreover, an optional Additional Protocol in the Area of Economic, Social, and Cultural Rights entered into effect in 1999 and boasted thirteen ratifications in mid-2005.[114] The OAS charter, in addition, commits all OAS member states to "devote their utmost efforts to accomplishing . . . basic goals," including, in pertinent part, fair wages, acceptable working conditions, and expansion of educational opportunities.[115] OAS member states also obligate themselves to "dedicate every effort" to the application of such "principles" as "a right to material well-being . . . and spiritual development under circumstances of liberty, dignity, equality of opportunity, and economic security"; work under conditions of "fair wages, that ensure life, health, and a decent standard of living"; and the right of association and collective bargaining.[116] Furthermore, the OAS charter requires member states to "exert the greatest efforts . . . to ensure the effective exercise of the right to education."[117]

The convention provides for two organs to enforce the rights set forth within it and within an additional protocol: the Inter-American Commission on Human Rights and the Inter-American Court of Human Rights. Both are potential tools for implementing the above-mentioned human rights norms in support of working children.

The commission is charged under the convention with promoting "respect for and defense of human rights."[118] In addition, as an organ also of the OAS charter, it is charged to "promote the observance and protection of human rights and to serve as a consultative organ of the [OAS] in these matters."[119] Thus, while the commission's authority under the convention is limited to those states parties to the *convention,* as an organ of the *charter* its purview includes the activities of all OAS member states, including those not party to the convention. The commission receives individual petitions against any state party and interstate petitions involving states parties, determines admissibility, conducts fact-finding, and attempts to reach friendly settlement of cases, whereupon it reports to the OAS secretary-general and the parties regarding the facts and friendly settlement. Such reports are made public. Under the convention, where friendly settlement is not achieved, the commission, after preparing a confidential report, may offer proposals and recommendations, and may submit the case to the Inter-American Court of Human Rights.

The court interprets and applies the convention via contentious and advisory jurisdiction. When exercising its contentious jurisdiction (as in the case of claims of human rights violations), the court may order compensation and/or issue injunctions, but then only with regard to states parties that have consented to such jurisdiction. The commission brings claims to the court, and the court's judgments are final and binding. Judgments are enforced via the OAS General Assembly, which may adopt whatever sanctions it deems appropriate.[120]

The African human rights system. Under the African Charter on Human and Peoples Rights, not only are civil/political and economic/social/cultural rights recognized, but so also are third generation community or solidarity rights.[121] Specifically, the charter binds the states parties to recognize and give effect to, inter alia, the rights to dignity and freedom from exploitation such as slavery, association, work under equitable and satisfactory conditions and equal pay for equal work, the best-attainable state of physical and mental health, education, and protection of morals[122]—all relevant, of course, to the safeguarding of the rights of working children. And this task is left to both an African Commission on Human and Peoples' Rights and, since January 2004, a new African Court on Human and Peoples' Rights. In addition to promotional functions (providing information, offering conferences and seminars, assisting national governments in formulating policy), the commission has both contentious and advisory jurisdiction to consider complaints lodged with it under the African charter. In contentious cases, the commission may resort to "any appropriate method of investigation," receive, investigate, report on, and make recommendations concerning alleged violations of the charter, pursuant to either interstate or individual communications involving any state party to the convention.[123] For its part, pursuant to the protocol that established it, the court may receive complaints submitted to it by the commission, by a state party that has lodged a complaint to the commission, by a state party whose citizen is an alleged victim of a human rights violation, or by one of the African intergovernmental organizations.[124] Further, the court is authorized to "entitle relevant Non Governmental organizations (NGOs) with observer status before the Commission, and individuals to institute cases directly before it" vis-à-vis states parties that have consented to such jurisdiction.[125] The court will hear cases, try to reach amicable settlement, and may order remedies/reparation,[126] deemed final and binding on the parties.[127] It remains, of course, to be seen how the court develops in practice. But clearly, given the high incidence of child labor in Africa, both the new court and the commission should be taken seriously and thoroughly explored in the struggle against African child labor.

Likewise relevant to the safeguarding of the rights of working children and therefore to be taken seriously is the African Charter on the Rights and Welfare of the Child, which entered into force in November 1999 and which obligates the parties to it to recognize, and take steps to give effect to, the rights enumerated in it.[128] Many of them, not surprisingly, are applicable to the problem of child labor generally, for example, rights to free association, education, rest and leisure, and the best attainable state of health.[129] But the charter also addresses child labor specifically, requiring states parties to take legislative and administrative measures to establish minimum ages of employment and regulation of hours and conditions,[130] and prohibiting the recruitment of children for armed conflict, their sexual exploitation, and their abduction and trafficking.[131]

To serve all these rights-based objectives, the charter establishes a Committee on the Rights and Welfare of the Child empowered to receive communications "from any person, group or non-governmental organization recognized by the [Organization of African Unity (OAU)][132] by a Member State, or the United Nations."[133] Like the African Commission on Human and Peoples' Rights, the committee may use "any appropriate method of investigating" matters brought to its attention, and, further, is required to report its activities to the Assembly of Heads of State and Government every two years.[134] Also, according to the charter's Article 42(a), the committee is empowered to (a) "interpret the provisions of [the Charter] at the request of a State Party, an Institution of the [AU] or any other person or institution recognized by the [AU], or any State Party"; (b) "monitor the implementation and ensure protection of the rights enshrined" in the charter; and (c) "where necessary give its views and make recommendations to Governments." All of which constitutes broad power to investigate violations of child labor–related human rights and both to report on such violations and to make specific recommendations to states parties on redressing them. However, the committee has only just begun operating in the last few years so that, as in the case of the African Court on Human and Peoples' Rights, only time will tell whether the committee lives up to its potential. A thoroughgoing commitment to child labor's abolition, however, would make sure that it does.

Concluding thoughts on the regional human rights systems. Notwithstanding the lofty goals espoused by the instruments establishing the regional human rights systems discussed above, each of these systems has been criticized for failing to protect human rights effectively or efficiently. In the case of the European system, for instance, huge backlogs and insufficient resources caused cases to drag out over years—providing the impetus for reforming the system with a single, full-time human rights court.[135] Similar criticism, coupled with charges of ineffectiveness, propelled the member states of the OAU (now the AU) to establish the Court of Human and Peoples' Rights.[136] Only time will tell whether these courts will become the effective and efficient arbiters of human rights contests that their architects hope for.

Despite the well-founded criticisms of the three regional systems, however, it is clear that, for reasons of cultural and geographic propinquity, these systems have had a positive effect on human rights promotion and protection in their respective regions. Indeed, it is fair to say that the enforcement of human rights at the regional level has proven generally more effective than at the global level. On the whole, states have responded cooperatively to the judgments of the regional tribunals, complying with their orders and changing their laws and practices as a result.[137] Moreover, the regional systems collectively encourage further development and improvement of the global human rights system via interaction and collaboration.[138] It thus is clear that the regional human rights systems are another potentially useful tool for addressing abusive, exploitive, or hazardous labor practices affecting children. Their enforcement or implementing potential in the anti–child labor struggle should be actively explored and invoked, in terms of both their direct impact and their catalytic ripple or demonstration effect.

Human Rights Action via "Extralegal" Means

As international lawyers, we naturally gravitate toward juridical solutions to the problem of child labor. However, though formal legal institutions and procedures created specifically to promote and protect human rights are indispensable components of a comprehensive strategy for the abolition of child labor, by no means are they the only components—indeed, possibly not even the most effective or important components in many instances. As previously stated, the abolition of child labor requires broad and deep social change, and for this is needed far more than the law and its formal arrangements, even when dedicated specifically to the promotion and protection of human rights. Legal solutions tend frequently to be "top-down" or "elitist," often suspect because they are inclined to overlook disparities in power—especially at points of conflict—between those who prescribe solutions and those who, typically less powerful, are on the receiving end of them. Though nonetheless indispensable, they are not likely to make much headway against abusive and exploitive child work without calling into collaborative service a host of more or less informal approaches to the problem. Many of these are "bottom-up" or "grassroots" approaches and generally of an "extralegal" (quasi- and nonlegal) sort that interface closely with education, international trade, and other such societal infrastructures—and commonly, too, with those who daily fight in the trenches on behalf of working and nonworking children: intergovernmental organizations such as the ILO and UNICEF; NGOs such as Anti-Slavery International, Save the Children, and Global March; and a host of others from civil society—trade unions, business enterprises, consumer groups, children's service providers, working children's groups/organizations, faith-based groups, women's organizations, academic institutions, and so forth.

The chapters that precede and follow in this volume treat many if not most of these "extralegal" considerations in a way that only experts specialized in them can do. We therefore limit ourselves here to outlining a multifaceted problem-solving/policy-implementing typology whose individual elements, we believe, hold out the potential for child labor's true abolition, especially when they are conceived in human rights terms (as detailed above)[139] and when they are acted upon as fully and with as much coherence and coordination as possible likewise in such normative terms. This is so even if these elements are not perceived by their owners as components of a comprehensive human rights strategy against child labor. If this be the case, it is simply that their owners have not yet fully understood or internalized the power of a human rights outlook on child labor, in which event human rights education becomes the first imperative. Indeed, given the necessity of social transformation in the child labor context, human rights education and particularly that kind of human rights education that, from the nuclear family to the cosmopolitan state, impels all levels of social organization and action to view human rights *as a way of life*[140] may be the single most important thing that anyone can do at this time. To each facet of each function recorded or capable of being recorded in our problem-solving/policy-implementing typology must be brought all of the conceptual and tactical elements we noted earlier that define what we mean by a human rights approach to the abolition of child labor.[141]

It is, at any rate, from this perspective that we identify in summary fashion the problem-solving/policy-implementing functions and their principal components that, including formal legal institutions and procedures, must be pursued if child labor is ever to be abolished or significantly reduced. The problem of child labor, we recognize, is a polychromatic problem that insists upon polychromatic solutions. In no way do we presume to have exhausted the options. Nor do we presume that our cataloging of them reflects an always precise, exclusive fit. What follows is meant to be heuristic, suggestive—*not* definitive or exhaustive.

Information retrieval and dissemination on behalf of working children's rights. Functions in this category include improved methodologies (case studies, correlation studies, experimental studies, prototypes, etc.) for the systematic gathering, analyzing, and processing of data about child labor and its impact on the child laborers, their families, and their communities, including increased reliance for such data upon working children themselves; expanded/strengthened NGO "watchdog" monitoring and trade union surveillance initiatives competent to retrieve, process, and disseminate accurate child labor data; enhanced methods of social accounting/auditing; improved/broadened curricular initiatives for K–12 and college-level courses; improved/broadened adult education programs, particularly for trade unions and business enterprises; improved/broadened mass media programming (including, e.g., documentary films); and improved/broadened artistic and other intuitive programming (e.g., "art" films, popular theater, photographic exhibits, etc.).

Promotion/advocacy on behalf of working children's rights. Functions in this category include improved coordination of anti–child labor agendas, definitions, and procedures among, inter alia, the UN, ILO, UNICEF, International Monetary Fund (IMF), World Bank, free trade associations (FTAs), and regional human rights systems; enhanced coordination/competition among longstanding and emerging NGO lobbies working to eradicate child labor; expanded/strengthened private sector lobbies specialized in particular child labor practices; expanded/strengthened trade union capacity to campaign against child labor; and enhanced mechanisms and opportunities for working children to speak and act in their own defense (including trade union organizing).

Prescription on behalf of working children's rights. Functions in this category include broadened/strengthened domestic (national and local) plans and legislation prohibiting child labor and related abusive practices, coupled with the creation of permanent governmental institutions competent in ensuring the effective implementation of human rights norms applicable to working children; expanded insinuation of "core labor standards" social clauses (prohibiting abusive/exploitive/hazardous children's work) in IMF/World Bank/World Trade Organization (WTO)/FTA agreements and rules; broadened/strengthened corporate codes of conduct prohibiting abusive/exploitive child labor; and broadened/strengthened industry codes of conduct prohibiting abusive/ exploitive child labor.

Invocation on behalf of working children's rights. Functions in this category include strengthened national and international (global and regional) complaint procedures (including shareholder and tort actions); expanded NGO "watchdog" monitoring groups, such as the US-based Fair Labor Association (FLA) and Worker Rights Consortium (WRC), competent to challenge violations of the rights of working children; and enhanced mechanisms and opportunities for working children and others to protest when norms for their protection are violated.

Application/enforcement on behalf of working children's rights. Functions in this category include expanded ratification and enforcement by states of international lawmaking instruments directed at the elimination of child labor; strengthened enforcement mechanisms and procedures among the UN, ILO, UNICEF, IMF, World Bank, FTAs, regional human rights systems, and other relevant IGOs; strengthened domestic law enforcement mechanisms and procedures, including the effective coordination of governmental institutions charged to implement human rights norms applicable to working children; enhanced economic strategies such as consumer boycotts, economic embargoes, and trade sanctions; and improved/expanded product/social labeling or certification schemes.

Termination on behalf of working children's rights. Functions in this category include broadened/strengthened national and international initiatives directed at the repeal of public laws and policies that encourage, support, or otherwise tolerate child labor; and enhanced interception and cancellation of private contractual and other social arrangements that encourage, support, or otherwise tolerate child labor.

Appraisal/recommendation on behalf of working children's rights. Functions in this category include strengthened evaluation of the short- and long-term effectiveness of anti–child labor norms, institutions, and procedures (local, national, and international) and revision or repeal of those proven misguided or unsuccessful, accompanied by concrete recommendations, both reformist and transformist in character, for enhanced performance in this regard.

   Reformist recommendations on behalf of working children's rights. These include strengthened developmental strategies (including debt relief and foreign assistance) that facilitate the rehabilitation and social integration (including education) of working children and their families; expanded/enhanced training of parents, teachers, social workers, medical authorities, police officials, and others responsible for protecting working children's best interests; income substitution via public subsidies targeted for families of working children; improved educational cost/opportunity/quality for children and enhanced support of them through education of families, employers, and communities; provision of real economic and social advancement opportunities for children and their families; broadened beneficial/nonexploitive work alternatives for children in need of income; and expanded/enhanced training of abused/exploited children to facilitate their social reintegration consistent with their individual dignity and potential.

Transformist recommendations on behalf of working children's rights. These include expanded strategies of humane governance that seek persuasively, both within and outside households, to change the myths and values that affect the way people think and act relative to abusive/exploitive/hazardous children's work, and that therefore commonly extend beyond the capacity of traditional enforcement means and mechanisms (e.g., innovative educational and work strategies that help children in their own efforts to change their life conditions, that help whole communities comprehend child labor in holistic public health terms, etc.); and broad and deep human rights education—both "top-down" and "bottom-up"—to encourage human rights as a way of life and thereby nurture a culture of respect for children's rights.

*   *   *

We repeat: a strategy worthy of child labor's abolition requires a multitude of mechanisms and techniques—from systematic research and documentation, to education and schooling, to domestic legislative programs, to national and international enforcement measures, to long-term initiatives of social transformation—and at all levels, from the most local to the most global, and on all fronts. It also must engage all elements of society (individuals, families, communities, academic institutions, trade unions, business enterprises, faith-based groups, nongovernmental organizations and associations, government agencies, intergovernmental organizations). Perhaps most important, it must proceed always self-consciously and proactively in the knowledge and determination that all the imagination and energy required to succeed must be applied in service to children's human rights as well as their human needs.

■ Conclusion

On final analysis, the abolition of child labor requires broad and deep initiatives of social transformation. A human rights understanding and approach to the problem of child labor, presupposing a holistic, multifaceted orientation to the individual child and society, are therefore indispensable. Conceptualizing child labor as a human rights issue alone "raises the stakes"; it changes the dynamic in positive ways and gives claims of abuse and exploitation greater legal and moral force.

However, reorienting one's worldview, while essential, is not sufficient to bring about the broad-based change we believe is required to eradicate the workplace abuse and exploitation of children. Thus we have sought to identify a wide range of practical mechanisms and measures, both legal and "extralegal," that may be adopted or adapted in the planning, creation, implementation, and assessment of anti–child labor initiatives. Some of these mechanisms and measures draw on the human rights vocabulary and vocation; others do not, though with appropriate imagination and resolve can be made to do so by reconceptualizing the task at hand and its solutions. Diverse mechanisms and measures drawn from multiple disciplines, founded on core human rights principles, maximally fine-tuned and coordinated, and guided by the values of transparency, accountability, participation, and nondiscrimination, offer, we believe, humankind's best hope for righting the wrong of child labor. And when one contemplates the brute statistics, and especially when one puts a child's face on them (for example, that of a little Cambodian girl in a red dress scavenging barefoot atop the huge Stung Meanchey garbage dump on the outskirts of Phnom Penh),[142] it becomes eminently clear that the time is long past due to take children's human rights seriously and abolish child labor without further delay. Nobel laureate Seamus Heaney says it just right:

> Two sides to every question, yes, yes, yes . . .
> But every now and then, just weighing in
> Is what it must come down to.[143]

▓ Notes

We are grateful to Gavin Boyles, Susan Bissell, Kenneth Cmiel, Dorian Gossy, Willam Myers, Marta Santos-Pais, Chivy Sok, and Marta Cullberg Weston for gracious, insightful counsel.

1. See pp. 6–18.

2. In this chapter, as in Chapter 1, we adopt the definition of "child labor" set forth in the introduction to this volume, in turn derived from Chapter 2, that is, "work done by children that is harmful to them because it is abusive, exploitive, hazardous, or otherwise contrary to their best interests—a subset of a larger class of children's work, some of which may be compatible with children's best interests (variously expressed as 'beneficial,' 'benign,' or 'harmless' children's work)."

3. Santos Pais, *A Human Rights Conceptual Framework for UNICEF,* p. 15.

4. Myers, "Valuing Diverse Approaches . . . ," pp. 30, 34, and 36.

5. See infra endnote 11 and accompanying text.

6. Leary, "Lessons from the Experience . . . ."

7. Haspels and Jankanish, eds., *Action Against Child Labour.*

8. Ibid., p. v.

9. See endnote 12 in Chapter 1.

10. See, generally, ILO, *Report of the Director-General: A Future Without Child Labour* . . . .

11. In his foreword to the 2002 report, ILO/IPEC's director put it thus: "The trafficking of human beings is unacceptable under any circumstances, but the trafficking of vulnerable children and young people is a violation of their rights to protection from exploitation, to play, to an education, and to health, and to family life." Röselaers, foreword to IPEC, *Unbearable to the Human Heart* . . . , p. v.

12. Myers, "Valuing Diverse Approaches . . . ," p. 41 (emphasis added).

13. See also United Nations, *Optional Protocol to the Convention on the Rights of the Child on the Involvement of Children in Armed Conflict* (2000); and United Nations, *Optional Protocol to the Convention on the Rights of the Child on the Sale of Children, Child Prostitution, and Child Pornography* (2000).

14. ILO, *Convention* (No. 182) *Concerning the Prohibition and Immediate Elimination of the Worst Forms of Child Labour* (1999).

15. ILO, *Convention* (No. 138) *Concerning Minimum Age for Admission to Employment* (1973).

16. Douzinas, *The End of Human Rights . . .* , p. 15.

17. Quoted from the Innocenti Research Center website, at http://www.unicef-icdc.org/aboutirc. See also Santos Pais, *A Human Rights Conceptual Framework for UNICEF.*

18. As detailed in "Contesting Resistance to Human Rights Strategy" in Chapter 1 in this volume.

19. As detailed in the conclusion to Chapter 1 in this volume.

20. *Vienna Declaration and Programme of Action . . . .*

21. See, for example, UNICEF, *The State of the World's Children 2004,* Annex B, pp. 91–93.

22. Ibid.

23. Ibid., p. 91, defining the process to include "assessment and analysis, programme planning and design (including setting of goals, objectives and strategies); implementation, monitoring and evaluation."

24. Ibid.

25. Ibid., p. 92.

26. Ibid.

27. Ibid., p. 93.

28. Such is the approach of the United Nations Development Programme (UNDP) in the context of development and from which we draw inspiration. See UNDP, *Integrating Human Rights with Sustainable Human Development . . .* ; and UNDP, *Guidelines . . . .* See also UNICEF, *A Human Rights Approach to UNICEF Programming . . . .*

29. Confirming this fact is, for pertinent example, the funding provided by the Bureau of International Labor Affairs of the US Department of Labor to The University of Iowa Center for Human Rights for an electronic database of national laws bearing upon child labor, designed to assist intergovernmental institutions, national governments, nongovernmental organizations, and others who seek to hold governments accountable for abusive and exploitive children's work. The electronic database may be found at http://www.childlaborlaws.org/projects/database/index.shtml. "At a click of a button, national policy-makers and decision-makers can examine and analyze existing legislation from throughout the world to develop their own laws. NGO activists and researchers in their respective countries can determine the extent to which their governments are in compliance with international obligations. Corporations can gain help to improve their corporate social responsibilities. And colleges and universities as well as other institutions can find guidance to uphold their codes of conduct."

30. See, in this connection, the so-called Paris Principles relating to the status, competence, and responsibilities of national institutions for the promotion and protection of human rights, annexed to United Nations, *General Assembly Resolution 48/134.*

31. United Nations, *Convention on the Rights of the Child* (1989) [hereinafter "CRC"], art. 43(1).

32. That is, the Committee on the Elimination of Racial Discrimination, established under Article 8 of the 1965 International Convention on the Elimination of All Forms of Racial Discrimination; the Human Rights Committee, established under Article 28 of the 1966 ICCPR; the Committee Against Torture, established under Article 17 of the 1984 Convention Against Torture and Other Cruel, Inhuman, or Degrading Treatment or Punishment; and the Committee on the Elimination of Discrimination Against Women, established under Article 1 of the 1999 Optional Protocol to the Convention on the Elimination of All Forms of Discrimination Against Women.

33. See ILO, *Report of the Second Session of the Committee on the Rights of the Child,* paras. 54–58.

34. CRC, art. 44(1).

35. Ibid., art. 44(4).

36. Ibid., art. 44(5).

37. Ibid., art. 45(a).

38. Ibid., art. 45(b)–(c).

39. For details, see the website of the Office of the UN High Commissioner for Human Rights, at http://www.unhchr.ch/html/menu2/6/crc/study.htm.

40. See supra endnote 13.

41. Ibid.

42. For a catalogue of these provisions in addition to CRC Article 32, see text accompanying endnotes 29–46 in Chapter 1 in this volume.

43. The CRC Committee on the Rights of the Child is reported to be "keen to establish a permanent mechanism for interaction with state parties, in addition to the reporting system called for under the CRC." UNICEF, *Report of the Expert Consultation* . . . .

44. See Article 1 of the 1999 Optional Protocol to the Convention on the Elimination of All Forms of Discrimination Against Women . . . .

45. For pertinent discussion, see "Contesting the Claimed Indeterminacy of Human Rights" in Chapter 1 in this volume.

46. *Economic and Social Council Resolution (1235)* . . . (1967) [hereinafter "ECOSOC Resolution 1235"].

47. *Economic and Social Council Resolution (No. 1503)* . . . (1970) [hereinafter "ECOSOC Resolution 1503"]. The procedures established under Resolution 1503 were reformed during the fifty-sixth session of the Commission on Human Rights in 2000. See http://www.unhchr.ch/html/menu2/8/1503.htm.

48. The procedures made possible by these resolutions broke new ground in the protection of human rights via the UN system at the time of their creation, significantly changing the functions of the UN Commission of Human Rights, which before 1967 had no power to take any action relative to complaints concerning human rights.

49. ECOSOC Resolution 1235, para. 2.

50. Rodley, "United Nations Non-Treaty Procedures . . . ," p. 63.

51. Ibid.

52. Ibid.

53. Farer, "The UN and Human Rights . . . ," p. 279.

54. Newman and Weissbrodt, *International Human Rights* . . . , p. 122. No less than the Bureau of the Commission on Human Rights has described the 1503 procedure as "increasingly ineffectual [and] highly cumbersome." See United Nations, *Report of the Bureau of the 54th Session* . . . . For convenient debate about the pros and cons of the 1503 procedure, see Steiner and Alston, *International Human Rights in Context* . . . , pp. 612–619.

55. ECOSOC Resolution 1503, paras. 6(a)–(b).

56. See Alston, "The Commission on Human Rights." Philip Alston concludes, at p. 151, that the "shortcomings" of the 1503 procedure "are so considerable, its tangible achievements so scarce, the justifications offered in its favour so modest, and the need for an effective and universally applicable petition procedure so great" that it should be either radically reformed or abolished.

57. See United Nations, *Annual Report of the Special Rapporteur (Dr. Katarina Tomasevski)* . . . . See also United Nations, *Report of the Special Rapporteur (Katarina Tomasevski)* . . . .

58. See United Nations, *Additional Report of the Special Representative of the Secretary-General (Olara A. Otunnu)* . . . .

59. See United Nations, *Report of the Special Rapporteur (Mr. Juan Miguel Petit)* . . . . See also United Nations, *Report of the Special Rapporteur (Mr. Juan Miguel Petit)* . . . .

60. Rodley, "United Nations Non-Treaty Procedures . . . ," pp. 80–81. The Bureau of the Commission on Human Rights has recommended collapsing the existing non-treaty structure for dealing with human rights violations into a single body of independent experts that would meet twice annually to determine the "situations" that should be referred to the commission. See United Nations, *Report of the Bureau of the 54th Session* . . . .

61. See "Contesting the Claimed Indeterminacy of Human Rights" in Chapter 1 in this volume.

62. See "Human Rights Action Within the United Nations System" in this chapter.

63. The ILO is composed of three organs: (1) the General Conference, comprising representatives of member states (the "International Labour Conference"); (2) the Governing Body; and (3) the International Labour Office.

64. Swepston, "Human Rights Complaint Procedures . . . ." We are indebted to the scholarship of Lee Swepston for the ILO summary provided here.

65. Exceptionally, the ILO also has adopted and supervises declarations and conventions dealing with the rights of indigenous and tribal peoples. See, for example, ILO *Convention* (No. 169) *Concerning Indigenous and Tribal Peoples in Independent Countries* (1989); and *Draft Declaration on the Rights of Indigenous Peoples* (1994).

66. See the ILO Constitution at http://www.ilo.org/public/english/about/iloconst. htm.

67. See, for example, ILO, *Declaration on Fundamental Principles and Rights at Work* (1998).

68. Since the follow-up to the 1998 ILO Declaration on Fundamental Principles and Rights at Work, there is in place a system of gathering information through the annual reports from those countries that have *not* yet ratified the relevant fundamental conventions, or through global reports on a specific theme each year. For example, child labor was the subject of the report presented to the ILO conference in June 2002.

69. According to Swepston, "Human Rights Complaint Procedures . . . ," p. 95, the FFCC may also examine complaints referred to it by ECOSOC against states that are not members of the ILO.

70. Ibid., p. 88.

71. Ibid., p. 95.

72. Swepston conveniently summarizes: "The principle of freedom of association includes, *inter alia:* the right of workers and employers to establish organizations; free functioning of such organizations; the right to join federations and confederations and to affiliate with international groupings of occupational organizations; the right of organizations not to be suspended or dissolved by administrative authorities; protection

against anti-union discrimination; the right to collective bargaining; the right to strike; and the right to basic civil liberties, which are necessary pre-conditions to the free exercise of trade union rights." Ibid., p. 96.

73. CRC, art. 12(1)–(2).

74. Swepston, "Human Rights Complaint Procedures . . . ," p. 100.

75. See generally, for example, IPEC, *IPEC Action Against Child Labour, 2002–2003*.

76. Ibid., pp. 14, 28.

77. See text accompanying endnote 79 in Chapter 1 in this volume.

78. United Nations, *International Covenant on Economic, Social, and Cultural Rights* (1966) [hereinafter "ICESCR"], art. 10(1).

79. Ibid., art 10(3).

80. Ibid.

81. Ibid.

82. Ibid.

83. See, for example, ibid., art. 6 (the right to work), art. 7 (the right to just and favorable conditions of work), art. 8 (the rights of workers to organize and bargain collectively), art. 11 (the right to an adequate standard of living), and art. 13 (the right to education).

84. The CESCR is the only human rights treaty body not created directly by its own treaty.

85. Office of the UN High Commissioner for Human Rights, *Fact Sheet No. 16 (Rev. 1)*, sec. 8 [hereinafter *"Fact Sheet No. 16"*].

86. See United Nations, *Draft Optional Protocol to the International Covenant on Civil and Political Rights* (1996).

87. *Fact Sheet No. 16,* sec. 8.

88. United Nations High Commissioner for Human Rights and the Committee on Economic, Social, and Cultural Rights, *Plan of Action . . . .*

89. For detailed clarification of the state reporting process, see Bayefsky, "How to Complain to the UN Human Rights Treaty System," chap. 8.

90. The Limburg Principles (1987) and the Maastricht Guidelines (1998) stipulate what may constitute a violation of the ICESCR.

91. *Fact Sheet No. 16,* sec. 6.

92. See United Nations, *International Convention on the Elimination of All Forms of Racial Discrimination* (1965), art. 8.

93. See United Nations, *Convention Against Torture and Other Cruel, Inhuman, or Degrading Treatment or Punishment* (1984), art. 17.

94. Norway established a commissioner, or ombud, with statutory rights to protect children and their rights in 1981 and was the first country in the world to do so. Since 1981, the ombudsman for children in Norway has worked continuously to improve national and international legislation affecting children's welfare. For details, see the ombudsman website, at http://www.barneombudet.no/english.

95. *European Convention for the Protection of Human Rights . . .* (1950) [hereinafter *"European Convention"*].

96. *European Social Charter (Revised)* (1996).

97. *Charter of the Organization of American States* (1948) [hereinafter *"OAS Charter"*].

98. *American Convention . . .* (1969).

99. *African Charter . . .* (1981).

100. *Charter on the Rights and Welfare of the Child* (1990).

101. For detailed discussion of the three regional human rights systems, see Shelton, "The Promise of Regional Human Rights Systems."

102. *Protocol No. 11* . . . (1994).

103. *European Convention* (1950), art. 2.

104. Ibid., art. 4.

105. See, for example, pt. I(2)–(7), (17), (22), (24), and (26) of the European Social Charter (Revised) meant to safeguard rights to just conditions of work; safe and healthy working conditions; fair remuneration sufficient for a decent standard of living; freedom of association; collective bargaining; special protection for children against physical and moral hazards; appropriate social, legal, and economic protection for children; a role in determining and improving working conditions and environment; protection in cases of termination; and dignity at work.

106. Ibid., pt. I, *chapeau.*

107. *Additional Protocol to the European Social Charter* . . . (1995).

108. Ibid., arts. 1–5.

109. Council of Europe, *Complaint No. 1/1998* . . . . For a convenient brief summary of this case and its disposition, see Churchill and Khaliq, "The Collective Complaints System . . . ," pp. 142–143, 148–149.

110. Ibid., arts. 6–8.

111. Ibid., art. 9.

112. *American Convention* . . . (1969), art. 26.

113. Ibid., arts. 4, 6, 16, 19.

114. *Additional Protocol in the Area* . . . (1988).

115. *OAS Charter* (1948), art. 33(g)–(h).

116. Ibid., art. 45(a)–(c).

117. Ibid., art. 49.

118. *American Convention* . . . (1969), art. 41.

119. *OAS Charter* (1948), art. 106.

120. Ibid., art. 9.

121. See endnotes 48–56 and accompanying text in Chapter 1 in this volume.

122. *African Charter* . . . (1981), arts. 5, 10, 15–17.

123. Ibid., arts. 45–59.

124. *Protocol to the African Charter on Human and People's Rights* . . . (1997), art. 5.

125. Ibid.

126. Ibid., arts. 6–9, 26–28.

127. Ibid., arts. 28, 30.

128. *African Charter on the Rights and Welfare of the Child* (1990), art. 1.

129. Ibid., arts. 8, 11, 12, 14.

130. Ibid., art. 15.

131. Ibid., arts. 22, 27, 29.

132. Now the African Union (AU).

133. *African Charter on the Rights and Welfare of the Child* (1990), art. 44.

134. Ibid., art. 45.

135. See *Protocol No. 11* . . . (1994).

136. *African Charter on the Rights and Welfare of the Child* (1990).

137. See Shelton, "The Promise of Regional Human Rights Systems," pp. 351–391.

138. Ibid., p. 391.

139. See also Chapter 1 in this volume.

140. For eloquent expression and advocacy of this notion of human rights education, see the website of the People's Movement for Human Rights Education, formerly the People's Decade for Human Rights Education, at http://www.pdhre.org/index.html.

141. See "Taking Working Children's Human Rights Seriously" in this chapter.

142. See the dedication page of this volume.

143. Heaney, "Weighing In," pp. 22–23.

11

Conceiving Child Labor in Human Rights Terms: Can It Mobilize Progressive Change?

David M. Post

How useful for generating progressive social change is a rights approach to child labor?[1] What's the *use* of using "rights" to eliminate abusive children's work or to help working children actualize themselves and thrive? Do such perverse questions—joining consequentialist language with a commandment to protect and empower children regardless of the consequence—really need to be asked?

The first goal in this chapter is to explain why we should concern ourselves with the practical results of a rights discourse for working children and their societies. To begin, I survey the theoretical approaches to children's rights that enable us to discuss progressive changes that may benefit working children. Next, I review four distinct perspectives on the ways in which social progress could be generated through a rights approach, with improved protection and advocacy for children as the result. Then, I offer an inventory of strategies that practitioners have used when trying to eliminate child labor or better the lot of working children. I link these strategies with theories about social change that predict the efficacy of each strategy. Next, I cite two examples of progressive change in national experiences that are explained to varying degrees by the above-mentioned social change theories. Finally, I offer my view about the progressive change potential of state-directed solutions to child labor, as compared with "bottom-up" efforts to promote children's rights through social mobilization by nonstate actors in civil society.

■ What Is the Question That Progressive Change Answers?

Today the freedom for human development is accepted as a maturation in thinking about public responsibility for children. A "right to development" as part of a "third generation of rights" is seen as progress rather than deviance from liberal conceptions of freedom from constraint, with their narrower focus on political liberty.[2] From this perspective, enabling human development becomes a concern not only of parents but also of a wider community, including the global community. And eliminating child labor fulfills a global obligation for children's development.

One impetus for this view has been the growing legitimacy—and as a result, the growing effectiveness—of international nongovernmental organizations (INGOs) such as Human Rights Watch, Save the Children, Amnesty International, PLAN, Anti-Slavery International, and many other secular and faith-based networks. INGOs have spread a new civil society through the grassroots at the same time that the United Nations Children's Fund (UNICEF) disseminated the 1989 United Nations Convention on the Rights of the Child (CRC)[3] to governments and the International Labour Organization (ILO) promoted its 1973 ILO Convention (No. 138) Concerning Minimum Age for Admission to Employment (ILO C138)[4] and 1999 ILO Convention (No. 182) Concerning the Prohibition and Immediate Elimination of the Worst Forms of Child Labour (ILO C182).[5] What has this mobilization around "second generation" and "third generation" rights achieved for working children? Conversely, what has global attention to working children accomplished for progressing global discussions of rights to the third generation? Posed in this way, the capability of a children's rights discourse to effect progressive change—an empirical question—assumes theoretical as well as substantive importance.

Our focus in this volume specifically on child labor offers us an opportunity to assess the efficacy of rights in an area where consequentialism——the evaluation of policies based on their consequences—had a long head start in mobilizing unions, welfare organizations, and economic development agencies. Until the 1990s, campaigns against children's work aimed to maximize social welfare by protecting adult wages from unfair competition and protecting children from harm. Evaluations of the effectiveness of these campaigns would naturally focus on their actual benefit in meeting children's needs. The regulation of children's work was designed to meet the needs of children through poverty reduction and through investment in their human capital. But questions about the usefulness of a rights discourse to reduce children's work and eliminate the exploitation of working children are germane today because the movement to a rights approach was made, in part, for strategic reasons. As UNICEF's 1999 *State of the World's Children* report put this strategy: "What were once seen as the needs of children have been elevated to something far harder to ignore: their rights."[6]

This elevation occurred in the face of serious objections. For example, ethicist Onora O'Neill has raised two key concerns about the usefulness of invoking children's rights.[7] First, she argues, the contemporary rhetoric on rights has been separated from its parent theories of natural law and human obligations. Rights make sense, according to O'Neill, only when they are derived from a larger theory of obligations. Within this larger theoretical framework, the child could arguably become a "claimant who demands what is owed and is wronged if a rightful claim is denied."[8] Merely to insist that ideals and goals for children are "rights" does not make them so unless there is also a corresponding "duty-bearer," a party responsible for the rights of the child. Without a corresponding bearer of the duty, insists O'Neill, there is only empty rhetoric. Invoking children's rights to live free of exploitation could even frustrate rather than advance social progress and welfare.[9]

Despite the theoretical problem of unidentified duty-bearers, O'Neill acknowledges that rights might be useful politically for *certain* groups in asserting their cause and building a mass movement. But, O'Neill wonders, are children among these groups? "Can appeals to children's fundamental rights be politically significant," she asks, "in the way that other appeals to rights have been? Do they or can they help empower children or their advocates to wring recognition and fulfillment of obligations from the powerful?"[10] In offering her tentative answer to this question, O'Neill is deeply skeptical that the dependence by children on adults is in any way analogous to the oppression of adults, who have been well served by a rhetoric of rights. No children's movement can be envisaged from this perspective, because the ranks of childhood are continuously depleted by entry to adulthood.

Might this problem reflect only a narrow vision by O'Neill? Yes, according to Michael Freeman and others, who have argued that it is indeed possible to envision a children's movement.[11] The empirical question now is whether, in the years since the diffusion of the 1989 CRC and its growing legitimacy, the facts have supported the views expressed either by O'Neill or by Freeman. As Philip Alston puts it, one's position on the concept and practice of children's rights is influenced by one's belief about the relations between international norms and national law, on the one hand, and national law and social change, on the other.[12] As a result of the CRC, what changed after 1989 for working children? Did children's mobilizations occur around their rights to participation and full development, and has this effected a consistent response to child labor issues? The question that progressive change answers is whether or not heightened concern for children's rights will be likely to force governments, employers, and parents to reduce child labor.

■ How Has a Rights Discourse Affected the Mobilization of Children and Their Public Voice?

Formal evaluations of the impact of the CRC remain piecemeal, considering its recent adoption. No attempts have yet been made to assess the global consequence of the convention for children's well-being, let alone its effect on child labor. Only one international attempt has been made to document the changes wrought in national laws and in NGO mobilization. After investigating six countries, Lisa Woll was able to report only a "sparse" impact of the CRC on civil society. And while the convention had affected the work of UNICEF and the INGOs, its effect on government was less profound; it "has not been wide or deep."[13]

Despite this dim view, there is little question that children's rights movements have become more visible since 1989. It is unclear whether this is because children today are better organized, more exploited, and more cognizant that exploitation violates the CRC, or whether adult organizations have used children's rights and children's organizations strategically to highlight long-standing welfare concerns. Brazil offers one of the best-known examples of this mobilization. Brazil's 1988 constitution reflected demands by a grass-roots movement of 1.4 million children and adolescents, who signed a petition in support of protections that were codified in Article 227.[14] "It is the duty of the family, of society, and of the State to assure children and adolescents, with absolute priority, the right to life, health, nutrition, education, recreation, vocational preparation, culture, dignity, respect, liberty, and family and community solidarity, over and beyond making them safe from neglect, discrimination, exploitation, cruelty and oppression."[15] After ratifying the CRC, Brazil codified its policies and the positive freedoms they bestow through its 1990 Statute on Children and Adolescents.

Several other examples could be cited to illustrate the range of issues and tactics used when children are mobilized. First, consider the press release by PLAN International, a global NGO, about its efforts to sensitize New Yorkers to the CRC:

> "Hello . . . I am Esther from Kenya. How do you support the UN Convention on the Rights of the Child?" These words were the first to appear on a computer screen in New York, beginning an hour-long Web chat between children and delegates at the United Nations and students in a PLAN program area counterpart in Kenya. The transcontinental linkup—in English, on computers provided by PLAN International, a child-focused development organization—gave children at both ends a chance to demonstrate their concern for children's rights issues, and their ability to discuss serious matters, such as "the right to a free basic education," with their leaders.[16]

Another example comes from the Child Rights Information Network (CRIN), which reports as well as helps to shape children's mobilization. Uchengamma is a fourteen-year-old girl who became president of the Bhima Sangha, India's national working children's union. Her personal testimony was disseminated worldwide by the CRIN newsletter:

> With the help of the Sangha, many children are now trying to participate, develop skills and stand on their own feet. Through my participation in Bhima

Sangha, many children who are members of the organization are actively participating in various fields, programs and discussions. As a result of the work of the organization, the situation of working children has improved in my area. Earlier, working children were never paid the right wages for their labor. Now they demand this as a right and have actually obtained better working conditions and better wages as a result. I also believe that because of our fight against child marriages, the situation of girls like me in our village has improved.[17]

Finally, consider an example of mobilization supported by trade unions as well as by the ILO's International Programme on the Elimination of Child Labour (IPEC). The "Global March Against Child Labour" led children from all continents to converge on several cities, among them Santiago, Chile. The record of their demonstration includes eloquent testimony of the pain caused by early work. The children's joint declaration states:

We, the boys and girls meeting in Santiago, representing Argentina, Uruguay, Colombia, Peru, Bolivia, Ecuador, Brazil and Chile, declare that: the governments of our nations must listen to us, the children; they must understand our reality; child labor exists, and it damages us physically and psychologically. Child labor takes no account of the value and dignity of children. All children like to read, play outside, share, listen to music, go to school, help in the home, play and take care of their younger brothers and sisters. But there are things that disgust us and hurt us, such as exploitation through hard labor; the lack of physical space to develop. Often our parents won't listen to us, and it is so hard to reach our dreams. We form part of a system that puts us down. We want child labor to disappear from the face of the earth, and for there to be new laws that respect our rights, that say fifteen years old is the minimum to work. Yes to the right to education! No to exploitation![18]

The previous anecdotes support the hope that mass mobilizations and movements of working children are indeed possible and that they can draw public attention. But children, like adults, rarely if ever speak in a single voice. Children who participate in discussions about their right to work usually do so with support from adult sponsoring organizations, and with no more consensus than is found among their sponsors.[19] Thus, as the preceding quotations illustrate, "listening to children" offers no clearer guide on the question of child labor than does listening to adults. By taking children seriously, we will not necessarily find clear direction on even the worst forms of child labor. For example, Heather Montgomery poses uncomfortable questions about sexual exploitation and consent in her study of young Thai children working as prostitutes. She writes that the CRC is "explicit in offering children protection from sexual exploitation, and yet many of the children I surveyed claimed not to be exploited. . . . Is it acceptable, given the international legal precedent of the Convention, to ignore children's voices or disregard their worldview?"[20]

▣   Theoretical Perspectives on Progressive Change

Scholars of political science and international relations have suggested four distinctive approaches to the ways in which human rights promote progressive change. Following Hans Schmitz and Kathryn Sikkink, these approaches can be described as "realist," "liberal," "institutionalist," and "constructivist."[21]

The Realist Approach

From the realist viewpoint, ideas about human rights are norms developed and diffused by powerful nation-states. From this perspective, there is no difference between norms expressed by nations and their national interests. As Condoleezza Rice declared, just prior to the election of George W. Bush, "[f]oreign policy in a Republican administration . . . will proceed from the firm ground of the national interest, not from the interests of an illusory international community."[22] The assumption underlying this view is that, in a tumultuous world without centralized authority, nations operate in uncertainty over their security. They establish armies and effect diplomatic agreements to advance their security interests, and they cooperate only if it is in their particular self-interest to do so. In this sense, the emerging international norms regulating the work of children are only manifestations of successful hegemony by dominant nations. But stronger nations are hesitant to accept human rights treaties in general—and those related to children's rights in particular—because this threatens state sovereignty.[23] Applied to the regulation of child labor, policies from this perspective would aim to defend US trade and economic interests rather than defend the values expressed by any international community, which are likely to reflect interests of competitor nations.

Why is the realist perspective on rights unable to accept mobilizations for change that are based in the common values of an "illusory international community"? Perhaps this is because the demand for human rights poses a qualitatively different type of problem for governments than do demands for social welfare, since the latter can be met using material resources and these can be easily evaluated in consequentialist terms. As Joe Foweraker concluded, based on his comparative study of Brazil and Chile, "material demands could be easily absorbed or diverted within political systems organized along clientelistic and corporatist lines. . . . But since demands for citizenship rights always have a universal content (insofar as the rights must apply equally and across the board to be rights at all), they necessarily challenge the particularism of the clientelistic power relations."[24] The threat to autonomy leads nations to embrace a particular human right only when this is in the national self-interest, and more powerful nations will be unlikely to accept these as rights at all.[25]

The realist approach to progressive change may explain the US disinterest in the CRC. As discussed below, this approach reflects some of the strategies used within the United States to address child labor, and strategies used by some Americans who seek to promote children's welfare in other countries. But this realist perspective fails to account for the widespread legitimacy the convention enjoys among most governments of the world. Outside the United States, the CRC has been instrumental in creating a "mobilization of shame."[26] Perhaps more than anything else, it was the prospect of negative publicity that led so many countries so rapidly to include items from the CRC in their constitutions and statutes.

The Liberal Approach

The voluntary acceptance by nations of constraints to their sovereignty through ratification of the CRC challenges the realist notion that the conception of human rights is merely a side product—an epiphenomenon—of power relations. The puzzle posed by this voluntary acceptance of constraint may be explained, at least in part, by liberal theories of international relations. From this viewpoint, according to Schmitz and Sikkink, "states have interests in entering international institutional arrangements to prevent sub-optimal outcomes of uncoordinated action."[27] Andrew Moravcsik has argued that adopting human rights conventions such as the CRC may be rational and in the national self-interest to strengthen domestic democracy. New democracies, in particular, can find the stability of international agreements to be a stabilizing force to avoid conflict.[28]

From the perspective of liberal theorists of human rights diffusion, such as David Forsythe, "it is states that create intergovernmental organizations, defining their authority and perhaps loaning them some elements of power."[29] According to Forsythe, nations harbor a self-image. From this perspective, too, it is the national *self-image* (not only self-interest) that leads to the application of sanctions, for example, by the United States against white minority rule in South Africa. National self-image can explain also the imposition of trade restrictions against the purchase by the US government of goods produced by child labor. The key actor is the nation-state, which alone has the power to implement or arrest progressive social change. The decisions made by national leaders and legislatures, especially those of liberal democracies, respond to public pressures. "But the state is hardly withering away," Forsythe continues, "even if its de facto independence is increasingly restricted by a variety of factors."[30]

Institutionalist and Constructivist Approaches

Liberal interpretations do not explain the force of ideas rallying partisans of human rights, nor do they explain the internal dynamics leading treaties such as the CRC to catalyze domestic change and socialization. As Michael Ignatieff has observed, "human rights has gone global not because it serves the interests of the powerful but primarily because it has advanced the interests of the powerless. Human rights has gone global by going local, imbedding itself in the soil of cultures and world views independent of the West, in order to sustain ordinary people's struggles against unjust states and oppressive social practices."[31] Ideational theories of social change grant the power of ideas. Such theories do not assume the state has withered away or become irrelevant. But they do see state action as endogenous, as the by-product of institutional normative change and of activism of extranational agents. The power of ideas is to legitimize the demand for human rights by nations and NGOs as well as individual citizens. Within this perspective are two variant strands of ideational theory, each of which downplays the state as the locus of action: institutionalism and constructivism.

Institutionalism. Institutionalist theories depart from Max Weber's insight that bureaucratic legitimacy develops from the bureaucracy itself, rather than from the original authority of the sacred or the exclusive body of expertise that happens to be regulated by the bureaucracy. The authority of the modern bureaucracy, according to Weber, spreads itself over new domains independently of the growth of these domains in themselves.[32] Seen in this light, the overall societal effects of education derive only partly from the socialization and training of individuals who become educated. Education affects societies much more pervasively than through changing merely the behaviors and capabilities of the individuals who are processed by schools as students. Historically, families came to recognize that the type of information that was legitimated officially through school credentials was "real" knowledge, while other types of knowledge left out of schooling were considered merely as "folklore," and their adherents were labeled as "undereducated." In this way, according to John Meyer, schools eventually came to affect individuals who do not attend them just as much as they change students who receive a formal education.[33] This conjecture has clear relevance to the value placed by societies on children who work rather than attend school, and the reasons for their stigmatization.

For institutionalist theorists, the rationalization of the worlds of work and schooling—and the divorce between these activities—is normative as well as administrative. It is normative because a growing proportion of the world's families voluntarily internalize, as an accepted norm, that authentic expertise should be centrally and legitimately certified through schooling. The historical process that is associated with the public's internalization of what it means to be a modern, educated person is independent of the plans by any particular government (witness the failure by many national education ministries in their attempts to promote nonformal education or vocational alternatives to university education). In the same way that blue jeans are taken for granted as the youth uniform of choice in diverse cultural settings, world norms of childhood are diffused globally. And yet, notwithstanding the diffusion of modern views about youth culture and what it means to be a modern citizen through popular channels and world media, the state is not irrelevant for institutionalists. Governments can reinforce world norms about childhood and apply them consistently throughout the population, including marginalized populations. From an institutionalist perspective, the symbolic value of compulsory school legislation and of legal sanctions against employers of children far exceeds the positive instrumental effects of these laws in changing family behavior. This symbolic value is the reason it is so rarely necessary to force parents or children to comply with child labor or compulsory school laws: merely the news of their adoption and promulgation is enough to effect compliance by most "hold-out" parents. By reinforcing the social stigma against deviations from modern views about appropriate activity, national labor codes and school laws tip the balance of public opinion about what is required for good parenting.

International organizations have been able to effect the progressive recognition of human rights by governments, despite the interest by nation-states in preserving sovereignty. For example, Martha Finnemore traces the campaign by Theodore Maunoir and the original committee members of the Red Cross.[34] Maunoir declared that he sought to "maintain an agitation . . . so that our views will be adopted by everyone, high and low, from the sovereigns of Europe to the people themselves."[35] Finnemore's research indicates that the actual progress of the Red Cross was mainly from the top down, rather than the bottom up. On a different front, Nitza Berkovitch recounts the strategies of the international women's movement, from its origins as a suffrage lobby.[36] By framing women's progress as the fulfillment of human rights, feminists were able to win attention from the ILO to women's work and to force governments to attend to sexism. The cases of the Red Cross and of the international women's movement are examples of the way that a global culture has emerged to restrict the unbridled authority of sovereign states.

Building on the work by Finnemore, Berkovitch, and others, John Boli has suggested three types of authority that are exercised by INGOs: autonomous authority, collateral authority, and penetrative INGO authority.[37] As an example of the first type of authority, scientific membership organizations exercise control over their members autonomously from the authority of any national government. By contrast, a second type of authority is exemplified by the International Committee of the Red Cross and various population-policy INGOs. These organizations have collateral authority along with willing government partners. International population groups such as the Population Council effect change in national population policies, but only when governments are persuaded that population control is in their best interests. The third type of authority suggested by Boli, and the one that is most clearly relevant to the rights discourse over child labor, is "penetrative" INGO authority. Some international organizations—for example, Save the Children, Casa Alianza, and Amnesty International—achieve their authority through "successful INGO penetration of the boundary-maintenance mechanisms shielding national and local polities from outside influence, as well as on the conscious effort by lower-level units to connect with INGO discourse and programs."[38] The form of penetrative authority depends on a rational-voluntaristic structure, in which governments voluntarily participate in and share authority over widely legitimated values. INGOs can set the agenda and priorities of sovereign states that recognize these shared values. Among these values is the sanctity of the individual child, not as a citizen of any nation but simply as a child, entitled to basic protections and rights, including the right to grow free from exploitation and abuse.

Constructivism. Constructivism is the fourth theoretical perspective on human rights that must be considered by advocates who are concerned with abusive children's work. Constructivist theorists of human rights, similar to the institutionalists, de-emphasize national sovereignty and autonomy. But constructivists differ with institutionalism because the latter theory de-emphasizes local political actors as change agents and tends to regard world culture as a totalizing, even homogenizing environment. By contrast, constructivists have traced back expressions of power and interest to local and transnational actors. For example, Keck and Sikkink recount the case of a Mexican human rights activist who testified to the importance of her training with Amnesty International,[39] which then became like an "exploding star" as it implanted local actors in Latin America who were able, through their NGOs, to mobilize around specific concerns, including children's rights, and to "socialize" governments about international human rights norms. From a constructivist perspective, local NGOs are not mere conveyor belts that carry Western human rights norms worldwide. Rather, interest groups are agents; they use local issues to connect with international organizations for their own particular needs and purposes. In particular, local NGOs seek to address issues and problems to make themselves indispensable and more capable of raising funds from international donors (the staff salaries paid in many such NGOs are far greater than university salaries).

Whatever the motives, the result is a socialization of world norms. Thomas Risse and Kathryn Sikkink find that "socialization processes start when actors adapt their behavior in accordance with the norm for initially instrumental reasons. Governments want to remain in power, while domestic NGOs seek the most effective means to rally the opposition. The more they 'talk the talk,' however, the more they entangle themselves in a moral discourse which they cannot escape in the long run."[40] The diffusion of international norms depends on the establishment and the sustainability of networks among domestic and transnational actors who succeed in linking with international regimes. "International contacts can 'amplify' the demands of domestic groups, prize open space for new issues, and then echo these demands back in the domestic arena."[41] As Schmitz and Sikkink observe, "moral argumentation rarely leads to direct behavioral change. Instead, state actors are forced to defend their human rights record in a social environment of world opinion and international institutions [creating a] 'corridor of narrowing choices for policy-makers.'"[42] Constituent and opposition national organizations lobby the national government and, in turn, are pressured by governments. But NGOs have powerful alliances outside of the national governance structure, and through these alliances they can leverage public policy change more effectively than through frontal assaults on the state because governments are more reluctant to retaliate against the United Nations Educational, Scientific, and Cultural Organization (UNESCO), UNICEF, or the ILO. In a "boomerang effect," pressures from civil society are thus exerted outward in particular nations through channels of transnational allies. But these pressures soon come back and bear forcefully on national governments. The self-image of the state is created by these pressures, in contradistinction to both the realist and liberal perspectives on human rights advocacy.

Theoretical Assumptions Underlying Progressive Change Practices

At this point it is useful to consider the wide range of actions that have been taken by states and NGOs to reduce child labor or otherwise improve the lot of working children. As already mentioned, many of the most prominent actions and actors do not rely on human rights arguments at all, but on welfare concerns and a realist perspective that human rights discourse is but a manifestation of national power. A possible explanation is that welfare concerns have been developed in political settings (e.g., the United States) where realist orientations to human rights give less traction to rights and more to alternative arguments to intervene against abusive children's work. The catalogue of strategies that follows can be instructive as to the reasons why human rights arguments are used because such a catalogue can help to identify the bases of particular practices that invoke human rights as the rationale for action against child labor.[43] To clarify the unique features of human rights activity against child labor, however, it is necessary to begin with examples of actions that do *not* use a human rights approach.

From an economic perspective on household decisionmaking, it is not the absence of rights but rather the absence of opportunity and any true alternative that impels parents to send their children to the work force instead of to full-time schooling; parents weigh the wages that children could earn and the value of the unpaid work that they would do against the benefits of going to school regularly and the money costs of that education. In Bangladesh, Brazil, and Mexico, to mention only three examples, targeted cash assistance therefore has been provided to families from the poorest regions of each country in exchange for parents sending their children to school. In Mexico, an important feature of the PROGRESA scholarship assistance to families in marginalized communities is that it offers a stipend for the school enrollment of daughters slightly greater than for sons. These scholarships were found to have been effective in promoting school attendance, especially by girls.[44] It is less certain that increased school attendance also reduces child labor among girls, although such evidence is beginning to emerge.[45]

Apart from strategies to reduce the cost to parents of educating their children, the other major welfare approach to ending child labor has been to increase the immediate benefit from sending children to school. To increase the immediate benefits, much attention has been given to increasing the relevance of the school curriculum, or to tailoring out-of-school education to the needs of workers. The goal is to make all children feel fulfilled and successful as students so that eventually they will not need to work. Beyond the improvements to the school curriculum, even small changes to school infrastructure (e.g., providing girls with safer and more sanitary toilets in Kenya) can decrease the risk of leaving school. Some parents are motivated to enroll children in school because of the immediate economic benefits that schooling provides to their families in the form of nutrition and supervision so that parents are free to work.[46]

From the perspective of the CRC, however, there are human rights arguments to improve the quality of schooling regardless of the consequences for reducing child labor.[47] Indeed, it would be surprising for any nation to undertake costly improvement of its school system only out of concern to improve conditions for working children, and there are few if any examples of social mobilizations for this purpose. Child labor has not been a major concern of the Education for All (EFA) movement. Nonetheless, school improvements resulting from the EFA movement, such as targeted subsidies, may operate synergistically with human rights movements to reduce abusive children's work.

Turning now to strategies that specifically invoke human rights among their motivating concerns, we can appreciate the growing efforts to grant children a voice.[48] In addition to the examples mentioned previously, we can observe the impact on the ILO and trade unions of the presence of children's organizations at international summits. For instance, in a conference on child labor hosted by the Netherlands in 1997, children representing the Peruvian working children's movement were in attendance. The Dutch minister for development cooperation welcomed Peru's delegates by declaring:

> We should not discuss child labor without involving the children themselves in the decision-making processes. An adult sitting behind a desk cannot for a moment imagine what it is like to be an undernourished, overworked child, stretched beyond the limits of its physical strength. We need inside informa-

tion and this can only be gained by involving the children themselves. Children are, moreover, perfectly capable of assessing their own situation and coming up with solutions.[49]

But labor organizations were unconvinced that NGOs representing working children ought to be represented in such discussions, and they urged that children not be included in the discussion of a new convention, scheduled to take place in Oslo later that same year. Peruvian organizations of working children responded by convening their own congress in Lima, this time *without* support from the ILO or UNICEF. The final declaration included the demand that the United Nations insert a new clause in the CRC, one that would provide for "[r]ecognition of the right to work as a human right based on the dignity of the child." This did not occur. It was viewed as a distraction rather than as a contribution by members of Peru's IPEC office, which would have preferred government action to institutionalize the programs it had developed to eliminate the most dangerous forms of child labor. Nevertheless, the mobilization of children (in this case by their adult sponsors in Peru) kept the focus on children's participation as agents.

Human rights have been considered by advocates who are concerned about child labor, independently of the CRC. One means for this advocacy, outside of the CRC framework, is through trade sanctions and consumer boycotts of goods produced by children. For example, although the United States is not a party to the CRC, President Bill Clinton, in 1999, signed Executive Order 13126, prohibiting federal procurement of goods that may be produced using forced or indentured child labor.[50] For several years, Senator Tom Harkin of Iowa attempted to introduce trade legislation that would restrict the importation of goods manufactured with "child labor." Additionally, the US Senate, in 1994, mandated annual reports from the US Department of Labor about child labor internationally. These reports were more than informational. By requiring governments to explain their policies and realities regarding child labor, the process appears to have led to a "mobilization of shame." On US university campuses, students protested against sweatshop conditions in overseas factories manufacturing athletic apparel bearing their university's logo, and these mobilizations have led to new coalitions with manufacturers and textile unions, such as the Global Alliance and SweatFree.[51]

Consumer and trade organizations have been sensitive to child labor abuse as a human rights issue outside the United States as well. RUGMARK, an organization that uses market pressures to help Western consumers fund educational opportunities for child carpet weavers,[52] licenses the right to sell carpets that are certified as free from child labor to registered dealers. A portion of the money raised from these sales supports free education in RUGMARK schools that serve former weavers on the Indian subcontinent. According to RUGMARK, 1,334 children have been liberated from looms in

India since 1995 and 1,172 former weavers attend four RUGMARK schools. Three schools in Pakistan are run directly by RUGMARK, which further supports an additional eight schools. In Nepal, 407 weavers have been rescued from carpet work, with 188 of them attending RUGMARK schools. Some critics of consumer-led interventions have decried their unintended consequences, which may cause children to leave the formal sector and to engage in even riskier employment in the informal sector. Such consequentialist analysis, though natural, represents a critique from outside the human rights perspective rather than an internal inconsistency. Consumers are sometimes less concerned with outcomes of their boycott than they are with the question, "Are my hands clean?" The consequentialist critique of consumer boycotts or trade embargoes could potentially help strengthen the moral foundations of a human rights perspective on child labor, if rights advocates will engage rather than disconnect with the consequences of such campaigns.[53]

Another way in which the CRC effects progressive change is through requiring the periodic reporting of children's situations—including labor situations—from states parties to the convention. The benefits of this process go beyond documentation, and there are several synergistic effects. First, the reporting schedule serves as a reminder to governments as parties to the convention about their commitments to children. In the cases of some governments, this reminder forces leaders to confront information about their nation's children for the first time. Such evidence may also focus more general public attention on the plight of working children. Second, there is an element of coercion involved in "shaming" governments, because the periodic reports of each government are disseminated widely, including through postings on the pervasive World Wide Web. Questions asked of governments frequently are critical, and it is always the Committee on the Rights of the Child that has the final word in these public exchanges. Third, the CRC explicitly recognizes NGOs as alternative sources of information to that of governments. This has the potential to extend the legitimacy of the United Nations and the Committee on the Rights of the Child to local NGOs, which take CRC reporting as an essential part of their public charter. In some cases—for example, in Indonesia's first official periodic report for the 1993–2000 interval—the legitimacy umbrella of the CRC forced the Indonesian government to include express input from several human rights NGOs in drafting its submission, an input that led to the public promise to implement the recently ratified ILO C182 (1999), on the "worst forms" of child labor, as well as to continue giving special attention to eliminating the risk that children will work on fishing platforms. In other cases—for example, Argentina in 2002—international NGOs like Amnesty International have taken the lead in filing alternative reports before the committee, and in still other cases a consortium of domestic NGOs has filed alternative reports. But even when uncoordinated presentations or reporting occur, as has been true for many countries, there can be benefits for progress. The periodic production of "alternative" reports can enrich civil society by promoting a diversity of interest groups that compete to establish themselves as advocates of children. The "bidding" among these groups to establish their reputations works also to establish the issues around which they organize; even more broadly, it disseminates the CRC view that children's rights must be protected. To the extent that local NGOs focus on child labor as a human rights issue, they bring this to the public eye without any direct intervention by international NGOs. In fact, international advocacy is key, for the coordination and archiving of NGO reports for the committee are maintained by Anti-Slavery International, one of the first organizations targeting abusive children's work. In sum, the human rights approach, and its institutionalization through the CRC, are much better explained by the constructivist theoretical approach than by alternative perspectives on progressive change.[54]

As the preceding discussion indicates, the act of gathering and documenting situations of working children is itself an intervention. In the United States, a parallel fact-finding function has also occurred, led both by the US Department of Labor and by the National Consumer League, which has surveyed state departments of labor to consolidate disparate information about inspections and enforcement of child labor laws. In the United States, in addition to increased documentation, such activity has increased the coordination between labor groups and child advocates. The American Center for International Labor Solidarity (ACILS) received funding from the American Federation of Labor–Congress of Industrial Organizations (AFL-CIO) and, during the Clinton administration, from the US Department of Labor and the US Agency for International Development (USAID) as well. Its goal has been to mobilize communities using the existing organizations of local trade unions. In Kenya, for example, the ACILS, in collaboration with trade unionists, raised awareness about child labor problems.

The usefulness of documentation and information gathering can be seen most clearly in the many creative curriculum projects that have been developed for children and adolescents since the CRC was adopted in 1989. In these curricula, there is clear evidence of NGO, government, and school collaboration. Several US examples may be cited:

- Scholastic Inc. is a private company with weekly access to over 30 million US students. It is the largest publisher of children's books in the world (including the Harry Potter series). In 2002, in collaboration with the International Labor Rights Fund and the National Consumer League, Scholastic Inc. devoted an in-depth series of its weekly magazine to child labor in Kenya (featuring programs of the ACILS) as well as Turkey, Mexico, and Indonesia. The series gave young US readers, typically in the twelve- to fourteen-year-old age range, an opportunity to contribute money to initiatives of the International Labor Rights Fund in Kenya.[55]

- With support from many of the above NGOs and a grant from both the US education and labor departments, the School for International Training in Brattleboro, Vermont, has created a Child Labor and Action curriculum for schools that is focused on children's rights. In March 2003 the project successfully coordinated a Vermont-wide day of teaching and student activities around child labor.[56]
- The American Federation of Teachers (AFT), through its International Affairs Office, has undertaken another labor collaborative initiative. "Lost Futures: The Problem of Child Labor" is a video produced by the AFT for use in US middle schools. In addition, "Child Labor Is Not Cheap," a widely hailed and well-received child labor curriculum that focuses specifically on the Americas, has been developed by a Minneapolis community-based organization, Resource Center of the Americas.[57]

Outside richer countries, curricula aimed at sensitizing teachers and students to child labor are likely to be even more effective in promoting change. This is so because, for poor and marginalized families, schools often represent the first point of contact with the dominant national culture and an official commitment to human rights norms. From the institutionalist perspective, the legitimacy that schools offer in their views about children's rights carries symbolic as well as technical or informational meaning to families as well as students. Even when parents do not themselves receive lessons on the hazards of child labor, parental awareness of the importance of this issue is likely to increase simply when schools demonstrate conspicuous concern about it. Although the ILO's International Programme on the Elimination of Child Labour (IPEC) has in general tended not to focus on formal education in its campaigns, it recently has undertaken a major project, "Mobilizing Educators, Teachers, and Organizations to Combat Child Labor."[58] As a result of this effort, teacher information kits are currently available from IPEC in Arabic, English, French, Spanish, and Swahili. They currently are being adapted for use in Brazil, Egypt, Indonesia, Nepal, Paraguay, Peru, the Philippines, and Tanzania.

A full inventory of programs used to curtail child labor from a human rights perspective would fill several volumes. The preceding examples are intended merely to identify a range of strategies in order to propose a preliminary taxonomy, as in Table 11.1. Taxonomies are analytically useful to the extent that ideas matter in practice. The assumption of the essays collected in this volume is that the rhetoric and ideas concerning children's rights do matter for the purpose of combating child labor and formulating coherent policy aimed at its prevention. The discursive space of this rhetoric could be imagined to have multiple dimensions, but two that are relevant here are those concerning the theoretical perspective on change and the type of strategy that is pursued to effect change. If we imagine this discursive space as a grid in Table 11.1, then it

Table 11.1 Theoretical Perspective on Human Rights Progress

Change Strategy	Realist	Liberal	Institutionalist	Constructivist
Family scholarships to reduce demand for children's work	Bolsa-Escola, Brazil; Progresa, Mexico			
School finance and quality improvement; meals to increase school demand	UN World Food Programme; EFA movement			
Trade sanctions from hegemons and multinational agreements		Harkin Bill; labor clause for WTO; Executive Order 13126		
Consumer boycotts led by international human rights and child advocacy		RUGMARK; Global Alliance; SweatFree		
NGO monitoring and official national reporting on implementation of CRC (1989)			Reports by states parties of CRC (1989); UN Ombudsman	
Officially, NGO-, and INGO-generated child labor curriculum			ILO teacher guides; Chile's Colegio de Professores; American Federation of Teachers; commercial publishers	
Alternative NGO reports to Child Rights Committee on local progress				Representations to governments of Ghana, Mexico, etc.

is instructive to identify which types of strategies rest on which theoretical foundations. By framing child labor strategies and human rights orientations in this way, we can observe the relation between ideas and actions.

Realist views of human rights, which are dominant in the US government, are most likely to support programs using legal codes and material incentives to withdraw children from the work force, and especially to enroll them in school by increasing the economic returns to education through better-quality or more relevant school experiences. Advocacy based on this approach does not necessarily deny that early, abusive labor violates children's rights, and re-alists may even invoke the vocabulary of human rights. But their underlying theory of change does not *require* acceptance of a rights perspective.

By contrast, liberal actions by states attempt to pressure and shame other governments into compliance with norms that are specified in international agreements. Rather than assert the national interest as a means to obtain compliance with these norms and conventions, liberal approaches invoke concern for the common global good. Liberal actions also include unilateral prohibitions on the purchase of goods manufactured by forced child labor, such as Executive Order 13126, signed by President Clinton.[59]

Ideational approaches to progressive change, in contrast to both realist and liberal perspectives, seek to promote actions that affect *all* working children, not only those who produce goods traded on the global market and not only those who forgo schooling to work. Such actions would include the school curriculum developed by the ILO in an attempt to institutionalize expectations of parents as well as employers. Trade union activity, such as the AFL-CIO's Solidarity Center, would come under this heading as well. How should we classify the periodic reporting by national governments about child labor abuses to the Committee on the Rights of the Child? Institutionalists would highlight the progress that occurs from the top down, that is, as governments voluntarily comply with global standards of behavior embodied by the committee. At the same time, as discussed in greater detail below, this process has other, more profound, and, in some cases, more widespread consequences through the legitimatizing role of the CRC for local NGOs that advocate for children. Constructivists would question how truly "voluntary" or conflict-free governmental compliance is with global standards. From this perspective, the roles of NGOs are critically important for creating the standards that are subsequently codified and institutionalized in regulatory bodies such as the Committee on the Rights of the Child.

■ Strategies in Action: Chile and Mexico Compared

To examine the effect of progressive change strategies, it is possible to identify four key policy events. First, in Latin America, we may consider two important incidences of progressive change in policy: the 1998 entry by Chile— a nation with very low rates of child labor—into the IPEC framework; and the passage by Mexico in 1999 of a new integrated code governing children's welfare. In each case, a mix of socializing and penetrative forces can be observed.

During a period of weak and often despotic national governments, Latin American NGOs assumed advocacy roles for children, borrowing legitimacy from the United Nations and the CRC. They thus began to reflect the "penetrative authority" of INGOs, in Boli's phrase.[60] As the Argentine child rights jurist Emilio García Méndez has observed:

During the 1980s a new type of non-governmental organization was born, committed to the cause of children and adolescents, and challenging public policies. These groups created a culture that was to continue long after the demise of the dictators, as they gradually improved their organization, expertise and technical knowledge. In addition, they began to work together and were able to exert influence both at regional and international levels. Because of the seriousness of the crisis and after the experience of authoritarian governments, these organizations moved away from the State, and lost interest in attempting to influence public policy.[61]

Chile's entry into IPEC was in many respects the legacy of an exceptionally broad coalition of human rights organizations, church groups, think tanks, and trade unions. The story begins in the late 1980s, when diverse interest groups forged a unity movement of the "concertación" to win the plebiscite necessary to force Augusto Pinochet from power. After Chile's return to democracy, education was prioritized to pay back the social deficit accumulated under the military. A broadly based national commission for educational modernization was appointed by President Eduardo Frei, one that included representatives from Catholic and Protestant church groups, unions, university students, and rectors. The commission called for greater and more equal investment in education, highlighting the differences in media participation rates by students from families of different wealth. As part of a subsequent reform, the Ministry of Education, in recognition of the difficulty of achieving an economy of scale in low-population rural areas, assisted rural schools to compete with nonrural schools by tripling the value of the per-pupil subventions allocated to schools serving rural children. This had the effect of promoting the supply of alternatives to rural work by Chilean children.

Synergistically with this expansion of school supply, and building on the missions of the many human rights NGOs operating under the dictatorship, children's rights gained visibility, and since the advent of civilian government in 1990, NGOs and human rights organizations must compete with one another to raise urgent issues for their causes. In this pluralist environment, child labor issues came to the fore. From a purely objective standpoint it may seem surprising that Chile entered IPEC. However, though Chile has one of the lowest rates of child labor in all of Latin America, the country's political dynamic raised the profile of children's rights far more prominently than in nations where child labor was a greater real problem, and in the process increased Chilean consciousness about working children. In part, it was the legacy of human rights activism, following the demise of the dictatorship, that created the conditions for a broad-based mobilization on behalf of children. Ultimately, as a result of his past employment by the ILO during the Pinochet regime, Chile's labor minister entered Chile into IPEC. And as constituents of this consortium, teachers proved to be key. The teaching profession lobbied successfully for an extension of the national school leaving age. Teacher's unions, in pushing for a lengthened period of compulsory schooling (from eight to twelve years), saw child labor as a surmountable obstacle to an objective that was clearly in their professional interest. The cause of child labor and children's rights became a cause that teachers connected to education. In the case of Chile, domestic politics reverberated with the language of rights, language invoked by government, the ILO, and UNICEF in a broad social consensus used to change social norms and expectations about children. Rates of youth employment instead of school fell further (although the rates of part-time employment by students probably rose). And the IPEC–Ministry of Labor relationship incorporated a broad national board, including representatives of business interest groups, teachers, unions, and human rights organizations.

The case of Chile's entry into IPEC shows a blurring of the distinction between "top-down" and "bottom-up" approaches to child labor.[62] By contrast with Chile, Mexico's history led to a greater challenge for human rights advocacy against child labor and, consequently, an uphill battle to create an integrated children's legal code. The code was passed finally into law in 1999, indicating both the power and the limitations of a human rights discourse to effect progressive change. Since the Mexican revolution, the interests of the country's individuals and families have been represented officially to the state through mass organizations, chiefly the labor and agriculture organizations that have constituted the ruling party coalition of the Partido Revolucionario Institucional (PRI; Revolutionary Institutional Party). Rather than openly contest positions taken by the PRI, opposition demands, up until the 1999 presidential race, were absorbed into the state apparatus. Reciprocal benefits were generated by the co-optation of new interest groups. Legitimacy was added to the PRI's control of the state through the co-optation of potential change-agents within the channels of the ruling party. Identity politics and conflicts between constituencies were thus contained, as the state coordinated the expressed pressures from its constituent organizations. Historically, many organizations that presented possible threats eventually were rewarded with offices and official places within the ruling bureaucracy.

From a rights perspective, a weakness of this system was that vulnerable families and working children were seldom organized, especially in Mexico's rural areas. The interests of working and out-of-school children were neither represented nor integrated within Mexico's corporativist arrangement. This social constitution helps to explain Mexico's resistance, until very recently, to single-interest, broad-based social mobilization outside the PRI structure. Historically, Mexico's official response to ILO or UNICEF pressures has been to represent a *collective* national interest of the Mexican people—that is, governments did not present themselves primarily as guardians, much less as advocates, of the "third generation" positive freedoms of *individuals*. Article 3 of Mexico's constitution has always guaranteed free education for all,[63] but until 1993 this guarantee was presented as the means to national progress rather than as an instrument for individual advancement. This stance changed in the wake of Mexico's ratification of the CRC, which required the government to present periodic reports to the UN Committee on the Rights of the Child, stating the progress of individual children's welfare and legal protection. Perhaps even more important, in Mexico the CRC lent legitimacy to NGOs that lobbied the government.

Thus, in June 1999, following Mexico's second official report to the Committee on the Rights of the Child and at the request of the Geneva-based group, Mexican NGO Comexani (Colectivo Mexicano de Apoyo a la Niñez) presented an alternative report on behalf of itself and numerous other Mexican NGOs; and thereafter, following the committee's review of the official report, it helped to formulate responses to Mexico's government. Based on Comexani's input, the committee first applauded Mexico's initiatives, including the National Program for Action for Children, the National Commission of Human Rights, and the National System for the Integral Development of the Family. At the same time, it called upon Mexico to initiate greater collaboration with NGOs and give further attention to ethnic and regional inequality. Most of all, the committee urged that a single body of law for children under eighteen years of age be developed in keeping with the requirements of the convention. These reactions by the committee were open for public inspection and they were quickly invoked by other human rights groups, child advocates, and opposition political parties.

This process was soon joined by initiatives of the opposition Partido de la Revolución Democrática (PRD; Party of the Democratic Revolution) in Mexico City (which controlled the mayor's office) and by UNICEF strategists who planned a commemoration of the tenth anniversary of Mexico's ratification of the CRC. The successful joining of these political forces led at last, at the end of 1999, to national legislation creating an integrated legal framework. Three legislators representing the three major parties (all women) coauthored a law to implement new constitutional responsibilities to protect the rights of children and adolescents. This law affirmed, first, the CRC's central tenet: the principle of the best interests of the child. Also, though the family was considered the "primordial space" for the development of children, the new law affirmed the coresponsibility of the Mexican state and society as a whole for protecting the legal rights and ensuring the full development of children. Further, relative to child labor specifically, the new law reaffirmed the prohibitions on contractual relations with children younger than age fourteen, as had been established previously in Mexico's federal labor law.[64]

What was most noteworthy about the new legal approach was its recognition of the need for interinstitutional collaboration and a shared responsibility between the federal and state governments. The success of the new law also reflected a desire by each of Mexico's three largest political parties to share credit for the protection of children's rights in the period leading to the presidential campaign. Jorge Valencia, of Comexani, characterized the new law as "a call to civil society to reassert . . . not only a defense of children's and adolescents' rights, but fundamentally to position them as social subjects with rights."[65] The call to protect children was also a call to illuminate "problems that formerly were invisible to the eyes of the majority of the population, as in this case were children and adolescents."[66] It is noteworthy that the energy for accomplishing this, evident in the modification of constitutional Article 4, came as part of a political process in which opposition political parties, NGOs, and labor syndicates were key players.[67]

◼ Conclusion: Top-Down Leadership Versus Grassroots Mobilization?

All four of the theoretical approaches and their associated strategies described above can be observed in the changes evident in Chile and Mexico. Within the array of strategies available to children's advocates, the chief lesson from this comparison is that context-specific choices are inevitable. Legal reform initiated by the mere ratification of the CRC is neither an essential nor a sufficient element in progressive change to eliminate child labor. However, when this reform serves as a focus for broadly based mobilization, it certainly can help. In Kenya, for example, alliances by child advocates with one another were assisted by international attention and pilot programming by international agencies, trade unions, and direct US support. In Mexico, these same factors achieved little progress until the country's dominant political party was at the point of losing power. The clear conceptual distinction between grassroots normative change and exogenously stimulated reform is blurred by close examination of these cases. But this may only prove the larger point by Ignatieff that rights have gone global by going local. The conceptual line between the top-down and bottom-up approach is useful precisely because it illustrates the way that world culture—including a culture embracing children's rights—has crossed the line to the local level. In a sense, this is not a new development. While there is today increased sensitivity to globalization, the penetration of external laws in local culture has occurred continuously, even without colonization. The rights vocabulary and consciousness, now omnipresent in the world, can make easier the task of the US Department of Labor, the ILO, the World Bank, and other actors that have formulated social welfare arguments against child labor. In fair exchange, consequentialist approaches to child labor can be useful to rights advocates by highlighting the shortcomings as well as the progress that ensues from attempts to generate progressive change using the principles of children's rights.

▒ Notes

1. In this chapter, I adopt the definition of "child labor" set forth in the introduction to this volume, in turn derived from Chapter 2, that is, "work done by children that is harmful to them because it is abusive, exploitive, hazardous, or otherwise contrary to their best interests—a subset of a larger class of children's work, some of which may be compatible with children's best interests (variously expressed as 'beneficial,' 'benign,' or 'harmless' children's work)."

2. Weston, "Human Rights." The classic argument for the incompatibility of negative and positive liberty is that of Isaiah Berlin, *Four Essays on Liberty.* For reviews of some of the many arguments for developmental freedom as the progressive outgrowth of negative liberty and liberalism, see MacPherson, *Democratic Theory;* and Post, "Jeffersonian Revisions of Locke . . . ."

3. United Nations, *Convention on the Rights of the Child* (1989) [hereinafter "CRC"].

4. ILO, *Convention* (No. 138) *Concerning Minimum Age for Admission to Employment* (1973).

5. ILO, *Convention* (No. 182) *Concerning the Prohibition and Immediate Elimination of the Worst Forms of Child Labour* (1999).

6. UNICEF, *The State of the World's Children 1999,* p. 19.

7. See O'Neill, "Children's Rights and Children's Lives."

8. Ibid., p. 35.

9. The irresolution of the question about who bears responsibility for ensuring children's rights—or whether it is even necessary to highlight the "duty-bearer"—is one reason for a disengagement during the 1990s between UNICEF and Swedish Save the Children over the issue of child labor. For a fascinating debate on the approaches of each organization in Latin America, see Pérez et al., "Comentario y Recomendaciones . . . ." More recently, the two organizations appear to be moving closer to one another on this issue. "Our goal, our understanding of children's work and our beliefs about appropriate responses are shaped by the UN Convention on the Rights of the Child (UNCRC) and a rights-based approach to programming. . . . In achieving this goal, we seek to ensure that governments, families and other 'duty-bearers' fulfill their obligations to address children's rights. We also seek to ensure that boys and girls fully and meaningfully participate in decisions which affect them. Children should be enabled to exercise their rights, and the opportunities available to them should be expanded so that work is a choice, not a necessity." Save the Children–UK, *Save the Children's Position on Children and Work.* This document also clarifies that Save the Children does not believe that the CRC grants children a right to work.

10. O'Neill, "Children's Rights and Children's Lives," p. 37.

11. Freeman, "Taking Children's Rights More Seriously," pp. 57–58.

12. See Alston, "Reconciliation of Culture and Human Rights," p. 22.

13. Woll, *The Convention on the Rights of the Child . . . ,* p. 26. See also Woll, "Organizational Responses to the Convention . . . ."

14. Discussed in detail in Chapter 9 in this volume.

15. See *Constitution of the Federative Republic of Brazil* (1988), art. 227.

16. Quoted at http://www.childreach.org/news/unspecial3pr.html.

17. Uchengamma, "Knowing Rights from Wrong . . . ."

18. IPEC and Marcha Global, *La Marcha Global,* p. 20.

19. As a further example of the divergent positions of children's mobilizations, consider the fact that, during roughly the same time period the ILO organized the "Global March" in South America, a Peruvian organization successfully lobbied its

government for a children's code that grants children over the age of eleven the right to work legally. This was seen as progress by Swedish Save the Children, but as a setback by the ILO. In the words of the movement's leaders: "We see children's work as a phenomenon worthy of more than general and superficial ethical censure or the sporadic, charitable gestures of some kind soul. For us, working children form a social group, and precisely because they work and have the status of workers, they can transform themselves into a collective subject, a movement and an organization which represents a new part of popular movement. . . . We set our hopes on their social protagonism, on the fact that working children could represent not only a pathological episode of Third World folklore, but an aware and active dynamic of the movement for liberation and social change." Quoted in Schibotto and Cussiánovich, *Working Children . . .* , p. 92.

20. Montgomery, "Imposing Rights? . . . ," p. 95.

21. See Schmitz and Sikkink, "International Human Rights."

22. Rice, "Promoting the National Interest," p. 62. See also Falk, *Human Rights Horizons . . .* , pp. 24–35; and Gourevitch, "International Relations Theories," pp. 7829–7832.

23. Accord, Chapter 1, pp. 8–9, 13–15, in this volume.

24. Foweraker, *Grassroots Movements . . .* , p. 5. See also the evidence from statistical analysis of rights and social movements in four countries in Foweraker and Landman, "Individual Rights . . . ," p. 312: "There is a dynamic two-way historical relationship between social movements and individual rights. In other words, the discourse of individual rights and social movements not only coexist in the public domain, but also condition each other's development and political trajectory. In its strongest form this proposition suggests that rights and movements are mutually constitutive, meaning that the one cannot develop without the other."

25. See Krasner, *Sovereignty . . . .*

26. See Drinan, *The Mobilization of Shame,* pp. 48–50.

27. Schmitz and Sikkink, "International Human Rights," p. 521.

28. Moravcsik, "Taking Preferences Seriously . . . ," pp. 513–553; Moravcsik, "The Origins of Human Rights Regimes," pp. 517–537.

29. Forsythe, *Human Rights and Comparative Foreign Policy,* p. 21.

30. Ibid.

31. Ignatieff, *Human Rights as Politics . . .* , p. 290.

32. "Once it is fully established, bureaucracy is among those social structures which are hardest to destroy. Bureaucracy is *the* means of carrying 'community action' over into rationally ordered 'societal action.' Therefore, as an instrument for 'societalizing' relations of power, bureaucracy has been and is a power instrument of the first order . . . . The rational bureaucratic structure of domination, as such, develops quite independently of the areas in which it takes hold." Gerth and Mills, *From Max Weber,* pp. 228, 240.

33. Meyer, "The Effects of Education . . . ." See also Fuller, *Growing Up Modern . . .* ; and Fuller and Rubinson, *The Political Construction of Education.*

34. Finnemore, "The Rules of War . . . ."

35. Quoted in ibid., p. 155.

36. See Berkovitch, "The Emergence and Transformation . . . ."

37. See Boli, "World Authority Structures . . . ," p. 273.

38. Ibid., p. 276.

39. Keck and Sikkink, *Activists Beyond Borders . . .* , pp. 89, 211.

40. Risse and Sikkink, "The Socialization of International Human Rights Norms . . . ," p. 16.

41. Ibid., p. 18.

42. Schmitz and Sikkink, "International Human Rights," p. 532. For a critical review of institutionalist perspectives, see Finnemore, "Norms, Culture, and World Politics . . . ." For a critical review of the constructivists and advocacy networks, see Lytle, "NGOs and the New Transnational Politics."

43. For reasons why human rights arguments should be used, see Chapter 1 in this volume, pp. 6–12.

44. Schultz, *What Are the Returns to Poverty Reduction?* . . . See also Post, "Can Targeted Assistance Make a Difference for Girls?"

45. See Arends-Kuenning and Amin, "School Incentive Programs . . . ."

46. See Easton and Fass, "Monetary Consumption Benefits . . ."; and Lloyd et al., "The Effects of Primary School Quality on School Dropout . . . ." For a comprehensive review, see Schiefelbein, "Incentivos Económicos . . . ."

47. "All the experience so far shows that the child-friendly school also provides the most effective learning. It is in that sense 'productive.' *But that is not the point.* Such a school would be good for children." Hammarberg, *A School for Children with Rights,* p. 28 (emphasis added).

48. See CRC, art. 12.

49. Excerpts from "Speech by Minister Pronk."

50. *Executive Order 13126: Prohibition of Acquisition of Products Produced by Forced or Indentured Child Labor.*

51. See, for example, the website of Global Alliance for Workers and Communities, at http://www.theglobalalliance.org/programs.htm.

52. See RUGMARK's website, at http://www.rugmark.org/about.htm.

53. For the disconnect between organizations and strategies using consequentialist versus human rights approaches—and their underlying images of working children—see Post, *Children's Work . . .* , chap. 2.

54. This approach is most evident in such comments as the following from UNICEF: "Creating a broad social alliance is a necessary condition for the elimination of child labor. It must reach from the highest levels of global power and influence to the hardest to reach, poorest and most powerless communities and families. This includes all branches and levels of government; civil society organizations, employers and trade unions, consumer groups, the media, families, children, teachers, health professionals, social workers, and street educators. The magic of social mobilization and one of its key challenges is ensuring that the impact of the effort is greater than the sum of various separate initiatives, and that all levels of society commit to a common goal." UNICEF, *Education and Child Labour,* p. 9.

55. For details, see the website of Scholastic, at http://teacher.scholastic.com/scholasticnews/indepth/child_labor.

56. For details, see the website of the Child Labor Education and Action Project, at http://clea.sit.edu.

57. For details, see the website of the American Federation of Teachers, at http://www.aft.org/international/child/instructional.html.

58. IPEC, "Broad-Based Multi-Sectoral Action Against Child Labour," box 7.

59. Supra endnote 49.

60. Boli, "World Authority Structures . . . ," p. 273.

61. García Méndez, *Child Rights in Latin America . . .* , p. 12.

62. Interviews with Francisco Rivas (ILO representative) and Frederico Alles (Chilean Ministry of Labor), Santiago, Nov. 12, 1999 (on file with the author); Salazar Negrón, *Trabajo Infantil y Educación . . . .* Chile's demographics played a role in this movement as well; the ratio of children to adults is far smaller than in nations where

the family and local economies depend on child labor. For more on the Chilean case, see Post, *Children's Work* . . . .

63. See The University of Iowa Center for Human Rights Child Labor Research Initiative legislative database, at http://db.uichr.org/docs/307.html.

64. Ibid.

65. Valencia, Jorge, *Derechos del Niño,* p. 1.

66. Ibid.

67. See ibid. See also Monge and Vivas, "Pobreza, Violencia y Caos Legislativo . . ."; and Galeana Cisneros, "El Trabajo Infantil en México . . . ." For further details on the politics of Mexican child labor advocacy, see Post and Sakurai, "Recognizing a Problem . . . ."

12

Working Children as Change Makers: Perspectives from the South

Victor P. Karunan

Child labor is rooted in poverty.[1] A complex problem that must be viewed against the complex macroeconomic and social backdrop of development, it is the clearest and worst manifestation of how "poverty has a child's face."[2] It is often also an elusive cross-border issue that requires cross-border agreements, legislation, and interstate cooperation to combat it effectively, especially in its most sensitive worst forms, which commonly are hidden and clandestine because they are linked to criminal cross-border trafficking, illegal drug trade, and armed conflict. Child labor is a dehumanizing phenomenon that "harms children's bodies and minds, their spirits and future . . . , a prison that withers both capabilities and potential."[3] In sum, child labor needs to be understood and acted upon in all its complexities. No simple or unilateral approaches that are confined primarily to the area of employment or the labor market will lead to its elimination. It is this challenge that confronts us, especially in the application of the 1989 United Nations Convention on the Rights of the Child (CRC) relative to child labor[4] and even more especially in the application of 1999 International Labour Organization Convention (No. 182) Concerning the Prohibition and Immediate Elimination of the Worst Forms of Child Labour (ILO C182).[5]

The central thesis of this chapter is that mainstream approaches to child labor, especially in the Global South, are grossly inadequate because they are premised on dominant Western conceptions of childhood and child development that tend generally to criminalize hazardous and exploitive work performed by children and therefore, in most cases, to neglect solutions to the problem on a lasting and sustainable basis. Partly in response to, but as a consequence also of an increasing trend toward a rights orientation in development, there has begun to emerge (as this volume itself bears witness) a human rights approach to working children and child labor. It puts the child at the center of policy planning and intervention and, in keeping with promoting "the best interests of the child," it favors the active involvement of children in the defense of their basic rights.

What has come to be known as a "child-centered approach to child labor" has emerged from this rights orientation. Specifically inspired by the spirit and key provisions of the 1989 CRC, this rights-oriented/child-centered approach has come increasingly to influence the vision and actions of a range of social actors, primarily in civil society, in the developing world. It has also influenced, and been influenced by, working children who have become organized and by working children's movements that have developed over two decades in many parts of the world. These organizations and movements have made it possible for working children to become effective advocates for this new approach. These perspectives and actions—most often at the grassroots level in the countries of the Global South—not only pose new challenges for mainstream orientations and programs against child labor, but they are beginning in practice to show relevant and effective alternatives to address the problem as a whole as well.

My central thesis is also that mainstream approaches to child labor are not adequate to its challenge because they fall short of valuing the full range of children's rights, which if taken seriously would do so. It is based on many years of experience with child labor in the Global South and on the perceptions and actions of nongovernmental organizations (NGOs) and other civil society organizations in this field, including organizations and movements of working children in developing countries, especially in Asia. Also, it is based on the perceptions and actions of working children relative to their everyday experiences of work and labor, and on their hopes and dreams for the future as well. These perceptions and actions have significantly influenced the human rights/child-centered approach as it has evolved in the Global South, Asia in particular, where two regional workshops were held in 1999–2000. The salient features of this alternative approach are discussed below. I argue that, at present, it is perhaps the most effective way to ensure that the full range of children's rights are respected in children's everyday lives. The fact that the majority of working children are to be found in poor countries and in the poor districts and regions of these countries makes it imperative that we base our perceptions, analyses, and actions on the reality and experience of working children in these countries of the Global South.

This chapter is divided into four main parts. First I argue the case for using a rights-based approach to child labor and point out the implications for policy and action. Second I review the new thinking that, based on the concrete everyday experiences of working children and their supportive NGOs and other civil society organizations, has shaped our understanding of "child work" and "child labor." Next I describe what has come to be known as the child-centered approach to working children, an approach that guides and inspires the processes of progressive intervention and change vis-à-vis child labor in the developing world. Finally, I consider the implications of these alternative approaches to current thought and action in the world of child labor and the lives of working children. Here I discuss some key factors that are helping to deal more strategically with the problem of child labor in the developing South, including a "new sociology of childhood" that addresses the structural context, focuses on intergenerational poverty, and takes a cultural approach that recognizes organized working children as social actors in their own right.

Toward a Rights Approach to Working Children and Child Labor

Conventional Approaches to Child Labor

Conventional approaches to child labor are premised on a labor market ideology that aims primarily to keep children away from the labor market and confined to schools. From this perspective, children's work is viewed largely as labor exploitation that must be abolished.

This approach has dominated child labor discourse for a long time and continues to inspire mainstream policies and programming for working children. The adoption of ILO C182, which mandates the identification and elimination of unacceptable and intolerable forms of work, is a step forward in the struggle to combat the detrimental effects of hazardous and exploitive work on children. By and large, policies and programs previously in place have failed to make a significant impact in eliminating these forms of children's work.[6] The reasons are many, but salient among them are the following:

- Most of these worst forms are hidden, clandestine, and illegal, largely inaccessible to policymakers (including governments) and field workers in international agencies.
- Policies and program interventions against the worst forms of child labor have not taken into account the general role of work in the lives of children, nor the cultural, social, and economic conditions and factors that compel children to earn a livelihood through labor.
- A general failure to address the root causes and structural conditions that perpetrate hazardous and exploitive child labor, particularly in the context of rapid globalization and international trade.
- A too narrow focus on removal and rescue operations of children in bondage and servitude in the worst forms of child labor, with too little attention and resources invested in providing sustainable alternative livelihoods for rescued children and their families, income generation, and improving the quality, relevance, and accessibility of education and the schooling system.

The prevalence of the worst forms of child labor in developing countries appears inevitable in situations where there is abject poverty and parents lack the income and abilities needed to meet basic needs;[7] where the labor market requires cheap, docile, and bonded labor for certain services; where unscrupulous employers and middlemen exploit children for illegal activities; where the system of education is inaccessible, expensive, and irrelevant; and where the local traditions and practices encourage—in some cases even endorse—the worst forms of child labor.[8] Thus the problem of child labor is based on a multicontextual set of complex variables that are structural to the societies in which it exists. The approach adopted to combat child labor must, therefore, take these variables into account.

Any approach to ending the worst forms of child labor must take into account also the attitudes of adults and society as a whole toward child labor. The very fact that children are involved in the worst forms of work is a reflection of mainstream adult and societal attitudes toward children, attitudes that are rooted in traditional social and cultural as well as modern practices that commodify children vis-à-vis the labor market. Adult attitudes as to why children should perform "worst forms" tasks and services are well summed up by an Indian district government official: "[For the employers], it's very easy to work . . . with children; you don't have any problem at all; you can just make them work all day, and they will not protest . . . ; you can really terrorize them [and] you will be paying much, much less than you will normally pay for an adult."[9]

As a starting point, then, the cultural reasons for children's work—not just the work itself—must be considered. As William Myers and Jo Boyden observe: "it [is] necessary to replace a narrow view of child work as a labor exploitation issue with a broader appreciation of it as a critical influence on the growth and development of perhaps most of the world's children."[10] The adoption of the 1989 CRC, with its emphasis on "the best interests of the child," reinforces this view.

The Rights-Based Approach to Child Labor

Conventionally, child labor programs have adopted a stereotyped "triple-R" strategy: removal, rescue, rehabilitation. This strategy is based on *needs* rather than *rights,* a welfare approach that results in piecemeal solutions that do not address the root causes of the problem or contribute to sustainable alternatives for the children and their families.

In contrast, a rights-based approach to child labor recognizes that children often forfeit their right to education and other rights to guarantee their holistic development irrespective of the kind of work they do. It aims, therefore, to

- redefine the concept of work and labor in the lives of children, taking into account the specific social, cultural, economic context of the society where it exists;

- understand and analyze children's lives "not just in terms of needs, or areas for development, but in terms of the obligation to respond to the rights of individuals . . . , [to empower] people to demand justice as a right and not as charity";
- listen to and incorporate children's views and opinions—their perceptions and experiences of work, of hazardous and exploitive labor, of work and school, and the like;
- address the centrality of exploitation in the lives of working children;
- involve children actively in the interpretation of circumstances of their work, in the design of policies and strategies aimed at identifying and eliminating intolerable forms of child work, and shaping interventions when seeking solutions to these problems;
- identify the structural conditions and factors that contribute to exploitive work performed by children;
- go beyond economic rights and address the full range of human rights of working children;
- develop coordinated multisectoral interventions in a variety of fields related to the effects of hazardous and exploitive work on children, namely education, health, nutrition, rest and relaxation, play, social security, and responsibilities of parents;[11] and
- finally, in all matters affecting working children, safeguard their best interests and their rights (as rights-bearers), on the one hand, and hold families, business enterprises, institutions, and governments accountable and responsible as duty-bearers to promote and protect children's rights, on the other.

Understood in this way, child labor is not simply a labor market concern; it is a human (child) rights problem.[12]

This fact has not been lost on children who work. Time and again, children have articulated their concerns and pleaded for a rights-based approach to combating child labor. As Joan Ranoy, a seventeen-year-old girl from the Philippines who worked for five years as a child domestic servant, put it in 1999 at the eighty-seventh session of the International Labour Conference (which adopted 1999 ILO C182): "We, as working children—boys and girls— are below 18 years of age, and in keeping with the spirit of the U.N. Convention on the Rights of the Child (Article 32), we have the right to be protected from exploitation and hazardous work and abuse."[13] In other words, the key to distinguishing between benign children's work and work that is harmful to their overall development is the nature and extent of exploitation involved.[14] Article 32 of the CRC guarantees "the right of the child to be protected from economic exploitation and from performing any work that is likely to be hazardous or to interfere with the child's education, or to be harmful to the child's health or physical, mental, spiritual, moral or social development."

It is this centrality of exploitation through work done by children that often is ignored in child labor discourse as well as in programming child labor interventions and actions. A rights-based approach helps us to address this centrality and to identify the conditions and factors that contribute to these forms of work prevalent in society. It also takes us beyond economic rights and helps us to address the full range of rights.[15]

Moreover, the programmatic implications of such a rights-based approach imply coordinated and multisectoral interventions in a variety of fields related to the effects of hazardous and exploitive work on children.[16] Child rights generate both entitlements and obligations and thus imply—indeed require—the building of strategic partnerships among children and between adults and children to confront this problem jointly and in combination. It means empowering children to participate actively in the improvement of their lives and developing solutions to their problems while at the same time empowering adults to fulfill their responsibility and duty to protect the rights of children.[17]

Thus, as entitlements provided to both children and adults and enshrined in the Universal Declaration of Human Rights (UDHR)[18] and other key instruments such as the CRC and ILO C182, rights are not just an abstract recognition of societal values. They have real and practical implications that hold governments and others accountable and thereby shape behavior and practice in society. They help to create the conditions in which children can effectively enjoy their rights; benefit from the actions of others—governments, family, community—to make these rights a reality in children's lives; recognize the increasing capacity of children to exercise their rights and to make valid claims on them; and impose a general duty and responsibility on everyone, including the state, to respect those rights and to refrain from any action that will prevent their enjoyment or violate them in any way.[19]

The family is the first line of protection for the child. It is the primary environment wherein children are introduced to the culture, and therefore the values and norms of society. It is also the first opportunity for the child to experience tolerance, mutual respect, and solidarity.[20] A rights-based approach to child labor recognizes this important place and role of the family in the lives of children. It calls upon the community and state to render appropriate support and assistance to parents and legal guardians in the performance of their child-rearing duties so as to facilitate the capacity of the family to protect the rights of children and their enhancement. It also means holding parents and guardians accountable for actions that put their children in harm's way by their induction, coercion, or sale for employment or services in the worst forms.

The rights-based approach, it can safely be said, is gaining recognition and beginning to challenge mainstream approaches and actions relative to child labor. The ILO acknowledges this fact in a recent report: "After the CRC (1989) was adopted, international NGOs began to reconsider their work with children to bring about a change from an essentially welfare-based, adult-focused, charitable approach to a more child-centered, rights-based approach."[21] While this approach and its application are spearheaded primarily by NGOs and other civil society organizations largely as a consequence of their reconsideration of the rights of children following the adoption of the CRC, they are beginning to influence key donors and international agencies. The time is past that the same rethinking can be undertaken by UN agencies and other key players in the field of child labor.

◼ The "World of Work" of Children: Toward a Redefinition

Using a rights-based approach to the world of children's work and the conditions that cause them to undertake dehumanizing work enables us to view work and labor from a radically different perspective; and the first point to be made is that participation by children in the labor market is commonly against the free will and choice of the children involved. Typically this is the case with prostitution, pornography, trafficking, bonded labor, and soldiering, for example. Because these services and tasks tend all too commonly to be accepted in the adult world, even if they are not always acceptable there, they enjoy a kind of unofficial legitimacy that tolerates the exploitation of children in ways that are usually beyond their control. Noi, a sixteen-year-old sex worker from Laos, put it this way: "I really hate this work. But I have to do it because I need the money. Sometimes I really don't like the client, but I have to sleep with him even if I don't like him. I don't think about myself. I don't really have an idea about the future. I just want to earn money to help my mother and my family."[22]

The work undertaken by children today is defined mainly in terms of economic activity that can be measured and counted in a labor market framework. When children undertake the same work that adults do in society, however, this work is often viewed differently. Why is this so?

For a long time, mainstream thinking and analysis relative to child labor have been dominated by social patterns that separate children from economic activity. In the Global North, as noted by Judith Ennew, children have been banned by law from the labor force, and their economic contribution to society is not accounted for in national budgets despite the fact that many of them are workers.[23] The implication is that they are working for pocket money or seeking to learn good work habits. Ennew notes that this perception is wholly inappropriate for many Southern contexts in which "children have economic and other responsibilities to fulfill within families and communities; are not the sentimental core of nucleus families but rather part of an inter-generational system of interchange and mutual responsibilities; and (in recent history at least) have often been important political protagonists."[24]

From a Southern child's perspective, work is learning, where the attitudes, knowledge, skills, and behavior relative to living and interacting in society are nurtured and developed, closely tied with the family and community. If work is learning, then it becomes an integral part of the educational and developmental process of the child and of the family's obligation toward child rearing and upbringing. Often a distinction is made between work that facilitates and *work that is detrimental* to child development. Children and families in the Global South see a clear difference between a child working in the fields side by side with her or his father or mother to learn the "skills of the trade" and a child required to do repetitive work in a factory setting or forced into hazardous work or abuse in the industrial or commercial sector. These two conceptions of work come from two different traditions that influence the way society views work (good) and labor (bad). The difference is revealed in the value society places on the tasks or services performed by children—in the case of "child labor," children become commodities that are bought and sold, traded, trafficked, and bonded into servitude for economic purposes. In other words, linking the concepts of child work and child labor to the market is significant because it often determines how we define them. A key complicating problem is whether the work or labor is in or out of the market sector, and whether it is formal or informal.[25]

Children's own perceptions of their work provide some useful insights into the relationship between them as children and the world of work and labor. They are therefore an important source of information and evidence on how work affects their lives and on whether and how it can cause harm to their development. The 1996–1997 Save the Children–Sweden study on child labor in South Asia and Central America and concerning children's perceptions of work revealed that, while many children may not be aware of certain detrimental effects of work on their lives, they may be acutely aware of other effects. The main findings of this study lend comprehensive insight into the world of work as lived and experienced by working children themselves, as demonstrated by the following summary of children's views and opinions of their working lives:[26]

- A few children felt they had been forced to work, but many felt they had made the choice to work within the constraints of their circumstances.
- Children believe they must work to help their families. Work is part of the family lifestyle, they are valued for it, and they are initiated at a very early age.
- Work is an important part of many children's self-respect—"we are helping our parents work even though we are young. We are not just another mouth to feed. We are helping the family survive."[27]
- Child workers are aware of many of the physical hazards of work.
- Working children are very sensitive about being stigmatized for their work.

- Children value many aspects of school and would like to combine work with school.
- Faced with new regulations preventing them from working, most groups would defy or evade the law.

In contrast, Northern perceptions and attitudes toward work often involve a separation between learning that is confined to formal classrooms and work or labor that involves skills and earnings (wages) in the workplace. This distinction is not only misleading but detrimental to the best interests of children. Based on this logic, an artificial distinction often is made between learning and education and work and employment.[28] As Piush Antony and V. Gayathri note in the Indian context:

> [W]hat is intriguing in an analysis of children's work is that those who are enrolled or attending the school are not considered for their involvement in activities, which are otherwise counted as work for out-of-school children. This omission, basically due to the dominant dichotomous framework of work/education in children's lives, has allowed for various misconstructions. First of all, it corroborates the class based construct of a childhood, in which education is a prerogative of some and work is a destined vocation for some others.[29]

The realities in the developing world show clearly that these constructions or distinctions are false and misleading; in the given social, economic, and cultural context of developing societies, they in fact blend into one and interface with each other in the daily lives of children, their families, and their communities.

▪ The Child-Centered Approach to Child Labor

This approach, which I call the "rights-based/child-centered approach," developed as a response to mainstream thinking and interventions on child labor that were driven by a labor market framework and "top-down" programming that often criminalizes children's work and seeks quick-fix solutions to complex problems.[30] Myers and Boyden discuss three key factors that have contributed to the development of a child-centered approach to child work issues: "the growing influence of the CRC (1989) on both national and international ideas about protecting children"; "the expanding quantity and quality of empirical information about child work and working children"; and "working children themselves [becoming] a quickly growing influence on thinking about child work."[31]

Using the CRC as its starting point and keeping the best interests of the child paramount, this approach seeks to restore the centrality of the child—her or his role, situation, problems, needs, capabilities, skills—in the discourse on child labor. "The holistic approach of the Convention addresses human rights while placing the child at the center of its considerations. This child-focused perspective guides its call for action and progress towards the realization of all the rights of the child, and stresses that the best interests of the child should always be a guiding reference."[32]

Three key elements characterize the child-centered approach to working children: a radical paradigm shift in our view of children and childhood, the resilience of working children, and working children's participation.

Paradigm Shift in Our View of Children and Childhood

A child-centered approach that is rights-based believes that children's knowledge and perspectives are shaped by the socioeconomic, historical, and cultural conditions of the family and community, which implies their active involvement and participation in all matters that affect their lives and well-being. It challenges us to accept a mind shift in the way we look at, and relate to, children in daily life.[33] This has implications for how we perceive childhood and child development.

Mainstream perceptions of childhood are based on a Western stereotype where "play, learning and schooling are staple topics, while work is rarely mentioned [and] masquerades as scientific knowledge about children's 'nature,' their 'normal' development, and their 'universal' needs."[34] In non-Western societies, on the other hand, the transition from childhood to adulthood is more fluid and less traumatic, where "the child's world and the adult's world [are] not separate and [are] characterized by greater inter-generational reciprocity. Play and work [are] also not such sharply delineated activities and mingled together in a manner that often it [is] difficult to distinguish the two. More importantly, the child is not viewed as separate from the larger unit, be it family, tribe, clan, etc."[35] Thus it is important that we recognize that there are different cultural traditions and concepts of childhood and that there is no one universal model that is applicable in all situations or that can be universally imposed. At the same time, we must be aware of those elements in our cultures and traditions that do not serve the best interests of the child or other children's rights. We need to be careful not to endorse discrimination and exploitation while harnessing the potentials in these cultures and traditions for promoting the rights of children.[36]

In addition, the concept of childhood and, by implication, how children are viewed in society and their relationship to work and labor, are constantly changing to keep pace with the rapid development of societies. Our own culturally determined concepts and perceptions of children, their childhood, and their roles and capabilities therefore need to change accordingly. We need constantly to question our own assumptions and attitudes about children.[37] As adults, we must bring into being a mind shift from traditional notions and values that we cherish about children as vulnerable and nonproductive to a child-centered approach that is rights-based, viewing children positively and as contributors to social development. We need to challenge traditional notions of childhood and child development that have become everyday cultural norms and practices in society. This is no easy task, as it entails a psychosocial or ideological shift that will alter fundamentally adult status, power, and control over children,[38] a shift that urgently calls for a new sociology of childhood (discussed below) that is based on a human (child) rights framework that is sensitive to the local social and cultural conditions prevailing in societies today.

Finally, and perhaps most important of all, a human rights/child-centered approach seeks to view working children as change makers. It locates children at the center of our perceptions, approaches, and actions. Its starting point is to view children not just as innocent, vulnerable, and susceptible beings, but also as active social actors who can make a positive contribution, as children, to social development and change. Children contribute based on their own abilities and capacities ("evolving capacities"), which are constantly developing.[39]

Resilience of Working Children

One of the significant outcomes of using the human rights/child-centered approach to comprehend children and their work has been a growing recognition of the resilience of many working children, based initially on experience with street and working children primarily in Latin America, where the coping mechanisms of these children were identified and their competencies documented.[40] In the Philippines, interest in resilience as a key concept in working with children came from dealing with children in especially difficult circumstances. A pioneering child-centered study conducted by the Program for Psychosocial Training of the University of the Philippines Center for Integrative and Development Studies aimed at understanding this concept from the experience and perspective of the children and their caregivers.[41] Titled "Working with Abused Children: From the Lenses of Resilience and Contextualization," the study involved the participation of twenty-five children from six NGOs who had suffered physical, sexual, emotional, and labor abuses. It identified four concrete guidelines designed to help identify and promote resilience among abused and exploited children:[42]

> *"I Have"*—the child's external supports and resources that endorse resilience. In most cases this refers to the child's access to survival and development services—food, clothing, and the like.
> *"I Can"*—the child's social and interpersonal skills, for example, communication, problem solving, managing feelings and impulses, seeking trusted relationships, and so forth.
> *"I Am"*—the child's internal, personal strengths, such as feelings, attitudes, and beliefs.

> *"I Will"*—the child's willingness, capacity, and commitment to do or to participate in matters affecting him or her.

Increasing knowledge and understanding of resilience among working children reinforced the need to pay attention to children's capacities, actual and potential, to deal with their situations and contribute toward change. This has informed the human rights/child-centered approach to working children, developed on the basis of pioneering research as well as many years of grassroots experience and lessons learned by NGOs and child labor organizations and networks, primarily in the Global South.

Working Children's Participation

"We as working children and our parents and communities, know best what is good and relevant for us," said Filipina Joan Ranoy, the seventeen-year-old former child domestic worker at the eighty-seventh session of the International Labour Conference in 1999.[43] "In many countries in Asia," she continued, "we are being actively supported and assisted by NGOs, community and civil society organizations that have promoted our best interests and protected us from abuse and exploitation. It is therefore imperative that working children themselves, families and communities, NGOs and civil society organizations are seen as active partners and collaborators in the national plans of action on the new Convention."

Working children, with their organizations and networks, have today entered the public stage of discourse on child labor and have come increasingly to be recognized as key social actors to be taken into serious account in policies and interventions on child labor. As Per Miljeteig notes, "[i]n fact, it could be claimed that the public appearance of working children and youth has helped to give child labor 'a face' and contributed to a more nuanced and diversified understanding of what 'child labor' is."[44]

A human rights/child-centered approach to working children is based on the principle of respecting children's views and opinions and involving them as active partners in seeking solutions to their problems. Being the most directly affected by the worst forms of work and child labor, it is only logical that they should be in the first line of participation and involved in efforts to address these issues and seek solutions. Four key principles or approaches are essential:

- Children have a right to be heard about matters that affect them.
- Children are not affected passively by their work—they are for the most part intelligent, active contributors to their social world, trying in their own way to make sense of their circumstances, the constraints and the opportunities available to them.

- Children are capable of expressing their feelings, concerns, and aspirations within a context that respects their abilities and is adapted to their interests and style of communication.
- Children are an important source of evidence on how work may harm their development, in the particular economic, family, community, and cultural context.[45]

Child respondents from the Philippines and Ethiopia identified the following three characteristics of participation by working children:[46]

- *Participation is both a right and a responsibility.* All children must be given the opportunity to express themselves. At the same time, it also implies taking responsibility for their actions.
- *Participation is an expression of capability.* Children have the capacity to stand up for what they believe in and accomplish what they intend to do. Children are active agents of change.
- *Participation is a process of growth.* Through participation, children become more aware of their own capacities and limitations. They can also acquire and develop skills and knowledge.

Participation, it thus must be added, is also a learning experience for the child. "In participation, children learn to express their own needs, consider those of others, and develop skills of cooperation, negotiation and problem-solving. In short, their participation provides children the opportunity to learn, develop and enhance skills that they would need to lead better lives."[47]

In mainstream approaches to child labor, there is a general tendency to view working children's participation as merely "taking into consideration children's views and opinions."[48] While this is an important step forward in promoting children's participation concerning their working conditions and experiences, it falls short of another key element of meaningful participation: involving children in all actions that affect their lives. As this chapter points out, there is sufficient successful experience among NGOs and other civil society organizations of meaningfully involving working children in programming and interventions at the ground level. Moreover, working children themselves have begun proactively to advocate for their involvement in all decisions and actions concerning their lives and future, supported by strong working children's organizations and movements that have developed in the regions of the Global South today.

For too long, working children have been viewed as a "default category."[49] It is time not only that they be recognized, but also that their voices be heard and that they be actively engaged as partners in the fight to combat the worst forms of child labor. This is a fundamental right of working children that needs to be promoted and guaranteed.

Implications for Progressive Social Change

A New "Sociology of Childhood"?

It is time that we develop a new sociology of childhood, for the developing world especially, to guide our responses to child labor that is based on the provisions and spirit of the CRC—a new discipline that, consistent with the rights-based/child-centered approach considered above, "takes children seriously as they experience their lives in the here and now as children."[50] It needs to take a comprehensive view of children and therefore to be interdisciplinary, drawing upon various academic and practice-based knowledge and research in the field, with a special emphasis on incorporating working children's own perceptions and experiences of child labor and child development. The subject matter of this new sociology should be, among other things, children in the context of family and community, viewed from a child-centered perspective that puts children's best interests first. It should recognize the positive contributions that children can make to the society around them and encourage their active participation in shaping and determining their own lives. A new sociology of childhood of this kind is critical as a foundational base to the human rights/child-centered approach to working children.

Addressing Structural Conditions and Factors

Today we know a fair amount about the numbers of children working, about their working conditions and environment, about their experiences of exploitation and abuse, and about their perspectives on alternatives. We know much less, however, about the structural conditions and factors that promote and maintain the exploitation of working children.[51] Mainstream approaches and interventions to exploitive child labor generally have failed to take these structural matters into account or to address them frontally with concrete remedies in hand. In this regard, a critical gap in child labor discourse today is the macroeconomic context of globalization and its direct and indirect influence on child labor in developing countries. If child labor is socially reproduced, then it is ever more important to focus on the structural context and factors that enable this reproduction. Unfortunately, however, structural matters have remained, so far, largely unchallenged and unaltered.

This neglect is alarming. Macroeconomic factors and structural changes directly impact child labor. The so-called Asian economic crisis of 1997 clearly showed this relationship. Thailand experienced massive "reversal migration" during the crisis in 1997–1998 from urban to rural areas. During that period, some 0.8 to 1.1 million children between eleven and fourteen years of age were child laborers, representing about 3 percent of the total 32 million labor force in the country. In 1998, more than 110,000 children from primary school grade six to secondary school grade nine were estimated to have entered the labor force, and among them over 80 percent were primary school students.[52] In the Philippines, the crisis contributed to an increase in the number of children working away from their homes, younger children working on agricultural farms, and an increase in the number of invisible children who work as child domestic workers.[53]

The macroeconomic conditions in most countries of the Global South today are characterized by stagnation in agriculture, handicrafts, and local industries; rapid erosion of control over land and its resources by the mass of peasantry, artisans, and fisherfolk; and an escalating commercialization of entire economies that is wiping out small producers and self-sufficient farmers.[54] It is this context and the resulting unequal relationship between rich and poor countries in international trade and commerce that are missing from the child labor discourse. The international campaign against child labor is focused largely on the manufacturing, commercial, and small-scale informal sectors, not on agriculture, where most of the child labor in the Global South is found and where the majority of laborers are women and children drawn from poor districts and regions. The World Bank acknowledges this direct connection between agriculture and child labor when it observes that "the best 'predictor' of child labor seems related to the structure of production: the higher the share of agriculture in GDP, the higher the incidence of child labor."[55] Implicitly, it acknowledges also the backward and forward nature of economic development in the agricultural sectors, which has a direct bearing on the incidence of child labor. As Vasanthi Raman laments, however: "The focus on child labor in these sectors tends to ignore the structural linkages both backwards (i.e., stagnating agriculture, etc., which ensures a steady supply of child laborers) and forwards (i.e., linkages with the international system)."[56]

Another structural determinant of child labor is inequality. A 2002 comparative study of child labor and child schooling in Nepal and Pakistan showed this relationship clearly: "First, high inequality provides demand for child labor from the more affluent households. Second, such inequality creates a pool of child labor from among children in the less affluent households. Third, high inequality implies that credit is siphoned off to the more affluent leaving the less affluent households to rely on child labor to smooth their income fluctuations."[57]

A rights-based approach to child labor must take into account the structural factors and conditions that impinge upon the kinds of exploitive work that children are subjected to. It must probe and unravel the problem in all its dimensions, especially in areas where it is most prevalent, such as agriculture, as well as establish links with the global macroeconomic context that shapes it.

Addressing Poverty and Child Labor

Poverty—or more precisely, income poverty—is viewed often as the primary if not sole cause of child labor. A number of other key factors determine the supply of child labor, however: vulnerability, poor educational services, lack of social security mechanisms, gender- and age-specific characteristics of some labor markets, consumerist pressures, and increasing population. Another key factor, one that has come increasingly to dominate entire political economies of poor countries, is international trade and the internationalization of production, which specifically create demand for cheap, unskilled labor, often child labor.[58]

In the developing world, in other words, poverty is a complex phenomenon that has broad and deep social, cultural, and political ramifications—in addition to direct economic ones. Working children in the Global South are confronted with situations that drive them to work to earn an income to support themselves and their families, and this of course keeps them from school. It is not income poverty alone that is the direct cause of child labor, as is well illustrated in the Indian context by the following comment of Vasanthi Ramachandran:

> In our country, economic poverty locks firmly with social poverty, political poverty and environmental poverty and drives children out of schools. The education system is driven by class and caste biases, and does not equip children to respond to other forms of poverty that play out in their lives. Schools defeat their own purpose. Reading and writing do not help when entire forest-based livelihoods get wiped away, or when teachers harass students for their lower-caste allegiances. . . . Given such a situation, a child's decision to work for the family rather than go to school is the most appropriate choice he can make.[59]

In most parts of the developing world, not just in India, the culture of poverty that prevails embraces a variety of important factors that define and determine the lives of children and families. Briefly put, income poverty or even economic poverty generally is but one among many important elements that define the circumstances of working children. Together with vulnerability, discrimination, deprivation, and other indignities, however, it can be a daunting barrier to change. It is this multifaceted challenge that confronts the problem of child labor and thwarts attempts to address and eliminate it, and thus one more reason why a holistic human rights/child-centered approach to child labor is imperative.

Culture and Working Children

As discussed above, working children tend to fall outside the Western conception of childhood and child development that dominates current child labor perceptions and interventions. It is not often acknowledged that this mainstream conception, though based on centuries of custom and tradition, runs up against complex cultural realities that, likewise based on centuries of custom and tradition, do not bend easily to it. If the right of children to have their best interests served is to be effectively realized, it therefore behooves us to approach childhood and child development in a manner that seeks to understand and interpret accurately the specific cultural environment (values, beliefs, practices) within which working children and their families/communities function—and thereby arrive at a definition of child labor that is relevant and support interventions that are sustainable. As Martin Woodhead reminds us, "we need to recognize that children's needs, and their process of meeting those needs, as well as protecting children from harmful influence, [are] profoundly shaped by beliefs and practices through which children are incorporated into their families and communities and which gradually become part of their own identity and self-esteem."[60]

An interesting anthropological angle is provided by Olga Nieuwenhuys in her discussion of child labor and anthropology.[61] Her main thesis is that modern society sets children apart ideologically as "a category of persons excluded from the production of value."[62] Given mainstream thinking that equates work with employment (i.e., paid work), it thus can be argued that any work that is performed outside this equation is not considered work at all, that work done by children produces no value. For this reason, Nieuwenhuys observes, "the disassociation of childhood from the performance of valued work has been increasingly considered a yardstick of modernity."[63] In developing countries, especially in poorer regions and provinces where the incidence of child labor is commonly higher, we know little about the production of value and the role of children in relation to it. As Nieuwenhuys rightly points out, there is need for more information and research that will uncover "how the need of poor children to realize self-esteem through paid work impinges upon the moral condemnation of child labor as one of the fundamental principles of modernity."[64]

Cultural traditions and practices have a strong influence on child-rearing and child development, and on what roles children play in the family, community, and society. Not all of them are benign, however. In South Asia, for example, caste factors influence how child work is viewed. In some cases, they endorse abuse and exploitation. A human rights/child-centered approach to child labor would identify and condemn such harmful traditions and practices. It also would address the factors that perpetuate them. Indeed, this is perhaps the greatest challenge for action against the worst forms of child labor. It directly confronts culturally sensitive attitudes, beliefs, and practices in families and communities, especially in the Global South, where child labor is widespread.

A human rights/child-centered approach to child labor needs therefore to evolve culturally sensitive strategies that facilitate the participation of working children and that develop interventions that are based on local conditions. As Miljeteig comments, "it is important to look for cultural and traditional experience that can ease the introduction of a concept that often feels alien in many societies, non-western and western alike. Here it is a need to draw on local expertise on cultural practices and local understandings of childhood and children's role in society."[65]

Organized Working Children as "Social Actors"

A human rights/child-centered approach to child labor values the positive contribution of children to their family, community, and society, and their resilience and capacity to contribute to change. It is no longer tenable to view children as "just innocent, vulnerable and susceptible," but as "active social actors who can make a positive contribution as children to social development."[66] Time and again, and notwithstanding the conditions of poverty and vulnerability, children have shown that they can affirm their role as social actors and display potentials that can be harnessed by society for development. As a 1998 study on child labor in the rural Philippines notes: "Rural children are active participants in the development process. They contribute in their own small way to the economy. . . . [A]lthough very vulnerable and exposed to the hazards of rural childhood, [they] have a role to play in rural development. They are not simply dependents and are not necessarily better off than their urban counterparts. They should be more active participants in development, if only for the reason that the future belongs to them and thus, even now, have a stake on current development initiatives."[67]

Working children have begun to organize themselves to defend their rights for better conditions and services.[68] A comprehensive study of working children's organizations in the world, published by Save the Children in 1999, surveyed selected organizations of street and working children in Latin America, Africa, and Asia.[69] The author, Anthony Swift, observed that

> the children's movements are leading exponents of the participation and organization of children. What the movements have done is build on children's ability to help protect themselves against the physical and psychological traumas that poverty and social exclusion expose them to. They have gone further, enabling children in varying degrees to become protagonists for their rights and for social change rather than victims of poverty.[70]

An excellent example of a local and indigenous working children's movement is Bhima Sangha in southern India, an independent grassroots organization of working children launched in 1990 and with a present membership of over 13,000 working children. The organization seeks to inform working children of their rights, the means available to them to change their situations, and the power of the trade union. "Members of Bhima Sangha feel that they are their own first line of defence and so have the right to organize themselves. They also believe that they are protagonists and can impact on social, political and economic structures in order to mould the society closer to their vision."[71]

The first-ever world movement of working children was launched in India in 1996, when working children from thirty-two countries in Africa,

Asia, and Latin America met for the first International Meeting of Working Children in Kundapur and adopted the Kundapur Declaration, the points of which laid down the perspective and demands of working children that are relevant today:

1. We want recognition of our problems, our initiatives, proposals and our process of organization.
2. We are against the boycott of products made by children.
3. We want respect and security for ourselves and the work that we do.
4. We want an education system whose methodology and content are adapted to our reality.
5. We want professional training adapted to our reality and capabilities.
6. We want access to good health care for working children.
7. We want to be consulted in all decisions concerning us, at local, national, and international levels.
8. We want the root causes of our situation, primarily poverty, to be addressed and tackled.
9. We want more activities in rural areas and decentralization in decision making, so that children will no longer be forced to migrate.
10. We are against exploitation at work but we are for work with dignity with hours adapted so that we have time for education and leisure.[72]

Similarly, in March 1998, working children representatives from Africa, Asia, Latin America, and the Caribbean (except Brazil) met in Dakar, Senegal, and formed the International Committee of Working Children's Movements, and though unable to participate in the ILO conference in June of that year (despite making a request to do so), issued a comparable statement:

Urging that working children's movements are consulted before processes concerning them are launched;

Declaring their opposition to such "intolerable forms of child labor" as prostitution, drug-trafficking and slavery but identifying them as crimes rather than forms of work;

Asserting that one day (when the causes that compel children to work have been tackled) children should have the choice of whether to work or not; [and]

Stating that the work children do should depend not on their age but on their development and capabilities.[73]

In addition, they explained "that their movements did not support the 'Global March Against Child Labour' because they could not 'march against their own jobs' and were not taken account of in the planning phase of the march."[74]

With the rapid growth of working children's organizations in the developing world and their successful efforts at international networking, advocacy, and influencing major international events and conferences in recent years, many international agencies and NGOs have today come to accept that working children are able to exercise their right to form associations and networks to protect their interests and advocate their rights. The International Save the Children Alliance, for example, in its recent position paper on children and work, reemphasizes that "[w]orking children's organizations help to achieve children's rights to participate and associate, and can help children to achieve their right to be free from harmful work. They can serve a variety of functions, including whistle-blowing, monitoring work places, providing mutual support and protection, and advocating for policy change. Girls and boys have the right to participation and association, and such organizations are to be encouraged."[75]

Notwithstanding these positive developments and a few pioneering studies on working children's organizations and networks, there remains, however, a seeming lack of in-depth research on, and understanding of, children's work force participation and its impact on societal change. Miljeteig notes that this lack of understanding is particularly related to what participation means in the case of working children; also that, if it is to be taken to its fullest meaning, it must include respect for the capacities and integrity of children and be culturally sensitive. He proposes a research agenda to address this gap that includes the following key issues and questions:

- Children's capacity for "participation" and "partnership," their competence, resilience, and other aspects of development that are relevant,
- Results and impact of working children's participation,
- How working children and youth perceive their roles and strategies when involved in programs or other activities related to child labor,
- Mechanisms that facilitate and complicate (or obstruct) children's participation,
- Local understandings and traditions that can be conducive to children's participation and respect their contribution to family and society,
- To what extent are programs that include working children actively more effective and sustainable, and what makes such programs replicable,
- Relationships and roles between children of different ages as well as between "children" and "adults," how to establish non-intrusive working relations between children of various ages and adults, [and]
- The role of adults involved—how do they balance their efforts to make a difference against the respect for children's integrity? How do they most effectively support the children without making them dependent on their constant presence?[76]

Bearing in mind the right of children, as provided in Article 12 of the CRC, "to express [their] views freely in all matters affecting [them]"and "in particular be provided the opportunity to be heard in any judicial and administrative proceedings affecting [them]," all of these issues and questions both inform and must be informed by the human rights/child-centered approach to the problem of child labor.

■ Conclusion

Work per se is not an issue for children. The issue is whether or not the work that children do is abusive and/or exploitive and/or deprives them of full human development. As Ben White puts it: "the problem [of child labor] is . . . best understood not as a problem of 'work' as such, but as an issue of the exploitation and abuse of children's capacity to work."[77]

Our concern, thus, is with the rights of children and how their economic exploitation is a violation of their fundamental rights. Child labor as defined herein prevents children from being recognized as legal subjects or rights-holders and denies them their work-related rights. Indeed, some have argued that it is not until these work-related rights are recognized that children will become legal subjects as rights-holders.[78] Hence the need for a rights-based approach to child labor that acknowledges that working children have rights and that they are therefore legal subjects whose rights need to be promoted and defended. As this chapter has argued, working children are able to exercise their rights and have proven that they can be responsible and effective change makers—with or without the aid of international legal instruments. Evidence shows—both from Bhima Sangha in Asia and Niños y Adolescentes Trabajadores in Latin America—that the first step toward successful advocacy by working children is their assertion of their self-identity as recognized legal subjects and rights-holders.

Some analysts have pointed out the danger of a polarized discourse in the child labor debate, putting human rights/child-centered advocates (primarily NGOs and other civil society organizations) at one end, and the "traditionalists" (primarily trade unions and the ILO) at the other.[79] Alec Fyfe argues that this polarization leads to false choices: "child-centered vs. traditional paternalism; work vs. education; public vs. private; local vs. global."[80] While this may be true given that child labor is an issue that has come to evoke passionate, emotional, and political sentiments among institutions and activists alike, there is enough evidence to suggest—some of it noted in this chapter—that today we are witnessing a comprehensive challenge to mainstream approaches and actions coming not only from grassroots civil society, but also from working children themselves. In this polarized situation, the real choices, I submit, reflected in the ideological and strategic positions taken in the current child labor discourse are adults vs. children, institutions vs. movements, top-down vs. bottom-up, and North vs. South.

The challenges we face in this complex realm can be surmounted only by building a broad-based social movement to combat the economic exploitation of children and especially the worst forms of child labor—a bottom-up social mobilization process that effectively identifies, acts upon, and eliminates the worst forms of exploitation of children by addressing root causes and structural conditions that perpetrate this situation. A rights-based approach enables us to meet this challenge—to address the structural factors and spearhead a broad social movement involving a strategic alliance of partners—with the working children and their movements as its center. At the same time, we need to ensure that our policies and actions are strategic in terms of results and outcomes, guided by the provisions and spirit of the CRC and ILO C182. A blanket abolitionist approach to children working is untenable with a rights-based approach and mitigates against protecting and promoting the rights of children. Moreover, "an unqualified ban . . . , without ensuring children's rights, can easily result in the eradication of the children itself."[81]

Kathy, a sixteen-year-old girl from Barbados, in her contribution to a global discussion on children and work on UNICEF's Voices of Youth, summed up well the problematic of child labor and the challenges ahead:

> The exploitation of child workers is a vicious global disease running rampant and unimpeded in our world today. Its monstrous tentacles know no boundaries, no limits. It snakes its way into every society regardless of race, religion or ethnicity leaving behind a gaping hole in the blanket of our humanity revealing the horror and terror; the abuse and agony that its victims must bear. I wish the answers were simple . . . to a child they are. . . . Tell me someone please what can YOU do when the kids who are exploited can look you in the eye and say "there is no other way, bills have to be paid, my brothers and sisters must eat, I have NO CHOICE." . . . Sadly the only solution I can find is to never stop, never stop trying to fight child exploitation even when all seems lost, never stop. FIGHT TO THE BITTER END, for to give up would mean the destruction of humanity itself.[82]

Notes

The views and opinions expressed in this chapter are my own and do not necessarily represent the official policies or views of the United Nations Children's Fund (UNICEF).

1. In this chapter, I adopt the definition of "child labor" set forth in the introduction to this volume, in turn derived from Chapter 2, that is, "work done by children that is harmful to them because it is abusive, exploitive, hazardous, or otherwise contrary to their best interests—a subset of a larger class of children's work, some of which may be compatible with children's best interests (variously expressed as 'beneficial,' 'benign,' or 'harmless' children's work)."

2. UNICEF, *Beyond Child Labour* . . . , p. 10.

3. Ibid., p. 1.

4. United Nations, *Convention on the Rights of the Child* (1989).

5. ILO, *Convention* (No. 182) *Concerning the Prohibition and Immediate Elimination of the Worst Forms of Child Labour* (1999).

6. See Hanson and Vandaele, "Working Children . . . ," pp. 73–146.

7. The results of a nine-country survey in Latin America showed that if teenage children did not work, poverty rates would increase by 10–20 percent. UNICEF, *Beyond Child Labour* . . . , p. 3.

8. Karunan, "Save the Children's Approach . . . ."

9. Sahu, *State of the World's Children*, p. 14.

10. Myers and Boyden, *Child Labor* . . . , p. 5.

11. See UNICEF, *Beyond Child Labour* . . . , p. 4.

12. UNICEF, *First Consolidated Donor Report* . . . , p. 4.

13. Ranoy, presentation . . . , p. 1.

14. See supra endnote 1.

15. See Chapter 1 in this volume, pp. 7–8. The rights-based approach embraces the "three generation rights," namely civil and political rights; economic, social, and cultural rights; and solidarity or community rights (e.g., the right to peace, to development, and to a clean and healthy environment).

16. UNICEF, *Beyond Child Labour* . . . , p. 4.

17. Santos Pais, *A Human Rights Conceptual Framework* . . . , p. 5; Chapter 1 in this volume, pp. 9–12.

18. United Nations, *Universal Declaration of Human Rights* (1948).

19. Santos Pais, *A Human Rights Conceptual Framework* . . . , p. 6. See also Chapter 1 in this volume.

20. Santos Pais, *A Human Rights Conceptual Framework* . . . , p. 13.

21. ILO, *A Future Without Child Labour* . . . , p. 25.

22. Quoted in UNICEF–UK, *End Child Exploitation* . . . , p. 22.

23. See Ennew, *Capacity Building and Maintenance* . . . .

24. Ibid., p. 7.

25. Karunan, "Children and Work in Southeast and East Asia . . . ," p. 21.

26. Woodhead, "Child Work and Child Development in Cultural Context . . . ," pp. 9–14.

27. Ibid., p. 21.

28. Ibid.

29. Antony and Gayathri, "Child Labor . . . ," pp. 1–12.

30. See Myers, "Valuing Diverse Approaches . . . ," pp. 27–48.

31. Myers and Boyden, *Child Labor* . . . , p. 6.

32. Santos Pais, *A Human Rights Conceptual Framework* . . . , p. 8; Chapter 10 in this volume, p. 238.

33. UNICEF's approach based on a human rights perspective signifies a radical shift in the way the agency views and works with children: "This approach reflects a general shift from a time when the most disadvantaged children were widely considered as objects of charity rather than holders of rights with valid claims on society. They are often perceived as problems to society rather than as individuals affected by society's failures to meet its obligations to all its children." UNICEF, *Programme Cooperation for Children and Women* . . . , p. 7, para. 21.

34. Woodhead, "Child Work and Child Development . . . ," p. 126.

35. Raman, "Politics of Childhood . . . ," p. 18.

36. See Karunan, "Participatory Action Research . . . ," p. 2.

37. See Theis, "Children and Participatory Appraisals . . . ," p. 25.

38. Karunan, "Participatory Action Research . . . ," pp. 13–14.

39. See Save the Children–Norway and Sweden, *Child-Centered Approaches* . . . , p. 33.

40. The experiences of working children's resilience in Latin America, Africa, and Asia were presented at a major international consultation organized in Oxford, England, on "Children in Adversity," Sept. 9–12, 2000. See http://www.childreninadversity.org.

41. See Program of Psychosocial Training and Human Rights, *Integrating Child-Centered Approaches* . . . .

42. Ibid., pp. 67–70.

43. Ranoy, presentation . . . , p. 1.

44. Miljeteig, *Creating Partnerships* . . . , p. 22.

45. Woodhead, "Child Work and Child Development . . . ," p. 127.

46. Program of Psychosocial Training and Human Rights, *Integrating Child-Centered Approaches* . . . , p. 33.

47. Quoted in Regional Working Group on Child Labor, *Handbook for Program Managers* . . . , p. 6.

48. Paragraph 2 of Recommendation 190 concerning ILO C182 (1999), not the main articles of ILO C182 (1999) itself, refers to this important point with some qualification as follows: "The programmes of action referred to in Article 6 of the Convention should be designed and implemented as a matter of urgency, in consultation with relevant government institutions and employers' and workers' organizations, *taking into consideration* the views of the children *directly affected* by the worst forms of child labour, their families *and, as appropriate, other concerned groups* committed to the aims of the Convention and this Recommendation" (emphasis added). ILO website, at http://www.ilo.org/ilolex/english/recdisp1.htm.

49. "Since 'working children' are primarily viewed as a default category (those who do not go to school), it follows that solutions being sought to address the issue also tend to be limited in their scope." Ramachandran and Saihjee, *Looking Back in Order to Look Ahead.*

50. Morrow and Richards, "The Ethics of Social Research . . . ," p. 11.

51. But see Chapters 5 and 6 in this volume.

52. Karunan, "Children: The Forgotten Victims," p. 4.

53. Ibid.

54. See generally, Chua, *World on Fire* . . . ; and Stiglitz, *Globalization and Its Discontents.*

55. Fallon and Tzannatos, *Child Labour* . . . , p. 3.

56. Raman, "Politics of Childhood . . . ," p. 22.

57. Ray, "Simultaneous Analysis . . . ," p. 5216.

58. Marcus and Harper, *Small Hands* . . . , p. 17.

59. Ramachandran, "Education, Work, and Rights," p. 31.

60. Woodhead, "Child Work and Child Development . . . ," p. 126.

61. Nieuwenhuys, "The Paradox of Anthropology and Child Labor," pp. 237–251.

62. Ibid., p. 246.

63. Ibid.

64. Ibid.

65. Miljeteig, *Creating Partnerships* . . . , p. 39.

66. Karunan, "Children and Work . . . ," p. 1.

67. Garcia and Molina, *Rural Children* . . . , p. 56.

68. Some of the well-known working children's organizations that have emerged in the developing world include, among others, the Movement of Working Children and Adolescents of Nicaragua (NATRAS), website at http://www.natras.kraetzae.de; the Movement of Working Children and Adolescents from Christian Working-Class Families (MANTHOC) in Peru, website at http://www.manthoc.50megs.com; the National Movement of Street Boys and Girls (MNMMR) in Brazil, website at http://www.mnmmr.org.br; Bhima Sangha in India, website at http://www.workingchild.org; and working children's organizations supported by ENDA Jeunesse Action in West Africa, website at http://www.enda.sn.

69. Swift, *Working Children Get Organised.*

70. Ibid., p. 7.

71. See the Concerned for Working Children, *Working Children as Protagonists.*
72. *Kundapur Declaration.*
73. Quoted in Swift, *Working Children Get Organised,* pp. 10–11.
74. Ibid., p. 11.
75. Save the Children, *Save the Children's Position on Children and Work.*
76. Miljeteig, *Creating Partnerships . . . ,* p. 37.
77. White, "Defining the Intolerable . . . ," pp. 133–144.
78. Hanson and Vandaele, "Working Children . . . ," pp. 73–146.
79. See Fyfe, "Child Labor and Education . . . ," p. 70.
80. Ibid., p. 83.
81. Quoted in Voices of Youth, *Young People Speak Out on Child Labour.*
82. Ibid.

13

Shifting Positions on Child Labor: The Views and Practice of Intergovernmental Organizations

Ben White

Regional and international organizations, in particular all United Nations bodies, as well as the Bretton Woods institutions and other multilateral agencies, should be encouraged to collaborate and play a key role in accelerating and achieving progress for children.
                                                    —*A World Fit for Children*[1]

Human rights standards contained in, and principles derived from, the Universal Declaration of Human Rights and other international human rights instruments guide all development cooperation and programming in all sectors and in all phases of the programming process.
                          —*The UN System Common Understanding on the Human Rights-Based Approach to Development Cooperation*[2]

This chapter reflects on the role of intergovernmental organizations (IGOs)[3] in debates and policies, both past and present, on problems of child labor.[4] The main focus is on the International Labour Organization (ILO), the United Nations Children's Fund (UNICEF), and the World Bank—the "big battalions"[5]— with some reference also to the United Nations Educational, Scientific, and Cultural Organization (UNESCO) and, for purposes of comparison, to some international nongovernmental organizations (INGOs) such as the Save the Children Alliance, Anti-Slavery International, and the international trade union federations. In view of the broader objectives of this volume,[6] one guiding theme is the extent to which ideas on (international) human rights and specifically child and youth rights have, do, or might inform the strategies and policies of these organizations in the future.

Never having worked in or for any of the IGOs or INGOs under consideration, I write from an outsider perspective, a position that has some advantages, but also disadvantages. It means, among other things, that I can provide no insider information on the detailed circumstances in which key strategic decisions are made within IGOs, or the internal dynamics and debates that gave rise to them.

IGOs influence the lives of the world's children and young people in various ways. Their direct influence on children's lives and work is rather modest due to their limited budgets, their limited field presence in member countries, and their limited authority to ensure effective compliance with the various international conventions, declarations, and other commitments signed, ratified, or otherwise subscribed to by governments under their auspices. This applies as much to the "core" UN bodies of global governance—whose capacity to govern global affairs is actually very limited—as it does to the specialized and humanitarian agencies of the UN system. The World Bank and the International Monetary Fund (IMF) are exceptions, since they work in a quite different way as providers of (large-scale) development finance and therefore have potentially greater power to make things happen.[7]

Through their important role in the "globalization of childhood,"[8] however, the potential indirect influence of IGOs is great, setting and sometimes shifting the terms of discourse and thereby the international construction of ideas about childhood, children's needs and interests, and the meaning of "child labor" itself. These ideas may in turn be adopted as authoritative discourse by other organizations and groups at international, national, and local levels to inform and legitimize their own approaches. If they are not subjected to continual rethinking, they can lose their function as tools for understanding and instead fixate our ways of seeing things, including, in turn, our ideas about appropriate policy directions. One key question therefore concerns the flexibility of IGOs and their capacity to stay at or near the cutting edge and to embrace, stimulate, or promote new knowledge and new ideas.

Two contrasting accounts of the IGO experience with child labor could be written, both of which would have an element of truth. One would be a story of achievement and promise, noting the pioneering historical role that IGOs like the ILO and later UNICEF have played in raising global awareness about child labor problems and bringing governments and other organizations to the table to discuss them, particularly in the last ten to fifteen years. The other would have a more somber flavor, noting that eighty-five years of intergovernmental attention and standard-setting on child labor have resulted in little progress toward realization of the human rights of the world's most poor and powerless children in the field of work and education. Recent ILO estimates suggest that more of the world's children are at work today than ever before (over 350 million),[9] while according to UNESCO, one in three children in developing countries does not complete five years of primary education (the minimum for achieving basic literacy), so that, after more than thirty years of international commitment to universal primary education, "the world is not on track to achieve Education For All by 2015."[10] While IGO discourse may be slowly shifting in more child-centered, rights-based directions, this has yet to produce concrete results in terms of access to education or protection from harmful work.[11]

Something is radically amiss with the global institutions of a world that, amid unprecedented material abundance and technological progress, still subjects nearly 180 million children to "unconditional worst forms of child labor" and "hazardous work"[12] and does not teach one-third of children in developing countries even to read and write.[13] For much of the past half century, IGOs were simply not very interested in these problems. Despite the greater attention to child labor problems in recent years and the global support given to interventions as a matter of children's rights by the 1989 United Nations Convention on the Rights of the Child (CRC),[14] the 1990s were not a time of significant progress in the reduction of widespread abuse of children's capacity to work or, indeed, other major forms of violation of child rights.[15]

Global and national policies on child labor should have two fundamental, but often insufficiently distinguished, objectives. One is the urgent, universally accepted, and so far largely unachieved goal of eliminating those unconditional worst forms of child labor, in which, according to ILO estimates, a small minority of some 2–3 percent of the world's working children are involved.[16] For the rest, child labor intervention is most fundamentally a question of promoting the historical shift from work to school as the principal occupation of young people.[17] These two issues—children's right to protection from harmful work and their right of access to good education—are inextricably bound up with each other,[18] and it is therefore a matter of concern that both discourse and policymaking on education and child labor in the IGOs (as also in many national contexts) have led largely segregated existences.[19] In this chapter, therefore, I try to consider IGO efforts toward the achievement of "Education for All" (EFA) as well as those directly promoting the elimination of abusive/harmful child work (i.e., "child labor").

While no organization is completely a prisoner of its own history, individual IGO histories do greatly influence the style and content of their present work and the discourse within which this is framed, and in particular their capacity to move with the times. Therefore, I have organized the rest of this chapter in broad historical sequence. First, I touch briefly on the period from the ILO's establishment at the end of World War I until the 1940s, in which the first international conventions and declarations on child work and child rights were adopted and some contradictory elements introduced into international discourse, which have persisted to the present day. Next I consider the Cold War period, from the end of World War II to the end of the 1980s, in which, despite the intention of 1973 ILO Convention (No. 138) Concerning Minimum Age for Admission to Employment (ILO C138) to achieve the "total abolition of child labor,"[20] very little international attention was paid in practice to issues of child work, while in contrast, considerable progress was made in extending access to education. Finally I discuss the important developments of the 1990s and early twenty-first century, in which—in my view—the 1989 CRC and the 1999 ILO Convention (No. 182) Concerning the Prohibition and Immediate Elimination of the Worst Forms of Child Labour (ILO C182)[21] offer the international community the opportunity and basis for a reorientation of IGO discourse, policy, and practice on child work and education in which children's needs and children's rights may play a more central role.

The reader is invited first to consider the following eight general propositions on IGOs, child work, and education, each of which is discussed further below:

1.   Although the language and perspectives of human rights and child rights can be found in some IGO discourse, rights-based arguments and strategies have been largely absent in the history of international standard-setting, policy, and practice on child work, with only some exceptions in very recent years.

2.   IGO discourse on child work has from its beginnings reflected and reinforced the confusion that arises from the use of the term "child labor" with multiple and contradictory meanings,[22] which in turn has reinforced a persistent, counterproductive, and largely unnecessary polarization between "abolitionist" and "protectionist" approaches to the problem of juvenile employment.

3.   The shifting historical thrust of global concern on child work should be seen in terms of successive waves or layers—abolitionism, protectionism, child labor as an international trade issue, child labor as a rights-based issue, and "first things first" approaches to child labor—that have not replaced each other but rather cumulated into an often uneasy coexistence.

4.   IGO policy discourses and interventions relating to problems of child work on the one hand, and access to education on the other, have operated largely in isolation from each other; this mirrors and strengthens a parallel segregation between government agencies at the national level.

5.   Arguments and policies promoting various combinations of education with child work were part of IGO policy discourse in the 1970s and 1980s, but since the early 1990s have virtually disappeared. Meanwhile, however, it has become clear that a large minority of the world's under-fifteen child workers do combine work and school attendance, and equally that a majority of school-going children in the developed countries are regularly employed (active in part-time labor markets) by the age of fifteen, suggesting that renewed attention to work-school combinations is warranted.

6. These realities suggest that the child's right to protection from economic exploitation, hazardous work, and work that interferes with their education (per Article 32 of the 1989 CRC) is not necessarily incompatible with notions of the child's right to work and to earn money, if he or she wants to or if he or she needs to.

7. ILO C182, despite many inadequacies of detail, is a very important step, establishing the legitimacy (previously much contested) of a differentiated approach to problems of child employment and opening up discourse on priorities for action. Since its adoption in 1999, the discourse around child labor has changed appreciably, even within the ILO.

8. The three main international commitments of the 1980s–1990s on child rights, child labor, and education, while not perfect, provide a workable basis for the reorientation of child labor policy and practice at international, national, and local levels in ways more attuned to the interests, needs, and rights of children. The problem now is to get governments, political elites, the general public, communities—and in some instances, it must be said, the IGOs themselves—to take them seriously and to act on them as a "a matter of urgency" (per Article 1 of ILO C182). So far, the IGOs have not made much headway in this regard.

This chapter should be read in conjunction with Chapter 2, by Judith Ennew, William Myers, and Dominique Plateau; Chapter 4, by Holly Cullen; and Chapter 15, by Susan Bissell. Cullen provides details on the evolution of global standard-setting on child work, in particular in ILO conventions and in the CRC, while Bissell provides background on IGO policies on both child labor and education. Ennew, Myers, and Plateau are particularly useful in showing how specific discourses on child labor are reflected in IGO practice in the context of a specific region. I have tried to avoid overlaps and will refer the reader to each of these chapters where necessary along the way.

▨ Beginnings: IGOs on Child Work and Education Prior to World War I

As already noted, one of the main roles of IGOs historically has been their standard-setting role. Table 13.1 sets out in summary form what various international conventions and declarations have had to say about child work and education, from 1919 to 2002. Child welfare in general, and child labor in particular, were first constituted as subjects of international relations with the founding of the League of Nations in 1919. In the League covenant, members pledged to protect the young and to "endeavor to secure fair and humane conditions of labor for men, women and children";[23] the same covenant provided

Table 13.1 Child Work and Education as Subjects of International Conventions or Declarations, 1919–2002 (selective list)

Convention/Declaration	On Employment	On Education
ILO C5, Minimum Age for Admission of Children to Industrial Employment (1919)	"Children under the age of 14 shall not be employed in any industrial enterprise"	Not mentioned
ILO C10, Age for Admission of Children to Employment in Agriculture (1921)	Children under 14 may not be employed in any public or private agricultural undertaking "save outside the hours of school attendance"	If children are employed outside school hours, "the employment shall not be such as to prejudice their attendance at school"
League of Nations Geneva Declaration on the Rights of the Child (1924)	". . . and must be protected against every form of exploitation"	"The child must be put into a position to earn a livelihood"
Universal Declaration of Human Rights (1948)	". . . and must be protected against every form of exploitation"	"The child . . . must receive a training which will enable it at the right time to earn a livelihood"
UN Declaration of the Rights of the Child (1959)	"The child shall not be admitted to employment before an appropriate minimum age; . . . in no case . . . to engage in any occupation or employment which could prejudice his health or education or interfere with his physical, mental or moral development"	"The child is entitled to receive education, which shall be free and compulsory, at least in the elementary stages"
UN's second development strategy (1971)	Not mentioned	1980 target for universal primary education
ILO C138, Minimum Age for Admission to Employment, and Minimum Age Recommendation 146 (1973)	Aimed to achieve the "total abolition of child labor" (preamble) Minimum age 15 for "employment or work in any occupation"; age 18 for hazardous work	No mention in preamble Art. 2.3: minimum age to be "not less than the age of completion of compulsory schooling" Rec. 1.2(e): "development & progressive extension of appropriate facilities for education and vocational orientation and training"
UN Convention on the Rights of the Child (1989)	"[T]he right of the child to be protected from exploitation and from performing any work that is likely to be hazardous or to interfere with the child's education, or to be harmful to the child's health or physical, mental, spiritual, moral or social development"	"States parties recognize the right of the child to education and . . . shall . . . make primary education compulsory and available to all, . . . make [secondary] education available to every child"

continues

Table 13.1 continued

Convention/Declaration	On Employment	On Education
Jomtien Declaration (1990)	Not mentioned	(basic) "Education for all by 2000" and 80 percent primary school completion rate
UN Population Fund's Cairo Action Program (1994)	Not mentioned	2015 as revised target for universal primary education
ILO C182, Prohibition and Immediate Elimination of the Worst Forms of Child Labour (1999)	"Prohibition and immediate elimination . . . as a matter of urgency" (to age 18) of slavery, trafficking, forced/bonded labor, prostitution/ pornography, and "any type of work which . . . is likely to jeopardize the health, safety or morals of children" (to be defined by each state party)	Preamble "recalling the CRC" and "taking into account the importance of free basic education" Art. 7.2(c): "access to free basic education . . . for all children removed from worst forms of child labour"
World Education Forum's Dakar Action Framework (2001)	Not mentioned	Confirms 2015 as EFA target; gender disparities in primary and secondary education to be eliminated by 2005
UN General Assembly's "A World Fit for Children" Declaration and Action Plan (2002)	"Take immediate and effective measures to eliminate the worst forms of child labor as defined in ILO C182 and elaborate and implement strategies for the elimination of child labor that is contrary to accepted international standards"	Confirms Dakar Action Framework's EFA targets; also "search for children who have dropped out or are excluded from school . . . especially girls and working children . . . and help them to attend and enroll in schools"

for the establishment of the International Labour Office, which was charged, as one of its most urgent tasks, with "the abolition of child labor and the imposition of such limitations on the labor of young persons as shall permit the continuation of their education and assure their proper physical development."[24] Comparing these two articles, we see an early example of the persistent confusion that arises from the plural use of the single term "child labor": first, as a neutral term more or less meaning, simply, "work done by children" (something that can be actually or potentially made "fair and humane" for children just as can be done relative to work done by adults); and second, as a prescriptively pejorative term (something that by its very nature demands "abolition").

The ILO's first convention on child employment, 1919 ILO Convention (No. 5) Fixing the Minimum Age for Admission of Children to Industrial Employment (ILO C5), stipulated that "children under the age of fourteen years shall not be employed for work in any public or private industrial undertaking other than an undertaking in which only members of the same family are employed."[25] Exceptions were made for Japan (allowing employment for children over twelve if they had completed elementary school) and for India (allowing employment for children under twelve in enterprises employing less than ten persons and not using powered machines). These and subsequent ILO conventions up to World War II were ratified mainly by (some) "Northern" countries, the main exceptions being Japan and various Latin American states.[26] However, children of the Global South—or at least those in the numerous colonial possessions of the metropolitan countries in Africa, Asia Pacific, and the Caribbean—were in theory covered by the conventions through the provisions of the Treaty of Versailles, which required member states to apply all ratified conventions to their colonies. Thus, ILO C5 required ILO member states with colonial possessions to apply the convention within them "except where owing to the local conditions its provisions are inapplicable; or subject to such modifications as may be necessary to adapt its provisions to local conditions."[27]

The process by which colonial powers such as Britain, France, the Netherlands, and Portugal adapted this and subsequent international conventions (such as 1921 ILO Convention [No. 10] Concerning the Age for Admission of Children to Employment in Agriculture [ILO C10]) to colonial conditions and priorities would make a fascinating comparative study. In British Tanganyika (now Tanzania), for example, after two decades of pressure from London, the resulting 1940 ordinance was such a watered-down version of the ILO conventions as to leave the employment of children under twelve years in export-crop estates, and the mass long-distance migration of children with their families to estate work, virtually undisturbed.[28] And in the Netherlands East Indies, pressure from plantation companies resulted in an ordinance (1924) that redefined both "employment" and "industrial workplace" and even the hours of night and daytime so as to permit child employment in precisely the (sub)sectors of production in which it was most common.[29]

In the discourse surrounding these labor conventions, there was no explicit notion of child rights, but rather of the child as "the future adult worker";[30] also, in some instances, arguments were about what is now called the "level playing field," that is, the elimination of "unfair" labor practices so as to promote "fair" competition in global markets. In contrast, the first International Declaration on the Rights of the Child (1924), also known as the Declaration of Geneva, declared that children, as a matter of rights, must be "put in a position to earn a livelihood and must be protected from every form of exploitation,"[31] thus initiating another dimension of child labor discourse that has continued to the present, namely the cleavage between "abolitionist" (minimum age prohibition) and "protectionist" approaches to the problem of child work.

■ Lost Decades? IGOs During the Cold War Period

The shifting historical thrust of global concerns about child work in the second half of the twentieth century may be pictured in terms of successive waves or layers of strategizing that have not replaced each other but cumulated: first, abolitionism (as reflected in minimum age legislation and ILO discourse); next, from the 1980s onward, the emergence of protectionism as the efficacy of abolitionist approaches was questioned and hotly debated; thereafter, in the 1990s, the evolution of child labor as both an international trade and human (child) rights issue.[32] To these we may add the beginnings, in the late 1990s, of "first things first" approaches (arguments to give priority to the worst forms of child labor, as articulated in 1999 ILO C182).[33] Likewise, the four analytic and diagnostic approaches to child labor identified by William Myers—the labor market, human capital, social responsibility, and child-centered perspectives[34]—emerged more or less in sequence, each with its distinctive logic, and without displacing those that came before; the result is the diversity of concepts and approaches we find today in (hopefully) creative tension with one another. While "total abolition" remains the official and ultimate pillar of the ILO's work and that of some INGOs as well (particularly the international trade union federations), all of these strategic orientations coexist today.

In terms of actual efforts directly aimed at problems of child labor, most of the Cold War period was characterized by relative inactivity, whether in the ILO or other IGOs. Wealthy countries considered their own child labor problems to have been solved. And in the late colonial or newly independent nations of Africa, Asia, and the Caribbean—most of which had some feeble version (if any at all) of 1919 ILO C5 on their national law books[35]—priority was given to other problems. The UN's establishment in 1971 of 1980 as the target year for achievement of universal primary education as part of the UN Second Development Decade was not seen as linked to efforts in the field of child work.

A little-acknowledged feature of this period was the achievement of virtually universal primary school enrollment and the disappearance of full-time and abusive forms of child work in the countries of the socialist bloc. This was achieved with little or no help from IGOs and INGOs. Where harmful and full-time child employment declined, on both sides of the Iron Curtain and in the nonaligned countries, it did so largely through progress in the provision and enforcement of (primary and later, secondary) education rather than through direct prohibition or regulation of juvenile employment.[36]

Another feature of this period is the emergence of two contradictory discourses within IGOs on the relation between child work and education. During the 1970s and 1980s, as Myers reminds us, "the idea of providing for both work and education in the development of children and youth was well received by many experts, by many international agencies such as UNESCO, the ILO and UNICEF, and by various NGOs promoting educational reform."[37] In the 1980s, a number of UNESCO and ILO publications explored various models fusing education and work in ways that emphasized "the dignity of work, both manual and intellectual, and the essential role of labor in the social and economic formation of both children and adults" and the potentials of earning while learning as an approach to protecting working children.[38]

In contrast, 1973 ILO C138, aimed explicitly at the "total abolition of child labor,"[39] articulated a rather rigid abolitionist approach. The convention amounts to a near-absolute prohibition on the employment of school-age children in all sectors, specifying a minimum age of not less than fifteen years (or the age of completion of compulsory schooling, whichever is higher) below which no child "shall be admitted to *employment or work in any occupation*."[40] Work and school are thus seen (implicitly) as fundamentally incompatible elements in the lives of children.[41] However, as observed by others in this volume,[42] the strategy of eliminating abusive child labor by eliminating *all* child labor, besides being largely unenforceable, tends to discourage protective legislation or other efforts to improve conditions of child work and to make the work of labor inspectors more difficult as all forms of child work become illegal and therefore go underground. Without insider knowledge, I do not speculate on why the ILO decided on this blanket prohibition and the rigid model of "child labor" it implicitly embodies, thus resulting in a convention that for decades could not secure widespread ratification. We should recall, however, that at the time neither the ILO nor other organizations had yet embarked on any serious research in this area and very little was known about the realities of child work anywhere in the world.

Serious and systematic research and discussion on child work and problems associated with it did not really begin until the issue of child exploitation reemerged in the context of the International Year of the Child (1979)—which was an initiative not of UNICEF or other IGOs but of a group of international children's NGOs.[43] Two research-based volumes emerging in the early 1980s pointed implicitly to some of the rigidities and contradictions inherent in ILO C138 and national legislation based on it,[44] which in principle increases the defenselessness of working children by excluding them from whatever protection and rights "legal" workers may have. In both volumes, one can discern the emergence of the notion—alongside other more rigid ones—that the abuse and exploitation of working children might be better addressed through approaches based on children's rights.[45]

▪ New Departures? IGOs in the Era of the CRC

After some decades of relative international neglect, the "long decade" of the 1990s (if we allow it to begin at 1989 and to stretch into the first year of the new millennium) has been a period crowded with new developments, new international actors, and new IGO initiatives in relation to child work and education. Among these one must include the 1989 CRC, the 1990 Jomtien Declaration on "Education for All"[46] (and renewed EFA commitments in Cairo 1994[47] and Dakar 2001[48]), 1999 ILO C182, and the reflection of all of these in the UN Millennium Goals of 2001.[49] It is also in this period that international donor funding for child labor interventions became available on a large scale; that the ILO became a major actor in programming interventions alongside its traditional role in standard-setting; that child labor became debated as an international trade issue; and that UNICEF and the World Bank declared themselves as important actors in the struggle against child labor.

Before considering these developments in more detail, it is useful to recall the changed global context in which they took place. With the ending of Cold War rivalry, the 1980s saw the rise of a new neoliberal economic orthodoxy based on the collapse of the idea of the developmental state in favor of the "Washington Consensus," requiring rollbacks in government spending (including spending for children, health, education, etc.). The neoliberal agenda was applied both to the restructuring of national economies, as reflected in IMF- and World Bank–led structural adjustment programs, and to the reorganization of the global economy supported by a powerful structure of international regulative authority in support of this model of development.[50] On the whole, these shifts were not good for children of the poor, on either side of the (former) Iron Curtain, as evidenced in the stagnation or decline of school enrollment and a corresponding increase in the numbers of children in full-time work in some regions. The 1990 World Conference on Education for All in Jomtien, Thailand, took place at the end of a decade of stagnation (and in sub-Saharan Africa, decline) in primary school enrollment under structural adjustment, and while that trend had been halted at the follow-up meeting five years later, new declines were occurring in the transitional (former socialist) economies of Europe and Asia.[51]

The 1989 CRC is a product of the same period. It is a remarkable human rights instrument, especially when we recall how it came into being, through a process of Cold War political maneuvering in which the needs, interests, and rights of the world's children were not always close to the top of the agendas driving the negotiating parties. Responding to the Eastern bloc initiative (in 1978) for a new convention, the UN General Assembly had established a working group, within the UN Commission for Human Rights, to embark on a drafting process. During the early 1980s, Western bloc governments (in particular the United States) first obstructed and slowed down the drafting process. Only when it became clear that the convention was gaining ground did they lobby for the inclusion of a full range of civil and political rights for children, although mainly to embarrass the other side.[52] UNICEF also first stayed on the margins of the process and came to embrace the convention fully only in 1987, after which its role in supporting the drafting process and mobilizing support became very important.[53] The outcome was an instrument going much further than the Polish government's original 1978 proposed text,[54] now including the "best interests" principle and various articles establishing children's rights to free expression and political participation; the mere fact of the CRC's existence and now near-universal ratification is a major human rights achievement that many would not have thought possible a decade earlier.[55]

Besides the CRC's important role in contributing to the formal basis for all international discourse on children's issues to be cast in a rights perspective, it also marked a turning point in UN discourse on child labor. As Björne Grimsrud correctly notes, previous conventions up to and including 1973 ILO C138 had defined the child labor problem simply in relation to the labor market.[56] With the arrival of the CRC, however, the problem became defined for the first time "not according to the activity but *according to the effect of the activity on the child*";[57] Article 32 established the right of the child to be protected from exploitation and (not from all work or employment, but) from work that is likely to harm the child. In defining the "child labor" problem as one of *harmful* work rather than of work itself, Article 32 follows the line taken by previous League of Nations and UN declarations on the rights of the child rather than of the ILO conventions, thus marking a shift away from rigid labor market approaches in international discourse. This shift was opposed throughout the 1990s by various international actors and initially by some actors within ILO itself.

The CRC has also provided support for a new, emerging discourse that picks up on earlier minority voices of the 1980s. The (mainly academic and NGO) proponents of this discourse argue that we should look at child labor and education issues from a child-centered and child rights perspective, and that we should listen to the voices of working children. They tend to argue also for the differentiated approach, distinguishing more and less harmful forms and conditions of work and questioning blanket prohibitions; they are interested in school-work combinations.[58]

Research provides growing evidence that education-with-work would meet a legitimate social demand, that it makes good educational sense, and that it is operationally feasible; and recent research shows clearly that it is this model that most working children in developing countries say they prefer.[59] It also shows that it is now the model that reflects what most young teenagers in many donor countries actually do.[60] Despite this evidence, however, from the early 1990s onward IGO interest in work-education combinations (which we have noted for the 1970s and 1980s) virtually disappeared, and the policy model based on the separation and incompatibility of school and work in children's lives has become part of the dominant international discourse on both child labor and education. Myers ventures three factors that may have contributed to this development: first, the end of the Cold War and the ascendancy of a globalized development model in which socialist ideas of the morally formative and humanizing character of work no longer have a place; second, the renewed attention to "Education for All" initiatives (since Jomtien), which paradoxically may deflect attention from issues of education relevance and quality (including discussion of beneficial links between work and education); and third, the difficulty of institutionalizing the somewhat radical change in education bureaucracies that work-education combinations require.[61]

The establishment of the ILO's International Programme for the Elimination of Child Labour (IPEC) in 1992 was an important step toward "moving child labor from the periphery to the center of the purposes of the ILO."[62] For those with a relatively recent acquaintance with the ILO's work, it is important to remember that in 1992 child labor really *was* quite marginal within the ILO, so much so that IPEC's initial donor, the German government, went first to UNICEF looking for an international organization to establish a program. At the time, as Alec Fyfe notes, the ILO had very little experience in country-level interventions in respect of child labor, having only one field project (in the Philippines).[63] UNICEF meanwhile had developed an early interest in street children (from the early 1980s) and in the mid-1980s included street and working children (along with abused and neglected children and child victims of armed conflict) as targets of activity under a program to address "children in especially difficult circumstances" (CEDC). In 1986, UNICEF also commissioned research to better determine and define "exploitative child labor." UNICEF's report to the board on CEDC took a line rather different from that of the ILO, arguing that exploitive and harmful work, not child work per se, was the problem: "It is largely through work . . . that children become socialized and learn adult skills and responsibilities. But child work becomes *exploitative* if it threatens his physical, mental, emotional or social development."[64]

The early and mid-1990s were a time of rapidly growing interest and debate in child labor, fueled not only by ILO's new program but also by the emergence of child labor as an international trade issue and involving such initiatives as the Harkin Bill, efforts toward international consumer boycotts of products made with juvenile labor, and proposals for the inclusion of child labor as one component of "social clauses" in international trade agreements. IPEC initiated a number of national and international programs, with considerable involvement of NGOs at the project level.

In its early years, IPEC did not appear to be actively promoting a rethinking of basic principles and strategies. Then at some point around 1995, it was decided within the ILO to work toward a new and quite different kind of convention, which for the first time would promote a differentiated approach to child work and attempt to establish priorities to deal with the most "intolerable" forms. The thinking behind this move is reflected in Assefa Bequele and William Myers's book *First Things First in Child Labor: Eliminating Work Detrimental to Children*,[65] and later in the ILO's 1996 report to the International Labour Conference, *Child Labour: Targeting the Intolerable,* which adopted much of Bequele and Myers's language.[66] However, the new draft convention made no reference to specific child rights and included only one perfunctory reference to the CRC in its preamble ("recalling the Convention on the Rights of the Child"). On the other hand, it did bring the ILO closer to the CRC's rights-based approach by defining the problem and the target for "immediate and effective action . . . as a matter of urgency," in terms of harm to children rather than of work or employment as such.

The various workshops and conferences accompanying the drafting process during 1996–1999 saw some quite polarized debates between proponents of abolitionist (labor market) and more differentiated approaches. In these debates, many Northern and international trade union federations, and on some occasions the ILO itself, showed considerable hostility toward arguments—sometimes made by working children themselves—that children should have the right not only to (good) education and protection from exploitation but also to "work with dignity." At various major international conferences (especially those held in Amsterdam, Trondheim, and Oslo in 1997), adult delegates were faced for the first time with representatives of organized working children, largely through the efforts of NGO networks (particularly the International Working Group on Child Labour and the Save the Children Alliance). The prospect of children exercising their participation rights under the CRC in this way was not welcomed by the various NGO, Northern government, and trade union groups that, commonly (and perhaps incorrectly) invoking ILO C138 in support of their essentially abolitionist position,[67] threatened to undermine or seriously dilute the new ILO initiative by insisting that *all* forms of child work are "intolerable."[68] Neither was it welcomed initially by the ILO itself, which for nearly eighty years had insisted correctly that workers be represented in its deliberations by their own representatives, but had applied this principle only to adult workers.[69]

UNICEF meanwhile responded to the new dynamism within the ILO with an extended statement on child labor, *The State of the World's Children 1997*.[70] This relatively progressive and balanced overview emphasized again that the target of concern and action should be harm rather than work itself: "in every country, rich and poor, it is the *nature* of the work children do that determines whether or not they are harmed by it—not the plain fact of their working."[71] Unlike the ILO's publications of this period, it also linked the child labor problem explicitly both to child rights and to education; it begins by arguing that "looking at children's work through the lens of children's rights and the CRC . . . offers not only new ways of understanding the problem of child labor but also provides new impetus and direction to the movement against it."[72] Additionally, it places major emphasis on education as a key part of the solution to exploitive child work.[73]

The World Bank also began to take an interest in issues of juvenile employment during the mid-1990s. During the five decades of its existence, the Bank has reinvented its general mission many times, causing some observers to wonder whether it now serves any useful purpose.[74] But one constant feature has been the Bank's considerable potential influence in the area of social development generally, and education and juvenile employment in particular, through its power as both lender (for development programs) and spender (for research). While its Articles of Agreement limit its power "to promote political human rights directly or to take political considerations into account in its decisions," the Bank claims both a large role in the protection and promotion of children's rights and to have "long recognized exploitative child labor as one of the most appalling manifestations of poverty."[75]

Although it has no formal policy on child labor, the Bank considers that its "projects focusing on increased enrollment in primary and secondary schools as well as on improved education through changes in curricula and more and better teachers and education tools . . . have . . . represented an important means of drawing children away from the labor markets."[76] Since the mid-1990s the Bank has sponsored a number of empirical studies and policy papers on child labor. In the early 1990s, its research work fed into the 1995 World Development Report, *Workers in an Integrating World,* which represented the Bank's major statement on global labor issues, including child labor. The report took a cautiously differentiated approach, noting that "some types of child labor are considered more harmful than others," mentioning types of labor that "most people would not condemn . . . so long as the child attends school."[77] It also noted the possibility of school-work combinations, citing the example of Kerala (India), which "indicates that school attendance does not eliminate child labor but does prevent its worst forms."[78]

It is noteworthy, however, that notions of child rights and children's agency are largely absent from the Bank's publications of this period even though undertaken in post-CRC years.[79] A subsequent World Bank position paper, aimed at summarizing what is known about the problem and clarifying the position of the Bank, also views the problem from what Myers calls the "human capital" perspective, a perspective based not on ideas of children's rights or even children's needs but rather on ideas of what national economies need their children to become.[80] Child rights are mentioned only once, and in connection with national legislative frameworks rather than as a guiding principle for the Bank's own policies.[81] The Bank's more recent (2003) position paper on education does not mention human or children's rights at all![82]

The polarization and tensions among different child labor discourses in the years leading to ILO C182 were further exemplified in the problems encountered by the "Global March Against Child Labour," a major worldwide publicity effort whose conclusion was planned to coincide with the ILO's 1999 conference in Geneva, at which the new convention would be adopted. Plans for this march, already quite advanced by 1997, were threatened by wide differences of opinion among the various NGO participants about what exactly was to be abolished. Interestingly, the common ground and "mission" eventually identified for the Global March drew its inspiration from the CRC: whatever the media and some participants may have thought, the Global March was not actually against the employment of children as such, but had the rights-centered aim "to mobilize worldwide efforts to protect and promote the rights of children, especially the right to receive a free, meaningful education and to be protected from economic exploitation and from performing any work that is likely to be damaging to the child's physical, mental, spiritual, moral or social development."[83]

While not in themselves productive, the debates of the late 1990s did help to expose and clarify the various coexisting perspectives on juvenile employment, and the contrasting implications of each for standard-setting and intervention. ILO C182, finally adopted in 1999,[84] has left the ILO with a difficult path, treading between two competing models and policy approaches to child work, one represented by 1973 ILO C138, the other by ILO C182 itself. In my view, ILO C182 is a very important step, not so much for the details of its definition of "harmful work" in the convention and its associated Recommendation 190 (about which many questions could be raised, and further debate is still needed),[85] but simply for the formal recognition it provides for the principle that it is both necessary and possible to distinguish between more and less intolerable and harmful forms and relations of juvenile work, and therefore to focus intervention on the most serious forms of abuse. This principle may now seem self-evident to many readers, but it is one that still is opposed by some national and international agencies, and until recently would have been opposed by the ILO itself.

▣ Taking Children's Rights More Seriously? IGOs and International Commitment in the New Millennium

"We can and must believe that the state of childhood will be improved if we are prepared to take children's rights more seriously, to transcend the rhetoric of international documents and domestic legislation. . . . Rights, of course, are never given but are fought for," writes human rights scholar Michael Freeman.[86] To what extent has his faith begun to be vindicated? When taken together, the three main international commitments of the 1980s–1990s on child rights, child work, and education—the CRC (1989); the commitments to "Education for All" made in Dakar and, most recently, in the UN Millennium Development Goals; and ILO C182 (1999)—do provide, however imperfectly, a workable basis for reorientation of child labor policy and practice at the international, national, and local levels in ways that are attuned to the interests, needs, and rights of children. And in May 2003, at a meeting attended by representatives of all the IGOs we have considered (and many more),[87] these commitments were reinforced by a further formal commitment to rights-based approaches in all the UN family's development programming by way of the UN Common Understanding on the Human Rights–Based Approach.[88] In other words, the formal frameworks, and the discourse of rights within which to frame them, are basically in place. The problem now is to promote the realization of these human (child) rights with action, to look beyond these instruments—on which so much effort has been spent in the 1990s, but which are, after all, only pieces of paper—and to get governments, political elites, the general public, communities—and in some instances, it must be said, the IGOs themselves—to take children's rights seriously and to act on them as "a matter of urgency" (per ILO C182).

So far, however, it must be said that most IGOs have not made much headway in this regard. While UNICEF has quite consistently adopted the language of rights in its position papers and programming, most other IGOs have not come that far. The fact is that most recent policy documents and position papers of the ILO, UNESCO, and the World Bank on child labor and education, far from trying to outline a rights-based approach to the problem, scarcely even mention the human rights or child rights dimension. The World Bank's recent position paper on education, as already noted, makes no mention at all of human or child rights,[89] and its policy paper on child labor mentions the CRC only once in passing, and then not in relation to the Bank's own work, but in a discussion of the legal frameworks within which national governments operate.[90] The

World Bank, UNESCO, and the ILO all seem more comfortable with utilitarian principles and arguments than with the language of rights. UNICEF is a lone exception, having for some years adopted the child rights discourse in its policy documents. But in trying to move beyond discourse to a practical understanding of what it actually means to develop and implement principles of rights-based programming in this field, even UNICEF tends to retreat into vague slogans—as, for example, in its recent publication *Beyond Child Labour: Affirming Rights*.[91]

Education is a good example. The right of children to free (at least at the primary level) and compulsory education has been on the international agenda since 1948 and is firmly and unambiguously established in the CRC.[92] As noted by the UN Special Rapporteur on the Right to Education, the right to education is crucial because it "operates as a multiplier. It enhances all other human rights and forecloses the enjoyment of most, if not all, when denied."[93] From the human rights viewpoint, education is not a means to achieving general societal (developmental) ends, and children are not "human capital." Thus, while it is interesting to study the economic costs and benefits of eliminating child labor and universalizing access to primary and lower secondary education as IPEC recently has done,[94] the outcomes of such utilitarian considerations should not affect the global commitment to act.

The World Bank is the largest global source of education finance. Also, it is bound by its statutes to support UN conventions and, as we have noted above, it claims a large role in the protection and promotion of children's rights. Since the early 1980s, however, the Bank has dropped all reference in its publications to education as a right (and as a corresponding public responsibility) and played a major role in the conversion of education from entitlement to commodity, from a public good protected by public law to a freely traded service, from a human right (a legally binding obligation, which one can claim now) into a "development goal" (a target that need not—and as we have seen, will not—be achieved).[95] If organizations in the UN family do this sort of thing, it is not surprising if national governments willingly follow suit. It is therefore important not to let international agencies and national governments off the hook with respect to the commitment to child rights, including especially the rights of the working child.

Taking children's rights seriously has another important dimension, reflected in Freeman's remarks (quoted above) on the need for rights to be "fought for." One lesson of history is that progress for children is not achieved through legislation and top-down enforcement efforts alone. Progress normally is achieved only when proreform actors who can exert pressure from above ally themselves with powerful social movements exercising pressure from below. This applies as much in lobbying for greater public resource allocation to education as in the identification and exposure of the most abusive kinds of child labor and the demand for heavy penalties for those who employ children in these "worst forms." This means that the IGOs must work toward a better relationship with international, national, and local NGOs and social movements. It would be naive to suggest that this will be easy. With the partial exception of UNICEF, IGO-NGO relations have rarely been smooth, and all IGOs have special problems with NGOs that engage in political advocacy and rights campaigns. However, it is precisely these agencies that in recent years have taken the lead in the development of basic principles and practical guidelines for (child) rights-based programming.[96]

Rights perspectives and rights-based programming can be important tools in shifting international activity from goal-setting to a more effective politics of getting things done, informed by a greater sense of urgency than is now apparent in IGO activity. This applies equally to the elimination of "unconditional worst forms" as to the shift from work to school as the principal occupation of children—the two fundamental objectives of child labor policies as outlined earlier in this chapter. IPEC's new "time-bound programs" strategy will perhaps help to underline the dimension of urgency, and its achievements and problems should be carefully watched and lessons learned; time-boundness hopefully will not result in too-rapid swings in donor support if and when initial achievements in these often intractable areas disappoint. Mention of donors here reminds us of another dimension of urgency: while large-scale funding to ILO-IPEC, the EFA initiatives, and other programs in this field may not yet have peaked, it will do so before long and there is a danger of losing momentum before "donor fatigue" sets in.

In some areas of work there are good grounds for loosening the present divide between IPEC "donors" on the one hand and "partners and affiliates" on the other. At present there is no overlap between the IPEC program's twenty donor governments and its seventy-four "participating" and "associated" countries;[97] in other words, no donor country has yet joined the IPEC program as a *participant.* In at least some areas—for example the trafficking of children and the use of children for prostitution or production of pornography[98]—there would be clear advantages for many donor countries in participating in the relevant IPEC time-bound programs besides the more general advantage of underlining that abusive and worst forms of child labor are truly a global problem.

Finally, please imagine that at some future time the Jomtien/Dakar commitments (on "Education for All") and the articles of 1999 ILO C182 (on "worst forms" of child labor) are universally honored and have been implemented in practice. The involvement of children in prostitution, forced labor, and all other forms of harmful work would then be a thing of the past, and the universal right of children to have access to education would have been realized. At which point it would be difficult to imagine that any blanket prohibition on child work would be needed. There actually would be nothing left to abolish.

▨ Notes

1. United Nations World Summit for Children, *A World Fit for Children.*
2. UNDP, *The UN System* . . . , p. 3.
3. Two points of clarification on terminology are necessary. First, the term "intergovernmental organizations" as used in this chapter and the volume as a whole includes and refers primarily to the United Nations agencies relevant to child labor, although these agencies often prefer to call themselves "multilateral," reserving the term "intergovernmental" for less inclusive groupings of governments on a regional or interest basis, such as the European Union (EU), the Association of Southeast Asian Nations (ASEAN), the Organization of American States (OAS), the Group of Eight (G8), and so forth. Second, while the ILO is included here for simplicity's sake under "IGO," it is of course much more than that, because of its unique tripartite structure within the UN system, in which its members are not only governments but also employer's and worker's organizations.
4. In this chapter, I adopt the definition of "child labor" set forth in the introduction to this volume, in turn derived from Chapter 2, that is, "work done by children that is harmful to them because it is abusive, exploitive, hazardous, or otherwise contrary to their best interests—a subset of a larger class of children's work, some of which may be compatible with children's best interests (variously expressed as 'beneficial,' 'benign,' or 'harmless' children's work)." But see endnote 22 below.
5. Fyfe, "Child Labour and Education . . . ," p. 73.
6. See Chapters 1 and 10 in this volume.
7. The WTO, as an IGO outside the UN system, is not further considered here because it is discussed in detail in Chapter 16 in this volume. See also Chapter 5.
8. Boyden, "Childhood and the Policy Makers . . . ," p. 190.
9. ILO, *Every Child Counts* . . . , p. 15.
10. UNESCO, *Education for All* . . . , p. 188. The reference is to the UN target for "Education for All" (EFA), revised again in 2001, after earlier targets—set at 1980 in 1972 and at 2000 in 1990—had proved hopelessly optimistic.
11. Accord, Chapter 10 in this volume, pp. 236–237.
12. ILO, *Every Child Counts* . . . , p. 25.
13. UNESCO, *Education for All* . . . , p. 188.
14. United Nations, *Convention on the Rights of the Child* (1989) [hereinafter "CRC"].
15. Summing up the achievements of the 1990s, the world's oldest and most influential child-focused INGO concludes that "these [international] commitments to children have not led to significant improvements in the everyday lives of millions of the world's children," and that children's rights have now to be given "a second chance." Save the Children, *Children's Rights* . . . , p. 2.
16. ILO, *Every Child Counts* . . . , p. 25.
17. Heywood, *A History of Childhood,* p. 155.
18. See, for example, Chapter 15 in this volume.
19. Fyfe, "Child Labour and Education . . . ," p. 68. There are indications of growing recognition of the links in recent years; see, for example, IPEC, *Child Labour: A Textbook* . . . , chap. 4.
20. ILO, *Convention* (No. 138) *Concerning Minimum Age for Admission to Employment* (1973) [hereinafter "ILO C138"], preamble.
21. ILO, *Convention* (No. 182) *Concerning the Prohibition and Immediate Elimination of the Worst Forms of Child Labour* (1999) [hereinafter "ILO C182"].

22. For this reason, although this chapter employs the common terminology adopted throughout this volume, my personal preference would have been to avoid use of the term "child labor" wherever possible, agreeing with William Myers that it "is now used to signify so many different things that it is almost useless except as an emotion-laden slogan." Myers, "The Right Rights? . . . ," p. 28. In my view, greater clarity is easily achieved (and problems of translation to other languages made much easier) by use of neutral terms like "work," "employment," and the like, modified as necessary with appropriate adjectives ("hazardous," "beneficial," "intolerable," and so on). See Lieten and White, "Children, Work, and Education . . . ," pp. 10–11. However, to facilitate coherence in this essay collection, I have accepted in this chapter the modified definitional approach adopted by Judith Ennew, William Myers, and Dominique Plateau in Chapter 2 in this volume. See supra endnote 4.

23. *Covenant of the League of Nations* (1919), art. 23(a).

24. See also Cunningham, "The Rights of the Child . . . ," p. 20; and Marshall, "The Construction of Children . . ." p. 105.

25. ILO, *Convention* (No. 5) *Fixing the Minimum Age for Admission of Children to Industrial Employment* (1919) [hereinafter "ILO C5"], art. 2.

26. Argentina, Brazil, Chile, Colombia, Cuba, the Dominican Republic, Nicaragua, Uruguay, and Venezuela all ratified 1919 ILO C5 during the 1920s or 1930s. The United States did not ratify ILO C5 or any of the ILO's subsequent minimum age conventions, before or after World War II, until the 1999 ILO C182.

27. ILO C5, art. 8.

28. Shivji, "Law and Conditions of Child Labour . . . ," p. 232. Similar examples are given for the Gold Coast, Nyasaland, and Southern Rhodesia in Chapter 3 in this volume.

29. White, "Childhood, Work, and Education . . . ," pp. 110–111. See also White, "Constructing Child Labour . . . ."

30. Cunningham, "The Rights of the Child . . . ," p. 20.

31. *Declaration of Geneva of the Rights of the Child* (1924). See also Marshall, "The Construction of Children . . . ," p. 129.

32. See Bessell, "The Politics of Child Labour in Indonesia . . ."; and Bessell, "The Politics of Children's Work in Indonesia . . . ."

33. The first major statement of a "first things first" approach emerging under IGO sponsorship is Bequele and Myers, *First Things First in Child Labour* . . . .

34. Myers, "Valuing Diverse Approaches . . . ."

35. See ILO C5.

36. Fyfe, *Child Labour*, p. 159.

37. Myers, "Can Children's Education and Work Be Reconciled?" p. 309.

38. Ibid., pp. 311–312.

39. ILO C138, preamble.

40. Ibid., art. 2 (emphasis added).

41. The only exceptions to the blanket prohibition in ILO C138 are (a) the possibility for governments to permit the employment of children aged thirteen to fifteen in "light work, which is not likely to be harmful to their health or development and not such as to prejudice their attendance at school"; and (b) work done by children over fourteen as "an integral part of a course of training" if approved by the competent authority and after consultation with organizations of workers and employers. See ILO C138, arts. 6–7.

42. See especially Chapter 4 in this volume.

43. Black, *Children First . . .* , p. 13.

44. See Rodgers and Standing, *Child Work* . . . ; and White, *Child Workers*. The first of these was sponsored by ILO, the second by the Anti-Slavery Society for the Protection of Human Rights (now Anti-Slavery International).

45. In particular, see Goddard and White, "Child Workers and Capitalist Development . . ."; and Morice, "The Exploitation of Children . . . ."

46. UNESCO, *World Declaration on Education for All*.

47. UNFPA, *International Conference* . . . , chap. XI.

48. UNESCO, *The Dakar Framework for Action* . . . .

49. United Nations, *Report of the Secretary-General: Road Map* . . . .

50. See Griffin, "Economic Globalization . . . ."

51. See Tomasevski, *Education Denied* . . . , p. 89.

52. Alston, "The Best Interests Principle . . . ," pp. 6–7.

53. Black, *Children First* . . . , pp. 22–25.

54. The original 1978 text was simply "the 1959 Declaration of the Rights of the Child recouched in legal parlance." Ibid., p. 22.

55. Freeman, "The Moral Status of Children," p. 3.

56. Grimsrud, "Too Much Work at Too Early an Age," p. 9.

57. Ibid., p. 10 (emphasis added).

58. Good examples of this approach are the publications of the Save the Children Alliance and the International Working Group on Child Labour (IWGCL) (an initiative of Defence for Children International and the International Society for the Prevention of Child Abuse and Neglect). IWGCL, *Have We Asked the Children?;* Save the Children, *Save the Children's Position on Children and Work*.

59. Woodhead, "Combating Child Labour . . ."; Woodhead, "The Value of Work . . . ."

60. While research on children's employment in Organization for Economic Co-operation and Development (OECD) countries is still rare, a number of studies have shown that regular involvement in labor markets is part of the experience of the majority of school-going children by age fifteen in such countries as Germany, the Netherlands, the United Kingdom, and the United States. Dorman, *Child Labour in the Developed Economies;* Hobbs and McKechnie, *Child Employment in Britain* . . . ; Liebel, *A Will of Their Own* . . . , chaps. 5–6; McKechnie and Hobbs, "Child Labour . . ."; NIBUD, *Bijbaantjes Van Scholieren;* White, "Childhood, Work, and Education . . ."

61. Myers, "Can Children's Education and Work Be Reconciled?" p. 313.

62. Smolin, "Strategic Choices . . . ," p. 946.

63. Fyfe, "Child Labour and Education . . . ," p. 74.

64. UNICEF, *Children in Especially Difficult Circumstances,* p. 132.

65. Bequele and Myers, *First Things First* . . . .

66. ILO, *Report VI (1)* . . . .

67. In this they were joined by some influential national NGOs. The most prominent and successful example is perhaps India's MV Foundation, which claims as one of its "nonnegotiable principles" that "all labor is hazardous and harms the overall growth and development of the child. There must be total abolition of child labor; any law regulating child work is unacceptable," and rejects any form of school-work combination. MV Foundation, "The Non-Negotiables," p. 2.

68. During the drafting process of ILO C182, the terminology for the forms of child work to be targeted changed twice, from "intolerable" and "most intolerable" in the initial formulation to "extreme" and "most extreme," and finally, after the June 1998 ILO conference, to "worst" forms of child labor. White, "Defining the Intolerable . . . ," p. 142.

69. At the closing of the 1997 Oslo conference, tripartite delegations leaving the conference hall were met by a row of representatives of working children's organizations, with their mouths taped shut in symbolic protest at their exclusion from the forum.

70. UNICEF, *The State of the World's Children 1997.*

71. Ibid., p. 18.

72. Ibid.

73. Ibid., esp. pp. 48–58 (the report's extended section on "The Power of Education").

74. Established with the original mission "to promote private foreign investment" by financing enabling infrastructure in the capital-starved world of the late 1940s, the World Bank has had to reinvent itself more than once since global capital markets recovered: first as a development aid agency through general lending for agriculture, health, education, and the like; more recently (with the decline of foreign aid) as an instrument to promote "sound" national policies (working with the IMF for structural adjustment and privatization programs); and most recently as a "knowledge bank." Griffin, "Economic Globalization . . . ," p. 803.

75. Shihata, "The World Bank's Protection . . . ," p. 403.

76. Ibid., pp. 404–405.

77. World Bank, *World Development Report 1995* . . . , pp. 72–73.

78. Ibid.

79. One notable exception is the sponsored review of the involvement of working children and youth in efforts to improve their own situation and to address issues of economic exploitation. See Miljeteig, *Creating Partnerships* . . . ; Miljeteig, "Establishing Partnerships . . . ."

80. Fallon and Tzannatos, *Child Labour* . . . .

81. Ibid., p. 6.

82. See World Bank, *Opening Doors* . . . .

83. "Global March Against Child Labour," p. 6.

84. The convention's details are discussed in many other chapters in this volume and therefore are not discussed here.

85. For example, Smolin argues that the substantive prioritization decisions represented in the convention and recommendations appear to have been based on a combination of "severity of need, visibility, political and ideological considerations" and in some respects may be considered irrational: "the Convention prioritizes and mobilizes in several areas where little is likely to be accomplished, while failing to mobilize in an area—particularly the provision of primary education—which is particularly likely to produce benefits"; and "as a matter of effective mobilization, it would have been easier if the ILO had concentrated its efforts on younger children, rather than adopting an inflexible age of majority which includes older teenagers often culturally and legally defined as adults." Smolin, "Strategic Choices . . . ," pp. 975, 979–980.

86. Freeman, "Taking Children's Rights More Seriously," p. 21.

87. Among those attending the Second Interagency Workshop on Implementing a Human Rights–Based Approach in the Context of UN Reform, in Stamford in May 2003, were representatives of the ILO, UNESCO, UNICEF, and the World Bank; also the Food and Agriculture Organization (FAO), the United Nations Industrial Development Organization (UNIDO), the United Nations High Commission for Refugees (UNHCR), the United Nations Office on Drug Control and Crime (UNOCD), the United Nations Development Programme (UNDP), the United Nations Population Fund (UNFPA), the United Nations Development Fund for Women (UNIFEM), the

United Nations System Staff College (UNSSC), the World Food Programme (WFP), and the World Health Organization (WHO). UNDP, *Report of the Second Interagency Workshop* . . . .

88. The text of the UN common understanding may be found in UNDP, *Human Rights–Based Reviews of UNDP Programmes* . . . , chap. 1.

89. See World Bank, *Opening Doors* . . . .

90. Fallon and Tzannatos, *Child Labour* . . . , p. 6.

91. Despite its interesting title, this publication does not provide the reader with an account of what a rights-based approach to child labor involves or how it differs from other approaches, beyond vague statements like "a human rights approach to child labour . . . permits, and indeed requires, responses that are as multifaceted as the affronts children endure and the conditions that give rise to them." UNICEF, *Beyond Child Labour* . . . , p. 4.

92. If not free, secondary education must be "available and accessible to every child [through] appropriate measures such as the introduction of free education and offering financial assistance in case of need." CRC, art. 28.

93. Tomasevski, *Education Denied* . . . , p. 1.

94. See IPEC, *Investing in Every Child* . . . .

95. Tomasevski, *Education Denied* . . . , chap. 5.

96. An early example is Save the Children, *An Introduction to Child Rights Programming* . . . .

97. The fifty-one "participating" countries have signed a memorandum of understanding (MOU) with IPEC; the twenty-three "associated" countries are those where IPEC has initiated activities with the government's permission, but an MOU has not yet been signed. See IPEC, "All About IPEC."

98. ILO C182, art. 3.

Nongovernmental Organizations in the Struggle Against Child Labor

Laurie S. Wiseberg

This chapter reviews the work of nongovernmental organizations (NGOs) in the struggle to combat child labor[1] and to assess the effectiveness of their efforts. The task is not easy because, on final analysis, the effectiveness of this children's rights movement must be measured by real change in the situation of children, not by the number of NGOs and networks that have been created, by the amount of activity they have generated (fact-finding, research, advocacy, educational campaigns and programs, or world congresses), or even by the international standards and national legislation they have helped draft and adopt. As Kailash Satyarthi, chairperson of the Global March Against Child Labour, has put it:

> On June 17, 1999, when the member states of the ILO unanimously voted to adopt Convention 182 on the Worst Forms of Child Labour, the world community made a commitment to stop the suffering of millions of children. It was recognised that ending the commercial exploitation of children must be one of humankind's top priorities. . . . Since then many governments, organisations, and individuals have stepped forward to meet this challenge. Governments have ratified Convention 182 at the fastest rate ever for an international treaty. NGOs, trade unions, and some businesses have launched innovative programs to protect children. . . . The real measure of success, however, is the difference being made in the lives of vulnerable children.[2]

It is from this perspective that I write. I begin with a general overview of the role played by NGOs in the protection and promotion of human rights. I then look more specifically at the universe of NGOs active in the area of child work. Next I examine the roles played by NGOs in combating child labor, and the strategies and tactics that have been designed specifically to attain a variety of objectives relative to the abolition of child labor. Finally, I return to the question of assessment and effectiveness.

▓ The Role of NGOs in the Protection and Promotion of Human Rights

An NGO is a private association of individuals and a key component of what today we call civil society. Its significant characteristic is its distinctiveness from the public sector; it is, or aspires to be, independent or autonomous from government.

A human rights NGO is a private association whose raison d'être derives from the promotion and/or protection of one or more internationally recognized human rights. Independence takes on added importance in this sphere given the inherent tension between the individual as the primary rights-holder and the state as the primary duty-bearer. Moreover, as the struggle for human rights has evolved in the past century, it has exposed the paradox of the state being at the same time the prime protector and prime violator of human rights. It is these human rights NGOs that have spearheaded the human rights movement, which began to coalesce into a major force in the late 1970s[3] and which has changed in a number of important respects over the past twenty-five years—from an initially Western-based movement to a truly universal one and from a concentration almost exclusively on civil and political rights, especially rights relating to the security of the person (torture, extrajudicial executions, political prisoners), to one encompassing also economic and social rights and even communitarian rights (right to peace, to development, to a sustainable environment).[4] In addition, it has become both more specialized and more complex, with a number of distinctive streams. Prominent among them are women's rights, the rights of indigenous peoples, and the rights of the child, which emerged in the context of the drafting of the 1989 United Nations Convention on the Rights of the Child (CRC).[5]

In the area of human rights promotion and protection, NGOs perform a myriad of roles or functions.[6] These include but are not limited to agenda-setting (getting governments and international organizations to pay attention to issues they consider important); standard-setting (assisting in the drafting of international human rights standards and amending national legislation to bring it into line with norms and principles elaborated in international and regional arenas); fact-finding and monitoring (primary research and analysis, particularly into situations where human rights violations are hidden or obscured); witnessing and advocacy (denouncing violations and advocating on behalf of the victims of violations in international, regional, national, and local arenas, which may involve lobbying for the adoption of specific recommendations at the national, regional, or global level); and petitioning and litigating (bringing cases and complaints before global bodies such as the UN Commission on Human Rights and its subcommission, the UN human rights treaty bodies, or regional tribunals such as the European Court of Human Rights or the Inter-American Court of Human Rights).[7] Human rights NGOs also facilitate international solidarity (by offering support to human rights defenders, particularly those at risk on the front lines of human rights work); engage in human rights education (by helping individuals to understand their rights and government representatives to understand their obligations under human rights treaties and declarations); and assist duty-bearers (by offering their expertise—both in developing policies and in delivering services—about how to respect, protect, and fulfill the human rights of those under their jurisdiction and by helping to ensure that the political systems remain open, democratic, and transparent).

▓ The Universe of NGOs Working on Child Labor

As one would expect, the universe of NGOs and networks currently working on the issue of child labor is both large and diverse, and the NGOs work at all levels—globally, regionally, nationally, and locally. The dimensions of the universe of course depend on one's definition of child labor.

Since the meaning, scope, and nature of child labor are discussed elsewhere in this volume,[8] here I merely draw attention to the typology suggested by Norwegian economist Björne Grimsrud, distinguishing among three main categories of child laborers: (1) those who work in their own households, in family businesses, or as a result of the employment relationship of their parents—the most common situation; (2) those who live with their families but work for someone not a member of their own household, the most traditional employment relationship; and (3) those where children have moved or been taken away from their parental household, or whose parents are dead or who have been integrated into and/or are being exploited by such new household relations.[9] The latter is numerically the smallest but typically the one that most often includes the worst forms of child labor as identified in 1999 International Labour Organization Convention (No. 182) Concerning the Prohibition and Immediate Elimination of the Worst Forms of Child Labour (ILO C182).[10]

Understandably, it is the worst forms of child labor that have attracted the highest level of attention from NGOs working in the area (e.g., bonded labor, commercial sexual exploitation of children, and child soldiers), followed by a focus on children employed in producing products for export (e.g., carpets, sports equipment, the garment industry), especially by multinational corporations. Children working under parental control—those who constitute the largest number of child laborers—have received the least attention, a fact that must be considered when evaluating the successes and failures of the movement.

International NGOs and Networks

At the international level, the universe of actors includes mainline human rights NGOs, though many have come somewhat late to the issue. For example, it was only in 1994, five years *after* the adoption of the 1989 CRC, that Human Rights Watch (HRW) established a Children's Rights Division to monitor and promote the human rights of children around the world, and it was only in 1996 that HRW issued its first report on child labor, *The Small Hands of Slavery: Bonded Child Labor in India.*[11] NGOs like Amnesty International (AI), the International Federation for Human Rights, and the International League for Human Rights have not made child labor a priority concern, although AI did issue two isolated publications on child labor in 1988[12] and made the specific issue of child soldiers one of its central concerns in the late 1990s.[13] Other NGOs have taken up the issue in the context of international conferences or campaigns.

Work at the global level includes of course international children's rights groups such as Defence for Children International (DCI),[14] which, relatively early on, set up a child labor desk and, together with the International Society for the Prevention of Child Abuse and Neglect (ISPCAN),[15] founded the International Working Group on Child Labour (IWGCL).[16] Also important is the NGO Group for the Convention on the Rights of the Child,[17] established by the NGOs that played an active role in drafting the children's rights convention to assist the Committee on the Rights of the Child to monitor the implementation of the convention.[18]

Another international NGO of note is the British-based Anti-Slavery International (ASI).[19] With roots in the nineteenth-century abolitionist movement, ASI focuses on contemporary forms of slavery, and has done pioneering work in the area of child labor. As early as 1975, ASI sent a fact-finding mission to Morocco to investigate stories that large numbers of children, mostly girls and some as young as five, were employed in carpet factories. It presented a report both to the government of Morocco and to the UN Group of Experts on Slavery.[20] Then, prompted by the fact that 1979 was declared the International Year of the Child, the tabling of a draft convention on the rights of the child by Poland, and the ILO's publication of an overview report, *Children at Work,*[21] the ASI decided to begin a major project on child labor.[22] By mid-1981, ASI had produced a series of country monographs on child labor[23] and had submitted nine reports on the subject to the UN.

Organizations of children or youth have engaged on this issue as well. Prominent among those that spotlighted the plight of bonded child workers is Canadian-based Free the Children, founded in 1995 by Craig Kielburger (then twelve years of age), who was moved by a newspaper story about the murder of freed child worker Iqbal Masih of Pakistan (also twelve at that time).[24] Free the Children reportedly has now spread to thirty-five countries, involving more than 100,000 youth in its activities.[25]

Another key actor on the global plane is the international trade union. According to Geir Myrstad, the struggle against child labor always has been part of the trade union agenda.[26] Myrstad notes that the abolition of child labor (together with freedom of association and shorter working hours) was among the core demands that sparked the birth of international workers' organizations, that is, the international trade secretariats set up from 1860 to around 1900, the forerunners of international trade unions. "As early as 1866," he writes, "the International Workers' Congress called for an international campaign against child labor. Workers continued to bring this issue to the international conference table in the last decades before the First World War and the decades after."[27] He points out that cooperation between trade unions and the ILO has been an important dimension in the worldwide movement against child labor, and "that today the child labour issue again finds itself near the top of the agenda, both for the ILO and the international trade union movement."[28]

Key among the trade unions has been the International Confederation of Free Trade Unions (ICFTU). In June 1994, the ICFTU launched the International Trade Union Campaign Against Child Labour, which was to become one of the most far-reaching child labor campaigns in decades. Said to have mobilized trade unions in developing and industrialized countries alike, the campaign was instrumental also in creating increased support for the engagement of the ILO in events like the Oslo International Conference on Child Labour in November 1997, which in turn brought the ILO and the United Nations Children's Fund (UNICEF) together in formalized cooperation on child labor research and influenced the World Bank to start its own child labor program. As well, the conference was the birthplace for the alliance between NGOs and trade unions that later organized the Global March Against Child Labour.[29]

The idea for a global march against child labor actually originated with the South Asian Coalition on Children in Servitude (SACCS). Its leader, Kailash Satyarthi, had used the protest march to draw attention to the plight of bonded child laborers since the early 1990s.

At the 1997 Oslo conference, which provided a venue for child rights activists to come together, the decision was made to launch a global march and to create an NGO involving both children and adult activists in Africa, Asia, the Americas, and Europe. The aim was to establish a worldwide movement to promote the rights of children relative to education and freedom from exploitive forms of work.[30]

In 1990, the Ecumenical Coalition on Third World Tourism and its partners in Southeast Asia established the Campaign to End Child Prostitution in Asian Tourism (ECPAT), which became ECPAT International, "a network of organisations and individuals working together to eliminate the commercial sexual exploitation of children."[31] The offices of ECPAT International are located in Bangkok, Thailand. Based on primary research into child prostitution conducted in the Philippines, Sri Lanka, and Thailand, the campaign was launched to create awareness about the phenomena of "sex tourism," specifically about wealthy foreigners who traveled to Southeast Asia to have sexual relations with children. In 1992, ECPAT held its first international conference in Bangkok, with 170 participants from the Northern "sending" countries and the Southern "receiving" countries. As a result of this meeting, other established NGOs, including Anti-Slavery International, Save the Children–UK, Christian Aid, and the Jubilee Campaign, began to involve themselves in the global campaign to end this egregious violation of the rights of the child. ECPAT was a lead organization in the development of the 2000 Optional Protocol on the Sale of Children, Child Prostitution, and Child Pornography.[32]

Still another noteworthy actor in the global struggle against the worst forms of child labor is the relatively new Coalition to Stop the Use of Child Soldiers, formed in May 1998 by six leading NGOs active in human rights— AI, HRW, International Federation Terre des Hommes, the Jesuit Refugee Service, the Quaker UN Office (Geneva), and Save the Children–Sweden— and now including Defence for Children International and World Vision International on the coalition's steering committee. The purpose of the coalition is to promote what became known as an absolute "straight-eighteen" ban on the use of children as soldiers—a ban on the recruitment of children under age eighteen by any armed force or group (governmental or nongovernmental) at any time, anywhere—and to ensure the demobilization and rehabilitation of all existing child soldiers.[33]

The coalition, with a small secretariat based in London, has built a world-wide network of NGOs, expert agencies, academic institutions, and national coalitions engaged in advocacy, campaigns, and public education in nearly forty countries, many of them with severe problems in child soldiering. These local campaigns have been organized in different ways, in some places formally constituted and in others through loose networks of organizations and individuals, bringing together global, regional, and local human rights and children's rights NGOs,[34] humanitarian and development agencies, peace and disarmament movements, veterans' associations and youth movements, teachers and students, religious groups and trade unions, academics, and other interested individuals. Numbering more than 500, these groups and organizations are at the very heart of the coalition's campaign and are a critical factor in its success, contributing to what probably is the coalition's greatest achievement to date: the creation of the 2000 Optional Protocol on the Involvement of Children in Armed Conflict.[35] The UN Special Representative on Children in Armed Conflict himself has stated that the United Nations "owes the success of the OP in large measure to the patient work, determination and all-out mobilization of the Coalition to Stop the Use of Child Soldiers."[36]

Thus, at the global level there now exists a substantial number of NGOs and networks working within the framework of the 1989 CRC and 1999 ILO

C182. They are focused on either the general issue of child labor or a specific aspect of the problem.

Regional, National, and Local NGOs and Networks
Equal if not more important in combating the exploitation of child labor are NGOs and networks at the regional, national, and local levels. Here we are dealing in the thousands, many of them, as we have seen, partners of organizations and networks working on the global level.

Regional. Prominently illustrative of such groups in the Asian region is Child Workers in Asia (CWA), established in 1985 as a support group for child workers.[37] From a small group of five organizations, it now brings together over sixty organizations and groups working on child labor in fourteen countries. CWA facilitates the sharing of expertise and experiences among NGOs and strengthens their capacity to respond jointly to the exploitation of working children in the region. In particular, CWA serves as a venue for the coordination, interaction, and strengthening of large and small NGOs in an effort to encourage and support the emergence of local actions for working children and for the promotion of children's rights. In recent years, CWA's network of national and local organizations has engaged in a broad range of activities: (1) providing information, support, and education to working children in different sectors; (2) caring for and educating children who are homeless, without parents, or otherwise at risk of entering exploitive employment; (3) caring for, rehabilitating, and educating children who previously have been dubiously employed; (4) facilitating community awareness and advocacy of the rights of children and the situation of children who are trafficked or who enter employment through other avenues; and (5) cooperating with governments to expand models of service and assistance available to working children through national programs.[38] If one is concerned with making a difference in the lives and futures of working children, particularly the largest segment of child workers—those who live with their own families—it is these local and national NGOs that hold out the hope of real transformation.

A second example is the African Network for the Prevention and Protection Against Child Abuse and Neglect (ANPPCAN), formed after the First African Conference on Child Abuse and Neglect, held in Enugu, Nigeria, in 1986.[39] Since then, ANPPCAN chapters have expanded to sixteen African countries. Headquartered in Nairobi, where ANPPCAN is registered as an international NGO, this regional network elevates the rights of children by enhancing the protection of children from all forms of maltreatment. Its philosophy holds that a community prepared to care for and protect its children requires a foundation of awareness. This includes both adequate knowledge of children's rights and sensitivity toward unacceptable violations. ANPPCAN therefore emphasizes research, advocacy, training, education, and participatory approaches toward child protection. And to these ends, ANPPCAN works collaboratively with its country partners to end physical and sexual abuse, economic and sexual exploitation, and other forms of abuse and exploitation such as child labor and prostitution. Further, ANPPCAN seeks to establish cooperative relationships with other organizations working in the field of children's rights, such as ASI, DCI, Global March, the International Society for the Prevention of Child Abuse and Neglect, as well as the African Union, UNICEF, and others.

National and local. A few examples must suffice to illustrate the diversity of NGOs engaged in the struggle against child labor and of their contributions at the national and local levels. In Serbia and Montenegro, the Youth Initiative's Anti-Trafficking Centre (ATC) focuses on preventing young women and girls from being lured into exploitive labor or trafficking by raising their awareness of the dangers of responding to advertisements and promises of good jobs in other cities or countries.[40] The ATC does this by going into high schools where such skills as hairdressing are taught and institutions where there is a concentration of girls at risk (e.g., orphanages, schools for disabled, girls' clubs) and talking about trafficking, its dangers, and what safety measures they can take if they are considering migrating to find work.

In Nepal, there is the Child Workers in Nepal Concerned Centre (CWIN). The first to raise the issue of child rights and child labor in Nepal, it runs a free hotline and emergency help services for child workers in Kathmandu.[41] The Nepal Trade Union Congress (NTUC) provides nonformal education programs to parents and children working in different industrial sectors.[42] The Children at Risk–Net Working Group (CAR-NWG), with twenty-five member NGOs, carries out a variety of research and action programs focusing on children's rights and conditions.[43]

Part 3 of this volume offers insight into the broad range of NGOs engaged in the children's rights movement in Tanzania, the Philippines, and Brazil, particularly in relation to child labor, and the phases through which the movement has progressed in these countries.

The Roles or Functions of NGOs in the Struggle Against Child Labor

As noted above, there are a myriad of functions that human rights NGOs perform, all of which are undertaken by NGOs working specifically in the area of child labor. In this section, I consider NGO anti–child labor activism in relation to what arguably are the most important functions that NGOs perform: agenda-setting, standard-setting, fact-finding and monitoring, and witnessing and advocacy. Then I look more specifically at a range of strategies that have been developed by NGOs to combat the exploitation of children's work.

Agenda-Setting

Among the most important results of NGO efforts has been the recognition of child labor as a problem. Getting an issue onto the legal/political agenda, whether at the global, regional, or national level, is often the first step in having it addressed. One scholar has remarked that, in the decade since the first UN special meeting on children in 1990, the global family has made real progress toward raising awareness about child labor, and about ways of tackling the problem: "Today, condemnations of child labor appear in places both obvious and obscure. 'Stop child labor' is a refrain at anti-globalization rallies around the world. Articles about child labor not only appear in mainstream news outlets but also in lighter fare, such as *Seventeen* and *People* magazines. Even Hollywood scriptwriters have gotten into the act, working the term 'child labor' into scripts for shows from 'The West Wing' to 'The Simpsons.'"[44]

NGOs have played a major role in getting the issue of child labor onto the agendas of the ILO, UNICEF, the UN Commission on Human Rights, and other global and also regional organizations. Increasingly in this area, they work in coalitions with intergovernmental organizations and governments to find solutions to a problem that has shown itself to be highly complex and multidimensional.

Above, I noted the pathbreaking work of the labor movement in first taking up the issue of child labor more than a century ago, as well as the pioneering work of Anti-Slavery International in the late 1970s and early 1980s. Similarly, ECPAT did groundbreaking work in its focus on child prostitution, child pornography, and the trafficking in children for sexual exploitation, while the Coalition to Stop the Use of Child Soldiers got many peace, religious, labor, and civic organizations to take up the tragic situation of children conscripted to kill.

In a world in which numerous concerns about order increasingly compete for public attention, however, children's rights activists have had to develop a variety of innovative techniques to win the headlines, such as the Global March Against Child Labour discussed above. The march started in Manila on January 17, 1998, gathered thousands as it traveled through fifty-six countries worldwide, and culminated in Geneva in time for the June 1988 session of the ILO's International Labour Conference (which was holding its first discussion on proposed ILO C182, on the "worst forms" of child labor). It is said to have "touched every corner of the globe, built immense awareness and led to high level participation from the masses." In the words of the organizers, it was "the largest social mobilisation in history for the benefit of children."[45] Participants in the Global March were permitted to address the ILO conference and its concerns were reflected in the draft convention. The unanimous adoption of ILO C182 the following year and the rapidity with which it has been ratified—153 of the 177 countries that are members of the ILO (86 percent) as of 2005[46]— prompt consideration of this unprecedented event as a true success.

Another technique used to good advantage has been the convening of a world conference, as with the first and second world conferences on commercial sexual exploitation of children in Stockholm (1996) and Yokahama (2001) or the Oslo International Conference on Child Labour (1997), where NGOs and governments came together to spotlight a critical issue. These meetings were organized specifically around key aspects of the problem of child labor.

NGOs also have utilized other existing international arenas to focus attention on the rights of working children, among them the UN Commission on Human Rights (UNCHR), where special rapporteurs or representatives (e.g., on the sale of children, on children in war, on violence against women) have targeted specific aspects of child labor in their annual reports to the UNCHR and the UN General Assembly; the Committee on the Rights of the Child, which reviews the periodic reports governments submit on their compliance with the 1989 CRC and which regularly receives the shadow reports of NGOs and invites NGOs to assist the committee in formulating appropriate questions to ask governments; and high-profile meetings such as the UN General Assembly Special Session on Children (May 10, 2002), which more than 1,700 NGO representatives from over eighty-eight countries attended. One should note, however, that NGO interventions are not always welcomed in such essentially statist settings and that the struggle to get items onto the agenda—and especially into negotiation sessions and policy documents—often meets resistance.[47]

Moreover, there are aspects of the child labor problem that have not yet been brought into focus. One—taken up at a panel discussion during the UN General Assembly Special Session on Children but not normally considered by child labor activists—is the issue of early or child marriage, described by one panelist as "child labor in its worst form."[48] Another is the situation of children working in agriculture in the rural sector, believed to make up the largest number of child laborers.

Standard-Setting

At the international level, NGOs have been instrumental in the drafting of much of the international law that exists to protect children from various forms of exploitation. In fact, the first piece of "international legislation" that called upon states to meet the basic needs of children was the Declaration of Geneva of the Rights of the Child adopted by the Council of the League of Nations Assembly in March 1924.[49] The declaration was essentially a restatement of the Charter for the Basic Care of Children, which originally was created by the International Union of Save the Children.[50] The 1989 CRC—considered the international legal framework for all subsequent efforts to protect children—was influenced very strongly by NGOs, whose representatives participated in the drafting process from the very beginning and at every subsequent stage of the process.[51]

Trade unions were instrumental in the adoption of early labor conventions such as 1930 ILO Convention (No. 29) Concerning Forced or Compulsory Labour (ILO C29) and 1973 ILO Convention (No. 138) Concerning Minimum Age for Admission to Employment (ILO C138).[52] As noted above, NGOs and trade unions were key players in pressing for the drafting, adoption, and ratification of ILO C182 (1999). In similar fashion, the Coalition to Stop the Use of Child Soldiers is credited with a key role in the adoption of the Optional Protocol to the Convention on the Rights of the Child on the Involvement of Children in Armed Conflict.[53] The coalition also successfully lobbied to get child soldiering included as one of the "worst forms" of child labor in ILO C182 and, as well, to get the new International Criminal Court to treat the use of child soldiers under age fifteen as a "war crime."[54]

At the national level, a great deal of energy often is directed by NGOs toward legislative reform—to provide a legal framework for regulating against the exploitation of child labor, and particularly to bring national legislation into line with international standards. Indeed, most countries now have adopted legislation specifying the minimum age of entry to employment, prohibiting child employment in certain occupations or activities, regulating such work where it is legally permitted, and making primary education compulsory.[55]

But enacting good law is only part of the problem. As the final report of the International Conference on Child Labour in Oslo stated: "Good and comprehensive legislation only has meaning when effectively enforced and implemented. Lack of enforcement is the biggest problem in many of our countries."[56] Madiha Murshed points out that "the passing of national laws has not resulted in an eradication of child labor" and that there is no clear correlation between laws making education compulsory and laws regulating the minimum age for work and the incidence of child labor, because the enforcement of the laws is grossly inadequate in many countries.[57] Law on the books is not necessarily law in fact. Murshed cites a 1997 ILO report, *Legislation and Enforcement,* that points to the weaknesses of labor inspectorates in developing countries: "understaffed and overburdened with many functions beyond child labor law enforcement."[58] It points out that many countries do not have inspectors trained in detecting child labor; that inspectors lack transportation to take them to establishments outside the major cities; that rural areas, which inspectors visit the least, have the largest number of working children and the greatest child exploitation; and that many workplaces (such as domestic homes and unregistered establishments that employ children) are inaccessible. Moreover, working children at high risk "are often not readily visible." Children working in rural areas, in the informal sector, and in domestic service "are out of the public eye"; they attract no public attention and therefore remain uninspected by the authorities.[59]

Fact-Finding and Monitoring

It is precisely because there is inadequate enforcement of legislation and because the rule of law is often more an ideal than a reality that fact-finding and monitoring are at the heart of human rights work. Active, free, and responsible media are often also key to exposing violations, but it is human rights organizations that continue to do the main systematic monitoring in most countries.[60] While information ("the facts") alone does not ordinarily produce change in behavior or policy, knowledge is a precondition for any effective action in rights protection.

In the area of child labor, systematic research and analysis have also been fundamental to understanding the nature and complexity of the issues. In this regard, NGOs have been strongly assisted by UNICEF, particularly the work of its Innocenti Research Centre in Florence, and by the ILO, particularly its International Programme for the Elimination of Child Labour (IPEC),[61] and NGOs and intergovernmental organizations (IGOs) alike have benefited from academic research.[62] Nonetheless, it remains true that international mechanisms such as the UN Special Rapporteur on the Sale of Children, Child Prostitution, and Child Pornography[63] and the Committee on the Rights of the Child (to which governments report on their compliance with the Convention on the Rights of the Child) depend heavily upon information and analysis provided by NGOs. Regarding the work of the Committee on the Rights of the Child, the director of UNICEF's Division for Evaluation, Policy, and Planning concluded that the participation of NGOs "has shown to be of a decisive relevance, in particular, in the light of their organization as an NGO Group" on the implementation of the convention.[64] Awa N'Dye Ouedraogo, one of the committee's experts, has noted that, for 90 percent of the state reports submitted, NGOs have provided alternative or "shadow" reports.[65]

While there are numerous examples of important monitoring and analysis being done by NGOs in the area of child labor, two should suffice to illustrate the point. First is the work done by ECPAT International in preparing for the Second World Congress Against Commercial Sexual Exploitation of Children in Yokohama, Japan, in December 2001. As cosponsor of the congress, ECPAT International commissioned a number of working papers, among them background studies on progress and problems in the implementation of programs to counter the sexual abuse and exploitation of children;[66] on the role and involvement of the private sector;[67] on the impact of international law in eliminating commercial sexual exploitation of children (CSEC);[68] and a comprehensive report evaluating the global campaign against child sex tourism.[69] Also prepared were reports from regional consultations for Africa and the Middle East; Asia and the Pacific; Latin America and the

Caribbean; North America; South Asia; and Western Europe, Eastern Europe, and Central Asia.[70] What is particularly interesting about this research is its attempt to evaluate the effectiveness of its own strategies and of the movement.

A second example is provided by the Coalition to Stop the Use of Child Soldiers, which in May 2001 published the first-ever global report on the subject, detailing military recruitment laws, practice, and (where appropriate) the use of child soldiers in conflict by both governments and nonstate actors in more than 180 countries, as well as information on the demobilization and reintegration of child soldiers. Of note here is the methodology that permits groups at the local and national levels to feed their information into an international study. (The coalition currently has networks in over forty countries with regional coordination on five continents.) The website of the coalition contains a research guide for the 2004 global report on child soldiers, with detailed instructions to NGOs or national coalitions that wish to contribute, whether by helping to gather information from existing sources, by conducting additional primary research, or by writing a full country entry. The coalition secretariat provides overall coordination for the global report project, including the final editing process to ensure a consistent style, content, and format among the report chapters.[71]

Witnessing and Advocacy

If fact-finding has been at the heart of human rights work, advocacy has been its driving force, its soul. The "name-shame-blame" strategy certainly has played a role in exposing and attempting to correct the most egregious forms of child labor. It has been used effectively to spotlight specific sweatshop conditions in which children have worked, in both the Global South and the Global North, and to target multinational corporations that have used child labor either directly in their own plants or indirectly through the subsidiary firms they contract out to. Earlier I cited reports issued by NGOs that focused on the exploitation of child workers in making knotted carpets, silks, or bricks, and there have been similar reports of children exploited for prostitution or pornography, of children mutilated and sold for begging or thieving, and of the brutalization of child soldiers.

Advocacy, however, is more than the publication of a report. It is, in many respects, the main NGO strategy for effecting change. It involves communicating with, lobbying, and influencing those who make and implement policy, and at all levels: mayors, parliamentarians, ministers or ministry staff, ambassadors, international civil servants, and so forth. Typically what is needed is the ability to change the views of those with the power to make a difference.

Advocacy often involves mobilizing others, whether the masses or members of the elite: workers (including child workers), trade unions, business executives, rotary associations, church constituencies, students, academics, other

NGOs—anyone who can pressure for change. Sometimes, too, "quiet diplomacy" is what is required to get the votes needed. More often than not, however, it is publicity or the fear of publicity that induces change. Thus, advocacy generally involves knowing how to use the media effectively—television, radio broadcasting, the print media—to focus attention on the demand for change, and persuasively getting across the message as to why others should support the measures being proposed. Today, this is likely to involve creating a website and developing and utilizing electronic mailing lists (listserves). In campaigning on behalf of the rights of children, NGOs often have been successful in attracting the support of stars and other celebrities (from the entertainment and sports worlds especially), whether for a concert, a protest demonstration, or a march.

Of course, advocacy does not need to have only an adversarial dimension; it can take on an educative role as well. In 2002, Anti-Slavery International published an advocacy handbook,[72] which in its preface drew attention to the fact that children working as domestics in the households of people other than their parents or close family members constitute a high proportion of child workers worldwide. It noted that, for girls, domestic work is by far the most common form of employment, paid or not, and that many of the practical characteristics of child domestic labor have features akin to slavery. This handbook followed up on an earlier ASI handbook[73] and represented a move forward from the stage of proposing and supporting research to the stage of promoting effective advocacy, based on newly generated information. This groundbreaking work on the part of ASI was undoubtedly one of the factors that led UNICEF to undertake its own research on the issue[74] and to conclude that "child domestic work is probably the most widespread, and at the same time the most neglected, form of child employment."[75]

In considering advocacy work, it is useful to note that, increasingly, advocacy against child labor is being developed as transborder campaigns rather than as strictly national or local ones. As discussed above, the battles to combat both the commercial sexual exploitation of children and child soldiering have given rise to international coalitions and regional networks and forums, where issues are discussed and different organizations and sectors dialogue to reach common understandings. This is not always easy. During the UN Special Session on Children in 2000, where approximately 125 organizations and caucuses contributed to the Child Rights Caucus (created to produce NGO recommendations for the text of the special session document), fierce battles ensued. Nonetheless, it is clear that unless NGOs are able to aggregate their diverse positions and articulate common positions, their efforts will be dissipated. In this regard, one should examine carefully the results of the youth-convened Children's World Congress on Child Labour, which took place in Florence, Italy, on May 10–13, 2004, to develop a platform for "worldwide youth-driven action to press international and national efforts toward integrating world resources and responses on poverty, child labor, and education."[76]

▓ Strategies and Tactics Specifically Designed to Combat Child Labor

In the work of the NGOs that are combating various forms of child labor, a number of specific campaign strategies present themselves. The first three described here—social labeling, codes of conduct, and boycotts—are related in that they target private sector manufacturers. Also, largely for this reason, they have generated controversy over their effectiveness and desirability.

Social Labeling

"The RUGMARK label is your best assurance that no illegal child labor was employed in the manufacture of a carpet or rug," states the website of RUGMARK, "a global nonprofit organization working to end child labor and offer educational opportunities for children in India, Nepal and Pakistan."[77] Its methodology seems straightforward. Carpet manufacturers who agree to adhere to RUGMARK's standard earn the RUGMARK label, which certifies that the rug has been made without the use of child labor.

Through regular and surprise inspections of carpet factories, each individual loom is checked for underage workers. If inspectors find child laborers who want to attend the RUGMARK school, the parents are asked for their permission and the job is offered to an adult family member. At factories licensed by RUGMARK, employees are paid at least minimum wage (locally defined). A portion of the companies' profits goes directly into rehabilitation programs for displaced child workers, which provide education and vocational training.

The RUGMARK concept actually was created by Indian child labor activists in the face of the failure of the Indian government to enforce its own laws banning children from working in the carpet industry (e.g., the Employment of Children Act of 1938).[78] The initiative began in the 1980s, when European media exposure of the abuse of child labor in the carpet industry in India led to calls for a consumer boycott. According to the International Labor Rights Fund (ILRF):

> Sensing the potential for disaster if a boycott were successful, and the even worse disaster for children if child labor continued to grow as a factor of production, far-sighted children's advocates teamed up with some carpet industry leaders to try to stem the use of child labor by a positive marketing scheme whereby consumers could be assured they were not investing in the blood and toil of children.[79]

Nonetheless, it took eleven years, until December 20, 1994, before the first licenses by exporters were accepted, and until March 1995 before the first carpets received their labels. By July 1996, however, more than 260,000 carpets had been individually labeled and exported,[80] and shortly thereafter the campaign spread to Nepal.

The RUGMARK strategy—giving a product a "good housekeeping seal" or stamp of approval—has both its advocates and its critics. The former promote the notion of ethical consumerism. The strategy is rooted in the belief that a substantial number of Western consumers—supported by churches, trade unions, and human rights groups—are prepared to pay more for a product in order to sleep with a better conscience.[81] Others argue, however, that there are many limitations to the RUGMARK strategy, and there has been quite sharp criticism from certain quarters.[82] In 1996, therefore, just a year after the RUGMARK initiative was actually launched in India, the ILRF was asked by the Child Labor Coalition in the United States to look into the complaints. On the basis of an investigation in India in April and May 1996, it examined several substantive criticisms, of which three merit mention.

The first arises from the geographic nature of India's carpet industry, with loomsheds comprising one to twenty looms each and scattered in villages across a 100,000-square-mile area, involving perhaps 90,000 looms and thus making monitoring of the industry extremely difficult if not impossible. RUGMARK, acknowledging the problem, makes no claims of being able to monitor the entire industry, but instead monitors only those firms, loomsheds, and exporters that voluntarily enter the program and submit to RUGMARK inspection. A year after the program was launched, it had as many as 13,000 looms under inspection.

A second and related criticism was whether the guarantee of "no child labor" was credible. The ILRF found that it was. "[I]nasmuch as a tight and effective system to prevent and punish non-compliance is in place, and after the labeling of more than 260,000 carpets," it concluded, "no case of mislabeling has been discovered or even charged."[83]

The third issue of concern was that, without accompanying rehabilitation and education programs for child laborers, the program would not work. This was a fact acknowledged by RUGMARK and to which it has responded by ensuring that children liberated from working at the looms are given the opportunity to attend school.[84]

Most interesting is the broader question the ILRF then posed and answered in the following terms:

> [T]he question of children released from the carpet looms is much larger than just the numbers found directly by RUGMARK inspectors. There are reportedly hundreds of thousands of children making carpets, according to the most reliable estimate. What we wanted to know has been the impact of

the RUGMARK program on this greater population of carpet children. Perhaps the most encouraging aspect of all our findings was to learn that during the past year, thousands of children have begun an exodus from the carpet belt in such numbers that the Bihar government has been led to establish forty new schools in one of the four districts in that state most responsible for sending children . . . to work the looms.[85]

The ILRF concluded: "The publicity given to child labor, plus the pressure of the RUGMARK program, have clearly had an impact. How large is impossible for us to estimate, but by all accounts from activists working in the region, it is significant."[86]

The idea of certifying a product as free of child labor has been taken up also in the sporting goods industry. One oft-cited success story concerns the pressure brought to bear on the Fédération Internationale de Football Association (FIFA; the International World Soccer Federation) when the Global March Against Child Labour launched its World Cup Campaign 2002.[87] FIFA was accused of ignoring children exploited by manufacturers of soccer balls in such countries as Pakistan, India, and China. These violations were reported in a document prepared by the India Committee of the Netherlands: *The Dark Side of Football: Child and Adult Labor in India's Football Industry and the Role of FIFA*.[88] As well, the movement was able to get thirty-three US senators to write letters to FIFA asking it to certify that the soccer balls used in competition were made without child labor, and high school students began to weigh in as well.[89] With the mobilization of such pressure, the international labor movement was able to negotiate an agreement whereby FIFA promised that it would no longer put its industry seal on soccer balls made by children. Adidas, Nike, Reebok, and other soccer ball manufacturers had to fall into line. Then, to put a positive spin on what had threatened to be a highly negative situation, FIFA, in partnership with UNICEF, launched a campaign to promote the rights of children. The World Cup Campaign 2002 used that occasion to urge FIFA to adopt transparent monitoring mechanisms to end child labor in the sporting goods industry.[90]

Codes of Conduct for Businesses

"Good housekeeping seal of approval" labeling often is closely related to "codes of conduct," a strategy that has been promoted by some child labor rights NGOs and taken up on a voluntary basis, with greater or lesser eagerness, by corporations in the private sector.[91] The concept of a voluntary code of conduct for business was popularized in the international arena by Reverend Leon Howard Sullivan, a pastor of the Zion Baptist Church in Philadelphia, who in 1977 developed the "Sullivan Principles" as a code of conduct for human rights and equal opportunity for companies operating in South Africa.[92] This voluntary code of conduct is credited by some as having effectively contributed to the dismantling of the South African apartheid regime, though others are skeptical about its impact. In the struggle to combat child labor via codes of conduct, a similar ambivalence exists.[93]

It is perhaps important to examine the issue of "codes of conduct" within the context of the broader Global Compact that UN Secretary-General Kofi Annan launched at the 1999 annual meeting of the World Economic Forum, calling upon individual corporations and representatives of business associations to support nine principles concerning human rights, labor, and the environment.[94] Principle 1 states that businesses "should support and respect the protection of international human rights within their sphere of influence"; Principle 2, that they "make sure their own corporations are not complicit in human rights abuses"; and Principle 5, that they should uphold "the effective abolition of child labour."

A recent study by the UN Office of the High Commissioner for Human Rights (OHCHR) found a proliferation of corporate codes of conduct aiming to protect the human and labor rights of workers employed by companies and their business partners and including human rights (as defined in the Universal Declaration of Human Rights)[95] among their global business principles.[96] Many of these codes are currently on the Web,[97] and a cursory review shows that a number now devote considerable attention to human rights and child labor.

Among the more conspicuously dedicated companies is Reebok International, which has made a public commitment to international human rights (especially of young people) through its annual Reebok Human Rights Awards, its cooperation with AI, and its grants for human rights work.[98] Reebok's code of conduct ("Reebok Human Rights Production Standards") begins as follows:

> The Reebok Human Rights Production Standards reflect the relevant covenants of the International Labor Organization, input from human rights organizations and academia, and our own experience. In developing this policy, we sought to use standards that are fair, appropriate to diverse cultures and that encourage workers to take pride in their work.[99]

The Reebok guide to the implementation of the code adds: "It is our experience that implementing these standards improves worker morale and results in a higher quality work environment and higher quality products."[100] And giving strength to these lofty introductory statements are code standards on nondiscrimination, working hours and overtime, forced or compulsory labor, fair wages and benefits, freedom of association, and a safe and healthy work environment. Specifically on the issue of child labor, the code says that "Reebok will not work with business partners that use child labor," defining the term "child" to mean "a person who is younger than 15 or younger than the age for completing compulsory education in the country of manufacture, whichever is higher."[101]

Nike's code of conduct, updated in January 2004, states:

> Nike partners with contractors who share our commitment to best practices and continuous improvement in: (1) management practices that respect the rights of all employees, including the right to free association and collective bargaining; (2) minimizing our impact on the environment; (3) providing a safe and healthy work place; (4) promoting the health and well-being of all employees.[102]

The Nike code also has clauses on forced labor; compensation; benefits; hours of work and overtime; environment, safety, and health; and documentation and inspection. On child labor, it says:

> The contractor does not employ any person below the age of 18 to produce footwear. The contractor does not employ any person below the age of 16 to produce apparel, accessories or equipment. If at the time Nike production begins, the contractor employs people of the legal working age who are at least 15, that employment may continue, but the contractor will not hire any person going forward who is younger than the Nike or legal age limit, whichever is higher. To further ensure these age standards are complied with, the contractor does not use any form of home work for Nike production.[103]

Other codes posted on the Web include that of the Body Shop, a natural cosmetics firm, which states emphatically that "[t]he Company does not engage in or support exploitive child labour."[104] The codes of conduct of Wal-Mart, The Gap, and Levi Strauss also ban child labor, but set the age at under fourteen.[105]

Meanwhile, during the July–August 2000 fifty-second session of the UN Sub-Commission on the Promotion and Protection of Human Rights, a draft human rights code of conduct for companies was considered.[106] Its Section E addresses slavery, forced labor, and child labor, reproducing the text of articles of international conventions, principles, guidelines, and codes of corporate conduct relevant to the prohibition on companies that use slave, forced, or compulsory labor; that allow any person under the age of eighteen to work under conditions that have been identified by ILO C182 as the worst forms of child labor; and that use child labor.

Mark Hecht, while evaluating codes of conduct in the context of the struggle against the commercial sexual exploitation of children, points out both their strengths and their weaknesses. On the plus side, "codes of conduct can build protective frameworks from the ground up. They can be used to identify holes in legislation, filling them with private obligations."[107] They can also help educate relevant parties about the underlying issues of commercial sexual exploitation of children, detrimental impacts of their actions, and their potential to participate in the elimination of CSEC.[108] On the minus side:

- codes of conduct are invariably voluntary and non-binding; they are "soft laws" which have no legislative force;
- codes of conduct are often under-inclusive and self-serving; private sector industries resist adhering to externally drawn codes—such as those drafted by NGOs—preferring to establish their own guidelines;
- compliance with such codes is often internally monitored, preventing public scrutiny of non-compliance;
- codes of conduct are often not widely distributed, particularly to employees, which supports the view that the codes are designed for the benefit of the market audience rather than for individuals who are ostensibly to be protected by the codes;
- these codes are often not obeyed—a study found that 80 percent of factories claiming to abide by US codes of conduct were in clear violation of these codes;
- finally, and perhaps most detrimentally, codes of conduct could serve as a disincentive for countries to strengthen their own laws. Southern NGOs have expressed a fear about the deleterious effects of child labor codes by industries working in their countries, explaining that such codes could serve to undermine the regulatory role of the state. The NGOs are concerned that actions of the private sector, in adopting such codes, may be an attempt to replace legislation, to privatize law enforcement and thus to evade standards. Furthermore, such codes could allow industries to justify working in countries with repressive regimes.[109]

It should be noted, however, that these weaknesses seem to be less about the use of codes of conduct in general than about codes designed and monitored by the companies they are supposed to regulate. And if one is to take what some companies say at face value, it may be that they are taking their social corporate responsibilities seriously.

Nike, for example, now issues an annual report on corporate responsibility, and the first one it issued, in October 2001, stated that Nike submits to "external independent monitoring."[110] "[W]e're committed to independent monitoring conducted by Fair Labor Association (FLA) approved monitoring organizations," said Maria Eitel, vice president and senior adviser for corporate responsibility. Other companies have begun to conduct systematic measures of their performance on human rights issues also, a development that, according to the OHCHR, must be seen as "part of a larger trend towards greater transparency on all aspects of corporate social responsibility."[111] This is a quite positive assessment. The OHCHR's 2000 report on business and human rights drew attention to "significant progress" in the past five years "as companies have worked to ensure that core labor standards are respected throughout their supply chains."[112] Stressing substantial progress in the development of innovative implementation efforts, it noted: "Once considered inappropriate by the private sector, independent monitoring of labor standards is fast becoming one of the primary measures of a company's efforts to ensure fair working conditions in its supply chain."[113] The OHCHR singled out several mixed partnerships of companies, NGOs, foundations, trade unions, and youth groups—for example, the US-based Global Alliance for Workers (GAW)[114] and Fair Labor Association (FLA),[115] and the UK-based Ethical Trading Initiative (ETI)[116]— created to promote, monitor, and improve (via codes of conduct and other devices) global supply-chain working conditions equal to or exceeding international core labor standards, including the prohibition on child labor. Additionally, the OHCHR report noted a host of independent verification projects involving toys, apparel, agriculture, and other products that have been launched in Africa, Asia, and Latin America, as well as efforts to ensure compliance with core labor standards not only from the multinational partner but also from the local supplier.

Two further remedies have been suggested relative to monitoring corporate practices. The first is that NGOs and working youth themselves participate both in the writing and in the monitoring of the codes of conduct. This would ensure more comprehensive codes that address the real needs of child workers and that also are objectively and impartially monitored. Second, one should promote industry-specific multistakeholder codes, rather than codes elaborated for and by individual corporations. Multistakeholder codes—so called because they are developed and promoted by governments, NGOs, and labor unions together with corporations—tend to mirror closely the provisions of international legal instruments[117] rather than being ad hoc (as evidenced in the provisions of the codes mentioned above). Further, they are more likely to address successfully the issue of independent monitoring and to impose penalties for noncompliance.[118]

Boycotts, Threats of Boycotts, and Trade Sanctions

Boycotts—which are closely associated with both labeling and codes of conduct—constitute another strategy that has been used by NGOs to pressure a corporation, an industry, or a government to change its behavior relative to the use of child labor. It is, in a sense, the penalty for noncompliance that the NGO community can impose on businesses that fail to cooperate or to live up to their commitments. Additionally, it is inherent in the movement for "socially responsible investment," which maintains a blacklist of companies that violate human rights, labor rights, and environmental standards. The Interfaith Center for Corporate Responsibility (ICCR), a coalition of religious investors that assists shareholders in advancing resolutions concerning global labor issues, has developed a set of principles for global corporate responsibility, recommending standards on human rights, labor rights, the environment, and sustainable community development.[119] One principle calls on companies to withdraw from a country "when there is a movement from within the country calling for withdrawal, in instances where there are gross and systematic violations of human rights."[120]

Boycotts may be of two sorts. One is the boycott that is declared by civil society and seeks to get the consumer to refuse to buy certain products for moral reasons. The second—and far more controversial—is the boycott that is declared by governments or even by intergovernmental organizations, more appropriately called a state sanction or embargo. This second category is beyond the scope of this chapter, however, and is therefore not addressed here.[121]

The boycott strategy was perhaps first effectively used for human rights purposes by Chicano activists in the United States in the late 1960s and early 1970s, when Cesar Chavez and Dolores Huerta were able to achieve a widespread boycott of California grape growers and wineries that were violating the rights of migrant workers. The socially conscious, both in the United States and abroad, refused to drink California wine in order to pressure for the legislation and enforcement of better and safer working conditions for the migrant workers. Indeed, for three decades, Cesar Chavez—a strong believer in the principles of nonviolent resistance practiced by Mahatma Gandhi and Martin Luther King Jr.—used boycotts as well as fasts, strikes, and pilgrimages to lead the fight for the rights of farmworkers to dignity, respect, fair wages, medical pensions, and humane living conditions. Against previously insurmountable odds, he led successful strikes and boycotts that resulted in the first industrywide labor contracts in the history of US agriculture and the establishment of the United Farm Workers of America.[122]

The boycott strategy was used also against the Nestlé Corporation from 1974 until 1984 for its refusal to support the breastfeeding policies of the World Health Organization (WHO) and its insistence on promoting baby formula in the third world despite prevalent unsanitary conditions in its use. Indeed, because of Nestlé's alleged continued defiance of WHO codes on advertising and promoting baby milk substitutes and supplements, the boycott was reinstituted in 1988 and is currently in effect.[123]

With increasing globalization, the strategy of boycott and trade sanctions has been recommended and actively pursued by some NGOs against corporations implicated in the exploitation of child labor: they believe that such a strategy can work because national actors have become increasingly vulnerable to external pressure from international movements, and because consumers in the Global North have evidenced a greater willingness to hold companies responsible for the conditions under which their products are produced.[124] Yet there have been serious reservations about boycotts in the movement to end child labor.

First, boycotts—at least those orchestrated at an international level—have been directed largely at corporations in the export sector. As the percentage of children actually employed by the export sector is small, this means that a lot of energy would be directed at a small part of the child labor problem.[125] This view is challenged, however, by Björne Grimsrud and Tim Noonan.[126] While they agree that production of internationally traded goods and services may only account for a small percentage of child labor worldwide, "export clusters and sectors in developing and transition countries are critically important to national development." Thus, along with ending the use of child labor in these sectors of the economy, "decent wages and conditions for the adult workers in export industries provide the basis for more widespread improvements and help guarantee that the children of these workers will complete their schooling."[127] A similar view is presented by Anjli Garg, who argues that, because the United States imports such a large proportion of the goods manufactured in the developing world for export to developed countries, the threat of denying a large and profitable market to child labor employers can encourage such companies to reevaluate their child labor practices.[128]

Others have reached a different conclusion. The UK Department for International Development (DFID), in a 1999 paper titled *Helping, Not Hurting Children,* reviews Western-driven consumer initiatives in South Asia and questions whether the consumer boycotts have been effective in tackling the issue. The DFID found that "the impact on children actually can be negative."[129] Sarah Bachman has reached a similar conclusion:

> Campaigns to ban the imports of child-made products don't always produce the effects activists intend. In 1992, under pressure from U.S. activists and politicians, Bangladeshi garment factories (which send 60 percent of their exports to the U.S.) fired about 50,000 of their child workers. UNICEF researchers found the children in other—often more dangerous—jobs, including prostitution.[130]

Journalist John Stackhouse of the Toronto *Globe and Mail* similarly reported: "[I]t was not the end of child labour, as most of the children simply fell deeper into the quagmire of despair, finding new work as stone crushers and prostitutes for less money than they earned in the relatively comfortable garment factories."[131]

The lesson to be learned from this experience is that campaigns to ban child labor must be linked to follow-up programs, particularly support for education for children and better wages for adults. The Canadian Labour Congress has adopted such a conditional approach, stating that it supports company boycotts only where the affected child laborers and adult workers have endorsed them. As two analysts have observed:

> Unlike their U.S. counterparts, Canadian unions have tended not to advocate a blanket import ban or consumer boycott of all goods produced by child labour. The Canadian Labour Congress (CLC) has taken a more nuanced ap-

proach, advocating that trade policy be linked to human and labour rights, supporting Fair Trade and child-labour-free labels and projects to rehabilitate child labourers, and "calling on the World Bank and the International Monetary Fund to forgive the debt of poorer countries and stop demanding structural adjustment programs that create poverty and deny educational opportunities."[132]

Supporting the Committee on the Rights of the Child in Monitoring the CRC

As noted above, NGOs played a significant role in drafting the 1989 CRC. As Geraldine Van Bueren notes in her review of the history of the CRC,[133] on some occasions the texts provided by NGOs were adopted as the basic working texts, and the contributions of the NGOs were acknowledged by the chair and by the state members of the working group. "The success of their work," says Van Bueren, "demonstrates that the formation of international law need not be a remote and closed process."[134] One of the results of the efforts of NGOs is that the convention includes a significant role for "other competent bodies"—apart from governmental and intergovernmental agencies—in monitoring its implementation in their countries.[135] This has meant that the Committee on the Rights of the Child can invite NGOs "to provide expert advice on the implementation of the Convention in areas falling within the scope of their respective mandates."[136]

As the committee has developed its working methods, it has not only proved willing to accept alternative or "shadow" reports prepared by NGOs but also actively encouraged NGOs to prepare such reports on progress being made (or lack thereof) in the countries under review. With assistance from the NGO Group for the Convention on the Rights of the Child,[137] many national coalitions have been established to draft such reports and to help the committee frame the questions that it directs toward a government. These can, and often do, include questions on the measures (legislative, administrative, social, and educational) being taken by a government to implement, per CRC Article 32, "the right of the child to be protected from economic exploitation and from performing any work that is likely to be hazardous or to interfere with the child's education, or to be harmful to the child's health or physical, mental, spiritual, moral or social development." Article 32 specifically asks states parties to provide a minimum age or minimum ages for admission to employment, appropriate regulations of the hours and conditions of employment, and appropriate penalties or other sanctions to ensure effective enforcement. As well, Article 34 provides the obligation of states "to protect the child from all forms of sexual exploitation and sexual abuse." These issues are matters of right, not charity, and NGOs are central to their clarification and enforcement.

Extraterritorial Legislation

Extraterritorial legislation on the part of wealthy nations in relation to their nationals who, attracted by sex tourism programs, travel to developing countries to exploit vulnerable women and children sexually is another strategy to which NGOs have given high priority. Without such legislation, exploiters generally are able to avoid prosecution, as they are beyond the jurisdiction of their home country and are easily able to evade prosecution in the country visited. Extraterritorial legislation enables a country to prosecute its citizens for crimes committed anywhere in the world. According to ECPAT International, there are about thirty-three countries that now have such extraterritorial legislation for the sexual exploitation of children.[138]

Extraterritorial legislation is not a new concept. It has been used for some years to fight drug trafficking, as well as to prosecute those who have committed war crimes. However, it was first introduced in the area of child protection only in 1992, at ECPAT International's first international meeting. At the First World Congress Against the Commercial Sexual Exploitation of Children, in Stockholm in 1996, the idea gained momentum with the vocal support of the International Criminal Police Organization (INTERPOL) and the European Police Organization (EUROPOL). Soon after, ECPAT International commissioned the ECPAT Europe Law Enforcement Group to prepare a report that reviewed successful prosecutions and best practices using extraterritorial legislation.[139] This was followed in 2000 by a sociolegal analysis, undertaken by Human Rights Internet (HRI), of jurisprudence on the commercial sexual exploitation of women and children.[140] Both reports highlighted the need for greater cooperation between the children's rights NGO community and law enforcement. The HRI report concludes as follows:

> The results of this report suggest that CSEC is a widespread and devastating international tragedy. . . . However, measures to eliminate CSEC, both at domestic and international levels, are growing. The legal framework is largely in place. . . . NGOs play a key role in promoting and evaluating these legal tools. As information-sharing continues and alliances of groups working to protect women and children expand, the ultimate elimination of CSEC is closer to becoming a reality.[141]

▪ Conclusion

Civil society has mobilized to combat child labor, particularly its worst forms, to an impressive degree in recent years, and increasingly, it seems, from a human rights perspective. In this struggle, new organizations have been created, coalitions have been forged, world conferences have been held, national legislation has been enacted, international agreements have been adopted, codes of conduct have been crafted, reports have been written, marches have been launched, violations have been denounced, and new strategies have been developed—all with NGOs centrally involved. Indeed, it has been said that most of the major innovations in combating child labor in the past twenty years have come from NGOs.[142] The proverbial bottom line remains, however: Has it made a difference? Has it altered the situation of children for the better?

To answer these questions, impact or outcome evaluations are needed. However, evaluating the effectiveness of NGOs in the human rights field is never easy because rarely if ever are NGOs the only actors in the field, and where change does occur it is hard to conclude with any degree of certainty that the outcome was the result of the NGO work.[143] There are yet other difficulties, however, when trying to evaluate whether NGO work is having a positive impact on the lives of child workers. Chief among them, as David Smolin observes, is the problem of the lack of clear definitions and of statistical data. The "explosion of world-wide interest in the child labor issue, particularly in the decade of the 1990s," he writes, "has occurred to a large degree without careful analysis of the underlying phenomena involved."[144] Smolin continues:

> The question of definition is critical not only for defining the activity forbidden by child labor convention, but also for gathering statistical information on child labor. This gathering of statistical information is, of course, fundamental to attempts to enforce international, national, and local child labor standards, and for monitoring the effects of programs to combat child labor. The ambiguities of the definition of "child labor" particularly haunt these statistical efforts.[145]

What this means is that baseline data against which to measure progress are particularly unreliable. Smolin points out that "the number of child laborers in India can, by varying methods, be determined to be somewhere between 11.3 and 105 million children."[146]

With respect to specific aspects of the child labor problematique—for example, the trafficking of children for sexual exploitation—there are also data problems. As Jane Warburton observed in her analysis for the Second World Congress Against the Sexual Exploitation of Children:

> Data on incidence of abuse is . . . beset with problems. Lack of consistency and clarity in the use of language and absence of precise definitions means that much of the data generated from research is not comparable, geographically or over time. . . . To ensure that children benefit from the protection international conventions have been designed to give, practical indicators are needed, based on reliable statistical data relevant to regional, national and local situations.[147]

Moreover, Warburton found that "information about outcomes of projects, measured in terms of preventing the sexual abuse of children and young people, protecting them, or aiding their recovery and reintegration, is particularly scarce."[148]

The type of "evaluations" one gets is illustrated by the website of the Coalition to Stop the Use of Child Soldiers,[149] which records among its achievements: "In just a few years the Coalition has generated considerable momentum towards its goals. It is credited internationally with having played an instrumental role in the adoption of the new Optional Protocol to the Convention on the Rights of the Child on the involvement of children in armed conflicts, in May 2000." Other achievements of the coalition at the global level include, inter alia (paraphrasing from the coalition's website):

- Mobilizing public pressure and political will to end the use of child soldiers and establish eighteen as the minimum age for all forms of military recruitment and participation in armed conflict.
- Organizing five regional conferences that produced strong political declarations, ongoing NGO networks, and practical recommendations for action.
- Publishing the first-ever report on child soldiers (May 2001).
- Publishing the "1379 Report" on child soldiers (November 2002).[150]
- Publishing advocacy documents, creating a website, and disseminating information to the media.

What we do not see here is whether this has led—or is leading—to a reduction in the number of child soldiers worldwide. That the impact of these activities will lead to this result is taken as a given, but nowhere demonstrated. To be fair, one can argue that not enough time has as yet elapsed to see this type of outcome. But there is always this act of faith in human rights advocacy, risky as it is.

I have noted in this chapter the three categories of child labor differentiated by Grimsrud: (1) those who work in their own households (the most common situation and incorporating much of the rural sector); (2) those who live with their families but work for an outside employer; and (3) those who have moved away or been taken away from their parental household (numerically the smallest category, but it includes the worst forms of child labor). This review of NGO activities confirms the observations made by a number of analysts that the movement against child labor has largely addressed the third category (worst forms) and the second category (particularly as this touches on products for export), but has largely ignored the first category.

This is understandable. The most visible and egregious violations—sexual exploitation, child soldiering, bonded child labor, sweatshop exploitation—are bound to attract the greatest attention. Moreover, in a world in which one catastrophe or tragedy competes with another for headline news, one can understand why these situations—as against the nonnewsworthiness of chronic poverty—appeal to both donors and NGOs. Yet if—as much evidence suggests—there is an inextricable link between poverty and lack of education, on the one hand, and abusive and exploitive child work, on the other, then one must ask what the movement to combat child labor actually will be able to achieve. Jay Mazur, analyzing the impact of globalization with reference to the United Nations Development Programme's 2000 *Human Development Report,* points in particular to the widening gap between rich and poor: "A world in which the assets of the 200 richest people are greater than the combined income of the more than 2 billion people at the other end of the economic ladder should give everyone pause."[151]

> Millions of workers are losing out in a global economy that disrupts economies and weakens the ability of governments to assist them. They are left to fend for themselves in failed states against destitution, famine and plagues. They are forced to migrate, offer their labor at wages below subsistence, sacrifice their children, and cash in their natural environments and often their personal health—all in a desperate struggle to survive.[152]

The 2002 *Human Development Report* also presents a sobering picture regarding the intractability of income poverty:

> To halve the share of people living on $1 a day, optimistic estimates suggest that 3.7% annual growth in per capita incomes is needed in developing countries. But over the past 10 years only 24 countries have grown this fast. Among them are China and India, the most populous developing countries. But 127 countries, with 34% of the world's people, have not grown at this rate. Indeed, many have suffered negative growth in recent years, and the share of their people in poverty has almost certainly increased.[153]

What all this suggests, of course, is that, while it is good to be developing international and national standards, laws, and programs to combat child labor (particularly its worst forms), until and unless one comes to moral and political grips with the reality of poverty and with the divide between the rich and the poor, the struggle against child labor will be a chimera.

From this perspective, the struggle against child labor must take place in arenas such as the World Trade Organization, where inadequate rules controlling world trade allow worker exploitation such as child labor.[154] One must confront the global economic deregulation that permits unscrupulous companies to increase their market share and profits by lowering labor costs through overworking, underpaying, and exploiting child and other workers. One must fight to defend trade unions, because where trade unions exist child labor does not; where trade unions are banned, there is no one to protect the rights of workers, either young or old.

From this perspective, too, the struggle against child labor must be a struggle also against governments in developing countries that spend grossly disproportionately on the military rather than primary education, against inadequate government legislation and corrupt officials who benefit from child labor. Evidence suggests that where there is a lack of affordable, accessible, and meaningful education, child labor is more common. This implies the need to monitor poverty reduction strategy programs—which all governments wanting concessional funding from the World Bank are now required to adopt—to ensure that education for all children is prioritized and that the minimal economic and social needs of the most vulnerable are addressed. One must, in other words, take a holistic approach to child labor and not see it as a discrete problem that can be tackled without reference to the broader socioeconomic setting in which it is rooted.

▨ Notes

I acknowledge with gratitude the contribution of Mark Erik Hecht to those portions of this chapter that pertain to the sexual exploitation of children and corporate social responsibility.

1. In this chapter, I adopt the definition of "child labor" set forth in the introduction to this volume, in turn derived from Chapter 2, that is, "work done by children that is harmful to them because it is abusive, exploitive, hazardous, or otherwise contrary to their best interests—a subset of a larger class of children's work, some of which may be compatible with children's best interests (variously expressed as 'beneficial,' 'benign,' or 'harmless' children's work)."

2. Satyarthi, *Out of the Shadows,* foreword.

3. I have discussed the development of this movement in other articles, including "The Role of Non-Governmental Organisations," *Defending Human Rights Defenders . . .* , and "Human Rights NGOs."

4. See, for example, Weston, "Human Rights."

5. United Nations, *Convention on the Rights of the Child* (1989) [hereinafter "CRC"].

6. See Wiseberg, "The Role of Non-Governmental Organizations (NGOs) in the Protection and Enforcement of Human Rights."

7. Cullen and Morrow, "International Civil Society in International Law," esp. pp. 19–21.

8. See supra endnote 1 and Chapter 2 in this volume.

9. Grimsrud, "Too Much Work at Too Early an Age," pp. 13–14.

10. ILO, *Convention* (No. 182) *Concerning the Prohibition and Immediate Elimination of the Worst Forms of Child Labour* (1999), art. 3.

11. Human Rights Watch, *The Small Hands of Slavery . . . .* In January 2003, Human Rights Watch published *Small Change: Bonded Child Labor in India's Silk Industry.*

12. See Amnesty International, *Patterns of Slavery . . .* ; and Cross, *Kashmiri Carpet Children . . . .*

13. See Amnesty International, "War: A Child's Game?"

14. See the DCI's website, at http://www.defence-for-children.org.

15. See ISPCAN's website, at http://www.ispcan.org.

16. See the IWGCL's website, at http://www.cwa.tnet.co.th/vol11-2&3/iwgcl. htm.

17. Originally created in 1983 as the Ad Hoc NGO Group on the Drafting of the Convention on the Rights of the Child, the group was renamed and formally constituted after the convention was adopted.

18. Based in Geneva, the group had about fifty NGO members in 2005.

19. See Montgomery, "The Anti-Slavery Society 1973."

20. Anti-Slavery Society for the Protection of Human Rights, *Anti-Slavery Reporter and Aborigines' Friend,* pp. 10–11. In 1978, the Anti-Slavery Society for the Protection of Human Rights published this report under the title *Child Labour in Morocco's Carpet Industry.*

21. ILO, *Children at Work.*

22. Email to Laurie Wiseberg from Leah Levin, who headed the ASI's Child Labor Project in the late 1970s to early 1980s (Mar. 25, 2003, on file with the author).

23. In addition to the report on Morocco's carpet industry, the following were published: Banerjee, *Child Labour in India;* Banerjee, *Child Labour in Thailand;* Ennew and Young, *Child Labour in Jamaica;* Searight, *Child Labour in Spain;* and Valcarengh, *Child Labour in Italy.*

24. See Harvey, *Crucifixion at Easter . . . .* See also Kielburger, *Free the Children.*

25. See the website of Free the Children, at http://www.freethechildren.org.

26. See Myrstad, "From Projects to Social Change." Geir Myrstad of Norway is a senior program officer in the ILO's International Programme on the Elimination of Child Labour (IPEC).

27. Ibid., p. 85.

28. Ibid.

29. Grimsrud, *The Next Steps,* pp. 6–7.

30. DCI, *Newsletter of Child Labour Desk.*

31. Quoted from ECPAT's mission statement on its website, at http://www .ecpat.net/eng/index.asp.

32. United Nations, *Optional Protocol to the Convention on the Rights of the Child on the Sale of Children . . .* (2000).

33. See the coalition's website, at http://www.child-soldiers.org.

34. Regional and national NGOs from Africa, Asia, Latin America, the Middle East, and the Pacific have come to play an active role in the coalition's work, with regional representation at steering committee meetings.

35. United Nations, *Optional Protocol to the Convention on the Rights of the Child on the Involvement . . .* (2000).

36. Quoted from the coalition's website, at http://www.child-soldiers.org.

37. See the CWA's website, at http://www.cwa.tnet.co.th.

38. Ibid.

39. See ANPPCAN's website, at http://www.anppcan.org.

40. The group is based in Belgrade, where in 2004 I was located and discussed their programs with them.

41. CWIN established the "CWIN Help-Line"—an emergency relief and counseling service for children at risk, on its twelfth anniversary, in 1998. See "About CWIN: History" on CWIN's website, at http://www.cwin-nepal.org.

42. The activities of Nepalese organizations combating child labor are described in IPEC, "Nepal: Situation of Child Ragpickers"; see esp. "Executive Summary" and p. 36.

43. Ibid.

44. Bachman, "A Stitch in Time" (discussing the involvement of students from Los Angeles's Monroe High Law and Government Magnet School).

45. Quotations from the Global March website, at http://www.globalmarch.org.

46. For the latest total, consult the ILO website, at http://www.ilo.org/ilolex/english/index.htm.

47. It was noticeably not welcomed, for example, during the UN General Assembly Special Session on Children in May 2002. As reported in *Special Session Update,* there was "[d]isappointment at the way non-governmental organisations (NGOs) were kept at a distance from the negotiations. This represents a backward step for governments and their representatives at the UN, for which they should be ashamed. More than 1,700 NGO representatives from over 88 countries attended, and the opening up of the UN process to NGOs, particularly at and since the 'Earth Summit,' is one of the most important advances made by the UN in recent years: it has brought greater expertise to the UN, more accountability, more transparency: It has brought the institution a little closer to the concept of 'we the people' and away from the idea of 'we the governments,' who know what's best and will fix it as we think best, in our own interests." In the words of Mary Diaz, cochair of the NGO Steering Group: "Governments must recognise that civil society needs to be present and consulted. Citizens are asked to participate in building strong societies and holding their governments accountable. In order to do so we must have access to policy-making work and negotiations like this one." *Special Session Update* (May 24, 2002), No. 6, available at the CRIN website, at http://crin.org/specialsession.

48. See Mian, "Early Marriage . . . ."

49. *Declaration of Geneva of the Rights of the Child* (1924).

50. See Save the Children–UK's website, at http://www.savethechildren.org.uk/scuk/jsp/aboutus/index.jsp?section=historytimeline&timeframe=1920.

51. Cohen, "The Role of Nongovernmental Organizations . . ."; Cantwell, "Nongovernmental Organizations . . . ."

52. ILO, *Convention* (No. 29) *Concerning Forced or Compulsory Labour* (1930); ILO, *Convention* (No. 138) *Concerning Minimum Age for Admission to Employment* (1973). The International Confederation of Free Trade Unions (ICFTU) has been active in the fight against child labor and in pressuring its members to have their governments sign and ratify relevant ILO conventions. For details, visit its website, at http://www.icftu.org.

53. Breen, "The Role of NGOs . . . ."

54. See, for example, Austin, "Small Victories . . . ."

55. Murshed, "Unraveling Child Labor . . . ," p. 180.

56. ILO, *Final Report of the International Conference on Child Labour,* sec. II ("Report from the Technical to the Political Session—Legislation").

57. Murshed, "Unraveling Child Labor . . . ," p. 181.

58. Ibid.

59. Ibid., pp. 181–182. Murshed cites Bequele and Myers, *First Things First . . . ,* but without a source provided in his or their bibliography to which this note refers.

60. In addition to, for example, the reports cited in supra endnotes 6, 20, 21, and 23, see the following: Human Rights Watch, *Children of Sudan . . .* ; Robertson and Mishra, *Forced to Plough . . .* ; Tucker, *Fingers to the Bone . . .* ; and Global March Against Child Labour, *Out of the Shadows . . . .*

61. See IPEC, *Annotated Bibliography on Child Labour.*

62. See, for example, the annual bibliographies (from 1988 to present) of child labor at the website of the Child Labor Resource Office of the University of Illinois at Urbana, Champaign School of Social Work, at http://childlabor.social.uiuc.edu.

63. The mandate of the special rapporteur was created in 1990 by the UN Commission on Human Rights (UNCHR) and has been renewed continually since that time. The special rapporteur presents annual reports to the UNCHR and to the General Assembly and may undertake on-site country visits with the agreement of the government concerned.

64. Santos Pais, "Monitoring Children's Rights . . . ," p. 135.

65. Ombudsman of British Columbia, "NGOs Support Children's Rights."

66. Prepared by Jane Warburton under the title "Prevention, Protection, and Recovery . . . ."

67. Hecht, "The Role and Involvement of the Private Sector."

68. Van Bueren, "Child Sexual Exploitation and the Law . . . ."

69. ECPAT, *Child Sex Tourism and Action Plan.* This is an internal ECPAT document; however, a synthesis report, *Child Sex Tourism Action Survey,* is publicly available from ECPAT.

70. See ECPAT's website, at http://www.ecpat.net.

71. See Coalition to Stop the Use of Child Soldiers, *Research Guide . . . .*

72. Black, *A Handbook on Advocacy . . . .*

73. Black, *Child Domestic Workers . . . .*

74. UNICEF, *Child Domestic Work.*

75. Ibid., p. 14.

76. Quoting from the website of the Children's World Congress on Child Labour, at http://stopchildlabor.org/cwc/about.htm.

77. See the RUGMARK Foundation website, at http://www.rugmark.org.

78. International Labor Rights Fund, *RUGMARK After One Year.*

79. Ibid.

80. Ibid.

81. See Garg, "A Child Labor Social Clause . . . ," p. 485.

82. See, for example, Levich, "Carpets and Caveats."

83. International Labor Rights Fund, *RUGMARK After One Year.*

84. Ibid.

85. Ibid.

86. Ibid.

87. For detailed discussion, see Schrage, *Promoting International Worker Rights . . . ,* pp. 13–60.

88. India Committee of the Netherlands, *The Dark Side of Football . . . .*

89. Bachman, "A Stitch in Time."

90. DCI, *Newsletter of Child Labour Desk;* "World Cup Notebook."

91. For extended discussion, see Schrage, *Promoting International Worker Rights . . . .*

92. The Sullivan Principles of Social Responsibility for businesses operating in apartheid South Africa were relaunched in 1999 as the Global Sullivan Principles for Corporate Social Responsibility. See *Global Sullivan Principles . . . .*

93. See, for example, Maquila Solidarity Network, "The Changing Terrain . . . ," and Status of Women Canada, "Codes of Conduct . . . ."

94. See the Global Compact website, at http://www.unglobalcompact.org.

95. United Nations, *Universal Declaration of Human Rights* (1948).

96. United Nations High Commissioner for Human Rights, *Business and Human Rights.*

97. The Human Rights Library of the University of Minnesota has over fifty codes posted on its website, at http://www1.umn.edu, and others can generally be found prominently displayed on the relevant corporate websites. See also the website

of Business for Social Responsibility, at http://www.bsr.org, especially its issue briefs on "Child Labor" and "Codes of Conduct."

98. See Reebok's website, at http://www.reebok.com/x/us/humanrights/index. html.

99. The Reebok Human Rights Production Standards (code of conduct) are available at http://www.reebok.com/x/us/humanrights/text-only/business/popup/standards. html.

100. *Guide to the Implementation of Reebok Human Rights Production Standards,* p. 1.

101. See supra endnote 99.

102. Nike's code of conduct is available at http://www.nike.com/nikebiz/nikebiz. jhtml?page=25&cat=code.

103. Ibid., para. 2.

104. See the Body Shop website, at http://www.thebodyshop.com/web/tbsgl/ images/tbs_supplier_code_of_conduct.pdf.

105. For Wal-Mart's code, see http://www1.umn.edu/humanrts/links/walmart. html; for The Gap, see http://www1.umn.edu/humanrts/links/gapcode.html; and for Levi Strauss, see http://www1.umn.edu/humanrts/links/levicode.html.

106. *Proposed Draft Human Rights Code of Conduct for Companies.*

107. Hecht, "The Role and Involvement of the Private Sector," p. 20.

108. Ibid.

109. Ibid., pp. 20–21.

110. "Nike Releases First Corporate Responsibility Report." Of course, this meant that, for the first three years, 90 percent of the factory base was not under independent scrutiny and that it would take at least another three years before the entire factory base would be independently monitored.

111. United Nations High Commissioner for Human Rights, *Business and Human Rights.*

112. Ibid.

113. Ibid.

114. See, generally, http://www.theglobalalliance.org.

115. For details, see the FLA website, at http://www.fairlabor.org. See also the website of the US-based Worker Rights Consortium (WRC), a nonprofit organization created by college and university administrations, students, and labor rights experts, at http://www.workersrights.org. As of June 30, 2005, there were more than 143 US colleges and universities affiliated with the WRC.

116. Details concerning the ETI may be found on its website, at http://www. ethicaltrade.org.

117. Hecht, "The Role and Involvement of the Private Sector," p. 21.

118. Ibid.

119. *Principles for Global Corporate Responsibility.*

120. Ibid., Principle 1.2.C.5.

121. Regarding multilateral trade sanctions to combat child labor, however, see Chapter 16 in this volume. See also Chapter 5.

122. See "Cesar E. Chavez: An American Hero" on the website of the Cesar E. Chavez Foundation, at http://www.cesarechavez.org; and "Dolores Huerta: Labor Movement Leader," at http://www.heroism.org/class/1970/huerta.html.

123. For details online, see "Information page on the Nestlé Boycott" at http:// homepages.ihug.co.nz/~stu/nestlmilk.htm; "Nestle's Record" on the website of Corporate Watch in Japanese, at http://www.jca.apc.org/web-news/corpwatch-jp/118. html; and Mary Assunta of the Third World Network, "International Boycott Against

Nestlé Continues," at http://www.thirdworldtraveler.com/boycotts/nestleboycott_cont. html.

124. See Murshed, "Unraveling Child Labor . . ." (citing Spar, "The Spotlight and the Bottom Line"). See also "Consumer Boycotts: Do They Work?" on the website of the British NGO No Sweat, at http://www.nosweat.org.uk/article.php?sid=736.

125. Murshed, "Unraveling Child Labor . . . ," pp. 179–180. According to UNICEF and the ILO, only about 5 percent of child laborers work on products for export. See Bachman, "A Stitch in Time."

126. Grimsrud and Noonan, "The Next Steps," pp. 113–123.

127. Ibid., p. 117.

128. Garg, "A Child Labor Social Clause . . . ," pp. 489–490.

129. See DFID, "Helping Not Hurting Children . . . ."

130. Bachman, "Label Conscience," p. 20. According to one commentator, the firing of the workers was seen as a direct response to Senator Tom Harkin's proposed US Child Labor Deterrence Act of 1992. Garg, "A Child Labor Social Clause . . . ," p. 491, cites this case, but positively: "[A]fter a threatened U.S.-led boycott by the Child Labor Coalition, Bangladeshi clothing manufacturers agreed to transfer children from factories to schools."

131. Stackhouse, "New Solutions Fashioned for Child Workers," p. A13.

132. Yanz and Jeffcott, "Eliminating Child Labour . . . ."

133. Van Bueren, *The International Law on the Rights of the Child.*

134. Ibid., p. 14.

135. CRC, art. 45(a).

136. Ibid.

137. See supra endnotes 17 and 18.

138. Information provided by Mark Hecht, who has worked closely with ECPAT International for the past several years.

139. Seabrook, *No Hiding Place . . . .*

140. HRI, *The Canadian Component of the Protection Project . . . .*

141. Ibid., p. 193.

142. James Silk, executive director of the Orville H. Schell Jr. Center for International Human Rights at the Yale Law School, in a comment to the author, July 9, 2003, at a research conference sponsored by The University of Iowa Center for Human Rights in Iowa City, July 8–10, 2003.

143. See, for example, Baehr, "Mobilization of the Conscience of Mankind . . . ."

144. Smolin, "Strategic Choices . . . ," p. 947.

145. Ibid., pp. 950–951.

146. Ibid., p. 954.

147. Warburton, "Prevention, Protection, and Recovery . . . ," pp. 8–10.

148. Ibid., p. 10.

149. See http://www.child-soldiers.org.

150. The number 1379 refers to UN Security Council Resolution 1379.

151. Mazur, "Labor's New Internationalism."

152. Ibid.

153. UNDP, *Human Development Report 2002,* p. 2.

154. On the potential of the WTO in this regard, see Chapter 16 in this volume. See also Chapter 5.

15

Earning and Learning: Tensions and Compatibility

Susan L. Bissell

Akram—The Egg Seller

Akram is probably 12 years old, but has no birth certificate so says he can-not be certain. I have chatted with him several times prior to the interview and he has been incessantly bubbly and cheerful, his eyes sparkling and full of mischief. When the interview begins he is instantly subdued, fidgets with his hands in the pockets of his tattered and dirty trousers, shuffling his bare feet under the bench we are seated on, refusing to make eye contact.

The early part of the interview seems more like I am administering a structured questionnaire than like the "conversations" I have had with the other children. Methodically, Akram tells me that he was born in Dhaka, not in a hospital but in the house. He has visited his village home a few times, accompanying his mother and father. In Dhaka, Akram lives with his par-ents, older brother, and younger sister. His elder sister is married and lives in her husband's home.

Akram relaxes as he begins to describe his father, who is a thela gari wala *(a push cart pusher) who works only sporadically depending on the weather and the availability of short-term contracts. Akram's mother works as a domestic servant in the home of a wealthy Bangladeshi family. Though his younger sister goes to school for a few hours each day, she spends most of her time bringing water to the one-room house from a nearby tap, wash-ing dishes and sweeping the packed-mud floors. Akram's older brother works in a garment factory, where he has been employed for only a few months and earns 2000 taka monthly.*

Before coming to the MOU [memorandum of understanding] school, Akram had never been to school. He worked in a garment factory for two years before he was fired, cutting threads in the "finishing section" of the factory. He "felt bad" because other children went to school and he did not, and also described being abused by the factory managers. Akram tells me that he wanted to go to school before he started to work in the garment fac-tory but his parents said: We are poor, how can we send you to school? *Ap-parently both his mother and father wanted to enroll him in school, but could*

377

afford neither the admittance fee required by the local government primary school, nor the tutors. Instead they took him to work in a garment factory where he earned 600 taka per month.

The per diem Akram now receives from the school is 300 taka per month. When asked how he manages with less money than he made in the garment factory, Akram proudly says he sells eggs after school. He found the job himself, and likes it better than garment work since no one mistreats him while he is selling eggs. If you give bad eggs to people what happens, do they not scold you? *To this Akram responds:* I tell them I did not go inside the eggs, how will I be able to tell?

In Akram's egg selling business he brings the eggs on credit at a whole-sale price and says: After I'm done selling at night, I keep my profits and pay the price for the eggs. *It is a good business, in Akram's opinion, since he can both work and go to school, something that garment work did not allow since the hours were long. He also says that he is more independent to some extent, only having to sell when he wants to, meandering through the market at his own pace, attracting customers, resting at will.*

When asked what happens when he is not keen to sell eggs, Akram hastens to explain that he sells balloons instead. Still, his preference is eggs: I like selling eggs. It is at night. In the summer I've to sell balloons in the day, in the hot sun. I feel very hot. I get sick sometimes. Besides, *he explains,* egg selling is more profitable than balloon selling. *All of the money, but for 5 taka he keeps as pocket money, is given to his mother who uses it to buy food for the family.*

If you can manage like this, why did you have to work in a garment factory before? *I ask Akram. He tells me that he was a garment worker when his brother was still looking for a job. Since his father's work was unde-pendable, and his mother's not particularly lucrative, Akram needed to provide support. Lately with his brother earning a good salary and with his own earnings from the egg selling, things are better.*

—Dhaka, February 11, 1998

For the past decade—arguably longer—scholars, practitioners, and activists have been in "opposing camps" relative to child labor prevention or elimina-tion and education.[1] To simplify, and fully understand that even within these camps there have been undefined "gray" areas of discourse, there are those who feel that combining work and school is an acceptable option for children living in conditions in which their economic contribution matters. The other camp believes that no combination of earning and learning is viable; all chil-dren should be in school, full-time, with no work of any sort permitted.

There are compelling reasons to occupy one or another of these camps. These reasons will be explored throughout this chapter. In addition to laying out the various arguments, however, I challenge both camps. The challenge is a simple one: to leave rigidly held positions and find some middle ground. There is mounting evidence of common ground between and among various thinkers and stakeholders, despite their adherence to positions that have been carved out over the years. Some of that common ground was articulated during a side meeting at the global education summit in Delhi late in 2003.[2] Commonality and what I refer to as "the shifted discourse" give us pause for reflection—and I think celebration—insofar as they are already ushering in a new type of programming for and with children, to prevent and eliminate their exploitation.

I have divided my own thinking in this chapter into three sections. The first examines the literature—in no way exhaustively—that considers the links between labor and education (essentially the literature around which the original camps formed). Thereafter, I discuss poverty and some of the economic issues relating to children working. Of particular interest is a brief discussion of the notion of social capital. In the third section, I focus on aspects of education quality that actually make children "available" for work. Finally, I argue that the complexity of the issue in a human rights (for children) context lies not in the incompatibility of earning and learning but in case and situation specificity. At the same time, I posit that if education quality were redressed effectively, then the numbers of abjectly poor children for whom education is immediately unaffordable would be small enough for a community (at all levels) to manage and "correct" in a manner sensitive to the best interests of the child, per Article 3 of the 1989 United Nations Convention on the Rights of the Child (CRC).[3] I conclude with a description of a human rights approach to child labor elimination that is championed by a growing number of stakeholders and shaping the new child labor discourse.[4]

▨ Linking Work and Education

There is a considerable literature on the linkages between child working and education.[5] These range from suggestions that primary education is a cure-all for child labor to assertions that with the introduction of compulsory primary education children will no longer be seen in the workplace.[6] Others note that working children are disinterested in education, commenting also on parental preference for placing children in working, rather than schooling, situations.[7] Finally, there is debate about the merits of nonformal education versus more formal systems.[8]

"The ILO," writes Alec Fyfe, "has long recognized the centrality of education in the fight against children labour."[9] Myron Weiner says that "[c]ompulsory primary education is the policy instrument by which the state effectively removes children from the labor force."[10] Neera Burra posits that "education alone can provide mobility to the socially and economically disadvantaged sections of society."[11] The arguments of all of these authors convey their confidence in compulsory primary education reducing demand for children in employment. Weiner bases his assertions on the experience of countries that "have removed children from the labour force and require that they attend school. They [these countries] believe that employers should not be permitted to employ child labour and that parents, no matter how poor, should not be allowed to keep children out of school."[12] While agreeing that, "through the introduction of compulsory primary education . . . at least 70 per cent, if not more, of children who are currently outside the school system, would go back to school,"[13] Burra argues that, in the case of India, even with compulsory primary education there would continue to be children in bonded and other forms of labor that would prohibit school attendance.[14]

Enforcement of compulsory education is a challenge in many countries, particularly in a country as vast and populous as India, Weiner's and Burra's focus.[15] Fyfe does not address enforcement, dismissing it as a matter of concern.[16] Weiner says that education laws are easier to enforce than labor laws, and that successful enforcement should be linked to attendance and retention.[17] On the one hand, this is Weiner's tacit admission that all laws are difficult to implement, some more difficult than others. On the other, Weiner is also admitting that enforcement of enrollment alone is not sufficient, that retention is critically important as well.[18]

Howard Brasted and Denis Wright, commenting on child labor in India, note that putting children in school, hence removing them from the work force, is not that simple:

> The education that is offered must convince parents that it is worthwhile. The political will must be present too, for not only do many new schools have to be built, but recurrent expenditure of education will have to increase dramatically and be kept up. In Kerala such an investment has been made: almost 100 percent of children attend school and illiteracy is almost nonexistent. But Kerala has not thereby become immune to child labour, since poverty remains a continuing, neutralising factor. In the last analysis, education can have an impact, but is no quick fix.[19]

Legislation calling for compulsory primary education is but one necessary prerequisite for child labor elimination. Reflecting on some of my own work, I would not privilege education over income substitution or generation schemes or social service interventions such as subsidized health care; nor would I ignore critical issues in the quality and type of education being offered. Education is part of the child labor solution, but it is not *the* solution.

Weiner, as Burra points out,[20] overlooks the fact that the countries he cites as having enforced compulsory primary education also allowed for a period of "school and work." The issues of poverty and need do not simply go away because a child is enrolled in school. The point relevant to education is that, without systemic redress of income poverty concerns, there is continuing financial pressure on poor families. While this may seem to be stating the obvious, it is something that often is sidelined in child labor prevention and elimination programs. I return to this below.[21]

Fyfe writes about linking labor and education in the policy and support programs of at least two global agencies: the United Nations Children's Fund (UNICEF) and the International Labour Organization (ILO).[22] He dates the history from the mid-1990s, but arguably in UNICEF the issues were much debated long before that. True, it was not until 1994 that the ILO and UNICEF tried to harmonize their positions and policies, agreeing on a common "policy framework."[23] This laid the foundation for a broader partnership among a number of multilateral institutions on the issue of child labor, among them the United Nations Educational, Scientific, and Cultural Organization (UNESCO), the World Bank, and the World Health Organization (WHO). After an international meeting on child labor in Oslo in 1997,[24] the ILO and UNICEF in particular started to work much more closely. For UNICEF, the Oslo conference was *the* opportunity to promote and support the provision of education as a child labor prevention strategy.[25]

The agency alignment and privileging of education in the "child labor solution" is important for a number of reasons. Though I later explore the role of multilateralism in what I refer to as the "shifting discourse and practice in child labor," a few comments are merited here. The multilateral actors, UNICEF and the ILO in particular, have had pivotal roles in determining the actions that many governments have been encouraged to take. "Earning and learning" is not something about which either agency has been particularly vocal publicly, but within UNICEF there have been lively discussions about formal and nonformal education and on the role of vocational education in the child labor context. "Earning and learning" as an approach to child labor appeared in UNICEF in Bangladesh following an exposé of child labor in the garment sector and the joint efforts of UNICEF, the ILO, and the Bangladesh Garment Manufacturers and Exporters Association to redress the problem.[26]

Advocates—including especially multilateral agencies—tend to focus on and privilege the application of legal instruments that relate to education (the ILO of course being inclined to reference its own conventions), but education legislation does not begin to address underlying economic causality. Moreover, even if school is compulsory, if it is not absolutely free of direct and indirect costs, children will not be able to attend, and families will not be able to fulfill their obligations under stringent education legislation.[27] Some of the costs of education include fees, books, uniforms, other learning materials, and of course the opportunity cost of the child being out of the workplace to attend school.[28]

There is a growing demand also for extracurricular tutoring of primary school children in the public system.[29] Private tutoring is expected if children are to be competitive with their peers. As Thérèse Blanchet relates in her work in South Asia, "teachers have little commitment to teach in the classroom. They impart their knowledge, but in private tutorship for an extra fee. Poor children born of illiterate parents, if in school at all, are likely to be . . . the first ones to drop out. They suffer discrimination . . . being unable to afford assistance which only money can buy."[30]

What are the real effects of education legislation on the nature and extent of child labor? Children who are in school may appear also in labor statistics, or they may be part of the labor force in the informal sector and be absent from official statistics but economically active nonetheless. Often forgotten, and possibly still working and attending school, are the millions of children who are "employed" but not earning wages, as in the case of girls caring for younger siblings, cooking, and cleaning in the family home. In short, the statistical picture provided by education legislation enforcement mechanisms is incomplete.

So What About Poverty Anyway?

A discussion of work, education, and children is incomplete without reference to the issue of poverty—in particular, poverty of income. This is highly contested in the literature, and even more contested among practitioners who are attempting to redress either poverty or child labor, sometimes though rarely coincidentally.

Poverty and Child Labor

Burra cites poverty as "the classic defence offered by apologists for child labour," and insists that "the prevalence and persistence of child labour itself reinforces, if not creates, poverty."[31] Weiner says that "there is historical evidence delinking mass education from the level of national and per capita income."[32] These same critics insist that parental claims of the high cost of education are simply rationalizations for their abuse and exploitation of children.

I find these arguments problematic on two levels. First, I consider dubious the assumption that poverty is homogeneous and that all countries go through precisely the same patterns of economic growth and social development. There is nothing homogeneous about poverty but for the fact that it describes a "lack" of something, or of several things. Even within economically poor communities there are differences between and among households. As difficult as it is to compare slums, and to compare households, so too is it difficult to compare the poverty of nations. Growth and development are relative terms, influenced by population, culture, political systems, stability or lack thereof, legislation, industry, and global trading relationships. No single measurement of growth and development among and between nations can allow for these variations and claim accuracy.[33]

The debate over which came first, child labor or poverty, is in any event immaterial when measured against the daily struggles of children and families trying to earn money for basic food and shelter.[34] Even if a convincing case can be made for child labor perpetuating poverty, what of the millions of children already living in abjectly poor conditions, for whom questions of "which came first" are academic and far from reality? Ignoring the poverty claims of working children and their families, I would argue, is tantamount to paternalism and disrespect. While I am not arguing that poverty needs to keep children from schools, or that being poor means that children should be exploited, evidence squarely demonstrates that families are struggling and that these struggles are legitimate.

There really are very divided opinions on the economic and livelihood dimensions of child labor. On the one hand, scholars and advocates argue that livelihood and poverty issues are of no concern in questions of protection of the child, and that, irrespective of economic status, no child should be exposed to the formal or informal workplace.[35] The contention is that parents and/or the state should be caring for the economic needs and human rights of children, and proponents of this position argue on what they regard as humanitarian grounds. On the other hand, poverty is commonly given as an excuse for child labor: if children do not work, family survival and self-preservation are at stake.[36] These positions are extreme and lead to extreme prescriptions for action.

There is very little empirical data on child labor and livelihoods. Elizabeth Kuznesof, for instance, points out that "the complicated relationship between household economy, child labour, the history of industrialization, and the history of public education has been insufficiently examined in any context."[37] Much of what is offered by way of "evidence" is garnered from the perspective of elites,[38] while still other material is anecdotal and impressionistic.[39] The literature in economics is speckled with contributions in the area of child labor,[40] but these tend to be based on strictly quantitative data, and on a series of assumptions that are "scientific" and distanced from social and cultural reality.

In reality, in interviews with nongovernmental organization (NGO) officers, teachers, employers, parents, and children, it is rare to hear poverty alone cited as a reason for children in the workplace. Children themselves comment on the economic pressures on their families, and how they participate in family-based livelihood strategies in the absence of viable social service or social support alternatives.[41] Their contributions to the household economy are considerable, though in some cases it may be possible to argue that they contribute little and that the family can survive without the contribution from the child.

This is consistent with the findings of Richard Anker and Helina Melkas in their examination of income substitution and child labor elimination globally.[42] In the case of girls, it also corroborates the work of Xiaoyan Liang, who examined the Bangladesh Female Secondary School Assistance Project; she concluded that "providing monetary incentives directly to girls can be an effective way of increasing their participation."[43] Though Liang was writing about girls, secondary school, and rural Bangladesh, her conclusions hold true for many children.

Livelihoods and Social Capital

In a world where childhood is socially constructed as an "ideal" place, where needs and human rights (for children) are met, a discussion of children's livelihoods would seem misplaced. However, for many of the world's children, the experience of childhood is not the idyllic world constructed in the West by the West, or by middle- and upper-middle-class advocates in the East. Nor is it the ideal childhood that is set out in the normative framework of the 1989 CRC. On the contrary, earning a living and making livelihood decisions and choices are very much a part of the childhood of millions of children the world over.

Discussions of livelihoods are closely related to emerging and evolving notions of social capital. For the most part, children have been left out of the social capital debate, irrespective of their roles in their families and communities. There are three possible reasons for their exclusion. First, "purists" undoubtedly would argue that children are a category separate from adults, and that livelihood and poverty issues are in the domain—or should be in the domain—of adults. Second, dependency theorists would consider children an appendage to, or an extension of, adult family members. Third, the active involvement of children in research, requiring a particular view of them as possessors of agentive capacity, is relatively new territory. In fact, children in poor communities are critical to any discussion of, or policy approach to, social capital formation and enhancement.

Geoffrey Wood describes social capital as a concept embodying the connections among social relationships, sustainable livelihood, and poverty elimination, and calls it a "contested area" where there are at least two views on its evolution and meaning.[44] Robert Putnam, for instance, views social capital as a culturally embedded and somewhat static entity.[45] Pierre Bourdieu and James Coleman have a comparatively pragmatic notion of social capital, insofar as it is a "controllable" entity, subject to political forces, and responsive to programs of growth.[46] Wood argues for a combination of Putnam, Bourdieu, and Coleman, where social capital is embedded and seen as neither positive nor negative, but where there is simultaneously a practical awareness that social mobilization can improve the lives of poor people.[47] He calls this social mobilization "social inclusion and integration" and points out the associated problems:

> In contexts of highly imperfect markets, corrupt state practices, and patriarchal norms, poor people (and especially women) face a problematic search for security, in income flows and stable access to stocks and services. They are obliged to manage vulnerability through investing in and maintaining various forms of social capital which produce various short-term, immediate outcomes and practical needs while postponing and putting at permanent risk more desirable forms of social capital which offer the strategic prospect of supporting needs and maintaining rights in the longer term.[48]

Children are, on two fronts, caught up in this social capital dilemma. First, they are players in the livelihood strategies of their parents, the adults described by Wood in the quotation above. Where children are sent to work instead of being sent to school, for instance, adults have determined priority interests that are immediate and do not involve sustained investments in education. Second, children are, in many cases, active participants in the maintenance of their own forms of social capital. This maintenance serves immediate interests, but puts longer-term strategies at risk. That is, the maintenance of social capital requires an investment of time and human resources that divert children from, for instance, attending full-time schooling. This means that, while social capital is formed and maintained, the greater and potentially longer-term benefits of learning and schooling are forgone. There are immediate and tangible gains from social capital formation. This is only rarely well countenanced with the longer-term good afforded by education, provided of course that education is of high quality, as discussed in other sections of this chapter.

As other researchers have noted, most studies on the livelihood and survival strategies of poor people and communities have had a rural focus.[49] The research also has had an adult focus, perhaps unintentionally overlooking the participation of children. In Dhaka, Sarah Salway and colleagues explored "the relationships between the environmental, social and material conditions of livelihoods," with a view ultimately to informing public policy in a way that "complements rather than substitutes for people's own effort to deal with contingencies . . . , a necessity if people are to become actors in the process of change rather than passive recipients of aid and relief."[50]

That the existing strategies of vulnerable populations need to be factored into understandings, which in turn inform policy, seems to me very persuasive. Such an approach gave substance to claims of "participation," not only in the research but in the development of future courses of policy and action. The assumed passivity and lack of agency of the children who participate in any form of work deny both the reality of their daily lives and their human rights. Just as with adults, a better understanding of the characteristics of the vulnerable livelihoods of children is crucial to the development of policies and interventions that acknowledge and incorporate their agency. As Olga Nieuwenhuys points out, in the short term at least, as long as this agency is denied, children will continue to be exploited.[51] Again, this is not to argue for sustaining the oftentimes difficult and harsh lives of working children. It is, rather, to understand, face, and deal with *what is* while at the same time addressing *what ought to be*.

Self-Exploitation

Sending children to work is an example of a self-exploitive coping strategy. "Self-exploitation" is a term coined by A. V. Chayanov in the context of Russian peasant farmers[52] and to which James Scott refers.[53] Scott says that "guaranteeing themselves a basic subsistence, an orientation that focuses unavoidably on the here and now, occasionally forces peasants to mortgage their own future."[54] Though writing about rural, Asian farmers, Scott's observations hold true in the context of many of the world's economically poor. Where children are abused in the workplace, self-exploitation is again an issue, since physical and psychosocial health of young minds and bodies is at risk. While an in-depth discussion of the health impacts of child labor are beyond the scope of this chapter, they are an important consideration in a discussion of why children work in the first place.[55] Parents and children knowingly put themselves in exploitive environments and do so out of a sense of duty to the family, to short-term needs, and to the compelling livelihood interests of family members.

Salway and colleagues write about the importance of nonkinship ties and how vital they are to obtaining work in urban poor areas.[56] Though immediate and extended family members draw rural nuclear families to cities, once there, little family contact or dependency is maintained. Accordingly, "the emergence of both exploitative and reciprocal relationships is evident. Dominant groups . . . mediate access to resources at a price. . . . (Slum) dwellers respond by seeking to establish relationships with neighbours, co-workers, and friends."[57]

There is little doubt that "survival" is part of the initial strategy behind families allowing and even encouraging their children to be employed. Supporters of such things as trade sanctions against communities and countries using child labor suggest that the survival of a few families will need to be "sacrificed" if the overall good of "the poor" is considered the ultimate goal.[58] This sort of thinking displays, in my view, an ignorance of the survival and livelihood strategies of poor families, as well as a complete misinterpretation of "adult labor substitutability." Poor families are singularly preoccupied with survival, and substituting adults for children in the workplace is impractical and in most situations impossible.

If You Build It, They Will Come, but Probably Drop Out

Together with livelihood issues, there are some aspects of education that need to be factored into an as-complete-as-possible understanding of working children. Of late, there are renewed efforts to examine these aspects of education, sometimes referred to as "quality," and to correct and improve them. The "quality" issues in education range from the attitudes of teachers to the children, to teaching skills, to facilities, to content of the curriculum. Globally, children report being ill-treated in the schools.[59] Abusive treatment by teachers is also reported among the most common reasons for children dropping out of school. I lead with this particular qualitative aspect of schooling as it is arguably the most pervasive.

Demand for quality education depends upon, among other things, the attitudes and aspirations of children and their parents, the long-term economic expedience of school attendance, confidence in the school system, and previous experience with education. The synergy of demand and education quality impinges on, and is impinged on by, immediate economic and other "events" at the household level.

Teachers

First, in economically poor communities, the pupil-to-teacher ratio tends to be very high. Certainly it will be too high to ensure that the teaching-learning transaction takes place effectively. Hence apathy, lethargy, dropping out, and—invariably—work. Typically, in South Asia for example, the pupil-to-teacher ratio at the primary level is seventy-one to one.[60] Second, teachers in areas of high child labor are seldom punctual or even present. There is a struggle, or ultimately a disinterest, in making the learning environment interesting and enjoyable. Third, teachers in government schools are almost universally poorly paid but nonetheless charged with responsibility for community and family "outreach."

Mahbub Haq and Khadija Haq explain that teacher motivation is linked to a number of factors.[61] Salary is of course one of them, with low salaries leading to poor teacher performance, absenteeism, and "early departure from the profession." The esteem in which the community holds teachers can be a powerful incentive—or a disincentive. Few people actually see teaching as an important or lucrative profession. Teaching in the nonformal sector is dismissed as even less important. Finally, there is the matter of classroom quality and teaching facilities, which undermines the motivation of teachers. Classrooms in economically deprived communities tend to be poorly resourced by any standard.

Girls

It is difficult to hold the lure of jobs solely responsible for girls dropping out of—or never attending—primary school. As has been discussed already, there are a variety of reasons that children and their families discourage or prohibit school attendance. Girls have attracted particular attention from those promoting education, since their circumstances are dramatically different from boys. Fyfe develops some strategic considerations concerning female working children.[62] He cites the following as particular constraints to a girl's learning:

- The direct costs of schooling such as fees, books, and uniforms.
- The opportunity costs of children's time in school—which in poor families are likely to be higher for girls, e.g., in Bangladesh, girls between 13 [and] 15

years, spend ten times as many hours as boys in household activities, but boys spend twice as much time on crop production and about five times as much time in wage work.

- The costs of observing cultural traditions and ensuring children's safety—again likely to be higher for girls—linked to special need for physical protection, and in some cultures, for seclusion.
- The neglect of girls' health and nutrition, especially in Asia, impacts on their capacity to learn.
- The limited economic opportunities that especially affect girls' earning potential and thus returns on their schooling.[63]

This is by no means an exhaustive list. Even these few considerations suggest, however, important gendered aspects of the challenges to education and working children.

Learning, Education, and Respect
In the mid-1990s, in Bangladesh, I and a colleague conducted research on child labor relative to 250 children who had been working in garment factories but who had lost their jobs at the threat of international trade sanctions. Prior to doing this research, it was my assumption that, though many of the children were out of school and in garment factories, they were nonetheless learning. Similarly, I thought that, in conversation with them, they would tell us that they learned things on the streets, in their homes, or in other workplaces. I was proven wrong. Any discussion of learning in the broad sense quickly turned, at the will of the children, to a discussion of their school-going experiences.

As noted earlier, statistics about the increasing levels of enrollment in primary school suggest that a high value is placed on education.[64] It would appear that "circumstances" intervene in a child's attempt to complete primary education. Given their obvious and well-articulated interest in learning (keeping in mind, of course, that the children themselves equate "learning" with a classroom), the tugs and pulls to seek paid employment must be very powerful. This is not to suggest that there is ambivalence about the value of, or need for, education. Rather, it is an acknowledgment that life is dynamic, full of changes and challenges, and that becoming educated is but one of these challenges—one that merits considerable investment.

Other Obstacles to Formal Education
A real obstacle to the provision of "appropriate and interesting" education, in particular to poor children, is the attitudes of a range of officials. In rural areas, the school-going population that is ultrapoor is likely also to suffer multiple exclusion, and for various reasons. For instance, while not having access to schools, or having lost confidence in the value and purpose of education, health services may be similarly wanting. Class, ethnicity, and even caste in some countries may come to bear. The linkages between the absence of social

services and children's school attendance are well-known; attendance and retention are poorest where, for instance, primary health care systems and services are dysfunctional or nonexistent.

In an urban context, the standard line has been that if education facilities and services for the urban poor are improved, expanded, and made more enticing, then ever more people will flock to already crowded cities. That this is a fallacious argument in the face of already staggering rates of rural-to-urban migration irrespective of social services is obvious to everyone but the officials putting forth the argument. Services are poor and life is difficult in urban areas, but people still leave their village homes, where there are even fewer prospects for a better future, and flock to cities.

There can be a stigma attached to nonformal education. In some countries, negative views of anything other than formal, government schools prevail. Nonformal education is seen generally as a substandard form of education, of which poor children avail themselves. If you have money, you don a uniform and go to a government primary school; you try to be like "the others." The assumption, and the signal that you give to the community, is that if you attend an NGO school you are poor, you are not receiving an "official" education, and you are less likely to get a good job later.

There is a vibrant and contemporary discourse on the repelling features of school.[65] The argument is that, with enrollment rates increasing globally, there continue to be soaring dropout rates. Something about "education," therefore, is making children available for work. This is a concrete example of what Jo Boyden, Birgitta Ling, and William Myers refer to as global "education-system problems and failures" that are a "major deterrent against school attendance."[66] Problems with teachers are cited as among the most critical, systemic issues. For instance: "The challenge in South Asia is to provide an adequate number of teachers for all primary school children, and to improve the capability of these teachers to deliver high quality education. At present South Asia has only 66 per cent of the teachers that are actually needed. Many of these teachers are poorly trained, remain absent from schools, and follow no in-service training programmes."[67]

In part because of the poor quality of teachers and teaching, and in part because of the school fees and the expense of uniforms, some children are tutored at home. As noted earlier, private tutoring is a virtual necessity if children are to perform well in their studies. It is particularly common in the case of girls, not least because at home they are "safe" and still under the watchful eye of parents.[68]

▪ Embracing the Complexity: A Real Human Rights (for Children) Approach

There are common threads that run through child labor experiences the world over. I recall "testing" this notion myself, comparing some research undertaken by UNICEF in Africa with a concurrent investigation in Asia. The similarities in the nature and extent, the causes and consequences, of child labor were remarkable. However, at the same time, there were striking differences in the types of responses required both to prevent and to eliminate existing child labor.

Herein lie the complexity and the tension. There are those who argue that child labor cannot reasonably and frugally be "dealt with" on a case-by-case basis. According to this line of reasoning, communities and governments need solutions that are systemic and sustainable. They need to preempt and resolve the exploitation of children in a manner—or manners—that benefit not individuals but masses of young people. What this implies is child labor prevention and elimination that is state or system driven.

Such is the view of the "moral high-grounders," and it is potentially not especially sensitive to human rights (for children). As discussed, the moral high-grounders claim that state-provided education is the solution to child labor. It is "nonnegotiable" because anything other than a clear demand for a single sector solution would give the state the opportunity to escape its obligation. There are a number of activists that have been articulating this view for some time, insisting on one message to government: all children have a right to a full-time education.

This position is further supported by a number of beliefs, among them that all work is detrimental and no children should be engaged in anything other than school or play. Linked to this is a particular view of children as dependents of the state and of the family. Children's views or ideas are, accordingly, immature and immaterial to resolving the child labor situation. In short, children have neither agency nor responsibility. Their only obligation is to go to, and stay in, a state-run school.

From a human rights (for children) perspective—informed by a range of human rights instruments, including the 1989 CRC—the moral high-ground position in the context of the education versus work paradox is troubling. It vests all responsibility in the state, and other actors (e.g., exploitive employers) are freed of obligations. In positing a single-sector response—that is, education as the answer to child labor elimination—moral high-grounders ignore the fact that other sectors owe a duty of care as well.[69] Accordingly, the CRC principle of the indivisibility of rights is ignored. Finally, the suggestion that only adults know what is good for children, that children do not know what is good for them, defies the CRC principle that children, according to their evolving capacity, have a right to be consulted in matters affecting them.

A real human rights (for children) approach to the elimination of child labor tackles the complexity of the issue, is true to the best interests principle of the CRC, and according to the evolving capacity of the children in question takes into account their views on what can and should be done. More succinctly, the foundation for preventing and eliminating child labor consists of a range of rights instruments and, in the case of the CRC, a range of indivisible human rights (for children) provisions.[70] By this I mean that building on this foundation of human rights (for children), the *process* of realizing it needs also to be rights-based. This combination of foundation and process dictates a "holistic" approach that will be articulated in detail below in terms of policy and "programmatic" principles.[71]

Marta Santos Pais articulated this orientation particularly well in her address at the Oslo meeting on child labor:

> The Convention [CRC] calls for the consideration of a holistic and child centered approach. It recognizes the fundamental rights of children and acknowledges the synergism of them. With the Convention we realize the natural relationship between all measures adopted to ensure the realization of children's rights, as well as the need for cooperation and coordination of activities between all bodies and mechanisms which are relevant to the lives of children. . . . [I]t is no longer sufficient to adopt dispersed or sectoral measures. A comprehensive and integrated agenda is required, based on an accurate assessment of the reality, guided by the best interests of the child.[72]

What is essential to recall—and to repeat—is that human rights for children are not optional, as emphasized by Burns Weston and Mark Teerink in Chapter 1 of this volume. If the adoption and ratification of human rights instruments like the CRC tell us anything, it is that there are rights obligations to children first and foremost because they are human. Those duties and obligations take on particular features because children are *special* human beings. They are evolving in their capacity to contribute to the realization of their own human rights. Also, they have a unique call on duty-bearers in the form of parents, community, and state apparatus. Even the international community is a partner for the protection, promotion, and propagation of the human rights of children. Finally, there is a sense of urgency that is unique with respect to children's human rights, simply because they are human, not because it is the charitable thing to do, or because it is expedient, or because "children are the future."

Policy

The first and key policy tenet in a human rights (for children) approach to preventing and eliminating child labor is that achievement of quality universal primary education and elimination of poverty are interlinked in a complex and cross-sector relationship. Though much professed, too little is known about this linkage. It certainly is clear that better policy research and the knowledge that research generates are required to eliminate child labor, fulfill the right of every child to a quality basic education, and achieve the Millennium Development Goal of eliminating extreme poverty.[73]

A human rights (for children) approach to child labor must face up to the connection between economic poverty and education. Privileging one over the other defies indivisibility vis-à-vis the CRC, to name but one reason. The CRC affords children the right to a certain standard of living, at the same time calling for laudable education outcomes. Nowhere does the CRC or any other human rights treaty suggest that there is anything sequential about the process. Moreover, as noted earlier, ignoring chronic, absolute poverty is perforce impractical; programs do not work if poverty is ignored. Hence the many interventions that offer economic incentives,[74] that offer alternative livelihood solutions, that relieve parents of direct and indirect education costs, are the ones that work.

Second, and related, it must be understood that while access to schools and quality education, according to a human rights (for children) approach, is key for the elimination of child labor, these policies are not sufficient in and of themselves. Polices in other sectors need consistently to address the economic poverty of families. It is essential that government policies also address the overall problems of the labor market and the lack of access that poor families have to affordable and effective ways to reduce their debt and prevent future indebtedness. In short, a range of state actors must be engaged, not simply those in the education and labor sectors. Those state actors need to rationalize their efforts irrespective of traditional, linear methods of working and interacting.

Third, government policies must address achieving the goal of universal primary education, and therefore also provide for special measures that will expedite the success of children in escaping from child labor and entering and succeeding in the mainstream of primary and then secondary education. The notion of special measures acknowledges that there is a continuum of human rights (for children) implementation, and that extraordinary effort needs to be made to reach all children, and to sustain that reach.

Fourth, policies must address the elimination of child labor within broader national frameworks, such as poverty reduction strategy papers (PRSPs),[75] so that there are stronger linkages with all socioeconomic features of the Millennium Development Goals.[76] To do so will require an overall strengthening of the strategy for partnerships among national and international partners, and government and nongovernmental partners, as called for in the Oslo Agenda for Action, which was unanimously adopted at the 1997 International Conference on Child Labour.[77]

Fifth, the success of the "fast-track initiative"[78] will depend on more effective identification and elimination of the barriers to the sustainable achievement of the Millennium Development Goal of universal basic education. Simply increasing access to schools is not enough; it is imperative also to reduce the barriers in schools to providing a quality, relevant basic education with satisfactory learning achievement for every child. It also is imperative to accelerate the mobilization of public opinion against child labor and in favor of increasing national and international resources to achieve the Jomtien Declaration's "Education for All" initiatives.

In short, the policy dimensions of a human rights (for children) approach to child labor prevention and elimination must be well articulated and coordinated. While aspects may be negotiated according to particular realities, certain policies—or processes related to policies—are consistent no matter what. Policy and process need to concurrently address labor and education, call to the fore a range of sectors beyond education and labor, have special measures, intertwine a range of national efforts, and fit within the broader development framework.

Programming Approaches: So What Do We Do?

There are particular actions that a human rights (for children) approach to child labor prevention and elimination must involve. Not all practitioners would agree on what those actions are, as noted at the outset of this chapter, but there is growing consensus. Below are what I call "programming approaches," though they could be equally well named the essential building blocks of a human rights approach. What differentiates them as being a human rights approach as opposed to a charity or needs approach is their consistency with the policy discourse above. In programming, as in policy, there needs to be a "whole" approach if it is to be human rights–based versus needs- or charity-based. "Whole" means quality improvements in the education system, concurrent transitional education to ensure special mechanisms to get children to the right level for their age, income substitution or debt poverty reduction or both, social mobilization to restore family and community faith in alternatives to current self-exploitation, and the application of legal instruments. A few of these merit closer consideration.

First, from a human rights perspective, it is vital to increase access of children to quality education and not to settle for low-quality education in the formal school system. The quality of education has to be a positive and powerful attraction for low-income families to grapple with the challenge and to have a real opportunity for their children to escape a life of poverty. Access to quality education means having child-friendly (and girl-friendly) schools—schools free of corporal punishment, schools with water and sanitation (an especially important factor for the education of girls), and schools with learning opportunities for children that they and their parents feel will help their children escape from poverty.

Second, efforts in creating "access" for excluded children to quality education need to be made more effective. Not least, efficient, speedy, and successful transition experiences into the school environment must be encouraged and acted upon so that marginalized and otherwise excluded children may succeed in appropriate age-for-grade learning before and shortly after they enter school. Special measures should address social barriers through "buddy systems" and other child peer support services so that children living in poverty are not stigmatized or discriminated against by school administrators, teachers, or even other children. To succeed at learning, children must have a genuine sense of self-esteem.

Third, nongovernmental organizations and civil society more generally have strategic and ongoing community roles to play in advocating to discourage child labor and encourage and rejuvenate the motivation of families and communities in human rights awareness, the elimination of poverty, and the realization of the right of every child to a quality basic education. True sustainability must be "programmed" to the elimination of child labor and poverty. In the end, programming sustainable education for all means that this goal is owned and protected by families and communities themselves.

Fourth, human rights programming means that poor families themselves must have the opportunity to form and manage their own self-help groups, as has been the case in a number of countries (for example, in Bangladesh through the Grameen Bank). They need the types of self-help groups, combined with institutional changes, that can address their credit and saving needs, that are key to family efforts to escape economic poverty, that earn self-respect, and ultimately, that make the kinds of social and even economic investments that can give children an "educational passport" to a brighter future.

Fifth, in the context of a country-by-country approach to education programming from a human rights perspective, governments and civil society must decide how and when to apply legal instruments, including civil society educational laws and laws related to the protection of children, the elimination of poverty, and achievement of compulsory, free basic education. This will necessitate a cross-sector effort with a number of public and nongovernmental institutions concerned with education, the health of children, civil education, and child protection in effective collaboration with communities and families. It also may demand action by way of legal reform.

◾ Conclusion

I return to "Akram—The Egg Seller" by way of conclusion. Akram is typical of the children who are central to the education-versus-labor discourse. He is typical also of children for whom an increasing number of financial resources are being generated for child labor elimination purposes. Akram started his life working, got an opportunity to go to school, but ultimately found that a combination of school and work "fit" his reality.

Taking a strictly charitable or even a "needs-based approach" to child labor, what would be said about Akram's situation? It would first be argued that he should not be working, that he needs to be in school full-time. There would be comments that his father should get a better job, or a better-paid job, and possibly even assertions that some other unemployed adult ought to do so as well, that Akram should not work because adults should be doing what he is doing, and that his labor is driving down wage rates, leading to an endless spiral of adult unemployment and underemployment and poverty. What Akram needs, accordingly, is an education. He needs also to be able to play, to be free to enjoy his childhood. Akram's views on what happens to him—or what should happened to him—are accordingly immaterial. He is, after all, a child and could not possibly know what is best for him now or in the future.

How is a human rights–based approach to Akram different? Most important, Akram has a right to specific services and other things simply because he is human, not because it would be kind to do so or because he is needy and wanting and the state or other actors feel compelled to respond. There is also the principle of indivisibility. Consider for a moment the following: Akram has no birth certificate, to which he has a right; Akram's father is underemployed and undoubtedly his mother underpaid, so there are "standard of living" concerns; Akram had been working and denied access to school not because of the work, but because free schooling was not really free; Akram combines work and school; and Akram has a pretty good idea of what is going on in his life, and the way he would like it to be.

Responding to Akram in keeping with a human rights (for children) approach requires that a number of concurrent actions be taken. He needs a birth certificate. Thinking more broadly, a system of civil registration has to be put in place. Akram's parents need more, better, and better-paid work. Again thinking more broadly, livelihoods and the labor market need redefinition and reform. In terms of education, Akram needs to be able to go to a school that is free and where he actually learns something. At twelve years of age, he probably needs some help to get to the same level as other school-going children his age. Thinking systemically, this means widespread education reform to ensure the universality of schooling for all children, including those who do not currently have appropriate age-for-grade skills. Finally, listening to Akram—as a human rights (for children) approach demands—it is clear that he has reflected and analyzed and come to the conclusion that, for him, "earning and learning" is both lucrative and meaningful for the moment.

Criticism of this approach as "too tailored to the individual child and too expensive" can be countered in three ways. First, for every required action, such as putting Akram in school, there is a systemwide response. "The many" benefit from realizing the rights of the individual, or even the rights of a few. Second, it is important to consider, in the case of the CRC in particular, that "the best interests of the child" prevail. It is not the best interest of *children* but of *the child,* of Akram. This belies an intention to fulfill rights en masse, recognizing the importance of the human rights of each and every child. As for this being costly, this is insufficient as a reason not to adopt such an approach. It is, I would argue, more costly *not* to adhere to this approach. We want to guarantee that child labor is prevented, and that children who are working are in school, learning, and free from exploitation at home or school to avoid the expense of "redoing" what has been done.[79] Ultimately, the success lies in fulfilling the rights of all children, in a way that responds to con-crete, real-life situations. As noted earlier, if the systemic responses re-quired—across a range of sectors—are truly effective, then, in fact, the num-ber of individuals needing "special" attention will actually be few.

There is evidence to suggest that the human rights (for children) approach is gaining momentum. This may in part be attributable to a discourse on child labor that is shifting as the moral high-grounders and the laissez-faire accep-tors are now actually speaking to each other. While each may continue to have a strongly held position, in debate there is, at the very least, a new willingness to consider embracing the complexity of the lives of laboring children. In a high-level meeting in Delhi in 2003, the World Bank, the ILO, Kailash Sat-yari of Global March, UNICEF, and a range of other stakeholders met to dis-cuss child labor, the Millennium Development Goals, and the global poverty eradication agenda. This is but one signal of a new willingness to accept re-sponsibility for complexity and intersectorality, two fundamental considera-tions coincident with a human rights approach to child labor. The ultimate re-sult for children in the face of these new approaches remains to be seen. One thing is very clear: in recognition of human rights obligation, the question of child labor elimination is no longer whether or even how to cease the ex-ploitation of children, but *how quickly.*

▓ Notes

The views and opinions expressed in this chapter are my own and do not necessarily rep-resent the official policies or views of the United Nations Children's Fund (UNICEF).

1. In this chapter, I adopt the definition of "child labor" set forth in the introduc-tion to this volume, in turn derived from Chapter 2, that is, "work done by children that is harmful to them because it is abusive, exploitive, hazardous, or otherwise contrary to their best interests—a subset of a larger class of children's work, some of which may be compatible with children's best interests (variously expressed as 'beneficial,' 'be-nign,' or 'harmless' children's work)."

2. In a roundtable discussion held in Delhi on November 13, 2003, and jointly organized by the ILO, UNESCO, the World Bank, and the Global March Against Child Labour, the interlinkages among the three key processes affecting the future of chil-dren were highlighted: poverty alleviation, "Education for All," and the elimination of child labor. For the first time, these different agencies clearly drew up together the need to tackle the triangular relationship among these processes at all levels of policy planning.

3. United Nations, *Convention on the Rights of the Child* (1989).

4. I would like to note the heavy reliance of this chapter on South Asian child labor "experiences." This is partly a function of my own lengthy tenure in Sri Lanka, Bangladesh, and India. It is also a reflection of the extent to which the region has at-tracted and fueled child labor elimination efforts.

5. See Ennew, *Learning or Labouring?* for a compilation of key texts on working children and education.

6. See Burra, *Born to Work . . .* ; Burra, "Exploitation of Children . . ."; and Weiner, *The Child and the State in India . . . .*

7. See Burra, "Exploitation of Children . . ."; and Ghosh, *Humananizing Child Labour.*

8. See Bacchus, "The Political Context . . ."; and Foster, "The Vocational School Fallacy . . . ."

9. Fyfe, *Educational Strategies . . .* , p. 2.

10. Weiner, *The Child and the State in India . . .* , p. 3.

11. Burra, *Born to Work . . .* , p. 230.

12. Weiner, *The Child and the State in India . . .* , p. 3.

13. Burra, *Born to Work . . .* , p. 245.

14. Ibid.

15. See Weiner, *The Child and the State in India . . .* ; and Burra, *Born to Work . . . .*

16. Fyfe, *Child Labour.*

17. Weiner, *The Child and the State in India . . .* , pp. 191–196.

18. See also Kumar, "What Can We Do?"

19. Brasted and Wright, "Why Worry About Child Labour?" p. 58.

20. Burra, *Born to Work . . .* , p. 245.

21. See "If You Build It, They Will Come, but Probably Drop Out" in this chapter.

22. Fyfe, *A Rights-Based Approach to Child Labour and Education . . .* , p. 4.

23. Ibid.

24. The International Conference on Child Labour, hosted by the Norwegian Ministry of Foreign Affairs, Oslo, Oct. 27–31, 1997.

25. UNICEF, background paper . . . .

26. The threat of US trade sanctions against countries employing underage workers led to thousands of Bangladeshi children losing their jobs (an estimated 50,000 to 200,000 underage workers were employed in the garment trade in the period between 1993 and 1995). When the retrenched workers appeared on Dhaka streets, local NGOs and others expressed their concern. This resulted in the signing and implementation of a memorandum of understanding (MOU) among UNICEF, the ILO's International Labour Office in Dhaka, and the Bangladesh Garment Manufacturers and Exporters Association. The MOU, which was designed to move children from their workplaces to schools established on their behalf, contained provisions for partial income substitution and promised vocational and skills training at a later date.

27. See also Espinola, Glauser, and Ortiz, *En la Calle . . .* , p. 94.

28. Wearing a uniform is a status symbol of sorts, though it is not necessarily an indication that a child is enrolled in an upper-class, fee-paying school.

29. In this discussion, "public" is understood to define a school that is established, funded, and maintained via public funding, state and central.

30. Blanchet, *Lost Innocence . . .* , p. 184.

31. Burra, *Born to Work . . .* , p. 243.

32. Weiner, *The Child and the State in India . . .* , p. 4.

33. For a useful discussion of absolute poverty, see Pryer, *Poverty and Vulnerability in Dhaka Slums . . . .*

34. For a helpful discussion of the impact of poverty on children, see Oppenheim and Harker, *Poverty: The Facts.*

35. Burra, "Exploitation of Children in Jaipur Gem Industry II . . . ."

36. See Bequele and Boyden, "Working Children . . ." (dismissing the economic value of child work); and Boyden, Ling, and Myers, *What Works for Working Children* (discussing "poverty as the main cause of child work and exploitation"), p. 127.

37. Kuznesof, "The Puzzling Contradictions of Child Labour . . . ," p. 225.

38. Ibid., p. 225.

39. My experience at a meeting in Delhi on child-centered social policy (July 1999) is a good illustration of non-evidence-based arguments. In the meeting, three prominent scholars and/or practitioners of child labor elimination on the Asian sub-continent argued against the importance of children's contributions to the household economy, but had no empirical data on which to base their claims.

40. See, for example, Basu and Van, *The Economics of Child Labor;* and Diamond and Fayed, "Evidence on Substitutability . . . ."

41. The absence of social services is a recurring theme in historical accounts of child labor. In their work on child labor in England in the eighteenth and nineteenth centuries, Sara Horrell and Jane Humphries note that the absence of a social support system offered parents no choice other than to put their children into the work force. Horrell and Humphries, "The Exploitation of Little Children . . . ." See also Cunningham, "The Employment of Children in England . . . ," pp. 115–150 (on working children in England); and Chapter 3 in this volume.

42. See Anker and Melkas, *Income Replacement and Substitution Activities* . . . .

43. Liang, *Bangladesh Female Secondary School Assistance Project,* p. 19.

44. See Wood, *Investing in Networks* . . . ; and Wood, "Security and Graduation . . . ."

45. Putnam, *Making Democracy Work* . . . .

46. Bourdieu, *Sociology in Question;* Coleman, *Foundations of Social Theory.*

47. Wood, "Adverse Incorporation . . . ," p. 1.

48. Ibid., p. 2.

49. See Salway, *Urban Livelihoods Study* . . . , p. 4.

50. Ibid.

51. Nieuwenhuys, "The Paradox of Anthropology and Child Labor."

52. See Thorner, *A. V. Chayanov on the Theory of Peasant Economy.*

53. See Scott, *The Moral Economy of the Peasant.*

54. Ibid., p. 14.

55. See Panter-Brick et al., "Growth Status of Homeless Nepali Boys . . ." (for measures of physical growth status in homeless Nepali boys); and Caesar-Leo, "Child Labour . . . ," pp. 80–82.

56. See Salway, *Urban Livelihoods Study* . . . .

57. Ibid., p. 108.

58. Rothstein, "The Case for Labour Standards."

59. See, among other sources, the Human Rights Watch website, at http://www.hrw.org/children/schools.htm.

60. Haq and Haq, *Human Development in South Asia,* p. 109.

61. Ibid., pp. 111–112.

62. Fyfe, *Letting Girls Learn* . . . , pp. 2–17.

63. Ibid., p. 5.

64. See *Public Report on Basic Education in India* for a discussion of positive parental attitudes to education, dispelling the myth that poor children's parents have neither interest nor faith in education and its value. See also Govinda, *India Education Report* . . . , pp. 2–5, for a discussion of increases in education enrollment.

65. See *Public Report on Basic Education in India,* which considers children's perceptions of schooling and various features that drive them away from school, rendering them available for work.

66. Boyden, Ling, and Myers, *What Works for Working Children,* p. 252.

67. Haq and Haq, *Human Development in South Asia,* p. 108.

68. Ibid., p. 109. See also Blanchet, *Lost Innocence* . . . .

69. For instance, what of health systems that function so badly that poor families pay for health care, and in a crisis "the need to pay" may mean that a child is sent to work instead of to school?

70. On the multidimensionality and indivisibility of human rights, see Weston, "Human Rights," pp. 5–9.

71. The balance of this chapter relies heavily on several recent documents: Gibbons, Huebler, and Loaiza, "Child Labor . . ."; *Child Labour . . .*; UNICEF, statement by Joe Judd . . . ; Santos Pais, *A Human Rights Conceptual Framework for UNICEF;* and Santos Pais, "The Question of Child Labour . . . ." They best convey this human rights (for children) approach and challenges to it. See also Chapters 1 and 10 in this volume.

72. Santos Pais, "The Question of Child Labour . . . ," pp. 71–79.

73. See United Nations, *Millennium Declaration.* See also United Nations, *Report of the Secretary-General: Road Map . . . .*

74. See, for example, Bissell and Schiefelbein, *Education to Combat Abusive Child Labour.*

75. PRSPs describe a country's macroeconomic, structural, and social policies and programs to promote growth and reduce poverty, as well as associated external financing needs. PRSPs are prepared by governments through a participatory process involving civil society and development partners, including the World Bank and the International Monetary Fund (IMF). See the World Bank website, at http://www. worldbank.org/poverty/strategies.

76. See United Nations, *Millennium Declaration.* See also the United Nations website, at http://www.un.org/millenniumgoals.

77. The International Conference on Child Labour, hosted by the Norwegian Ministry of Foreign Affairs, Oslo, Oct. 27–31, 1997.

78. This initiative is a partnership of developing countries and donors created to help low-income countries achieve the Millennium Development Goal of universal completion of primary education by 2015. In the spirit of the Monterrey global compact, the fast-track initiative bridges global commitments and local implementation around a set of reciprocal obligations: for the low-income countries to develop and implement sound education programs, and for donors to support such programs with finance and with enhanced efforts at harmonization, coordination, and acceleration.

79. See, for example, Psacharopoulos, *Economic Justification for Investment in Education.*

16

Trade-Based Strategies for Combating Child Labor

Frank J. Garcia and Soohyun Jun

From a regulatory standpoint, the problem of distinguishing between good and bad child work takes on special significance: Which practices are appropriate targets for legal (and extralegal) sanction and which are not? Many contributors to this volume have responded skillfully to this definitional challenge. We defer to that work and assume here that abusive and exploitive child work (hereinafter "child labor") is the appropriate regulatory target.[1]

While domestic strategies are central to any effective elimination or reduction of child labor, complementary international strategies of cooperation and coordination are required as well. Given the competing interests and values involved, it cannot be assumed by the world community that child labor will be eradicated solely through domestic law mechanisms and procedures. Such is the nature of our Westphalian system of international relations. Yet despite widespread recognition of human rights doctrines, principles, and rules, there currently is no effective multilateral regime requiring states to eliminate child labor in a manner that subjects them to binding, enforceable sanctions for failure to do so. The need for international cooperation and coordination to ensure that the rights of working children will be effectively enforced remains a global policy priority of the highest magnitude.

Recognizing such coordination and enforcement problems allows us to situate properly the role of trade-based strategies to address child labor. Reform-minded states can use trade to address *extraterritorially* the problem of child labor occurring within other jurisdictions. For example, they can offer trade preferences to child labor states that are conditioned on compliance with international labor standards pertinent to child labor (hereinafter "child labor standards").[2] This approach alters the policy incentives of the target state, by linking *its* domestic enforcement of child labor standards to eligibility for attractive trade preferences. Alternatively, reform-minded states can follow a more punitive trade-based strategy by using trade sanctions to impose bans on the importation of products produced through the use of child labor.

Trade-based strategies can be seen as specific instances of a market-oriented regulatory strategy to child labor—in contrast to other regulatory strategies that subject perpetrators to criminal or civil penalties or private causes of action (in tort, for example).[3] Manipulating information or incentives relevant to investment, production, and consumption decisions, market-oriented strategies operate *indirectly* to alter the commercial behavior of producers or consumers in relation to the manufacture or purchase of child labor products and thereby, it is hoped, discourage the demand for child labor. Trade sanctions are intended to eliminate or reduce producer incentives to use child labor by eliminating or reducing through law demand for their products. Social labeling, corporate codes of conduct, and other such private sector initiatives likewise seek to alter commercial conduct, but in a voluntary manner.[4] And conditional trade preferences, also a market-oriented approach but operating in the state-to-state market for trade advantages, use the promise of preferential trade terms to cause states to alter *their* behavior—in the present context, relative to the more aggressive domestic enforcement of child labor standards. By their very indirection, of course, trade strategies may play a limited role in combating child labor. Sanctions are effective only with child labor industries that export. Social labeling and other voluntary approaches rely on public goodwill. And conditional trade preferences depend on the degree to which the target state's economy needs the preferences, supervisory and enforcement efforts are vigorous, and compliance is not waived for extrinsic political reasons. Nevertheless, trade strategies play an important role, offering readily available methods to address extraterritorial child labor problems in the absence of more effective transnational mechanisms.

In this chapter, we discuss the structure and legality of trade-based strategies for addressing child labor. In doing so, we focus primarily on unilateral trade sanctions, specifically import bans, as the most aggressive and therefore most controversial of the trade-based strategies.[5] We do not argue for the effectiveness of trade sanctions in economic or political terms, however. Nor do we offer a moral argument favoring or opposing the use of unilateral sanctions. Though we touch upon both issues, we assume the desirability and propriety of this trade-based strategy and address its legality. By their very nature, trade sanctions interfere with the free movement of goods, so proponents of such measures must address their compatibility with the international trade regulatory system. Does World Trade Organization (WTO) law permit this trade-restrictive measure? At the core of the WTO system are two antidiscrimination principles: most-favored-nation (MFN) treatment (barring discrimination between exporting countries) and national treatment (barring discrimination between imports and domestic goods). As will be discussed further below, trade sanctions are prima facie violations of these two rules, and therefore must be justified through recourse to the policy exceptions listed in the General Agreement on Tariffs and Trade (GATT).[6]

This leads to a larger question regarding the role of the WTO in addressing child labor, and international human rights generally. Conflicting views reflect the ongoing tension between the goals of liberalizing trade and of protecting other social values such as human rights. We presuppose that there is a direct, fundamental, and appropriate relationship between international trade and the protection of human rights, including the rights of working children.[7] The real question is not whether there is a linkage between human rights and trade, but *how* this linkage should be managed by the international community in theory and practice.[8] Institutionally, this can be reduced to two questions: (1) Is the WTO as an institution capable of addressing child labor or human rights issues more generally? (2) More specifically, does WTO case law offer interpretative room for allowing unilateral child labor–based trade sanctions? While we do not focus directly on the first question,[9] we hope through our analysis of the second question to suggest both strategies for the reconciliation of trade liberalization and the protection of working children at the dispute resolution level and, more broadly, a general positive view on the question of the WTO's potential human rights contributions.

We begin by evaluating the legality of trade sanctions as a response to child labor. We first review the arguments for and against trade sanctions based on child labor practices in target countries, and consider the question of the effectiveness of such sanctions. We then introduce contemporary US law banning the importation of forced child labor products as an example of a trade-based strategy.

Next we probe the compatibility of US trade sanction law and WTO case law, reviewing major cases under GATT Article I (MFN treatment) and Article III (national treatment), and the general problem of production process method (PPM)–based trade measures (of which a child labor import ban is an example). We then examine cases under GATT Article XX, the provision setting forth exceptions under which deviations from other GATT obligations may be justified. In particular, we focus on the meaning and potential use of the Article XX(a) public morals exception and the Article XX(b) human life and health exception in justifying a trade-based strategy. Through a review of the interpretative techniques used by WTO dispute settlement panels and certain developments in the case law, we determine that there indeed may be room within trade rules for legitimate child labor sanctions, and make further proposals for a reform-oriented interpretation of the relevant provisions.

Finally, we conclude that the use of import bans to address child labor practices is in compliance with the WTO system if certain conditions are met. Thereafter, we recommend that trade-based strategies be accepted as a dynamic part of a comprehensive blend of public and private efforts to eliminate the worst forms of child labor.

▓ Trade Sanctions Based on Child Labor Practices

The purpose of sanctions is to change the behavior of states.[10] For this reason, if sanctions are to succeed in whole or in part, they must be recognized as legitimate in moral and legal terms.[11] In this respect, a multilateral trade sanctions regime is better than a unilateral one because of its enhanced legitimacy. If, for lack of a multilateral alternative, a state is driven to take unilateral trade action to modify another state's behavior—say, in its use or tolerance of forced child labor—it will have squarely to face contentious debate and potential retaliation.

Arguments For and Against Trade Sanctions Opposed to Child Labor

When is it justifiable to impose trade sanctions to prevent the exploitation of working children or otherwise protect them? The answer to this question depends in part on the normative traditions of the sanctioning state. In a liberal state favoring Kantian notions of human autonomy, children's rights will be seen as inalienable (belonging to them simply for being human), and trade sanctions in defense of children's rights therefore as moral (assuming a meaningful link between the sanction and the infringed right). Of course, the target state may have a quite different normative tradition than the sanctioning state. For this reason, sanctions critics argue on relativist grounds that a country should not restrict trade access for internal moral reasons. Jagdish Bhagwati and T. N. Srinivasan, for example, find inappropriate "GATT sanctioning of the use of unilateral state action to suspend other countries' trade access, or . . . their trading rights under the GATT 'treaty,' unless one's choice of ethical concerns is adopted by others through implicit harmonization in one's direction."[12]

Even granting this objection, however, sanctions opposing child labor cannot be easily condemned outright. Beyond the liberal community, international law ensures that certain human rights attain universal status as positive law because of their widespread recognition in consensual instruments such as International Labour Organization (ILO) conventions and other international agreements.[13] Within international law, the goal of prohibiting certain child labor practices, for example, indentured or exploitive child labor, is widely recognized in custom and treaties. This amounts to "explicit" harmonization and justifies sanctions even against cultural relativism objections.

Nevertheless, the cultural relativism/cultural autonomy objection to unilateral sanctions is frequently cited and thus deserves fuller consideration.[14] Bhagwati and Srinivasan argue that the imposition of morally grounded sanctions is improper principally for two interrelated reasons: (1) the "culture specificity" of values and (2) asymmetries in power—the first of these resulting in acts of "unjustified moral militancy that is itself ethically offensive"; the second allowing the Global North to impose "idiosyncratic moral preferences" on the Global South, among others.[15] These arguments, the second especially, highlight that the range of attitudes toward the regulation of child labor through externally imposed trade measures tends to divide along development lines. While some feel that the labor standards (including child labor standards) prevailing in the developing world can be improved only through sanctions, others maintain that cultural differences justify alternative standards and that concerns for labor rights in developing countries are "paternalistic or culturally patronizing."[16] Developing countries in particular have criticized the trade-labor rights linkage as "protectionist" and "imperialist."[17]

The international regulation of child labor requires more than emotive responses to the value systems shaping different societies' perceptions of the socioeconomic issues that are embedded in labor standards.[18] To begin with, the debate surrounding sanctions on imports produced with child labor must address the degree to which the child labor policies in question actually implicate harmful child labor.[19] Free trade advocates often contend that child labor sanctions are in fact competition-based, a subterfuge designed to "level the playing field"[20] (i.e., eliminate differences in labor standards among countries) so as to deprive developing countries of the comparative advantage they enjoy from low labor costs—in other words, rank protectionism.[21] Of course, free traders are right to challenge any invocation of the rights of working children on purely protectionist grounds. Trade sanctions that are justified by reference to child labor but that in reality serve protectionist interests do not by virtue of their claims to legitimacy acquire genuine moral validity. Kantian liberalism requires, after all, that any trade measures that are geared to the protection of working children must strive to treat the children as ends in themselves, not as means to serve sanctioning country economic or political goals.[22] Indeed, the 1998 ILO Declaration on Fundamental Principles and Rights at Work expressly provides that labor standards should not be used for protectionist purposes or for questioning a country's comparative advantage.[23]

On the other hand, it must not be assumed categorically that all invocations of child worker rights are thus motivated. Nevertheless, if the Global North wants to escape the criticism that it is using child labor as a "moral shield" to disallow imports from developing countries that enjoy a competitive advantage through cheap labor, it needs to design regimes that are tailored clearly to benefit the children and not the domestic industries of the sanctioning state.[24] Conversely, developing countries that seek to defend alternative labor standards relative to working children must take care that their justifications are grounded in cultural traditions that demonstrably benefit all the people involved: the children, their families, and their communities. Too often such relativist claims are trumpeted by authoritarian leaders whose policies do not serve as a whole the people they claim to benefit or by industry representatives whose motives and practices are often best explained via Western concepts of greed rather than by reference to other cultural traditions.[25]

Some free traders argue also that an increased focus on reformist social policies will result automatically from rising incomes through market forces in international trade.[26] This economic determinism ignores, however, the historical political struggle that took place in industrialized countries to win the labor standards that exist today.[27] Others argue that contemporary free trade orthodoxy is itself the threat; workers would be much better off, it is argued, without the neoliberal policies of trade liberalization, deregulation of the economy, privatization, and the free market ideology that force wages down and deny people work.[28] While this argument is a legitimate global economic policy debate, we cannot wait for its resolution to implement strategies to address child labor, a necessary response within *any* global economic paradigm, particularly in relation to child labor's "worst forms."

Critics of a trade sanctions approach to child labor in particular perceive this strategy also as too simplistic; they believe that import bans only drive employed children from the formal to the informal sector, where they are less exposed to scrutiny and more vulnerable to infringement of their rights.[29] At the opposite extreme is the argument that any trade sanction is justified once the child labor practice in question is deemed illegal or immoral, and regardless of its actual impact on the children or whether the sanction actually reduces the offending practice[30]—a contention that raises the central question of the effectiveness of child labor sanctions, independent of their legitimacy. Before implementing measures that are designed to ensure that children's interests are protected, one must consider whether linking labor rights to trade actually can improve the conditions of child workers (in the developing world especially) or can eliminate child labor where it should not exist.[31] In other words, are sanctions effective or useful in protecting children against abusive and exploitive labor?[32]

We do not undertake to answer this question definitively here. However, we do recommend some relevant considerations. Generally it is agreed that for sanctions to be justifiable it must be possible to demonstrate that they can be more or less effective in addressing the root concern. There is less agreement as to the definition of effectiveness. A simple measure would be the elimination or substantial reduction of child labor practices in the target industry. However, this metric is by itself inadequate to measure the effectiveness of child labor trade sanctions because it fails to take a comprehensive view of the problem. Where the effect of an import ban is to increase the number of working children in the sector producing goods for domestic consumption rather than exports, or in the informal economy, in which their rights are even less subject to protection, it could be argued that the sanction has failed.[33] Moreover, if the number of children in the sector producing for domestic consumers increases, the wages may dwindle, adversely affecting all workers.[34]

These "static" effects must be considered along with "dynamic" ones, however.[35] A trade sanction alone may have some positive effects on improving the rights of working children in target countries, but these effects can be enhanced in a dynamic way if combined with such alternatives as providing children with education, social labeling, and other "grassroots" initiatives.[36] Conversely, if sanctions fail, poverty rates may be accelerated, as may also the rate of child workers shifting into less supervised informal sectors.

Regardless of how one measures effectiveness, however, questions of "market leverage" and "industry leverage" are essential considerations (market leverage being the power the sanctioning state can exert over the target state; industry leverage being the power afforded by the ratio of child labor industries in the target state that are export-sensitive to child labor industries in the target states as a whole). In terms of market leverage, a trade sanction imposed consistently by a country with a large market for child labor products would have the strongest effects,[37] although without multilateral support such a sanction might fail anyway because the target country can then easily find noncooperating substitute markets.[38] In terms of industry leverage, if the majority of child labor industries are not export-sensitive, then a sanctions strategy will have limited, albeit potentially laudable, effects in addressing target state child labor practices.

Case Study: US Child Labor Trade Sanctions Law

To understand better the legal and policy issues raised by a trade-based strategy opposed to child labor, we explore here a particular trade sanctions law with child labor ramifications: Section 307 of the US Tariff Act of 1930, also known as the US "forced labor statute."[39] Section 307 has been amended to include forced child labor, and is therefore the leading US statute on point,[40] and given the sway of the United States worldwide, of obvious significance to any trade-based approach to human rights enforcement.

Section 307 prohibits the importation of all goods produced wholly or in part in any foreign country by forced labor, and authorizes the secretary of the treasury to prescribe such regulations as may be necessary for the enforcement of the provision. Amendments to Section 307 in 1997 barred the use of customs service funds for the importation into the United States of any goods produced by forced or indentured child labor.[41] Additional amendments in 2000 inserted a definition of forced labor, which explicitly included forced child labor.[42] If a customs officer has reason to believe that any merchandise being imported or likely to be imported into the United States is produced in any foreign country with the use of forced child labor, he or she must report this belief to the commissioner of customs.[43] If the commissioner conclusively determines that the merchandise is subject to the import ban, the burden is on the importer to establish by satisfactory evidence that the merchandise was not produced in any part with the use of forced child labor, in order to have the merchandise released from custody.[44]

In conjunction with Section 307 of the Tariff Act of 1930, and in order to further enforce US laws on forced labor, President Bill Clinton, in 1999, issued an executive order to prevent federal agencies from buying products made with forced or indentured child labor.[45] "Forced child labor" is defined as "involuntary work or service rendered by a person under the age of eighteen,"[46] and under the executive order, the Department of Labor, in cooperation with the Department of Treasury and the Department of State, is required to publish a list of products that it reasonably believes might have been produced by forced child labor.[47] If the contracting officer of an executive agency reasonably believes that forced child labor has been used, the head of the agency will initiate an investigation.[48] If it is found that the contractor has furnished products produced by forced child labor or uses forced child labor and has submitted a false certification or has failed to cooperate, the head of an executive agency may terminate a contract or debar or suspend a contractor from eligibility for federal contracts.[49] This order does show a determination on the part of the executive branch to enforce laws relating to child labor practices in foreign countries.[50]

Application of Section 307 has been episodic and, from a child labor perspective, disappointing. During the 1990s, Section 307 of the Tariff Act was invoked to prohibit the importation of certain Mexican products produced with prison or forced labor and was used to ban the importation of leather imports and iron pipe fittings determined by the US Customs Service to have been produced with convict or prison labor from China.[51] However, since the 1997 amendment to Section 307 affecting child labor, petitions have been filed to halt importation of rugs from South Asia knotted by children, and cocoa picked by children in Côte d'Ivoire, with no action taken in either case.[52]

WTO Case Law on GATT Articles I, III, and XX: Room for Justifiable Child Labor Sanctions?

Those who claim the WTO downplays adult workers' rights may also conclude that the GATT contains nothing for working children.[53] In this section, we seek to demonstrate that WTO case law allows room for distinguishing nondiscriminatory and justified child labor measures from protectionist measures purportedly based on child labor, and that therefore it can accommodate a trade-based strategy of import sanctions to protect working children's rights while also safeguarding core trade liberalization principles.

When the WTO was established in 1994, it incorporated into its governing agreements the original 1947 GATT, supplemented by various agreements and understandings.[54] However, unlike the 1948 Havana Charter, the blueprint for the International Trade Organization, the WTO's stillborn predecessor, neither the WTO agreement nor the GATT contained any explicit provision permitting trade sanctions against unfair labor conditions.[55] Furthermore, at their first meeting at Singapore in 1996, the WTO Conference of Ministers, in their Singapore Declaration, expressed their commitment to the observance of internationally recognized core labor standards and, in so doing, acknowledged the ILO as the competent body to set and deal with these standards and supported the ILO's work in promoting them.[56] In addition, they explicitly rejected any use of labor standards for protectionist purposes, particularly those directed at neutralizing comparative advantage (i.e., leveling the playing field), stating that comparative advantage in low-wage developing countries may in no way be questioned, thereby leaving room for trade measures of a legitimate, nonprotectionist nature.[57] The Singapore Declaration does not formally assign the role of dealing with labor-related trade issues to the ILO, and it does note the importance of existing collaboration with the ILO.[58] Nevertheless, under the current division of labor, the WTO's chief role is to adjudicate all trade-labor disputes.

Ongoing experience with the WTO's dispute settlement understanding (DSU),[59] the system for panel and appellate body reports, and resulting case law have led to a more effective and credible system for resolving differences among WTO member countries.[60] We examine here how this improvement in WTO practice may be enhanced in the child labor context, particularly with reference to the exceptions of GATT Article XX. Despite the WTO's unwillingness to assume any policymaking role in respect of trade sanctions relating to labor rights, the WTO's positive impact in this realm would be substantial should a trade sanction based on child labor practices ever successfully come before it due to the preeminence of its dispute settlement mechanism.

Substantive GATT Rules

The GATT regime for reviewing the legality of trade-restrictive measures is bifurcated. A complaining party must first establish that a measure violates one or more GATT trade rules, such as Articles I, III, and XI. If a violation is established, the responding party may then argue that the violation is permitted under one of a number of recognized exceptions to the GATT rules, most often those enumerated in Article XX. We proceed here accordingly.

Article I: MFN treatment. GATT Article I provides for unconditional most-favored-nation treatment with respect to tariffs, charges, and other measures. In other words, a member may not provide more favorable treatment to some members than to others with respect to "like products,"[61] a principle well established in WTO case law. Generally, WTO case law reflects a very rigid interpretation of MFN treatment, emphasizing likeness of product, rejecting differentiation based on other factors.[62] In particular, WTO case law suggests that differences in the production and process method used to manufacture the product in question (such as the use of child labor) are wholly irrelevant to a "like products" analysis.[63]

Article III: National treatment, and Article XI: Elimination of quantitative restrictions. GATT Article III allows the importing country to impose its regulations and requirements on imported products as long as they are given treatment no less favorable than that accorded to like products of national origin. Article III covers internal taxation and measures affecting internal sale, offering for sale, purchase, transportation, distribution, or use. Therefore, if the United States bans the sale within the US market of child labor products, such as imported rugs knotted by exploited children, and *also* prohibits the sale of domestically produced child labor rugs, it would seem to follow that there would be no violation of the national treatment principle, since like products are treated equally.

However, two unadopted GATT panel reports on tuna caught with dolphin-unfriendly methods *(Tuna-Dolphin I* and *II)*[64] created a distinction between regulatory measures on products and measures relating to the PPMs, removing the latter category from Article III. The reasoning in these cases was that Article III dealt only with measures on products, not measures based on PPMs, and that therefore the US ban on tuna caught with dolphin-unfriendly methods could not be evaluated for simple evenhandedness as a domestic regulation under Article III, but instead constituted an embargo, prohibited in all cases under GATT Article XI.[65] Had Article III applied, the issue would have been whether imported tuna produced in a dolphin-unfriendly manner was afforded a less favorable or worse treatment than domestically produced tuna caught in a dolphin-unfriendly manner, and the US measure might have succeeded.[66] Although unadopted pre-WTO panel reports have uncertain legal status, the product-process distinction has been both influential and controversial.

The status of the PPM distinction regarding the scope of Article III is critical to the viability of any trade-based social welfare legislation, including child labor measures. Such measures, if deemed reviewable under Article III and evenhanded between domestic and foreign goods, might not violate Article III and therefore would survive a GATT challenge. If, however, *Tuna-Dolphin*'s distinction between "product" and "PPM" were to be followed relative to a child labor import ban, such a ban would be held "GATT-inconsistent" at all times.[67]

On account of this potentially broad preclusive effect, the subject of PPM-based measures has been the subject of much scholarly debate. Commentators have observed that WTO treaty law as a whole does not per se prohibit PPMs that impinge on trade[68] and have argued strenuously that the distinction between products and PPMs in the context of Article III has no basis, especially given that the two *Tuna-Dolphin* reports were not adopted, and therefore not binding upon the states involved.[69] Moreover, a recent Appellate Body decision, *European Communities: Measures Affecting Asbestos and Asbestos-Containing Products*,[70] seems to look beyond the narrow physical characteristics of the products, stating that "the health risks associated with a product may be pertinent in an examination of likeness under Article III:4."[71]

Together, these lines of scholarly and legal development suggest that an import ban based on who makes the product might succeed to the extent it is origin-neutral, that is, it applies to any foreign or domestic producer in any foreign country that employs forced or indentured child labor, and does not impose a policy standard on a foreign government.[72] But given the current law, the more likely scenario is that these aspects of the regime would have to be analyzed under the exceptions in Article XX because, under traditional analysis, the product is not differentiated *as a product* by use of child labor, and the ban would therefore violate Articles I, III, and/or XI.

Guiding a Trade-Based Strategy Through GATT Article XX

Assuming that all efforts to reinterpret GATT principles in Articles I and III have failed, Article XX provides for situations in which a WTO member may deviate from its GATT obligations for certain designated policy reasons.[73] A three-step inquiry is required to determine whether an otherwise "GATT-illegal" measure is justified under Article XX.[74] First, the stated policy must come within the scope of one of the categories listed under Article XX—for example, as a measure to protect public morals, or human, animal, or plant life, or health. Second, the measure complained of must be either "necessary" or "related" to the policy allegedly being furthered, depending on the paragraph. Finally, the *chapeau* (i.e., preamble or introductory clause) of Article XX requires that the application of any measure that otherwise meets the first two tests must not constitute a means of arbitrary or unjustifiable discrimination between countries where the same conditions prevail, or a disguised restriction on international trade is present. In other words, Article XX permits policy-driven discrimination between countries as long as it is not arbitrary or unjustifiable.

Finding the right exception. The first step in evaluating the legality of a child labor sanction under Article XX is to determine which of the enumerated exceptions best covers the regulatory goal of the measure in question, here child labor. There are three immediate possibilities: Article XX(a) for measures protecting public morals, Article XX(b) for measures protecting human life or health, and Article XX(e) for measures banning importation of the products of prison labor. Despite the obvious similarities between products of prison labor and products of forced child labor, Article XX(e) will not be developed here as a suitable exception under which to mount the defense of a child labor trade sanction. It is our judgment that the language and negotiating history of the provision are too narrowly tied specifically to prison labor to allow extension to other forms of forced labor.[75] This leaves two other options: Articles XX(a) and XX(b).

Article XX(a): Public morals exception. Surprisingly there is no GATT or WTO case law on the public morals exception. Some have argued against interpreting this exception to cover labor rights violations on the grounds that both the reference to prison labor in Article XX(e) and the fact that the Havana Charter included explicit language on labor rights suggest that the drafters did not intend for Article XX to cover labor rights (or children's rights had they envisioned regulating child labor).[76] A powerful counterargument to this view is that as in the case of constitutional interpretation, it is reasonable and appropriate not to be bound by the drafters' "original intent." Instead, altogether consistent with the international law of treaty interpretation, one should take into account the evolution of thinking about the intersection of trade and human rights in the years intervening, which has developed to include the prohibition of certain labor practices that violate universal human rights, for example, the prohibition on child labor.[77]

This being said, the hard question remains as to how to resolve what constitutes "public morals" and whose public morals count. It is clear that the provision is intended to protect the public morality of the importing/sanctioning country. Controversy arises, however, when that country, on the basis of its own sense of public morality, seeks, through "outwardly directed" trade measures, to protect foreigners outside its jurisdiction.[78] The US law banning goods made with forced child labor via "outwardly directed" trade measures is arguably illustrative in that it attempts to protect working children in other countries from practices the United States considers immoral and/or illegal.

Although there has been no case under the public morals exception in the fifty-odd years of the GATT, there is relevant case law interpreting the rest of Article XX. With respect to the "outwardly directed" problem, the *Tuna-Dolphin* cases once again raise issues, given that both panels objected to the measures in question as outwardly directed and coercive. At the same time, it bears noting again that neither panel report was adopted. It also can be argued that the United States may be *encouraging* the target countries to design certain preferred child labor practices but is *not coercing* them to adopt a particular set of laws or regulations.

If we view international law as an evolving system, then one could read into Article XX(a) the core labor rights stipulated in the ILO Declaration on Fundamental Principles and Rights at Work, including the elimination of child labor.[79] This reflects the Appellate Body's approach in *Shrimp-Turtle,* in which it ruled that the meaning of "exhaustible natural resources" had evolved in light of developments in international law and policy and that even if the exception at issue did not include living species during the drafting stage, it should be interpreted as so now.[80] In addition, the Appellate Body took account of the preamble to the WTO agreement, which refers to the objective of sustainable development. The same preamble recognizes that trade relations and economic endeavor should be conducted with a view to raising standards of living and ensuring full employment.[81]

On this textual basis, a parallel could be used to elicit the meaning of public morals in Article XX(a) as including the protection of working children.[82] The content of public morals should have a universal and evolutionary character as manifested by the increasing number of international agreements with widespread ratifications among states, and by the ILO declaration setting forth core labor rights.[83]

Finally, the drafting history of GATT between 1945 and 1948 shows little other than the possibility of covering alcohol.[84] Nevertheless, Steve Charnovitz, examining other trade agreements containing moral exceptions prior to 1948,[85] concludes that public morals concerns were both outwardly directed and based on "beliefs about morality and rectitude."[86]

At a minimum, then, the protection of public morals outside the importing/sanctioning country is not precluded from Article XX(a). However, a stronger—and in our view equally valid—argument is that a trade sanction opposed to child labor is not outwardly directed at all. Instead of basing a sanction against child labor on the theory that the child labor *production process* in the target country violates our sense of public morality, one could instead base the sanction on the theory that the presence of the child labor *product* in our own jurisdiction violates our public morality, in much the same way that the presence of pornographic material or illegal arms or drugs *in our jurisdiction* endangers our public morality. A child labor trade sanction thus would be no different from any of the other types of sanctions traditionally understood as falling within the ambit of Article XX(a). The difficulty with this argument lies in its novel interpretation of the child labor product as itself being "tainted" with the abusive practices underlying its production, or as representing a moral "temptation" to the consumer in the importing/sanctioning country to choose lower-cost products that are cheap due to the labor of children. This approach would represent a departure from the traditional view, although not without basis in the environmental cases that "dolphin-unfriendly" tuna should not be considered a "like product" to dolphin-friendly tuna.

Article XX(b): Human life and health exception. It is not difficult to argue initially that a measure aimed at eradicating forced child labor would be a measure aimed at protecting human life or health. The case law interpreting Article XX(b), however, interposes some juridical hurdles on the way to this conclusion, such as the question of the provision's jurisdictional scope and whether it covers only products harmful to human life and health or whether it includes processes and production methods as well.[87]

In this connection, it is important to recall that the WTO panel in the *Tuna-Dolphin* litigation did not on final analysis limit the jurisdictional scope of the life or health to be protected by the trade-restricting measure involved in those cases.[88] Similarly, while the Appellate Body in *Shrimp-Turtle* also found the measure in question inconsistent with the GATT, it did not object to the extraterritoriality of the measure.[89]

Thus, if a measure protecting the life and health of animals outside the jurisdiction of the importing country is covered by Article XX(b), there appears to be no reason for excluding an extraterritorial child labor measure for that reason alone. It was the discriminatory application of the US measure in *Shrimp-Turtle,* not its extraterritoriality, that led the Appellate Body to find the import ban to be GATT-illegal.[90]

The necessity test.   Once it has been determined that a measure falls within the scope of an enumerated exception, the WTO panel would turn to examine what is usually termed the "trade-off" mechanism embedded in the particular exception. The GATT uses a variety of trade-off mechanisms—such as "rational relation" or "necessity"—which together indicate the weight or balance to be given to trade versus nontrade values at stake in the adjudication. Paragraphs (a) and (b) of Article XX both employ the "necessity" test.

The interpretation of "necessity" or "necessary" has been strict and has come to mean use by the state of the "least trade-restrictive measure available to achieve the policy goal."[91] In the Article XX(b) context, the panels in *Tuna-Dolphin I* and *II* first considered the meaning of "necessary"[92] and noted that the United States had not exhausted all options reasonably available to it in pursuit of its dolphin protection objectives. Additionally, they reasoned that a measure (the import ban) that depends for its success (protecting dolphins) on forcing changes in target state practices (such as tuna harvesting methods) could not by definition ever be "necessary" in itself to the protection of animal life.[93]

In *Shrimp-Turtle,* the Appellate Body rejected this interpretation of "necessary," reasoning that to deem measures requiring exporting countries to comply with certain policies prescribed by the importing country to be a priori incapable of justification under Article XX would render most Article XX exceptions useless, a result that the Appellate Body characterized as "abhorrent to the principles of interpretation [the Appellate Body is] bound to apply."[94] Accordingly, the fact that the success of a child labor import ban implicitly depends on exporting countries adopting measures to protect children or to ban child labor does not automatically render the defense under Article XX(a) or (b) hopeless.

GATT application of the necessity test is subject to several additional criticisms. First, the word "necessary" is part of a purpose clause, with its object the protection of a social good, such as public morals.[95] However, the "least trade-restrictive" construction of this language makes the provision incapable of relating to a social good such as the protection of "public morals" or "human life or health"; instead it asks whether the sanction would be a necessary departure from the GATT, seemingly a misconstruction of the text.[96] If this interpretation is taken literally, it suggests that there may be a less trade-restrictive alternative (for instance, in the child labor context, social labeling or compensation to the target exporting country for use of educating children) and that therefore the import ban based on child labor practices would be "GATT-inconsistent" and not saved by the Article XX interpretive techniques thus far employed.

If this interpretive judgment is correct, then the best alternative approach (and the only one capable of rescuing a trade-based strategy) is for the Appellate Body to develop through its case law a requirement that, to give meaning to Article XX(a) and (b), panels inquire into the actual effectiveness or feasibility of alternatives for the protection of public morals or human life or health.[97] Instead of judging the necessity of such protection according to its effects on trade, a panel should find a "significantly less effective" alternative measure protecting public morals to be *not* "reasonably available," thereby paving the way to validation of the measure.[98]

This approach is confirmed in the context of human life and health, through the WTO Agreement on Sanitary and Phytosanitary Measures (SPS Agreement).[99] Under the SPS Agreement, members may take measures necessary to protect human and animal health[100] subject to the standard that the measures must "not be more trade-restrictive than required to achieve their appropriate level of protection"—thereby granting to members the right to choose their own level of protection.[101] The measure would not be more trade restrictive than required unless there is another measure reasonably available or feasible that would achieve the same goal.[102] Thus, if, for example, financial compensation, social labeling, or voluntary corporate codes of conduct would not do the job as effectively as the import ban on child labor products, the sanction would be held necessary.

Recent case law suggests moderation of the rigors of the necessity test where important social goals are at stake. In the *Asbestos* case, for example, the first to have found that a measure satisfied Article XX(b), the Appellate Body asked "whether there is an alternative measure that would achieve the same end and that is *less restrictive* of trade than a prohibition."[103] It concluded in the negative, upholding the French ban, and in so doing, was highly concerned to respect France's chosen level of protection from asbestos, thereby importing concepts more fully developed under the SPS Agreement. This deference to national regulatory autonomy in determining what possible "less trade-restrictive" measures are deemed in fact "reasonably available" could bode well for the viability of a child labor import ban if such a ban is ever litigated.

The chapeau. If a child labor measure survives the first two prongs of the Article XX analysis, it must surmount, finally, the *chapeau* test (which looks at how the measure is actually applied). Although "unjustifiable discrimination," "arbitrary discrimination," and "disguised restriction on international trade" seem to intermingle with each other, they have been construed as separate though interrelated. According to the Appellate Body in *Shrimp-Turtle,* for example, it is not necessarily "GATT-illegal" to impose a government policy extraterritorially provided one is "sensitive" to the conditions in each country and the resulting administrative process meets minimum standards of transparency and procedural fairness.[104] The Appellate Body stressed the need to treat equally the countries where the same or similar conditions prevail and to treat differently the countries where different conditions exist.[105]

Following this logic, a US sanction opposing forced or indentured child labor will be justified if it applies the definition of forced or indentured child labor evenhandedly to countries faced with similar situations. Also, the United States would have to take into account special circumstances in individual target countries. For example, a sanction based on forced and indentured child labor would be permissible where domestic equivalent practices are also prohibited. However, taking agriculture as an example, in view of the differences between the agrarian sectors of the US economy and those in many developing countries, a sanction used in response to the "traditional, non-exploitive use of underage workers in small, family-based agriculture" could constitute unjustifiable discrimination, even if similar practices are prohibited in the United States.[106]

Finally, several WTO panels suggest that the existence and extent of prior multilateral negotiations are important factors in determining whether a unilateral extraterritorial measure will survive the *chapeau.*[107] Given that labor conventions are typically negotiated internationally, including agreements covering child labor, this does not mean that fresh multilateral negotiations are necessarily an absolute requirement of a unilateral child labor sanction. However, when a country such as the United States has a poor record of ratifications of international human rights conventions (for example, only one of eight fundamental ILO conventions in the case of the United States), a dispute resolution panel might view the imposition of a unilateral labor-related import ban by such a country as inconsistent with its record of multilateral efforts.[108] Furthermore, any selectivity in the administration of a trade sanction by a country prone to unilateralism would likely undermine international respect, because the sanction might be considered to be promoting only the "human rights du jour" of the sanctioning country.[109] Therefore, in the case of the United States at least, maintaining consistency is critical for the legitimacy and justifiability of the child labor–based sanction.[110]

WTO Law and US Tariff Act Section 307

Since international organizations tend generally to lack human rights enforcement mechanisms beyond the "mobilization of shame," the WTO stands out as an attractive if not the ideal arena in which to confront fundamental violations of internationally recognized labor rights, including the rights of working children. It is unlikely that a targeted WTO member country would protest a sanction issue in a WTO dispute settlement proceeding, lest it publicize its child labor practices. Nevertheless, since legality is central to international legitimacy independent of whether or not the measure ever will be litigated, it is important to consider the trade law issues discussed above when designing and implementing a child labor trade sanction.

Taking Section 307 of the US Tariff Act of 1930 as our model, we have analyzed the key features of a trade sanction that raise issues under WTO standards. Based on this analysis, we conclude that Section 307 is capable of surviving a WTO challenge. The fact that trade sanctions such as Section 307 are targeted at a production process and not at a product per se raises important interpretive issues, but we conclude that such sanctions are not or should not be a problem under current WTO law. The more difficult question is whether child labor sanctions can be excused under the existing public morals or human life and health exceptions of the GATT. As argued above, it is reasonable and appropriate to conclude that they do come within the scope of the exceptions.

The most serious issue is unilateralism. Section 307 is unilateral in nature since it allows the United States to act essentially on its own determination.[111] While a unilateral sanction is inherently controversial, such sanctions can prove to be multilateral de facto[112] when there is a multilateral legal or moral consensus underlying a de jure unilateral ban. This is to the good, given that, as discussed above, a multilateral approach to trade sanctions is to be preferred over a unilateral one. The most troubling scenario, implying that there exists no international consensus whatsoever, would be a sanction that is unilateral in both law and fact. This issue presents the greatest risk to Section 307 and similar trade sanctions. In interpreting the Article XX *chapeau,* the WTO Appellate Body has indicated that it expects sanctioning countries to engage in bona fide multilateral negotiations before resorting to unilateral action. Section 307 is not a response by the United States to failed multilateral negotiations, but international standards prohibiting forced or indentured child labor do confer a de facto multilateralism on Section 307.

Given the spotty US record relative to multilateral human rights instruments, it remains to be seen if this conferral would be enough under WTO law. A fully multilateral trade sanctions regime would be subject to less opposition and create less criticism on "culture specificity" and "power asymmetry" grounds, but de facto multilateralism at least is preferable to pure unilateralism.

■ Conclusion

Trade sanctions that take aim at child labor practices to enhance the human rights of working children, such as Section 307 of the US Tariff Act of 1930, have a role to play in the internationalization of fundamental values. Sanctions can influence producers in particular child labor sectors, they can attract foreign attention to the importance of protecting exploited children in various parts of the world, and they can increase multilateral pressure on the target country. In sum, they can move states and private actors "from one-time grudging compliance to habitual internalized obedience."[113]

Since a trade-based strategy must work within the rules of the GATT, the means employed to address child labor through trade sanctions must be designed carefully. We have argued that, if correctly legislated and enforced, the use of unilateral child labor sanctions such as Section 307 can be justified under the GATT. Since 1995, WTO case law addressing Article XX has evinced progressive development in its interpretation of specific exceptions, the necessity test, and in the utilization of the *chapeau,* shedding light on how to reconcile human rights values and trade values that may at the outset appear in conflict.

Given the fact that child labor enforcement efforts under Section 307 have so far been fruitless, it is disappointing that the WTO as currently constituted has no active role to play in compelling any state to enforce international child labor standards. However, by ruling positively on any unilateral child labor sanction statute that comes before them, future WTO panels *can* play an important continuing role in shaping the interpretation of GATT provisions to promote fundamental human rights, in particular the human rights of working children.

One conclusion that emerges forcefully from this volume is that child labor is a complex social phenomenon with many causes. Many of the social factors contributing to child labor, including ignorance, avarice, and prejudice, may be addressed effectively through trade sanctions, supplemented by consciousness-raising strategies. However, the efforts of reform-minded states must not end with the imposition of trade sanctions. Child labor sanctions alone are inadequate to address the root causes and extent of child labor, because there always is the risk that children who lose employment in a targeted sector will move to another area, perhaps into a potentially more dangerous informal economy. Sanctioning states must look beyond trade measures to find all variety of effective market-oriented strategies that can persuade producers, consumers, and investors to pursue policies protecting children. If possible, such measures should be pursued prior to, and in tandem with, the imposition of any trade sanction. Skillfully designed trade sanctions, consumer education and boycotts involving child labor products, social labeling, consumer boycotts, socially responsible investing, corporate self-discipline, and union consolidation around the rights of working children—all and more are needed to ensure the successful furthering of children's rights.[114]

One cautionary note: the fact that poverty is a leading cause of child labor should lead to caution in designing regulatory responses that do not contain a poverty-reduction component. It does little to advance the protection of children's rights if sanctions and other market-oriented strategies lead to the elimination of legitimate, albeit marginal, industries employing children, who then are forced by poverty into the even riskier informal economy. This does not mean that sanctions have no place; they are a necessary tool for realigning both producer and consumer interests toward the pursuit of more difficult, but ultimately necessary, societal reforms. Trade sanctions by themselves, and indeed market-oriented strategies as a whole, are nevertheless unlikely to constitute an adequate response unless coupled with broader measures aimed at alleviating poverty. This multifaceted approach is essential for protecting the rights of working children and for resolving social and economic problems that compelled the children to enter the workplace in the first place.

◼ Notes

1. In this chapter, I adopt the definition of "child labor" set forth in the introduction to this volume, in turn derived from Chapter 2, that is, "work done by children that is harmful to them because it is abusive, exploitive, hazardous, or otherwise contrary to their best interests—a subset of a larger class of children's work, some of which may be compatible with children's best interests (variously expressed as 'beneficial,' 'benign,' or 'harmless' children's work)."

2. This is the approach taken to labor rights generally in existing trade preference programs, such as the US Generalized System of Preferences (GSP). Because such programs are discretionary under the law of the World Trade Organization (WTO), states are free to engage in such conditionality, although it raises problematic issues. See infra endnote 6.

3. A comprehensive regulatory approach would use all three strategies, rendering child labor illegal, subjecting perpetrators to civil liability for compensation of their victims, and interdicting the flow of their products.

4. See, generally, Schrage, *Promoting International Worker Rights* . . . .

5. The *most* aggressive approach would be, of course, a total import ban or embargo against all products of a child labor country. We deem this scenario highly implausible and so do not address it further here. Also, we focus on unilateral sanctions. While conditionality, that is, the practice of linking trade and other economic benefits to changes in domestic policies, is certainly controversial as a policy, trade conditionality and labor rights, such as the US practice of linking multilateral GSP to adherence to core labor rights, are *legal* and therefore less controversial than unilateral sanctions. Other forms of human rights conditionality, such as linking WTO membership to ratification of core labor and human rights treaties, may be still less problematic. See Garcia, "Integrating Trade and Human Rights . . . ."

6. See infra endnote 56 and accompanying and subsequent text.

7. See, generally, Garcia, *Trade, Inequality, and Justice*. See also Garcia, "Trade and Justice . . . ," pp. 414–415. A justice perspective of the linkage discourse "requires recognition of the fact that conflicts between traditional trade policy and other areas of social policy involve branches of *the same tree,* and that this tree is the construction of *a just society*" (emphasis added). Ibid., p. 425.

8. See Garcia, "The Global Market and Human Rights . . . ," pp. 85–86.

9. For an overview of institutional issues raised by the WTO's general role in human rights enforcement, see Garcia, "Trade, Constitutionalism, and Human Rights

. . . ." For a discussion of the political factors confronting any move to give the WTO a stronger standard-setting role, see Chapter 5 in this volume.

10. See Cleveland, "Norm Internationalization and U.S. Economic Sanctions," p. 5.

11. The use of trade sanctions may conflict with the principle of nonintervention, rules of territorial jurisdiction, and GATT trade liberalization principles. Ibid., p. 6. On the other hand, as Sarah Cleveland further points out, the UN Charter does not bar the use of "nonforcible, economic measures to promote human rights adherence and the principle of nonintervention does not necessarily apply to economic sanctions to further human rights." Ibid., p. 52.

12. Bhagwati and Srinivasan, "Trade and the Environment . . . ," p. 180.

13. See Leary, "Workers' Rights and International Trade . . . ," pp. 214–219 (claiming that the standards adopted by the ILO are the "best reference for defining 'internationally recognized worker rights'").

14. On the relativist-universalist debate generally, see Weston, "The Universality of Human Rights . . . ."

15. Bhagwati and Srinivasan, "Trade and the Environment . . . ," p. 180.

16. Howse, "The World Trade Organization . . . ," p. 133.

17. Cleveland, "Norm Internationalization and U.S. Economic Sanctions," p. 35. See also Leary, "Workers' Rights and International Trade . . . ," pp. 180–197.

18. Cleveland, "Norm Internationalization and U.S. Economic Sanctions," p. 40.

19. See ibid. See also Mehta, "Child Labour . . . ," pp. 41–42.

20. Howse, "The World Trade Organization . . . ," p. 133.

21. Mehta, "Child Labour . . . ," p. 40.

22. Garcia, "Building a Just Trade Order . . . ," p. 1025.

23. ILO, *Declaration on Fundamental Principles and Rights at Work* (1998), art. 5.

24. See Mehta, "Child Labour . . . ," p. 41 (suggesting that it may be poverty and survival rather than choice that forces children to work and arguing that in some cases these children, though poverty-stricken, may be cared for with love and affection).

25. See, for example, Weston, "The Universality of Human Rights . . . ," p. 73 (citing criticisms of pretextual invocation of cultural relativism).

26. See Naiman, "'Rightsizing' the IMF . . . ," p. 98; and Howse, "The World Trade Organization . . . ," pp. 132–133.

27. Naiman, "'Rightsizing' the IMF . . . ," pp. 98–99 and n. 5 (repudiating economic determinism by reference to the fact that the United States took over 100 years of protracted social struggle to secure national legislation limiting the working day).

28. Bullard, "The World Workers Need Solidarity . . . ," pp. 33–34.

29. See Ray, "Child Labor . . . ," p. 365. See also Alston, "Labor Rights Provisions in U.S. Trade Law," pp. 76–77 (arguing that linking child labor with legislation is inadequate and citing ILO study on India that the application of legislation "may not be in the best interest of the families concerned and . . . of the nation at large").

30. Robert Howse writes that such "results-blind moralism" is rare. Howse, "The World Trade Organization . . . ," p. 152.

31. See Bullard, "The World Workers Need Solidarity . . . ," p. 31.

32. Empirical studies on the effectiveness of trade sanctions for the protection of child workers are rare. However, for a general and theoretical analysis of welfare and other effects of the harmonization of labor standards in the trade context, see, generally, Brown, Deardorff, and Stern, "International Labor Standards and Trade . . . " (concluding that the case for international harmonization of labor standards is weak and that the harmonization of standards will have negative consequences for those who are meant to be protected).

33. Brown, Deardorff, and Stern, "International Labor Standards and Trade . . . ," pp. 154–155.

34. Ibid., p. 155.

35. Ibid.

36. Ibid. See also the conclusion to this chapter.

37. See Brown, Deardorff, and Stern, "International Labor Standards and Trade . . ." ("global demand will . . . be met through production that complies with the standards in question").

38. See Stirling, "The Use of Trade Sanctions . . . ," p. 43.

39. *US Tariff Act of 1930.*

40. For US legislation concerning child labor linking it to trade introduced but not enacted, see Tsogas, *Labor Regulation in a Global Economy,* chap. 4 ("Unilateral Application of Labor Standards in Trade Relations").

41. *Treasury, Postal Service, and General Government Appropriations Act of 1998.*

42. Ibid. The regulation does not speak only in terms of "child labor" per se; it includes "convict labor, forced labor and indentured labor under penal sanctions" and explicitly provides for "forced child labor or indentured child labor penal sanctions."

43. Moreover, any person outside the US Customs Service with reason to believe that such merchandise is being or is likely to be imported into the United States *may* communicate this belief to the commissioner. 19 CFR sec. 12.42(a).

44. 19 CFR sec. 12.42(g).

45. *Executive Order 13126* . . . , sec. 1. This order speaks directly to the prohibition of acquisition of products produced by forced or indentured "child labor."

46. *Executive Order 13126* . . . , sec. 6(c). Forced child labor in this section is defined as "all work or service exacted from any person under the age of 18 under the menace of any penalty for its nonperformance and for which the worker does not offer himself voluntarily." The order does not apply to the countries party to the North American Free Trade Agreement (NAFTA) or the WTO. Ibid., sec. 5(b)(1).

47. *Executive Order 13126* . . . , sec. 2.

48. Ibid., sec. 3(b).

49. Ibid., sec. 3(c)(1)–(3).

50. However, it does not grant any party rights against the United States, its agencies, or officers to compel enforcement of the order itself. Ibid., sec. 7. This means there is no judicial review for violation of this order and that the United States is immune from suit by any party under it. Section 7 is explicit in that the order is intended only to improve the internal management of the executive branch. Ibid.

51. See Cleveland, "Norm Internationalization and U.S. Economic Sanctions," p. 46 and nn. 280–281.

52. See ibid., pp. 46–47. See also ISCA, *Child Labor in the Cocoa Industry* (reviewing unsuccessful Section 307 enforcement efforts by the International Labor Rights Fund on behalf of working children).

53. In the words of George Becker, president of the United Steelworkers of America, "[t]here is nothing in it [GATT] for working people. Nothing. That law exists to support multinationals. It is not for workers. There is no way that you can put a comma here or change a word there to make it compatible. It is not our law. Scrap it." Quoted in Bullard, "The World Workers Need Solidarity . . . ," p. 34.

54. Collectively, these instruments are referred to as GATT 1994 and constitute a separate annex to the WTO agreement. For present purposes and to minimize confusion, we refer to the agreement simply as "GATT."

55. The only possible exception to this is Article XX(e), permitting embargoes of prison labor products, but the emphasis here is on competitiveness concerns rather than unfair labor practices. See Charnovitz, "The Influence of International Labor Standards . . ." and the sources cited therein.

56. See *Singapore Ministerial Declaration* (1996), para. 4.

57. Ibid.

58. Ibid. See also ibid., para. 6 (rejecting all forms of protectionism).

59. *WTO Understanding on Rules and Procedures* . . . .

60. See *Singapore Ministerial Declaration* (1996), para. 9 (in which WTO members affirm satisfaction with operation of DSU). See also Hudec, "The New WTO Dispute Settlement Procedure . . ." (evaluating the success of the DSU).

61. *General Agreement on Tariffs and Trade* (1994) [hereinafter "GATT"], art. I.

62. The key to the interpretation of Article I is what constitutes "like products," which will depend on the physical characteristics and end uses of the product. A fairly recent panel ruling held that Article I excludes any measure that makes MFN treatment conditional on criteria unrelated to the imported product, again stressing physical characteristics and end uses. *Indonesia: Certain Measures Affecting the Automobile Industry*, paras. 14.143–14.147. Howse concedes that the panel's focus on physical characteristics and end uses was "not unreasonable" but states that "conditions concerning how a product is produced are *clearly related* to that product, even when they do not affect its physical properties." Howse, "The World Trade Organization . . . ," p. 138, n. 24.

63. See Schoenbaum, "International Trade and Protection of the Environment . . . ," p. 291 (arguing that any attempt to allow panels to adopt a more lenient test by taking PPMs into consideration and to balance the legitimacy of the protected value with the disruption to trading interests is unsuited to WTO panels whose ad hoc judges would be delegated "extraordinary discretion"); and Charnovitz, "The Law of Environmental 'PPMs' in the WTO . . . ," p. 101 (arguing the same). It may be that the *Asbestos* case's holding that the health effects of a product are relevant to its likeness might be a step toward broadening this analysis. See *European Communities: Measures Affecting Asbestos and Asbestos-Containing Products* [hereinafter *"European Communities Asbestos"*].

64. *GATT Dispute Panel Report* . . . (Aug. 16, 1991) [hereinafter *Tuna-Dolphin I*] and *GATT Dispute Panel Report* . . . (June 16, 1994) [hereinafter *Tuna-Dolphin II*].

65. GATT art. XI prohibits nontariff border restrictions such as embargoes, quotas, and import licenses.

66. See Howse, "The World Trade Organization . . . ," pp. 138–142.

67. Some have suggested that the WTO redefine "like products" in Article III so that products could be considered "unlike" on the basis of PPMs. See, for example, Snape and Lefkovitz, "Searching for GATT's Environmental Miranda . . . ," pp. 782–792. The current interpretation of "like products" turns mainly on physical characteristics, end uses, and tariff classifications. The case that details the factors that will be considered for the determination of "like products" is *Japan: Taxes on Alcoholic Beverages* [hereinafter *"Japan Alcoholic Beverages"*].

68. Charnovitz, "The Law of Environmental 'PPMs' in the WTO . . . ," pp. 60–62.

69. Howse argues that this distinction between products and PPMs neither has a textual basis nor is supported by the legislative history of the GATT. Howse, "The World Trade Organization . . . ," p. 139.

70. *European Communities Asbestos*.

71. Ibid., paras. 113, 192.

72. Charnovitz, "The Law of Environmental 'PPMs' in the WTO . . . ," pp. 83–85.

73. GATT, art. XX.

74. See *United States: Standards for Reformulated and Conventional Gasoline* ... (1996) [hereinafter *"Gasoline Standards"*]. The party asserting Article XX as a defense has the burden of showing that the exception applies. *Gasoline Standards* is the first case that provides an authoritative interpretation of the *chapeau;* also the first case where an environmental PPM could fit one of the exceptions in Article XX.

75. See Stevenson, "Pursuing an End to Foreign Child Labor Through U.S. Trade Law ... ," pp. 163–164. But see Diller and Levy, "Child Labor, Trade, and Investment ... ," pp. 683–685; and Stirling, "The Use of Trade Sanctions ... ," pp. 36–39 (arguing that Article XX[e] can serve as the basis for a human rights exception in the GATT).

76. See, for example, Howse, "The World Trade Organization ... ," p. 142.

77. This evolutionary interpretive approach in fact reflects the way in which WTO panels have treated the definition of "exhaustible natural resources" in the context of Article XX(g) determinations. See ibid.

78. See Charnovitz, "The Moral Exception in Trade Policy," p. 696.

79. Howse, "The World Trade Organization ... ," pp. 142–143.

80. *United States: Import Prohibition of Certain Shrimp and Shrimp Products,* para. 129 [hereinafter *"Shrimp-Turtle"*]. The case concerned the US import ban of shrimp caught in a manner threatening to sea turtles. See also GATT art. XX(g), an exception for the conservation of exhaustible natural resources.

81. *Final Act Embodying the Results of the Uruguay Round* ....

82. The Appellate Body has stated that while not binding in subsequent disputes, *adopted* panel reports should be taken into account by panels where relevant. See *Japan Alcoholic Beverages,* p. 15.

83. Howse, "The World Trade Organization ... ," p. 169.

84. See Charnovitz, "The Moral Exception in Trade Policy," pp. 704–705.

85. Ibid., pp. 705–710 and n. 123 (listing trade agreements containing moral or humanitarian exceptions).

86. Ibid., p. 713.

87. See, generally, Diller and Levy, "Child Labor, Trade, and Investment ... ."

88. See *Tuna-Dolphin II,* paras. 5.15–5.16.

89. *Shrimp-Turtle,* para. 2.16. The case concerned the US import ban of shrimp caught in a manner threatening to sea turtles.

90. Charnovitz, "The Law of Environmental 'PPMs' in the WTO ... ," p. 94.

91. *Thailand: Restrictions on Importation of and Internal Taxes on Cigarettes,* para. 74.

92. See *Tuna-Dolphin I.*

93. Ibid., para. 5.28.

94. *Shrimp-Turtle,* para. 121.

95. See Schoenbaum, "International Trade and Protection of the Environment ... ," p. 276 (outlining criticisms of the panel's "least trade restrictive" interpretation in Article XX[b]).

96. See ibid.

97. See Howse, "The World Trade Organization ... ," pp. 144–145. See also Garcia, "Building a Just Trade Order for a New Millennium," p. 1058. This approach can be supported by reference to the necessity test in the WTO Agreement on Sanitary and Phytosanitary Measures, which explicitly requires such a comparative evaluation.

98. See Garcia, "Building a Just Trade Order for a New Millennium," pp. 1058, 1060–1061. A necessity test should require that a panel find a less trade-restrictive alternative measure "equally effective" in protecting human rights to be disqualified as a justified measure. Ibid., p. 1061. Therefore, if negotiation among countries, social labeling,

private actors' collective actions, or financial compensation for target countries are deemed not *as effective as* a trade sanction, the sanction would pass the necessity test.

99. *WTO Agreement on the Application of Sanitary and Phytosanitary Measures* (hereinafter *"SPS Agreement"*). This agreement deals with measures relating to additives, contaminants, toxins, and disease-carrying organisms in imported food, seeking to protect life or health *within* the importing country, and thereby excluding any non-product-related PPMs from coverage.

100. *SPS Agreement,* arts. 2.1–2.2.

101. Ibid., art. 5.6.

102. Ibid., art. 5.6, n. 3.

103. *European Communities Asbestos,* para. 172.

104. *Shrimp-Turtle,* paras. 177–182; Charnovitz, "The Law of Environmental 'PPMs' in the WTO . . . ," p. 96.

105. See *Shrimp-Turtle,* paras. 161–176.

106. Howse, "The World Trade Organization . . . ," p. 145.

107. See Charnovitz, "The Law of Environmental 'PPMs' in the WTO . . . ," p. 108.

108. See Cleveland, "Norm Internationalization and U.S. Economic Sanctions," pp. 69–73 (analyzing the criticisms of US unilateralism).

109. Ibid., p. 74.

110. Ibid., p. 85.

111. See ibid., pp. 23–24 (explaining that countries without a formal measure could provide de facto "low-profile support" for a de jure US sanction or threat, as imposed on Iraq after the Gulf War, for example).

112. Ibid., pp. 24–25.

113. Koh, "Why Do Nations Obey International Law?" pp. 2646, 2655.

114. For convenient discussion of these "extralegal" initiatives, see Chapters 4, 10, and 14 in this volume. In addition, see, for example, Macklem, "Labor Law Beyond Borders"; Schrage, *Promoting International Worker Rights Through Private Voluntary Initiatives . . .* ; and US Department of Labor, *By the Sweat and Toil of Children,* vols. 3–4.

Part 5

Conclusion:
Contributors' Consensus

17

Bringing Human Rights to Child Labor: Guiding Principles and Call to Action

Burns H. Weston

The following guiding principles and call to action constitute a consensus statement based on shared understandings among the authors contributing to this book on child labor and human rights.[1] It outlines important foundational principles of a practical human rights approach to child labor and the protection of working children, and it suggests also an agenda for future action. It is hoped that these recommendations will be taken into serious account by national governments, nongovernmental organizations, academic and research institutions, and international organizations seeking to end the workplace abuse and exploitation of children.

▓ Why a Human Rights Approach to Child Labor Is Needed

Experience, research, and international debate in recent years have revealed that conventional ways of thinking about and acting upon child labor are not adequate to the challenges of the present. While the vast majority of working children today work without recompense, for family members, and in agriculture and the maintenance of households, traditional child labor policies were developed primarily for children working for keep or wages for non-family employers, and in industrially organized services and manufacturing. Currently important issues such as cross-border trafficking, domestic child work, and the military recruitment of children now challenge old child labor concepts and prescriptions not designed to address them. Child labor seems to persist beyond national and international capacity not only to control it, but even to identify and understand it. In neither industrialized nor developing countries have child labor policies kept pace with rapid social and economic change, and traditional paradigms inherited from the nineteenth and early

427

twentieth centuries have become outmoded even in the places for which they were developed.

While many old verities have proved irrelevant, unworkable, or even counterproductive, no new policy consensus has yet arisen to replace them. Except when dealing with its worst forms, there is not even agreement on precisely what child labor is, let alone what to do about it. What makes sense in one place or circumstance is shown to be senseless in another. Traditionally prescribed interventions against child labor based on Northern approaches have been imposed as universal standards with mixed results at best. For example, excluding children below a legal minimum age from all economic participation has in many cases proved more disastrous for children than was the work in which they were engaged prior to the exclusion. Blanket prohibition of work based only on age is today opposed by many child defense advocates and often the very children that minimum age laws were intended to protect. The shards of a shattered paradigm cannot be reassembled as they are. Something new is needed. Clearly the time has come to entertain fresh ideas and policies, and to search for grounds of new consensus appropriate to the moment and the future.

Modern concepts of human rights and the application of a rights-based approach to child labor can help fill the present vacuum and provide the foundation for a new intellectual and policy consensus about child labor. This approach puts the internationally recognized rights of children at the center of child labor discourse and policy, and places them in a supportive framework of more general human rights treaties and declarations constituting international law, including those that constitute the "International Bill of Human Rights": the 1948 Universal Declaration of Human Rights; the 1966 International Covenant on Economic, Social, and Cultural Rights; and the 1996 International Covenant on Civil and Political Rights.[2] It thus usefully addresses two aforementioned problems that now bedevil child labor policy. First, it provides credible international criteria for defining child labor and for determining which children merit special attention. Second, it forestalls cures worse than the disease by demanding that child labor interventions observe the rights and welfare of children as scrupulously as should any acceptable child work. By laying a credibly protective legal foundation that various intervention strategies to eliminate child labor can build upon, a human rights approach to child labor can make a crucial contribution to the protection of working children, promoting their dignity and value as it also contributes to the social and economic progress of their families, communities, and countries.

Under a rights-based framework, the labor exploitation of children is viewed from a radically different perspective that revolutionizes the way society regards and engages with both working children and their social context. From this perspective, children are recognized to be rights-holders with the potential to make valuable contributions to their own present and future well-being as well as to the social and economic development of society. No longer merely dependent objects of outside intervention, children under a human rights approach become empowered as citizens, for powerlessness is not compatible with human rights. Their right to express their observations and opinions and to participate meaningfully in defining and implementing sustainable solutions to their problems is appreciated as an important social asset that can enrich action against child labor by making policies and programs more just and effective for all.

A human rights approach to child labor affirms not only the rights of working children, but also the duties of governments and of society as a whole to secure those rights in practice. Rights and duties go hand in hand. Governments and other social duty-bearers should be held accountable toward working children and their rights. A human rights approach enables a society—including its advocates for children—to monitor its own progress in protecting children according to national and international commitments, and it permits international tracking of the performance of countries in ensuring meaningful improvement in the lives of their working children. It presents both opportunity and challenge, and it is the task of the human rights community to awaken the world to the opportunity for greater social justice through a human rights orientation to child labor, and to encourage governments and societies to accept the challenge of bringing it to reality in the lives of millions of children around the world.

A big part of this challenge is to relate human rights principles to specific children and situations in ways that well serve both adherence to international human rights standards and safeguarding of the well-being of children. Meeting this challenge requires a two-way accountability: children's work must be governed according to human rights principles, and human rights interventions in children's work must be judged according to how they affect the well-being and development of the children involved. Neither can be considered a success without the other; children's rights and children's welfare are two faces of the same coin whose value is appreciated from both aspects.

■ Foundational Principles of a Human Rights Approach to Child Labor

Start from International Human Rights Instruments

A human rights approach to child labor must be solidly rooted in the key international treaties and declarations that guide the definition and application of human rights, with special emphasis on the rights of children. Although these instruments are far from perfect—they are the inevitably flawed products of bargaining between countries with varied levels of concern and motives that are not always high-minded—they carry significant authority as official agreements about the kind of world countries at least claim they want to live in and about the rules and obligations to which they say they will commit to bring that vision into reality. As statements of rough international consensus, at least rhetorically, the texts of these treaties and declarations constitute the fragile but indispensable political and legal foundation of human rights, and they define the rights of children, including the right not to be abused in and through their work. Two sorts of rights instruments must be involved in protecting children from abusive work: those specific to children and those setting forth general human rights for all citizens in society. The two complement each other through a relationship in which core rights pertaining specifically to children are embedded in, and linked to, a supportive structure of general human rights that pertain to everyone.

Place Children and Their Rights at the Center

From a human rights perspective, "child labor" is best defined as work that is detrimental to children who perform it—impairing their overall physical and social development and inhibiting their ability to exercise their rights fully. One reason is that it makes the well-being of working children rather than their economic or labor market behavior the central issue, thereby emphasizing their status as bearers of rights. Another is that it reflects the thrust of two recent, widely ratified international conventions that provide for the protection of children against abusive work. The first is the 1989 United Nations Convention on the Rights of the Child (CRC), which guarantees "the right of the child to be protected from economic exploitation and from performing any work that is likely to be hazardous or to interfere with the child's education, or to be harmful to the child's health or physical, mental, spiritual, moral or social development."[3] This convention, which applies the gamut of internationally accepted human rights to the specific case of children, is the most widely ratified human rights convention ever and therefore the generally accepted standard for national and international policy for nurturing and protecting children. The second instrument implying this definition is the 1999 International Labour Organization Convention (No. 182) Concerning the Prohibition and Immediate Elimination of the Worst Forms of Child Labour (ILO C182),[4] which makes work injurious to children the top priority for national and international child labor intervention.

Together, these two mutually supportive conventions placing the well-being of children at the center of concern and affirming the right of children to protection from abusive and exploitative work constitute a nearly unanimous consensus of governments that should be universally respected as the reigning international legal standard. The great advantage of these two conventions is that, by focusing on children, they bring them more firmly and explicitly under human rights protection. Together, they imply a child labor policy that privileges children's best interests over other objectives and that concentrates effort on the worst forms of child labor. At the same time, even the best international human rights treaties and declarations need periodic revision to correct mistakes or to keep pace with new knowledge, new vision, or changing world conditions. The CRC and ILO C182 are no exception. Their provisions need constantly to be evaluated according to how they affect the welfare of the children they seek to protect. Those found to undermine children's well-being should be repealed or improved.

Link the Special Rights of Children to the Broader Context of General Human Rights

A focus on children alone is not by itself sufficient to penetrate the deeply entrenched obstacles and complexities of child labor. Close links between child labor and poverty, corruption, exploitation, discrimination, ignorance, injustice, oppression, disease, and violence suggest that solving this social problem involves addressing the human rights not only of children but also of an entire society. To combat the abuse of children through their work successfully, the central focus on children's rights must be embedded within a more general vision of the human rights of everyone. Ultimately, the rights of children cannot be guaranteed in isolation from the rights of the adults in their families and communities, which are officially enshrined in the 1948 Universal Declaration of Human Rights, and the two 1966 United Nations covenants and numerous other human rights treaties and lawmaking declarations. Situating specific children's rights within the context of more general human rights not only mobilizes the political resources necessary to attack the causes and structures of child labor, but also helps ensure that the principles articulated specifically for the young do not vitiate or trivialize fundamental human rights intended to protect everyone regardless of age. While an effective human rights approach to child labor will espouse core values and principles articulated in the CRC and ILO C182, it will, in implementing those values and principles, also draw upon the full range of rights contained in other human rights lawmaking instruments to which most countries have by now officially committed themselves in word if not yet in deed.

View and Treat Working Children Holistically

Just as a comprehensive perspective on the social roots of child labor is necessary to identify and attack the causes that perpetuate it, so is a holistic view of the children involved required to ensure that public and private action ostensibly intended to benefit them does in fact serve their best interests. Children are much more than workers, and the work they do must be understood in the full context of their broader lives. Working children should be viewed and treated in the light of their growth and development processes, their aspirations, their own views about their work, their education both in and outside of school, their family and other important relationships, and their realistic options for survival and advancement. Failure to understand working children and the work they do in situational context sufficiently can lead to misguided interventions that perversely leave children worse rather than better off. Attention to the full complement of rights guaranteed to children by the CRC promotes an appropriately holistic view of children.

Address Child Labor Situations Empirically and Comprehensively

Thinking more holistically about working children and more contextually about child labor moves intervention policy and programs away from a simplistically narrow sectoral focus—treating child labor too exclusively as a labor, economic, family relations, occupational health, or education issue, for instance—and toward sophisticated multidimensional consideration of the people and situations involved. Many now question whether responsibility for child labor policy should continue to be lodged primarily in ministries of labor, which treat it as primarily a labor issue, rather than in other structures that encourage cross-sectoral cooperation. A comprehensive perspective also emphasizes the importance of basing interventions against child labor on the facts of the situation and the everyday life experiences of working children rather than on untested assumptions or ideological preconceptions. Indeed, rapidly accumulating experience and research today demonstrate the need to found policy and action on sophisticated, nuanced understanding of child labor problems. More heed should be paid to rigorously empirical findings that arise from program evaluation, from evolving social science insight into children and childhoods (including children's work), and from recent trends in economic and social development theory that stress the centrality of human factors, notably including human rights. A critical perspective born of experience and research should be utilized not only to help improve the practical implementation of existing rights concepts, but also to correct and improve the conceptualization and formulation of rights as they apply to child labor.

▨   A Call to Future Action

1. All countries should ratify both the UN Convention on the Rights of the Child (CRC) and ILO Convention (No. 182) Concerning the Prohibition and Immediate Elimination of the Worst Forms of Child Labour (ILO C182), and bring their national legislation into compliance with them. Where these most basic international conventions establishing the right of children to be protected against abusive and exploitive work have not been ratified or implemented into national law, human rights organizations should campaign to secure their recognition and observance. In all countries, both government and the general public should be made familiar with the basic precepts of the CRC and ILO C182.

2. The elimination of abusive and exploitive children's work should be accorded high priority, especially by the human rights community. It should be made an important element in campaigns for social and economic justice, and its links to other human rights issues should be publicized to both government and the general public. Elimination of child labor can be accomplished by removing children from detrimental work, by changing the nature or conditions of work to remove its harmful aspects and to make it safe for children, and by preparing children and others to defend themselves against exploitation and other abuses effectively.

3. Everyone should respect and promote the right of working children to organize. To help end the exploitation of children, human rights organizations should devote special effort to ending the systematic denial by government and labor organizations of working children's clear human right to form their own organizations or to join trade unions in their own defense against abusive and exploitive work and working conditions.

4. In every country, rigorous scientific research should be undertaken to help identify children in abusive and exploitive forms of work and to take a holistic view of them and their situation. Some such studies already have been accomplished in drafting national action plans against the worst forms of child labor required under ILO C182. However, many such plans are either empirically weak or have yet to be completed. Human rights advocates should monitor and review the national plans of action to ensure that they have been properly conducted and that they reflect the provisions of the CRC, ILO C182, and other relevant international human rights lawmaking instruments. They also should ensure that public sector interventions in child labor be decided only in full view of the facts of the situation and with the best interests of the children involved as the primary objective.

5. Special efforts should be made to learn and apply lessons from existing experience in applying human rights to child labor issues. In some places and in some parts of the human rights community, a considerable repository of innovative experience in applying human rights to child labor already exists, but needs to be systematically documented and reviewed for what can be learned from it. This is especially true in the child rights sector of the human rights movement. Numerous national and international child advocacy and defense organizations have for well over a decade been applying rights criteria and developing innovative oriented strategies and tools to assist working children and to address child labor issues. Some of them (e.g., the United Nations Children's Fund, international nongovernmental organizations such as the Save the Children Alliance, and many regional, national, and grassroots organizations and networks in developing countries) are guided by an explicit child rights policy and program framework. Almost unnoticed, they have become the primary locus of practical child labor experience within the human rights community. In the past several years, these groups, as well as the ILO and other labor-oriented organizations, have been orienting their child labor efforts by the objectives and criteria of the CRC and by ILO C182, which increasingly is treated as an important child rights instrument. While considerable research, publication, and workshop effort has been expended to learn from the accumulating experience in utilizing child rights to address child labor, much more is needed.

6. The human rights community should develop practical tools and strategies for applying the full range of human rights to the issue of child labor. Universities, research institutes, advocacy organizations, and other major promoters of human rights have unique research and development capacity to devise and test systematically practical means for making human rights a reality for working children, their families, and their communities. It is not sufficient for the human rights community merely to denounce child labor abuses, which may already be well-known and recognized. In many cases, straightforward application of existing law is not the solution, but neither is it clear how to move against child labor abuse in reliable ways that can be expected to improve rather than complicate the situation of the children involved. The human rights community should take an active role in developing effective strategies and tools to apply human rights instruments to the problem of child labor, promoting its elimination in ways that are consistent with all the rights of the children involved.

7. Human rights groups should be educated about strategies, methods, and instruments available to them for combating child labor. Groups and individuals now wielding only a limited range of human rights tools to combat child labor should be equipped to understand and make use of the full body of human rights principles, instruments, arguments, and strategies. The many organizations and individuals already applying children's rights as articulated in the CRC to child labor are not fully aware of how also to make effective use of a broader gamut of human rights instruments. They should be provided with training and information that will increase their ability to mobilize a wide range of human rights tools in the defense of children. Similarly, activists attacking child labor primarily from other human rights perspectives often are unskilled in the application of child rights instruments and unaware of the considerable work already done to apply them to child labor. They should be familiarized with child rights approaches to child work issues. Exchange of expertise that can unify the human rights community is needed not only in the field, but also in academic and advocacy institutions that prepare and support human rights workers.

8. A concentrated effort should be made to inform children—especially those who work—about their general human rights, their special rights as children, and their rights as workers, and to engage their full participation in realizing those rights. Such efforts must involve not only outreach to children but also training of adults in how to work with working children as partners. Lessons learned from the various places and programs where such education and participation already occur should be made readily available to everyone. Policymakers need to be informed that the participation of children in public decisions concerning them is not only required by the CRC but also found through experience in many places and settings to be pragmatically necessary for long-term success against child labor.

9. Multilateral organizations and bilateral donors concerned with child labor should adopt policies and strategies that are aimed primarily at promoting the full human rights of children. They should review their standards, policies, programs, and procedures to ensure that they provide working children with maximum possible access to general human rights protection as well as to defend their rights as children. The fundamental human rights envisioned by the Universal Declaration of Human Rights and related instruments for all people should not be abridged when applied to working children—even when permitted under the CRC—except as a last resort when rigorous investigation has empirically demonstrated it to be necessary to protect them against work seriously detrimental to them. Similarly, rights specific to children should be implemented only in ways that promote their overall development and facilitate their access to the full spectrum of human rights, thereby respecting their status as young citizens in society. The worth and rights sensitivity of child labor interventions should be tested according to whether the current well-being and future prospects of children involved have been tangibly improved. No intervention that decreases their welfare or narrows their options for survival and advancement should be considered consistent with either their general human rights or their special rights as children.

Conclusion

Although most—but certainly not all—worrisome child labor is today found in developing countries, to date, most international norms for defining and attacking it have come from rich countries. The ethnocentric imposition of Northern intervention models on countries where they are plainly ill-adapted does not derive from a dearth of good ideas from developing regions. In fact, many developing country innovations in understanding and combating child labor have been amply documented but so far unable to influence mainstream thinking and action because of severe power inequalities that may themselves represent a violation of human rights. A human rights approach to child labor implies greater international openness to new ideas and paradigms arising from the experience of countries where child labor problems are now most common. Some of these run against the grain of prevailing rich-country positions, policies, and models. However, the relative impotence of conventional approaches to stem a rising tide even of particularly vicious forms of child labor—such as the trafficking of children for prostitution and armed combat—suggests that the time has come to open the way to experiment with fresh ideas coming out of the societies that best know the problems and have to confront them directly. A human rights approach to child labor must emphasize engaged listening and partnership over detached condemnation and preaching, and it will search out and respect the constructive ideas of all concerned parties, especially including children who work.

▨ Notes

I take pleasure in thanking Victor Karunan and William Myers, who graciously assembled and recorded this consensus of experience and minds. They did so from those contributors to this volume who attended a colloquium ("Using the Human Rights Framework to Combat Abusive Child Labor") hosted by The University of Iowa Center for Human Rights (http://www.uichr.org) in July 2003 and thereafter from those who were unable to attend but who nonetheless commented.

1. In this "Contributors' Consensus," we adopt the definition of "child labor" set forth in the Introduction to this volume, in turn derived from Chapter 2, that is, "work done by children that is harmful to them because it is abusive, exploitive, hazardous, or otherwise contrary to their best interests—a subset of a larger class of children's work, some of which may be compatible with children's best interests (variously expressed as 'beneficial,' 'benign,' or 'harmless' children's work)."

2. See the bibliography for the official citations to each of these leading human rights instruments.

3. United Nations, *Convention on the Rights of the Child* (1989), art. 32(1). See also United Nations, *Optional Protocol to the Convention on the Rights of the Child on the Involvement of Children in Armed Conflict* (2000); and United Nations, *Optional Protocol to the Convention on the Rights of the Child on the Sale of Children, Child Prostitution and Child Pornography* (2000).

4. ILO, *Convention* (No. 182) *Concerning the Prohibition and Immediate Elimination of the Worst Forms of Child Labour* (1999).

Abbreviations
and Acronyms

AAAS	American Association for the Advancement of Science
ACILS	American Center for International Labor Solidarity
ADB	Asian Development Bank
AFL	American Federation of Labor
AFL-CIO	American Federation of Labor–Congress of Industrial Organizations
AFT	American Federation of Teachers
AI	Amnesty International
AMWCY	African Movement of Working Children and Youth
ANDI	Agência de Notícias dos Direitos da Infância (News Agency for Children's Rights) (Brazil)
ANPPCAN	African Network for the Prevention and Protection Against Child Abuse and Neglect
ASEAN	Association of Southeast Asian Nations
ASI	Anti-Slavery International
ATC	Anti-Trafficking Centre
AU	African Union
BFSP	British and Foreign State Papers
BISD	Basic Instruments and Selected Documents
CAH	Department of Child and Adolescent Health and Development (of the WHO)
CAR-NWG	Children at Risk–Net Working Group
CEDAW	Convention on the Elimination of All Forms of Discrimination Against Women (1967)
CEDC	children in especially difficult circumstances
CERD	Committee on the Elimination of Racial Discrimination (of the UN)

CESCR	Committee on Economic, Social, and Cultural Rights (of the UN)
CFA	Committee on Freedom of Association (of the ILO)
CFR	Code of Federal Regulations
CHODAWU	Conservation, Hotels, Domestic, and Allied Workers Union (Tanzania)
CIO	Congress of Industrial Organizations
CNSP	children in need of special protection
COBET	Complementary Basic Education (Tanzania)
CONAETI	Comissão Nacional de Erradicação do Trabalho Infantil (National Commission for Child Labor Eradication) (Brazil)
CONANDA	Conselho Nacional dos Direitos da Criança e do Adolescente (National Council for Child and Adolescent Rights) (Brazil)
CONTAG	Confederação dos Trabalhadores na Agricultura (Agricultural Workers Confederation) (Brazil)
CRC	Convention on the Rights of the Child (1989)
CRIN	Child Rights Information Network
CSC	Coalition to Stop the Use of Child Soldiers
CSEC	commercial sexual exploitation of children
CSPD	Child Survival and Protection Development (Tanzania)
CUT/CEAP	Central Única dos Trabalhadores Brasileiros (National Trade Union) (Brazil)
CWA	Child Workers in Asia
CWIN	Child Workers in Nepal Concerned Centre
DCI	Defence for Children International
DFID	Department for International Development (UK)
DSU	dispute settlement understanding
ECA	Estatuto da Criança e do Adolescente (Statute of the Child and Adolescent) (Brazil)
ECLIPSE	Exodus from Child Labor to Integration, Play, Socialization, and Education
ECOSOC	Economic and Social Council (of the UN)
ECPAT	Campaign to End Child Prostitution in Asian Tourism
EDC	Education Development Center (Tanzania)
EFA	Education for All
ESC	Economic and Social Council (of the UN)
ESDP	Education Sector Development Program (Tanzania)
ETI	Ethical Trading Initiative
ETS	European Treaty Series
EU	European Union
EUROPOL	European Police Organization

FAO	Food and Agriculture Organization
FFCC	Fact-Finding and Conciliation Commission on Freedom of Association (of the ILO)
FIFA	Fédération Internationale de Football Association
FLA	Fair Labor Association
FLSA	Fair Labor Standards Act (1938)
FNPETI	Fórum Nacional de Prevenção e Erradicação do Trabalho Infantil (Brazilian National Forum on the Prevention and Eradication of Child Labor)
FOIL	Forum of Indian Leftists
Forum DCA	Forum Nacional Permanente de Organizações Não-Governamentais de Defesa dos Direitos da Criança e do Adolescente (Permanent National Forum of Nongovernmental Organizations in Defense of Children's Rights) (Brazil)
FTA	free trade association
FUNBEM	National Foundation for the Welfare of Minors (Brazil)
GATT	General Agreement on Tariffs and Trade
GAW	Global Alliance for Workers
GCLP	Global Child Labour Program
GDP	gross domestic product
GECTIPA	Grupos de Combate ao Trabalho Infantil e Proteção ao Trabalho do Adolescente (Special Group for the Combat of Child Labor and the Protection of the Work of Adolescents) (Brazil)
G8	Group of Eight
GMACL	Global March Against Child Labour
GSP	Generalized System of Preferences
HIPC	Highly Indebted Poor Countries Initiative
HRI	Human Rights Internet
HRW	Human Rights Watch
HURIDOCS	Human Rights Information and Documentation Systems
IBGE	Fundação Instituto Brasileiro de Geografia e Estatísticas (Brazilian Institute of Geography and Statistics)
ICCPR	International Covenant on Civil and Political Rights (1966)
ICCR	Interfaith Center for Corporate Responsibility
ICESCR	International Covenant on Economic, Social, and Cultural Rights (1966)
ICFTU	International Confederation of Free Trade Unions
IGO	intergovernmental organization
IGTLWF	International Garment, Textile, and Leather Workers Federation
ILM	International Legal Materials

ILO	International Labour Organization
ILO C5	International Labour Organization Convention (No. 5) Fixing the Minimum Age for Admission of Children to Industrial Employment (1919)
ILO C10	International Labour Organization Convention (No. 10) Concerning the Age for Admission of Children to Employment in Agriculture (1921)
ILO C29	International Labour Organization Convention (No. 29) Concerning Forced or Compulsory Labour (1930)
ILO C33	International Labour Organization Convention (No. 33) Concerning the Age for Admission of Children to Non-Industrial Employment (1932)
ILO C87	Convention (No. 87) Concerning Freedom of Association and Protection of the Right to Organize (1948)
ILO C98	Convention (No. 98) Concerning the Application of the Principles of the Right to Organize and to Bargain Collectively (1948)
ILO C100	Convention (No. 100) Concerning Equal Remuneration for Men and Women Workers for Work of Equal Value (1951)
ILO C105	International Labour Organization Convention (No. 105) Concerning the Abolition of Forced Labour (1957)
ILO C111	Convention (No. 111) Concerning Discrimination in Respect of Employment and Occupation (1958)
ILO C138	International Labour Organization Convention (No. 138) Concerning Minimum Age for Admission to Employment (1973)
ILO C182	International Labour Organization Convention (No. 182) Concerning the Prohibition and Immediate Elimination of the Worst Forms of Child Labour (1999)
ILRF	International Labor Rights Fund
IMF	International Monetary Fund
INGO	international nongovernmental organization
INTERPOL	International Criminal Police Organization
IPEC	International Programme on the Elimination of Child Labour (of the ILO)
IPER	Institute of Psychological and Educational Research
ISCA	International Save the Children Alliance
ISO	International Standards Organization
ISPCAN	International Society for the Prevention of Child Abuse and Neglect

ITGLWF   International Textile, Garment, and Leather Workers
           Federation
IWGCL   International Working Group on Child Labour
JORF   Journal Officiel de la République de France
KIWOHEDE   Kiota Women's Health and Development (Tanzania)
LNTS   League of Nations Treaty Series
MANTHOC   Movement of Working Children and Adolescents from
           Christian Working-Class Families (Peru)
MFN   most favored nation
MNMMR   Movimento Nacional de Meninos e Meninas de Ruas
           (Brazilian National Movement of Street Boys and Girls)
MOU   memorandum of understanding
MPT   Ministério Público do Trabalho (Procurator-General for
           Labor) (Brazil)
NACP   National AIDS Control Programme (Tanzania)
NAFTA   North American Free Trade Agreement
NAPC   National Anti-Poverty Council (Philippines)
NATRAS   Movement of Working Children and Adolescents of
           Nicaragua
NCLC   National Child Labor Committee
NGO   nongovernmental organization
NIRA   National Industrial Recovery Act
NISC   National Intersectoral Coordination Committee (Tanzania)
NLRB   National Labor Relations Board
NPACL   National Program Against Child Labor (Philippines)
NTUC   Nepal Trade Union Congress
OAS   Organization of American States
OASTS   Organization of American States Treaty Series
OAU   Organization of African Unity
OECD   Organization for Economic Cooperation and Development
OHCHR   Office of the High Commissioner for Human Rights (United
           Nations)
OIT Brasil Organização Internacional do Trabalho (Brazilian office of
           the ILO)
OJEC   Official Journal of the European Communities
PEDP   Primary Education Development Plan (Tanzania)
PETI   Programa Erradicação do Trabalho Infantil (National
           Program for Child Labor Eradication) (Brazil)
PNETI   Plano Nacional de Prevenção e Erradicação do Trabalho
           Infantil (National Plan for the Prevention and Eradication
           of Child Labor) (Brazil)
PPM   production process method

PRD	Partido de la Revolución Democrática (Party of the Democratic Revolution) (Mexico)
PRI	Partido Revolucionario Institucional (Revolutionary Institutional Party) (Mexico)
PRS	poverty reduction strategy
PRSP	poverty reduction strategy paper
REPOA	Research on Poverty Alleviation (Tanzania)
SACCS	South Asian Coalition on Children in Servitude
SAI	Social Accountability International
SAS	Secretaria de Assistência Social do Ministério da Previdência e Assistência Social (Social Action Secretariat of the Ministry of Social Security and Action) (Brazil)
SENAC	Sistema Nacional de Aprendizagem Comercial (National System for Commercial Apprenticeship) (Brazil)
SENAI	Sistema Nacional de Aprendizagem Industrial (National System for Industrial Apprenticeship) (Brazil)
SIMPOC	Statistical Information and Monitoring Programme on Child Labour (of the ILO)
SPS Agreement	Agreement on Sanitary and Phytosanitary Measures (of the GATT)
Stat.	United States Statutes at Large
TACAIDS	Tanzania AIDS Commission
TBP	time-bound program
TS	Treaty Series (US Department of State)
UDHR	Universal Declaration of Human Rights (1948)
UICHR	University of Iowa Center for Human Rights
UK	United Kingdom
UKTS	United Kingdom Treaty Series
UN	United Nations
UNCHR	United Nations Commission on Human Rights
UNDP	United Nations Development Programme
UNESCO	United Nations Educational, Scientific, and Cultural Organization
UNFPA	United Nations Population Fund
UNHCHR	United Nations High Commission for Human Rights
UNHCR	United Nations High Commission for Refugees
UNICEF	United Nations Children's Fund
UNIDO	United Nations Industrial Development Organization
UNIFEM	United Nations Development Fund for Women
UNJYB	United Nations Juridical Yearbook
UNODC	United Nations Office on Drug Control and Crime
UNSSC	United Nations System Staff College
UNTS	United Nations Treaty Series

US	United States Reports
USAID	US Agency for International Development
VETA	Vocational Education Training Authority (Tanzania)
WFP	World Food Programme
WHO	World Health Organization
WRC	Worker Rights Consortium
WTO	World Trade Organization
YBUN	Yearbook of the United Nations

Appendix:
Selected Provisions of
Key Instruments

■ **ILO Convention (No. 138) Concerning Minimum Age for Admission to Employment**

Adopted at the fifty-eighth session of the International Labour Conference, Geneva, June 26, 1973.
Entered into force June 19, 1976.
1015 UNTS 297, 2 ILO CR 1030, reprinted in Weston and Carlson, *International Law and World Order: Basic Documents,* vol. 3, III.O.5.

* * *

Article 1
Each Member for which this Convention is in force undertakes to pursue a national policy designed to ensure the effective abolition of child labor and to raise progressively the minimum age for admission to employment or work to a level consistent with the fullest physical and mental development of young persons.

Article 2
1. Each Member which ratifies this Convention shall specify, in a declaration appended to its ratification, a minimum age for admission to employment or work within its territory and on means of transport registered in its territory; subject to Articles 4 to 8 of this Convention, no one under that age shall be admitted to employment or work in any occupation.

* * *

3. The minimum age specified in pursuance of paragraph 1 of this Article shall not be less than the age of completion of compulsory schooling and, in any case, shall not be less than 15 years.

4. Notwithstanding the provisions of paragraph 3 of this Article, a Member whose economy and educational facilities are insufficiently developed may, after consultation with the organizations of employers and workers concerned, where such exist, initially specify a minimum age of 14 years.

*   *   *

Article 3

1. The minimum age for admission to any type of employment or work which by its nature or the circumstances in which it is carried out is likely to jeopardize the health, safety or morals of young persons shall not be less than 18 years.

2. The types of employment or work to which paragraph 1 of this Article applies shall be determined by national laws or regulations or by the competent authority, after consultation with the organizations of employers and workers concerned, where such exist.

3. Notwithstanding the provisions of paragraph 1 of this Article, national laws or regulations or the competent authority may, after consultation with the organizations of employers and workers concerned, where such exist, authorize employment or work as from the age of 16 years on condition that the health, safety and morals of the young persons concerned are fully protected and that the young persons have received adequate specific instruction or vocational training in the relevant branch of activity.

Article 4

1. In so far as necessary, the competent authority, after consultation with the organizations of employers and workers concerned, where such exist, may exclude from the application of this Convention limited categories of employment or work in respect of which special and substantial problems of application arise.

2. Each Member which ratifies this Convention shall list in its first report on the application of the Convention . . . any categories which may have been excluded in pursuance of paragraph 1 of this Article, giving the reasons for such exclusion, and shall state in subsequent reports the position of its law and practice in respect of the categories excluded and the extent to which effect has been given or is proposed to be given to the Convention in respect of such categories.

3. Employment or work covered by Article 3 of this Convention shall not be excluded from the application of the Convention in pursuance of this Article.

Article 5

1. A Member whose economy and administrative facilities are insufficiently developed may, after consultation with the organizations of employers

and workers concerned, where such exist, initially limit the scope of application of this Convention.

* * *

3. The provisions of the Convention shall be applicable as a minimum to the following: mining and quarrying; manufacturing; construction; electricity, gas and water; sanitary services; transport, storage and communication; and plantations and other agricultural undertakings mainly producing for commercial purposes, but excluding family and small-scale holdings producing for local consumption and not regularly employing hired workers.

* * *

Article 6
This Convention does not apply to work done by children and young persons in schools for general, vocational or technical education or in other training institutions, or to work done by persons at least 14 years of age in undertakings, where such work is carried out in accordance with conditions prescribed by the competent authority, after consultation with the organizations of employers and workers concerned.

* * *

Article 7
1. National laws or regulations may permit the employment or work of persons 13 to 15 years of age on light work which is—

(a) not likely to be harmful to their health or development; and
(b) not such as to prejudice their attendance at school, their participation in vocational orientation or training programs approved by the competent authority or their capacity to benefit from the instruction received.

2. National laws or regulations may also permit the employment or work of persons who are at least 15 years of age but have not yet completed their compulsory schooling on work which meets the requirements set forth in subparagraphs (a) and (b) of paragraph 1 of this Article.

3. The competent authority shall determine the activities in which employment or work may be permitted under paragraphs 1 and 2 of this Article and shall prescribe the number of hours during which and the conditions in which such employment or work may be undertaken.

4. Notwithstanding the provisions of paragraphs 1 and 2 of this Article, a Member which has availed itself of the provisions of paragraph 4 of Article 2 may, for as long as it continues to do so, substitute the ages 12 and 14 for the ages 13 and 15 in paragraph 1 and the age 14 for the age 15 in paragraph 2 of this Article.

Article 8

1. After consultation with the organizations of employers and workers concerned, where such exist, the competent authority may, by permits granted in individual cases, allow exceptions to the prohibition of employment or work provided for in Article 2 of this Convention, for such purposes as participation in artistic performances.

2. Permits so granted shall limit the number of hours during which and prescribe the conditions in which employment or work is allowed.

*   *   *

▪ Convention on the Rights of the Child

Adopted by UN General Assembly Resolution 44/25 of November 20, 1989.
Entered into force September 2, 1990.
1577 UNTS 3, reprinted in Weston and Carlson, *International Law and World Order: Basic Documents,* vol. 3, III.D.3.

The States Parties to the present Convention,

Considering that, in accordance with the principles proclaimed in the Charter of the United Nations, recognition of the inherent dignity and of the equal and inalienable rights of all members of the human family is the foundation of freedom, justice and peace in the world,

Bearing in mind that the peoples of the United Nations have, in the Charter, reaffirmed their faith in fundamental human rights and in the dignity and worth of the human person, and have determined to promote social progress and better standards of life in larger freedom,

Recognizing that the United Nations has, in the Universal Declaration of Human Rights and in the International Covenants on Human Rights, proclaimed and agreed that everyone is entitled to all the rights and freedoms set forth therein, without distinction of any kind, such as race, colour, sex, language, religion, political or other opinion, national or social origin, property, birth or other status,

Recalling that, in the Universal Declaration of Human Rights, the United Nations has proclaimed that childhood is entitled to special care and assistance,

Convinced that the family, as the fundamental group of society and the natural environment for the growth and well-being of all its members and particularly children, should be afforded the necessary protection and assistance so that it can fully assume its responsibilities within the community,

Recognizing that the child, for the full and harmonious development of his or her personality, should grow up in a family environment, in an atmosphere of happiness, love and understanding,

Considering that the child should be fully prepared to live an individual life in society, and brought up in the spirit of the ideals proclaimed in the Charter of the United Nations, and in particular in the spirit of peace, dignity, tolerance, freedom, equality and solidarity,

Bearing in mind that the need to extend particular care to the child has been stated in the Geneva Declaration of the Rights of the Child of 1924 and in the Declaration of the Rights of the Child adopted by the General Assembly on 20 November 1959 and recognized in the Universal Declaration of Human Rights, in the International Covenant on Civil and Political Rights (in particular in articles 23 and 24), in the International Covenant on Economic, Social and Cultural Rights (in particular in article 10) and in the statutes and relevant instruments of specialized agencies and international organizations concerned with the welfare of children,

Bearing in mind that, as indicated in the Declaration of the Rights of the Child, "the child, by reason of his physical and mental immaturity, needs special safeguards and care, including appropriate legal protection, before as well as after birth,"

Recalling the provisions of the Declaration on Social and Legal Principles relating to the Protection and Welfare of Children, with Special Reference to Foster Placement and Adoption Nationally and Internationally; the United Nations Standard Minimum Rules for the Administration of Juvenile Justice (The Beijing Rules); and the Declaration on the Protection of Women and Children in Emergency and Armed Conflict,

Recognizing that, in all countries in the world, there are children living in exceptionally difficult conditions, and that such children need special consideration,

Taking due account of the importance of the traditions and cultural values of each people for the protection and harmonious development of the child,

Recognizing the importance of international co-operation for improving the living conditions of children in every country, in particular in the developing countries,

Have agreed as follows:

Part I

Article 1

For the purposes of the present Convention, a child means every human being below the age of eighteen years unless under the law applicable to the child, majority is attained earlier.

Article 2

1. States Parties shall respect and ensure the rights set forth in the present Convention to each child within their jurisdiction without discrimination

of any kind, irrespective of the child's or his or her parent's or legal guardian's race, colour, sex, language, religion, political or other opinion, national, ethnic or social origin, property, disability, birth or other status.

2. States Parties shall take all appropriate measures to ensure that the child is protected against all forms of discrimination or punishment on the basis of the status, activities, expressed opinions, or beliefs of the child's parents, legal guardians, or family members.

Article 3

1. In all actions concerning children, whether undertaken by public or private social welfare institutions, courts of law, administrative authorities or legislative bodies, the best interests of the child shall be a primary consideration.

2. States Parties undertake to ensure the child such protection and care as is necessary for his or her well-being, taking into account the rights and duties of his or her parents, legal guardians, or other individuals legally responsible for him or her, and, to this end, shall take all appropriate legislative and administrative measures.

3. States Parties shall ensure that the institutions, services and facilities responsible for the care or protection of children shall conform with the standards established by competent authorities, particularly in the areas of safety, health, in the number and suitability of their staff, as well as competent supervision.

Article 4

States Parties shall undertake all appropriate legislative, administrative, and other measures for the implementation of the rights recognized in the present Convention. With regard to economic, social and cultural rights, States Parties shall undertake such measures to the maximum extent of their available resources and, where needed, within the framework of international co-operation.

Article 5

States Parties shall respect the responsibilities, rights and duties of parents or, where applicable, the members of the extended family or community as provided for by local custom, legal guardians or other persons legally responsible for the child, to provide, in a manner consistent with the evolving capacities of the child, appropriate direction and guidance in the exercise by the child of the rights recognized in the present Convention.

Article 6

1. States Parties recognize that every child has the inherent right to life.

2. States Parties shall ensure to the maximum extent possible the survival and development of the child.

Article 7

1. The child shall be registered immediately after birth and shall have the right from birth to a name, the right to acquire a nationality and, as far as possible, the right to know and be cared for by his or her parents.

2. States Parties shall ensure the implementation of these rights in accordance with their national law and their obligations under the relevant international instruments in this field, in particular where the child would otherwise be stateless.

Article 8

1. States Parties undertake to respect the right of the child to preserve his or her identity, including nationality, name and family relations as recognized by law without unlawful interference.

2. Where a child is illegally deprived of some or all of the elements of his or her identity, States Parties shall provide appropriate assistance and protection, with a view to re-establishing speedily his or her identity.

Article 9

1. States Parties shall ensure that a child shall not be separated from his or her parents against their will, except when competent authorities subject to judicial review determine, in accordance with applicable law and procedures, that such separation is necessary for the best interests of the child. Such determination may be necessary in a particular case such as one involving abuse or neglect of the child by the parents, or one where the parents are living separately and a decision must be made as to the child's place of residence.

* * *

Article 11

1. States Parties shall take measures to combat the illicit transfer and non-return of children abroad.

2. To this end, States Parties shall promote the conclusion of bilateral or multilateral agreements or accession to existing agreements.

Article 12

1. States Parties shall assure to the child who is capable of forming his or her own views the right to express those views freely in all matters affecting the child, the views of the child being given due weight in accordance with the age and maturity of the child.

2. For this purpose, the child shall in particular be provided the opportunity to be heard in any judicial and administrative proceedings affecting the child, either directly, or through a representative or an appropriate body, in a manner consistent with the procedural rules of national law.

Article 13

1. The child shall have the right to freedom of expression; this right shall include freedom to seek, receive and impart information and ideas of all kinds, regardless of frontiers, either orally, in writing or in print, in the form of art, or through any other media of the child's choice.

2. The exercise of this right may be subject to certain restrictions, but these shall only be such as are provided by law and are necessary:

(a) For respect of the rights or reputations of others; or

(b) For the protection of national security or of public order (ordre public), or of public health or morals.

Article 14

1. States Parties shall respect the right of the child to freedom of thought, conscience and religion.

2. States Parties shall respect the rights and duties of the parents and, when applicable, legal guardians, to provide direction to the child in the exercise of his or her right in a manner consistent with the evolving capacities of the child.

3. Freedom to manifest one's religion or beliefs may be subject only to such limitations as are prescribed by law and are necessary to protect public safety, order, health or morals, or the fundamental rights and freedoms of others.

Article 15

1. States Parties recognize the rights of the child to freedom of association and to freedom of peaceful assembly.

2. No restrictions may be placed on the exercise of these rights other than those imposed in conformity with the law and which are necessary in a democratic society in the interests of national security or public safety, public order (ordre public), the protection of public health or morals or the protection of the rights and freedoms of others.

Article 16

1. No child shall be subjected to arbitrary or unlawful interference with his or her privacy, family, home or correspondence, nor to unlawful attacks on his or her honour and reputation.

2. The child has the right to the protection of the law against such interference or attacks.

Article 17

States Parties recognize the important function performed by the mass media and shall ensure that the child has access to information and material from a diversity of national and international sources, especially those aimed at the promotion of his or her social, spiritual and moral well-being and physical and mental health. . . .

* * *

Article 18

1. States Parties shall use their best efforts to ensure recognition of the principle that both parents have common responsibilities for the upbringing and development of the child. Parents or, as the case may be, legal guardians, have the primary responsibility for the upbringing and development of the child. The best interests of the child will be their basic concern.

2. For the purpose of guaranteeing and promoting the rights set forth in the present Convention, States Parties shall render appropriate assistance to parents and legal guardians in the performance of their child-rearing responsibilities and shall ensure the development of institutions, facilities and services for the care of children.

3. States Parties shall take all appropriate measures to ensure that children of working parents have the right to benefit from child-care services and facilities for which they are eligible.

Article 19

1. States Parties shall take all appropriate legislative, administrative, social and educational measures to protect the child from all forms of physical or mental violence, injury or abuse, neglect or negligent treatment, maltreatment or exploitation, including sexual abuse, while in the care of parent(s), legal guardian(s) or any other person who has the care of the child.

2. Such protective measures should, as appropriate, include effective procedures for the establishment of social programmes to provide necessary support for the child and for those who have the care of the child, as well as for other forms of prevention and for identification, reporting, referral, investigation, treatment and follow-up of instances of child maltreatment described heretofore, and, as appropriate, for judicial involvement.

Article 20

1. A child temporarily or permanently deprived of his or her family environment, or in whose own best interests cannot be allowed to remain in that environment, shall be entitled to special protection and assistance provided by the State.

* * *

Article 22

1. States Parties shall take appropriate measures to ensure that a child who is seeking refugee status or who is considered a refugee in accordance with applicable international or domestic law and procedures shall, whether unac-

companied or accompanied by his or her parents or by any other person, receive appropriate protection and humanitarian assistance in the enjoyment of applicable rights set forth in the present Convention and in other international human rights or humanitarian instruments to which the said States are Parties.

* * *

Article 23

1. States Parties recognize that a mentally or physically disabled child should enjoy a full and decent life, in conditions which ensure dignity, promote self-reliance and facilitate the child's active participation in the community.

* * *

Article 24

1. States Parties recognize the right of the child to the enjoyment of the highest attainable standard of health and to facilities for the treatment of illness and rehabilitation of health. States Parties shall strive to ensure that no child is deprived of his or her right of access to such health care services.

* * *

Article 26

1. States Parties shall recognize for every child the right to benefit from social security, including social insurance, and shall take the necessary measures to achieve the full realization of this right in accordance with their national law.

2. The benefits should, where appropriate, be granted, taking into account the resources and the circumstances of the child and persons having responsibility for the maintenance of the child, as well as any other consideration relevant to an application for benefits made by or on behalf of the child.

Article 27

1. States Parties recognize the right of every child to a standard of living adequate for the child's physical, mental, spiritual, moral and social development.

2. The parent(s) or others responsible for the child have the primary responsibility to secure, within their abilities and financial capacities, the conditions of living necessary for the child's development.

3. States Parties, in accordance with national conditions and within their means, shall take appropriate measures to assist parents and others responsible for the child to implement this right and shall in case of need provide material assistance and support programmes, particularly with regard to nutrition, clothing and housing.

4. States Parties shall take all appropriate measures to secure the recovery of maintenance for the child from the parents or other persons having financial responsibility for the child, both within the State Party and from abroad. In particular, where the person having financial responsibility for the

child lives in a State different from that of the child, States Parties shall promote the accession to international agreements or the conclusion of such agreements, as well as the making of other appropriate arrangements.

Article 28

1. States Parties recognize the right of the child to education, and with a view to achieving this right progressively and on the basis of equal opportunity, they shall, in particular:

(a) Make primary education compulsory and available free to all;

(b) Encourage the development of different forms of secondary education, including general and vocational education, make them available and accessible to every child, and take appropriate measures such as the introduction of free education and offering financial assistance in case of need;

(c) Make higher education accessible to all on the basis of capacity by every appropriate means;

(d) Make educational and vocational information and guidance available and accessible to all children;

(e) Take measures to encourage regular attendance at schools and the reduction of drop-out rates.

*   *   *

Article 29

1. States Parties agree that the education of the child shall be directed to:

(a) The development of the child's personality, talents and mental and physical abilities to their fullest potential;

(b) The development of respect for human rights and fundamental freedoms, and for the principles enshrined in the Charter of the United Nations;

(c) The development of respect for the child's parents, his or her own cultural identity, language and values, for the national values of the country in which the child is living, the country from which he or she may originate, and for civilizations different from his or her own;

(d) The preparation of the child for responsible life in a free society, in the spirit of understanding, peace, tolerance, equality of sexes, and friendship among all peoples, ethnic, national and religious groups and persons of indigenous origin;

(e) The development of respect for the natural environment.

*   *   *

Article 30

In those States in which ethnic, religious or linguistic minorities or persons of indigenous origin exist, a child belonging to such a minority or who is indigenous shall not be denied the right, in community with other members of his or her group, to enjoy his or her own culture, to profess and practise his or her own religion, or to use his or her own language.

Article 31

1. States Parties recognize the right of the child to rest and leisure, to engage in play and recreational activities appropriate to the age of the child and to participate freely in cultural life and the arts.

2. States Parties shall respect and promote the right of the child to participate fully in cultural and artistic life and shall encourage the provision of appropriate and equal opportunities for cultural, artistic, recreational and leisure activity.

Article 32

1. States Parties recognize the right of the child to be protected from economic exploitation and from performing any work that is likely to be hazardous or to interfere with the child's education, or to be harmful to the child's health or physical, mental, spiritual, moral or social development.

2. States Parties shall take legislative, administrative, social and educational measures to ensure the implementation of the present article. To this end, and having regard to the relevant provisions of other international instruments, States Parties shall in particular:

(a) Provide for a minimum age or minimum ages for admission to employment;

(b) Provide for appropriate regulation of the hours and conditions of employment;

(c) Provide for appropriate penalties or other sanctions to ensure the effective enforcement of the present article.

Article 33

States Parties shall take all appropriate measures, including legislative, administrative, social and educational measures, to protect children from the illicit use of narcotic drugs and psychotropic substances as defined in the relevant international treaties, and to prevent the use of children in the illicit production and trafficking of such substances.

Article 34

States Parties undertake to protect the child from all forms of sexual exploitation and sexual abuse. For these purposes, States Parties shall in particular take all appropriate national, bilateral and multilateral measures to prevent:

(a) The inducement or coercion of a child to engage in any unlawful sexual activity;

(b) The exploitative use of children in prostitution or other unlawful sexual practices;

(c) The exploitative use of children in pornographic performances and materials.

Article 35

States Parties shall take all appropriate national, bilateral and multilateral measures to prevent the abduction of, the sale of or traffic in children for any purpose or in any form.

Article 36

States Parties shall protect the child against all other forms of exploitation prejudicial to any aspects of the child's welfare.

Article 37

States Parties shall ensure that:

(a) No child shall be subjected to torture or other cruel, inhuman or degrading treatment or punishment. Neither capital punishment nor life imprisonment without possibility of release shall be imposed for offences committed by persons below eighteen years of age;

(b) No child shall be deprived of his or her liberty unlawfully or arbitrarily. The arrest, detention or imprisonment of a child shall be in conformity with the law and shall be used only as a measure of last resort and for the shortest appropriate period of time;

(c) Every child deprived of liberty shall be treated with humanity and respect for the inherent dignity of the human person, and in a manner which takes into account the needs of persons of his or her age. In particular, every child deprived of liberty shall be separated from adults unless it is considered in the child's best interest not to do so and shall have the right to maintain contact with his or her family through correspondence and visits, save in exceptional circumstances;

(d) Every child deprived of his or her liberty shall have the right to prompt access to legal and other appropriate assistance, as well as the right to challenge the legality of the deprivation of his or her liberty before a court or other competent, independent and impartial authority, and to a prompt decision on any such action.

Article 38

1. States Parties undertake to respect and to ensure respect for rules of international humanitarian law applicable to them in armed conflicts which are relevant to the child.

2. States Parties shall take all feasible measures to ensure that persons who have not attained the age of fifteen years do not take a direct part in hostilities.

3. States Parties shall refrain from recruiting any person who has not attained the age of fifteen years into their armed forces. In recruiting among those persons who have attained the age of fifteen years but who have not attained the age of eighteen years, States Parties shall endeavour to give priority to those who are oldest.

4. In accordance with their obligations under international humanitarian law to protect the civilian population in armed conflicts, States Parties shall take all feasible measures to ensure protection and care of children who are affected by an armed conflict.

Article 39

States Parties shall take all appropriate measures to promote physical and psychological recovery and social reintegration of a child victim of: any form of neglect, exploitation, or abuse; torture or any other form of cruel, inhuman or degrading treatment or punishment; or armed conflicts. Such recovery and reintegration shall take place in an environment which fosters the health, self-respect and dignity of the child.

*   *   *

ILO Convention (No. 182) Concerning the Prohibition and Immediate Action for the Elimination of the Worst Forms of Child Labour

Adopted at the eighty-seventh session of the International Labour Conference, Geneva, June 17, 1999.
Entered into force November 19, 2000.
38 ILM 1207 (1999), reprinted in Weston and Carlson, *International Law and World Order: Basic Documents,* vol. 3, III.D.4.

The General Conference of the International Labor Organization,

Having been convened at Geneva by the Governing Body of the International Labor Office, and having met in its 87th Session on 1 June 1999, and

Considering the need to adopt new instruments for the prohibition and elimination of the worst forms of child labor, as the main priority for national and international action, including international cooperation and assistance, to complement the Convention and the Recommendation concerning Minimum Age for Admission to Employment, 1973, which remain fundamental instruments on child labor, and

Considering that the effective elimination of the worst forms of child labor requires immediate and comprehensive action, taking into account the importance of free basic education and the need to remove the children concerned from all such work and to provide for their rehabilitation and social integration while addressing the needs of their families, and

Recalling the resolution concerning the elimination of child labor adopted by the International Labor Conference at its 83rd Session in 1996, and

Recognizing that child labor is to a great extent caused by poverty and that the long-term solution lies in sustained economic growth leading to social progress, in particular poverty alleviation and universal education, and

Recalling the Convention on the Rights of the Child adopted by the United Nations General Assembly on 20 November 1989, and

Recalling the ILO Declaration on Fundamental Principles and Rights at Work and its Follow-up, adopted by the International Labor Conference at its 86th Session in 1998, and

Recalling that some of the worst forms of child labor are covered by other international instruments, in particular the Forced Labor Convention, 1930, and the United Nations Supplementary Convention on the Abolition of Slavery, the Slave Trade, and Institutions and Practices Similar to Slavery, 1956, and

Having decided upon the adoption of certain proposals with regard to child labor, which is the fourth item on the agenda of the session, and

Having determined that these proposals shall take the form of an international Convention;

adopts this seventeenth day of June of the year one thousand nine hundred and ninety-nine the following Convention, which may be cited as the Worst Forms of Child Labor Convention, 1999.

Article 1
Each Member which ratifies this Convention shall take immediate and effective measures to secure the prohibition and elimination of the worst forms of child labor as a matter of urgency.

Article 2
For the purposes of this Convention, the term *child* shall apply to all persons under the age of 18.

Article 3
For the purposes of this Convention, the term *the worst forms of child labor* comprises:

(a) all forms of slavery or practices similar to slavery, such as the sale and trafficking of children, debt bondage and serfdom and forced or compulsory labor, including forced or compulsory recruitment of children for use in armed conflict;

(b) the use, procuring or offering of a child for prostitution, for the production of pornography or for pornographic performances;

(c) the use, procuring or offering of a child for illicit activities, in particular for the production and trafficking of drugs as defined in the relevant international treaties;

(d) work which, by its nature or the circumstances in which it is carried out, is likely to harm the health, safety or morals of children.

Article 4

1. The types of work referred to under Article 3(d) shall be determined by national laws or regulations or by the competent authority, after consultation with the organizations of employers and workers concerned, taking into consideration relevant international standards, in particular Paragraphs 3 and 4 of the Worst Forms of Child Labor Recommendation, 1999.

2. The competent authority, after consultation with the organizations of employers and workers concerned, shall identify where the types of work so determined exist.

3. The list of the types of work determined under paragraph 1 of this Article shall be periodically examined and revised as necessary, in consultation with the organizations of employers and workers concerned.

Article 5

Each Member shall, after consultation with employers' and workers' organizations, establish or designate appropriate mechanisms to monitor the implementation of the provisions giving effect to this Convention.

Article 6

1. Each Member shall design and implement programs of action to eliminate as a priority the worst forms of child labor.

2. Such programs of action shall be designed and implemented in consultation with relevant government institutions and employers' and workers' organizations, taking into consideration the views of other concerned groups as appropriate.

Article 7

1. Each Member shall take all necessary measures to ensure the effective implementation and enforcement of the provisions giving effect to this Convention including the provision and application of penal sanctions or, as appropriate, other sanctions.

2. Each Member shall, taking into account the importance of education in eliminating child labor, take effective and time-bound measures to:

(a) prevent the engagement of children in the worst forms of child labor;
(b) provide the necessary and appropriate direct assistance for the re-

moval of children from the worst forms of child labor and for their rehabilitation and social integration;

(c) ensure access to free basic education, and, wherever possible and appropriate, vocational training, for all children removed from the worst forms of child labor;

(d) identify and reach out to children at special risk; and

(e) take account of the special situation of girls.

3. Each Member shall designate the competent authority responsible for the implementation of the provisions giving effect to this Convention.

Article 8

Members shall take appropriate steps to assist one another in giving effect to the provisions of this Convention through enhanced international cooperation and/or assistance including support for social and economic development, poverty eradication programs and universal education.

* * *

Bibliography

AAAS (American Association for the Advancement of Science) and Science and Human Rights Program in cooperation with HURIDOCS (Human Rights Information and Documentation Systems). *Economic, Social, and Cultural Rights Violations Project Handbook.* Washington, DC, 2000.

Abbott, Grace. *The Child and the State.* Vol. 1. Westport, CT: Greenwood Press, 1938, reprinted 1968.

ADB (Asian Development Bank). "Child Protection." Available at http://www.adb .org.

———. "Labor Standards and Development." Available at http://www.adb.org.

———. *Social Protection Strategy.* Manila, 2001.

———. *Working with Street Children: Exploring Ways for ADB Assistance.* Manila, 2003.

Addams, Jane. "Child Labor and Pauperism." In *Proceedings of the National Conference of Charities and Corrections.* Boston: Press of George Ellis, 1903, pp. 114–121.

Additional Protocol in the Area of Economic, Social, and Cultural Rights. Nov. 17, 1988. OASTS 69. Reprinted in 28 ILM 156 (1989) and Weston and Carlson, *International Law and World Order,* infra vol. 3, III.B.25.

Additional Protocol to the European Social Charter Providing for a System of Collective Complaints. Nov. 9, 1995. ETS 158.

AFL-CIO (American Federation of Labor–Congress of Industrial Organizations). "This Is the AFL-CIO." Available at http://www.aflcio.org/aboutaflcio/about/ thisis/index.cfm.

African Charter on Human and Peoples Rights. June 27, 1981. OAU Doc. CAB/LEG/ 67/3 Rev. 5. Reprinted in Weston and Carlson, *International Law and World Order,* infra vol. 3, III.B.1.

African Charter on the Rights and Welfare of the Child. July 1990/Nov. 29, 1999. OAU Doc. CAB/LEG/153/Rev. 2 (1990).

African Movement of Working Children and Youth. *"A World Fit for and by Children" : Our Point of View as African Working Children.* Dakar: Enda TM, 2001.

Agarwal, Manish, and Ravi Tewari. *Eradicating Child Labor While Saving the Child.* Research report. Jaipur: Centre for International Trade, Economics, and Environment, 1999.

Alfred [Samuel H. G. Kydd]. *The History of the Factory Movement.* 2 vols. New York: Augustus M. Kelley, 1857, reprinted 1966.

Allison, James, and Alan Prout, eds. *Constructing and Reconstructing Childhood: Contemporary Issues in the Sociological Study of Childhood.* 2nd ed. London: RoutledgeFalmer, 1997.

Alston, Philip, ed. *The Best Interests of the Child: Reconciling Culture and Human Rights.* New York: Oxford University Press, 1994.

———. "The Best Interests Principle: Towards a Reconciliation of Culture and Human Rights." In Alston, *The Best Interests of the Child . . .* , supra pp. 1–25.

———. "The Commission on Human Rights." In Alston, *The United Nations and Human Rights . . .* , infra pp. 126–210.

———. "Labor Rights Provisions in U.S. Trade Law." In Compa and Diamond, *Human Rights, Labor Rights, and International Trade,* infra pp. 71–95.

———. "Peace as a Human Right." *Bulletin of Peace Proposals* (1980), 11(4): 319–330.

———. "The Right to Development and the Need for an Integrated Human Rights Approach to Development." In *Experts Discuss Some Critical Social Development Issues.* UN Division for Social Policy and Development, UN Doc. ESA/DSPD/BP.2 (May 1999), pp. 71–88.

———. *The United Nations and Human Rights: A Critical Appraisal.* Oxford: Clarendon Press.

Alston, Philip, Stephen Parker, and John Seymour, eds. *Children, Rights, and the Law.* New York: Oxford University Press, 1992.

American Convention on Human Rights. Nov. 22, 1969. 1114 UNTS 123, OASTS 36. Reprinted in Weston and Carlson, *International Law and World Order,* infra vol. 3, III.B.24.

Amnesty International. *Kashmiri Carpet Children: Exploited Village Weavers.* London, 1988.

———. *Patterns of Slavery: India's Carpet Boys.* London, Jan. 1, 1988.

———. *2002 in Focus: Economic, Social, and Cultural Rights.* Available at http://web.amnesty.org/report2003/focus2002_10-eng.

———. "War: A Child's Game?" Available at http://web.amnesty.org/pages/childsoldiers-index-eng.

Anderson, C. Arnold, and Mary Jean Bowman, eds. *Education and Economic Development.* Chicago: Aldine, 1965.

Anderson, Kym. "Environmental and Labor Standards: What Role for the WTO?" In Krueger, *The WTO as an International Organization,* infra pp. 231–255.

Anderson, Sarah, and John Cavanaugh. *Foreign Policy in Focus: World Trade Organization.* Washington, DC: Institute for Policy Studies and Interhemispheric Resource Center, n.d.

ANDI (Agência de Notícias dos Direitos da Infância). *Análise do Clipping No. 471.* Brasília: ANDI, Apr. 16–22, 2003.

———. *Criança na Mídia 1999.* Brasília: ANDI, 2000.

Andvig, Jens Chr. "Child Labour in Sub-Saharan Africa: An Exploration." *Forum for Development Studies* (1998), 2:327–362.

Anker, Richard, and Helina Melkas. *Economic Incentives for Children and the Families Intended to Eliminate or Reduce Child Labour.* Geneva: ILO, 1995.

———. *Income Replacement and Substitution Activities Intended to Eliminate or Reduce Child Labour.* Unpublished draft survey report. Geneva, 1995 (on file with Susan Bissell).

Anti-Slavery Society for the Protection of Human Rights. *Anti-Slavery Reporter* (Dec. 1981), 13(1).

———. *Anti-Slavery Reporter and Aborigines' Friend* (Nov. 1976), 12(5):10–11.

———. *Child Labour in Morocco's Carpet Industry*. Child Labour Series No. 1. London: Anti-Slavery Society, 1978.

———. "Child Labour Marches Up the International Agenda." *Anti-Slavery Newsletter* (June 1994).

———. *Debt Bondage*. London, 1988.

———. "Success on Child Jockeys." *Anti-Slavery Newsletter* (Feb. 1994).

Antony, Piush, and V. Gayathri. "Child Labor: A Perspective of Locale and Context." *Economic and Political Weekly* (Dec. 28, 2002), 37:1–28.

Arends-Kuenning, Mary, and Sajeda Amin. "School Incentive Programs and Children's Activities: The Case of Bangladesh." *Comparative Education Review* (2004), 48:380–415.

Ashagrie, Kebebew. *Economically Active Children in 1995/6: Description of Methods Used for Global and Regional Estimates*. Geneva: ILO/IPEC/SIMPOC, 2001.

———. *Methodological Child Labour Surveys and Statistics*. Geneva: ILO, 1997.

———. *Statistics on Working Children in Brief*. Geneva: ILO, 1998.

Asian American Free Labor Institute. *Child Labor in Cambodia*. Phnom Penh: Asian American Free Labor Institute, 1996.

Atleson, James. "'An Injury to One . . .': Transnational Labor Solidarity and the Role of Domestic Law." In Gross, *Workers' Rights as Human Rights,* infra pp. 160–182.

Austin, Karen. "Small Victories: Children's Rights Under the International Criminal Court." *Human Rights Tribune* (Sept. 1998), 5(4). Available at http://www.hri.ca/tribune/viewArticle.asp?id=2476.

Bacchus, Kazim. "The Political Context of the Vocationalization of Education." In Lauglo and Lillis, *Vocationalizing Education . . .* , infra pp. 31–44.

Bachman, S. L. "Label Conscience." *Mother Jones* (Mar.–Apr. 1999).

———. "A New Economics of Child Labor: Searching for Answers Behind the Headlines." *Journal of International Affairs* (Spring 2000), 53(2):545–572.

———. "A Stitch in Time." *Los Angeles Times,* Sept. 16, 2001.

Baehr, Peter R. "Mobilization of the Conscience of Mankind: Conditions of Effectiveness of Human Rights NGOs." Presentation at a UN University public forum on human rights and NGOs, Tokyo, Sept. 18, 1996. Available at the Global Policy Forum website, http://www.globalpolicy.org.

Baker, Russell. "Why Credit Is Tight." *New York Times,* Nov. 30, 1993.

Banerjee, Sumanta. *Child Labour in India*. London: Anti-Slavery Society, 1976.

———. *Child Labour in Thailand*. London: Anti-Slavery Society, 1980.

Barkan, Joel D. *Beyond Capitalism and Socialism in Kenya and Tanzania: East African Education*. Boulder: Lynne Rienner, 1994.

———. "Divergence and Convergence in Kenya and Tanzania: Pressure for Reform." In Barkan, *Beyond Capitalism and Socialism . . .* , supra pp. 1–46.

Barnet, Richard J., and Ronald E. Müller. *Global Reach: The Power of Multinational Corporations*. New York: Simon and Schuster, 1974.

Basu, Kaushik, and Pham Hoang Van. *The Economics of Child Labor*. Ithaca: Cornell University, Department of Economics, 1998.

Bayefsky, Anne F. "How to Complain to the UN Human Rights Treaty System." 2002. Available at http://www.bayefsky.com/tree.php/id/9237.

Becker, Jo. "If the US Opposes Child Labor, Why Not Child Soldiers?" Human Rights Watch, 1999. Available at http://www.hrw.org/editorials/1999/child-soldiers-jo.htm.

Becker, Saul, Chris Dearden, and Jo Aldridge. "Children's Labour of Love: Young Carers and Care Work." In Mizen, Pole, and Bolton, *Hidden Hands . . .* , infra pp. 70–87.

Beigbeder, Yves. *New Challenges for UNICEF: Children, Women, and Human Rights.* Basingstoke: Palgrave, 2001.

Belleville, M. A., S. H. Pollack, J. G. Godbold, and P. J. Landrigan. "Occupational Injuries Among Working Adolescents in New York State." *Mount Sinai Journal of Medicine* (1992), 59(6):2754–2759.

Benedek, Wolfgang, Minna Nikolova, et al., eds. *Understanding Human Rights: Manual on Human Rights Education.* Graz, Austria: Human Security Network, 2003.

Benjamin, Judea. "A Critique of the Fair Labor Association." Available at http://www.globalwatch.org.

Bequele, Assefa, and Jo Boyden. "Working Children: Current Trends and Policy Responses." *International Labour Review* (1988), 127(2):153–172.

Bequele, Assefa, and William E. Myers. *First Things First in Child Labour: Eliminating Work Detrimental to Children.* Geneva: International Labour Office, 1995.

Berg, M., and P. Hudson. "Rehabilitating the Industrial Revolution." *Economic History Review* (1992), 14:24–50.

Berger, L. R., M. Belsey, and P. M. Shah. "Medical Aspects of Child Labor in Developing Countries." *American Journal of Industrial Medicine* (1991), 19:697–699.

Berkovitch, Nitza. "The Emergence and Transformation of the International Women's Movement." In Boli and Thomas, *Constructing World Culture . . .* , infra pp. 100–126.

Berlau, John. "Exploiting Children: The Paradox of Child-Labor Reform." *Insight on the News 1997.* Available at http://www.insightmag.com/news/1997/11/24/nation/exploiting.children.the.paradox.of.childlabor.reform-213759.shtml.

Berle, Adolf A., Jr. *The 20th Century Capitalist Revolution.* New York: Harcourt, Brace, and World, 1954.

Berlin, Isaiah. *Four Essays on Liberty.* London: Oxford University Press, 1969.

Bessell, Sharon. "The Politics of Child Labour in Indonesia: Global Trends and Domestic Policy." *Pacific Affairs* (1999), 72(3):353–371.

———."The Politics of Children's Work in Indonesia: Child Labour in Domestic and Global Contexts." PhD diss., Clayton, Monash University, 1998.

Best, Geoffrey. *Mid-Victorian Britain 1851–75.* London: Weidenfeld and Nicolson, 1971.

Betten, Lammy. *International Labour Law: Selected Issues.* Deventer, Netherlands: Kluwer Law and Taxation, 1993.

Bhagwati, Jagdish, and Mathias Hirsch, eds. *The Uruguay Round and Beyond: Essays in Honour of Arthur Dunkel.* New York: Springer-Verlag, 1998.

Bhagwati, Jagdish, and Robert E. Hudec, eds. *Fair Trade and Harmonization.* London: MIT Press, 1996.

Bhagwati, Jagdish, and T. N. Srinivasan. "Trade and the Environment: Does Environmental Diversity Detract from the Case for Free Trade?" In Bhagwati and Hudec, *Fair Trade and Harmonization,* supra vol. 1, pp. 159–223.

Bhima Sangha. *Work We Can and Cannot Do.* Bangalore: The Concerned for Working Children, 1999.

Bissell, Susan, and Ernesto Shiefelbein. *Education to Combat Abusive Child Labour.* Washington, DC: USAID Bureau for Economic Growth, Culture, Agriculture, and Trade, Office for Education, 2003.

Black, Maggie. *Child Domestic Workers: A Handbook for Research and Action.* London: Anti-Slavery Society, 1997.

————. *Child Domestics.* London: Anti-Slavery Society, 1996.

————. *Children First: The Story of UNICEF, Past and Present.* Oxford: University Press, 1996.

————. *A Handbook on Advocacy: Child Domestic Workers—Finding a Voice.* London: Anti-Slavery Society, 2002.

————. *Opening Minds, Opening Up Opportunities: Children's Participation in Action for Working Children.* London: Save the Children, 2004.

Blagbrough, Johnathan, and Edmund Glynn. "Child Domestic Workers: Characteristics of the Modern Slave and Approaches to Ending Such Exploitation." *Childhood* (1999), 6(1):51–56.

Blanchet, Thérèse. *Lost Innocence: Stolen Childhoods.* Dhaka: University Press, 1996.

Blanpain, Roger, ed. *Multinational Enterprises and the Social Challenges of the XXIst Century.* The Hague: Kluwer Law International, 2000.

Blunt, Liz. "The Bitter Taste of Slavery." *BBC News,* Sept. 28, 2000. Available at http://news.bbc.co.uk/1/hi/world/africa/946952.stm.

Blustein, Paul. *The Chastening: Inside the Crisis That Rocked the Global Financial System and Humbled the IMF.* New York: PublicAffairs, 2001.

Bobo, Kimberley. "Religion-Labor Partnerships: Alive and Growing in the New Millennium." *Working USA* (2003), 6:71–83.

Bodin, Jean. *On Sovereignty: Four Chapters from the Six Books of the Commonwealth.* New York: Cambridge University Press, 1992.

Boli, John. "World Authority Structures and Legitimations." In Boli and Thomas, *Constructing World Culture . . . ,* infra pp. 267–302.

Boli, John, and George Thomas, eds. *Constructing World Culture: International Nongovernmental Organizations Since 1875.* Stanford: Stanford University Press, 1999.

Bourdieu, Pierre. *Sociology in Question.* Trans. Richard Nice. London: Sage, 1993.

Bourdieu, Pierre, and Loïc J. D. Wacquant. *An Invitation to Reflexive Sociology.* Cambridge: Polity Press, 1992.

Bourdillon, Michael, ed. "Children at Work on Tea and Coffee Estates." In Bourdillon, *Earning a Life . . . ,* infra pp. 147–172.

————. *Earning a Life: Working Children in Zimbabwe.* Harare: Weaver Press, 2000.

Boyden, Jo. "Childhood and the Policy Makers: A Comparative Perspective on the Globalization of Childhood." In Allison and Prout, *Constructing and Reconstructing Childhood . . . ,* supra pp. 190–229.

————. *The Relationship Between Education and Child Work.* Innocenti Occasional Papers, Child Rights Series No. 9. Florence: UNICEF International Child Development Centre, 1994.

Boyden, Jo, Birgitta Ling, and William E. Myers. *What Works for Working Children.* Stockholm: UNICEF and Radda Barnen, 1998.

Boyden, Jo, and William E. Myers. *Exploring Alternative Approaches to Combating Child Labour: Case Studies from Developing Countries.* Innocenti Occasional Papers, Child Rights Series No. 8. Florence: UNICEF International Child Development Centre, 1995.

Boyle, Alan E., and Michael R. Anderson, eds. *Human Rights Approaches to Environmental Protection.* Oxford: Clarendon Press, 1998.

Brasil, Congresso Nacional. *Estatuto dos Direitos da Criança e do Adolescente* [Child and Adolescent Act]. Federal Law No. 9.069 (1990). Available at http://www.uichr.org.

Brasted, Howard, and Denis Wright. "Why Worry About Child Labour?" *Asian Studies Review* (1996), 19(3):53–58.

Breen, Claire. "The Role of NGOs in the Formulation of and Compliance with the Optional Protocol to the Convention on the Rights of the Child on Involvement of Children in Armed Conflict." *Human Rights Quarterly* (2003), 25(2):453–481.

Breman, Jan. *Footloose Labor: Working in India's Informal Economy.* Cambridge: Cambridge University Press, 1996.

———. *The Laboring Poor in India: Patterns of Exploitation, Subordination, and Exclusion.* New Delhi: Oxford University Press, 2003.

———. Prologue to Breman and Das, *Down and Out . . . ,* infra pp. 2–11.

———. "The Study of Industrial Labour in Post-Colonial India: The Formal Sector—An Introductory Review." In Parry et al., *The Worlds of Indian Industrial Labour,* infra pp. 1–41.

———. "The Study of Industrial Labor in Post-Colonial India: The Informal Sector—A Concluding Review." In Parry et al., *The Worlds of Indian Industrial Labor,* infra pp. 407–431.

Breman, Jan, and Arvind Das. *Down and Out: Laboring Under Global Capitalism.* New Delhi: Oxford University Press, 2000.

Bremner, Robert H. *From the Depths: The Discovery of Poverty in the United States.* New York: New York University Press, 1956.

Brown, Drusilla K., Alan V. Deardorff, and Robert M. Stern. "International Labor Standards and Trade: A Theoretical Analysis." In Bhagwati and Hudec, *Fair Trade and Harmonization,* supra vol. 1, pp. 227–280.

———. "Pros and Cons of Linking Trade and Labor Standards." Paper prepared for the Murphy Institute conference "The Political Economy of Policy Reform," Tulane University, Nov. 9–10, 2001, revised May 6, 2002.

Bullard, Nicola. "The World Workers Need Solidarity, Not Sanctions." *Development* (June 2000).

"Burma: Death Sentences for Contacting the ILO." International Confederation of Free Trade Unions (ICFTU) press release. Mar. 18, 2004. Available at http://www.icftu.org./displaydocument.asp?index=991219095&lLanguage=en.

Burra, Neera. *Born to Work: Child Labour in India.* Delhi, Oxford: Oxford University Press, 1995.

———. "Exploitation of Children in Jaipur Gem Industry II: Health Hazards of Gem Polishing." *Economic and Political Weekly,* Jan. 23, 1988.

Caesar-Leo, Michaela. "Child Labour: The Most Visible Type of Child Abuse and Neglect in India." *Child Abuse Review* (1999), 8:75–86.

Call, Kathleen T. "Adolescent Work as 'An Arena of Comfort.'" In Mortimer and Finch, *Adolescents, Work, and the Family . . . ,* infra pp. 129–166.

———. "The Implications of Helpfulness for Possible Selves." In Mortimer and Finch, *Adolescents, Work, and the Family . . . ,* infra pp. 63–96.

Cantwell, Nigel. "Nongovernmental Organizations and the United Nations Convention on the Rights of the Child." In *Bulletin of Human Rights: The Rights of the Child,* vol. 91/2. New York: United Nations, 1992, pp. 16–24.

Carlsnaes, Walter, Thomas Risse, and Beth Simmons, eds. *Handbook of International Relations.* London: Sage, 2002.

Carter Center. *Human Rights, the United Nations, and Nongovernmental Organizations: A Report of the International Human Rights Council.* Atlanta, 1997.

Cassel, Douglass. "International Human Rights in Practice: Does International Human Rights Law Make a Difference?" *Chicago Journal of International Law* (2001), 2:121–135.

Castermans, Alex Geert, et al., eds. *The Role of Non-Governmental Organizations in the Promotion and Protection of Human Rights: Symposium Organized on the Occasion of the Award of the Praemium Erasmianum to the International Commission of Jurists.* Leiden: Stichting NJCM-Boekerij, 1989.

Caufield, Catherine. *Masters of Illusion: The World Bank and the Poverty of Nations.* New York: Holt, 1996.

Cervini, Rubens, and Freda Burger. "O Menino Trabalhador no Brasil Urbano dos Anos 80." In Cervini and Fausto, *O Trabalho e a Rua . . .*, infra pp. 17–46.

Cervini, Rubens, and Ayrton Fausto. *O Trabalho e a Rua: Crianças e Adolescentes no Brasil Urbano dos Anos 80.* São Paulo: UNICEF/FLACSO/CBIA Editora Cortez, 1991.

Chambers, Robert. *Whose Reality Counts? Putting the First Last.* London: Intermediate Technology, 1997.

Charlesworth, Hilary. "Author! Author! A Response to David Kennedy." *Harvard Human Rights Journal* (2002), 15:127–131.

Charlesworth, Hilary, and Christine Chinkin. *The Boundaries of International Law: A Feminist Analysis.* Manchester: Manchester University Press, 2000.

Charlesworth, Hilary, Christine Chinkin, and Shelley Wright. "Feminist Approaches to International Law." *American Journal of International Law* (1991), 85:613–645.

Charnovitz, Steve. "The Influence of International Labor Standards on the World Trading System: A Historical Overview." *International Labour Review* (1987), 126: 565–584.

———. "The Law of Environmental 'PPMs' in the WTO: Debunking the Myth of Illegality." *Yale Journal of International Law* (2002), 27:59–110.

———. "The Moral Exception in Trade Policy." *Virginia Journal of International Law* (1998), 38:689–745.

Charter of the Organization of American States. Apr. 30, 1948. 119 UNTS 3. Reprinted in Weston and Carlson, *International Law and World Order,* infra vol. 1, I.B.14.

Charter of the United Nations. 1976 YBUN 1043 (1945). Reprinted in Weston and Carlson, *International Law and World Order,* infra vol. 5, I.A.1.

Charter on the Rights and Welfare of the Child. July 11, 1990. OAU Doc. CAB/LEG/ 24.9/49.

"Child Labour: The Benetton Case in Turkey." European Industrial Relations Observatory Online. Available at http://www.eiro.eurofound.ie.

Chirwa, Wiseman Chijere. "Child and Youth Labour on the Nyasaland Plantations, 1890–1953." *Journal of Southern African Studies* (1993), 19:662–680.

Chirwa, Yotamu, and Michael Bourdillon. "Small-Scale Commercial Farming: Working Children in Nyanyadzi Irrigation Scheme." In Bourdillon, *Earning a Life . . .*, supra pp. 127–146.

Chowdhry, Geeta, and Mark Beeman. "Challenging Child Labor: Transnational Activism and India's Carpet Industry." *Annals of the American Academy of Political and Social Science* (2001), 575:158–175.

Chua, Amy. *World on Fire: How Exporting Free Market Democracy Breeds Ethnic Hatred and Global Instability.* New York: Anchor Books, 2003.

Churchill, Robin R., and Urgan Khaliq. "The Collective Complaints System of the European Social Charter: An Effective Mechanism for Ensuring Compliance with Economic and Social Rights?" *European Journal of International Law* (2004), 15(3):417–456. Available at http://www.ejil.org/journal/vol15/no3/chh301.pdf.

Claude, Richard Pierre, and Burns H. Weston, eds. *Human Rights in the World Community: Issues and Action.* Philadelphia: University of Pennsylvania Press, 1992.

Clean Clothes Campaign. *Code of Labor Practices for the Apparel Industry Including Sportswear.* Feb. 1998. Available at http://www.cleanclothes.org/codes/ccccode. htm#2.

Cleveland, Sarah H. "Norm Internationalization and U.S. Economic Sanctions." *Yale Journal of International Law* (2001), 26:1–102.

Coalition to Stop the Use of Child Soldiers. *Research Guide for the Child Soldiers Global Report 2004.* Available at http://www.child-soliders.org.

Cohen, Cynthia Price. "The Role of Nongovernmental Organizations in the Drafting of the Convention on the Rights of the Child." *Human Rights Quarterly* (1990), 12(1):137–147.

Coleman, James S. *Foundations of Social Theory.* Cambridge: Harvard University Press, 1990.

Compa, Lance A., and Tashia Hinchliffe Darricarrère. "Private Labor Rights Enforcement Through Corporate Codes of Conduct." In Compa and Diamond, *Human Rights, Labor Rights, and International Trade,* infra pp. 181–198.

Compa, Lance A., and Stephen F. Diamond, eds. *Human Rights, Labor Rights, and International Trade.* Philadelphia: University of Pennsylvania Press, 1996.

Compa, Lance A., and Jeffrey S. Vogt. "Labor Rights in the Generalized System of Preferences: A 20-Year Review." *Comparative Labor Law and Policy Journal* (2001), 22:199–238.

The Concerned for Working Children. *Working Children as Protagonists.* Available at http://www.workingchild.org.

———. *Working Children's Report: India 1998.* Bangalore: Books for Change, 1998.

Constitution of the Federative Republic of Brazil. 1988. Available at http://legis. senado.gov.br/con1988/con1988_05.10.1988/art_227_.htm.

Constitution of the International Labour Organization. June 28, 1919. 1920 JORF 506, 10723; 1919 UKTS 4, UK Command Papers (1919–1956) 153, 112 BFSP 191; 48 Stat. 2712, TS 874.

———. Preamble to Part XIII of the Treaty of Versailles. June 28, 1919. 49 Stat. 2712, 15 UNTS 35. As amended and reprinted in ILO, Constitution of the International Labour Organization and Standing Orders of the International Labour Conference 5–24 (1980). Available at http://www.ilo.org/public/english/about/iloconst.htm.

Constitution of the Republic of the Philippines. 1987. Available at http://www. chanrobles.com/philsupremelaw.htm.

Corlett, Celeste. "Impact of the 2000 Child Labor Treaty on United States Child Laborers." *Arizona Journal of International and Comparative Law* (2002), 19: 713–739.

Costa, Antônio Carlos G. *O Estatuto da Criança e do Adolescente e o Trabalho Infantil.* São Paulo: Editora Ltr/OIT, 1994.

———. "O Novo Direito da Criança: Dez Anos de Travessia." In *Revista Conjuntura Social.* São Paulo: Fundação Ayrton Sena, 1999.

Cottier, Thomas, ed. *Trade and Human Rights.* Ann Arbor: University of Michigan Press, 2005.

Coulibaly, Pierre Marie, and Dibou Faye. "Le Programme AEJT–ENDA–Gouvernement–IPEC/BIT au Sénégal." Dakar: ENDA Tiers-Monde, 1999.

Council for the Welfare of Children and UNICEF. *Guidelines Mainstreaming Child Rights in Local Development Planning.* Philippines, 2001.

Council of Europe. *Complaint No. 1/1998 by the International Commission of Jurists Against Portugal.* Sept. 9, 1999. Available at http://www.coe.int/t/e/human_rights/ esc/4_collective_complaints/list_of_collective_complaints/rc1_on_merits.pdf.

Covenant of the League of Nations. June 28, 1919. Repinted in Clive Parry, ed., *Consolidated Treaty Series* (1969–), 225:195.

Cowan, Jane K., Marie-Bénédicte Dembour, and Richard A. Wilson, eds. *Culture and Rights: Anthropological Perspectives.* Cambridge: Cambridge University Press, 2001.

Creighton, Breen. "Combating Child Labour: The Role of International Labour Standards." *Comparative Labor Law Journal* (1997), 18:362–388.

Cross, Peter. *Kashmiri Carpet Children: Exploited Village Weavers.* ASS Child Labour Series No. 11. Ed. Alan Whittaker. London: Anti-Slavery International, 1991.

Cullen, Holly. "The Right of Child Workers to Protection from Environmental Hazards." In Fitzmaurice and Fijalkowski, *The Right of the Child to a Clean Environment,* infra pp. 35–59.

Cullen, Holly, and Karen Morrow. "International Civil Society in International Law: The Growth of NGO Participation." *Non-State Actors and International Law* (2001), 1:7–39.

Cunningham, Hugh. *Children and Childhood in Western Society Since 1500.* London: Longman, 1995.

———. *The Children of the Poor: Representations of Childhood Since the Seventeenth Century.* Oxford: Blackwell, 1991.

———. "The Decline of Child Labor: Labor Markets and Family Economies in Europe and North America Since 1830." *Economic History Review* (2000), 53(3): 409–428.

———. "The Employment and Unemployment of Children in England, c. 1680–1851." *Past and Present* (Feb. 1990), 126:115–150.

———. "The Rights of the Child and the Wrongs of Child Labor: An Historical Perspective." In Lieten and White, *Child Labour . . . ,* infra pp. 13–26.

———. "The Rights of the Child from the Mid-Eighteenth to the Early Twentieth Century." *Aspects of Education* (1994), 50:2–16.

Cunningham, Stephen. "The Problem That Doesn't Exist? Child Labor in Britain 1918–1970." In Lavalette, *A Thing of the Past? . . . ,* pp. 139–172.

Das, Arvind. Epilogue to Breman and Das, *Down and Out . . . ,* supra pp. 150–156.

Davidson, Mary Gray. "The International Labour Organization's Latest Campaign to End Child Labor: Will It Succeed Where Others Have Failed?" *Transnational Law & Contemporary Problems* (2001), 11:203–224.

DCI (Defence for Children International). *Newsletter of Child Labour Desk* (Nov.–Dec. 2001), No. 1.

de Araújo, Braz, org. *Crianças e Adolescentes no Brasil: Diagnósticos, Políticas e Experiências.* São Paulo: Fundação Cargill, 1997.

de Coninck-Smith, Ning, Bengt Sandin, and Ellen Schrumpf, eds. *Industrious Children: Work and Childhood in the Nordic Countries, 1850–1990.* Odense, Denmark: Odense University Press, 1997.

de la Cruz, Protacio, et al. *Trust and Power: Child Abuse in the Eyes of the Child and the Parent.* University of the Philippines Center for Integrative Studies, Save the Children–UK, and UNICEF, 2000.

de Oliveira, Oris. *O Menino, o Trabalho e a Lei.* Rio de Janeiro: FUNABEM/Projeto Alternativas, 1987.

———. *Trabalho da Criança e do Adolescente.* São Paulo: Editora Ltr/OIT, 1994.

Dearden, Chris, and Saul Becker. "The Experiences of Young Carers in the United Kingdom: The Mental Health Issues." *Mental Health Care* (1999), 21(8): 273–276.

———. *Young Carers in the United Kingdom*. London: Carers National Association, 1998.

Declaration by the National Movement of Working Children and Adolescents of Peru (MNNATSOP) on the New ILO Convention Concerning Child Labour. Available at http://www.tu-berlin.de/fak1/gsw/pronats/doku/mnnastop.html.

Declaration of Geneva of the Rights of the Child. Adopted by the Council of the League of Nations Assembly, 5th Assembly, Sept. 26, 1924. Official Journal–5, League of Nations OJ Spec. Supp. 23, at 177 (1924). Reprinted in Weston and Carlson, *International Law and World Order*, infra vol. 3, III.D.1.

DFID (Department for International Development). "Helping Not Hurting Children: An Alternative Approach to Child Labour." Press release, 1999. Available at http://www.tgwu.org.uk/tgwuinternated/textiles/dfid_news1.htm.

———. *Liberating Children: Combating Hidden and Harmful Child Labour*. London: DFID, 2002.

Diamond, Charles, and Tammy Faye, eds. "Evidence on Sustainability of Adult and Child Labour." *Journal of Development Studies* (1998), 34(3):62–70.

Diller, Janelle M., and David A. Levy. "Child Labor, Trade, and Investment: Toward the Harmonization of International Law." *American Journal of International Law* (1997), 91:663–696.

Donnelly, Jack. *The Concept of Human Rights*. New York: St. Martin's Press, 1985.

———. *Universal Human Rights in Theory and Practice*. Ithaca: Cornell University Press, 1989.

Dorman, Peter. *Child Labour in the Developed Economies*. IPEC working paper. Geneva: ILO, 2001.

dos Santos, Benedito R. "A Cidadania de Crianças e Adolescentes: Legislação de Proteção às seus Direitos." In de Araújo, *Crianças e Adolescentes no Brasil . . .* , supra pp. 295–334.

———. "A Cidadania Regulada de Crianças e Adolescentes." *Estudos: Revista da UCG (Universidade Católica de Goiás)* (1999), 26:7–32.

———. "Da 'Virtude' à Violação de Direitos: O Agendamento Contra o Trabalho Infantil no Brasil—Uma Perspectiva Histórico-Analítica." In Gomes Sousa, *Infância, Adolescência e Família*, infra pp. 69–101.

———. *Mobilização Empresarial pela Erradicação do Trabalho Infantil: Um Estudo das Estratégias Desenvolvidas pela Fundação Abrinq Pelos Direitos da Criança*. São Paulo: UNICEF/Abrinq, 1997.

———. "A Regulamentação do Trabalho Educativo." In *Cadernos Abong-Subsídos para II Conferência Nacional dos Direitos da Criança e do Adolescente: Por uma Agenda de Compromissos*, No. 18. São Paulo: ABONG/UNICEF, 1997, pp. 10–22.

———. "Trabalho Infantil no Brasil: Discussão e Balanço das Principais Estratégias de Erradicação." In de Araújo, *Crianças e Adolescentes no Brasil . . .* , supra pp. 295–334.

———. "Ungovernable Children: Runaways, Homeless Youths, and Street Children in New York and São Paulo." PhD diss., University of California at Berkeley, 2002.

dos Santos, Benedito R., et al. *Report: O Trabalho Infantil no Brasil—Um Estudo das Estratégias e Políticas para sua Eliminação*. Mimeo. São Paulo: International Working Group on Child Labour, ISPICAN, DCI, Feb. 1996.

Douzinas, Costas. *The End of Human Rights: Critical Legal Thought at the Turn of the Century*. Oxford: Hart, 2000.

Draft Declaration on the Rights of Indigenous Peoples. Aug. 26, 1994. UN Doc. E/CN.4/1995/2; E/CN.4/Sub.2/1994/56 (Oct. 28, 1994). Reprinted in Weston and Carlson, *International Law and World Order,* infra vol. 3, III.F.4.

Drinan, S. J., Robert F. *The Mobilization of Shame.* New Haven: Yale University Press, 2001.

Dubofsky, Melvyn. *The State and Labor in Modern America.* Chapel Hill: University of North Carolina Press, 1994.

Dugard, John. "Reconciliation and Justice: The South African Experience." In Weston and Marks, *The Future of International Human Rights,* infra pp. 399–432.

Dugger, Celia W. "To Help Poor Be Pupils, Not Wage Earners, Brazil Pays Parents." *New York Times,* Jan. 3, 2004.

Dworkin, Ronald. *Taking Rights Seriously.* London: Duckworth, 1977.

Easterly, William. *The Elusive Quest for Growth: Economists' Adventures and Misadventures in the Tropics.* Cambridge: MIT Press, 2002.

Easton, Peter, and Simon Fass. "Monetary Consumption Benefits and the Demand for Primary Schooling in Haiti." *Comparative Education Review* (1989), 33:176–193.

Economic and Social Council Resolution (No. 1235) Concerning Questions of the Violation of Human Rights and Fundamental Freedoms, Including Policies of Racial Discrimination and Segregation and of Apartheid, in All Countries, with Particular Reference to Colonial and Other Dependent Countries and Territories. ESC Res. 1235, UN ESCOR, 42nd Sess., Supp. No. 1, at 17. UN Doc. E/4393 (1967). Reprinted in Weston and Carlson, *International Law and World Order,* infra vol. 3, III.T.3.

Economic and Social Council Resolution (No. 1503) Concerning Procedures for Dealing with Communications Relating to Violations of Human Rights and Fundamental Freedoms. ESC Res. 1503, UN ESCOR, 48th Sess., Supp. 1A, at 8. UN Doc E/4832/Add.1 (1970). Reprinted in Weston and Carlson, *International Law and World Order,* infra vol. 3, III.T.6.

Economic and Social Research Foundation. *Summary of the Participatory Poverty Assessment Presented During the Poverty Policy Week.* Dar es Salaam, October 2003.

ECPAT (End Child Prostitution in Asian Tourism). *Child Sex Tourism and Action Plan.* Group development report, 2001.

ECPAT International. *Annual Report 2001–2002.* Available at http://www.ecpat.net/eng/ecpat_inter/annual_report/index.asp.

Effah, Josephine. *Modernised Slavery: Child Trade in Nigeria.* Lagos: Constitutional Rights Project, 1996.

Elliott, Kimberly A. "Getting Beyond No . . . ! Promoting Workers' Rights *and* Trade." In Schott, *The WTO After Seattle,* infra pp. 187–204.

Elmhirst, Rebecca, and Ratna Saptari, eds. *Changing Labour Relations in Southeast Asia.* London: RoutledgeCurzon, 2004.

Enda Tiers-Monde. *Les Mbindaam sans Mbindou: Études avec les Petites Bonnes à Dakar (Jeuda 99).* Dakar: Enda Tiers-Monde, 1996.

———. *Quatrième Rencontre Régionale des Enfants et Jeunes Travailleurs d'Afrique, Popenguine, Senegal, do 17 au 27 Février 1998 (Jeuda 101).* Dakar: Enda Tiers-Monde, 1999.

———. *Working Children of Africa.* Dakar: Equipe Jeunesse Action, 1999.

Ennew, Judith. *Capacity Building and Maintenance in Measuring and Monitoring Child Labor.* Concept paper. New York: UNICEF Centre for Family Research, 1999.

————, ed. *Learning or Labouring? A Compilation of Key Texts on Child Work and Basic Education.* Florence: UNICEF International Centre for Child Development, 1995.

Ennew, Judith, and Pansy Young. *Child Labour in Jamaica.* London: Anti-Slavery Society, 1981.

Ermacora, Felix. "Non-Governmental Organizations as Promoters of Human Rights." In Mascher and Petzold, *Protecting Human Rights . . .* , infra pp. 171–180.

Escott, T. H. S. *England: Its People, Polity, and Pursuits.* London: Chapman and Hall, 1885.

Espinola, Basilica, Benno Glauser, and Rosa Maria Ortiz. *En la Calle: Menores Trabajadores de la Calle en Asunción: Un Libra para Acción.* Asunción: Impr. el Grafico, 1987.

Ethical Trading Initiative. "The Base Code." Available at http://www.ethicaltrade.org/pub/publications/basecode/en/index.shtml.

European Communities: Community Directive 94/33 on Young Workers. OJEC L216/12 (1994).

European Communities: Measures Affecting Asbestos and Asbestos-Containing Products. Report of the Appellate Body. WT/DS135/Appellate Body/R, Mar. 12, 2001.

European Communities: Measures Concerning Meat and Meat Products (Hormones). Report of the Appellate Body. WT/DS26 & 48/AB/R, Jan. 16, 1998.

European Convention for the Protection of Human Rights and Fundamental Freedoms. Nov. 4, 1950. 213 UNTS 221, ETS 5. Reprinted in Weston and Carlson, *International Law and World Order,* infra vol. 3, III.B.2.

European Social Charter (Revised). May 3, 1996. ETS 163. Reprinted in Weston and Carlson, *International Law and World Order,* infra vol. 3, III.B.4.

Executive Order 13126: Prohibition of Acquisition of Products Produced by Forced or Indentured Child Labor. 64 Fed. Reg. 32383. June 12, 1999. Available at http://www.dol.gov/ilab/regs/eo13126/main.htm.

Fair Wear Foundation. *The Fair Wear Code of Labor Practices.* May 2002. Available at http://www.fairwear.nl/policy%20document.pdf.

Falk, Richard A. *Human Rights Horizons: The Pursuit of Justice in a Globalizing World.* New York: Routledge, 2000.

Fallon, Peter, and Zafiris Tzannatos. *Child Labour: Issues and Directions for the World Bank.* Washington, DC: World Bank, Social Protection Human Development Network, 1998.

Farer, Tom. "The UN and Human Rights: At the End of the Beginning." In Roberts and Kingsbury, *United Nations, Divided World . . .* , infra pp. 240–296.

Farías, Vilmar. "A Montanha e a Pedra: Limites da Política Social Brasileira e os Problemas da Infância e de Juventude." In Cervini and Fausto, *O Trabalho e a Rua . . .* , supra pp. 195–226.

Feinstein, Charles. "Pessimism Perpetuated: Real Wages and the Standards of Living in Britain During and After the Industrial Revolution." *Journal of Economic History* (1998), 58:625–658.

Felt, Jeremy P. *Hostages of Fortune: Child Labor Reform in New York State.* Syracuse, NY: Syracuse University Press, 1965.

Fernando, Jude L. "Children's Rights: Beyond the Impasse." *Annals of the American Academy of Political and Social Science* (2001), 575:8–24.

Field, Norma. "The Child as Laborer and Consumer: The Disappearance of Childhood in Contemporary Japan." In Stephens, *Children and the Politics of Culture,* infra pp. 51–78.

Final Act Embodying the Results of the Uruguay Round of Multilateral Negotiations. Apr. 15, 1994. *Legal Instruments: Results of the Uruguay Round* (1994). Reprinted in 33 ILM 1125 (1994) and Weston and Carlson, *International Law and World Order,* infra vol. 4, IV.C.2.

Final Act of the Conference on Security and Co-operation in Europe: Declaration on Principles Guiding Relations Between Participating States, Respect for Human Rights and Fundamental Freedoms, Including the Freedom of Thought, Conscience, Religion, or Belief. Aug. 1, 1975. Reprinted in 14 ILM 1292 (1975) and Weston and Carlson, *International Law and World Order,* infra vol. 1, I.D.9.

Final Appeal of Children and Young People. Second World Congress Against Commercial Sexual Exploitation of Children, Yokohama, Japan, Dec. 17–20, 2001. Available at http://www.ecpat.net/eng/ecpat_inter/projects/monitoring/wc2/final_appeal_of_young_people.pdf.

Final Declaration of the Second Meeting of the World Movement of Working Children and Adolescents. Berlin, Apr. 19–May 2, 2004. Available at http://66.102.9.104/search?q=cache:zvizaigkhzuj:www.teimun.nl/2004/forum/final%2520declaration%2520berlin.doc+final+declaration+2nd+meeting+of+the+world+movement+of+working+children+and+adolescents+2004&hl=en.

Finnemore, Martha. "Norms, Culture, and World Politics: Insights from Sociology's Institutionalism." *International Organization* (1996), 50:325–347.

————. "The Rules of War and the War of Rules: The International Red Cross and the Restraint of State Violence." In Boli and Thomas, *Constructing World Culture,* supra pp. 149–165.

Fischer, Rosa Maria. "Estudo Avalia Selos Socias." Administraçâo em Pauta. Launch leaflet. São Paulo: Abrinq, 1995.

Fitzmaurice, Malgosia, and Agata Fijalkowski, eds. *The Right of the Child to a Clean Environment.* Aldershot: Ashgate, 1999.

FNPETI (Fórum Nacional de Prevenção e Erradicação do Trabalho Infantil). *Proposta de Trabalho.* Mimeo. Brasília, Nov. 1994.

FOIL (Forum of Indian Leftists). *Those That Be in Bondage: Child Labor and the IMF Strategy in India.* Pamphlet No. 1. Hartford, Fall 1996.

Foner, Nancy. *From Ellis Island to JFK: New York's Two Great Waves of Immigration.* New Haven: Yale University Press, 2000.

Forster, M., ed. *Selected Poems of Elizabeth Barrett Browning.* London: Chatto and Windus, 1998.

Forsythe, David P., ed. *Human Rights and Comparative Foreign Policy.* Tokyo: United Nations University Press, 2000.

Forsythe, John S. "Legislative History of the Fair Labor Standards Act." *Law and Contemporary Problems* (Summer 1939), 6:464–490.

Fortin, Jane. *Children's Rights and the Developing Law.* 2nd ed. London: Butterworths, 2003.

Foster, Phillip J. "The Vocational School Fallacy in Development Planning." In Anderson and Bowman, *Education and Economic Development,* supra pp. 155–157.

Foweraker, Joe. *Grassroots Movements, Political Activism, and Social Development in Latin America.* Geneva: United Nations Research Institute for Social Development, 2001.

Foweraker, Joe, and Todd Landman. "Individual Rights and Social Movements: A Comparative and Statistical Inquiry." *British Journal of Political Science* (1999), 29:291–322.

Franck, Thomas M. "Are Human Rights Universal?" *Foreign Affairs* (Jan.–Feb. 2001), 80(1):191–204.

Frank, Andre Gunder. *Capitalism and Underdevelopment in Latin America: Historical Studies of Chile and Brazil.* New York: Monthly Review Press, 1967.

———. *The Underdevelopment of Development.* Stockholm: Bethany Books, 1991.

Frank, J., C. Tatum, and S. Tucker. *On Small Shoulders.* London: London Children's Society, 1999.

Fraser, Steve. *Labor Will Rule: Sidney Hillman and the Rise of American Labor.* New York: Free Press, 1991.

Freeman, Michael D. A. *Human Rights: An Interdisciplinary Approach.* Cambridge: Polity Press, 2002.

———. "The Moral Status of Children." In Freeman, *The Moral Status of Children* . . . , infra pp. 1–17.

———, ed. *The Moral Status of Children: Essays on the Rights of the Child.* The Hague: Martinus Nijhoff, 1997.

———. "Taking Children's Rights More Seriously." In Alston, Parker, and Seymour, *Children, Rights, and the Law,* supra pp. 52–71.

Freestone, David, ed. *Children and the Law.* Hull, UK: Hull University Press, 1990.

Fuchs, Estelle, ed. *Youth in a Changing World: Cross-Cultural Perspectives on Adolescence.* The Hague: Mouton, 1976.

Fukui, Lia. "A Questão do Trabalho Infantil na Grande Imprensa Paulista na Década de 70." *Revista Bras. Est. Pedagógicos* (Jan.–Apr. 1985), 66(152):28–46.

———. "Por que o Trabalho de Crianças é Tolerado?" In *Bibliografia Sobre o Trabalho de Crianças no Brasil.* São Paulo: SCFBES, 1994, pp. 21–39.

Fuller, Bruce. *Growing Up Modern: The Western State Builds Third-World Schools.* New York: Routledge, 1991.

Fuller, Bruce, and Richard Rubinson. *The Political Construction of Education.* New York: Praeger, 1992.

Fuller, Raymond G. "Child Labor." In Seligman, *Encyclopedia of the Social Sciences,* infra pp. 412–424.

Fundação Abrinq Pelos Direitos da Criança. "Child Friendly Company." Launch leaflet. São Paulo: Abrinq, 1995.

Fyfe, Alec. "Child Labor and Education: Revisiting the Policy Debate." In Lieten and White, *Child Labour* . . . , infra pp. 67–84.

———. *Child Labour.* Cambridge: Polity Press, 1989.

———. *Educational Strategies for Street and Working Children.* WHO conference paper, unpublished mimeo. Geneva, 1994 (on file with Susan Bissell).

———. *Letting Girls Learn: Strategic Considerations Concerning Female Working Children in Bangladesh.* Unpublished mimeo. Dhaka: UNICEF Bangladesh, 1996 (on file with Susan Bissell).

———. *A Rights-Based Approach to Child Labour and Education: Moving from Rhetoric to Reality.* Unpublished mimeo. New York: UNICEF, 2003 (on file with Susan Bissell).

Gaer, Felice D. "Reality Check: Human Rights Non-Governmental Organizations Confront Governments at the United Nations." Paper presented to the conference "Nongovernmental Organizations, the United Nations, and Global Governance," Academic Council on the United Nations System, Apr. 1995.

Galeana Cisneros, Rosaura. "El Trabajo Infantil en México, Balance de una Década." In Valencia, *Avances y Retrocesos* . . . , infra pp. 291–319.

Galtung, Johan. *Human Rights in Another Key.* Cambridge: Polity Press, 1994.

Galtung, Johan, and Anders H. Wirak. *Human Needs, Human Rights, and the Theories of Development in Indicators of Social and Economic Change and Their Applications.* Reports and Papers in Social Science No. 37. Paris: UNESCO, 1976.

Garcia, Frank J. "Building a Just Trade Order for a New Millennium." *George Washington International Law Review* (2001), 33:1015–1062.

———. "The Global Market and Human Rights: Trading Away the Human Rights Principle." *Brooklyn Journal of International Law* (1999), 25:51–97.

———. "Integrating Trade and Human Rights in the Americas." In Cottier, supra.

———. "Trade and Justice: Linking the Trade Linkage Debates." *University of Pennsylvania Journal of International Business Law* (1998), 19:391–434.

———. "Trade, Constitutionalism, and Human Rights: An Overview." *Proceedings of the 96th Annual Meeting, American Society of International Law* (2002), 96: 132–134.

———. *Trade, Inequality, and Justice.* Ardsley, NY: Transnational, 2003.

Garcia, Leonora S., and Ma. Theresa Molina. *Rural Children: Poverty and Hazards of Childhood.* Manila: Philippine Network-Research and Development Institute, 1998.

García Méndez, Emilio. *Child Rights in Latin America: From "Irregular Situation" to Full Protection.* Working Paper No. 8. Florence: UNICEF Innocenti Research Centre, 1998.

Garg, Anjli. "A Child Labor Social Clause: Analysis and Proposal for Action." *New York University Journal of International Law and Politics* (1999), 31:473–534.

GATT Dispute Panel Report on U.S. Restrictions on Imports of Tuna. 30 ILM 1594 (Aug. 16, 1991) *[Tuna-Dolphin I].* Unadopted.

———. 33 ILM 839, 885 (June 16, 1994) *[Tuna-Dolphin II].* Unadopted.

General Agreement on Tariffs and Trade (GATT). Oct. 30, 1947. 55 UNTS 194, 61 Stat. A-11, TIAS 1700. Reprinted in Weston and Carlson, *International Law and World Order,* infra vol. 4, IV.C.1.

———. Annex 1A, *Agreement Establishing the World Trade Organization.* Apr. 15, 1994. In *Final Act Embodying the Results of the Uruguay Round of Multilateral Negotiations,* supra. Reprinted in 33 ILM 28 (1994).

Gerth, H. H., and C. Wright Mills, eds. *From Max Weber.* New York: Oxford University Press, 1946.

Gewirth, Alan. *The Community of Rights.* Chicago: University of Chicago Press, 1996.

Ghosh, Arun. *Humanizing Child Labour.* Report on the Institute of Psychological and Educational Research (IPER) Project on Child Labour. Calcutta: IPER, 1983–1985.

Ghosh, B. N. *Dependency Theory Revisited.* Aldershot: Ashgate, 2001.

Gibbons, Elizabeth, Friedrich Huebler, and Edilberto Loaiza. "Child Labour, Education, and the Principal of Non/Discrimination." Paper prepared for the conference "Human Rights and Development: Towards Mutual Reinforcement," sponsored by the Ethical Globalization Initiative and the Center for Human Rights and Global Justice, New York University School of Law, Mar. 1, 2004.

Gilman, Nils. *Mandarins of the Future: Modernization Theory in Cold War America.* Baltimore: Johns Hopkins University Press, 2003.

Glasinovich, Walter A. "Trabajar o Estudiar: Un Falso Dilema." In *Entr Calles y Plazas: El Trabajo de los Niños en Lima.* Peru: IEP, UNICEF, and ADEC/ATC, 1991. Translated extract in Ennew, *Learning or Labouring? . . . ,* supra pp. 80–82.

Global Compact. *The Nine Principles.* Available at http://www.unglobalcompact.org/portal/default.asp.

Global March Against Child Labour. "About Us." Available at http://globalmarch. org/index.php.

———. *Anti-Slavery Reporter* (1998), VIII.4(1):6–9.

———. *Out of the Shadows: Domestic Child Servitude.* New Delhi, 2001. Available at http://globalmarch.org/index/html.

Global Rights.org—Partners for Justice Online. "About Global Rights." Available at http://www.hrlawgroup.org/who_we_are/about_global_rights.

Global Sullivan Principles of Social Responsibility. Available at http:// globalsullivanprinciples.org/principles.htm.

Goddard, Victoria, and Ben White. "Child Workers and Capitalist Development: An Introductory Note and Bibliography." *Development and Change* (1982), 13(4):465–477.

Goldman, Wendy Z. *Women, the State, and Revolution: Soviet Family Policy and Social Life, 1917–1936.* Cambridge: Cambridge University Press, 1993.

Golub, Stephen C. "Are International Labor Standards Needed to Prevent Social Dumping?" *Finance and Development* (Dec. 1997).

Gomes Sousa, Sônia M. *Infância, Adolescência e Família.* Goiânia: Cânone Editorial, 2001.

Gonzales, David. "Latin Sweatshops Pressed by U.S. Campus Power." *New York Times,* Apr. 4, 2003.

Gourevitch, Peter. "International Relations Theories." In *International Encyclopedia of the Social and Behavioral Sciences.* Amsterdam: Elsevier, 2001, pp. 7829–7832.

Gourlay, Steve, LICADHO, and RCG Labour Inspectorate Staff. *Child Labour Matrix.* Phnom Penh: LICADHO, 2002.

Government of the Philippines. *Commercial Sexual Exploitation in the Philippines.* Department of Social Welfare and Development, and UNICEF, 1999.

———. *Philippine National Plan of Action Against Sexual Exploitation of Children, 1999–2003.* Department of Labor and Employment, 1999.

———. *Philippine National Plan of Action for Children for the Year 2000 and Beyond.* Department of Labor and Employment, 1999.

———. *Redefining the Strategic Directions and Thrusts of the National Program Against Child Labor.* Department of Labor and Employment, 2000.

———. *Survey of Children 5 to 17 Years Old.* National Statistics Office, 2001.

Government of the Philippines and UNICEF. *Country Programme of Cooperation for Child Survival, Development, Protection and Participation: Master Plan of Operations V, 1999–2003.* 1998.

Government of Zimbabwe. *Inter-Census Demographic Survey, 1997.* Harare: Central Statistics Office, 1998.

———. *Zimbabwe 1999 National Child Labour Survey Country Report.* Harare: Central Statistics Office, 1999.

Governo Brasileiro. CONANDA (Conselho Nacional dos Direitos da Criança e do Adolescente). *Plano Nacional de Erradicação do Trabalho Infantil.* Brasília: CONANDA, 2003.

———. IBGE (Fundação Instituto Brasileiro de Geografia e Estatísticas). *Crianças e Adolescentes: Indicadores Sociais.* Vol. 3. 1994.

———. Ministério da Justiça. *Plano Nacional de Enfrentamento da Violência Sexual Infanto-Juvenil.* Brasília: MJ/SEDH/DCA, 2002.

———. Ministério da Previdência e Assistência Social. *Manual Operacional do Programa de Erradicação do Trabalho Infantil–PETI.* Brasília: MPAS, 1999.

————. Ministério do Trabalho e Emprego. *Trabalho Infantil no Brasil.* Available at http://www.mte.gov.br/temas/fiscatrab/combatetrabalhoinfantil/contendo/537.pdf.

Govinda, R. *India Education Report: A Profile of Basic Education.* New Delhi: Oxford University Press, 2002.

Graitcer, P. L., and L. B. Lerer. *Child Labor and Health: Quantifying the Global Health Impacts of Child Labor.* Working Paper No. 19021. Washington, DC: World Bank, 1998.

Gray, Alexander. *The Development of Economic Doctrine: An Introductory Survey.* London: Longmans, 1931.

Gray, Laurence. *Just How Clean Are Your Shoes?* London: CAFOD, 1997.

Green, Duncan. "Child Workers of the Americas." *Nacla Report on the Americas* (1999), 32(4):21–27.

Green, Lora A. "The Global Fight for the Elimination of Child Labor in Pakistan." *Wisconsin International Law Journal* (2001), 20:177–196.

Green, Maria. "What We Talk About When We Talk About Indicators: Current Approaches to Human Rights Measurement." *Human Rights Quarterly* (2001), 23(4):1062–1097.

Greene, Julia. *Pure and Simple Politics: The American Federation of Labor and Political Activism, 1881–1917.* New York: Cambridge University Press, 1998.

Griffin, Keith. "Economic Globalization and Institutions of Global Governance." *Development & Change* (2003), 34(6):789–807.

Grimsrud, Björne, ed. *The Next Steps: Experiences and Analysis of How to Eradicate Child Labour.* Oslo: Fafo, 2002.

————. "Too Much Work at Too Early an Age." In Grimsrud, *The Next Steps . . . ,* supra pp. 9–23.

Grimsrud, Björne, and Tim Noonan. "The Next Steps." In Grimsrud, *The Next Steps . . . ,* supra pp. 113–123.

Grootaert, Christiaan, and Harry Anthony Patrinos. *The Policy Analysis of Child Labor: A Comparative Study.* New York: St. Martin's Press, 1999.

Gross, James A. "The Broken Promises of the National Labor Relations Act and the Occupational Safety and Health Act: Conflicting Values and Conceptions of Rights and Justice." *Chicago-Kent Law Review* (1998), 73:351–387.

————. "Conflicting Statutory Purposes: Another Look at Fifty Years of NLRB Law Making." *Industrial and Labor Relations Review* (Oct. 1985), 39:7–18.

————. "A Human Rights Perspective on United States Labor Relations Law: A Violation of the Right of Freedom of Association." *Employer Rights & Employment Policy Journal* (1999), 3:65–103.

————. "A Human Rights Perspective on U.S. Education: Only Some Children Matter." *Catholic University Law Review* (Summer 2001), 50:919–956.

————. "A Long Overdue Beginning: The Promotion and Protection of Workers' Rights as Human Rights." In Gross, *Workers' Rights as Human Rights,* infra pp. 1–22.

————. "Worker Rights as Human Rights: Wagner Act Values and Moral Choices." *University of Pennsylvania Journal of Labor and Employment Law* (Spring 2002), 4:479–492.

————, ed. *Workers' Rights as Human Rights.* Ithaca: Cornell University Press, 2003.

Guide to the Implementation of Reebok Human Rights Production Standards. Ver. 3. Available at http://www.reebok.com/x/us/humanrights/pdf/reebokhr_guide.pdf.

Gupta, Shakuntala, and Sangeeta Nagaich. "Child Labor in India: Extent and Causes— A Case Study." In Rao, *Exploited Children . . . ,* infra pp. 74–83.

Hammarberg, Thomas. *A School for Children with Rights: The Significance of the United Nations Convention on the Rights of the Child for Modern Education Policy*. Florence: UNICEF, 1997.

Hancock, Graham. *Lords of Poverty: The Power, Prestige, and Corruption of the International Aid Business*. New York: Atlantic, 1989.

Hannum, Hurst, ed. *Guide to International Human Rights Practice*. 3rd ed. Ardsley, NY: Transnational, 1999.

Hansen, Stephen A. *Thesaurus of Economic, Social, and Cultural Rights: Terminology and Potential Violations*. 2000. Available at http://shr.aaas.org/ethesaurus.html.

Hanson, Karl, and Arne Vandaele. "Working Children and International Labour Law: A Critical Analysis." *International Journal of Children's Rights* (2003), 11(1):73–146.

Haq, Mahbub ul, and Khadija Haq. *Human Development in South Asia*. Delhi: Oxford University Press, for the Mahbub ul Haq Human Development Center, 1998.

Harris, David, and John Darcy. *The European Social Charter*. 2nd ed. Ardsley, NY: Transnational, 2001.

Harvey, Pharis J. *Crucifixion at Easter: The Redemptive Death of a 12-Year Old Boy*. 1995. Available at http://www.laborrights.org.

Haspels, Nilien, and Michele Jankanish, eds. *Action Against Child Labor*. Washington, DC: Brookings Institution, 2000.

Hayek, Friedrich A. *The Mirage of Social Justice*. Chicago: University of Chicago Press, 1976.

Heady, Christopher. *What Is the Effect of Child Labour on Learning Achievement? Evidence from Ghana*. Working Paper No. 79. Florence: UNICEF Innocenti Research Centre, 2000.

Heaney, Seamus. "Weighing In." In Heaney, *The Spirit Level*. New York: Faber and Faber, 1996.

Hebinck, Paul, and Michael Bourdillon, eds. *Rural Livelihoods in Southeastern Zimbabwe*. Harare: Weaver Press, 2002.

Hecht, Mark Erik. "The Role and Involvement of the Private Sector." Theme paper for the Second World Congress Against Commercial Sexual Exploitation of Children, Yokohama, Japan, Dec. 17–20, 2001.

Heilbroner, Robert. *The Worldly Philosophers*. New York: Simon and Schuster, 1986.

Henn, Stephen. "Child Labor Unions." Markteplace Radio, Jan. 21, 2003. Available at http://www.marketplace.org/shows/2003/01/21_mpp.html.

Hensman, Rohini. *The Impact of Globalisation on Employment in India and Responses from the Formal and Informal Sectors: Changing Labor Relations in Asia (CLARA)*. Working Paper No. 15. Amsterdam: International Institute of Social History, 2001.

Heywood, Colin. *A History of Childhood*. Cambridge: Polity Press, 2001.

———."The Market for Child Labor in Nineteenth-Century France." *History* (1981), 66(1):34–49.

Hie-Joang, Che. "Children in the Examination War in South Korea: A Cultural Analysis." In Stephens, *Children and the Politics of Culture,* infra pp. 141–168.

Higgott, Richard A., Geoffrey R. D. Underhill, and Andreas Bieler. *Non-State Actors and Authority in the Global System*. London: Routledge, 2000.

Hilton, Margaret, ed. *Monitoring International Labor Standards: Quality of Information—Summary of a Workshop*. Washington, DC: National Academies Press, 2003.

Hindman, Hugh D. *Child Labor: An American History*. Armonk, NY: M. E. Sharpe, 2002.

Hobbs, Sandy, and Jim McKechnie. *Child Employment in Britain: A Social and Psychological Analysis.* Edinburgh: Stationery Office, 1997.

Hobbs, Sandy, Jim McKechnie, and Michael Lavalette, eds. *Child Labor: A World History Companion.* Santa Barbara, CA: ABC-CLIO, 1999.

Horan, Patrick M., and Peggy G. Hargis. "Children's Work and Schooling in the Late Nineteenth-Century Family Economy." *American Sociological Review* (1991), 56(5):583–596.

Horner, Leonard. *On the Employment of Children in Factories.* Shannon: Irish University Press, 1840, reprinted 1971.

Horrell, Sara, and Jane Humphries. "The Exploitation of Little Children: Child Labour and the Family Economy in the Industrial Revolution." *Explorations in Economic History* (Oct. 1995), 32(4):485–516.

Howard, Alan. "Partners in Sweat." *The Nation,* Nov. 29, 1998.

Howard-Hassmann, Rhoda. "The Second Great Transformation: Human Rights Leapfrogging in the Era of Globalization." *Human Rights Quarterly* (Feb. 2005), 27: 1–40.

Howse, Robert. "The World Trade Organization and the Protection of Workers' Rights." *Journal of Small and Emerging Business Law* (1999), 3:131–172.

Howse, Robert, and Makau Mutua. "Protecting Human Rights in a Global Economy: Challenges for the World Trade Organization." Available at http://www.ichrdd. ca/english/commdoc/publications/globalization/wtorightsglob.html.

HRI (Human Rights Internet). *The Canadian Component of the Protection Project: A Socio-Legal Analysis of International Jurisprudence on the Commercial Sexual Exploitation of Women and Children.* Ottawa, July 2000.

Hudec, Robert E. "The New WTO Dispute Settlement Procedure: An Overview of the First Three Years." *Minnesota Journal of Global Trade* (1999), 8:1–53.

———. "The Role of the GATT Secretariat in the Evolution of the WTO Dispute Settlement Procedure." In Bhagwati and Hirsch, *The Uruguay Round and Beyond* . . . , supra pp. 101–120.

———. "The World Trade Organization and the Protection of Workers' Rights." *Minnesota Journal of Global Trade* (1999), 8:1–53.

Hulme, David, and Michael Edwards. "NGOs, States, and Donors: An Overview." In Hulme and Edwards, *NGOs, States, and Donors: Too Close for Comfort?* New York: St. Martin's Press, 1997, pp. 3–22.

Human Rights First. "Protecting Worker Rights." Available at http://www. humanrightsfirst.org/workers_rights/workers_rights.htm.

Human Rights Watch. *Children of Sudan: Slaves, Street Children, and Child Soldiers.* New York, 1995. Available at http://www.hrw.org/reports/1995/sudan.htm.

———. "Does Human Rights Watch Work on Social, Cultural, and Economic Rights?" In *Some Frequently Asked Questions About Human Rights Watch.* Available at http://hrw.org/about/faq/#9.

———. *Fingers to the Bone: United States Failure to Protect Child Farmworkers.* New York, 2000.

———. *Small Change: Bonded Child Labor in India's Silk Industry.* New York, Jan. 2003. Available at http://www.hrw.org/reports/2003/india.

———. *The Small Hands of Slavery: Bonded Child Labor in India.* New York, 1996. Available at http://www.hrw.org/reports/1996/India3.htm.

———. *Unfair Advantage: Workers' Freedom of Association in the United States Under International Human Rights Standards.* New York, 2000.

ICFTU (International Confederation of Free Trade Unions). "WTO Ignoring Workers' Rights in a Race to the Bottom." Jan. 9, 2003. Available at http://www.icftu. org/displaydocument.asp?index=991218382&language=en.

Ignatieff, Michael. *Human Rights as Politics, Human Rights as Idolatry.* Tanner Lectures on Human Values. Salt Lake City: University of Utah Press, 2001.

IGTLWF (International Garment, Textile, and Leather Workers Federation). "Linking Trade and Workers Rights: Agenda for Action." Available at http://www.itglwf.org.

ILO (International Labour Organization). "About the Declaration." Available at http://www.ilo.org/dyn/declaris/declarationweb.aboutdeclarationhome?var_ language=en.

———. *Background Document Prepared for the Amsterdam Child Labour Conference.* Geneva, 1997.

———. *Baseline and Attitude Surveys on Child Labour in Tanzania.* Dar es Salaam, 2002.

———. "Child Labour: What Is to Be Done?" *Document for Discussion at the Informal Tripartite Meeting at the Ministerial Level.* Geneva, 1996.

———. *Children at Work.* Geneva, 1970.

———. *Convention* (No. 5) *Fixing the Minimum Age for Admission of Children to Industrial Employment.* Nov. 28, 1919. 38 UNTS 81. [Revised by ILO Convention No. 59 (1937) and ILO Convention No. 138 (1973), infra.]

———. *Convention* (No. 6) *Concerning Night Work of Young Persons (Industry).* Nov. 28, 1919. 38 UNTS 93. [Revised by ILO Convention No. 90 (1948), infra.]

———. *Convention* (No. 7) *Fixing the Minimum Age for Admission of Children to Employment at Sea.* July 9, 1920. 38 UNTS 109. [Revised by ILO Convention No. 58 (1936) and ILO Convention No. 138 (1973), infra.]

———. *Convention* (No. 10) *Concerning the Age for Admission of Children to Employment in Agriculture.* Nov. 16, 1921. 38 UNTS 143. [Revised by ILO Convention No. 138 (1973), infra.]

———. *Convention* (No. 29) *Concerning Forced or Compulsory Labour.* June 28, 1930. 39 UNTS 55. Reprinted in Weston and Carlson, *International Law and World Order,* infra vol. 3, III.H.2.

———. *Convention* (No. 33) *Concerning the Age for Admission of Children to Non-Industrial Employment.* Apr. 30, 1932. 39 UNTS 133. [Revised by ILO Convention No. 138 (1973), infra.]

———. *Convention* (No. 58) *Fixing the Minimum Age for the Admission of Children to Employment at Sea (Revised).* Oct. 24, 1936. 40 UNTS 205. [Revising ILO Convention No. 7 (1920), supra; revised by ILO Convention No. 138 (1973), infra.]

———. *Convention* (No. 59) *Fixing the Minimum Age for Admission of Children to Industrial Employment (Revised).* June 22, 1937. 40 UNTS 217. [Revising ILO Convention No. 5 (1919), supra; revised by ILO Convention No. 138 (1973), infra.]

———. *Convention* (No. 60) *Concerning the Age for Admission of Children to Non-Industrial Employment (Non-Industrial Employment) (Revised).* June 22, 1937. 78 UNTS 181. [Revising ILO Convention No. 33 (1932), supra; revised by ILO Convention No. 138 (1973), infra.]

———. *Convention* (No. 77) *Concerning Medical Examination for Fitness for Employment in Industry of Children and Young Persons.* Oct. 9, 1946. 78 UNTS 197.

———. *Convention* (No. 78) *Concerning Medical Examination of Children and Young Persons for Fitness for Employment in Non-Industrial Occupations.* Oct. 9, 1946. 78 UNTS 213.

————. *Convention* (No. 79) *Concerning the Restriction of Night Work of Children and Young Persons in Non-Industrial Occupations.* Oct. 9, 1946. 78 UNTS 227.

————. *Convention* (No. 87) *Concerning Freedom of Association and Protection of the Right to Organize.* July 9, 1948. 68 UNTS 17. Reprinted in Weston and Carlson, *International Law and World Order,* infra vol. 3, III.O.1.

————. *Convention* (No. 90) *Concerning the Night Work of Young Persons Employed in Industry (Revised).* July 10, 1948. 91 UNTS 3.

————. *Convention* (No. 98) *Concerning the Application of the Principles of the Right to Organize and to Bargain Collectively.* July 1, 1949. 96 UNTS 257. Reprinted in Weston and Carlson, *International Law and World Order,* infra vol. 3, III.O.2.

————. *Convention* (No. 100) *Concerning Equal Remuneration for Men and Women Workers for Work of Equal Value.* June 29, 1951. 165 UNTS 303. Reprinted in Weston and Carlson, *International Law and World Order,* infra vol. 3, III.O.3.

————. *Convention* (No. 105) *Concerning the Abolition of Forced Labour.* June 25, 1957. 320 UNTS 291. Reprinted in Weston and Carlson, *International Law and World Order,* infra vol. 3, III.H.4.

————. *Convention* (No. 111) *Concerning Discrimination in Respect of Employment and Occupation.* June 25, 1958. 362 UNTS 31. Reprinted in Weston and Carlson, *International Law and World Order,* infra vol. 3, III.O.4.

————. *Convention* (No. 112) *Concerning Minimum Age for Admission to Employment as Fishermen.* June 19, 1959. 413 UNTS 147. [Revised by ILO Convention No. 138 (1973), infra.]

————. *Convention* (No. 123) *Concerning the Minimum Age for Admission to Employment Underground in Mines.* June 22, 1965. 610 UNTS 79. [Revised by ILO Convention No. 139 (1973), infra.]

————. *Convention* (No. 138) *Concerning Minimum Age for Admission to Employment.* June 26, 1973. 1015 UNTS 297. [Revising ILO Conventions nos. 5, 7, 10, 15, 33, 58, 59, 60, 112, and 123, supra.] Reprinted in Weston and Carlson, *International Law and World Order,* infra vol. 3, III.O.5.

————. *Convention* (No. 139) *Concerning Prevention and Control of Occupational Hazards Caused by Carcinogenic Substances and Agents.* June 24, 1974. 1010 UNTS 5. [Revising ILO Convention No. 123 (1965), supra.]

————. *Convention* (No. 169) *Concerning Indigenous and Tribal Peoples in Independent Countries.* June 27, 1989. 2 ILO Conventions & Recommendations 1919–66, at 1436, 72 ILO Off. Bull. 59 (1989). Reprinted in Weston and Carlson, *International Law and World Order,* infra vol. 3, III.F.2.

————. *Convention* (No. 182) *Concerning the Prohibition and Immediate Elimination of the Worst Forms of Child Labour.* June 17, 1999. Reprinted in 38 ILM 1207 (1999) and Weston and Carlson, *International Law and World Order,* infra vol. 3, III.D.4.

————. *Current International Recommendations on Labour Statistics.* Geneva, 2000.

————. *Declaration Concerning the Aims and Purposes of the International Labour Organization.* 26th Sess., 1944.

————. *Declaration on Fundamental Principles and Rights at Work.* June, 18, 1998. Reprinted in Weston and Carlson, *International Law and World Order,* infra vol. 3, III.O.7.

————. *Economically Active Population, 1950–2010.* STAT working paper. Geneva: ILO Bureau of Statistics, 1997.

————. *Every Child Counts: New Global Estimates of Child Labour.* Geneva, 2001. Available at http://www.ilo.org/public/english/standards/ipec/simpoc/others/globalest.pdf.

————. *Final Report of the International Conference on Child Labour.* Oslo, 1997. Available at http://www.ilo.org/public/english/comp/child/conf/oslo/report.htm.

————. *Follow-Up Action on the Declaration on Fundamental Principles and Rights at Work and Its Follow-Up.* GB 273/3. Governing Body, 273rd Sess., Nov. 1998.

————. *A Future Without Child Labour: Global Report Under the Follow-Up to the ILO Declaration on Fundamental Principles and Rights at Work.* Report of the director-general to the International Labour Conference. 90th Sess., Report I-B, 2002. Available at http://echo.ilo.org/pls/declaris/declarationweb.globalreportdetails?var_language=en&var_publicationsid=37&var_reporttype=report#.

————. "ILO Welcomes New Foundation to Eliminate Abusive Child and Forced Labour Practices in Cocoa Farming." Press release, July 1, 2002. Available at http://www.ilo.org/public/english/bureau/inf/pr/2002/34.htm.

————. *International Labour Standards and Human Rights: International Labour Standards.* Available at http://www.ilo.org/public/english/standards/norm/index.htm.

————. *Recommendation (No. 41) Concerning the Age for Admission of Children to Non-Industrial Employment.* 1932. Available at http://www.ilo.org/ilolex/english/recdisp1.htm.

————. *Recommendation (No. 52) Concerning the Minimum Age for Admission of Children to Industrial Employment in Family Undertakings.* 1937. Available at http://www.ilo.org/ilolex/english/recdisp1.htm.

————. *Recommendation (No. 96) Concerning the Minimum Age of Admission to Work Underground in Coal Mines.* 1953. Available at http://www.ilo.org/ilolex/english/recdisp1.htm.

————. *Recommendation (No. 124) Concerning the Minimum Age for Admission to Employment Underground in Mines.* 1965. Available at http://www.ilo.org/ilolex/english/recdisp1.htm.

————. *Recommendation (No. 146) Concerning Minimum Age for Admission to Employment.* 1973. Available at http://www.ilo.org/ilolex/english/recdisp1.htm.

————. *Recommendation (No. 190) Concerning the Prohibition and Immediate Action for the Elimination of the Worst Forms of Child Labour.* June 17, 1999. Available at http://www.ilo.org/ilolex/english/recdisp1.htm.

————. *Report of the Director-General: A Future Without Child Labour—Global Report Under the Follow-Up to the ILO Declaration on Fundamental Principles and Rights at Work.* International Labour Conference, 90th Sess., Report I (B). Geneva: International Labour Office, 2002.

————. *Report IV: General Report—Sixteenth International Conference of Labour Statisticians.* ICLS/16/1998/IV (1998).

————. *Report IV (2A): Child Labour—Reply Received from the United States.* 87th Sess., 1999.

————. *Report VI (1): Child Labour—Targeting the Intolerable, Sixth Item on the Agenda.* 86th Sess., 1998.

————. *Report VI (2).* 86th Sess., 1998. Available at http://www.ilo.org/public/english/standards/ipec/publ/law/ilc/ilc86/repvi/index.htm#summary.

————. *Report of the Committee on Child Labour, International Labour Conference.* 86th Sess., June 1998. Available at http://www.ilo.org/public/english/standards/ipec/publ/law/ilc/ilc86/com_chil/index.htm.

————. *Report of the Committee on Child Labour, International Labour Conference.* 87th Sess., June 1999. Available at http://www.ilo.org/public/english/standards/ipec/publ/law/ilc/ilc87/com_chil/index.htm.

————. *Report of the Second Session of the Committee on the Rights of the Child.* Oct. 19, 1992. Sessional/annual report of the committee. CRC/C/10.

————. *Stopping Forced Labour.* Geneva, 2001.

ILO and United Republic of Tanzania. *Project Document: Supporting the Time Bound Programme on the Worst Forms of Child Labour in Tanzania.* Dar es Salaam, Oct. 2001.

IMF (International Monetary Fund). *Articles of Agreement.* July 22, 1944. 2 UNTS 39. Reprinted in Weston and Carlson, *International Law and World Order,* infra vol. 4, IV.A.3.

India Committee of the Netherlands. *The Dark Side of Football: Child and Adult Labor in India's Football Industry and the Role of FIFA.* June 2000. Available at http://www.indianet.nl/iv.html.

Indonesia: Certain Measures Affecting the Automobile Industry. Panel report. WT/DS54/R (Feb. 7, 1998).

International Human Rights Internship Program and Asian Forum for Human Rights and Development. *Circle of Rights: Economic, Social, and Cultural Activism—A Training Resource.* 2000.

International Labor Rights Fund. *RUGMARK After One Year.* Report of the International Labor Rights Fund on behalf of the US Child Labor Coalition. Oct. 1996. Available at http://www.laborrights.org.

International Labour Office (Bureau of Workers' Activities). "International Labor Law." In *Globalization and Workers Rights.* Available at http://www.itcilo.it/english/actrav/telearn/global/ilo/law/lablaw.htm#ilo_instruments.

Invernezzi, Antonella, and Brian Milne. "Are Children Entitled to Contribute to International Policy Making? A Critical View of Children's Participation in the International Campaign for the Elimination of Child Labor." *International Journal of Children's Rights* (2002), 10:403–431.

IPEC (International Program on the Elimination of Child Labour). "All About IPEC." Available at http://www.ilo.org.public/english/standards/ipec/about/countries/t_country.htm.

————. *Annotated Bibliography on Child Labour.* Geneva: International Labour Office, Dec. 2002.

————. "Broad-Based Multi-Sectoral Action Against Child Labour." In *IPEC Implementation Report 1998–99: IPEC Action Against Child Labour—Achievements, Lessons Learned, and Indications for the Future.* Geneva: ILO, Oct. 1999. Available at http://www.ilo.org/public/english/standards/ipec/publ/imprep99/report4.htm.

————. *Child Labour: A Textbook for University Students.* Geneva: ILO, 2004.

————. "Child Labour in Commercial Agriculture in Africa." In *Report of the Technical Workshop on Child Labour in Commercial Agriculture in Africa, Dar es Salaam, the Republic of Tanzania, Aug. 27–30, 1996.* Geneva: ILO, 1997.

————. *Eliminating the Worst Forms of Child Labour: An Integrated and Time-Bound Approach—A Guide for Governments, Employers, Workers, and Other Stakeholders.* Geneva: ILO, April 2001. Available at http://www.ilo.org/public/english/standards/ipec/timebound/manual.pdf.

————. *Investing in Every Child: An Economic Study of the Costs and Benefits of Eliminating Child Labour.* Geneva: ILO, 2004. Available at http://www.ilo.org/public/english/standards/ipec/index.htm.

————. *IPEC Action Against Child Labour: Achievements, Lessons Learned, and Indications for the Future, 1998–1999.* Geneva: ILO, 1999. Available at http://www.ilo.org/public.english/standards/ipec/publ/imprep99/report.pdf.

————. *IPEC Action Against Child Labour: Implementation Report 2002–03.* Geneva: ILO, 2003. Available at http://www.ilo.org/public/english/standards/ipec/index.htm.

————. *IPEC Action Against Child Labour, 2002–2003: Progress and Future Priorities.* Geneva: ILO, Jan. 2004. Available at http://www.ilo.org/public/english/standards/ipec/publ/download/implementation_2003_en.pdf.

————. "Nepal: Situation of Child Ragpickers: A Rapid Assessment." In *Investigating the Worst Forms of Child Labour.* No. 4. Geneva: ILO, Nov. 2001.

————. *TBP Map Guide Book II: Time-Bound Programmes for the Elimination of the Worst Forms of Child Labour—An Introduction.* Available at http://www.ilo.org/public/english/standards/ipec/themes/timebound/downloads/gudbk2en.pdf.

————. *Unbearable to the Human Heart: Child Trafficking and Action to Eliminate It.* Geneva: International Labour Office, 2002. Available at http://www.ilo.org/public/english/standards/ipec/publ/childtraf/unbearable.pdf.

————. *Working Paper 2000: Social Labeling Against Child Labour—Brazilian Experiences.* Universidade de São Paulo, Fundação Instituto de Administração, Centro de Estudos em Administração do Terceiro Setor (CEATS-USP). Available at http://www.ilo.org/public/english/standards/ipec/publ/policy/papers/brasil/report.pdf.

IPEC and Marcha Global. *La Marcha Global.* Santiago, 1998 (on file with David Post).

ISCA (International Save the Children Alliance). *Child-Centered Policies and Programmes for Working Children in South and Central Asia.* Katmandu, Dec. 2000.

————. *Child-Centered Policies and Programmes for Working Children in Southeast Asia, East Asia, and the Pacific Region.* Bangkok, Sept. 20–23, 1999.

————. *Child Labor in the Cocoa Industry.* June 2003. Available at http://www.laborrights.org/projects/childlab/cocoa.htm.

————. *Save the Children's Position on Children and Work.* London, Jan. 2003.

IWGCL (International Working Group on Child Labour). *Have We Asked the Children?* Discussion paper. Bangalore, 1997.

Jacobs, Antoine. "Child Labour." In Blanpain, *Multinational Enterprises . . . ,* supra pp. 199–205.

Jain, Mahaveer. *Child Labor in India: A Select Bibliography.* New Delhi: National Labor Institute, 1994.

Janis, Mark W. *An Introduction to International Law.* 4th ed. New York: Aspen, 2003.

Japan: Taxes on Alcoholic Beverages. Panel report of the WTO, WT/DS8/R; report of the Appellate Body, WT/DS8/Appellate Body/R (Oct. 4, 1996).

Jay, Bruce. "ILO Resolution on Burma Could Set Precedent for Further Sanctions." 2000. Available at http://www.americasnet.net/commentators/bruce_jay/jay_15.pdf.

Jennings, Marianne M., and Jon Entine. "Business with a Soul: A Reexamination of What Counts in Business Ethics." *Hamline Journal of Public Law and Policy* (1998), 20(1):1–88.

Johnson, Victoria, Edda Ivan-Smith, Gill Gordon, Pat Pridmore, and Patta Scott, eds. *Stepping Forward: Children and Young People's Participation in the Development Process.* London: Intermediate Technology, 1998.

Karunan, Victor P. "Children: The Forgotten Victims—The Impact of the Asian Economic Crisis on Working Children in Southeast Asia." Paper presented at the International Conference on Child Labour in the Context of Globalization: Outline of Problem and Action Points, German NGO-Forum on Child Labour, Hattingen, Sept. 26–28, 2003 (on file with Victor P. Karunan).

———. "Children and Work in Southeast and East Asia: Issues, Trends, and Challenges—The Need for a Paradigm Shift." Paper presented at the International Save the Children Alliance workshop "Child-Centered Policies and Programmes for Working Children in Southeast Asia, East Asia, and the Pacific Region," Bangkok, Sept. 1999 (on file with Victor P. Karunan).

———. "The Impact of Macro-Economic Policies and the Corporate Sector on Working Children in Asia: Towards a Child-Centered Approach and Strategy." Paper presented at the International Save the Children Alliance regional workshop "Child-Centered Policies and Programmes for Working Children in South and Central Asia," Katmandu, 1999 (on file with Victor P. Karunan).

———. "Participatory Action Research on Children and Work in Southeast Asia: Conceptual and Methodological Issues and Challenges." Paper presented at the IREWOC and University of Amsterdam Child Labor Workshop, Nov. 15–17, 1999 (on file with Victor P. Karunan).

———. "Save the Children's Approach and Strategy on Child Labor." Paper presented at the ILO/Japan Asia Regional High-Level Meeting on Child Labor, Jakarta, Mar. 8–10, 2000 (on file with Victor P. Karunan).

———. "The Social Impact of the Macro-Economic Crisis on Child Labor." *Child Workers in Asia* (Bangkok) (1999), 14(3) and 15(1):36–39.

Keck, Margaret, and Kathryn Sikkink. *Activists Beyond Borders: Advocacy Networks in International Politics.* Ithaca: Cornell University Press, 1998.

Keeble, Alexandra, ed. *In the Spirit of Wandering Teachers: The Cuban Literacy Campaign, 1961.* Melbourne: Ocean Press, 2001.

Keeling, Frederic. *Child Labor in the United Kingdom.* London: P. S. King and Son, 1914.

Keil, Thomas J., and Wayne M. Usui. "The Family Wage System in Pennsylvania's Anthracite Region: 1850–1900." *Social Forces* (1988), 67(1):185–207.

Keller, Morton. *Affairs of State: Public Life in Late Nineteenth-Century America.* Cambridge: Harvard University Press, 1977.

Kelly, John. "For Some, an Uncomfortable Fit." *Washington Post,* May 14, 2002.

Kelly, Mark, and Heilena Melkas. *Child Labour and Education: Income Substitution Schemes as a Mechanism to Reduce Child Labour and Increase Schooling.* Draft report. Florence: UNICEF International Child Development Centre, 1995.

Kennedy, David. *The Dark Sides of Virtue: Reassessing International Humanitarianism.* Princeton: Princeton University Press, 2004.

———. *Freedom from Fear: The American People in Depression and War, 1929–1945.* New York: Oxford University Press, 1999.

———. "The International Human Rights Movement: Part of the Problem?" *Harvard Human Rights Journal* (2002), 15:102–125.

Kessler-Harris, Alice. *In Pursuit of Equity: Women, Men, and the Quest for Economic Citizenship in Twentieth-Century America.* New York: Oxford University Press, 2001.

———. *Out to Work: A History of Wage-Earning Women in the United States.* New York: Oxford University Press, 1982.

Kielburger, Craig. *Free the Children.* New York: HarperPerennial, 1998.

———. *Free the Children: A Young Man Fights Against Child Labor and Proves That Children Can Change.* New York: HarperCollins, 2000.

King, Martin Luther. "I've Been to the Mountaintop." In Lauter, *The Heath Anthology of American Literature,* infra pp. 2487–2494.

Kirby, Peter. *Child Labour in Britain, 1750–1870.* Basingstoke: Palgrave Macmillan, 2003.

Koh, Harold Hongju. "Why Do Nations Obey International Law?" *Yale Law Journal* (1997), 106:2599–2659.

Korey, William. *NGOs and the Universal Declaration of Human Rights.* New York: St. Martin's Press, 1998.

Korgaokor, Chandra, and Geir Myrstad. "Child Labour in the Diamond and Gemstone Industry in India." In *Protecting Children in the World of Work,* No. 108. Geneva: ILO, Labour Education, 1997.

Krasner, Stephen. *Sovereignty: Organized Hypocrisy.* Princeton: Princeton University Press, 1999.

Krueger, Anne O. "An Agenda for the WTO." In Krueger, ed., *The WTO as an International Organization.* Chicago: University of Chicago Press, 1998, pp. 401–410.

Krugman, Paul R., and Maurice Obstfeld. *International Economics: Theory and Policy.* 6th ed. Reading: Addison-Wesley, 2002.

Kumar, Dharma. "What Can We Do?" *Seminar* (New Delhi) (Oct. 1988), 350:34–35.

Kundapur Declaration ("Our Story, Our Dreams: Micro and Macro Influences on Child Labour"). June 12, 1997. Available at http://www.workingchild.org/htm/dreams.htm.

Kuttner, Robert. "The Poverty of Economics." *Atlantic Monthly* (Feb. 1985).

Kuznesof, Elizabeth Anne. "The Puzzling Contradictions of Child Labour, Unemployment, and Education in Brazil." *Journal of Family History* (1998), 23(3): 225–239.

Kydd, Samuel H. G. [Alfred Kydd, pseud.]. *The History of the Factory Movement.* New York: Augustus M. Kelley, 1857, reprinted 1966.

"Labor Summary." Global Trade Negotiations home page, Center for International Development, Harvard University. Available at http://www.cid.harvard.edu/cidtrade/issues/labor.html.

Landrigan, Philip J. "Child Labor: A Re-emergent Threat." *American Journal of Industrial Medicine* (1993), 24(3):267–268.

Landrigan, P. J., S. H. Pollack, M. A. Belville, and J. G. Godbold. "Child Labor in the United States: Historical Background and Current Crisis." *Mount Sinai Journal of Medicine* (1992), 59(6):498–503.

Landy, E. A. *The Effectiveness of International Supervision: Thirty Years of ILO Experience.* London: Stevens and Sons, 1966.

Lane, Robert E. *The Market Experience.* Cambridge: Cambridge University Press, 1991.

Lao PDR Ministry of Labour and Social Welfare, Department of Social Welfare. *Street Children and Child Beggars: Lao PDR.* Vientiane: Ministry of Labour and Social Welfare and UNICEF, 2001.

Lauglo, Jon, and Kevin Lillis, eds. *Vocationalizing Education: An International Perspective.* Oxford: Pergamon Press, 1988.

Lauter, Paul, ed. *The Heath Anthology of American Literature.* 2nd ed. Lexington: D. C. Heath, 1994.

Lavalette, Michael. *Child Employment in the Capitalist Labour Market.* Aldershot: Avebury, 1994.

———, ed. *A Thing of the Past? Child Labor in Britain in the Nineteenth and Twentieth Centuries.* Liverpool: Liverpool University Press, 1999.

Leary, Virginia A. "Lessons from the Experience of the International Labour Organization." In Alston, *The United Nations and Human Rights . . . ,* supra pp. 580–619.

———. "The Paradox of Workers' Rights as Human Rights." In Compa and Diamond, eds., *Human Rights, Labor Rights, and International Trade,* supra pp. 22–47.

———. "The Right to Health in International Human Rights Law." *Health and Human Rights* (1994), 1(1):24–56.

———. "Workers' Rights and International Trade: The Social Clause (GATT, ILO, NAFTA, U.S. Laws)." *Fair Trade and Harmonization: Legal Analysis* (1996), 2:177–230.

———. "The WTO and the Social Clause: Post-Singapore." *European Journal of International Law* (1997), 8(1):118–122.

Levich, Gerald. "Carpets and Caveats." *Globe and Mail* (Toronto), Sept. 5, 1996.

Liang, Xiaoyan. *Bangladesh Female Secondary School Assistance Project.* Draft report. Washington, DC: World Bank, Human Development Department, 1996.

Lichtenstein, Nelson. "The Rights Revolution." *New Labor Forum* (2003), 12:61–73.

Liebel, Manfred. *A Will of Their Own: Cross-Cultural Perspectives on Working Children.* London: Zed Books, 2004.

Lieten, G. K. "Child Labor and Poverty: The Poverty of Analysis." *Indian Journal of Labor Economics* (2002), 5(45):451–465.

Lieten, Kristoffel. "Child Labor: Questions of Magnitude." In Lieten and White, *Child Labour . . .* , infra pp. 49–65.

Lieten, Kristoffel, and Ben White. "Children, Work, and Education: Perspectives on Policy." In Lieten and White, eds., *Child Labour: Policy Options.* Amsterdam: Aksant, 2001, pp. 1–11.

Lim, Hoe. "The Social Clause: Issues and Challenges." In International Labour Office (Bureau for Workers' Activities), *Globalization and Workers' Rights.* Available at http://www.itcilo.it/english/actrav/telearn/global/ilo/guide/hoelim.htm.

Lim, Lin Leam. "Child Prostitution." In Lim, ed., *The Sex Sector: The Economic and Social Bases of Prostitution in Southeast Asia.* Geneva: ILO, 1998, pp. 170–205.

Limburg Principles on the Implementation of the International Covenant on Economic, Social, and Cultural Rights. UN Doc. E/CN.4/1987/17 (Annex).

Lindsay, Samuel McCune. *The Work, Policy, and Plans of the National Child Labor Committee.* 1907.

Lippman, Matthew. "Multinational Corporations and Human Rights." In Shepherd and Nanda, *Human Rights and Third World Development,* infra pp. 250–272.

Lloyd, Cynthia B., Barbara S. Mensch, and Wesley H. Clark. "The Effects of Primary School Quality on School Dropout Among Kenyan Girls and Boys." *Comparative Education Review* (2000), 44:113–147.

Lloyd, Cynthia B., Sahar El Tawila, Wesley Clark, and Barbara Mensch. "The Impact of Educational Quality on School Exit in Egypt." *Comparative Education Review* (2003), 47:444–467.

Lopez-Hurtado, Carlos. "Social Labeling and WTO Law." *Journal of International Economic Law* (2002), 5:719–746.

Lotz, Linda. "'All Religions Believe in Justice': Reflections on Faith Community Support for Worker Organizing." In Gross, *Workers' Rights as Human Rights,* supra pp. 183–202.

Lucy, William. "Controversy over Children's Rights." In Freestone, *Children and the Law,* supra pp. 213–242.

Lytle, Mark H. "NGOs and the New Transnational Politics." *Diplomatic History* (2001), 25:121–128.

Maastricht Guidelines on Violations of Economic, Social, and Cultural Rights. Reprinted in *Human Rights Quarterly* (1998), 20:691–704.

Macaulay, Thomas Babbington. *The History of England from the Accession of James II.* Vol. 1. London: J. M. Dent, 1848, reprinted 1906.

Macklem, Patrick. "Labor Law Beyond Borders." *Journal of International Economic Law* (2002), 5:605–645.

MacPherson, C. B. *Democratic Theory.* New York: Oxford University Press, 1973.

Malcolm X. "The Ballot or the Bullet." In Lauter, *The Heath Anthology of American Literature,* supra pp. 2496–2509.

Mangoma, Jaquie, and Michael Bourdillon. "The Work of Children in Impoverished Families." In Hebinck and Bourdillon, *Rural Livelihoods in Southeastern Zimbabwe,* supra pp. 13–35.

Manning, Wendy D. "Parenting Employed Teenagers." *Youth and Society* (1990), 22(2):184–220.

Mannion, Jenne. "Lobby Groups Open Ethical Attacks." *Sunday Business,* Dec. 9, 2001.

Mante, James, and Loree Mante. *Overall Assessment: National Program Against Child Labor.* Philippines Department of Labor and Employment, 2000.

Mapedzahama, Virginia, and Michael Bourdillon. "Working Street Children in Harare." In Bourdillon, *Earning a Life . . . ,* supra pp. 25–44.

Maquila Solidarity Network. "The Changing Terrain in the Code Debate." Codes Memo No. 9. Nov. 2001. Available at http://www.maquilasolidarity.org/resources/codes/memo9.htm.

Marcus, Rachel, and Caroline Harper. *Small Hands: Children in the Working World.* Working Paper No. 16. London: Save the Children–UK, 1996.

Markham, Edwin. "The Hoe Man in the Making." *Cosmopolitan Magazine* (1906), 41:482–487.

Marks, Stephen P. "Emerging Human Rights: A New Generation for the 1980s?" *Rutgers Law Review* (1981), 33:435–452.

———. "The Human Right to Development: Between Rhetoric and Reality." *Harvard Human Rights Journal* (2004), 17:137–168.

———. "The United Nations and Human Rights: The Promise of Multilateral Diplomacy and Action." In Weston and Marks, *The Future of International Human Rights,* infra pp. 291–350.

Marshall, David. "The Construction of Children as an Object of International Relations: The Declaration of Children's Rights and the Child Welfare Committee of the League of Nations, 1900–1924." *International Journal of Children's Rights* (1999), 7:103–147.

Mascher, Franz, and Herbert Petzold, eds. *Protecting Human Rights: The European Dimension.* Cologne: Carl Heymanns Verlag, 1988.

Maskus, Keith. *Should Core Labor Standards Be Imposed Through Trade Policy?* Policy Research Working Paper No. 1817. Washington, DC: World Bank, 1997.

Mayall, Berry, ed. *Children's Childhoods: Observed and Experienced.* London: Farmer Press, 1994.

Mazur, Jay. "Labor's New Internationalism." *Journal of Foreign Affairs* (Jan.–Feb. 2000). Available at http://www.globalpolicy.org/socecon/global/labor.htm.

McDougal, Myres S. "Perspectives for an International Law of Human Dignity." In McDougal et al., *Studies in World Public Order,* infra pp. 987–1019.

McDougal, Myres S., Harold D. Lasswell, and Lung-Chu Chen. *Human Rights and World Public Order: The Basic Policies of an International Law of Human Dignity.* New Haven: Yale University Press, 1980.

McDougal, Myres S., et al. *Studies in World Public Order.* New Haven: Yale University Press, 1960.

McElrath, Roger, ed. *Monitoring International Labor Standards: Summary of Domestic Forums.* Washington, DC: National Academies Press, 2003.

McKechnie, Jim, and Sandy Hobbs. "Child Labour: The View from the North." *Childhood* (1999), 6(1):89–100.

McKechnie, Jim, Niamh Stack, and Sandy Hobbs. "Work by Secondary School Students in Scotland." *International Journal of Education Policy, Research, and Practice* (2001), 2(3):287–305.

McMillan, Margaret. "Child Labour." In Oliver, *Dangerous Trades,* infra pp. 90–97.

Mehta, Pradeep. "Child Labour: A Different Perspective." *Development* (June 2000).

Meron, Theodor, ed. *Human Rights in Law: Legal and Policy Issues.* Oxford: Clarendon Press, 1984.

Merry, Sally Engle. "Changing Rights, Changing Culture." In Cowan, Dembour, and Wilson, *Culture and Rights . . . ,* supra pp. 31–55.

Meyer, John W. "The Effects of Education as an Institution." *American Journal of Sociology* (1977), 83:55–77.

Mian, Khawlah. "Early Marriage Is 'Child Labor in Its Worst Form.'" *On the Record for Children* (June 5, 2002), 3(16). Available at http://www.ngosatunicef.org/old_site/otr/v3/16.html.

Miljeteig, Per. *Creating Partnerships with Working Children and Youth.* Social Protection Discussion Paper Series. Washington, DC: World Bank, Social Protection Unit, 2000.

———. "Establishing Partnerships with Working Children and Youth." In Lieten and White, *Child Labour . . . ,* supra pp. 117–129.

Minow, Martha. *Between Vengeance and Forgiveness: Facing History After Genocide and Mass Violence.* Boston: Beacon Press, 1999.

Mishra, H. K. "Multi-Dimensional Approach to Child Labor in India." In Rao, *Exploited Children . . . ,* infra pp. 28–45.

Mishra, Lakshmidhar. *Child Labor in India.* New Delhi: Oxford University Press, 2001.

Mizen, Phillip, Angela Bolton, and Christopher Pole. "School Age Workers: The Paid Employment of Children in Britain." *Work, Employment, and Society* (1999), 13(3):423–438.

Mizen, Phillip, Christopher Pole, and Angela Bolton, eds. *Hidden Hands: International Perspectives on Children's Work and Labour.* London: Routledge Farmer, 2001.

Mock, William B. T. "Human Rights, Corporate Responsibility, and Economic Sanctions: Corporate Transparency and Human Rights." *Tulsa Journal of Comparative and International Law* (2000), 8:15–26.

Mokyr, Joel. *The British Industrial Revolution: An Economic Perspective.* Boulder: Westview, 1999.

Monge, Raúl, and María Luisa Vivas. "Pobreza, Violencia y Caos Legislativo, Verdugos de Infancia Mexicana." *Proceso* (1999), 1204:15–20.

Monshipouri, Mahmood, Claude E. Welch Jr., and Evan T. Kennedy. "Multinational Corporations and the Ethics of Global Responsibility: Problems and Possibilities." *Human Rights Quarterly* (2003) 25:965–989.

Montgomery, Heather. "Imposing Rights? A Case Study of Child Prostitution in Thailand." In Cowan, Dembour, and Wilson, *Culture and Rights . . . ,* supra pp. 80–101.

———. *Modern Babylon? Prostituting Children in Thailand.* Oxford: Berghahn Books, 2001.

Montgomery, Patrick. "The Anti-Slavery Society 1973." *Contemporary Review* (Aug. 1973), 223:1291.

Moravcsik, Andrew. "The Origins of Human Rights Regimes." *International Organization* (2000), 54:217–252.

———. "Taking Preferences Seriously: A Liberal Theory of International Relations." *International Organization* (1997), 51:513–553.

Morice, Alain. "The Exploitation of Children in the 'Informal Sector': Proposals for Research." In Rodgers and Standing, *Child Work . . .* , infra pp. 131–158.

Morrow, Virginia. "Responsible Children? Aspects of Children's Work and Employment Outside School in Contemporary U.K." In Mayall, *Children's Childhoods . . .* , supra pp. 128–143.

Morrow, Virginia, and Martin Richards. "The Ethics of Social Research with Children: An Overview." *Children and Society* (1996), 10:90–105.

Mortimer, Jeylan T., and Michael D. Finch. "Work, Family, and Adolescent Development." In Mortimer and Finch, eds., *Adolescents, Work, and the Family: An Intergenerational Developmental Analysis.* London: Sage, 1996, pp. 1–24.

Muncy, Robyn. *Creating a Female Dominion of Reform, 1890–1935.* New York: Oxford, 1991.

Murshed, Madiha. "Unraveling Child Labor and Labor Legislation." *Journal of International Affairs* (Fall 2001), 55(1):169–188.

Mutisi, Martha, and Michael Bourdillon. "Vendors at a Rural Growth Point." In Bourdillon, *Earning a Life . . .* , supra pp. 75–94.

MV Foundation. "The Non-Negotiables." In *M. Venkatarangaiya Foundation: Making Education a Reality for Every Child.* Bangalore: MV Foundation. Available at http://www.mvfindia.org.aboutmvf.htm.

Myers, William E. "Can Children's Education and Work Be Reconciled?" *International Journal of Education Policy, Research, and Practice* (2001), 2(3):307–330.

———, ed. *Protecting Working Children.* London: Zed Books, 1991.

———. "The Right Rights? Child Labour in a Globalizing World." *Annals of the American Academy of Political and Social Sciences* (May 2001), 575:38–55.

———. "Valuing Diverse Approaches to Child Labour." In Lieten and White, *Child Labour . . .* , supra pp. 27–48.

Myers, William E., and Jo Boyden. *Child Labor: Promoting the Best Interests of Working Children.* London: Save the Children–UK, 1998.

Myrdal, Gunnar. *An American Dilemma: The Negro Problem and Modern Democracy.* New York: Harper and Brothers, 1944.

Myrstad, Geir. "From Projects to Social Change." In Grimsrud, *The Next Steps . . .* , supra pp. 85–93.

Naiman, Robert. "'Rightsizing' the IMF, the World Bank and the WTO." *Development* (June 2000).

Nangia, Parveen. *Child Labour: Cause-Effect Syndrome.* New Delhi: Janak, 1996.

Nardinelli, Clark. *Child Labor and the Industrial Revolution.* Bloomington: Indiana University Press, 1990.

Nasaw, David. *Children of the City at Work and at Play.* New York: Oxford University Press, 1996.

National Resource Centre on Child Labor. *Child Labor in India: An Overview.* Delhi, 2001.

Newman, Frank C., and David S. Weissbrodt. *International Human Rights: Law, Policy, and Process.* Cincinnati: Anderson, 1990.

NIBUD. *Bijbaantjes van Scholieren* [Part-Time Employment of School Children]. Utrecht: Nationaal Institutut voor Budgetvoorlichting, 2000.

Nichols, Philip M. "GATT Doctrine." *Virginia Journal of International Law* (1996), 36:379–466.

Nieuwenhuys, Olga. "The Paradox of Anthropology and Child Labour." *Annual Review of Anthropology* (1966), 25:237–251.
"Nike Releases First Corporate Responsibility Report." Nike press release. Oct. 9, 2001. Available at http://www.nike.com/nikebiz/news/pressrelease.jhtml?year=2001&month=10&letter=e.
Nilsen, Ann C. E. "Negotiating Children's Work: A Comparative Study of Children's Work in Norway and Zimbabwe." Unpublished postgraduate thesis, University of Bergen, Department of Sociology, 2002.
Noble, Charles. *Liberalism at Work: The Rise and Fall of OSHA.* Philadelphia: Temple University Press, 1986.
Nussbaum, Martha C. "Capabilities and Human Rights." *Fordham Law Review* (1997), 66:273–300.
———. "Capabilities, Human Rights, and the Universal Declaration." In Weston and Marks, *The Future of International Human Rights,* infra pp. 25–99.
Nussbaum, Martha, and Amartya Sen, eds. *The Quality of Life.* Oxford: Clarendon Press, 1993.
O'Connell, Helen. *Women and the Family.* London: Zed Books, 1994.
Odell, John. "Problems in Negotiating Consensus in the World Trade Organization." Paper presented at a conference at Beijing University, July 10, 2001, and at the annual convention of the American Political Science Association, San Francisco, Aug. 30, 2001.
Oeter, Stefan. "International Human Rights Law and National Sovereignty in Federal Systems: The German Experience." *Wayne Law Review* (2001), 47:871–889.
Office of the UN High Commissioner for Human Rights. *Business and Human Rights: A Progress Report.* Available at http://www.unhchr.ch/business.htm.
———. *Fact Sheet No. 16 (Rev. 1): The Committee on Economic, Social, and Cultural Rights.* Available at http://www.unhchr.ch/html/menu6/2/fs16.htm.
OIT Brasil (Organização Internacional do Trabalho). *Boas Práticas de Combate ao Trabalho Infantil: Os 10 Anos do IPEC no Brasil.* Brasília, 2003. Available at http://www.ilo.org/public/portugue/region/ampro/brasilia/#.
———. *IPEC—Relatório de Atividades no Brasil (Biênio 2/93).* Brasília, 1995.
———. *Pela Abolição do Trabalho Infantil: A Política da OIT e Suas Implicações para as Atividades de Cooperação Técnica.* Brasília, 1993.
Oliveira, Alvaro, João Ripper, Gianne Carvalho, Giuliano Cedroni, and Simone Bieher Mateos. "Nossas Crianças: A Sucata do Progresso." *Revista Atenção* (Dec. 1995–Jan. 1996), 1(2):8–16.
Oliver, Thomas, ed. *Dangerous Trades.* London: John Murray, 1902.
Oloka, Beatrice O. "Children's Work in Urban Nigeria: A Case Study of Young Lagos Street Traders." In Myers, *Protecting Working Children,* supra pp. 11–23.
Ombudsman of British Columbia. "NGOs Support Children's Rights." In *Annual Report 1997.* Available at http://www.ombud.gov.bc.ca.
O'Neill, Onora. "Children's Rights and Children's Lives." In Alston, Parker, and Seymour, *Children, Rights, and the Law,* supra pp. 24–42.
Oppenheim, Carey, and Lisa Harker. *Poverty: The Facts.* 3rd ed., rev. and updated. London: Child Poverty Action Group, 1996.
Orford, Anne. "Contesting Globalization: A Feminist Perspective on the Future of Human Rights." In Weston and Marks, *The Future of International Human Rights,* infra pp. 157–185.
Panter-Brick, Catherine, et al. "Growth Status of Homeless Nepali Boys: Do They Differ from Rural and Urban Controls?" *Social Science and Medicine* (1996), 43(4):441–451.

Paparella, Domenico. *Agreement to Combat Child Labour in the Leather and Suede Industry.* 1998. European Industrial Relations Observatory Online. Available at http://www.eiro.eurofound.ie/1998/03/inbrief/it9803153n.html.

Parry, Jonathan F., et al., eds. *The Worlds of Indian Industrial Labor.* New Delhi: Sage, 1999.

Patel, S. K., and R. C. Talati. "Child Labor in India: A Multi-Dimensional Problem." In Rao, *Exploited Children . . . ,* infra pp. 46–73.

Paust, Jordan J. "Human Rights Responsibilities of Private Corporations." *Vanderbilt Journal of Transnational Law* (2002), 35:802–810.

Pereira, Irandi, et al. *Trabalho do Adolescente: Mitos e Dilemas.* São Paulo: IEE/PUC, UNICEF, Fundacentro, Forja Editora, 1993.

Pérez, Jaime Jesús, Roger Hart, Jim Himes, and Gerison Lansdown. "Comentario y Recomendaciones para las Iniciativas de Unicef y Rädda Barnen Relativas al Derecho del Niño a la Participación." In UNICEF, *La Participatión des Niños y Adolescentes . . . ,* infra pp. 47–57.

Pflug, Bharati. *An Overview of Child Domestic Workers in Asia.* Geneva: ILO, 1995. Available at http://www.ilo.org/public/english/standards/ipec/publ/childdomestic/overview_child.pdf.

Philippine Child and Youth Welfare Code. Presidential Decree No. 603 (1974). Available at http://www.chanrobles.com/childandyouthwelfarecodeofthephilippines.htm.

Philippine Social Reform and Poverty Alleviation Act. Republic Act No. 8425 (1997). Available at http://www.chanrobles.com/republicactno8425.htm.

Polanyi, Karl. *The Great Transformation: The Political and Economic Origins of Our Time.* Boston: Beacon Press, 1957.

Polaski, Sandra. *Trade and Labor Standards: A Strategy for Developing Countries.* Washington, DC: Carnegie Endowment for International Peace, 2003.

Post, David. "Can Targeted Assistance Make a Difference for Girls?" *Gender and Society* (2001), 15:468–489.

———. *Children's Work, Schooling, and Welfare in Latin America.* Boulder: Westview, 2001.

———. "Jeffersonian Revisions of Locke: Education, Property-Rights, and Liberty." *Journal of the History of Ideas* (1986), 47:147–157.

Post, David, and Riho Sakurai. "Recognizing a Problem: The Impact of Global Politics on Child Labor Advocacy in Mexico." *International Journal of Educational Policy, Research, and Practice* (2001), 3:120–155.

Prepared Statement of Alexis M. Herman, U.S. Secretary of Labor. Hearing on ILO Convention on the Worst Forms of Child Labour, U.S. Senate Committee on Foreign Relations, 106th Cong., Federal Document Clearing House, Oct. 21, 1999 (unpublished; on file with James A. Gross).

Prepared Testimony of Ambassador Thomas M. T. Niles, President United States Council for International Business. Hearing on ILO Convention for the Elimination of Child Labour, US Senate Committee on Foreign Relations, 106th Cong., Federal News Service, Oct. 21, 1999 (unpublished; on file with James A. Gross).

Principles for Global Corporate Responsibility. Available at http://www.bench-marks.org/1_2.html.

Proceedings: Changing Our Lives—International Conference on Young People's Participation Against Commercial Sexual Exploitation of Children. Markina City, Philippines: National Reports, May 2000.

Proceedings of National Anti-Poverty Council: Children Basic Sector Assessment Workshop. Cebu City, Philippines, Sept. 1–2, 2000.

Program of Psychosocial Training and Human Rights. *Integrating Child-Centered Approaches in Children's Work.* Manila: University of the Philippines Center for Integrative and Development Studies and Save the Children–UK, 2002.

Proposed Draft Human Rights Code of Conduct for Companies. Working paper prepared by David Weissbrodt for the Sessional Working Group on the Working Methods and Activities of Transnational Corporations of the Sub-Commission on the Promotion and Protection of Human Rights. UN Doc. E/CN.4/Sub.2/2000/WG.2/WP.1/Add.1 (May 25, 2000).

Protocol Against the Smuggling of Migrants by Land, Sea, and Air, Supplementing the United Nations Convention Against Transnational Organized Crime. Nov. 15, 2000. GA Res. 55/25 (Annex III), UN GAOR, 55th Sess., Supp. No. 49, at 65. UN Doc. A/RES/55/25 (2000). Reprinted in 40 ILM 335, at 384 (2001) and Weston and Carlson, *International Law and World Order,* infra vol. 3, III.I.8.

Protocol for the Growing and Processing of Cocoa Beans and Their Derivative Products in a Manner That Complies with ILO Convention 182 Concerning the Prohibition and Immediate Action for the Elimination of the Worst Forms of Child Labour. Sept. 19, 2001. Available at http://www.chocolateandcocoa.org/images/protocol.pdf.

Protocol No. 11 to Be the 1950 European Convention for the Protection of Human Rights and Fundamental Freedoms. May 11, 1994. ETS 155. Reprinted in Weston and Carlson, *International Law and World Order,* infra vol. 3, III.B.16a.

Protocol to Prevent, Suppress, and Punish Trafficking in Persons, Especially Women and Children, Supplementing the United Nations Convention Against Transnational Organized Crime. Nov. 15, 2000. GA Res. 55/25 (Annex II), UN GAOR, 55th Sess., Supp. No. 49, at 43. UN Doc A/RES/55/383 (2000). Reprinted in 40 I.L.M. 335 (2001) and Weston and Carlson, *International Law and World Order,* infra vol. 3, III.C.19.

Protocol to the African Charter on Human and Peoples' Rights on the Establishment of an African Court on Human and Peoples' Rights. Dec. 12–13, 1997. OAU/LEG/MIN/AFCHPR/PROT 1, Rev. 2 (1997). Reprinted in Weston and Carlson, *International Law and World Order,* infra vol. 3, III.B.1a.

Pryer, Jane. *Poverty and Vulnerability in Dhaka Slums: The Urban Livelihoods Study.* Hampshire, UK: Ashgate, 2003.

Psacharopoulos, George. *Economic Justification for Investment in Education.* Washington, DC: World Bank, 1994.

Public Report on Basic Education in India (PROBE). New Delhi: Oxford University Press, 1999.

Purvis, Andrew. "Loaded: Why Supermarkets Are Getting Richer and Richer." *The Observer* (London), Jan. 25, 2004. Available at http://observer.guardian.co.uk/foodmonthly/story/0,9950,1127912,00.html.

Putnam, Robert D. (with Robert Leonardi and Raffaella Y. Nanetti). *Making Democracy Work: Civic Traditions in Modern Italy.* Princeton: Princeton University Press, 1993.

Ramachandran, Vimala. "Education, Work, and Rights." Unpublished paper. Bangalore: The Concerned for Working Children, Dec. 29, 2000 (on file with Victor P. Karunan).

Ramachandran, Vimala, and Aarfti Saihjee. *Looking Back in Order to Look Ahead: An External Review.* New Delhi/Jaipur: The Concerned for Working Children, Education Research Unit, Nov. 14, 2001.

Raman, Vasanthi. "Politics of Childhood: Perspectives from the South." *Economic and Political Weekly* (Bombay) (Nov. 11–17, 2000), 35(46):1–36.

Ranoy, Joan. Presentation to the eighty-seventh session of the International Labour Conference, Geneva, June 1–17, 1999 (on file with Victor Karunan).

Rao, M. Koteswara, ed. *Exploited Children: A Comprehensive Blueprint for Child Labor Rehabilitation.* New Delhi: Kanishka, 2000.

Raphael, Alison. "Eliminando o Trabalho Infantil no Brasil." In *Cadernos de Direitos da Criança e do Adolescente.* Brasília: UNICEF, 1996, pp. 1–28.

Ratner, Steven R. "Corporations and Human Rights: A Theory of Legal Responsibility." *Yale Law Journal* (2001), 111:443–545.

Rawls, John. *The Law of Peoples.* Cambridge: Harvard University Press, 1999.

———. *Political Liberalism.* New York: Columbia University Press, 1993.

———. *A Theory of Justice.* Oxford: Clarendon Press, 1972.

Ray, Ranjan. "Child Labor, Child Schooling, and Their Interaction with Adult Labor: Empirical Evidence for Peru and Pakistan." *World Bank Economic Review* (May 2000), 14(2):347–367.

———. "Simultaneous Analysis of Child Labor and Child Schooling: Comparative Evidence from Nepal and Pakistan." *Economic and Political Weekly* (Bombay) (Dec. 28, 2002), 37:35–48.

Regional Working Group on Child Labor. *Handbook for Program Managers: Facilitating Children's Participation in Programs Addressing Child Labor in Asia.* 2nd draft, rev. Prepared by the Psychosocial Trauma and Human Rights Program, Center for Integrative and Development Studies, University of the Philippines. Bangkok, Dec. 16, 2002.

Rehman, M. M., Kanta Rehman, and S. Mahartaj Begum. *Child Labour and Child Rights: A Compendium.* Delhi: Manak, 2002.

Reisman, W. M., and B. Weston, eds. and contribs. *Toward World Order and Human Dignity.* New York: Free Press.

Report of National Consultation on Child Labor in Commercial Plantations. Davao City, Philippines, Sept. 2002.

Report on Children's Forum and Regional Consultation Against the Most Intolerable Forms of Child Labor. Bangkok, Sept. 1997.

Revista Claudia. *Responsabilidade Social.* São Paulo: Editora Bloch, Feb. 2000.

Reynolds, Pamela. *Dance Civet Cat: Child Labour in the Zambezi Valley.* London: Zed Books, 1991.

Rice, Condoleezza. "Promoting the National Interest." *Foreign Affairs* (2000), 79:1.

Richter, Elihu D., and Janice Jacobs. "Work Injuries and Exposures in Children and Young Adults: Review and Recommendations for Action." *American Journal of Industrial Medicine* (1991), 19(6):747–796.

Richter, Linda, and Jill Swart-Kruger. "Society Makes Survival a Crime." *Child Youth Care* (1996), 14(6):17–19.

Risse, Thomas, Stephen Ropp, and Kathryn Sikkink, eds. *The Power of Human Rights: International Norms and Domestic Change.* New York: Cambridge University Press, 1999.

Risse, Thomas, and Kathryn Sikkink. "The Socialization of International Human Rights Norms into Domestic Practices." In Risse, Ropp, and Sikkink, *The Power of Human Rights . . .*, supra pp. 1–38.

Roberts, Adam, and Benedict Kingsbury, eds. *United Nations, Divided World: The U.N.'s Roles in International Relations.* 2nd ed. Oxford: Clarendon Press, 1993.

Robertson, Adam, and Shisham Mishra. *Forced to Plough: Bonded Labour in Nepal's Agricultural Economy.* London: Anti-Slavery International, 1997.

Robinson, Robert V. "Economic Necessity and the Life Cycle in the Family Economy of Nineteenth-Century Indianapolis." *American Journal of Sociology* (1993), 99(1):49–74.

———. Foreword to Marta Santos Pais, *A Human Rights Conceptual Framework for UNICEF*, Innocenti Essay No. 9. Florence: UNICEF International Child Development Centre, May 1999.

Rodgers, Gerry, and Guy Standing. *Child Work, Poverty, and Underdevelopment.* Geneva: ILO, 1981.

Rodley, Nigel S. "United Nations Non-Treaty Procedures for Dealing with Human Rights Violations." In Hannum, *Guide to International Human Rights Practice,* supra pp. 61–84.

Rogoff, Kenneth. "The IMF Strikes Back." *Foreign Policy* (Jan.–Feb. 2003).

Rome Statute of the International Criminal Tribunal. July 17, 1998. UN Doc. A/CONF.183/9 (1998). Reprinted in 37 ILM 999 (1998) and Weston and Carlson, *International Law and World Order,* infra vol. 1, I.H.13.

Rorty, Richard. "Human Rights, Rationality, and Sentimentality." In Shute and Hurley, *On Human Rights,* infra pp. 111–134.

Röselaers, Frans. Foreword to IPEC, *Unbearable to the Human Heart . . . ,* supra.

Rotberg, Robert I., and Dennis Thompson, eds. *Truth v. Justice: The Morality of Truth Commissions.* Princeton: Princeton University Press, 2000.

Rothstein, Richard. "The Case for Labour Standards." *Boston Review* (1995–1996). Available at http://www.princeton.edu/~speac/html/case_for_labor_standards.html.

Rurevo, Rumbidzai, and Michael Bourdillon. *Less Visible Street Children.* Harare: Weaver Press, 2003.

Ryan, Mary. *The Cradle of the Middle Class: The Family in Oneida County, New York, 1790–1865.* New York: Cambridge University Press, 1981.

Sachs, Jeffrey D. "Globalization and the Rule of Law." Yale Law School address, Oct. 16, 1998. Available at http://www.earth.columbia.edu/about/director/index.html.

Sahu, Supriya (Indian district government official). *State of the World's Children.* Interview by UNICEF, videocassette (1997), quoted in UNICEF-UK, *End Child Exploitation . . . ,* infra pp. 14–15.

Salazar, María C., and Walter A. Glasinovich, eds. *Better Schools, Less Child Work: Child Work and Education in Brazil, Colombia, Ecuador, Guatemala, and Peru.* Florence: UNICEF, 1998.

Salazar Negrón, Miriam. *Trabajo Infantil y Educación: Experiencia en Prevención y Erradicación.* Santiago: Colegio Nacional de Profesores, 2000.

Salway, Sarah, Ataur Rahman, Shahana Rahman, Matthew Kiggins, and Jane Pryer. *Urban Livelihoods Study: Preliminary Findings from the Quantitative Panel Survey.* Unpublished report. Dhaka: Proshika, 1997 (on file with Susan Bissell).

Santoro, Michael. "Beyond Codes of Conduct and Monitoring: An Organizational Integrity Approach to Global Labor Practices." *Human Rights Quarterly* (2003), 25:407–424.

Santos Pais, Marta. *A Human Rights Conceptual Framework for UNICEF.* Innocenti Essay No. 9. Florence: UNICEF International Child Development Centre, May 1999. Available at http://www.unicef.org/crc/essay-9.pdf.

———. "Monitoring Children's Rights: A View from Within." In Verhellen, *Monitoring Children's Rights,* infra pp. 129–143.

———. "The Question of Child Labour in a Child Rights Perspective." Paper presented at the Oslo Conference on Child Labour, Oct. 27–31, 1997 (on file with Susan Bissell).

Sassen, Saskia. *Globalization and Its Discontents*. New York: New Press, 1998.

Satyarthi, Kailash. *Out of the Shadows: Global March Against Child Labour.* Nov. 2000. Available at http://www.globalmarch.org/worstformsreport/foreword.html.

Save the Children. *Children's Rights: A Second Chance.* London: International Save the Children Alliance, 2001.

————. *An Introduction to Child Rights Programming: Concept and Application.* London: Save the Children, 2001.

————. *Save the Children's Position on Children and Work.* London: International Save the Children Alliance, 2001.

Save the Children and Child Workers in Asia. *Invisible Children: Child Work in Asia and the Pacific.* Bangkok, 1997.

Save the Children and South and Central Asia's Children. *Working with Working Children.* Katmandu, 1999.

Save the Children–Norway and Sweden. *Child-Centered Approaches to Child Work Issues.* Conference report, Oslo, Apr. 20–21, 1999.

Save the Children–UK. *Big Business, Small Hands: Responsible Approaches to Child Labour.* London: Save the Children Fund, 2000.

————. *Children in the Informal Mining Sector in Zimbabwe.* Harare: Save the Children–UK, 2000.

————. *Save the Children's Position on Children and Work.* London: International Save the Children Alliance, 2003. Available at http://www.savethechildren.org.uk/temp/scuk/cache/cmsattach/411childwork.pdf.

————. *Stitching Footballs: Voices of Children in Sialkot, Pakistan.* London: Save the Children Fund, 1997.

Sawyer, Roger. *Children Enslaved.* London: Routledge, 1988.

Schibotto, Giangi, and Alejandro Cussiánovich. *Working Children: Building an Identity.* Lima: Movimiento de Adolescentes y Niños Trabajadores Hijos de Obreros Cristianos (MANTHOC), 1994.

Schiefelbein, Ernesto. "Incentivos Económicos a la Ascuela en América Latina." *Realidad y Utopía* (1997), 2:33–67.

Schmitz, Hans Peter, and Kathryn Sikkink. "International Human Rights." In Carlsnaes, Risse, and Simmons, *Handbook of International Relations,* supra pp. 517–537.

Schoenbaum, Thomas J. "International Trade and Protection of the Environment: The Continuing Search for Reconciliation." *American Journal of International Law* (1997), 91:268–231.

Schott, Jeffrey J. *The WTO After Seattle.* Washington, DC: Institute for International Economics, July 2000.

Schrage, Elliot J. *Promoting International Worker Rights Through Private Voluntary Initiatives: Public Relations or Public Policy?* Report to the US Department of State. Iowa City: Global Workplace Research Initiative, University of Iowa Center for Human Rights, Jan. 2004. Available at http://www.uichr.org.

Schrumpf, Ellen. "Attitudes Towards Child Work in Industry: An Argument Against the History of Misery." *Norwegian Journal of History* (1993), 2:209–222.

————. "From Full-Time to Part-Time: Working Children in Norway from the Nineteenth to the Twentieth Century." In de Coninck-Smith, Sandin, and Schrumpf, *Industrious Children . . . ,* supra pp. 47–78.

Schultz, T. Paul. *What Are the Returns to Poverty Reduction? Evaluation of Progresa in Mexico.* Working paper. New Haven: Yale University, Department of Economics, 2001.

Schumacher, E. F. *Small Is Beautiful: Economics As If People Mattered.* New York: Perennial Library, 1989.

Schwarz, Solomon H. *Labour in the Soviet Union.* London: Cresset Press, 1953.

Scott, Catherine V. *Gender and Development: Rethinking Modernization and Dependency Theory.* Boulder: Lynne Rienner, 1995.

Scott, James. *The Moral Economy of the Peasant.* New Haven: Yale University Press, 1976.

Seabrook, Jeremy. *No Hiding Place: Child Sex Tourism and the Role of Extraterritorial Legislation.* London: ECPAT Europe Law Enforcement Group, Zed Books, 2000.

Searight, Susan. *Child Labour in Spain.* London: Anti-Slavery Society, 1980.

Seligman, Edwin R. A. *Encyclopedia of the Social Sciences.* 15 vols. New York: Macmillan, 1930.

Sen, Amartya K. "Capability and Well-Being." In Nussbaum and Sen, *The Quality of Life,* supra pp. 30–31.

———. *Choice, Welfare, and Measurement.* Oxford: Blackwell, 1982.

———. *Commodities and Capabilities.* Amsterdam: North Holland, 1985.

———. *Development and Freedom.* New York: Anchor Books, 2000.

———. *Equality of What?* Tanner Lectures on Human Values. Cambridge: Cambridge University Press, 1980.

Sen, Amartya K., and John Muelbauer. *The Standard of Living.* Tanner Lectures on Human Values. Cambridge: Cambridge University Press, 1987.

Sengupta, Arjun. "On the Theory and Practice of the Right to Development." *Human Rights Quarterly* (2002), 24:837–889.

Shaw, Malcolm N. *International Law.* Cambridge: Cambridge University Press, 1997.

Shell, G. Richard. "Trade Legalism and International Relations Theory: An Analysis of the World Trade Organization." *Duke Law Journal* (1995), 44:829–927.

Shelton, Dinah. "The Promise of Regional Human Rights Systems." In Weston and Marks, *The Future of International Human Rights,* infra pp. 351–398.

———. "Protecting Human Rights in a Globalized World." *Boston College International and Comparative Law Review* (2002), 25:273–322.

Shepherd, George W., Jr., and Ved P. Nanda, eds. *Human Rights and Third World Development.* Westport: Greenwood Press, 1985.

Sheppard, Anne. "Child Soldiers: Is the Optional Protocol Evidence of an Emerging 'Straight-18' Consensus?" *International Journal of Children's Rights* (2000), 8: 37–70.

Shihata, Ibrahim. "The World Bank's Protection and Promotion of Children's Rights." *International Journal of Children's Rights* (1996), 4:383–405.

Shivji, Issac. "Law and Conditions of Child Labour in Colonial Tanganyika, 1920–1940." *International Journal of the Sociology of Law* (1985), 13:221–235.

Shotwell, James T., ed. *The Origins of the International Labor Organization.* 2 vols. New York: Columbia University Press, 1934.

Shute, Stephen, and Susan Hurley, eds. *On Human Rights.* New York: Basic Books, 1993.

Singapore Ministerial Declaration. Dec. 13, 1996. WTO Doc. WT/MIN(96)/DEC (1996). Reprinted in 36 ILM 218 (1997).

Singh, A. N. *Child Labor in India: Socio-Economic Perspectives.* Delhi: Shipra, 1990.

Skocpol, Theda. *Protecting Soldiers and Mothers: The Political Origins of Social Policy in the U.S.* Cambridge: Harvard University Press, 1992.

Skowronek, Stephen. *Building the New American State: The Expansion of National Administrative Capacities, 1877–1920.* New York: Cambridge University Press, 1982.

Slavery Convention. Sept. 25, 1926 (as amended by protocol of Dec. 7, 1953). 60 LNTS 253 (convention), 182 UNTS 51 (protocol), 212 UNTS 17 (consolidated). Reprinted in Weston and Carlson, *International Law and World Order,* infra vol. 3, III.H.1.

Slye, Ronald C. "International Human Rights Law in Practice: International Law, Human Rights Beneficiaries, and South Africa: Some Thoughts on the Utility of International Human Rights Law." *Chicago Journal of International Law* (2001), 2:59–79.

Smillie, Ian. *The Alms Bazaar: Altruism Under Fire—Non-Profit Organisations and International Development.* Ottawa: IDRC, 1995.

———. "Changing Partners: Northern NGOs, Northern Governments." In Smillie and Helmich, *Non-Governmental Organizations and Governments . . . ,* infra pp. 13–44.

Smillie, Ian, and Henry Helmich, eds. *Non-Governmental Organizations and Governments: Stakeholders for Development.* Paris: OCED, 1993.

Smith, George. *The Cry of the Children from the Brickyards of England.* London: Simpkin Marshall, 1871.

Smith, Joan M. "North American Free Trade and the Exploitation of Working Children." *Temple Political and Civil Rights Law Review* (1994), 4:57–116.

Smolin, David M. "Strategic Choices in the International Campaign Against Child Labor." *Human Rights Quarterly* (2000), 22:942–987.

Snape, William J., III, and Naomi B. Lefkovitz. "Searching for GATT's Environmental Miranda: Are 'Process Standards' Getting 'Due Process'?" *Cornell International Law Journal* (1994), 27(3):777–817.

Social Accountability International. *SA8000 Standard Elements.* Available at http://www/cepaa.org/sa8000/sa8000.htm.

Socialist Republic of Vietnam. "Interministerial Circular 09/TT-LB 1995 Between Ministry of Labour, Invalids, and Social Affairs and the Ministry of Health." Quoted in Socialist Republic of Vietnam, *National Report on the Implementation of the CRC 1993–1998.* Hanoi, 1999, p. 47.

———. *National Report on Two Years Implementation of the UNCRC.* Hanoi: Committee for the Protection and Care of Children, 1992.

Spar, Debora L. "The Spotlight and the Bottom Line." *Foreign Affairs* (1998), 77(2): 7–12.

"Speech by Minister Pronk." Minister for Development Cooperation. Netherlands, Amsterdam Child Labour Conference, Workshop 1 on International and Regional Cooperation. Feb. 27, 1997. Available at http://pangaea.org/street_children/world/labor2.htm.

Stackhouse, John. "New Solutions Fashioned for Child Workers." *Globe and Mail* (Toronto), Feb. 26, 1996.

Statement by Ms. Louise Arbour, High Commissioner for Human Rights, to the Open-Ended Working Group Established by the Commission on Human Rights to Consider Options Regarding the Elaboration of an Optional Protocol to the International Covenant on Economic, Social, and Cultural Rights. Jan. 14, 2005. Available at http://www.unhchr.ch/huricane/huricane.nsf/newsroom.

Statement of Senator Jesse Helms, Chairman, Senate Committee on Foreign Relations. Hearing on ILO Convention for the Elimination of Child Labour, US Senate

Committee on Foreign Relations, 106th Cong. (Oct. 21, 1999), Federal News Service, Oct. 21, 1999 (unpublished; on file with James A. Gross).

Statistics South Africa. *Child Labour in South Africa: Summary Report*. Pretoria: ILO and South African Department of Labour, 2000.

Status of Women Canada. "Codes of Conduct and Independent Monitoring: Tools to Challenge Sweatshop Practices Internationally." In *Policy Options to Improve Standards for Women Garment Workers in Canada and Internationally,* Mar. 19, 2004. Available at http://www.swc-cfc.gc.ca/pubs/0662273834/199901_0662273834_8_e.html#1.

Steinberg, L. D., S. Fergley, and S. M. Dornbusch. "Negative Impact of Part-Time Work on Adolescent Adjustment: Evidence from a Longitudinal Study." *Developmental Psychology* (1993), 29(2):171–180.

Steiner, Henry J. *Diverse Partners: Non-Governmental Organizations in the Human Rights Movement*. Cambridge: Harvard Law School Human Rights Program and Human Rights Internet, 1991.

Steiner, Henry J., and Philip Alston. *International Human Rights in Context: Law, Politics, Morals*. 2nd ed. Oxford: Clarendon Press, 2000.

Stephens, Sharon, ed. *Children and the Politics of Culture*. Princeton: Princeton University Press, 1995.

Stern, Robert M. *Labor Standards and Trade*. Discussion Paper No. 459. Ann Arbor: University of Michigan, Research Seminar in International Economics, Feb. 17, 2000.

Stern, Robert M., and Katherine Terrell. *Labor Standards and the World Trade Organization: A Position Paper*. Discussion Paper No. 499. Ann Arbor: University of Michigan, Research Seminar in International Economics, Aug. 2003.

Stevenson, Benjamin J. "Pursuing an End to Foreign Child Labor Through U.S. Trade Law: WTO Challenges and Doctrinal Solutions." *UCLA Journal of International Law and Foreign Affairs* (2002), 7:129–167.

Stiglitz, Joseph E. *Globalization and Its Discontents*. New York: W. W. Norton, 2003.

Stiles, Kendall W. "Grassroots Empowerment: States, Non-State Actors and Global Policy Formulation." In Higgott, Underhill, and Bieler, *Non-State Actors and Authority in the Global System,* supra pp. 32–47.

Stirling, Patricia. "The Use of Trade Sanctions as an Enforcement Mechanism for Basic Human Rights: A Proposal for Addition to the World Trade Organization." *American University Journal of International Law* (1996), 11(1):1–46.

Stockholm Declaration and Agenda for Action. First World Congress Against Commercial Sexual Exploitation of Children, Stockholm, Aug. 27–31, 1996. Available at http://www.csecworldcongress.org/pdf/en/stockholm/outome_documents/stockholm%20declaration%201996_en.pdf.

Stolee, Margaret K. "Homeless Children in the USSR, 1917–1957." *Soviet Studies* (1988), 40:64–83.

Street, B. V. *Literacy in Theory and Practice*. Cambridge: Cambridge University Press, 1984.

Stromquist, Shelton. *Reinventing "The People" : The Progressive Movement, the Class Problem, and the Origins of Modern Liberalism*. Urbana: University of Illinois Press, 2005.

Subida, R. *Defining Hazardous Undertakings for Young Workers Below 18 Years of Age: A Country Report*. Manila: IPEC, 1997.

Summers, Clyde. "The Battle in Seattle: Free Trade, Labor Rights, and Societal Values." *University of Pennsylvania Journal of International Economic Law* (2001), 22:61–90.

Swepston, Lee. "Human Rights Complaint Procedures of the International Labor Organization." In Hannum, *Guide to International Human Rights Practice,* supra pp. 85–101.

Swift, Anthony. *Working Children Get Organised.* London: International Save the Children Alliance, 1999.

Swinarski, C., ed. *Studies and Essays on International Humanitarian Law and Red Cross Principles.* Geneva: Committee of the International Red Cross, 1984.

Symonides, Janusz, ed. *Human Rights: International Protection, Monitoring, Enforcement.* Paris: UNESCO, 2003.

Taylor, P. *The Texts of Paulo Freire.* Buckingham: Open University Press, 1993.

Tengey, Wilbert. *Convention on the Rights of the Child Impact Study: Ghana.* Accra: Save the Children Fund–UK, 1998.

Thailand: Restrictions on Importation of and Internal Taxes on Cigarettes. GATT BISD (37th Supp.) 200 (Nov. 7, 1990).

Theis, Joachim. "Children and Participatory Appraisals: Experiences from Vietnam." Participatory Learning Appraisal Notes No. 25. London: International Institute for Environment and Development (IIED), 1996.

Thompson, Edward P. *The Making of the English Working Class.* London: Victor Gollancz, 1963.

Thorner, Daniel, Basile Kerblay, and R. E. F. Smith, eds. *A. V. Chayanov on the Theory of Peasant Economy.* Madison: University of Wisconsin Press, 1986.

Tolfree, David. *Old Enough to Work, Old Enough to Have a Say: Different Approaches to Supporting Working Children.* Stockholm: Save the Children–Sweden, 1998.

Tomasevski, Katarina. *Education Denied: Costs and Remedies.* London: Zed Books, 2003.

Trachtman, Joel P. "The Domain of WTO Dispute Resolution." *Harvard International Law Journal* (1999), 40:333–377.

Trattner, Walter I. *Crusade for the Children: A History of the National Child Labor Committee and Child Labor Reform in America.* Chicago: Quadrangle Books, 1970.

Treasury, Postal Service, and General Government Appropriations Act of 1998. Pub. L. No. 105-61, sec. 634, 111 Stat. 1272 (1997).

Treaty of Versailles. June 28, 1919. 49 Stat. 2712, 15 UNTS 35, Preamble–Part XIII.

Tsogas, George. *Labor Regulation in a Global Economy.* Armonk, NY: M. E. Sharpe, 2001.

Tucker, Lee. *Fingers to the Bone: United States Failure to Protect Child Farmworkers.* New York: Human Rights Watch, 2000. Available at http://www.hrw.org/reports/2000/frmwrkr.

Tuttle, Carolyn. *Hard at Work in Factories and Mines: The Economics of Child Labor During the British Industrial Revolution.* Boulder: Westview, 1999.

Uchengamma. "Knowing Rights from Wrong: Child Workers Learn to Fight Back." *CRIN Newsletter* (Oct. 2002), 16:31–32.

Udombana, N. J. "The Third World and the Right to Development: Agenda for the New Millennium." *Human Rights Quarterly* (2000), 22:753–787.

Ulewicz, Monica, ed. *Monitoring International Labor Standards: Human Capital Investment—Summary of a Workshop.* Washington, DC: National Academies Press, 2003.

UNDP (United Nations Development Programme). *Guidelines for Human Rights–Based Reviews of UNDP Programmes.* New York, Oct. 1, 2002.

———. *Human Development Report 2002.* New York, 2002.

————. *Human Rights–Based Reviews of UNDP Programmes: Working Guidelines.* New York, 2003. Available at http://www.undp.org/governance/docshurist/ 030617guidelines.doc.

————. *Integrating Human Rights with Sustainable Human Development: A UNDP Policy Document.* New York, 1998.

————. *Report of the Second Interagency Workshop on Implementing the Human Rights–Based Approach in the Context of UN Reform.* New York, 2003.

————. *The U.N. System: Common Understanding on the Human Rights–Based Approach to Development.* New York, 2003.

UNDP Philippines. *Training Manual: Rights-Based Approach to Development Programming.* Draft report. 2002.

UNESCO (United Nations Educational, Scientific, and Cultural Organization). *The Dakar Framework for Action: Education for All: Meeting Our Collective Commitments.* Paris, 2001.

————. *Education for All: Is the World on Track?* Paris, 2002.

————. *World Declaration on Education for All.* Paris, 1990.

UNFPA (United Nations Population Fund). *International Conference on Population and Development (Cairo, Sept. 1994): Summary of the Programme of Action.* New York, 2004.

UNICEF (United Nations Children's Fund). *Atlas of Children in South East Asia and the Pacific.* Bangkok: UNICEF Regional Office for South East Asia and Pacific, 2003.

————. Background paper for Oslo Conference, Oct. 27–31, 1997 (on file with Child Protection Section, Programme Division, UNICEF headquarters, New York).

————. *Beyond Child Labour: Affirming Rights.* New York, Mar. 2001. Available at http://www.unicef.org/publications/index_4302.html.

————. *Child Domestic Work.* Innocenti Digest No. 5. Florence: UNICEF International Child Development Centre, 1999.

————. *Children and Their Families in a Changing Thai Society.* Bangkok: UNICEF Thailand Country Office, 1997.

————. *Children and Women: Situation Analysis.* Hanoi: UNICEF Vietnam Country Office, 1994.

————. *Children in Especially Difficult Circumstances.* Report to UNICEF Executive Board. New York, 1986.

————. *Children in Need of Special Protection.* Bangkok: UNICEF Regional Office for East Asia and the Pacific, 2002.

————. *Children on the Edge.* Bangkok: UNICEF Office for East Asia and Pacific, n.d.

————. *Country Programme 2002–2006.* Dar es Salaam, 2001.

————. *Education and Child Labor.* Background paper for Oct. 1997 Oslo Conference. New York, 1997.

————. *First Consolidated Donor Report on the UNICEF Global Child Labour Programme: Accomplishments and Lessons Learnt, 1999.* New York: UNICEF Programme Division, Child Protection Section, June 2000.

————. *A Human Rights Approach to UNICEF Programming for Children and Women: What It Is, and What Changes It Will Bring.* Available at http://coe-dmha.org/ unicef/hpt_introreading01.htm.

————. *Human Rights for Children and Women: How UNICEF Helps Make Them a Reality.* June 1999. Available at http://www.unicef.org/mozambique/human rightseng.pdf.

————. *Implementation Handbook on the Convention on the Rights of the Child.* Geneva, 1998.

————, ed. *La Participatión des Niños y Adolescentes en el Contexto de la Convención Sobre Derechos del Niño.* Bogatá, 1998.

————. *Making a Difference: A Review of UNICEF-Supported Initiatives Against Child Labour.* Philippines, 2001.

————. *National Child and Youth Participation Framework: A Practical Guide for Promoting Child and Youth Participation in the Philippines.* Draft report. UNICEF Philippines, March 2003.

————. *Programme Cooperation for Children and Women from a Human Rights Perspective.* UNICEF Executive Board, 1999 Annual Session. Doc. E/ICEF/1999/11 (Apr. 5, 1999).

————. *Report of the Expert Consultation on the Impact of the Implementation Process of the Convention on the Rights of the Child.* Florence: UNICEF Innocenti Research Centre, Apr. 6–7, 2004.

————. *Speaking Out! Voices of Children and Adolescents in Asia and the Pacific—A Regional Opinion Survey.* Bangkok, 2001.

————. *The State of the World's Children 1997.* Oxford: Oxford University Press, 1997. Available at http://www.unicef.org/sowc97.

————. *The State of the World's Children 1999.* New York, 1999. Available at http://www.unicef.org/org/sowc99/summary2.htm.

————. *The State of the World's Children 2004.* New York, 2003. Available at http://www.unicef.org/sowc04/index.html.

————. Statement by Joe Judd at the Global Conference on Education, New Delhi, 2003, unpublished (on file with Susan Bissell).

————. *Towards a Region Fit for Children: An Atlas for the Sixth East Asia and Pacific Ministerial Consultation.* Bangkok: UNICEF EAPRO, 2003.

————. *Viet Nam: Children and Women—A Situation Analysis 2000.* Hanoi, 2000.

UNICEF International Child Development Centre. *Child Domestic Work.* Innocenti Digest No. 5. Florence, 1999.

UNICEF–UK. *End Child Exploitation: Faces of Exploitation.* London, Jan. 2003.

United Nations. *Additional Report of the Special Representative of the Secretary-General (Olara A. Otunnu) for Children and Armed Conflict.* UN Commission on Human Rights, 58th Sess., Provisional Agenda Item 13, at 1. UN Doc. E/CN.4/2002/85 (2002). Available at http://www.hri.ca/fortherecord2002/documentation/commission/e-cn4-2002-85.htm.

————. *Annual Report of the Special Rapporteur (Dr. Katarina Tomasevski) on the Right to Education.* Commission on Human Rights, 58th Sess., Provisional Agenda Item 10, at 1. UN Doc. E/CN.4/2002/60 (2002). Available at http://www.unhchr.ch/huridocda/huridoca.nsf/testframe/ff9709c1d502132ec1256b810058ca6d?opendocument.

————. *Charter of Economic Rights and Duties of States.* Dec. 12, 1974. GA Res. 3281 (Annex), UN GAOR, 29th Sess., Supp. No. 31, at 50. UN Doc. A/9631, 28 UNJYB 403. Reprinted in 14 ILM 251 (1975) and Weston and Carlson, *International Law and World Order,* infra vol. 4, IV.F.5.

————. *Commentary on the Norms on the Responsibilities of Transnational Corporations and Other Business Enterprises with Regard to Human Rights.* UN Doc. E/CN.4/Sub.2/2003/38/Rev.2 (2003).

————. *Convention Against Torture and Other Cruel, Inhuman, or Degrading Treatment or Punishment.* Dec. 10, 1984. 1465 UNTS 85. Reprinted in Weston and Carlson, *International Law and World Order,* infra vol. 3, III.K.2.

————. *Convention Against Transnational Organized Crime.* Nov. 15, 2000. GA Res. 55/383 (Annex I), UN GAOR, 55th Sess., Supp. No. 49, at 43. UN Doc. A/RES/55/383 (2000). Reprinted in 40 ILM 335, at 377 (2001), and Weston and Carlson, *International Law and World Order,* infra vol. 3, III.M.9.

————. *Convention for the Suppression of the Traffic in Persons and of the Exploitation of the Prostitution of Others.* Mar. 21, 1950. 96 UNTS 271. Reprinted in Weston and Carlson, *International Law and World Order,* infra vol. 3, III.C.7.

————. *Convention on the Rights of the Child.* Nov. 2, 1989. 1577 UNTS 3. Reprinted in 28 ILM 1448 (1989) and Weston and Carlson, *International Law and World Order,* infra vol. 3, III.D.3.

————. *Copenhagen Declaration on Social Development and Programme of Action for the World Summit for Social Development.* In *Report of the World Summit for Social Development.* UN Doc. A/Conf.166/9 (Apr. 19, 1995).

————. *Draft Optional Protocol to the International Covenant on Economic, Social, and Cultural Rights.* Dec. 18, 1996. UN Doc. E/CN.4/1997/105 (Annex). Reprinted in Weston and Carlson, *International Law and World Order,* infra vol. 3, III.A.6.

————. *General Assembly Declaration on the Establishment of a New International Economic Order.* May 1, 1974. GA Res. 3201, UN GAOR, 6th Special Sess., Supp. No. 1, at 3. UN Doc A/9559; 128 UNJYB 324. Reprinted in 13 ILM 715 (1974) and Weston and Carlson, *International Law and World Order,* infra vol. 4, IV.F.3.

————. *General Assembly Declaration on the Preparation of Societies for Life in Peace.* Dec. 15, 1978. GA Res. 33/73, UN GAOR, 33rd Sess., Supp. No. 45, at 55. UN Doc. A/33/45 (1979). Reprinted in Weston and Carlson, *International Law and World Order,* infra vol. 3, III.S.1.

————. *General Assembly Declaration on the Right of Peoples to Peace.* Nov 12, 1984. GA Res. 39/11 (Annex), UN GAOR, 39th Sess., Supp. No. 51, at 22. UN Doc. A/39/51 (1985). Reprinted in Weston and Carlson, *International Law and World Order,* infra vol. 3, III.S.2.

————. *General Assembly Declaration on the Right to Development.* Dec. 4, 1986. GA Res. 41/128 (Annex), UN GAOR, 41st Sess., Supp. No. 53, at 186. UN Doc. A/41/53 (1987). Reprinted in Weston and Carlson, *International Law and World Order,* infra vol. 3, III.R.2.

————. *General Assembly Declaration on the Rights of the Child.* Nov. 20, 1959. GA Res. 1386, UN GAOR, 14th Sess., Supp. No. 16, at 19. UN Doc. A/4354 (1960).

————. *General Assembly Resolution 49/134* (on National Institutions for the Promotion and Protection of Human Rights). Dec. 20, 1993. GA Res. 49/134, UN GAOR, 48th Sess., Supp. No. 49, at 9. UN Doc. A/RES/48/134 (1994).

————. *Global Compact: Human Rights, Labour, Environment.* Available at http://www.unglobalcompact.org/portal/default.asp.

————. *International Convention on the Elimination of All Forms of Racial Discrimination.* Dec. 21, 1965. 660 UNTS 195. Reprinted in Weston and Carlson, *International Law and World Order,* infra vol. 3, III.I.1.

————. *International Covenant on Civil and Political Rights.* Dec. 16, 1966. 993 UNTS 171. Reprinted in Weston and Carlson, *International Law and World Order,* infra vol. 3, III.A.3.

————. *International Covenant on Economic, Social, and Cultural Rights.* Dec. 16, 1966. 993 UNTS 3. Reprinted in Weston and Carlson, *International Law and World Order,* infra vol. 3, III.A.2.

————. *Millennium Declaration.* Sept. 18, 2000. GA Res. 55/2, UN GAOR, 55th Sess., Supp. No. 49, at 4. UN Doc A/RES/55/2 (2000). Reprinted in Weston and Carlson, *International Law and World Order,* infra vol. 3, III.U.4.

————. *Optional Protocol to the Convention on the Elimination of All Forms of Discrimination Against Women.* Oct. 15, 1999. GA Res. 54/4 (Annex), UN GAOR, 54th Sess., Supp. No. 49, at 4. UN Doc. A/54/4 (1999). Reprinted in 39 ILM 281 (2000) and Weston and Carlson, *International Law and World Order,* infra vol. 3, III.C.16.

————. *Optional Protocol to the Convention on the Rights of the Child on the Involvement of Children in Armed Conflict.* May 25, 2000. GA Res. 54/263 (Annex I), UN GAOR, 54th Sess., Supp. No. 49, at 7. UN Doc. A/RES/54/263 (2000). Reprinted in Weston and Carlson, *International Law and World Order,* infra vol. 3, III.D.5.

————. *Optional Protocol to the Convention on the Rights of the Child on the Sale of Children, Child Prostitution, and Child Pornography.* May 25, 2000, GA Res. 54/263 (Annex II), UN GAOR, 54th Sess., Supp. No. 49, at 6. UN Doc. A/RES/54/263 (2000). Reprinted in Weston and Carlson, *International Law and World Order,* infra vol. 3, III.D.6.

————. *Optional Protocol to the International Covenant on Civil and Political Rights.* Dec. 16, 1966. GA Res. 2200 (Annex), 999 UNTS 171, 999 UNTS 302. Reprinted in Weston and Carlson, *International Law and World Order,* infra vol. 3, III.A.4.

————. *Program of Action on the Establishment of a New International Economic Order.* May 1, 1974. GA Res. 3202, UN GAOR, 6th Special Sess., Supp. No. 1, at 5. UN Doc. A/9559. Reprinted in 13 ILM 720 (1974) and Weston and Carlson, *International Law and World Order,* infra vol. 4, IV.F.4.

————. *Report of the Bureau of the 54th Session of the Commission on Human Rights Pursuant to Commission Decision 198/112.* UN Doc. E/CN.4/1999/104 (1999).

————. *Report of the Secretary-General: Children and Armed Conflict.* UN Doc. A/55/163 (July 19, 2000).

————. *Report of the Secretary-General: Road Map Towards the Implementation of the United Nations Millennium Declaration.* Sept. 6, 2001. UN Doc. A/56/326 (2001).

————. *Report of the Special Rapporteur (Dr. Katarina Tomasevski) on the Right to Education.* Commission on Human Rights, 59th Sess., Provisional Agenda Item 10, at 1. UN Doc. E/CN.4/2003/9 (2003). Available at http://www.unhchr.ch/huridocda/huridoca.nsf/allsymbols/4550cac4b8a69c0cc1256cf0002fa69d/$file/g0310495.doc?openelement.

————. *Report of the Special Rapporteur (Mr. Juan Miguel Petit) on the Sale of Children, Child Prostitution and Child Pornography.* Commission on Human Rights, 58th Sess., Provisional Agenda Item 13, at 1. UN Doc. E/CN.4/2002/88 (2002). Available at http://ods-dds-ny.un.org/doc/undoc/gen/G02/105/92/pdf/g0210592.pdf?openelement.

————. *Report of the Special Rapporteur (Mr. Juan Miguel Petit) on the Sale of Children, Child Prostitution, and Child Pornography.* Commission on Human Rights, 59th Sess., Provisional Agenda Item 13, at 1. UN Doc. E/CN.4/2003/79 (2003). Available at http://ods-dds-ny.un.org/doc/undoc/gen/G03/100/90/pfd/G0310090.pdf?openelement.

————. *Report of the Special Rapporteur (Ms. Ofelia Calcetas-Santos) on the Optional Protocol to the Convention on the Rights of the Child, Sale of Children, Child Prostitution, and Child Pornography in Accordance with Commission on Human Rights Resolution.* UN Doc. E/CN.4/1999/71 (Jan. 29, 1999).

————. *Report of the Special Representative of the Secretary-General (Mr. Olara A. Otunnu) of Children Affected on the Optional Protocol to the Convention on the*

Rights of the Child on the Involvement of Children in Armed Conflict to the General Assembly: Protection of Children Affected by Armed Conflict. UN Doc. A/53/482 (Oct. 12, 1998), UN Doc. A/54/430 (Oct. 1, 1999), UN Doc. A/55/442 (Oct. 3, 2000), UN Doc. A/56/453 (Oct. 9, 2001), UN Doc. A57/402 (Sept. 25, 2002).

————. *Report of the Special Representative of the Secretary-General (Mr. Olara A. Otunnu) on the Involvement of Children Affected on the Optional Protocol to the Convention on the Rights of the Child on the Involvement of Children in Armed Conflict to the Commission on Human Rights.* UN Doc. E/CN.4/2003/77 (Mar. 3, 2003).

————. *Security Council Resolution 1325* (on Women and Peace and Security). Oct. 31, 2000. UN SCOR, 4213rd meeting, at 177. UN Doc. S/RES/1325 (2000). Reprinted in Weston and Carlson, *International Law and World Order,* infra vol. 2, II.D.4c.

————. *Security Council Resolution 1379* (on Children and Armed Conflict). UN SCOR, 4423rd meeting, at 18. UN Doc. S/RES/1379 (2001).

————. *Supplementary Convention on the Abolition of Slavery, the Slave Trade, and Institutions and Practices Similar to Slavery.* Sept. 7, 1956. 266 UNTS 40. Reprinted in Weston and Carlson, *International Law and World Order,* infra vol. 3, III.H.3.

————. *Universal Declaration of Human Rights.* GA Res. 217A, UN GAOR, 3rd Sess., Pt. I, Resolutions, at 71. UN Doc. A/810 (1948). Reprinted in Weston and Carlson, *International Law and World Order,* infra vol. 3, III.A.1.

United Nations Children's Fund and Social Welfare Department. *Reaching the Most Vulnerable Children: The Process.* New York, 2003.

United Nations Economic and Social Council. *Review of UNICEF Policies and Strategies in Child Protection.* UN Doc. E/ICEF/1996/14 (Apr. 1996).

United Nations High Commissioner for Human Rights. *Business and Human Rights: A Progress Report.* Jan. 2000. Available at http://www.unhchr.ch/business.htm.

United Nations High Commissioner for Human Rights and the Committee on Economic, Social, and Cultural Rights. *Plan of Action to Strengthen the Implementation of the International Covenant on Economic, Social, and Cultural Rights.* Available at http://www.unhchr.ch/html/menu2/6/action.htm.

United Nations Secretariat. "Secretary-General Calls Partnership of NGOs, Private Sector, International Organizations and Governments Powerful Partnership for Future." Press Release SG/SM/6973. Remarks of Kofi Annan at the NGO Forum on Global Issues, Berlin, Apr. 29, 1999.

United Nations Sub-Commission on the Promotion and Protection of Human Rights. *Norms on the Responsibilities of Transnational Corporations and Other Business Enterprises with Regard to Human Rights.* UN Doc. E/CN.4/Sub.2/2003/12/ Rev.2 (2003), approved Aug. 13, 2003, by Resolution 2003/16, UN Doc. E/CN.4/ Sub.2/2003/L.11, at 52 (2003). Available at http://www.unhchr.ch/huridocda/ huridoca.nsf/0/64155e7e8141b38cc1256d63002c55e8?opendocument.

United Nations World Summit for Children. *A World Fit for Children.* GA Res. A/ RES/S-27/2, 27th Special Sess., May 10, 2002. Available at http://www.unicef .org/specialsession/wffc/index.html.

United Nations World Summit for Social Development. *Report of the World Summit for Social Development.* UN Doc. A/Conf.166/9 (Apr. 19, 1995).

United Republic of Tanzania. *Demographic Health Survey.* Dar es Salaam: National Bureau of Statistics, 1996.

————. *The Education Sector Development Programme.* Dar es Salaam, 2001.

———. *The Education Sector Development Programme.* Dar es Salaam, 2001.

———. *His Excellence Benjamin William Mkapa, at the Special High-Level Session of the International Labour Conference on the Launch of the Time-Bound Programme on the Worst Forms of Child Labour.* Address by the president. Geneva, 2002.

———. *Household Budget Survey.* Dar es Salaam: National Bureau of Statistics, 2001.

———. *Integrated Labour Force Survey.* Dar es Salaam: National Bureau of Statistics, 2001.

———. *The National Employment Policy.* Dar es Salaam, 1997.

———. *Non-Formal Education Strategy.* Dar es Salaam, 2001.

———. *Poverty and Human Development Report.* Dar es Salaam, 2002.

———. *Poverty Reduction Strategy Paper* (PRSP). Dar es Salaam, 2000.

———. *Primary Education Development Plan, 2002–2006.* Dar es Salaam, 2001.

———. Prime Minister's Office. *National Multi-Sectoral Strategic Framework on HIV/AIDS, 2003–2007.* Dar es Salaam, 2003.

———. *Tanzania Development Vision 2025.* Dar es Salaam, 2001.

United States: Import Prohibition of Certain Shrimp and Shrimp Products. Report of the Appellate Body, WT/DS58/Appellate Body/R (Oct. 12, 1998).

United States: Imports of Certain Automotive Spring Assemblies. GATT BISD (30th Supp.) 107 (May 26, 1983).

United States: Prohibition of Imports of Tuna and Tuna Products from Canada. GATT BISD (29th Supp.) 9 (Feb. 22, 1982).

United States: Standards for Reformulated and Conventional Gasoline. Report of the Appellate Body, WT/DS2/Appellate Body/R (Apr. 29, 1996).

US Council for International Business. "Business Representative Explains ILO's Action Against Myanmar." Press release, Nov. 21, 2000. Available at http://www.uscib.org/index.asp?documentid=1135.

US Department of Labor. *By the Sweat and Toil of Children.* Vol. 3, *The Apparel Industry and Codes of Conduct: A Solution to the International Child Labor Problem?* Washington, DC, 1996.

———. *By the Sweat and Toil of Children.* Vol. 4, *Child Labor Consumer Labels and Child Labor.* Washington, DC, 1997.

———. *By the Sweat and Toil of Children.* Vol. 5, *Efforts to Eliminate Child Labor.* Washington, DC, 1998.

US Tariff Act of 1930. Chap. 497, Title III, sec. 307 (codified as amended at 19 USCA sec. 1307). St. Paul, MN: West, 2002.

Valcarengh, Marina. *Child Labour in Italy.* London: Anti-Slavery Society, 1981.

Valencia, Jorge, ed. *Avances y Retrocesos: Informe Sobre los Derechos y la Situación de le Ninéz.* Mexico City: Comexani, 2000.

———. *Derechos del Niño.* Mexico City, 2000 (mimeo; on file with David Post).

Valticos, Nicolas, and Geraldo von Potobsky. *International Labour Law.* 2nd ed. Deventer, Netherlands: Kluwer Law and Taxation, 1995.

Van Boven, Theo C. "Survey of the Positive Law of Human Rights." In Vasak, *The International Dimensions of Human Rights,* infra pp. 87–110.

Van Boven, Theo C., Cees Flinterman, and Ingrid Westendorp, eds. "The Maastricht Guidelines on Violations of Economic, Social, and Cultural Rights." In *Netherlands Institute of Human Rights SIM Special No. 20.* Utrecht, 1988.

Van Bueren, Geraldine. "Child Sexual Exploitation and the Law: A Report on the International Legal Framework and Current National Legislation and Enforcement

Responses." Theme paper for the Second World Congress Against Commercial Sexual Exploitation of Children, Yokohama, Japan, Dec. 17–20, 2001.

———. "Combating Child Poverty: Human Rights Approaches." *Human Rights Quarterly* (1999), 21(4):680–706.

———. *The International Law on the Rights of the Child.* International Studies in Human Rights, vol. 35. Dordrecht, Netherlands: Kluwer Academic, 1995.

Van der Waal, C. S. "Rural Children and Residential Instability in the Northern Province of South Africa." *Social Dynamics* (1996), 22(1):31–53.

Van Hear, Nick. "Child Labor and the Development of Capitalist Agriculture in Ghana." *Development and Change* (1982), 13(4):499–514.

Vasak, Karel, ed. *The International Dimensions of Human Rights.* Vol. 1. Revised and edited for the English translation by Philip Alston. Westport, CT: Greenwood Press, 1982.

———. "Pour une Troisième Génération des Droits de l'Homme." In Swinarski, *Studies and Essays . . . ,* supra pp. 837–845.

Verhellen, Eugeen, ed. *Monitoring Children's Rights.* The Hague: Kluwer Law International, 1996.

Vidyasagar, R. "Issues Relating to Children and Work in South Asia." Unpublished paper. Katmandu, n.d. (on file with Victor P. Karunan).

Vienna Convention on the Law of Treaties. May 3, 1969. UNTS 331. Reprinted in Weston and Carlson, *International Law and World Order,* infra vol. 1, I.E.1.

Vienna Declaration and Programme of Action of the World Conference on Human Rights. UN Doc. A/Conf.157/24, at 20–46 (June 25, 1993). Reprinted in 32 ILM 1661 (1993) and Weston and Carlson, *International Law and World Order,* infra vol. 3, III.U.2.

Voices of Youth. *Young People Speak Out on Child Labour.* UNICEF, 2003. Available at http://www.unicef.org/voy/news/news.2003-08.pdf.

Vongsavath, Nikone. "Lao People's Democratic Republic Country Paper." ILO-Japan Asian Regional Meeting on Trafficking of Children for Labour and Sexual Exploitation, Manila, Oct. 11–12, 2001 (on file with Judith Ennew, William Myers, and Dominique Pierre Plateau).

Walters, Pamela Barnhouse, and David R. James. "Schooling for Some: Child Labor and School Enrollment of Black and White Children in the Early Twentieth-Century South." *American Sociology Review* (1992), 57(5):635–650.

Warburton, Jane. "Prevention, Protection, and Recovery: On Progress and Problems in the Implementation of Programmes to Counter the Sexual Abuse and Exploitation of Children." Theme paper for the Second World Congress Against Commercial Exploitation of Children, Yokohama, Japan, Dec. 17–20, 2001.

Wasserstrom, Richard. "Rights, Human Rights, and Racial Discrimination." *Journal of Philosophy* (1964), 61(20):628–641.

Wazir, Rekha. *Getting Children out of Work and into School.* Secunderabad: MV Foundation, 2002.

Weiner, Myron. *The Child and the State in India: Child Labor and Education Policy in Comparative Perspective.* Princeton: Princeton University Press, 1991.

Weiner, Myron, and Omar Noman. *The Child and the State in India and Pakistan: Child Labor and Education Policies in Comparative Perspective.* Karachi: Oxford University Press, 1995.

Weinstein, James. *The Corporate Ideal of the Liberal State, 1900–1918.* Boston: Beacon Press, 1968.

Weiss, Edith Brown. *In Fairness to Future Generations: International Law, Common Patrimony, and Intergenerational Equity.* Ardsley, NY: Transnational, 1989.

Weissbrodt, David. "The Contribution of International Non-Governmental Organizations to the Protection of Human Rights." In Meron, *Human Rights in Law . . . ,* supra pp. 403–438.

Welch, Claude E., ed. *NGOs and Human Rights: Promise and Performance.* Philadelphia: University of Pennsylvania Press, 2002.

Weldon, Kristin, "Piercing the Silence or Lulling You to Sleep: The Sounds of Child Labor." *Widener Law Symposium Journal* (Spring 2001), 7:227–250.

Weston, Burns H. "Human Rights." *Encyclopædia Britannica.* Chicago, IL: Encyclopædia Britannica, Inc., 2005. Available at http://www.britannica.com/eb/article?tocId-219350 and http://www.uichr.org/features/eb/encybrit.pdf.

———. "The Role of Law in Promoting Peace and Violence: A Matter of Definition, Social Values, and Individual Responsibility." In Reisman and Weston, *Toward World Order and Human Dignity,* supra pp. 114–131.

———. "The Universality of Human Rights in a Multicultured World: Toward Respectful Decision-Making." In Weston and Marks, *The Future of International Human Rights,* infra pp. 65–99.

Weston, Burns H., and Jonathan C. Carlson, eds. *International Law and World Order: Basic Documents.* 5 vols. Ardsley, NY: Transnational, 1994– .

Weston, Burns H., and Stephen P. Marks, eds. *The Future of International Human Rights.* Ardsley, NY: Transnational, 1999.

White, Ben, ed. *Child Workers.* Special issue of *Development and Change* (1982), 13(4).

———. "Childhood, Work, and Education, 1900–2000: The Netherlands and Netherlands Indies/Indonesia Compared." *Brood & Rozen: Tijdschrift voor de Geschiedenis van Sociale Bewegingen* (2001), 4:105–119.

———. "Children, Work, and 'Child Labour': Changing Responses to the Employment of Children." *Development and Change* (1994), 25(4):849–878.

———. "Constructing Child Labour: Attitudes to Juvenile Work in Indonesia, 1900–2000." In Elmhirst and Saptari, *Changing Labour Relations in Southeast Asia,* supra pp. 77–105.

———. "Defining the Intolerable: Child Work, Global Standards, and Cultural Relativism." *Childhood* (1999), 6(1):133–144.

———. "The Economic Importance of Children in a Javanese Village." In Fuchs, *Youth in a Changing World . . . ,* supra pp. 187–206.

White, Ben, and Indrasari Tjandraningsih. *Child Workers in Indonesia.* Bandung: Akatiga, 1998.

Whittaker, Alan, ed. *A Pattern of Slavery: India's Carpet Boys.* Child Labour Series No. 9. London: Anti-Slavery Society, 1988.

WHO (World Health Organization). "Child and Adolescent Rights." Available at http://www.who.int/child-adolescent-health/right.htm.

Wilber, Charles K. *An Inquiry into the Poverty of Economics.* Notre Dame, IN: University of Notre Dame Press, 1983.

Williams, Bernard. "The Standard of Living: Interests and Capabilities." In Hawthorn, Sen, and Muelbauer, *The Standard of Living,* supra pp. 94–102.

Winstanley, Michael. *Working Children in Nineteenth-Century Lancashire.* Lancaster: Lancashire County Books, 1995.

Wiseberg, Laurie S. *Defending Human Rights Defenders: The Importance of Freedom of Association for Human Rights NGOs.* Essays on Human Rights and Democratic Development No. 3. Montreal: International Centre for Human Rights and Democratic Development, 1993.

———. "Human Rights NGOs." In Castermans et al., *The Role of Non-Governmental Organizations* . . . , supra pp. 23–44.

———. "The Internet: One More Tool in the Struggle for Human Rights." In Welch, *NGOs and Human Rights* . . . , supra pp. 238–247.

———. "The Role of Non-Governmental Organisations." In *Put Our World to Rights*. London: Commonwealth Human Rights Initiative, 1991, pp. 151–172.

———. "The Role of Non-Governmental Organizations (NGOs) in the Protection and Enforcement of Human Rights." In Symonides, *Human Rights* . . . , supra pp. 347–368.

Woll, Lisa. *The Convention on the Rights of the Child Impact Study.* Stockholm: Save the Children, 2000.

———. "Organizational Responses to the Convention on the Rights of the Child: International Lessons for Child Welfare Organizations." *Child Welfare* (2001), 80:668–679.

Wood, Geoffrey. "Adverse Incorporation: Another Dark Side of Social Capital." Presentation notes for meeting on 2001 World Development Report on Poverty, Oxford, 1999 (on file with Susan Bissell).

———. *Investing in Networks: Livelihoods and Social Capital in Dhaka Slums.* Bath, UK: Center for Development Studies, University of Bath, 1998.

———. "Security and Graduation: Working for a Living in Dhaka's Slums." *Discourse* (1998), 3.

Wood, Stephen B. *Constitutional Politics in the Progressive Era: Child Labor and the Law.* Chicago: University of Chicago Press, 1968.

Woodhead, Martin. "Child Work and Child Development in Cultural Context: A Study of Children's Perspectives in Selected Countries in Asia, Africa and Central America." In Johnson et al., *Stepping Forward* . . . , supra pp. 126–148.

———. "Combating Child Labour: Listen to What the Children Say." *Childhood* (1999), 6(1):27–50.

———. "The Value of Work and School: A Study of Working Children's Perspectives." In Lieten and White, *Child Labour* . . . , supra pp. 103–116.

World Bank. "Education Lending." Available at http://www.worldbank.org.

———. "The Global Child Labour Program Update 2003." Available at http://www.worldbank.org.

———. *Opening Doors: Education and the World Bank.* Washington, DC: Human Development Network, World Bank, 2003.

———. *Participatory Poverty Assessments from Four Sites in Viet Nam: Lao Cai, Ha Tinh, Tra Vinh, and Ho Chi Minh City—Submission to the World Development Report 2000 by Vietnam-Sweden Mountain Rural Development Programme.* Washington, DC, 1999.

———. "World Bank Forum on Child Labor: A Dialogue with the ILO and Other Partners." Apr. 29, 2004. Available at http://www.worldbank.org.

———. *World Development Report 1995: Workers in an Integrating World.* New York: Oxford University Press, 1995.

World Cocoa Foundation. *Progress Report.* May 27, 2003. Available at http://www.chocolateandcocoa.org/news/lprogress%20report.htm.

"World Cup Notebook." *Globe and Mail,* June 7, 2002.

WTO (World Trade Organization). "Joint Communiqué." Eleventh Summit of the Heads of State and Government of the Group of Fifteen, Jakarta, May 30–31, 2001. Available at http://www.sto.org/english/news_e/news_e.htm.

———. *Singapore Ministerial Declaration.* Dec. 13, 1996. WTO Doc. WT/MIN(96)/DEC (1996). Reprinted in 36 ILM 218 (1997). Available at http://www.wto.org/english/thewto_e/minist_e/min96_e/wtodec_e.htm.

WTO Agreement on the Application of Sanitary and Phytosanitary Measures. Apr. 15, 1994. In *Final Act Embodying the Results of the Uruguay Round of Multilateral Negotiations,* supra. Reprinted in 33 ILM 1153 (1994).

WTO Understanding on Rules and Procedures Governing the Settlement of Disputes. Apr. 15, 1994. WTO Agreement, Annex 2. Reprinted in 33 ILM 1226 (1994).

Yanz, Lynda, and Bob Jeffcott. "Eliminating Child Labour: Not as Simple as It Seems." *Briarpatch* (June 1998), 27(5). Available at http://maquilasolidarity.org/resources/child/briarpatch.htm.

Yellowitz, Irwin. *Labor and the Progressive Movement in New York State, 1897–1916.* Ithaca: Cornell University Press, 1965.

Zalami, Fatima Badry. *Forgotten on the Pyjama Trail: A Case Study of Garment Workers in Méknès* [Morocco] *Dismissed from Their Jobs Following Foreign Media Attention.* Amsterdam: International Working Group on Child Labour, 1998.

Zia-Zarifi, Saman. "Suing Multinational Corporations in the U.S. for Violating International Law." *UCLA Journal of International Law and Foreign Affairs* (1999), 4:81–147.

Zinn, Howard. *The Zinn Reader: Writings on Disobedience and Democracy.* New York: Seven Stories Press, 1997.

The Contributors

S. L. Bachman is assistant director and chief reporter at Child Labor and the Global Village: Photography for Social Change. An independent journalist, she previously was an editorial writer and reporter at the *San Jose Mercury News*. Her articles about child labor have appeared in many academic journals and news media.

Susan L. Bissell is senior project officer, Child Protection, UNICEF, based at the Innocenti Research Centre in Florence, Italy. For many years, she managed UNICEF programs in Bangladesh, India, and Sri Lanka for children in especially difficult circumstances (CEDC). Bissell coproduced a television documentary titled *A Kind of Childhood,* which screened at the 2003 Human Rights Watch Festival in London and received critical acclaim in North America and Europe.

Michael F. C. Bourdillon is emeritus professor of sociology at the University of Zimbabwe. His most recent publications include *The Children's Advisory Board: Initial Experiences* and *Girls on the Street*. Bourdillon has for many years, in association with nongovernmental organizations, worked with street children and other working children.

Holly Cullen is reader in law and deputy director at the European Law Institute at Durham University. She has published numerous articles on international labor law in various academic journals, and is currently completing her book *The Role of International Law in the Elimination of Child Labor.*

Hugh Cunningham is emeritus professor of social history at the University of Kent, Canterbury. His most recent publications include *Children and Childhood in Western Society Since 1500* and *Child Labour in Historical Perspective,*

1800–1985: Case Studies from Europe, Japan, and Colombia (coeditor with Pier Paolo Viazzo).

Judith Ennew is senior research associate at the Centre for Family Research, University of Cambridge. An activist and researcher in children's rights since 1979, Ennew specializes in child workers, street children, and child sexual exploitation. Presently in Bangkok, she concentrates on developing skills for research with children among students, academics, and fieldworkers in Southeast and East Asia. In 2000 she was elected to the Academy of Learned Societies in the Social Sciences.

Frank J. Garcia is professor of law and director of the Law and Justice in the Americas Program, Boston College. His recent publications include *Trade, Inequality, and Justice.* His current research focuses on the effects of globalization on the formation of social policy, and he speaks and writes frequently on trade and human rights and on trade and development topics.

Soohyun Jun is a lawyer currently in practice in Boston. A former research fellow at Boston College Law School, she holds an M.A. degree in international law from the Graduate School of International Studies at Sogang University (Seoul), a J.D. degree from Boston College Law School, and an LL.M. degree from Boston University School of Law. Previously she served as a legal consultant to Sang-Yong Park of the UN Sub-Commission on Human Rights.

Victor P. Karunan is senior adviser for adolescent development and participation in the program division of UNICEF headquarters in New York. Formerly project officer for participation and partnerships in the UNICEF regional office for East Asia and the Pacific in Bangkok, Karunan has worked for the past twenty years in South and Southeast Asia in policy research and program development in child protection, children and macroeconomics, social policy, and NGO capacity building.

Donald Mmari is consultancy coordinator for Research on Poverty Alleviation (REPOA), an NGO involved in research and policy on poverty and development, based in Dar es Salaam, Tanzania. An economist, Mmari led a REPOA team to carry out a baseline and attitude survey on the worst forms of child labor in Tanzania as part of an IPEC time-bound program, and recently carried out a review of the country's national child labor monitoring system.

William E. Myers is visiting scholar in the Department of Human and Community Development, University of California at Davis, and an international consultant on child labor and other child rights and protection issues. Since retiring from the ILO and UNICEF, he has published widely on children and child labor.

Dominique Pierre Plateau is regional adviser on prevention of child abuse and exploitation for Save the Children–Sweden, Southeast Asia. His recent publications include *Child Labour: Getting the Message Across* (with Judith Ennew). A communications specialist, Plateau previously worked in the Vietnamese and Cambodian repatriation efforts of the UNHCR.

David M. Post is professor of education policy and of human development and family studies at Pennsylvania State University. He has published widely in the area of social stratification and inequality, and is coeditor of the *Comparative Education Review*. Recently, Post directed a cross-national study of Latin American education policies and their impact on children's work.

Victoria V. Rialp is an independent consultant on child protection issues with the ILO and UNICEF. Previously a UNICEF program officer in the Philippines, Brazil, and New York, she has contributed major working papers and chapters on child-related issues to ILO and UNICEF publications, and has helped to organize national-level, regional, and global seminars and training workshops on street and working children.

Benedito Rodrigues dos Santos is professor of anthropology at the Catholic University of Goiás State, Brazil. His recent publications include *Guia Escolar: Métodos para Identificação de Sinais de Abuso e Exploração Sexual de Crianças e Adolescentes* (with Rita Ippólito) (School Guide: Methods for the Identification of Signs of Child Abuse and Sexual Exploitation) and *Mobilizing Business Companies for Eradication of Child Labor: A Study on Strategies Developed by the Abrinq Foundation for Children's Rights*. Dos Santos is also a cofounder and member of the Brazilian National Movement of Street Boys and Girls (MNMMR).

Shelton Stromquist is professor of history at The University of Iowa, specializing in US social and labor history. His major recent publications include *Reinventing "The People": The Progressive Movement, the Class Problem, and the Origins of Modern Liberalism* and *Solidarity and Survival: An Oral History of Iowa Labor in the Twentieth Century*. Stromquist is presently working on a new comparative labor history titled *Social Democracy in the City: Politics, Ideology and Reform in Comparative Perspective, 1980–1920*.

Mark B. Teerink is a senior associate at Miller & Company, P.C., in Kansas City, Missouri, where he specializes in international trade law. A former Peace Corps volunteer in Sierra Leone and graduate of The University of Iowa College of Law, Teerink has a long-standing interest in international human rights. Previously he served as an election registration and polling supervisor for the Organization for Security and Cooperation in Europe in Bosnia and Herzegovina and as a member of the faculty of law at Makerere University in Kampala, Uganda, where he advised on human rights.

Burns H. Weston is Bessie Dutton Murray Distinguished Professor of Law Emeritus at The University of Iowa, founding and former director of that university's Center for Human Rights, and now senior scholar there. His most recent book is *The Future of International Human Rights* (with Stephen P. Marks). Forthcoming are new editions of *Human Rights in the World Community: Issues and Action* (with Richard Pierre Claude); *International Law and World Order: A Problem-Oriented Coursebook* (with Richard Falk, Hilary Charlesworth, and Andrew Strauss); and *International Environmental Law and World Order: A Problem-Oriented Coursebook* (with Jonathan C. Carlson and Geoffrey W. R. Palmer).

Ben White is professor of rural sociology and director of the International Centre for Child and Youth Studies at the Institute of Social Studies, The Hague, and professor of social sciences at the University of Amsterdam. His authored and edited books include *Child Labour: Policy Options* (with Kristoffel Lieten) and *Child Workers in Indonesia*. White's current research focuses on the impact of Indonesia's recent economic and political crisis on different groups in Indonesian society, including children and youth. He is also at work on a new collaborative study titled *Redefining Childhood: New and Emerging Needs of Children and Youth*.

Laurie S. Wiseberg is minority rights adviser in the Office of Returns and Communities of the Office of the Special Representative of the Secretary-General (SRSG) for the United Nations Mission in Kosovo. Founder and former executive director of Human Rights Internet (HRI), she has written extensively on the role of nongovernmental organizations in the protection and promotion of human rights and done pioneering work in the areas of information, documentation, and education in human rights.

▩   Assisting Contributor

Mark Erik Hecht is a member of the Law Society of Upper Canada and the International Bar Association, national coordinator for the Canadian Information Network on Child and Youth Rights, and senior legal counsel to Beyond Borders: Ensuring Global Justice for Children. Hecht also sits on the executive committee of ECPAT, the international campaign to end child prostitution, child pornography, and the trafficking of children for sexual purposes.

Index

About the Book

The International Labour Organization estimated in 2000 that, of the approximately 246 million children engaged in labor worldwide, 171 million were working in situations hazardous to their physical and psychosocial development. *Child Labor and Human Rights* provides a comprehensive overview of the phenomenon of child labor from a human rights perspective.

The authors consider the connections between human rights and abusive child labor, the pros and cons of a rights-based approach to the problem, and specific strategies for effective change. They make an indispensable contribution to the growing effort to abolish abusive and exploitive child labor practices.

Burns H. Weston is Bessie Dutton Murray Distinguished Professor of Law Emeritus and senior scholar of The University of Iowa Center for Human Rights (UICHR), which he founded and directed for six years. His numerous works in the field of human rights include *Human Rights in the World Community: Issues and Action* and *The Future of International Human Rights*. He also is a member of the Editorial Review Board of *Human Rights and Human Welfare* and honorary editor of the *American Journal of International Law*.